THE SUPREME COURT OF PENNSYLVANIA

THE SUPREME COURT

OF PENNSYLVANIA

Life and Law in the Commonwealth,
1684–2017

Edited by John J. Hare

THE PENNSYLVANIA STATE UNIVERSITY PRESS

UNIVERSITY PARK, PENNSYLVANIA

Library of Congress Cataloging-in-Publication Data

Names: Hare, John J., editor.
Title: The Supreme Court of Pennsylvania: life and law in the Commonwealth,
    1684–2017 / edited by John J. Hare.
Description: University Park, Pennsylvania : The Pennsylvania State University
    Press, [2018] | Includes bibliographical references and index.
Identifiers: LCCN 2017033576 | ISBN 9780271080116 (cloth : alk. paper)
Summary: "A narrative history of the Supreme Court of Pennsylvania. Explores
    the court's notable decisions and why they matter in the broader context of
    Pennsylvania and American law and history"—Provided by publisher.
Subjects: LCSH: Pennsylvania. Supreme Court—History. | Law—Pennsylvania—
    History.
Classification: LCC KFP512 .P46 2018 | DDC 347.748/035—dc23
LC record available at https://lccn.loc.gov/2017033576

The Pennsylvania State University Press is a member of the Association of American University Presses.

It is the policy of The Pennsylvania State University Press to use acid-free paper. Publications on uncoated stock satisfy the minimum requirements of American National Standard for Information Sciences—Permanence of Paper for Printed Library Material, ANSI Z39.48-1992.

Contents

Section 2: Tort Law

Foreword

The Pennsylvania Supreme Court predates the Commonwealth itself by more than a century and fairly claims to be the oldest court in North America. Given Pennsylvania's prominence in American history—it acquired the motto "the Keystone State" for good reason—its High Court has been routinely called on to address novel and fundamental questions about our structure of government and the way citizens and organizations relate to the government and each other. The Supreme Court's answers to those questions tell us a great deal about our history, even as they shaped that history.

But the Supreme Court's remarkable story has never been told in a comprehensive fashion. The most scholarly works to date are a 1994 book and an unpublished 1960 PhD dissertation, both of which ended their coverage more than two centuries ago.[1] This incomplete historical record prompted Chief Justice Thomas G. Saylor to initiate the project that led to this book. Without his steady guidance, the book would not exist. Others who made invaluable contributions include Dean R. Phillips, a pillar of the Pennsylvania Bar who played a key role in organizing the project and providing his advice throughout, and C. Dale McClain, a past president of the Pennsylvania Bar Association who gave generously of his good offices and arranged the financing for the book's publication. Thomas B. Darr, the court administrator of Pennsylvania, also facilitated access to the Court's archival resources and lent us the talents of Justin P. Scott, the Court's multimedia specialist, whose keen eye produced the photographs in this book.

The contributing authors are leading jurists, deans, law and history professors, and practicing attorneys. They teach at or are alumni of all eight Pennsylvania law schools, among many others, and all are specialists in their subjects. The parts begin with an introduction by Duquesne University president and former law dean Kenneth G. Gormley, the noted constitutional scholar and *New York Times* best-selling author. Mr. Gormley sets the stage for the chapters that follow by introducing readers to the Supreme Court's rich history and the people and events that have allowed it to evolve into one of the most influential courts in the nation. The introduction poses the question, How have the Court and its justices shaped life and law in Pennsylvania and beyond? The remainder of the book answers this question from a number of perspectives.

The sections and chapters that follow are organized topically, rather than chronologically, to highlight the authors' expertise in discrete legal subjects and historical events. The first part includes seven chapters that describe the structure and powers of the Supreme Court. They discuss, in particular, the controversial subject of judicial elections, the Supreme Court's sweeping King's Bench and rulemaking powers, and its broad authority to regulate and discipline judges and lawyers—all of which make the Court one of the most powerful state high courts in the nation. The first section concludes with a description of the Court's forward-thinking embrace of technology to foster unification of the Commonwealth's sprawling judicial system.

The second part focuses on the Court's work in deciding notable cases in the areas of constitutional law, civil rights, torts, criminal law, labor law, and administrative law. In each of these areas, the Court decided cases of historical significance that developed and clarified Pennsylvania law and often influenced jurisprudence nationally. For instance, the authors describe the context in which the Court adjudicated new and complex issues arising from some of the most notable events and tragedies in American history, including the struggle for religious liberty in colonial Pennsylvania, the Revolutionary War, slavery, the Johnstown Flood, the Homestead Steel Strike, both world wars, and more recently, the dramatic rise of criminal procedural rights and the expansion of tort law. The Supreme Court's reputation as a preeminent judicial body was built primarily through its work in these areas.

The book ends with an afterword by Chief Justice Saylor, in which he describes the many roles of the modern Supreme Court. The Court's most commonly known function is the resolution of discretionary appeals selected from among the three thousand petitions the Court receives each year, but it also exercises original jurisdiction over death penalty appeals and other significant cases, and it supervises a judiciary that includes sixty districts, more than one thousand lower court judges, and many thousands of employees. In his afterword, Chief Justice Saylor discusses and appreciates the Court's work in performing these and other functions.

Although this book covers a broad swath of the Court's history, it is impossible to be truly comprehensive in any single volume, especially given the Court's age. By way of comparison, the 1960 dissertation mentioned earlier spent nearly a thousand pages covering fifteen years of the Court's history. Applying such an approach to the Court's whole history would not be practical or publishable, so this book sacrifices some depth for breadth. As a result, notable parts of the Court's history are inevitably omitted. It is also regrettable that the remarkable men and women who have populated the Court, many of national prominence, are not given the biographical coverage they deserve. Despite these limitations, the chapters offer a fascinating and highly readable assessment of the Court's efforts to develop and adapt Pennsylvania law in an ever-changing historical context.

Finally, while many of the chapters are celebratory, others are not. Like any group of human beings addressing difficult issues, the Court has rendered decisions that are open to criticism. Authors offer strong and thoughtful critiques, for instance, of the Court's jurisprudence regarding freedom of expression, gender equality, and felony murder. Not surprisingly, the Court's work in other contentious areas has drawn praise from some and criticism from others, as illustrated by the two chapters on product liability law that draw starkly different conclusions from the same body of case law. In this regard, we have declined to follow the praise-only model of other court histories. Fairness requires objectivity, so the chapters both compliment and criticize. What follows, then, is a fair-minded assessment of the Court's central role in shaping law and history over the past three centuries.

John J. Hare

NOTES

John J. Hare is a shareholder at Marshall Dennehey Warner Coleman & Goggin.

1. *See* G. S. Rowe, *Embattled Bench: The Pennsylvania Supreme Court and the Forging of a Democratic Society, 1684–1809* (Newark: University of Delaware Press, 1994); *see also* Thomas R. Meehan, "The Pennsylvania Supreme Court in the Law and Politics of the Commonwealth, 1776–1790" (PhD diss., University of Wisconsin, Madison, 1960), on file with the editor.

Introduction

The History of a Time-Honored Court

The Pennsylvania Supreme Court is one of the most significant, esteemed judicial bodies in the history of the United States, and, indeed, in the civilized world.

There has been some debate, however, about whether Pennsylvania's Supreme Court—often dubbed "the oldest court in North America"—can legitimately claim that distinction. One renowned legal historian, writing in 1972 to mark the 250th anniversary of the act that formally established the Pennsylvania Supreme Court, provided the best analysis of the matter.[1] Erwin C. Surrency, professor of law, librarian at Temple University, and founder of the *American Journal of Legal History*, confirmed that the Court can trace its roots to the establishment of a provincial court in 1684.[2] This body sat in Philadelphia and consisted of five judges "who were required to go on circuit into each county to try titles to land and all suits in law and equity which were outside the jurisdiction of the county courts then held by the justices of the peace."[3]

The complicated part of the Court's history, however, resides in the period between 1684 and 1722, before the Court was formally created by statute. During that time, the statutory definition of the courts changed as a result of the need to send legislation to the Privy Council in England for review.[4] During this four-decade stretch, the British Crown repeatedly "disallowed" efforts by William Penn and the General Assembly of the colony to establish a permanent judicial system.[5] For instance, in 1690, the Pennsylvania legislature sought to create a provincial court of five judges with broad jurisdiction and the ability to take appeals from county courts.[6] This act was disallowed by the Crown. After Governor John Evans (1704–9) issued an ordinance pressing for the creation of a permanent judicial system with a high court seated atop the pyramid, the Crown eventually permitted such a change. The Judiciary Act of 1722 established a "Supream Court" composed of three justices "of known Integrity and Ability," with one presiding as chief justice.[7] The three-member court consisted of a chief justice (David Lloyd, 1717–31) and two associate justices (George Roche and Robert Assheton). The Court's jurisdiction, while not as sweeping as it would eventually become, nonetheless encompassed "a large charter."[8] As Professor Surrency correctly noted, the practical effect of the Judiciary Act of 1722 was that "it combined both trial and appellate functions" in the Supreme Court, which "stood above all other courts of the Province."[9]

Thus it is a fair claim that the Supreme Court of Pennsylvania is the oldest court in North America. Yet it is also true that the Court did not function continuously during its earliest stages due to ongoing battles with the Crown. When it finally emerged in 1722 as a permanent judicial body, however, it was unlike any other court in the history of America. Indeed, one distinguished member of the Pennsylvania Bar—who spoke at the celebration marking the Supreme Court's 250th anniversary, held at Independence Hall in Philadelphia—observed that this judicial body reflected the ambitious dream of William Penn himself: Penn had hoped to create a court with broad jurisdiction to handle matters across the length and breadth of his new colony. This new court not only fulfilled that vision; it became "the prototype" for the Framers of the US Constitution a half century later when they created the US Supreme Court in Article III of that document.[10]

I. THE PENNSYLVANIA CONSTITUTION SHAPES THE COURT

The Pennsylvania Supreme Court has undergone significant changes over the course of the past three centuries. Most of these have been tied to the evolution of the Pennsylvania Constitution itself, which assigns the Supreme Court a special place in the state's governmental structure. Thus the history of our Supreme Court is indissolubly linked to that of the state's fundamental charter.

Pennsylvania's first Constitution, approved in September 1776, was adopted in the midst of the Revolutionary War, twelve years before the US Constitution came into being. It thus served as a rallying point for colonists determined to break ties with the British. A secret resolution adopted by the Second Continental Congress in May 1776 had authorized the colonies to establish their own frameworks of government. In Philadelphia, four thousand Pennsylvanians swarmed into a public meeting place and, with "three rousing cheers," endorsed the notion of drafting their own Constitution.[11]

The elderly statesman Benjamin Franklin was selected as chair of the Pennsylvania constitutional convention. That body gathered in Carpenter's Hall in Philadelphia on July 5, 1776, finished its drafting, and approved the Pennsylvania Constitution on September 28, 1776. Chapter II of that document ("Plan or Frame of Government") provided for the creation of a Supreme Court. Section 20 of the Constitution provided that the president of the Supreme Executive Council (SEC) and the short-lived Council of Censors would appoint judges rather than leaving the matter to recurring elections.[12] Section 23 stated that "judges of the supreme court of judicative" would be commissioned for seven years.[13] All judges—including those on the Supreme Court—were given "fixed" salaries so that they would not be beholden to a legislature that might increase, decrease, or abolish their pay.[14] Thus the Pennsylvania Constitution created a uniquely independent judiciary—the first of its kind.

When it convened on April 10, 1776, just before the Declaration of Independence was formalized, the Pennsylvania Supreme Court was still conducting proceedings under the caption the "reign of our Sovereign, George the Third."[15] By its next session in September 1778, the caption had been changed to read, "The Commonwealth of Pennsylvania."[16] Thus the Provincial Court had formally ended; a new court, not beholden to the Crown, had come into existence. It was presided over by Chief Justice Thomas McKean (1777–99). A leading public figure, McKean was a signer of the Declaration of Independence, president of the Continental Congress, and later governor of Delaware; he has rightly been described as the "father of the judicial system in Pennsylvania."[17]

II. THE COURT'S FUNCTIONS

During the pre-Revolutionary period, the Supreme Court possessed a mishmash of functions designed to establish a loosely constructed judicial system in the sprawling territory. It had the ability to issue writs of error, writs of certiorari, and writs of habeas corpus.[18] In criminal cases, the Supreme Court possessed trial court functions and could preside over trials.[19]

During the period of British rule, appeals had been permitted from the Pennsylvania Supreme Court to the Privy Council in England (a body that represented the sovereign). Briefly, following independence, appeals were allowed to a "High Court of Errors and Appeals" (a body consisting of judges, the president of the SEC, and others). By 1806, the High Court of Errors and Appeals was abolished entirely, and the Supreme Court became the final court of review in Pennsylvania.[20] For the most part, the laws and procedures established during the colonial era "were continued without change."[21]

Justices of the Supreme Court rode circuit across the state, with sessions regularly held in Philadelphia (covering counties in the eastern district), Pittsburgh (the western district), and Sunbury in Northumberland County (the middle district). After the practice of riding circuit was temporarily halted in 1809, the Court held sessions in Philadelphia, Pittsburgh, Lancaster, Chambersburg, and Sunbury. By 1834, when the practice of riding circuit was resumed, sessions were added in the new state capital at Harrisburg.[22] The Constitution of 1874 abolished the Court's *nisi prius* duties in Philadelphia, thereby making it exclusively an appellate court.[23]

III. SIZE OF THE COURT

The Supreme Court's size has fluctuated over the years. Pursuant to the Judiciary Act of 1722, it initially consisted of three justices, including a chief justice. By 1767, it was increased to four justices; that number ended up being embodied in the original state Constitution. In 1809, after the Court's circuit duty was temporarily eliminated, the number of justices dropped back down to three; it then bounced up to five in 1826, after circuit duties resumed. With the adoption of the Constitution of 1873, the Supreme Court was given jurisdiction over the entire state—by appeal, certiorari, and/or writ of error—"in all cases, as is now or hereafter be provided by law." Concurrent with this change, the number of justices was increased to seven, including the chief justice.[24] This number has remained fixed since 1873. It recognizes the breadth of the Court's work and the importance of ensuring a variety of perspectives on this supreme judicial body in order to properly address the Commonwealth's (and its citizens') most pressing issues.

IV. AMENDMENTS TO THE CONSTITUTION

The original Pennsylvania Constitution of 1776 has been overhauled four times. In each instance, the changes have impacted and shaped the evolution of the Supreme Court.

In 1790, the Constitution was totally rewritten. Certain radical features, particularly the failed unicameral legislature and the Council of Censors, were abolished. Under the 1776 Constitution, justices had been appointed for a "fixed term" of seven years with reappointment possible. Now all judges—including Supreme Court justices—were to be appointed by the governor and could serve for life "during good behavior." Simultaneously, an impeachment provision was added to allow jurists to be removed for misbehavior, and the governor could request the legislature to remove any judge "for any reasonable cause, which shall not be sufficient ground of impeachment,"[25] upon the vote of two-thirds of each house of the legislature.

In 1838, in response to popular demand for a more liberal, more democratic Constitution, the state's charter was again revised. With respect to the judiciary, the provision for life tenure was eliminated. There was a strong push for the popular election of judges, yet this effort failed. Supreme Court justices were still appointed by the governor, with the advice and consent of the Senate, but their terms were fixed to a period of fifteen years.[26] There was no provision for renewal beyond the fifteen-year term. Additionally, a provision was added requiring that all judges and justices be "learned in the law," ensuring that only individuals with formal legal training could fill seats on the High Court.

An 1850 constitutional amendment made the state judiciary elective for the first time in 1851.[27] Pursuant to this provision, the justices of the Supreme Court kept the fifteen-year term of office. However, the justices first chosen under this system were phased in over time; they were required to draw lots to determine the number of years each would hold office (three, six, nine, twelve, or fifteen), with the jurist drawing the shortest term serving as chief justice.

In 1872, responding to outcry over corruption in government and the proliferation of "local and special" laws designed to favor special interests (particularly corporations), the

Constitution was once again rewritten. Popular election of judges continued. However, the term of judges was increased from fifteen to twenty-one years. Additionally, the number of justices on the High Court was increased from five to seven.[28]

Finally, in 1968, the Pennsylvania Constitution was revised through a limited constitutional convention. While the provisions relating to the judiciary were amended in a number of respects, the structure of the Supreme Court remained largely intact. Yet for the first time, the Constitution created a Unified Judicial System (UJS), and the Supreme Court was given supervisory power over the entire state judiciary; it was also given power to promulgate rules of procedure.[29] In addition, the Superior Court and Commonwealth Court, the former created in 1895 and the latter slated to be created in 1970, were deemed to be constitutional courts pursuant to these changes.[30]

V. HISTORIC CASES

The Pennsylvania Supreme Court is not only a historic body in terms of its origin and structure. Since its inception, it has also been a leading force among judicial bodies throughout the United States. In a host of landmark cases, the Court has helped shape the jurisprudence of the United States and the formation of the nation itself.

While George Washington was still president, in 1796, the Pennsylvania Supreme Court issued a historic opinion in *Hubley's Lessee v. Madison*, endorsing the notion of judicial review over acts of the state legislature. This decision was handed down by the Court seven years before the US Supreme Court and Chief Justice John Marshall, in *Marbury v. Madison*,[31] established the principle of judicial review as a matter of federal constitutional law. In *Hubley's Lessee*,[32] the Supreme Court stated in a per curiam opinion that a 1792 statute regulating the sale of unappropriated lands was unconstitutional because it "abridged the judicial power of the courts."[33] A quarter century later, in *Eakin v. Raub*,[34] Chief Justice William Tilghman of the state's High Court reaffirmed that notion of judicial review. Tilghman stated with eloquence, "I adhere to the opinion which I have frequently expressed, that when a judge is convinced, beyond doubt, that an act has been passed in violation of the constitution, he is bound to declare it void, by his oath, by his duty to the party who has brought the cause before him, and to the people, the only source of legitimate power."[35]

Interestingly, Justice John Bannister Gibson issued a strong dissent in *Eakin v. Raub*, challenging the historical and philosophical basis of the notion of judicial review. He went so far as to challenge the US Supreme Court's landmark decision in *Marbury v. Madison*. In Justice Gibson's view, the judiciary was limited to interpreting statutes and pronouncing what the law was—it did not have the authority to second-guess acts of the legislature.[36] Ironically, Gibson's iconoclastic position came back to haunt him: many commentators believe that he was later passed up for a seat on the US Supreme Court because of his strident criticism of judicial review and of Chief Justice John Marshall's historic decision in *Marbury*.[37]

In other areas, the Pennsylvania Supreme Court blazed new paths. When it came to the subject of the legality (and morality) of slavery, the state High Court was a major force in changing the national dialogue. As early as 1789, in *Republica v. Negroe Betsey*,[38] the Court upheld the Act for the Gradual Abolition of Slavery (1780).[39] This was the first law of its kind designed to abolish slavery in the new nation. In the *Negroe Betsey* case, the Supreme Court decision granted freedom to three children born to a slave mother prior to passage of the act.

Similarly, when it came to "fugitive" slaves, the Pennsylvania Supreme Court issued a brief but historic ruling in the case that eventually became *Prigg v. Pennsylvania*,[40] enforcing the state's Personal Liberty Law. The Pennsylvania High Court upheld the kidnapping conviction of Edward Prigg—a white citizen of Maryland—after he traveled to Pennsylvania and forcibly removed Margaret Morgan, a black woman, and her children to Maryland without complying with the state's law designed to protect fugitive slaves.[41] Thus in the period leading up to the Civil War, the Pennsylvania Supreme Court played a key role in upholding laws designed to protect freed slaves and their families.[42]

The Court in 1896 also bucked the federal trend in directing the prothonotary of Philadelphia to administer the prescribed oath to a female—Carrie Burnham Kilgore—admitting her to practice as an attorney of the Supreme Court.[43] It thus became one of the earliest courts in the nation to admit women to practice law. Significantly, the *Kilgore* ruling was handed down in the shadow of the US Supreme Court's decision in *Bradwell v. State*,[44] which had upheld an Illinois law that refused to grant women licenses to practice law in that state and had declared that such a provision did not violate the federal Constitution.

Likewise, during an era in which the US Supreme Court was permitting states to employ child labor—as part of its interpretation of the Commerce Clause and its recognition of an implied liberty of contract under the federal Constitution[45]—the Pennsylvania Supreme Court in *Commonwealth v. Wormser*[46] upheld a 1915 statute that imposed stiff regulations on the employment of minors. The Court concluded that this act was a reasonable exercise of the Commonwealth's police power to protect the health, safety, and welfare of its citizens—in this case, a boy under the age of sixteen who had been employed long hours without a proper employment certificate.

As early as 1891, in *Robb v. Carnegie Bros. & Co.*[47]—an action brought by a farmer for the injury done to his crops from the gas fumes and smoke emanating from Andrew Carnegie's coke oven located on adjoining land—the Court laid the foundation for the doctrine of strict liability in Pennsylvania. Shifting its focus from the social utility of Carnegie's industrial activity to the farmer's plight, the Court refused to consider Carnegie's manufacture of coke at the site to be the natural and necessary consequence of development and upheld the farmer's right to recover damages for his losses without proving fault.

During the Great Depression, in 1937, the Supreme Court upheld a law that created a state commission to provide relief to unemployed individuals and their families[48] well before the federal Social Security Act of 1935 was signed into law by President Franklin D. Roosevelt.

VI. LEADER IN STATE CONSTITUTIONAL DEVELOPMENT

In more recent years, the Pennsylvania Supreme Court has been a national leader in developing groundbreaking new areas of jurisprudence under its state Constitution, serving as a model for other states that have rediscovered the rich historical traditions of their own state charters.[49] Chief Justices Michael J. Eagen (1977–80), Henry X. O'Brien (1980–83), and Samuel J. Roberts (1983–86) all had records of tackling difficult issues under the state Constitution[50] well before it was fashionable to do so. Chief Justice Robert C. Nix Jr. (1986–96) and Chief Justice John P. Flaherty (1996–2001) authored influential opinions—including *Commonwealth v. Sell*[51] and *Commonwealth v. One (1) Z-28 Camaro Coupe*,[52] respectively—that served as pillars for the rebirth of state constitutional jurisprudence in Pennsylvania.

Chief Justice Ralph J. Cappy (2003–8) authored a landmark decision in *Commonwealth v. Edmunds*,[53] which established a four-part protocol that lawyers and litigants were strongly encouraged to follow in briefing and arguing all state constitutional issues (including criminal procedural issues). As Judge Thomas Hardiman of the US Court of Appeals for the Third Circuit has written, *Edmunds* played a "seminal role in the development of new judicial federalism" nationwide; indeed, the *Edmunds* framework has become a model for state supreme courts and jurists around the country.[54] Moreover, *Edmunds* has continued to shape constitutional jurisprudence within Pennsylvania in a dramatic fashion since it was decided in 1993.

Chief Justice Ronald D. Castille (2008–15), a former district attorney in Philadelphia who tended to resist expanding state constitutional rights in the criminal sphere, nonetheless made giant strides in solidifying the independence of Pennsylvania constitutional jurisprudence in other areas, pushing that jurisprudence to new levels of sophistication.[55] In cases such as *Pap's A.M. v. City of Erie* (free speech),[56] *Holt v. 2011 Legislative Reapportionment Commission* (legislative redistricting),[57] and *Robinson Twp. v. Commonwealth* (environmental rights),[58] Chief Justice Castille authored pioneering, courageous decisions that elevated Pennsylvania constitutional jurisprudence to an unprecedented level of excellence.

Current Chief Justice Thomas G. Saylor (2015–present), a constitutional scholar in his own right, has written widely on state constitutional topics[59] and has authored thoughtful opinions exploring the boundaries of independent state constitutional jurisprudence.[60]

Thus virtually every chief justice of Pennsylvania in modern times—and many justices who have occupied seats on the state's High Court[61]—has actively contributed to creating a new body of state constitutional jurisprudence in the Commonwealth, thus helping define the scope and fabric of Pennsylvania's fundamental charter.

VII. CONCLUSION

In a wide array of areas, far beyond the important realm of state constitutional decision making, the Pennsylvania Supreme Court has made lasting contributions that have shaped Pennsylvania as a polity and influenced the evolution of jurisprudence across the United States. As pointed out in the foreword, not every decision of this Court—or of any judicial body—can escape criticism. Yet that is the essence of a system of laws that seeks to attain the highest manifestation of common good through an incremental process of deliberation, debate, and reasoned decision making over the span of decades and centuries.

In the 290-plus years since the Supreme Court formally came into existence through the Judiciary Act of 1722, that body has forged a rich legacy that remains unparalleled in American history. This book brings to life those historic contributions that continue to make the oldest court in North America a shining example of the very best features of our American democracy.

Kenneth G. Gormley

NOTES

Kenneth G. Gormley is the president of Duquesne University, a former dean and professor at Duquesne University School of Law, and editor of *The Pennsylvania Constitution: A Treatise on Rights and Liberties* (Philadelphia: George T. Bisel, 2004).

1. Erwin C. Surrency, "The Court's Place in History," *Pennsylvania Bar Association Quarterly* 43 (1972): 440–53. For a more current review of the Pennsylvania colonial judiciary, *see* Scott Douglas Gerber, *A Distinct Judicial Power: The Origins of an Independent Judiciary, 1606–1787* (Oxford: Oxford University Press, 2011), 267–87.

2. When William Penn received a royal charter from King Charles II in 1681 and was appointed proprietor of Pennsylvania, a judicial body known as the Court of Assizes (of Dutch origin) was already functioning in the territory.

Kenneth G. Gormley, "Overview of the Pennsylvania Constitution," in *The Pennsylvania Constitution: A Treatise on Rights and Liberties*, ed. Kenneth G. Gormley et al. (Philadelphia: George T. Bisel, 2004), 1.

3. Surrency, "Court's Place," 440, 444 (citing John Blair Linn, *Charter to William Penn and the Laws of the Province of Pennsylvania, Passed Between the Years 1862 and 1700, Preceded by Duke of York's Laws in Force from the Year 1676 to the Year 1682, with an Appendix Containing Laws Relating to the Organization of the Provincial Courts and Historical Matter* [Harrisburg, Pa.: Lane S. Hart, 1879], 168).

4. During this period prior to independence, the Crown established a Privy Council in England that was essentially the court of last resort. This body reviewed colonial legislation and had appellate jurisdiction over the decisions of

the highest court in the colonies. King Charles II's charter to William Penn included the provision that all laws had to be reviewed by the Privy Council within five years of enactment (Section 7). *See* Robert L. Cable, *The Statutes at Large of Pennsylvania from 1682 to 1700* (Harrisburg, Pa.: Legislative Reference Bureau, 2001), 303, 307–8. For the judicial function, *see* Sharon Hamby O'Connor and Mary Sarah Bilder with the assistance of Charles Donahue Jr., *Appeals to the Privy Council from the American Colonies: An Annotated Digital Catalogue* (Cambridge, Mass.: Ames Foundation, 2014).

5. Surrency, "Court's Place," 440–41; Linn, *Charter to William Penn*. Appendix A contains the "Compilation of the Laws and Ordinances Establishing the Several Courts of Judicature of the Province of Pennsylvania with an Introduction by Staughton George," 295–409. *See also* Thomas F. Gordon, *The History of Pennsylvania from Its Discovery by Europeans to the Declaration of Independence in 1776* (Philadelphia: Carey, Lea & Carey, 1829), 546–47.

6. Surrency, "Court's Place," 440–41, citing Linn, *Charter to William Penn*, 312–13.

7. Surrency, "Court's Place," 441.

8. Ibid., quoting J. Woodward in Chase v. Miller, 41 Pa. 403, 411 (1862).

9. Surrency, "Court's Place," 443–44.

10. Henry Thomas Dolan, "A Call to Remembrance," *Pennsylvania Bar Association Quarterly* 43 (1972): 432, 434. Attorney Dolan noted that James Wilson of Pennsylvania became a chief architect of the US Constitution and went on to serve as one of President George Washington's first appointees to the US Supreme Court. Of course, other colonies served as a model for the Framers of the US Constitution when they created a supreme court or court of appeals. For instance, Delaware created a "Supreme Court" in its constitution on September 21, 1776, seven days before Pennsylvania adopted its Constitution.

11. Gormley, "Overview of the Pennsylvania Constitution," 2. John Adams later wrote in his personal diary that he believed the secret resolution of May 1776 constituted the true act of independence, more so than the formal declaration two months later on July 4, 1776. Adams called it "the most important Resolution that was ever taken in America." John Ferling, *John Adams: A Life* (Oxford: Oxford University Press, 2010), 146.

12. The Pennsylvania Constitution of 1776 provided that "[t]he supreme executive power shall be vested in a president council" (Pa. Const. [1776], ch. II, § 3). The president was a member of the council, chosen annually; this official had little power. J. Paul Selsam, *The Pennsylvania Constitution of 1776: A Study in Revolutionary Democracy* (Philadelphia: University of Pennsylvania Press, 1936), 194–95. The Council of Censors was a novel body that was to meet every seven years "to determine whether the legislative and executive branches of the government have performed their duties as guardians of the people." Lewis H. Meader, "The Council of Censors," *Pennsylvania Magazine of History and Biography* 22, no. 3 (1898): 265–300.

13. Pa. Const. (1776), ch. II, § 23. The provision went on to state that judges were "capable of re-appointment at the end of that term, but removable for misbehavior at any time by the general assembly."

14. Selsam, *Pennsylvania Constitution*, 196–97.

15. Surrency, "Court's Place," 445–46.

16. Pa. Const. (1776), ch. II, § 27 concluded, "The style of all process hereafter in this state shall be, The commonwealth of Pennsylvania."

17. Surrency, "Court's Place," 444. He was assisted on the Supreme Court by Judges William A. Atlee and John Evans. After his term as chief justice, McKean became the governor of Pennsylvania from 1799 to 1807.

18. The Court was given civil jurisdiction, yet it remained unclear whether civil suits could be initiated there.

19. Surrency, "Court's Place," 442–43. Sometimes these trials took place in the county where the case originated, and sometimes (e.g., in cases involving capital offenses) they took place in the Court's seat in Philadelphia.

20. Ibid., 447, citing Act of February 24, 1806, sec. XI, 4 SM. L.272; 18 St. L., 61, 64. For a brief description, *see* Frank M. Eastman, *Courts and Lawyers of Pennsylvania: A History 1623–1923*, vol. 1 (New York: American Historical Society, 1922), 279–81.

21. Surrency, "Court's Place," 446.

22. Ibid., 451. Harrisburg became the state capital in October 1812.

23. Pa. Const. (1874), art. V, § 21.

24. Surrency, "Court's Place," 452.

25. Rosalind L. Branning, *Pennsylvania Constitutional Development* (Pittsburgh: University of Pittsburgh Press, 1960), 20; Pa. Const. (1790), art. V, § 2.

26. Branning, *Pennsylvania Constitutional Development*, 30; Pa. Const. (1838), art. V, § 2.

27. Thomas Raeburn White, *Commentaries on the Constitution of Pennsylvania* (Philadelphia: T. & J. W. Johnson, 1907), 316, 317n14.

28. Branning, *Pennsylvania Constitutional Development*, 77–86; Pa. Const. (1873), art. V, §§ 2, 15.

29. Pa. Const. (1968), art. V, §§ 1, 10. Section 1 provided for the UJS, Section 2 provided for the Supreme Court, and Section 10 provided for the supervisory and administrative authority that the Supreme Court had over the whole court system.

30. Pa. Const. (1968), art. V, §§ 3, 4.

31. 5 U.S. 137 (1803).

32. 2 Yeates 133 (Pa. 1796).

33. Ibid., 147 (citations omitted).

34. 12 S. & R. 330 (Pa. 1825).

35. Ibid., 340.

36. Ibid., 344–58 (Gibson, J., dissenting). For more on Gibson, *see* Stanley I. Kutler, "John Bannister Gibson and the 'Positive State,'" *Journal of Public Law* 4 (1965): 181–97; John Harrison, "The Constitutional Origins and Implications of Judicial Review," *Virginia Law Review* 84 (1998): 333–87.

37. Roger K. Newman and John Bannister Gibson, *The Yale Biographical Dictionary of American Law*, ed. Roger K. Newman (New Haven: Yale University Press, 2009), 219.

38. 1 Dall. 469 (Pa. 1789). *See* Paul Finkelman, "Human Liberty, Property in Human Beings, and the Pennsylvania Supreme Court," *Duquesne Law Review* 53 (2015): 453, 468–70. Alexander James Dallas was the first court reporter for Pennsylvania state cases and the US Supreme Court. The first four volumes of Dallas's reports are the same first four volumes of the *United States Reports*. Volume 1 contains only Pennsylvania court cases from 1754 to 1788. In volumes 2 to 4, Dallas added the US Supreme Court and Circuit Court cases from 1789 onward as well as the Pennsylvania court cases. Volume 5 of the *United States Reports* and onward contain no Pennsylvania cases. *See* Joel Fishman, "The Reports of the Supreme Court of Pennsylvania," *Law Library Journal* 87 (1995): 643–93. *See also* Morris L. Cohen and Sharon Hanby O'Connor, *A Guide to the Early Reports of the Supreme Court of the United States* (Littleton, Colo.: F. B. Rothman, 1995), 17–22.

39. 10 St. L. 67–73; 1 Sm.L. 492 (1780).

40. 41 U.S. 539 (1842).

41. *See also* Commonwealth ex rel. Johnson v. Holloway, 2 S. & R. 305 (Pa. 1816), pursuant to an earlier case protecting the child of a fugitive slave pursuant to the 1780 Act for the Gradual Abolition of Slavery.

42. *But see* Hobbs v. Fogg, 6 Watts 553 (Pa. 1847), in which the Court, per Chief Justice John Bannister Gibson, held that the Pennsylvania Constitution did not grant a "free negro or mulatto" the right to vote. For a recent study on fugitive slaves in south-central Pennsylvania, *see* David G. Smith, *On the Edge of Freedom: The Fugitive Slave Issue in South Central Pennsylvania, 1820–1870* (New York: Fordham University Press, 2013).

43. In re Application of Kilgore, 5 A. 872 (Pa. 1896).

44. 83 U.S. 130 (1872).

45. Hammer v. Dagenhart, 247 U.S. 251 (1918).

46. 260 Pa. 44 (Pa. 1918).

47. 22 A. 649 (Pa. 1891).

48. Commonwealth ex rel. Schnader v. Liveright, 161 A. 697 (Pa. 1932).

49. Kenneth G. Gormley, "A New Constitutional Vigor for the Nation's Oldest Court," *Temple Law Review* 64 (1991): 215, 219. The Kentucky Supreme Court, recognizing that Pennsylvania's Declaration of Rights served as the basis for the Kentucky Bill of Rights in its first constitution of 1792, stated in a landmark decision in 1993, "Decisions of the Pennsylvania Supreme Court interpreting like clauses in the Pennsylvania Constitution are uniquely persuasive in interpreting our own." Commonwealth v. Wasson, 842 S.W.2d 487, 492, 498 (Ky. 1992).

50. *See* Gormley, "New Constitutional Vigor," 215, 219. *See also* Commonwealth v. Campana, 314 A.2d 854 (Pa. 1974), *cert. denied*, 417 (Roberts, J.); Commonwealth v. Tate, 432 A.2d 1382 (Pa. 1981) (Roberts, J.); Commonwealth v. Bussey, 404 A.2d 1309 (Pa. 1979) (Eagen, C.J.); Commonwealth v. Triplett, 341 A.2d 62 (Pa. 1975) (O'Brien, J.).

51. 470 A.2d 457 (Pa. 1983) (adopting "automatic standing" rule under Article I, Section 8 of Pennsylvania Constitution, reversing prevailing rule under federal constitutional precedent).

52. 610 A.2d 36 (Pa. 1992) (holding that plaintiffs are entitled to jury trial in in rem article forfeiture actions pursuant to Article I, Section 6, notwithstanding federal precedent to contrary).

53. 586 A.2d 887 (Pa. 1991) (Cappy, J.) (rejecting federal "good faith exception to exclusionary rule" as matter of state constitutional jurisprudence).

54. *See* Thomas M. Hardiman, "New Judicial Federalism and the Pennsylvania Experience: Reflections on the Edmunds Decision," *Duquesne Law Review* 42 (2009): 503, 526.

55. *See generally* Thomas G. Saylor, "A Tribute to Chief Justice Castille and State Constitutional Law," *Duquesne Law Review* 53 (2015): 301–566.

56. 812 A.2d 591 (Pa. 2002) (finding that ordinance banning nude dancing in Erie violated free speech provision contained in Article I, Section 7 of the state Constitution).

57. 67 A.3d 1211 (Pa. 2013) (Castille, C.J.) (striking down state legislative reapportionment plan as violative of Article II, Section 16 of state Constitution, which mandated creating districts as nearly equal in population "as practicable").

58. 83 A.3d 901 (Pa. 2013) (Castille, C.J.) (invalidating several provisions of Act 13, which had sought to preempt local zoning laws as they applied to oil and gas exploration, as violative of environmental protection provision contained in Article I, Section 27 of state Constitution).

59. *See* Thomas G. Saylor, "Prophylaxis in Modern State Constitutionalism: New Judicial Federalism and the Acknowledged, Prophylactic Rule," *N.Y.U. Annual Survey of American Law* 59 (2003): 283–328; Thomas G. Saylor, "On the Nature of Judging," *Widener Law Journal* 20 (2011): 681–96; Thomas G. Saylor, "Power and Prerogative: Reflections on Judicial Suspension of Laws," *Widener Law Journal* 21 (2012): 259–84; Thomas G. Saylor, "Fourth Amendment Departures and Sustainability in State Constitutionalism," *Widener Law Journal* 22 (2012): 1–27; Thomas G. Saylor, "Death-Penalty Stewardship and the Current State of Pennsylvania Capital Jurisprudence," *Widener Law Journal* 23 (2013):1–46; Thomas G. Saylor, "Tribute to the Honorable Ronald D. Castille," *Duquesne Law Review* 53 (2015): 301–3.

60. *See, e.g.*, Commonwealth v. Zhahir, 751 A.2d 1153 (Pa. 2000) (embracing "plain touch" exception to warrant requirement under Pennsylvania constitutional law); Commonwealth v. Gary, 91 A.3d 102, 138 (Pa. 2014) (Saylor, J., concurring); Philadelphia v. Commonwealth, 838 A.2d 566 (Pa. 2003) (Saylor, J.) (finding that legislation seeking to reorganize Pennsylvania Convention Center violated single subject rule of Article III, Section 3); Commonwealth v. Laventure, 894 A.2d 109 (Pa. 2006) (Saylor, J.) (finding that criminal complaint and arrest warrant violated particularity requirement of Article I, Section 8); Commonwealth ex rel. Kearney v. Rambler, 32 A.3d 658 (Pa. 2011) (finding that federal felony offense to which defendant pleaded guilty was "infamous crime" pursuant to Article II, Section 7, regardless of how state legislative sought to categorize it); Commonwealth v. Batts, 66 A.3d 286 (Pa. 2013) (Saylor, J.) (holding that prohibition of "cruel punishments" in Article I, Section 13 did not necessitate a categorical ban on sentences of life imprisonment without parole for juvenile offenders, so long as age-related factors of Miller v. Alabama, 132 S. Ct. 2455 [2012] were considered).

61. *See, e.g.*, Applewhite v. Commonwealth, 54 A.3d 1 (Pa. 2012) (per curiam) (holding that state voter ID law, as implemented, was inconsistent with the right to vote under the Pennsylvania Constitution); Mesivtah Eitz Chaim of Boboy, Inc. v. Pike Co., 44 A.3d 3 (Pa. 2012) (Eakin, J.) (exploring constitutional meaning of "purely public charity" for purposes of real estate tax exemptions, pursuant to Article VIII, Section 2); In re Interest of JB, 107 A.3d 1 (Pa. 2014) (Baer, J.) (noting Sex Offender Registration and Notification Act violates juvenile offenders' due process reputational rights pursuant to Article I, Section 1); Commonwealth v. Molina, 104 A.3d 430 (Pa. 2014) (Baer, J.) (use of prearrest silence as substantive evidence of guilt violates nontestifying defendant's constitutional rights under Article I, Section 9 relating to self-incrimination); Commonwealth v. Nieman, 84 A.3d 603 (Pa. 2013) (Todd, J.) (Act 152, making myriad amendments to the Judicial Code, violates "single subject" rule of Article III, Section 3); Commonwealth v. Johnson, 86 A.3d 182 (Pa. 2014) (opinion by Chief Justice Castille, joined by Justices Saylor, Eakin, Baer, and Todd, holding that evidence seized by police incident to arrest based solely on invalid, expired warrant violated Article I, Section 8).

PART 1

The Structure and Powers of the Supreme Court

CHAPTER 1

(S)electing Judges in Pennsylvania

CHARLES L. BECKER AND

RUXANDRA M. LAIDACKER

[W]hen all is said, there is hardly one Frame of Government
in the World so ill design'd by its first Founders, that in good
hands would not do well enough; and Story tells us, the best in
Ill Ones can do nothing that is great or good.

—*The Frame of the Government of the
Province of Pennsilvania, in America* (1682)

The cradle of the oldest appellate court in the nation, Pennsylvania has engaged in a continuing democratic experiment of refining its judicial institutions since 1684. The earliest colonial laws intended "[t]hat all Courts shall be open, and Justice shall neither be sold, denied or delayed."[1] The same governing promise appears today in Section 11 of Pennsylvania's Bill of Rights.[2] Pursuit of this ideal created momentum from time to time to reconsider the method by which the several judicial officers who serve on the Commonwealth's trial and appellate benches come to office. This chapter chronicles the history of the process by which Pennsylvanians select members of the state's judiciary.

As described in the introduction, the Pennsylvania Supreme Court traces its heritage to the institutions of William Penn's colonial province of Pennsylvania. In 1681, Charles II of England granted William Penn by royal charter large land holdings in America as repayment for debts owed to Penn's father.[3] The charter of the province of Pennsylvania granted Penn power to establish a government and laws for the benefit of the province's inhabitants.[4] Penn provided for a General Assembly and a Provincial Council, whose members were elected.[5]

Penn also had explicit authority to establish courts and appoint judges, justices, magistrates, and other judicial officers.[6] The hearing and determination of appeals from any judgment made in the province were "reserve[ed]" to the king and the English judiciary.[7] Early documents offered little insight into Penn's plans for the province's courts, their forms, or their practices. Penn's personal legal troubles and incarceration in England, and the religious and political aspirations for the new colony he derived from those experiences, provided strong indications that Penn did not intend to replicate either the laws or the legal institutions and practices of that country.[8]

In practice, Penn charged Deputy Governor William Markham, who preceded him to Pennsylvania, with the task to "[e]rect Courts[,] make Sheriffs, Justices of the Peace & other requisite Inferiour officers that Right may be Done, the Peace Kept & all vice Punished without Partiallity according to the good laws of England."[9] In 1683, Penn and the General Assembly clarified the status of existing county courts (for counties now part of Delaware) and established new county courts in Philadelphia, Chester, and Bucks.[10] These courts had jurisdiction over civil and most criminal matters.[11] No efforts were made to create a supreme or appellate tribunal or to identify candidates for judicial appointment to such a court.[12] The court system so established did not have the capability to try capital felonies (like murder and treason) or to decide appeals in either civil or criminal matters.[13]

Yet before leaving England, Penn appointed William Crispin, the husband of his first cousin Rebecca Bradshaw, as the first chief justice of Pennsylvania. In October 1681, Penn informed Markham, recommending Crispin as one whose "skill, experience[,] Industry & Integrety are well Known to me, & perticulerly in Court keeping &c: so that it is my will & pleasure, that he be as cheif Justice to keep the seal, the Courts & Sessions; & he shall be accountable to me for it."[14] Whether Crispin would serve as chief justice of a supreme court was unclear. He died in late 1681 or early 1682, before he arrived in Pennsylvania and before he exercised any function of his office. On Crispin's death, Penn did not name a successor.[15]

In 1683, the General Assembly vested appellate authority in the governor and the Provincial Council. The assembly also empowered the council with exclusive original jurisdiction over manslaughter, murder, treason, and other serious crimes.[16] The notion of a Superior Provincial Court crystallized in 1684.

In March of that year, Penn proposed to the council a bill that would establish a Provincial Court. The bill gave authority to the proprietor of the province to appoint the five members of the Court, one of whom would be designated "first," or "pryor," judge.[17] The judges would ride circuit yearly.[18] The council approved the bill and sent it to the General Assembly for ratification at the meeting in New Castle in May 1684. Assembly representatives contested the wisdom of the proprietor appointing judicial officers but ultimately approved the creation of the court.[19]

The first men to serve on the Provincial Court were appointed from among Philadelphia's "merchant elite."[20] On August 19, 1684, Penn appointed Dr. Nicholas More as chief justice of the Provincial Court and four prominent Quakers as associate judges.[21] The Provincial Court judges were commissioned for two years, although none of the judges served their full terms.[22] Chief Justice More, for instance, was impeached less than a year after he was commissioned.[23] The Provincial Council commissioned other justices, but "[m]en with the requisite training and character to serve effectively as Provincial Court justices were scarce. Penn was particularly sensitive to the need for identifying and appointing men of great talent and reputation."[24]

Many of the powers of the Provincial Court and of the individual judges remained largely undefined and at the center of political power struggles between the General Assembly and the Provincial Council and religious power struggles between Quakers and Anglicans.[25] The composition of the Provincial Court changed often to reflect shifts in political power.[26]

By the beginning of the eighteenth century, the Provincial Court had been restructured several times in an effort to strengthen its role.[27] For instance, in October 1701, the General Assembly passed an act of comprehensive judicial reform, under which much of the appellate jurisdiction of the Provincial Council was shifted to a renamed Supreme Provincial Court.[28] The act called for a fixed number of judges—five, appointed by the governor.[29] The Crown—which had veto power over all colonial legislation—intervened to disallow the act in 1705.[30] This was followed by intense debate on the shape of Pennsylvania's judiciary over the next decade.[31] In 1706, Provincial Governor John Evans offered an ordinance that called for a Supreme Provincial Court that consisted of a chief justice and two or more associates.[32] The ordinance did not address judicial tenure, and decisions on compensation were left to the General Assembly.[33] The Court would decide cases taken up on writs of habeas corpus, certiorari, or error.[34] The General Assembly resisted powers on which Governor Evans insisted, including permitting the provincial governor to remove all judges at pleasure rather than only for misbehavior in office.[35] While the executive-legislative stalemate over control of the judiciary persisted, Governor Evans and his successor, Governor Charles Gookin, assembled the courts by proclamation.[36]

In 1710, a compromise was reached and a bill was passed.[37] Among other things, the act created a Supreme Court with power to hear appeals at law or in equity.[38] This Supreme Court would be composed of four judges appointed by the governor.[39] The system remained in place until 1713, when the 1710 act was also disallowed by the Crown.[40] The provincial government would subsequently restructure essential parts of this act.[41] Some suggest that the repeated failures to obtain the Crown's sanction for legislative acts devising a judicial system for the province were caused by the proprietor's displeasure with a bill that did not represent its interests.[42] Having returned to England, Penn died in 1718.[43]

In May 1722, the General Assembly adopted yet another judiciary act, which would be sanctioned by the Crown in 1727.[44] Many of its provisions remained law until the Revolution.[45] The Act of 1722 provided for a "Supreme Court of Pennsylvania."[46] The act stated "that there shall be three persons of known integrity and ability" appointed by the governor to be judges of the Supreme Court.[47] By later amendment, the number of justices was raised to four.[48] One of the appointees would be specially commissioned "chief justice."[49] Although theirs were lifetime appointments, with the exception of the Supreme Court justices, few of the commissioned judicial officers remained in office that long.[50] Some, like Benjamin Franklin, who served briefly on the trial court, recognized that doing the job well required specialized knowledge that he neither had nor was willing to spend time acquiring. Others were dissatisfied with the amount and reliability of compensation.

The Act of 1722 enumerated the powers of the Supreme Court: except in limited instances, the Court acted in cases on writ and exercised appellate jurisdiction over all inferior courts in criminal and civil cases more than fifty pounds in value; the Court had no original jurisdiction in civil cases.[51] In addition, the Act of 1722 provided for a role in which the Court "generally shall minister justice to all persons, and exercise the jurisdictions and powers hereby granted concerning all and singular the premises according to law, as fully and amply, to all intents and purposes whatsoever, as the justices of the court of King's Bench, common pleas and exchequer at Westminster, or any of them, may or can do."[52]

While the structure of the court system did not change again until 1776, the character of the judicial institutions continued to be challenged. The question of judicial independence from the executive branch came to the fore in the debates prompted by the Judiciary Act of 1759.[53] In that year, the General Assembly was acting to implement instructions from the Crown directing the governor and Provincial Council to hear appeals, and subsequent appeals would be taken to the Crown in Privy Council.[54] At the debate, Benjamin Franklin invoked William Penn's 1682 *Frame of Government of Pennsylvania* to argue in favor of an independent judiciary and the immediate issue of judicial tenure during good behavior: "It was certainly the import and design of th[e 1682 royal charter] grant, that the courts of judicature should be formed, and that the *judges* and officers that hold their commissions, in a manner not repugnant, but agreeable, to the laws and customs of England; that thereby they might remain free from the influence of persons in power, the rights of the people might be preserved, and their properties effectually secured."[55] But the proprietors successfully resisted the effort and, as a result, by some accounts, Pennsylvania's judiciary continued to be "a subordinate institution" of Pennsylvania's other branches of government.[56]

In 1776, the proprietorship of the Penns came to an end. A general convention was elected for the purpose of devising the first Constitution for the newly independent Commonwealth.[57] The convention met in Philadelphia on Monday, July 15, 1776, and elected Dr. Benjamin Franklin as president.[58] The task of drafting a Constitution was completed on September 28, 1776.[59] The chief architects of the document were Judge George Bryan and James Cannon, a college professor.[60] Bryan served both in the General Assembly and as a judge who, by some accounts, argued to preserve the existing provincial structures to which the assembly was the centerpiece.[61] Cannon, a "radical" with "a strong dislike for checks on the natural impulses of the people," provided most of the language of the 1776 Constitution.[62]

That document structured government around the legislative and executive branches, much as earlier founding documents had. Chapter II, which described the frame of government, provided for the "Supreme" legislative and executive powers to be vested "in a house of representatives" and "in a president and council," respectively.[63] Representative and council membership would be elective offices, filled annually.[64] The president and vice president would be chosen from among council members by the General Assembly and council members.[65] Each council member served, by virtue of his office, as "a justice of the peace for the whole commonwealth."[66]

Courts of justice were created in Philadelphia and in every county of the Commonwealth.[67] The president in council had "the power to appoint and commissionate judges."[68] The judges of the Supreme Court were commissioned for seven years, with the possibility of reappointment at the end of the term.[69] Eligible voters in each city and county would elect candidates for justices of the peace, and from among them, the president and council would commission persons for the offices for terms of seven years.[70] Judicial officers could be removed by the General Assembly for "misbehaviour at any time" and were liable for impeachment before the president and council.[71] Judges of the Supreme Court were prohibited from holding any other office; justices of the peace were prohibited from holding legislative office.[72] Salaries for judicial offices were fixed by the General Assembly.[73] The power to review the constitutionality of legislative and executive acts was reposed in a Council of Censors, elected and constituted every seven years.[74] The Council of Censors also had subpoena power and the authority to call a constitutional convention.[75]

This first Constitution went into effect on September 28, 1776, as soon as its drafting had been completed.[76] Although support for a change in government was substantial, by the end of October 1776, meetings were held at the State House to oppose the Constitution, which had not yet been submitted to the people for ratification.[77] A particular call was for the separation of powers, denoting the dependency of the judiciary on the General Assembly for their salaries, the duration of their commissions, and their removal from office.[78] One resolution explained that the legislature "may remove any judge from his office *without trial*, for anything they may please to call 'misbehavior.'"[79]

Various claims of legislative encroachment on the courts, such as attempting to overrule a judicial decision and granting divorces, were substantiated when, in November 1783, the first Council of Censors met in Philadelphia.[80] A report of the council was read to the House on January 2, 1784, which concluded that some articles of the Constitution of 1776 were defective and required amendment.[81] Among the proposed amendments were the reconstitution of the General Assembly as a bicameral legislature and the vesting of executive power in a governor.[82] The governor would have the power to appoint judges to serve during good behavior and with fixed salaries.[83] But on September 25, 1784, attempts to call a constitutional convention failed and the Council of Censors adjourned.[84]

By 1790, a second Council of Censors stood to be elected. An act proposed to the General Assembly in March 1789, however, brought the question of a constitutional convention to the people instead.[85] The measure passed the House, and members of the convention were elected at the general election of that year.[86] The members of the convention met in Philadelphia in November 1789. On December 21, 1789, the committee assigned to draft a document embraced the reforms suggested by the Council of Censors in 1783–84.[87]

The Constitution of the Commonwealth of Pennsylvania, ratified in 1790, laid the foundations of Pennsylvania's modern form of government. Notably, the Commonwealth's government was reconstituted, with a bicameral legislature and a governor exercising executive powers. Article V of the 1790 Constitution vested the judicial power of the Commonwealth in a Supreme Court, inferior courts, justices of the peace, and other courts that could be established by the legislature.[88] Judicial officers would be appointed by the governor to hold their offices for their lifetimes during "good behaviour."[89] The governor retained the authority to remove all judicial officers with the consent of the legislature.[90]

By the turn of the nineteenth century, however, dissatisfaction was growing, with aspects of the Constitution of 1790 viewed as undemocratic and conducive to patronage and corruption by the governor:[91] "It was openly charged that this broad power of patronage had formed the basis for re-election of governors."[92] In 1810, initial efforts at constitutional reform failed, and the concerns persisted for another quarter century.[93]

In 1835, the General Assembly submitted to a vote the issue of calling another constitutional convention, which was popularly approved by a narrow margin.[94] Members were elected and the convention assembled on May 2, 1837, lasting nearly seven months.[95] Conservative anti-Masons and Whigs captured a majority of the delegates—fifty-two and fifteen, respectively—while Democratic Republicans calling for a liberalization of the Constitution elected sixty-six candidates.[96]

Among chief reforms debated were the governor's powers of appointment, tenure of office, and the method of selecting judges.[97] A majority of the committee formed to address the article on the executive proposed a limited amendment by which the governor retained the power of appointing all state officers—with, however, the advice and consent of the Senate.[98] Thaddeus Stevens, chairman of the committee, authored a minority report that proposed the election of certain officers (prothonotaries, clerks of court, registers of wills, and recorders of deeds).[99] Others prepared minority reports generally limiting the purview of Senate involvement.[100] Although Democrats had long supported the election of judges, with a minority in the convention, they advanced the alternative with no success.[101] Their efforts at reform concentrated on limiting the tenure of judges.[102] The majority report supported continuing to provide for lifetime appointments on good behavior; the minority proposed ten-year terms for Supreme Court judges, seven-year terms for Common Pleas judges, and five-year terms for associate Common Pleas judges.[103] The debates centered on the importance of life tenancy to judicial independence and, as a counterweight, the accountability of judges to the people.[104]

The task of the convention was completed in February 1838, and the new Constitution was ratified by the electorate in a very close vote of 113,971 to 112,759.[105] The result was a partial overhaul of the judicial system. Notably, the 1838 Constitution provided that members of the Supreme Court, the Courts of Common Pleas, and any other courts established by law would be nominated and, with the consent of the Senate, appointed and commissioned by the governor.[106] Judges of the Supreme Court would serve "for the term of fifteen years, if they shall so long behave themselves well."[107] President judges of the Courts of Common Pleas would serve ten-year terms, and associate judges of the Courts of Common Pleas would serve five-year terms, on conditions of good behavior.[108] The Constitution also called for adequate compensation fixed by law, which would not be diminished during the judge's tenure in office.[109] These provisions regarding tenure and compensation were intended to foster judicial independence, and they remain part of our Constitution today.[110]

The 1838 Constitution remained the basic charter of the Commonwealth for the next thirty-six years, until January 1, 1874. In that period, it was amended four times, most notably in 1850. The 1850 amendment provided for the election of all judges in the Commonwealth.[111] Judges of the Supreme Court would be chosen by qualified electors of the Commonwealth at large for a term of fifteen years, the office to be held on good behavior.[112] The term limitations from the 1838 Constitution also continued for the inferior courts.[113] The amendment of 1850 provided for a removal process by the governor on the consent of two-thirds of each chamber of the legislature.[114] Any judicial vacancies resulting from death, resignation, or otherwise would be filled by the governor to continue until the first Monday of December following the next general election.[115]

The convention that drafted the 1874 Constitution focused on reforming the legislature, driven by distrust of that body and the growing influence of railroads and other corporations.[116] The structure of the judiciary was also crafted in some detail. Like its predecessor after the 1850 amendment, the 1874 Constitution provided for the election of judges.[117] The new Constitution fixed the number of judges on the Supreme Court at five, to hold the office for one term of twenty-one years.[118] The number of judges was increased to seven in 1909.[119] The first commissioned judge would be chief justice, succeeded to that office by the next commissioned judge.[120] This Constitution also abolished the office of associate judge of the Court of Common Pleas, which had permitted men without a legal education to serve as jurists, while increasing the number of judges on the Common Pleas bench.[121] Vacancies in judicial offices caused by death, resignation, or otherwise would be filled by appointment of the governor, to continue until the first Monday in January following the first general election occurring three or more months after the happening of such a vacancy.[122]

Selection of judges by election remains the law today, although efforts continue to be made to improve the system. For instance, in 1913, Pennsylvania briefly experimented with nonpartisan judicial elections. Legislation was passed that provided for candidates to be listed without party affiliation on ballots for the Supreme Court and Superior Court (the latter created by legislation in 1895).[123] However, because of continued partisan involvement in the electoral process, which undermined the law for practical purposes, the act was repealed in 1921 and partisan elections were reinstated.[124]

The idea of nonpartisan selection persisted and reemerged in the 1940s and 1950s. In 1957, the General Assembly created a commission on constitutional revision, chaired by the

Honorable Robert E. Woodside. In 1959, the Woodside Commission sent a report to the General Assembly and Governor William Scranton that called for the appointment of trial and appellate judges by the governor from a list submitted by a nominating commission.[125] At the end of a jurist's appointed term, the jurist would be eligible for either reappointment or retention in a nonpartisan up-or-down vote.[126] These recommendations were part of the so-called Pennsylvania Plan.[127] In 1963, Governor Scranton appointed a commission that proposed thirteen discrete amendments to the Constitution, among which was an endorsement of selecting judges by appointment.[128] Questions of reform relating to the judiciary were rejected by the electorate and deferred.

The next attempt to move away from judicial elections occurred in the late 1960s, against the background of significant modernization of Pennsylvania's basic charter. In 1967, the General Assembly called the latest constitutional convention, with the assent of Governor Raymond P. Shafer, after several necessary constitutional reforms failed to clear the legislature.[129] The convention that met in Harrisburg on December 1, 1967, consisted of eighty-eight Republicans and seventy-five Democrats.[130] Their task was limited to four areas of reform: the judiciary, state finance, local government, and legislative reapportionment.[131] Several proposals came out of the subcommittees, including one from the Pennsylvania Bar Association (PBA) to establish a Unified Judicial System (UJS) in Pennsylvania premised on Supreme Court rules.[132] The Supreme Court was explicitly referred to as the highest court of the Commonwealth, in which the "supreme judicial power" of the Commonwealth was reposed.[133]

The convention called for the "merit" selection of judicial officers.[134] At the primary election in 1969, the people were given the opportunity to replace the elective system with one of appointment by the governor from a list of qualified persons submitted to him by a Judicial Qualifications Commission.[135] Appointments did not require the consent of the Senate.[136] The Judicial Qualifications Commission would be a new body, composed of four nonlawyer electors appointed by the governor and three nonjudge members of the bar appointed by the Supreme Court.[137] No more than four members would be from the same party.[138] They would serve for terms of seven years.[139] Further, the convention called for reform of judges' tenure. One aspect was to standardize the terms of office to ten years for justices and judges and to six years for the minor judiciary.[140] Judges were eligible for retention at the expiration of the term.[141] The convention also recommended mandatory retirement at age seventy, with the possibility for continued service as a senior judge on appointment by the Supreme Court.[142]

These proposals were subject to a popular referendum in April 1968 and received wide support.[143] The question of judicial selection, which had been a most contested issue during the convention, was separately posed to the people in May 1969 and was rejected by a vote of 643,960 to 624,453.[144]

The 1968 Constitution created our modern judicial system. The implementation of the concept of a UJS remained for decades subject to concerns over funding.[145] Other concerns expressed themselves as renewed efforts to transcend partisan politics in the judicial selection process by adoption of a qualifications-driven appointment process. For instance, in 1981, former Supreme Court justice Thomas W. Pomeroy Jr. chaired the Committee to Study Pennsylvania's UJS, which recommended selection of Pennsylvania's appellate court judges only by the governor.[146] After an initial appointment for a term of two years, the jurists would then stand for a retention vote.[147]

Then in July 1987, Governor Robert P. Casey issued an executive order by which a Judicial Reform Commission was appointed to revisit questions surrounding the selection of judges in Pennsylvania, the financing of judicial campaigns, and others.[148] The commission was chaired by the Honorable Phyllis W. Beck (coauthor of chapter 12 in this book). In its report, the Beck Commission recommended a hybrid system in which the elective system would continue operating for trial courts, and an appointive method would be put into place for appellate judges.[149] The Beck Commission's report led to increased efforts over the next ten years in the General Assembly to adopt a constitutional amendment for appointive selection of appellate judges. Bills endorsing the appointive system have been repeatedly introduced in the General Assembly but have been unsuccessful.[150] As recently as January 2015, members of the House and Senate issued a joint resolution proposing constitutional amendments for the selection of appellate judges by appointment of the governor on recommendation of a nominating commission.[151]

Today, financing and the role of partisan politics in judicial campaigns continue to spur debate over the selection of judges in Pennsylvania. Whether these issues will drive additional innovation in the realm of judicial selection in the Commonwealth remains to be seen.

NOTES

Charles L. Becker is a partner at Kline & Specter, P.C., and a lecturer in law at the University of Pennsylvania Law School. Ruxandra M. Laidacker is an associate at Kline & Specter, P.C., and a former law clerk to Pennsylvania Supreme Court Chief Justice Ronald D. Castille.

1. "Laws Agreed Upon in England," ¶ V (London, 1682).
2. Pa. Const. art. I, § 11 (1967).
3. "Charter of the Province of Pennsylvania," ¶¶ 1–3 (London, 1681).
4. Ibid., ¶¶ 4–5.
5. Ibid., ¶ 4.
6. Ibid., ¶ 5.
7. Ibid.
8. G. S. Rowe, *Embattled Bench: The Pennsylvania Supreme Court and the Forging of a Democratic Society, 1684–1809* (Newark: University of Delaware Press, 1994), 22–24.
9. Ibid., 25.
10. Ibid., 27.
11. Ibid., xx.
12. Ibid., 24–25.
13. Ibid., 25.
14. Ibid., 26.
15. Ibid., 26.
16. Ibid., 27.
17. Ibid., 27.
18. Ibid., 27.
19. Ibid.
20. Ibid., 31.
21. Ibid., 28.
22. Ibid., 28, 31.
23. Ibid., 32.

24. Ibid., 33.

25. Ibid., 39–40, 44, 46.

26. Ibid., 40–41, 44.

27. Ibid., 36, 44–45.

28. Ibid., 48.

29. William H. Loyd, *The Early Courts of Pennsylvania*, University of Pennsylvania Law School Series no. 2 (Boston: Boston Book Company, 1910), 29.

30. Ibid., 30–31; Rowe, *Embattled Bench*, 52.

31. Rowe, *Embattled Bench*, 52.

32. Loyd, *Early Courts*, 31; Rowe, *Embattled Bench*, 53–54.

33. Scott D. Gerber, *A Distinct Judicial Power: The Origins of an Independent Judiciary, 1606–1787* (Oxford: Oxford University Press, 2011), 275.

34. Rowe, *Embattled Bench*, 53–54.

35. Ibid., 55.

36. Ibid., 55–56. For additional details about the struggle for control over the Pennsylvania judiciary between the legislative and executive branches, *see also* Thomas F. Gordon, *The History of Pennsylvania from Its Discovery by Europeans to the Declaration of Independence in 1776* (Philadelphia: Carey, Lea & Carey, 1829), 140–55, 161.

37. Rowe, *Embattled Bench*, 57; Gordon, *History of Pennsylvania*, 161.

38. Loyd, *Early Courts*, 31–32.

39. Ibid.

40. Ibid.; Gordon, *History of Pennsylvania*, 166–67.

41. Loyd, *Early Courts*, 33.

42. *See* Gordon, *History of Pennsylvania*, 140–55.

43. Gerber, *Distinct Judicial Power*, 275.

44. Loyd, *Early Courts*, 37–38.

45. Ibid.

46. 1 Smith Laws 131.

47. Ibid.

48. Loyd, *Early Courts*, 41.

49. 1 Smith Laws 131.

50. Loyd, *Early Courts*, 41.

51. Ibid.; *see also* Commonwealth ex rel. O'Hara v. Smith, 4 Binn. 117, 1811 WL 1551, *4 (Pa. 1811); Gordon, *History of Pennsylvania*, 548.

52. 1 Smith Laws 131. The Supreme Court's King's Bench powers are addressed in the next chapter by William S. Stickman IV. For a case discussing those powers, *see generally* In re Bruno, 101 A.3d 635 (Pa. 2014).

53. Gerber, *Distinct Judicial Power*, 277.

54. Ibid., 277n45.

55. Ibid., 277.

56. Ibid., 279.

57. Ibid., 281; Gordon, *History of Pennsylvania*, 529–30.

58. Pa. Const. (1776), pmbl.; Gordon, *History of Pennsylvania*, 539.

59. Pa. Const. (1776), pmbl.

60. Gerber, *Distinct Judicial Power*, 281.

61. Ibid.

62. Ibid.

63. Pa. Const. (1776), ch. II, §§ 2, 3.

64. Ibid., §§ 9, 19.

65. Ibid., § 19.

66. Ibid.

67. Ibid., § 4.

68. Ibid., § 20.

69. Ibid., § 23.

70. Ibid., § 30.

71. Ibid., §§ 22, 23, 30.

72. Ibid., §§ 23, 30.

73. Ibid., §§ 23, 30.

74. Ibid., § 47.

75. Ibid.

76. Gerber, *Distinct Judicial Power*, 283.

77. Ibid.

78. Ibid.

79. Ibid., emphasis in original.

80. Ibid., 283–84; Lewis Hamilton Meader, *The Council of Censors: Papers from the Historical Seminary of Brown University* (Providence, R.I.: Privately published, 1899), 23.

81. Meader, *Council of Censors*, 24.

82. Ibid.

83. Ibid.

84. Ibid., 28–31.

85. Ibid., 31–32.

86. Ibid., 32.

87. Ibid., 34.

88. Pa. Const. (1790), art. V, § 1.

89. Pa. Const. (1790), art. II, § 8; Pa. Const. (1790), art. V, §§ 2, 10.

90. Pa. Const. (1790), art. V, §§ 2, 10.

91. Rosalind L. Branning, *Pennsylvania Constitutional Development* (Pittsburgh: University of Pittsburgh Press, 1960), 21, 24.

92. Ibid., 24.

93. Ibid.

94. Ibid.

95. Ibid., 22–23.

96. Ibid., 22.

97. Ibid.

98. Ibid.

99. Ibid.

100. Ibid.

101. Ibid., 24.

102. Ibid.

103. Ibid.

104. Ibid., 24–25; *see also* Roy A. Schotland, "To the

Endangered Species List, Add: Nonpartisan Judicial Elections," *Willamette Law Review* 39 (2003): 1397, 1400.

105. Branning, *Pennsylvania*, 29, 31.
106. Pa. Const. (1838), art. V, § 2.
107. Ibid.
108. Ibid.
109. Ibid.
110. For an application of the current provision against diminishment of judicial compensation during the officer's tenure, *see* Stilp v. Commonwealth, 905 A.2d 918 (Pa. 2006).
111. Pa. Const. (1838) (amended 1850), art. V, § 2.
112. Ibid.
113. Ibid.
114. Ibid.
115. Ibid.
116. Branning, *Pennsylvania*, 37.
117. Pa. Const. (1874), art. V, § 2.
118. Ibid.
119. Pa. Const. (1874) (amended 1909), sched. no. 1, § 10.
120. Pa. Const. (1874), art. V, § 2.
121. Pa. Const. (1874), art. V, § 5.
122. Pa. Const. (1874), art. V, § 25.
123. Act 457 of July 24, 1913.
124. Acts 198 and 199 of May 10, 1921; Schotland, "Endangered Species," 1414.
125. Commission on Constitutional Revision, Report, 33–37 (1959).
126. Ibid.
127. Ibid.
128. Governor's Commission on Constitutional Revision, Report, §7 (1964); *see also* Pennsylvania Bar Association, Proposed New Judiciary Article (1964).
129. Act 2 of March 16, 1967.
130. Ibid.
131. Ibid.
132. Kerry L. Moyer and Mark W. Podvia, "A Citizens' Guide to a Modern Constitutional Convention," *Civic Research Alliance* (2009): 35, http://www.palwv .org/wp-content/uploads/2014/03/133 _CitizensGuideModernConstitutional Convention.pdf.
133. Pennsylvania Constitutional Convention,

"Constitutional Proposals Adopted by the Convention," April 23, 1968, http://www.duq.edu /Documents/law/pa-constitution/_pdf /conventions/1967-68/constitutional -prop.pdf. For additional explanation of this authority, *see* In re Bruno, 101 A.3d 635 (Pa. 2014).
134. Moyer and Podvia, "A Citizens' Guide to a Modern Constitutional Convention," 31–32.
135. Ibid.
136. Ibid., 32.
137. Ibid.
138. Pennsylvania Constitutional Convention, "Constitutional Proposals," 32.
139. Ibid.
140. Ibid.
141. Ibid., 33.
142. Ibid.
143. Robert E. Woodside, *Pennsylvania Constitutional Law* (Sayre, Pa.: Murelle Print, 1985), 558. For a description of the reasoning behind the proposed reforms, *see generally* Driscoll v. Corbett, 69 A.3d 197 (Pa. 2013). For a description of how the drafters described to the people the measure for ratification of a majority of these reforms at the April 23, 1968, primary election, *see* Friedman v. Corbett, 72 A.3d 255, 261 (Pa. 2013) (Castille, C.J., concurring).
144. Philip S. Klein and Ari A. Hoogenboom, *A History of Pennsylvania* (University Park: Pennsylvania State University Press, 1980), 523; Darren M. Breslin, "Judicial Merit-Retention Elections in Pennsylvania," *Duquesne Law Review* 48 (2010): 891, 897–900.
145. *See generally* Pennsylvania State Ass'n of Cty. Comm'rs v. Commonwealth, 52 A.3d 1213 (Pa. 2012).
146. The Committee to Study Pennsylvania's Unified Judicial System, Report, 81, 89–92 (1981). *See also* Breslin, "Judicial Merit-Retention," 901.
147. The Committee to Study Pennsylvania's Unified Judicial System, Report, 81, 89–92.
148. Governor's Judicial Reform Commission, Report, iv (1988).
149. Ibid., 147–48.
150. Breslin, "Judicial Merit-Retention," 903.
151. S. 44, 114th Cong. (2015–16); H.R. 1336, 114th Cong. (2015–16).

CHAPTER 2

The King's Bench Powers

WILLIAM S. STICKMAN IV

I. INTRODUCTION

No comprehensive work on the Pennsylvania Supreme Court is complete without an examination of the Court's King's Bench powers. Those powers have their foundation in the deepest history of the common law yet remain an important tool for the Court in the twenty-first century.

The very name "King's Bench powers" calls forth images of bewigged judges in ermine-lined scarlet robes dispensing judgment in some medieval English castle. Perhaps it should. The Pennsylvania Supreme Court predates the independence of the United States by nearly a century and has formally possessed the King's Bench powers since 1722. Moreover, the nature of the powers is based on the jurisdiction of the even more ancient royal courts of England. The jurisdiction of these courts developed over the course of centuries, from the very dawn of the common law.

Perhaps more than any other area of Pennsylvania law, an understanding of what is meant by the "King's Bench powers" and what they include requires an understanding of the historical development of those powers. This brief exploration of the King's Bench powers will, therefore, explore how the Supreme Court came to be vested with these powers nearly three centuries ago. It will show that the powers include three primary authorities: (1) plenary supervisory authority over the administration of all Commonwealth Courts and the practice of law, (2) the authority to review any action pending before any tribunal of this Commonwealth, and (3) the authority to exercise original jurisdiction over any matter of public importance arising in the Commonwealth. Finally, it will examine the development of the powers and real-life examples of where the Court exercised them in each of those areas.

II. CONSTITUTIONAL AND STATUTORY SOURCES OF THE KING'S BENCH POWERS

The King's Bench powers derive their name from the language of Section 502 of the Judicial Code.[1] The statute outlines the general powers of the Supreme Court, stating,

The Supreme Court shall have and exercise the powers vested in it by the Constitution of Pennsylvania, including the power generally to minister justice to all persons *and to exercise the powers of the court, as fully and amply, to all intents and purposes, as the justices of the Court of King's Bench, Common Pleas and Exchequer, at Westminster, or any of them, could or might do on May 22, 1722.* The Supreme Court shall also have and exercise the following powers:

1) All powers necessary or appropriate in aid of its original and appellate jurisdiction which are agreeable to the usages and principles of law.
2) The powers vested in it by the statutes, including the provisions of this title.[2]

Section 502 references a date, May 22, 1722, because it is nearly a verbatim reenactment of certain provisions of the Judiciary Act of 1722.[3] As such, these provisions predate all the state constitutions and are among the oldest laws still substantially in effect in this Commonwealth.

What type of authority does this cryptic statute confer? How broad of a grant of authority does it provide to the Court? These questions can be answered only by exploring what constituted the powers of "the justices of the Court of King's Bench, Common Pleas and Exchequer, at Westminster" on May 22, 1722.

III. THE POWERS OF THE ENGLISH COMMON-LAW COURTS

Justice Oliver Wendell Holmes wrote that "a page of history is worth a volume of logic."[4] This adage applies fully in our context because the Supreme Court's King's Bench powers can be understood only by appreciating the historical context—and the common-law courts—from which those powers arose.

A. The Court of King's Bench

The formal title of the Court of King's Bench was the court *coram ipso rege*, or "before the king himself."[5] This title reflects the origin of the Court as part of the *aula regia*, or the king's royal court—that is, his council of courtiers, advisors, and retainers.[6] Indeed, in the court's earliest history, the king himself, as the origin and source of justice, personally sat and dispensed justice.[7] Henry Bracton, the thirteenth-century judge and legal commentator, observed that "the King has many councils in which diverse types of action are decided and he himself takes possession of these councils, *such as the aula regia*."[8]

Because of its close relation with the person of the king, the Court of King's Bench did not have a regular place of sitting but rather followed the king's travels around England.[9] Accompanying the perambulating royal household, the court had ready access to the king's council for the determination of particularly difficult cases. Likewise, the king had ready access to the court, where he might occasionally join the judges and participate in the operation of the court particularly as his own.[10]

The court acquired a distinct character of a court of law by the thirteenth century and, beginning in 1234, started to keep its own records, the *Coram Rege* rolls.[11] This reflects the gradual development of the convention whereby the king ceded the power to decide cases in the King's Bench to the justices that he appointed to that court: "[T]hough the king himself used to sit in this court, and is still supposed so to do, he did not, neither by law is he empowered to, determine any cause or motion, but by the mouth of his judges, to whom he has committed his whole judicial authority."[12]

In his *Commentaries on the Laws of England*, William Blackstone provides a comprehensive summary of the powers and jurisdiction of the Court of King's Bench. Although Blackstone's *Commentaries* were published in 1765, forty-three years *after* the Pennsylvania Supreme Court had been invested with the powers of the Courts of King's Bench, Common Pleas, and Exchequer, there is no indication that the powers of those courts changed in any appreciable manner in those years. Moreover, Blackstone's *Commentaries* were foundational to the development of the American common law and, as such, provide insight into how the Pennsylvania Supreme Court has historically viewed its King's Bench powers.

Blackstone recognized that the Court of King's Bench was "the supreme court of common law in the kingdom."[13] He further observed, "The jurisdiction of this court is very high and transcendent. It **keeps all inferior jurisdictions within the bounds of their authority**, and may either **remove their proceedings** to be determined here, or **prohibit their progress below**. It superintends all civil corporations in the kingdom, it commands magistrates and others to do what their duty requires, in every case where there is no specific remedy. It **protects the liberty of the subject by speedy and summary interposition**. It takes cognizance both of criminal and civil causes; the former in what is called the crown-side or crown office; the latter in the plea-side of the court."[14] Blackstone pointed out that the Court of King's Bench "is likewise a court of appeal, into which may be removed by writ of error all determinations of the court of common pleas, and of all inferior courts of record in England."[15]

A century before Blackstone, Edward Coke, legal commentator and himself Chief Justice of the Court of King's Bench, described the powers of the Court in his treatise, *Institutes of the Laws of England*.[16] Coke described five general areas of the Court's jurisdiction:

1. "All pleas of the Crowne."[17]
2. "Regularly **to examine and correct all and all manner of errors in fact, and in law, of all the Judges and Justices of the Realm in their judgments, processe, and proceeding in the Courts of record** and not only in pleas of the Crowne, but in all pleas, reall and personall."[18]

3. "This Court hath not only jurisdiction to *correct errors in judicial pro-ceeding, but other errors and misdemeanours extra judicial tending to the breach of the peace or oppression of the subjects, or raising of fac-tion, controversy, debate, or any other manner of misgovernment so that no injury, either public or private, can be done*, but that this shall be reformed or punished in one Court or other by due course of law . . . *It granteth prohibitions* to Courts Temproall and Ecclesiastical, to keep them within their proper jurisdiction."[19]

4. "This Court may hold pleas by Writ out of the Chancery of all trespasses done vi & armis, of Replevins, of Quare impedit, &c."[20]

5. "This Court hath power to hold plea by Bill for debt, detinue, covenant, promise, and all other personall actions, ejections and the like, against any officer, minister or clerke of the Court."[21]

Finally, relative to the authority of the King's Bench to remove actions of inferior courts, Coke remarked, "And so supreme is the jurisdiction of this Court, that if any Record be removed into this Court, it cannot be remanded back, unless it be by Act of Parliament."[22]

To summarize, at the time the Pennsylvania Supreme Court was vested with the powers of the King's Bench, those powers included

- the power to superintend all other courts, including the ability to prohibit further proceedings therein and correct errors there rendered;
- the authority to remove a case from any court and immediately exercise jurisdiction over it;
- original jurisdiction over all crown pleas; and
- the authority to protect the liberty of the subject and grant timely vindi-cation of his or her rights.

As will be discussed further in the following sections, these powers—particularly the first two—are most frequently cited when Pennsylvania litigants invoke the King's Bench powers.

B. The Court of Common Pleas

The colloquial use of the term "King's Bench authority" when describing the inherent common-law powers of the Supreme Court makes it easy to forget that the 1722 Judiciary Act and its successors also vest the Court with the powers of the Court of Common Pleas. This court was an important part of the English system of jurisprudence and is a necessary area of exploration in examining the powers of the Supreme Court.

The Court of Common Pleas has its roots in 1178, when King Henry II appointed five judges to sit as a permanent court to hear all pleas arising under any royal writ.[23] The Court of Common Pleas was specifically mentioned in the Magna Carta. Significantly, the Magna Carta provided not only that the court be permanent but, unlike the King's Bench, that it be stationary: "The Common Pleas does not follow the King's court, but is to be held in a single, certain place."[24] That place was the palace of Westminster.[25]

The Court of Common Pleas' authority was to exercise jurisdiction over all civil actions.[26] As Blackstone explained, the Court "hear[s] and determine[s] all matters of law arising in civil causes, whether real, personal, or mixed and compounded of both."[27] Coke described the breadth of cases addressed by the court: "This Court is the lock and key of the Common Law in common pleas, for herein are reall actions whereupon fines and recoveries (the Common assurances of the Realm) do pass, and all other reall actions by original writ are to be determined, and also of all common pleas mixt or personall."[28]

The Court of Common Pleas exercised both original jurisdiction and appellate jurisdiction over such actions arising in the inferior courts.[29] A litigant could appeal a determination of the Common Pleas to the King's Bench by a writ of error.[30]

Above and beyond its role in deciding cases, Blackstone observed that the stationary nature of the Common Pleas led to it becoming the overseer of the legal profession—including legal education. He stated, "Which critical establishment of this principal court or common law, at that particular juncture and that particular place, gave rise to the inns of court in it's neighborhood; and thereby collecting together the whole body of the common lawyers, enabled the law itself to withstand the attacks of the canonists and civilians, who labored to extirpate and destroy it."[31]

C. The Court of Exchequer

The Court of Exchequer was one of the oldest centralized courts in the kingdom, being established by William the Conqueror.[32] It was, however, inferior in rank to both later creations—the King's Bench and the Court of Common Pleas.[33] While initially directed to the mundane tasks of ordering revenues and recovering the king's debts, it was nevertheless significant in that it developed into a court of both common law and equity.[34]

The common-law side of the Exchequer permitted subjects to sue one another for money damages based on a legal fiction that the plaintiff, being a tax debtor to the king, would be unable to pay unless he obtained the sought judgment.[35] In effect, this gave the Exchequer concurrent jurisdiction with the Common Pleas over most civil actions for money.

The Exchequer also possessed equitable jurisdiction. Blackstone observed that "[t]he court of equity is held in the exchequer chamber before the lord treasurer, the chancellor of the exchequer, the chief baron, and three puisne ones."[36] An appeal from a decision of the Exchequer was directed immediately to the House of Lords.[37] By the time of the 1722

Judiciary Act, the Exchequer had faded to a position of least prominence among the three common-law courts at Westminster—being surpassed on the law side by the Common Pleas and on the equity side by the Chancery.[38]

IV. THE SUPREME COURT OBTAINS KING'S BENCH POWERS

Our Supreme Court obtained the King's Bench authority only as a result of a decades-long struggle to develop a permanent and independent judiciary for the colony. From its institution in 1684 as the Provincial Court, the Court's jurisdiction had been periodically enlarged and contracted by a series of ad hoc bills governing the nascent colonial judiciary.[39] As time progressed and the population of the colony increased, so too did the need for some permanent guidance on the relative jurisdiction and interaction of Pennsylvania's courts.

As early as 1706, Pennsylvania's colonial governor, John Evans, sought to strengthen the Supreme Court and provide for its independence from both the office of the governor and the colonial assembly.[40] Governor Evans advocated for a bill that would provide the Supreme Court with the authority of the English Queen's Bench and the Court of Common Pleas.[41] The assembly, on the other hand, favored a more narrow statement of the Court's jurisdiction.[42] Ultimately, the governor and the colonial assembly were unable to reach agreement and a stalemate ensued, preventing any permanent resolution of the issue. Finally, in 1715, an "Act for erecting a Supreme or Provincial Court of Law & Equity" was passed, which gave the Supreme Court broad original jurisdiction over all matters "cognizable in any other court."[43] This bill was, however, disallowed by the Crown.[44]

Ultimately, the colonial authorities managed to pass the 1722 Judiciary Act. This act is generally significant in that it provided a permanent statement of the Court's jurisdiction.[45] It was this act that provided the King's Bench authority to the Court in a manner that remains essentially unchanged today. The act gave the Supreme Court the authority to issue all common-law writs[46] and sit in both original and appellate jurisdiction[47] and provided that it "[g]enerally shall minister justice to all persons, and exercise the jurisdictions and powers hereby granted concerning all and singular the premises according to law, as fully and amply, to all intents and purposes whatsoever, as the justices of the court of King's Bench, common pleas and exchequer at Westminster, or any of them, may or can do."[48] This language survives nearly unchanged in the current Judiciary Code, 42 Pa.C.S. §502.

In providing the Supreme Court with all powers of the Courts of King's Bench, Common Pleas, and Exchequer, the 1722 Judiciary Act conferred extremely broad powers on the Court. As explored previously, those powers included authority to exercise original jurisdiction over all criminal and civil actions at law as well as suits in equity. It also conferred the authority to hear appeals of lower courts and exercise general superintendency over lower courts. It also conferred, at least in theory, the less-defined authority to address extrajudicial situations "tending to the breach of the peace or oppression of the subjects, or raising of faction, controversy, debate, or any other manner of misgovernment so that no injury, either public or private, can be done."[49] These powers were not only conferred on the Supreme Court by reference in the 1722 Judiciary Act but also subsequently confirmed in a variety of statutory and constitutional provisions. The Court's enunciation of those powers developed on a case-by-case basis throughout the following centuries.

V. THE SUPREME COURT EXPLORES THE CONTOURS OF ITS KING'S BENCH POWERS

The Supreme Court's use and development of its King's Bench powers developed throughout the nineteenth century as the Court itself developed from its roots as a colonial court to a modern state supreme court. As early as 1803, the Court explained that it had jurisdiction to entertain an appeal from proceedings before a justice of the peace, even absent express statutory authority to do so. In *Burginhofen v. Martin*, the Court explained that "[t]o prevent gross injustice in a variety of instances, the power of reviewing the acts of inferior tribunals must necessarily be exercised by the Supreme Court."[50] In so holding, the Court explained that the King's Bench "is not ousted of its jurisdiction but by express words."[51]

Half a century later, in *Commonwealth v. Ickhoff*, the Court examined the meaning of its King's Bench authority in the context of the Court's appointment of one of its justices to preside over Oyer and Terminer[52] proceedings in place of a Common Pleas judge who had recused himself.[53] The Court explained that it had the authority to do so pursuant to the Judiciary Act of 1836, which, in turn, referred back to the Judiciary Act of 1722.[54] The Court observed that "our judicial institutions appear to have grown naturally out of prior institutions, whose jurisdiction is to be studied in the history of jurisprudence."[55] Exploring that history, the Court stated the following:

> The justices of the King's Bench are the supreme and general justices of the kingdom, these terms indicating both the order and extent of their jurisdiction; that they are the supreme and general justices of Oyer and Terminer and jail delivery, and conservators of the peace; and that they hold courts of Oyer and Terminer and jail delivery, not as ordinary justices do; that is by virtue of special commissions for that purpose; *but by virtue of their offices as justices of the King's Bench. These are inherent authorities of their office, and are not given to them by any writ, patent, or commission, as in the case of other judges.*[56]

As in the earlier *Burginhofen* case, the Supreme Court explained that it has the *inherent* authority pursuant to its King's Bench authority to exercise jurisdiction over cases independent of any express statutory grant of jurisdiction.

In *Commonwealth v. Balph*, the Court undertook a lengthy exploration of its authority to remove a pending case from a Court of Common Pleas for trial.[57] There, the defendant petitioned the Court to remove his case from the lower court because of the inability of the judge to be impartial.[58] The Court reiterated its King's Bench authority under the 1722 Judiciary Act and subsequent legislation and explored whether it had the ability to issue a writ of certiorari to the lower court to remove the case and assume jurisdiction. In doing so, the Court explored the extent of the common-law authority of the Court of King's Bench and stated that "[i]t possesses the inherent power of removing by certiorari the record and proceedings of any criminal case from the inferior courts at any stage of the proceedings."[59]

This trio of nineteenth-century cases demonstrates the Supreme Court's understanding that it possesses the inherent authority, through its King's Bench powers—and without express statutory grant—to entertain appeals from lower courts, exercise supervision over original jurisdiction proceedings in lower courts, and even remove a pending case from a lower court. These are the essential elements of the "basket" of authorities that constitute the current understanding of the King's Bench jurisdiction.

Two cases in the mid-twentieth century show the Court's continuing use and understanding of its King's Bench powers. In *In re Carbon County Judicial Vacancy*, the Court held that its King's Bench powers included the right to fill a Carbon County judicial vacancy by assigning the judge of a neighboring judicial district to act as a president judge in that county.[60] The Court's per curiam order/opinion cited the 1722 Judiciary Act conferring the King's Bench authority and held the following:

> It cannot be doubted that if in 1722, the occasion required such a course, the judges of the king's bench of England either could have presided over any other court of lower degree, or, if they had deemed it necessary so to do, could have sent another judge of proper rank to sit in such court. The lastmentioned [*sic*] power is the one here invoked, and we have no doubt of our right to exercise it. The authority of a tribunal in the relative position of the Supreme Court of Pennsylvania over other tribunals of less degree can be taken away only by express words or irresistible implication, and we have not thus been deprived of any of the general powers granted to this court by the thirteenth section of the act of 1722.[61]

In *Carpentertown Coal & Coke Co. v. Laird*,[62] the Court considered whether it had the authority to enter a writ of prohibition. One of the parties argued that the Supreme Court lacked the authority to do so because Article V, Section 3 of the Pennsylvania Constitution provided the Court with original jurisdiction "in cases of injunction where a corporation is a party defendant, of habeas corpus, of mandamus to courts of inferior jurisdiction, and of quo warranto as to all officers of the Commonwealth whose jurisdiction extends over the state, but shall not exercise any other original jurisdiction."[63] The Court responded to this argument, stating, "[T]he justification for the court's exercise of such power is to be found in the Act of May 22, 1722, which vested in the Supreme Court all the jurisdictions and powers of the three superior courts at Westminster, namely, the King's Bench, the Common Pleas and Exchequer. Inherent in the Court of King's Bench was the power of general superintendency over inferior tribunals, a power which was of ancient inception and recognized by the common law from its very beginning."[64] The Court explained that "[i]n the exercise of its supervisory powers over subordinate tribunals[,] the Court of King's Bench employed the writ of prohibition and such right and practice accordingly passed to the Supreme Court. The provision of the Constitution limiting original jurisdiction of the court did not affect the existence of this right."[65]

By the mid-twentieth century, the Court's King's Bench authority was well established to encompass three primary authorities: (1) supervisory authority over all lower tribunals in the Commonwealth, (2) discretionary immediate jurisdiction over any case, and (3) authority to remove cases pending in lower tribunals. The Court has used, and continues to use, these authorities in a variety of interesting cases, all with the ultimate aim of the efficient and just resolution of cases and the uniform administration of justice.

Finally, the 1967–68 constitutional convention considered the structure and power of the judicial branch and the Supreme Court. The convention proposed current Article V, Section 2, which provides that the Court "shall be the highest court of the Commonwealth and in this court shall be reposed the supreme judicial power of the Commonwealth." Moreover, the Court "shall have such jurisdiction as shall be provided by law."[66] The delegates confirmed that they intended the Supreme Court to continue to possess the powers that it had hitherto exercised, including the King's Bench authorities: "[The proposed amendment] deals with the jurisdiction of the Supreme Court of the State and you will notice on the proposal that the Supreme Court is granted such jurisdiction as shall be provided by law. In the schedule to the proposal it also gives to the Supreme Court the power it now has. This is a point I believe we have to consider, that the Supreme Court will have the kingsmen's power and this has been agreed to by counsel and by the Chairman of the Judiciary Committee."[67]

As a result, the King's Bench authority survived the 1968 constitutional amendments unscathed. Indeed, the statutory revisions of the Judicial Code following the amendments retain at Section 502 the King's Bench authority nearly verbatim from the 1722 legislation.

VI. RECENT EXAMPLES OF THE COURT'S EXERCISE OF ITS KING'S BENCH POWERS

The Supreme Court's King's Bench powers are not just a historic curiosity for academic study. Rather, they continue to present the Court and litigants with an effective tool for seeking timely review of issues of great importance. Cases since the 1968 constitutional convention, where the Court used its King's Bench powers, illustrate their continued usefulness and importance.

In 1992, the Court used the powers to help resolve a transit strike that had caused considerable public disruption in Allegheny County.[68] On March 16, 1992, the union representing the Port Authority of Allegheny County's drivers went on strike. By the end of March, the City of Pittsburgh sought to intervene in the dispute and obtain an injunction against the strike due to the hardship that it posed to the citizens of Pittsburgh and Allegheny County.[69] Pittsburgh Mayor Sophie Masloff filed a petition with the Supreme Court to exercise its King's Bench powers to find that the city had standing to seek an injunction.[70] The city chose to seek relief under the King's Bench powers because of the immediate impact that the strike was having on the city. Indeed, "there were some very sad, some scary and some almost tragic stories evolving from this bus strike."[71]

The Supreme Court unanimously agreed to exercise immediate jurisdiction over the matter and determined that the city did have standing to intervene in the strike.[72] The Court referred the matter to the Commonwealth Court for expedited proceedings and disposition.[73] The Commonwealth Court immediately assigned the matter to a judge who, on April 10, 1992, granted permanent injunctive relief and ordered the Port Authority workers to end the strike.[74] This use of the King's Bench powers enabled the Supreme Court to avoid protracted litigation and effectuate a swift resolution of a matter of immediate public importance.

More recently, the Court's exercise of its King's Bench powers in *In re Interbranch Commission on Juvenile Justice*[75] provides another example wherein the Court granted immediate review of a matter of great public importance. The case arose from the Commonwealth's official inquiry into the tragic "kids for cash" scandal, which investigated allegations that certain judges in Luzerne County were unnecessarily placing children in juvenile detention centers in exchange for kickbacks. The Interbranch Commission on Juvenile Justice was constituted to investigate the misconduct and the response to the allegations of misconduct. As part of its investigation, the commission issued subpoenas for testimony of the counsel of the Judicial Conduct Board (JCB) and for records of complaints made to the JCB regarding the conduct of the implicated jurists and the board's response to those complaints.[76] The subpoena was issued on November 4, 2009, for testimony at a hearing scheduled for November 9, 2009.[77] The JCB took the position that the requested testimony and documents would violate the constitutional privilege set forth at Pa. Const. art. V, §18(a)(8), as well as the deliberative process privilege and the attorney client privilege.[78]

In light of the importance of the subject matter and the short time frame, the JCB filed an emergency application asking the Supreme Court to exercise its King's Bench jurisdiction and grant immediate review. The Court granted the request[79] and allowed in part and denied in part the relief sought by the board. A separate opinion by Justice Baer concurring in part and dissenting in part summed up the rationale of the Court's exercise of its King's Bench jurisdiction: "I concur in the invocation of this Court's King's Bench powers, recognizing the need for expediency and efficiency in resolving any disputes, current or future, between the Judicial Conduct Board (JCB) and the Interbranch Commission on Juvenile Justice (ICJJ)."[80]

In light of the importance of the subject matter to the Commonwealth's citizenry and the short time frame posed by the ongoing investigation into the judicial misconduct, the Court's exercise of immediate review provided a definitive resolution to the dispute without requiring the proceeding to wend its way through typical litigation channels.

In addition, the Court's *ability* to exercise immediate jurisdiction over a matter of importance can clear up any doubt that would otherwise exist as to the Court's invocation of its jurisdiction. In *The Pennsylvania Gaming Control Board v. City Council of Philadelphia*,[81] the Court reviewed the actions of the city, which permitted a referendum as to whether to permit gaming facilities within certain areas of Philadelphia for which the Pennsylvania Gaming Control Board had already granted licenses for the construction and operation of casinos.[82] The Court undertook its review of the case pursuant to a provision of the Gaming Act, which, it held, conferred on the Court exclusive jurisdiction of the matters in question.[83] In light of strong opposition from Philadelphia to the Court's exercise of original jurisdiction, the Court removed any doubt as to the legitimacy of its review by stating, "Although we have concluded as a matter of statutory construction that §1506 vests this Court with jurisdiction over Petition I, we would be remiss in failing to note that this matter also clearly merits the invocation of our King's Bench powers.... Petition I concerns the Gaming Act, a statute that has widespread importance, and one that has generated and continues to generate substantial public attention."[84]

The Court's King's Bench powers continue to provide it with all the authority necessary to oversee and administer the judicial system of the Commonwealth. In *In re Merlo*,[85] the Court invoked its King's Bench powers to affirm the interim suspension of a Magisterial District judge. The JCB had filed charges against the district judge, charging her with violating numerous provisions of the Rules Governing the Standards of Conduct of Magisterial District Judges.[86] After the JCB filed charges, the Supreme Court entered an order suspending the district judge until further order of the Court. The district judge petitioned to strike the suspension, arguing that the Court had no authority under the Constitution to issue interim suspensions but could only review decisions of the Court of Judicial Discipline (CJD), a separate body created to adjudicate cases involving allegations of judicial misconduct.[87]

The Court dismissed the petition, explaining that it has plenary authority over the administration of the judicial system: "The Pennsylvania Constitution provides that this Court shall exercise general supervisory and administrative authority over all the courts. This is a broad authority. This Court is entrusted with safeguarding the integrity of the judicial system; even the appearance of judicial impropriety can be cause for exercise of our King's Bench jurisdiction."[88]

The Court has also recently held that its King's Bench authority extends to resolving disputes within a Court of Common Pleas about judicial assignments[89] and that the Court has the inherent authority to appoint two of its justices to oversee the budgetary restructuring and administrative reformation of a Court of Common Pleas.[90] Thus, in addition to conferring on the Court the authority to exercise plenary jurisdiction over cases of importance, the King's Bench powers also give it broad administrative oversight of the entire judicial system of the Commonwealth.

Finally, the Supreme Court provided a magisterial examination of the contours of its King's Bench powers in the case *In re Magisterial District Judge Mark K Bruno*.[91] There, the Court held that the King's Bench powers provide plenary supervisory authority over the judiciary—and jurists. As such, even though the CJD has the constitutional jurisdiction to discipline jurists, the Supreme Court *also* possesses that authority and, to the extent that an order of the Supreme Court conflicts with that of the CJD, the Supreme Court's determination must control.[92] In other words, not only did the creation of the JCB and CJD not divest the Supreme Court of jurisdiction over the discipline of a jurist; the Supreme Court's jurisdiction and disciplinary authority will supersede any action by the other bodies.[93] The Court explained, "From its adoption by the Commonwealth's colonial government, the power of the King's Bench was intended to be supreme and general, and was understood to transcend forms of procedure and requirements of action upon particular writs. Such a broad articulation of the King's Bench power obviously admits the use of the Court's supervisory authority to inquire into issues affecting the lower courts and to suspend jurists, where that remedy is deemed necessary and appropriate."[94]

Only months after the *Bruno* decision, the Court called on its King's Bench powers to suspend one of its own members on allegations of misconduct, another example of the broad scope of the powers.[95]

VII. CONCLUSION

For nearly three hundred years, the Pennsylvania Supreme Court has been vested with the ancient powers of the great common-law courts of England. These powers have served and continue to serve as a basis on which the Court can efficiently and effectively fulfill its role as the head of Pennsylvania's judicial branch. They also provide litigants and the Court with an efficient means to resolve matters of great public importance. As the Court moves ahead in its fourth century of existence, the King's Bench powers will continue to serve as important tools in its arsenal of justice.

NOTES

William S. Stickman IV is a partner at Del Sole Cavanaugh Stroyd LLC and a former law clerk to Pennsylvania Supreme Court Chief Justice Ralph J. Cappy (2006–7).

1. 42 Pa.C.S. § 502.
2. Ibid.
3. *See* 1 Smith Laws 140 (1810).
4. New York Trust Co. v. Eisner, 256 U.S. 345, 349 (1921).

5. William Blackstone, *Commentaries on the Laws of England*, 1st ed., vol. 3 (Oxford: Clarendon Press, 1765), 41. The translation of the Latin term is the author's.

6. Ibid.

7. Ibid.

8. "Habet Rex plures Curias in quibus diversae actions terminantur, et illarum curiarum habet unam propriam, sicut aulam regiam, et jusiciarios capitals qui proprias gaufas regias terminant, et aliorum omnium, per querelam, vel per privilegium, sive libertatem." Henry Bracton, Lib. 3, cap. 7, fol. 105(b), cited by Edward Coke, *The Fourth Part of the Institutes of the Laws of England*, 1st ed., vol. 4 (London: M. Flesher, 1658), 70. The translation of the Latin phrase is the author's.

9. Ibid.

10. Arthur R. Hogue, *Origins of the Common Law* (Bloomington, Ind.: Liberty Fund, 1986), 158.

11. Ibid.

12. Blackstone, *Commentaries*, 41. Blackstone observed that King James I (r. 1603–25) sat in person in the King's Bench "but was informed by his judges that he could not deliver an opinion."

13. Ibid.

14. Ibid., 42, emphasis added.

15. Ibid., 43.

16. *See* Coke, *Fourth Part*, 70–77.

17. Ibid., 71.

18. Ibid., emphasis added.

19. Ibid., emphasis added.

20. Ibid. Trespass "vi & armis" was a common-law form of action for damages resulting from intentional injury to a person or property. Bryan A. Garner, *Black's Law Dictionary*, 7th abr. ed. (Eagan, Minn.: West Publishers, 2000), 1221.

21. Ibid.

22. Coke, *Fourth Part*, 73.

23. Hogue, *Origins*, 153.

24. "Communia placita non sequantur curiam regis, sed teneantur in alioquo loco certo." Blackstone, *Commentaries*, 38 (citing Magna Carta, ch. 11, author's translation).

25. Hogue, *Origins*, 153.

26. Ibid.

27. Blackstone, *Commentaries*, 40.

28. Coke, *Fourth Part*, 99.

29. Blackstone, *Commentaries*, 40. The inferior courts included the various county courts. Ibid., 35–36.

30. Ibid., 40.

31. Ibid., 39.

32. Ibid., 43.

33. Ibid.

34. Ibid.

35. Ibid., 45.

36. Ibid., 44.

37. Ibid., 46.

38. Ibid. *See also* Hogue, *Origins*, 153.

39. G. S. Rowe, *Embattled Bench: The Pennsylvania Supreme Court and the Forging of a Democratic Society, 1684–1809* (Newark: University of Delaware Press, 1994), 30–46.

40. Ibid., 52–55.

41. Ibid., 53. The Court is alternately referred to as the "King's Bench" or "Queen's Bench," depending on the gender of the English monarch. In 1706, Queen Anne was the reigning monarch.

42. Ibid.

43. Ibid., 58.

44. Rowe, *Embattled Bench*, 58.

45. William H. Loyd, *The Early Courts of Pennsylvania*, University of Pennsylvania Law School Series no. 2 (Boston: Boston Book Company, 1910), 93.

46. Ibid., 95.

47. Ibid.

48. Ibid.

49. Coke, *Fourth Part*, 71.

50. 3 Yeates 479, 1803 WL 763 (Pa. 1803).

51. Ibid., n. a1. The Court referred to the BR (Bench Regis; i.e., King's Bench).

52. The court of oyer and terminer handled common-law criminal proceedings held in the Courts of Common Pleas until the Constitutional reform of 1968.

53. 33 Pa. 80 (1859).

54. Ibid.

55. Ibid.

56. Ibid., emphasis added.

57. 3 A. 220 (Pa. 1886).

58. Ibid., 222. The Court pointed out that, inter alia, the Common Pleas judge might be unable to serve impartially because of "excitement and prejudice" against the defendant in Warren County.

59. Ibid., 226.

60. 141 A. 249 (Pa. 1928). The vacancy was created by the death of the sitting president judge, the only judge from that judicial district.

61. Ibid., 303 (internal citations omitted).

62. 61 A.2d 426 (Pa. 1948).

63. Ibid., 427–28.

64. Ibid., 428 (internal citations omitted).

65. Ibid. The Court further explained that the writ of prohibition is not even, per se, an exercise of either original or appellate jurisdiction but rather a tool used in the Court's supervisory authority to ensure that lower courts stay within their own authority.

66. Pa. Const. art. V, § 2(c).

67. Debates of the Pennsylvania Constitutional Convention 1967–68, vol. 2, 1457, http://www.duq.edu/academics/gumberg-library/pa-constitution/historical-research/constitutional-convention-1967-1968.

68. Jonathan D. Silver, "How the '92 Transit Strike Ended," *Pittsburgh Post-Gazette*, November 23, 2008, http://www.post-gazette.com/news/transportation/2008/11/23/How-92-transit-strike-ended/stories/200811230263.

69. Ibid.

70. Ibid. Specifically, the city invoked the Court's Extraordinary Jurisdiction under 42 Pa. C. S. § 726. *See* Masloff v. Port Auth. of Allegheny Cnty., 613 A.2d 1186 (Pa. 1992). As explained previously, although separately codified, the authority of the Court to exercise immediate jurisdiction over any matter pending in the Commonwealth stems from and is in the nature of the King's Bench powers.

71. Silver, "How the '92 Transit Strike Ended," quoting Joseph Sabino Mistick, a Duquesne University School of Law professor who had served as an advisor to Mayor Masloff and was the architect of the strategy to invoke the Court's King's Bench powers.

72. Masloff, 613 A.2d at 1187–88.

73. Ibid., 1188.

74. Ibid.

75. 988 A.2d 1269 (Pa. 2010).

76. Ibid., 1270–71.

77. Ibid.

78. Ibid., 1271.

79. Ibid., 1270.

80. Ibid., 1283.

81. 928 A.2d 1255 (Pa. 2007).

82. Ibid., 1258–59.

83. Ibid., 1263–64.

84. Ibid., 1264n6.

85. 17 A.3d 869 (Pa. 2011).

86. Ibid., 870.

87. Ibid., 871.

88. Ibid.

89. In re Assignment of Judge Bernard J. Avellino, 690 A.2d 1138 (Pa. 1997).

90. In re Petition of Hon. Edward Blake, 593 A.2d 1267 (Pa. 1991).

91. In re Bruno, 101 A.3d 635 (Pa. 2014)

92. Petitioner Bruno had argued that the 1993 amendment to the Pennsylvania Constitution (Article V, Section 18) creating the two-tiered Judicial Conduct Board and Court of Judicial Discipline placed exclusive jurisdiction over the discipline of judges in those tribunals, divesting the Supreme Court of the authority to discipline jurists. Bruno conceded that the Supreme Court retained administrative authority but claimed that discipline had been carved out of administration.

93. The In re Bruno decision makes absolutely clear that even though one of the Court's traditional, common-law King's Bench powers has been codified by the Constitution or statute, the ultimate genesis of that authority is the common-law power—not the codification. *See* Bruno, 101 A.3d at 666–69.

94. Ibid., 679.

95. In re Mr. Justice Seamus P. McCaffery of the Supreme Court of Pennsylvania, No. 430 Judicial Administration Docket (October 20, 2014).

CHAPTER 3

The Power of Rulemaking

RENÉE COHN JUBELIRER, ROBERT L. BYER,

AND MEREDITH E. CARPENTER

I. INTRODUCTION

Pennsylvania procedural law underwent a major change with the ratification of the 1968 amendments to Article V of the Pennsylvania Constitution. Before the 1968 constitutional revision, procedural law in Pennsylvania was governed by a combination of legislatively enacted statutes and procedural rules promulgated by the Supreme Court. But, as was the case in the federal system, statutes controlled over court rules in the event of any conflict.[1]

For many years, there was a growing national recognition, spurred by Roscoe Pound and other reformers, that necessary or desirable procedural reform required that the judiciary have primary responsibility for judicial procedure, with legislation being relegated a more minor role.[2] These reformers believed that because court procedures are inherently matters that affect the courts, separation of powers requires that the legislature not be able to impose "a strait-jacket of statutory procedure" on the courts.[3] They further believed that vesting courts with the power to control their own procedure would ensure a "simple effective procedure," which could be continually and gradually reshaped in response to changing practice, rather than having to wait for legislative intervention if the legislature were the holder of this power.[4] The reformers also saw an advantage in vesting the courts with procedural rulemaking power because they believed that when the judiciary is in control of procedure, it will tend to elevate substantive law over procedure, as those who create the procedure are clear on how that procedure should be applied and do not need to devote resources to its interpretation.[5]

At that time in Pennsylvania, members of the bar particularly desired "autonomy in court administration," believing that court administrative functions should "lie solely in the hands of the courts themselves," outside of legislative control.[6] This desire for "judicial administrative independence from the executive branch"[7] motivated the 1968 Pennsylvania constitutional convention to adopt what now is Article V, Section 10(c) of the Constitution,[8] which provides the following:

The Supreme Court shall have the power to prescribe general rules governing practice, procedure and the conduct of all courts, justices of the peace and all officers serving process or enforcing orders, judgments or decrees of any court or justice of the peace, including the power to provide for assignments and reassignment of classes of actions or classes of appeals among the several courts as the needs of justice shall require, and for admission to the bar and to practice law, and the administration of all courts and supervision of all officers of the Judicial Branch, if such rules are consistent with this Constitution and neither abridge, enlarge nor modify the substantive rights of any litigant, nor affect the right of the General Assembly to determine the jurisdiction of any court or justice of the peace, nor suspend nor alter any statute of limitation or repose. All laws shall be suspended to the extent that they are inconsistent with rules prescribed under these provisions.

This constitutional provision grants the Supreme Court the exclusive power to adopt rules regulating practice and procedure and to suspend statutes that are inconsistent with those rules. In granting this power to the Supreme Court, the constitutional revision spurred a shift in the understanding of separation of powers as between the legislative branch and the judiciary, recharacterizing procedural rules not as law, within the sphere of the legislature, but as judicial matters, within the sphere of the courts.[9]

The 1968 amendments thus resulted in significant changes, including the establishment of a statewide practice and solidification of the supremacy of rules over statutes. Prior to 1968, the General Assembly had granted rulemaking authority to the judiciary. Through the Enabling Act of 1937,[10] the Supreme Court had procedural rulemaking authority for civil actions, and procedural rules promulgated by the Supreme Court had the full force of law.[11] However, before the 1968 revision, it was not clear whether this power was inherent in the courts or solely resulted from the statutory grant.[12] While prior case law had overruled certain laws that affected judicial rules, finding them to unconstitutionally infringe on the judiciary as a matter of separation of powers,[13] the 1968 amendments clarified the primacy of the judiciary in making procedural rules, basing the source of this authority on the Constitution rather than a statute.[14] According to some, this has resulted in Pennsylvania's Supreme Court having more power than any other state supreme court in the United States.[15]

II. THE ROLE OF STATUTES AND THE SUPREME COURT'S EXERCISE OF POWER TO SUSPEND LAWS

As indicated, the ratification of the revisions to the Pennsylvania Constitution in 1968 radically changed the structure of Pennsylvania's judicial system and the Supreme Court's authority over rulemaking. Faced with the question of who should reign supreme over matters of procedure and practice, the judiciary or the legislative branch, Pennsylvania chose the Supreme Court. In eliminating the need for enabling legislation, "the Pennsylvania Constitution gives the state's supreme court exclusive power to establish rules of procedure for state courts," and "the legislature . . . is without power to control procedure."[16] The Supreme Court has interpreted its constitutional rulemaking authority as exclusive, ensuring that no procedural and evidentiary rules in Pennsylvania can be promulgated or amended without the Supreme Court's express approval.

Pennsylvania's state interbranch balance is the opposite of the federal balance, and the 1968 revision represented Pennsylvania breaking with the federal model of how procedural rules are promulgated.[17] Under the US Constitution, Congress is vested with ultimate federal rulemaking authority, which it has delegated to the courts through the Federal Rules Enabling Act as amended in 1988[18] and the Civil Justice Reform Act of 1990. In this statutory authorization, however, Congress has retained substantial legislative authority over procedural rulemaking. Unlike in Pennsylvania, where the Supreme Court has exclusive *constitutional* rulemaking authority, in the federal system, the US Supreme Court only has *statutory* rulemaking authority under the Rules Enabling Act. While the Pennsylvania Supreme Court's rules are final and binding, after the US Supreme Court promulgates rules, Congress has the power to reject, modify, or defer the pending rules.[19] Congress asserted this power with respect to the Federal Rules of Evidence, refusing to allow them to go into effect after they were approved by the Supreme Court in 1973 until Congress made significant changes and enacted them as legislation.[20]

The experience with the Federal Rules of Evidence demonstrates how the allocation of rulemaking power between the judiciary and the legislature implicates important issues of judicial independence and the separation of powers and how it can create tension between the legislative and judicial branches of government. In Pennsylvania, the Supreme Court has the power to suspend statutes enacted by the General Assembly that interfere with its rulemaking authority.[21] Indeed, the Supreme Court has described Article V, Section 10(c) as imposing on the Court "an *affirmative* obligation . . . to suspend any statute which is inconsistent with pre-existing procedural rules promulgated by this Court."[22]

While Article I, Section 12 of the Pennsylvania Constitution states that the authority to suspend laws is reserved to the legislature,[23] the Pennsylvania Supreme Court has concluded that its exclusive authority under Article V, Section 10(c) of the Pennsylvania Constitution to prescribe rules governing court practice, procedure, and conduct[24] also authorizes it to suspend "[a]ll laws . . . to the extent that they are inconsistent with rules prescribed under" that provision.[25] The Supreme Court has opined that laws infringing on the Court's exclusive authority to enact procedural rules represent an attempt by the legislature to intrude on the essential functioning of the judiciary and that such "intrusion[s] into that power must be viewed with the greatest skepticism."[26] Thus the Supreme Court has suspended laws (1) requiring the Court and other judicial agencies to comply with

Section 1703 of the Public Agency Open Meeting Law[27] when meeting to consider promulgating or amending court procedural rules,[28] (2) setting rates for prejudgment interest that differed from the Pennsylvania Rules of Civil Procedure,[29] (3) establishing procedures for filing medical malpractice actions,[30] (4) creating new procedures for courts to follow in the administration of capital cases,[31] (5) establishing reporting and disclosure requirements for lobbyists,[32] (6) setting forth requirements that an attorney must certify that an action is not frivolous,[33] and (7) restricting former government attorneys from practicing before their former agencies for a period of time.[34]

Still, the Supreme Court has recognized that its suspension power is not absolute, because its authority extends only to "procedural" rules and not "substantive" rules.[35] While the Supreme Court may promulgate procedural rules, those procedural rules may not "abridge[,] enlarge[,] or modif[y] any substantive rights" of the parties.[36] Instead, the procedural rules must solely "govern [the] elements of practice and procedure."[37] The Supreme Court, however, has explained that "this analytic determination would only be useful if 'substance' and 'procedure' were two 'mutually exclusive categories with easily ascertainable contents.' Rather, '[t]he demarcation between procedure and substantive rights frequently is shadowy and difficult to determine.'"[38] Noting that most rules of procedure will eventually impact the substantive rights of the parties, the Supreme Court has indicated that such overlap does not render rulemaking on a particular topic inappropriate.[39] Nevertheless, some question whether the Supreme Court's promulgation of rules in these overlapping areas supports the conclusion that the General Assembly should "be allowed leeway to impact procedure in furtherance of substantive" matters.[40] Nevertheless, the Supreme Court continues to guard its constitutional rulemaking authority by using, when it concludes it is legally necessary, its power to suspend laws that infringe on that authority.

III. DEVELOPMENT OF THE RULES OF CIVIL PROCEDURE

A. The Migration from Statutory and Common Law to Rule-Based Procedures

Even before the 1968 constitutional revision vesting the Supreme Court with exclusive procedural rulemaking power, Pennsylvania's courts had promulgated rules of procedure pursuant to statutory authority delegated by the General Assembly. In 1937, the Enabling Act gave the Supreme Court the right to create procedural rules for civil actions that would have all the force and effectiveness of legislative acts.[41] The Enabling Act followed the trend of the federal system, which had recently embarked on revamping the federal civil procedural rules, resulting in the promulgation of the Federal Rules of Civil Procedure in 1938.[42] Pursuant to the Enabling Act's authority, the Supreme Court undertook to change Pennsylvania's rules governing civil procedure, looking to the federal experience as a guide. The Supreme Court promulgated Pennsylvania's rules through a long, deliberative process[43] led by the Procedural Rules Committee, in which lawyers and bar associations—chiefly the Pennsylvania Bar Association (PBA)—debated not only specific procedural requirements but also the main philosophical question of whether Pennsylvania should adopt the Federal Rules of Civil Procedure.[44]

Similar to the federal reformers, the Pennsylvania Procedural Rules Committee was tasked with creating rules that would be "definite enough to work yet flexible enough to do justice."[45] The federal reformers addressed this dilemma by creating a set of rules that were intended to be less comprehensive and more general, allowing courts broader discretion in application.[46] For example, the Federal Rules of Civil Procedure simplified federal civil practice by removing the distinction between law and equity and by merging all forms of civil action into one form. Instead of separate rules governing separate types of actions, one broad set of rules was created to apply to all situations.

In contrast, the Pennsylvania reformers addressed the "definite enough yet flexible enough" dilemma by creating a comprehensive set of rules that would cover all possible situations, leaving the courts little discretion in applying them.[47] Reformers such as Philip A. Amram and George Ross Hull supported the break from the federal model, arguing that a comprehensive set of rules like Pennsylvania's could be beneficial because they would clarify the exact boundaries of a trial court's discretion.[48] They believed that detailed and specific rules could guide litigants along in the proceedings, providing them with the exact procedure they must follow at each step, ensuring that their matters would be resolved efficiently, without being slowed by procedural missteps.[49] These advocates of a comprehensive set of rules also argued that detailed rules were preferable because they would prevent the "horror" cases that could result without enough specificity,[50] and they would also prevent needless litigation over the interpretation of overly general procedural rules.[51]

Critics of Pennsylvania's overly detailed set of rules, such as Ella Graubart, urged the Procedural Rules Committee to follow the federal model, voicing their opinion that the simplicity of the federal rules was preferable and would lead to better results in practice because "too many [rules] hamper and impede our movements."[52] These critics believed that a more streamlined and simplistic system would be more stable and efficient[53] and that Pennsylvania's existing civil rules were too numerous.[54] Critics also urged the Procedural Rules Committee to abolish the separate forms of common-law actions to simplify proceedings, arguing that no matter how an action is styled, the plaintiff is still asking the court for relief against a defendant.[55] These critics additionally proposed following the federal model of merging law and equity, arguing that such a merger would not change the parties' substantive rights but merely simplify the form of actions.[56]

Ultimately, the Procedural Rules Committee and the Supreme Court conceptualized Pennsylvania as unique, with particular needs that the federal rules could not satisfy.[57] Persuaded by the fact that Pennsylvania practice was based on a modified common law procedure, while the federal rules were based on the practices of code states that did not translate over into Pennsylvania's experience,[58] Pennsylvania rejected the federal model.

As Charles Alan Wright noted, the unique aspects of Pennsylvania's model might have been warranted because "[p]rovisions no longer required in other jurisdictions may be responsive to local needs which no outsider can gauge."[59]

In rejecting the federal rules, the Procedural Rules Committee maintained separate rules for different forms of civil actions, determining that "it is absolutely impossible to adopt a set of rules dealing with process, venue and pleadings that are identical regardless of the type of action."[60] The committee believed that because these separate actions had long existed and practitioners understood the practice in these different actions, any change would bring about litigation.[61] As such, they believed that the best course would be to keep the separate actions and only make changes to the extent necessary to meet a particular inadequacy or to achieve a specific improvement.[62] The Pennsylvania Rules of Civil Procedure thus kept separate forms of action, and they also preserved the distinction between law and equity.

The Supreme Court also rejected the push to move toward notice pleading, which the federal rules had adopted, adhering instead to fact pleading.[63] Advocates of the federal model welcomed a less stringent pleading system, where plaintiffs could wait until discovery to produce all the facts.[64] They argued that Pennsylvania's system of fact pleading resulted in forcing plaintiffs to set forth all possible theories for their causes of action in order to preserve those theories, even though they might not yet have enough facts to determine which claim is most meritorious.[65] As a result, they argued that pleadings in fact-pleading jurisdictions do not provide the court or the parties with any more information than they would have received through notice pleading.[66] Supporters of the federal system also believed that notice pleading was simpler and that it was desirable for "the requirements of pleading [to] be so simple and brief that a complaint can be dictated in an hour."[67] However, the advocates of fact pleading (and the victors on this issue) believed that the more specific pleading requirements provide parties with better knowledge of the other party's claim and what the opponent intended to assert in the proceeding, requiring less in the way of discovery.[68] They argued that notice pleading would tend to fail to define the issues, requiring parties to be prepared to meet all assertions that could possibly be made.[69] Adhering to existing practice, the committee kept the established fact-pleading rules, requiring a complaint to set forth the "material facts on which a cause of action or defense is based."[70]

The resulting Pennsylvania Rules of Civil Procedure thus did not follow the federal rules' modernized procedural system. As Charles Alan Wright noted, "Of the states which have undergone large scale procedural reform [after the adoption of the Federal Rules], Pennsylvania has been influenced the least by the new concepts and improved techniques first suggested in the Federal Rules."[71] Instead, the Pennsylvania Procedural Rules Committee believed it had "modernize[d] procedure without sacrificing established Pennsylvania traditions which are of proven merit."[72]

After the 1968 constitutional revision, the Rules of Civil Procedure that had been promulgated under the Enabling Act remained in effect. The Supreme Court issued an order under its new constitutional powers to continue the pre-1969 procedural rules that were already in effect, stating, "All statutes and rules governing practice and procedure in actions and proceedings in the Courts of record and Courts not of record of this Commonwealth in force on December 31, 1968, shall continue in force until suspended, revoked or modified, pursuant to Article V of the Constitution of Pennsylvania."[73] The General Assembly later repealed the Enabling Act through the Judiciary Act Repealer Act of 1978.[74]

The Supreme Court's primacy over Pennsylvania's procedural rules is reflected in the current Rules of Civil Procedure. These rules clarify that "[a]ll laws shall be suspended to the extent that they are inconsistent with rules prescribed under the Constitution of 1968"[75] and that "[t]he principle that laws in derogation of the common law are to be strictly construed, shall have no application to the rules promulgated by the Supreme Court."[76] Moreover, the Court specifically requires the lower courts to interpret the rules consistent with its own intentions, providing that the "object of all interpretation and construction of rules is to ascertain and effectuate the intention of the Supreme Court."[77]

B. The Gradual Influence of the Federal Model and the Continuing Unique Aspects of Pennsylvania Civil Practice

Notwithstanding the 1968 constitutional revision that gave the Supreme Court primary authority over statewide procedural rules, including the power to suspend laws (the opposite of the federal model), Pennsylvania has gradually adopted some of the innovations found in the federal rules.[78] For example, in 1983, the Supreme Court eliminated many of the separate forms of action in civil cases in favor of a generic civil action.[79] In addition, in 2003, the Supreme Court abolished the separate actions at law and in equity, merging the procedure for the two into one set of rules.[80] The Court has also relaxed fact pleading to a certain extent, finding that plaintiffs do not need to plead legal theories but only enough facts to formulate the issues involved.[81] In civil rights cases, plaintiffs have been allowed to assert fewer facts in their complaints, which has skewed these cases more toward notice pleading.[82]

Despite the gradual influence of certain characteristics of the federal model, Pennsylvania civil practice still retains a number of unique aspects. For example, although it has somewhat relaxed the pleading standards, Pennsylvania still remains largely a fact-pleading state.[83] Indeed, some of the more recent developments in the federal courts seem to be moving toward the Pennsylvania model, requiring heightened pleading. For example, in *Bell Atlantic Corp. v. Twombly* and *Ashcroft v. Iqbal*, the US Supreme Court required that a complaint in federal court must include enough facts to state a claim for relief that is "plausible on its face" rather than just raising a "sheer possibility" of entitlement to relief.[84]

Additionally, although the Pennsylvania Supreme Court consolidated many of the separate forms of civil actions into a generic civil action, it has retained separate procedural rules governing other common-law forms of action. Separate rules still apply to ejectment actions,[85] quiet title actions,[86] replevin actions,[87] and mandamus actions.[88] Still, the rules governing these separate forms of action are somewhat flexible, as Rule 1033 allows a party to "change the form of action" at any time by leave of court or consent of the adverse party,[89] and Rule 126 authorizes a court to "disregard any error or defect of procedure which does not affect the substantial rights of the parties."[90]

While the Supreme Court consolidated actions at law and equity under the same procedural rules in 2003, law and equity still remain separate to the extent that Pennsylvania has not adopted the US Supreme Court's approach to determining the right to jury trial. In Pennsylvania, the question of whether a jury must find the facts in a case is primarily determined by whether the remedy sought is a remedy at law (in which case there is a right to a jury trial) or a remedy administered in equity (in which case there is no right to a jury trial).[91]

Pennsylvania's amendments to the Rules of Civil Procedure to address discovery of electronically stored information ("e-discovery") have also resisted the federal model. Unlike the federal model, Pennsylvania's e-discovery rules are intended to be streamlined with traditional discovery rules.[92] Pennsylvania's rules do not require electronically stored information to be treated differently than traditional information, and they maintain the proportionality standard for discovery of electronically stored information.[93] This approach differs from the federal model by providing courts with wide discretion in resolving e-discovery disputes.[94] Also, Pennsylvania's e-discovery rule prefers, but does not require, that the parties meet and confer before commencing e-discovery, which is different from the federal e-discovery rule's requirement that parties confer and create a proposed discovery plan.[95]

Additionally, Pennsylvania's sanction rules for e-discovery violations are not comparable to the "Safe Harbor" provision contained in Rule 37(e) of the Federal Rules of Civil Procedure. Federal Rule 37(e) discourages sanctions for the loss of electronically stored information "as a result of the routine, good-faith operation of an electronic information system."[96] Pennsylvania's discovery rules contain no such provision,[97] in part because of the belief that routine good-faith actions should not expose parties to sanctions under Pennsylvania's rules.[98] As a result, where parties do not comply in good faith with e-discovery, recent case law suggests that Pennsylvania courts may impose sanctions.[99]

IV. PENNSYLVANIA'S RULES OF APPELLATE PROCEDURE

A. How Constitutional and Societal Changes Resulted in the Adoption of the Appellate Rules

Pennsylvania's rules of appellate procedure were also shaped by the ratification of the Pennsylvania Constitution of 1968. More than sixty years ago, Philip Amram, a leading authority in the area of Pennsylvania procedure, wrote that "there is no doubt that Pennsylvania lawyers look upon their established traditions with considerable pride and admiration. This has been particularly true in the field of procedural law."[100] Since that time, Pennsylvania has undergone a transformation in its approach to appellate practice and procedure.

Prior to the creation of Pennsylvania's current appellate rules, the General Assembly set the stage by enacting legislation in 1953 empowering the Supreme Court and the Superior Court to adopt rules of procedure governing appeals, subject only to the restriction that the rules "be consistent with the Constitution of the Commonwealth and . . . neither abridge, enlarge, nor modify . . . the jurisdiction of any of the said courts, nor affect any statute of limitations."[101] The Supreme Court appointed a special committee to draft the rules. Minutes from 1955 describe the committee's efforts to "reduce the cost of appeals and shorten the time lag between the final judgment of the court below and the disposition of the appeal," which were issues of real concern to the bar.[102]

As a result of these efforts, the Supreme Court and Superior Court separately adopted their own appellate rules. Although the two sets of rules were substantially the same, it was understood that the rules of practice need not remain similar and could become radically different. In fact, legislation mandated that appellate practice in the Superior Court was not governed by the Supreme Court's appellate rules. Even at the time, though, both courts recognized that the better practice for the appellate system would be to adopt one basic set of rules, with such special differences as needed.

In revising the Constitution in 1968, Pennsylvania created a Unified Judicial System (UJS) that constitutionally established the Superior Court (which had only been a creature of statute before then)[103] and the Commonwealth Court.[104] The UJS consolidated the administration of the court systems, with the Supreme Court at the helm. Under this system, the Supreme Court now directly supervises and administers the courts in the Commonwealth. While previously the Supreme Court's rules only applied to the Supreme Court, after the creation of the UJS, the Court can now develop rules applicable to all courts in the Commonwealth.[105] The Supreme Court has, however, allowed the lower courts to establish rules and internal operating procedures to the extent that they do not conflict with the general rules. At the same time, the Constitution of 1968 created a constitutional right to appeal, which increased the number of appeals.[106] In addition to more courts and more appeals, more laws and more regulations were enacted during the 1960s and 1970s, which likewise led to increased litigation and more appeals. In Pennsylvania and across the country, these pressures ushered in progressive judicial reform of the development of rules of court, spurred by pragmatists' and legal realists' conceptualization of rules as instruments that could guide a pragmatic decision-making process and serve a disciplining function in the legal system.[107]

B. The Philosophy Behind the Appellate Rules

Against this backdrop, the newly created Advisory Committee on Appellate Court Rules (now known as the Appellate Court Procedural Rules Committee) met in 1974. Reducing costs and delay and improving the administration of appellate procedures in ways that provide clear guidance to courts and the bar have long been undisputed goals of the procedural rules. How to best accomplish those objectives, however, has not been without differences of opinion, even in Philip Amram's day. Similar to the debate surrounding the promulgation of the Rules of Civil Procedure, the drafters of the current Appellate Rules of Procedure faced great debate and had to make a philosophical choice. On one side stood those like William Zeiter, the secretary and first executive director of the committee, who believed that the rules should be modernized and reformed to make law fair and accessible—like a cookbook—so that anyone could open the rule book and see what had to be done.[108] On the other side were those who believed it was unfair to draft the rules in a way that placed a first-year lawyer on par with an experienced and sophisticated attorney who had spent his or her career developing knowledge of the practice and customs of the courts. William Zeiter won that debate. An example of his approach can be seen in Rule 1112 of the Pennsylvania Rules of Appellate Procedure, Appeals by Allowance, in which US Postal Service Form 3817 is reproduced in the note to the rule, with an explanation of how to properly mail the petition, including specifying that the petition "should be taken *unsealed* to the Post Office, the Form 3817 Certificate of Mailing . . . from which the date of deposit can be verified should be obtained, cancelled and attached to the petition and the envelope should only then be sealed. . . . It is recommended that the petitioner obtain a duplicate copy of the Form 3817 [in case it is] lost in the mail . . . [and] counsel will be expected to follow up . . . by telephone inquiry to the appellate prothonotary."[109] No client should go hungry if an attorney had this cookbook!

The Rules of Appellate Procedure unified the procedure for all three appellate courts, "draw[ing] together into a single authoritative text the legal principles governing appellate practice."[110] Appellate procedure was Pennsylvania's first modernized procedure, and the consolidation of procedure for all appellate courts was intended to represent "the best practice in this area."[111] Of course, the creation of the UJS itself was a progressive innovation; where the appellate tribunal and the court of first instance are branches of one court, cases can be transferred to reduce "litigation over the forum and the venue at the expense of the merits."[112] Chapter 15 of the appellate rules, governing judicial review of governmental determinations, demonstrates this modern approach. In petitioning for review of governmental determinations, parties do not have to worry about the form or whether the relief sought was original jurisdiction or an appeal.[113] The general petition for review was intended to replace the great writs of quo warranto, mandamus, and others.[114]

How best to draft the appellate rules still remains the product of debate, animated by philosophy, experience, and practice. The appellate rules must simultaneously provide a road map to bring cases before the appellate courts for a decision on the merits of the appeal and control the traffic so that judges can efficiently administer justice. Thus the rules must be simple, practical, convenient, and fair so that litigants have their day in court, which also requires minimizing the risk of "waiver traps." However, the administration of justice also needs to be efficient and orderly, because justice delayed can be justice denied. Where the rules are not followed, administrative burdens are created for the courts and other litigants.

Appeals arise from all types of proceedings—Criminal, Civil, Domestic, Juvenile, and Orphans' Court matters—and the appellate procedural rules must provide instructions for all these different types of cases. A process that makes perfect sense to attorneys in civil proceedings might have terrible consequences for those litigating criminal cases. Drafting rules that are specific enough to be understood and applied, yet general enough to apply across different factual and legal situations, is both art and craft. This balance might be achieved by designing a list, as in Appellate Rule 311, which identifies many possible types of "interlocutory appeals as of right," some of which apply generally, while others apply only to certain types of appeals.[115]

Because the Supreme Court is vested with rulemaking authority, it can respond where necessary to resolve serious problems with current practice, or misapplication of a rule, and it can dynamically respond to changing times and reality. The Appellate Court Procedural Rules Committee assists the Court by monitoring case law, applying the rules, and evaluating suggestions and concerns received from any of the courts or their judges, the organized bar, individual attorneys, and others. Where procedure ends and substance begins is not always a clear divide, and there can be real substantive effects from procedural choices.

V. PENNSYLVANIA'S RULES OF EVIDENCE

As previously mentioned, one example of an overlapping area of substantive and procedural rules was the development of the Pennsylvania Rules of Evidence. The adoption by Congress of the Federal Rules of Evidence in 1975 created a nationwide movement toward the codification of evidence rules.[116] Beginning in the early 1990s, the Pennsylvania Senate Judiciary Committee began to develop an evidence code for Pennsylvania that was closely modeled after the Federal Rules of Evidence.[117] By the time the Pennsylvania Senate began working on an evidence code, Pennsylvania's existing evidence rules had become an anachronistic and outdated patchwork of evidence rules based on common law and statutes.[118] Pennsylvania's scheme of evidence rules made it difficult for lawyers, judges, and litigants to gain a firm understanding of the regulations.[119] The proposed code of evidence attempted to bring Pennsylvania into the modern era by using a widely understood national standard while preserving some of the unique aspects of Pennsylvania's evidence rules.[120]

At the same time that the Pennsylvania General Assembly was attempting to legislate an evidence code, the Supreme Court was working on a parallel effort to develop rules of evidence. The Supreme Court appointed an ad hoc committee, which drafted the Pennsylvania Rules of Evidence.[121] The rules "closely follow[ed] the format, language, and style of the Federal Rules of Evidence" while maintaining some of the common-law rules of evidence developed by Pennsylvania's courts.[122] The ad hoc committee modeled the Pennsylvania Rules of Evidence on the federal rules because the federal rules were a proven model and widely adopted in other jurisdictions. Moreover, the committee wanted to develop rules of evidence that would be consistent and uniform with other jurisdictions.

The parallel efforts of the ad hoc committee and the Senate Judiciary Committee set the stage for a conflict between the legislative and judicial branches. The Supreme Court questioned the constitutionality of the Senate effort, deeming the development of the Rules of Evidence a prerogative of the Court, under the Court's procedural rulemaking powers. Eventually the chair of the Senate judiciary committee and chief sponsor of the Senate bill, Senator Stewart J. Greenleaf, agreed to hold up the Senate bill in order to avoid taking any actions that would be declared unconstitutional by the Supreme Court.[123] Finally, in May 1998, the Supreme Court promulgated the Pennsylvania Rules of Evidence for use in Pennsylvania courts.[124] In promulgating the Rules of Evidence, the Court focused on procedure and attempted to avoid issuing rules that would be considered substantive law.[125] For example, the Court declined to issue a rule protecting alleged rape victims from being questioned about sexual history, preferring to rely on the Rape Shield Law already passed by the General Assembly.[126] Following talks between them, Supreme Court Justice Ronald D. Castille and Senator Greenleaf agreed that the General Assembly would study the new Rules of Evidence and enact any legislation where changes to substantive law were necessary.[127] The Supreme Court avoided addressing evidence rules involving substantive law due to its recognition that substantive legal issues were best left to the purview of the General Assembly.

The clash between the legislative and judicial branches over the Rules of Evidence has occasionally resurfaced since their promulgation. In *Gillard v. AIG Insurance Company*, the Supreme Court was faced with the question of whether the attorney-client privilege only applies to communications from the client to the attorney or whether the privilege also applies to communications from the attorney to the client.[128] Based on the language of Section 5928 of the Judicial Code,[129] the appellee in the case argued that the attorney-client privilege only applies to communications initiated by the client.[130] Several amici in the case argued that even if the General Assembly intended for the statute to create a narrow attorney-client privilege, Article V, Section 10(c) of the Pennsylvania Constitution allocates the decisional authority for deciding the scope of attorney-client privilege with the Court.[131] Therefore, as argued in the relevant amici brief, because Article V, Section 10(c) does not allow the General Assembly to preempt or cabin the Court's power for determining the scope of attorney-client privilege, the Court could overrule the statute.[132] While the Court determined that the General Assembly was not attempting to cabin its involvement in determining the scope of the attorney-client privilege, the Court agreed with the amici that "under the Pennsylvania Constitution[,] [the] Court does maintain a role beyond the mere construction of statutes in determining the appropriate scope of testimonial privileges."[133] According to the Court, just as it promulgated the Pennsylvania Rules of Evidence governing admissibility and the Rules of Civil Procedure establishing the framework and scope of discovery, the Court also has the authority under the Pennsylvania Constitution to determine the scope of the attorney-client privilege.[134] Thus in *Gillard*, the Supreme Court established itself as the preeminent authority for determining Pennsylvania's evidence rules insomuch as they involve procedural rather than substantive law.

VI. THE SUPREME COURT'S LEADERSHIP AND ROLE IN RULEMAKING

As stated by Chief Justice Thomas Saylor, "Although the constitution does not say so expressly, the Supreme Court of Pennsylvania, like a number of other state supreme courts, has maintained that its regulatory powers over court procedures, attorneys, and court administration are exclusive."[135] The Supreme Court has exercised its exclusive authority over rulemaking in Pennsylvania by establishing procedural and evidentiary rules committees to advise the Court and make procedural rule recommendations.[136] Members of the rules committees are appointed by the Supreme Court and serve on a voluntary basis, typically for one or two three-year terms.

When a new rule or an amendment to an existing rule is proposed, the rules committees are guided by the rulemaking process set forth in Pennsylvania Rule of Judicial Administration 103.[137] This process generally requires that recommendations be published for public comment before the Supreme Court takes action unless prompt action is required, a proposed rule change is technical or perfunctory in nature, or the Supreme Court, in its discretion, determines that such action is unnecessary in the interest of justice or efficient administration.[138] A rule change is then implemented by an order of the Supreme Court.[139] By interpreting the Pennsylvania Constitution as granting it exclusive rulemaking authority, the Supreme Court has ensured that all procedural and evidentiary rules in Pennsylvania cannot be promulgated or amended without the Supreme Court's express approval.

The 1968 revision to Article V of the Pennsylvania Constitution gave the Supreme Court the last word on matters of practice and procedure, granting it exclusive authority in this area, including the power to suspend statutes enacted by the General Assembly. This interbranch balance is the opposite of the federal balance pursuant to the Federal Rules Enabling Act, as amended in 1988, and the Civil Justice Reform Act of 1990, in which Congress asserted substantial authority over procedural rulemaking. The allocation of this power between the court and legislature implicates important issues of judicial independence unique to Pennsylvania.

The Honorable Renée Cohn Jubelirer is a judge on the Commonwealth Court of Pennsylvania. Robert L. Byer is a partner at Duane Morris LLP. Meredith E. Carpenter is an associate at Duane Morris LLP.

1. *See* In re 42 Pa.C.S. § 1703, 394 A.2d 444, 449 (Pa. 1978).

2. *See* Roscoe Pound, "The Rulemaking Power of the Courts," *American Bar Association Journal* 12 (1926): 599, 601; A. Leo Levin and Anthony G. Amsterdam, "Legislative Control over Judicial Rule-Making: A Problem in Constitutional Revision," *University of Pennsylvania Law Review* 107 (1958): 1, 3, 10, stating the following benefits of vesting the courts with procedural rulemaking power:

> Legislatures have neither the immediate familiarity with the day-by-day practice of the courts which would allow them to isolate the pressing problems of procedural revision nor the experience and expertness necessary to the solution of these problems; legislatures are intolerably slow to act and cause even the slightest and most obviously necessary matter of procedural change to be long delayed; legislatures are subject to the influence of other pressures than those which seek the efficient administration of justice and may often push through some particular and ill-advised pet project of an influential legislator while the comprehensive, long-studied proposal of a bar association molders in committee; and legislatures are not held responsible in the public eye for the efficient administration of the courts and hence do not feel pressed to constant reexamination of procedural methods.

Charles W. Joiner and Oscar J. Miller, "Rules of Practice and Procedure: A Study of Judicial Rule-Making," *Michigan Law Review* 55 (1957): 623, 643–44, listing additional benefits of vesting the courts with procedural rulemaking power, including the following: "(1) courts are better able to and have more interest in promulgating rules that will efficiently administer justice; (2) courts who have rulemaking power tend to base their decisions more on substantive law than procedural questions; (3) courts who have rulemaking power periodically reexamine their rules to improve them; and (4) when the same group that promulgates rules also interprets them, the rules are interpreted to adhere more closely to their intent."

3. Pound, "Rulemaking Power," 601–2 ("[P]rocedure of courts is something that belongs to the courts rather than to the legislature. . . . Analytically, there is no more warrant for the legislature's imposing a straitjacket of statutory procedure upon the courts than for its doing the like with the executive. . . . The legislature ought to leave judicial procedure to the judiciary as the judiciary must leave legislative procedure [except as prescribed sometimes by state constitutional provisions] to the legislature.").

4. Ibid., 602; Levin and Amsterdam, "Legislative Control," 11.

5. Pound, "Rulemaking Power," 602–3; *see also* Joiner and Miller, "Rules of Practice," 643 ("[A] random comparison of decisions by courts exercising rule-making power before and after their court rules were adopted indicates that there are fewer decisions turning on procedural questions after the rules were adopted.").

6. The Preparatory Committee, *The Judiciary: Reference Manual No. 5* (1967–68), 222 (hereafter *Reference Manual No. 5*), http://www.duq.edu /assets/Documents/law/pa-constitution/_pdf /conventions/1967-68/reference-manuals /reference-manual05.pdf; *see also* William J. Brennan Jr., "Efficient Organization and Effective Administration for Today's Courts: The Citizen's Responsibility," *Journal of the American Judicature Society* 48 (1964): 145, 148 (analogizing the operation of courts to the job of running a business and suggesting that only the courts can knowledgeably establish court policy and procedures, posing the following question: "Can anyone in business imagine what it could mean if the processes and procedures for running his business were formulated not by his board of directors but by some outside agency?"); Robert C. Finley, "Constitutional Responsibility and Authority for Court Administration," *Journal of the American Judicature Society* 47 (1963): 30, 31 ("Obviously,

in either public or private administration or management, responsibility and authority must go hand in hand, and should be vested in one executive position or office.").

7. *Reference Manual No. 5*, 222.

8. Pa. Const. art. V, § 10(c).

9. *See, e.g.,* Pound, "Rulemaking Power," 601 (explaining that the reason the legislature had previously taken over control of court procedural rules was because members of the legal profession had come to believe that court procedure was intrinsically part of the law and that the legislature "must prescribe judicial procedure or abdicate control over the law"); John M. Mulcahey, "Separation of Powers in Pennsylvania: The Judiciary's Prevention of Legislative Encroachment," *Duquesne Law Review* 32 (1994): 539, 540 (noting that post-Constitutional revision, Pennsylvania's "separation of powers doctrine prohibits the legislative branch from enacting any law that affects the judicial branch"); Charles Gardner Geyh, "Highlighting a Low Point on a High Court: Some Thoughts on the Removal of Pennsylvania Supreme Court Justice Rolf Larsen and the Limits of Judicial Self-Regulation," *Temple Law Review* 68 (1995): 1041, 1054–61 (describing the intent and interpretation of Article V, Section 10[c]).

10. Act of June 21, 1937, P.L. 1982, No. 392, as amended by the Act of March 30, 1939, P.L. 14, and the Act of August 25, 1959, P.L. 751, formerly codified at 17 P.S. § 61 and repealed by Section 2 of the Judiciary Act Repealer Act, No. 1978-53.

11. Dombrowski v. City of Philadelphia, 245 A.2d 238, 241 (Pa. 1968).

12. *See* Sweet v. Pennsylvania Labor Relations Board, 316 A.2d 665, 669 (Pa. Cmwlth. 1974) (indicating that Article V, Section 10[c] had granted the judiciary more power than it previously had); Kotch v. Middle Coal Field Poor District, 197 A. 334, 339 (Pa. 1938) (stating that the General Assembly has jurisdiction over all matters for which legislation is not prohibited); In re Likins' Petition, 72 A. 858, 860 (Pa. 1909) (stating that the General Assembly may do whatever the Constitution does not prohibit).

13. *See, e.g.,* Greenough v. Greenough, 11 Pa. (Jones) 489, 494 (1849) (noting that "the judicial power of the Commonwealth is its whole judicial power; and it is so distributed that the legislature cannot exercise any part of it. Under the constitution, therefore, there is no mixed

power—party legislative and partly judicial"); Commonwealth ex rel. Johnson v. Halloway, 42 Pa. (6 Wright) 446, 448 (1862) (declaring that an act that allowed for the reduction in an incarcerated person's prison term violated the doctrine of separation of powers because the "whole" judicial power was "vested" in the judiciary and "[n]ot a fragment of [the judicial power] belongs to the legislature").

14. *See* Ballou v. State Ethics Commission, 424 A.2d 983, 986 (Pa. Cmwlth. 1981) ("When the judiciary Article of the Pennsylvania Constitution was revised in 1968, the Supreme Court's inherent and exclusive power, until then implicit as a fundamental matter, was made explicit by Article V Section 10[c].").

15. Mulcahey, "Separation of Powers," 552; Dana Stuchell, "Constitutional Crisis in Pennsylvania: Pennsylvania Supreme Court v. Pennsylvania General Assembly," *Dickinson Law Review* 102 (1997): 201, 226 ("[The Pennsylvania Supreme Court] has increasingly used the 1968 amendments to the Pennsylvania Constitution to tip the balance of powers in its favor and isolate itself from the other two branches to such an extent that it has become virtually unaccountable."); Melissa Lennon Walsh, "Quis Custodiet Ipsos Custodes? Who Shall Keep the Keepers?," *Temple Law Review* 68 (1995): 1527, 1534 ("[B]ecause the supreme court had the power to govern the practice and procedure of *all* courts, the supreme court combined these provisions to assert more control over the judicial branch and other branches.").

16. Garrett v. Bamford, 582 F.2d 810, 814 (3d Cir. 1978), emphasis added.

17. *See* Stuchell, "Constitutional Crisis," 227, 227n124 (noting that "[n]either the federal courts nor the vast majority of state courts have asserted [the] authority" that the Pennsylvania Supreme Court has asserted over laws that affect the operation of the judicial branch, and that "[i]n most states, as well as in the federal system, the legislature and the courts are considered to have concurrent jurisdiction over judicial administration and rule-making").

18. 28 U.S.C. §§ 2071–77.

19. Ibid.

20. Act of March 30, 1973, P.L. No. 93-12, 87 Stat. 9 (allowing more time for congressional review of the draft Rules of Evidence the Supreme Court had submitted to Congress for approval under the Rules Enabling Act); Act of January 2, 1975, P.L. No. 93-595, 88

Stat. 1926 (enacting the Federal Rules of Evidence).

21. Pa. Const. art. V, § 10(c).

22. In re Suspension of the Capital Unitary Review Act, 722 A.2d 676, 677 (Pa. 1999).

23. Pa. Const. art. I, § 12 ("No power of suspending laws shall be exercised unless by the Legislature or by its authority.").

24. Pa. Const. art. V, § 10(c) ("The Supreme Court shall have the power to prescribe general rules governing practice, procedure and conduct of all courts . . . if such rules are consistent with this Constitution and neither abridge, enlarge nor modify the substantive rights of any litigant. . . . All laws shall be suspended to the extent that they are inconsistent with rules prescribed under these provisions.").

25. In re 42 Pa.C.S. § 1703, 394 A.2d 444, 447, 451 (Pa. 1978).

26. In re 42 Pa.C.S. § 1703, 394 A.2d at 448.

27. 42 Pa.C.S. § 1703.

28. In re 42 Pa.C.S. § 1703, 394 A.2d at 444.

29. Laudenberger v. Port Authority of Allegheny County, 436 A.2d 147 (Pa. 1981).

30. Supreme Court Per Curiam Order of January 17, 1997, 27 Pa. B. 581 (February 1, 1997) (suspending Sections 812-A[d], [e], and [f]; 813-A, 821-A-826-A of the Health Care Services Malpractice Act, 40 P.S. §§ 1301.812-A[d], [e], and [f], 1301.813-A, 1301.821-A-1301.826-A, repealed by Act of March 20, 2002, P.L. 154).

31. In re Suspension of the Capital Unitary Review Act, 722 A.2d 676. The Capital Unitary Review Act (CURA) established the "procedure by which the courts were to administer capital cases, from the time the sentence of death was imposed by the jury until the time of its implementation," proceedings that rendered the Court's preexisting rules (Pa.R.A.P. 1941, and Pa.R.Crim.Pro. 1501) wholly inoperative. The Supreme Court therefore suspended CURA because it "encroache[d] into the procedural domain of the judicial system, but also conflict[ed] with pre-existing procedural rules duly promulgated by th[e] Court."

32. Gmerek v. State Ethics Commission, 807 A.2d 812 (Pa. 2002).

33. 42 Pa.C.S. § 8355, suspended absolutely by Pa.R.C.P. No. 1023.1(e).

34. Shaulis v. Pennsylvania State Ethics Commission, 833 A.2d 123 (Pa. 2003).

35. Laudenberger v. Port Authority of Allegheny County, 436 A.2d 147 (Pa. 1981).

36. Ibid., 149 (citation omitted).

37. Ibid.

38. Ibid., 150 (footnote omitted; alteration in original). Quoting Sibbach v. Wilson & Co., 312 U.S. 1, 17 (1941) (dissenting opinion by Frankfurter, J., in which Black, Douglas, and Murphy, J.J., concurred).

39. Laudenberger, 436 A.2d at 155.

40. Thomas G. Saylor, "Power and Prerogative: Reflections on Judicial Suspension of Laws," *Widener Law Journal* 21 (2012): 259, 276–79.

41. Act of June 21, 1937, P.L. 1982, No. 392, formerly codified at 17 P.S. § 61, as amended by the Act of March 30, 1939, P.L. 14, and the Act of August 25, 1959, P.L. 751, and repealed by Section 2 of the Judiciary Act Repealer Act, No. 1978-53.

42. *See* Christo v. Tuscany, Inc., 533 A.2d 461, 466 (Pa. Super. 1987) (noting that "[m]any states, including Pennsylvania, promulgated new rules of civil procedure, intended to govern both law and equity actions, in response to the federal rules").

43. The extended deliberation that went into the process was a subject of critique. Ella Graubart noted that Pennsylvania's "Committee was appointed in 1937. It has been working for four years . . . but its work is far from completed. . . . In contrast to this experience it is interesting to learn that in one jurisdiction the Supreme Court of that state appointed a committee which in four months recommended a set of complete rules modeled on the Federal system." Ella Graubart, "A Critic Replies," *Pennsylvania Bar Association Quarterly* 13 (1941): 23, 27.

44. *See* George Ross Hull, "A Critic 'Views with Alarm': Comments on 'Pennsylvania Is Moving Backwards,'" *Pennsylvania Bar Association Quarterly* 12 (1941): 146 (noting that Pennsylvania's Procedural Rules Committee first considered whether it should recommend adopting the Federal Rules, "with only such minor changes and additions as were absolutely necessary to adapt them to Pennsylvania practice"). Because of the lengthy deliberations that went into the promulgation of the rules, Pennsylvania's Rules of Civil Procedure were issued little by little, rather than as a complete set, beginning on May 1, 1939.

45. Hull, "Critic 'Views,'" 147 (quoting Clark on code pleading).

46. Ibid.

47. Ella Graubart, "Pennsylvania Is Moving Backwards," *Pennsylvania Bar Association Quarterly* 12 (1941): 137.

48. Charles Alan Wright, "Modern Pleading and the Pennsylvania Rules," *University of Pennsylvania Law Review* 101 (1953): 909, 913.

49. Hull, "Critic 'Views,'" 148–49 ("[W]henever the procedural step to be taken is of material consequence, a single rule that is easily found, clearly expressed and certain of application, is to be preferred to the uncertain conclusion which may be reached by a judge in his discretion. . . . The best and most satisfactory guide is to be found in rules which are reasonably comprehensive, logically arranged, easily found and clearly expressed.").

50. Philip A. Amram, "A Reply to Professor Wright," *University of Pennsylvania Law Review* 101 (1953): 948, 953.

51. Hull, "Critic 'Views,'" 151–52.

52. Ibid., 139.

53. Ibid.

54. "Report of the Commission on Procedural Rules of the Pennsylvania Bar Association," *Annual Report of the Pennsylvania Bar Association* 51 (1945): 90, 91.

55. Ella Graubart, "Comments on the Proposed Rules of Civil Procedure Governing Actions at Law," *Pennsylvania Bar Association Quarterly* 17 (1946): 210.

56. Ibid., 211.

57. *See, e.g.*, Amram, "Reply to Professor Wright," 948 (stating that the Pennsylvania Bar is "distinguished and scholarly" and that "perhaps partly because of its scholastic eminence, it is more conscious of 'established Pennsylvania traditions' than lawyers of some other states,'" and "[t]here is no doubt that Pennsylvania lawyers look upon their established traditions with considerable pride and admiration[,] . . . particularly . . . in the field of procedural law"); Hull, "Critic 'Views'"; Graubart, "Pennsylvania Is Moving," 145.

58. Philip A. Amram, "The New Procedural Rules," *Annual Report of the Pennsylvania Bar Association* 45 (1939): 56, 60.

59. Wright, "Modern Pleading," 910.

60. Charles E. Kenworthey and Ronald A. Anderson, "The New Procedural Rules," *Pennsylvania Bar Association Quarterly* 18 (1946): 59.

61. "Report of the Commission," *Annual Report of the Pennsylvania Bar Association* 51 (1945): 90, 91–92.

62. Ibid.

63. Charles E. Kenworthey, "The Proposed Pleading Rules," *Pennsylvania Bar Association Quarterly* 14 (1943): 201, 211.

64. Wright, "Modern Pleading," 926–27.

65. Ibid., 928–29.

66. Ibid., 929–31 (noting that while the Pennsylvania rules "'are drawn on the theory that the issues for trial can be narrowed through the use of sworn pleadings stating the facts which each side proposes to prove' . . . even in Pennsylvania pleadings do not accomplish as much as people like to imagine" [quoting 1 Goodrich-Amram §§ 1017–11]).

67. Ella Graubart, "Baron Surrebutter Walks Again," *Pennsylvania Bar Association Quarterly* 17 (1946): 126, 131.

68. *See* "Report of the New Procedural Rules Committee," *Annual Report of the Pennsylvania Bar Association* 55 (1949): 95, 101; Kenworthey, "Proposed Pleading," 212 (noting that the "philosophy of *fact-pleading* is that the result is accomplished by the pleadings alone or with a minimum amount of assistance from a pretrial conference and pretrial discovery," whereas the "philosophy of *notice-pleading* is that the result is accomplished by the pretrial conference and pretrial discovery with a minimum amount of assistance from pleadings").

69. Kenworthey, "Proposed Pleading," 214.

70. Pa.R.C.P. No. 1019(a).

71. Wright, "Modern Pleading," 910.

72. Ibid., quoting Charles E. Kenworthey, "Discovery Under the Proposed New Rules," *Pennsylvania Bar Association Quarterly* 20 (1948): 17, 21.

73. 204 Pa. Code § 29.1 ("Continuation of Pre-1969 Statutes and Rules").

74. Judiciary Act Repealer Act, No. 1978-53, 42 Pa.C.S. § 1722.

75. Pa.R.C.P. No. 133.

76. Pa.R.C.P. No. 130.

77. Pa.R.C.P. No. 127.

78. *See* Vincent L. McKusick, "State Courts' Interest in Federal Rulemaking: A Proposal for Recognition," *Maine Law Review* 36 (1984): 253 ("Even those states such as Illinois, Michigan, New York, and Pennsylvania that have not modeled their civil procedure generally on the federal rules have nonetheless adopted comparable provisions to govern certain matters as, for example, joinder of parties, class actions, or discovery.").

79. Pa.R.C.P. No. 1001, as amended (merging actions of assumpsit and trespass).

80. Pa. Supreme Court, No. 402 Civil Procedural Rules Docket No. 5, In re Consolidation of the Action in Equity with the Civil Action: Order, Rule, and Explanatory Comment, 34 Pa.B. 9

(Dec. 16, 2003); *see* Official Note to Pa.R.C.P. No. 1001(b) ("The procedural distinctions between the forms of action in assumpsit, trespass and equity are abolished."); Official Note to Pa.R.C.P. No. 1501 ("The action in equity has been abolished. Equitable relief may be obtained through a civil action, Rule 1001 et seq."); In re Scheidmantel, 868 A.2d 464, 477n6 (Pa. 2005) ("On December 17, 2003, amendments to the Pennsylvania Rules of Civil Procedure were promulgated abolishing the separate action in equity and merging claims for equitable relief into the civil action.").

81. *See, e.g.,* Gavula v. ARA Servs., Inc., 756 A.2d 17, 22 (Pa. Super. 2000) (even though the relevant counts were not specifically identified as "negligence" counts in a plaintiff's complaint, those counts that were "clearly intended to be a claim for negligence" were to be treated as such); McClellan v. Health Maint. Org. of Pa., 604 A.2d 1053, 1060 (Pa. Super. 1992) ("The obligation to discover the cause or causes of actions is on the court: the plaintiff need not identify them."); Weiss v. Equibank, 460 A.2d 271, 275 (Pa. Super. 1983) (noting that while a complaint must include the facts on which a plaintiff's claims are based, "a plaintiff is not obliged to identify the legal theory underlying his complaint").

82. *See* Thomas O. Main, "Procedural Uniformity and the Exaggerated Role of Rules: A Survey of Intra-state Uniformity in Three States That Have Not Adopted the Federal Rules of Civil Procedure," *Villanova Law Review* 46 (2011): 311, 345–53.

83. *See* Pa.R.C.P. No. 1019(a) ("The material facts on which a cause of action or defense is based shall be stated in a concise and summary form."); *see also* Alpha Tau Omega Fraternity v. University of Pennsylvania, 464 A.2d 1349, 1352 (Pa. Super. 1983) ("Pennsylvania is a fact pleading state. . . . A complaint must not only give the defendant notice of what the plaintiff's claim is and the grounds upon which it rests, but it must also formulate the issues by summarizing those facts essential to support the claim."); Philadelphia v. Kane, 438 A.2d 1051, 1052 (Pa. Cmwlth. 1982) ("The Pennsylvania system of fact pleading requires that the pleading must define the issues, and every act or performance essential to that end must be set forth in the complaint.").

84. Ashcroft v. Iqbal, 556 U.S. 662, 678–79 (2009) (requiring a complaint to include enough facts "to state a claim to relief that is plausible on its face," which must do more than just raise "a sheer possibility" of entitlement to relief); Bell Atlantic Corp. v. Twombly, 550 U.S. 544, 555 (2007) (requiring a complaint to allege facts that, if proven, would support the relief requested and to show that the alleged facts were "enough to raise a right to relief above the speculative level, on the assumption that all the allegations in the complaint are true [even if doubtful in fact]").

85. Pa.R.C.P. Nos. 1051–58.

86. Pa.R.C.P. Nos. 1061–68.

87. Pa.R.C.P. Nos. 1071–88.

88. Pa.R.C.P. Nos. 1091–1100.

89. Pa.R.C.P. No. 1033.

90. Pa.R.C.P. No. 126; *see also* Pomerantz v. Goldstein, 387 A.2d 1280, 1282 (Pa. 1978) ("Rule 126 not only expresses the reasons why our rules are to be liberally construed—to ensure that justice is accorded the parties to a lawsuit—but also permits us to disregard procedural errors which do not affect substantial rights.").

91. *See* Pa.R.C.P. No. 1038.3 ("In any case in which there is a claim for equitable relief, the court on its own motion or upon the petition of any party may submit to trial by jury any or all issues of fact arising from that claim. The advisory verdict of the jury shall be in the form of answers to specific questions and shall not be binding upon the court."). Official Note to Pa.R.C.P. No. 1038.3 states, "Rule 1038.3 does not confer a right to trial by jury if the right did not exist prior to the consolidation of the action in equity with the civil action. The rule preserves the practice under former Equity Rule 1513 of allowing a court in its discretion to submit such claims to trial by jury for an advisory verdict." Rule 128 of the Pennsylvania Rules of Civil Procedure also provides, "In ascertaining the intention of the Supreme Court in the promulgation of a rule, the courts may be guided by the following presumptions among others: . . . That no rule shall be construed to confer a right to trial by jury where such right does not otherwise exist." *See also* Advanced Telephone Systems, Inc. v. Com-Net Professional Mobile Radio, LLC, 846 A.2d 1264, 1275–76 (Pa. Super. 2004) ("[T]he Pennsylvania analysis of whether there is a right to a jury trial differs from the federal analysis. . . . [T]he primary inquiry is whether the cause of action existed at common law at the time the Pennsylvania Constitution was adopted. In

contrast, 'federal case law examines whether the statutory cause of action is analogous to a common law claim for which there was a right to trial by jury, with focus . . . on the relief provided.'" [Quoting Wertz v. Chapman Twp., 741 A.2d 1272, 1278 (Pa. 1999)]).

92. Compare Pa.R.C.P. No. 4009.1 and Fed. R. Civ. P. 26.

93. Pa.R.C.P. No. 4009.1; Explanatory Comment—Electronically Stored Information, In re Amendment of Rules 4009.1, 4009.11, 4009.12, 4009.21, 4009.23, and 4011 of the Pennsylvania Rules of Civil Procedure, No. 564 Civil Procedural Rules Docket (June 6, 2012), http://www.pacourts.us/assets/opinions /Supreme/out/564civ.rpt.pdf?cb=1 ("No Importation of Federal Law—Though the term 'electronically stored information' is used in these rules, there is no intent to incorporate the federal jurisprudence surrounding the discovery of electronically stored information. The treatment of such issues is to be determined by traditional principles of proportionality under Pennsylvania law.").

94. Explanatory Comment—Electronically Stored Information.

95. See Fed. R. Civ. P. 26(f).

96. Fed. R. Civ. P. 37(f), Committee Notes on Rules—2006 Amendment.

97. Pa.R.C.P. No. 4019(a); Explanatory Note to Pa.R.C.P. No. 4019 ("Willfulness of course may be a factor in determining the extent of the sanction but it will not be an essential condition precedent to the power to impose a sanction.").

98. See Gonzales v. Procaccio Bros. Trucking Co., 407 A.2d 1338, 1341 (Pa. Super. 1979) (noting that as general rule, Pennsylvania courts will not impose sanctions absent some willful disregard or disobedience of court order or an obligation expressly required by the Rules of Civil Procedure).

99. See Solara Ventures IV, LLC v. PNC Bank, National Association (Pa. Super. 2014), unpub., LEXIS 1725 (Pa. Super. Aug. 7, 2014).

100. Amram, "Reply to Professor Wright," 948.

101. Act of July 29, 1953, P.L. 1012, No. 259, 17 P.S. § 67, entitled "An Act Authorizing and Empowering the Supreme Court of Pennsylvania to Prescribe, by General Rule, the Practice and Procedure Governing Appeals to the Supreme Court of Pennsylvania"; Act of July 29, 1953, P.L. 1025, No. 264, 17 P.S. § 2071.1, entitled "An Act Authorizing and Empowering the Superior Court of Pennsylvania to Prescribe, by General Rule, the Practice and Procedure Governing Appeals to the Superior Court of Pennsylvania."

102. Report of the Appellate Rules Committee (1955), 3.

103. 1895 Pa. Laws 212.

104. Pa. Const. art. V, §§ 1–4.

105. Pa. Const. art. V, § 10.

106. Pa. Const. art. V, § 9 ("There shall be a right of appeal in all cases to a court of record from a court not of record; and there shall also be a right of appeal from a court of record or from an administrative agency to a court of record or to an appellate court.").

107. See David Marcus, "The Federal Rules of Civil Procedure and Legal Realism as a Jurisprudence of Law Reform," Georgia Law Review 44 (2010): 433.

108. See "New Appellate Rules for Pennsylvania," Pennsylvania Bar Association Quarterly 47 (1976): 201 ("The members of the bar should have rules which are as uniform as is possible and which will guide even the most inexperienced lawyer through the appellate process step by step in chronological form. Finally, the litigants deserve a procedure designed to dispose of their cases as speedily as is consistent with thoughtful consideration, and to eliminate any pitfalls or ambiguities that may deprive them of review or cause any missteps and delay.").

109. Pa.R.A.P. 1112.

110. Explanatory Note to the Pennsylvania Rules of Appellate Procedure, 42 Pa.C.S., 1984 Rules of Appellate Procedure Pamphlet.

111. Ibid.

112. Charles W. Eliot, "Preliminary Report on Efficiency in the Administration of Justice, 1914 Report," cited in Dosal et al., "'Administration of Justice Is Archaic'—the Rise of Modern Court Administration: Assessing Roscoe Pound's Court Administration Prescriptions," Indiana Law Journal 82 (2007): 1293, 1297.

113. Pa.R.A.P. 1501 et seq.

114. Pa.R.A.P. 1502 & Official Note ("The appeal and the original jurisdiction actions of equity, replevin, mandamus and quo warranto, the action for a declaratory judgment, and the writs of certiorari and prohibition are abolished insofar as they relate to matters within the scope of a petition for review under this chapter. The petition for review, insofar as applicable under this chapter, shall be the exclusive procedure for judicial review of a determination of a government unit.").

115. Pa.R.A.P. 311.

116. David P. Leonard, "Foreword: Twenty Years of the Federal Rules of Evidence," *Loyola of Los Angeles Law Review* 28 (1995): 1251.

117. Edward D. Ohlbaum, *Ohlbaum on Evidence* (Newark, N.J.: LexisNexis, 2009), xi.

118. Pa. Legis. Journal No. 33, 869 (1993).

119. Ibid.

120. Ibid.

121. Ohlbaum, *Ohlbaum on Evidence*, xi.

122. Pa. R. Evid. Explanatory Comments.

123. Michael A. Riccardi, "Supreme Court Releases Evidence Code; Greenleaf: Legislature to Add Final Touches," *Legal Intelligencer* 218 (1998): 4.

124. Ibid.

125. Ibid.

126. Ibid.

127. Ibid.

128. Gillard v. AIG Insurance, Co., 15 A.3d 44 (Pa. 2011).

129. Section 5928 of the Judicial Code states, "In a civil matter counsel shall not be competent or permitted to testify to confidential communications *made to him by the client*, nor shall the client be compelled to disclose the same, unless in either case this privilege is waived upon the trial by the client." 42 Pa.C.S. § 5928, emphasis added.

130. Gillard, 15 A.3d at 46.

131. Ibid., 54.

132. Brief for Association of Corp. Counsel et al., as Amici Curiae Supporting Appellants 15–16, Gillard v. AIG Insurance Co., 15 A.3d 44 (2011) (No. 10 EAP 2010).

133. Gillard, 15 A.3d at 58.

134. Ibid., 58n14.

135. Saylor, "Power and Prerogative," 264 (citing In re 42 Pa.C.S. § 1703, 394 A.2d 444, 448 [Pa. 1978], reasoning that "there is simply no substantial support for the proposition that the grant of authority in [a]rticle V, § 10[c] is anything other than exclusive").

136. These committees currently consist of (1) Appellate Court Procedural Rules Committee, (2) Civil Procedural Rules Committee, (3) Criminal Procedural Rules Committee, (4) Committee on Rules of Evidence, (5) Domestic Relations Procedural Rules Committee, (6) Juvenile Court Procedural Rules Committee, (7) Minor Court Rules Committee, and (8) Orphans' Court Procedural Rules Committee.

137. Pa.R.J.A. No. 103.

138. Ibid.

139. Ibid.

CHAPTER 4

The Supreme Court's Singular Criminal Procedure Work in a Pivotal Era

JAMES A. SHELLENBERGER

AND JAMES A. STRAZZELLA

In the long and rich history of the Pennsylvania Supreme Court, the pivotal era that stretched from the early 1970s through the mid-1980s was a uniquely challenging one for the Court's work in criminal procedure. In addition to other legal developments, the era coincided with the emerging impact of the 1968 Pennsylvania Constitution. This crucial period required the Court to deal with a confluence of urgent pressures on the Commonwealth's entire criminal justice system and on the Court itself. The Court's response was impressive.

Beyond the Court's need to deal with significant new attention to criminal procedure in its appellate case decisions, the time period presented a demonstrably new role for the Court to play in the overall procedural arena and in Pennsylvania's judicial administration. The era implicated delicate new structural interactions with the legislature as well as with the disparate trial courts of a large and diverse Commonwealth. These pressing, voluminous, converging currents included a number that were constitutional and mandatory, some federal and some Commonwealth; some were initiated by the US Supreme Court and some by Pennsylvania court decisions. In addition, some nonmandated changes were simply driven by the Court's desire to improve, streamline, standardize, and unify the Commonwealth's body of criminal procedure, as well as make it more accessible. Among these emerging currents were

- the need to revise state procedure because of an unprecedented constitutional expansion of federally mandated procedural rights;
- a dramatic expansion of the federal judicial remedies available in criminal cases, remedies that would significantly impact state cases;

- procedural revision needs driven by the Supreme Court's own decisions interpreting the Commonwealth's Constitution or other law; and
- an expansion of the Court's judicial administrative role.

I. THE NEED TO ACCOUNT FOR EXPANDED FEDERAL CONSTITUTIONAL RIGHTS

A substantial imperative of this pivotal period was the exceptional "Due Process Revolution" that broadened state criminal defendants' rights by applying an expansive list of federal rights to the states through the Fourteenth Amendment "Due Process" clause. This period was overlaid with a massive amount of changing law embedded in complicated case decisions. These new decisions were the product of case-by-case, fact-oriented, multi-judge decision making with all the ambiguities common in US Supreme Court opinions. The case limits were of uncertain contours and application, yet they were critical in areas that routinely affected everyday trial courts and magisterial actions. Some of the new federal decisions were also unclear in their retroactive application to past police conduct, past court rulings, or past convictions. All typically required at least some procedural clarification and adjustment for the future. All required careful and time-consuming assessment of how the new fundamental federal procedural rights were to be constitutionally superimposed onto existing state processes—whether they called for subtle or wholesale revision of proceedings set out in state case law, statutory law, rules of procedure, or local practice. The era thus called for the translation of complicated case law imperatives into workable, interlocking, expanded, and concrete Pennsylvania rules of everyday procedure.

The newly declared federal rights were made mandatorily applicable in state litigation in the pretrial, trial, and review processes, including the Pennsylvania Supreme Court's own now more complicated docket. It is worth underscoring that the overwhelming majority of criminal cases—approximately 95 percent of felonies—are prosecuted in state courts.[1] As a result, the vast percentage of criminal cases are typically charged and prosecuted by noncentralized, largely independent, elected state district attorneys prosecuting the cases in front of elected Commonwealth judges of all levels, from magisterial through appellate. State prosecutions occur before judges who are required to integrate into their state trials and appeals the body of state constitutional law, state legislation, and court rules; the judges are also required to integrate any overlaying, applicable federal case imperatives, which may limit state law. Among other consequences, then, the Due Process Revolution's newly incorporated federal procedural rights had a much larger opportunity to arise and be tested—and to be tested in a wider variety of fact patterns—than was previously the situation when such rights were only applied to federal crimes. The newly enunciated federal constitutional rights also had an impact beyond the immediacy of the Commonwealth's trial courts. Not only could more federal constitutional issues involved in state trials survive for possible state court appellate review, but they could now survive for *federal* court review (including habeas corpus).

Significantly, the expansion of the right to counsel[2] also required greater attention to ensuring applications of that right. Waiver and forfeiture issues—pervasive in procedure matters generally—became a greater matter for record clarity in connection with counsel decisions.

II. THE NEED DERIVED FROM THE ERA'S SIMULTANEOUS, DRAMATIC EXPANSION OF THE FEDERAL JUDICIAL REMEDIES THAT IMPACT STATE CASES

At the same time procedural rights were themselves being expanded, there was a notable expansion of available federal mechanisms by which to assert those broadened procedural rights. This dramatic criminal procedure remedial force afforded more direct appeal claims and, importantly, afforded broader posttrial review of federal claims. This broadening extended finality concerns and required clearer state process records to demonstrate whether rights had been afforded in trial and appellate courts. Moreover, developing notions of ineffective assistance of counsel claims also allowed more issues to be raised, despite possible forfeitures (e.g., failures to comply with contemporaneous objection rules), and to thus test finality.[3] This too led to efforts to create clearer trial court records regarding procedural default issues.

The expanding federal habeas corpus law, and the view that the prosecution bore the burden of proving waiver of constitutional rights (and by a standard of knowing, intelligent, and voluntary waiver, usually by the defendant personally), called for clearer and more express trial-level recording of decisions to forgo certain claims.[4] Not only was this pressure derived from federal Supreme Court cases; the assessment also required practical state court attention to lower-level federal court interpretations, which (given the more likely threat of ultimate habeas corpus collateral review) added pressure on state courts to both take up possible federal posttrial claims and interpret the federal Constitution similarly to the federal circuit cases.

III. PROCEDURAL REVISION NEEDS DRIVEN BY THE SUPREME COURT'S OWN DECISIONS INTERPRETING THE COMMONWEALTH CONSTITUTION OR OTHER LAW

Pennsylvania court decisions such as these had the power to extend rights beyond the minimum rights set out as the federal Constitution's protective floor. At the same time, even without a constitutionally driven need for modification, there was much in Pennsylvania law that called for updating or addressing.

As the ramifications of the 1968 Constitution emerged, its vision of the Unified Judicial System (UJS) that gave the Court pervasive structural administrative power over the lower courts became more influential.[5] It was a feature of the fact that the Commonwealth is a large and diverse state with different-size counties (now "judicial districts") long accustomed to disparate practices. A significant number of the judicial districts were then presided over by a single judge; all counties but one contained multiple police departments (and police procedures), while another had scores of judges with a county containing one centralized police force and a city border coterminous with the border of the judicial district (county). In between, the size and the practicalities of the judicial districts can vary widely.

A. Criminal Procedural Rulemaking

These dramatic changes naturally required the Court's serious and time-consuming attention and called for unifying solutions. In the common law tradition, the case-by-case adjudication of issues—wrestling with the meanings and reach of federal case law in opinions—traditionally awaited the pressing of an issue in some trial court and then its advancement on appeal. Yet despite its advantages, the narrow case-law system was hard-put to deal with the era's fast pace of change and provide the clarity, uniformity, and prompt resolution necessary for those involved in the criminal law process. Much of the Court's assessment of the new procedural needs, and of best responses in a complicated Commonwealth, was thus carefully handled through the Court's procedural rulemaking authority under the Pennsylvania Constitution of 1968.

As described in more detail in the previous chapter, the Judiciary Article, Article V of the Pennsylvania Constitution of 1968, created the UJS and entrusted the Supreme Court with responsibility over that system. In order to fulfill that responsibility, the Court needed authority to establish the procedures for court proceedings within the UJS. Article V, Section 10(c) explicitly provides the Court with the power "to prescribe general rules governing practice, procedure and the conduct of all courts," as long as those rules "are consistent with this Constitution and neither abridge, enlarge nor modify the substantive rights of any litigant." This section also states, "All laws shall be suspended to the extent that they are inconsistent with rules prescribed under these provisions," thereby empowering the Court to suspend legislation that prescribes procedural matters. As the head of the judicial branch, responsible for the UJS under Article V, the Court uses its plenary authority over the rules governing the system, separate from the legislature or the executive.[6]

In responding to the complex challenges of this pivotal era, much of the Supreme Court's work involved the use of this Article V, Section 10(c) rulemaking authority and the Court's Criminal Procedural Rules Committee. The comprehensive rulemaking process allowed procedural issues to be debated, focused, and handled beyond narrow (and possibly too untimely) reliance on case-by-case decision making. As a result, the Court was able to deal with broad matters that needed prompt guidelines in all counties, establishing readily available rules setting forth sustainable, realistic procedures. The advantages of this rulemaking process include the ability to go beyond immediate case facts and issues to coordinate interrelated matters and principles and provide a uniform solution to statewide procedural problems. In addition, because the Court does not have to wait for issues to be presented in a particular appealed case, rulemaking allows the Court to anticipate problems and respond to them promptly while fixing effective dates for rules (and rule amendments) to provide litigants adequate notice and the opportunity to comply with the rules.

Not unexpectedly, the Court's general rulemaking power has been the subject of debate.[7] Some commentators, and occasionally legislators, have suggested that the General Assembly should be more involved in the rulemaking process—at least being given the power to approve or disapprove rules promulgated by the Court, as in the federal system, where Congress has ultimate authority over rules of procedure. Others have taken a contrary view, among other things comparing the judiciary's familiarity with the issues and their own processes in solving procedural issues, as well as the imperative to quickly and effectively deal with needed procedural changes and constant amendments.[8] In fact, the Court has approached its rulemaking power with care (as has its committee), respectful of the nonjudicial branches of the Commonwealth government.

As noted, much of the Court's work has involved the use of its Criminal Procedural Rules Committee. That committee was originally appointed in 1957, with the first rules promulgated in 1964.[9] However, given the aforementioned driving imperatives, the Rules Committee also burgeoned in the pivotal era of the 1970s and 1980s. The committee's makeup went on term limits and was rounded out to approximately five judges, five prosecutors, five defense attorneys, a law professor, and notably, a legislator; it was supported by a small, excellent staff that prepared thorough need assessments, analyses, and drafts for full committee consideration. In the committee, extensive debate took place as to the need, content, and workability of proposed rules and rule amendments in the wide variety of Pennsylvania counties. It was typical for the full committee to meet for a day and a half, in some particularly pressing periods, on a nearly monthly basis. Moreover, for more complicated matters, subcommittees were created to focus on the issues and to prepare an initially vetted proposal for the committee's ultimate consideration and decision. An abbreviated list affords a flavor of some rule matters that engaged the committee: prompt trial rules, discovery, guilty plea practice, prosecutorial control of the charging function, bail, pretrial diversion, procedures under a new death penalty statute, sentencing processes, suppression motions, joinder and severance, posttrial motions, investigating grand juries, citations in lieu of arrests, venue, recording of court proceedings, summary cases, search warrants, and local rules review.

The rulemaking process is, of course, informed by specific cases that have arisen; the process is also informed by many other issues arising in the trial courts and the intermediate appellate courts, even in unreported decisions, as well as problems communicated from the bench and bar. The Criminal Rules Committee and its staff research and analyze the issues and make recommendations based on a wealth of information and experience. The makeup of the committee members provides familiarity with day-to-day criminal practice and procedure, from which ideas for rules and rules revisions naturally develop. The members' broad experience also allows for a balanced analysis of the need for rules, the particular provisions that the rules should include, and the specific language that will effectively deal with issues that have already arisen and those that can be anticipated. The committee's staff drafts each rule proposal and presents it to the committee, supported by a detailed legal memorandum. The proposals are then considered by and discussed among the members, often at more than one meeting, with the staff drafting revisions between meetings. Thus each proposal is fully aired within the committee and then published for general comments by the bench, bar, and public pursuant to Pa. R. Jud. Admin. 103. The publication process allows for additional and widespread input from around the Commonwealth before rule proposals are finalized and presented to the Court.

Potential rules and rule revisions are also suggested to the Court, committee members, and the committee's staff by the bench and bar. Periodically, of course, the committee has surveyed and investigated areas on its own to determine whether rules might be necessary. Rules often draw on the rules of other states, or even the federal rules,[10] but the disparate nature of Pennsylvania and its long legal history means that the rules need to be tailored particularly to this Commonwealth, not just copied wholesale from other states or the Federal Rules of Procedure (which, of course, were themselves evolving). The work of the Court's Criminal Procedural Rules Committee also meant that the justices had to devote more agenda time for consideration of rule proposals and supporting material—beyond the Court's existing (and continuing) case-oriented docket. This expanded agenda for criminal procedure matters mirrored the Court's whole agenda as its administrative and rulemaking role expanded to deal with a substantial body of other procedural rules, including its consideration of important Civil Procedure Rules and others (among them the addition of Judicial Administration Rules, Appellate Rules, and an array of other developing rules and other administrative matters).

B. The Court's Control of the Rulemaking Process

As part of its Article V, Section 10(c) rulemaking power, the Court regulates and controls the process by which its rules of procedure are promulgated. This has led to periodic tension with the General Assembly, although meetings between the committee leadership and legislators tended to ameliorate that tension to some degree. In the Judiciary Act Repealer Act (JARA) of 1978,[11] the legislature provided that the Court's rulemaking would be subject to the Commonwealth's Public Agency Open Meeting Law,[12] which would require the Court to, among other things, open to the public any meetings related to the exercise of its rulemaking authority. Any rules promulgated without open public meetings would be invalidated, and any persons who participated in a meeting that was not open would be guilty of a summary offense. Although the Court concluded that this provision was not constitutional under Article V, it also made sure that its rulemaking process would be suitably open and participatory.

In order to respond to JARA's attempt to subject the procedural rule process to the Open Meeting Law, the Court chose an extraordinary approach by submitting a letter directly to the governor and other high state officials declaring the statute unconstitutional.[13] In choosing this vehicle, the Court was concerned that waiting for "an adversary challenge to our failure to follow the Open Meeting Law . . . would risk creating and prolonging unnecessary tension between our branches of government."[14] In its letter, the Court reasoned that the JARA provision was not constitutional because Article V, Section 10(c) gives the Court exclusive rulemaking authority, and the power to prescribe rules must include the power to decide how they are to be prescribed. The Court explained that the rulemaking power *is* judicial power, and any attempt by the legislature to limit or regulate that power would amount to an attempt to assume some of it, which is inconsistent with the judiciary being a separate, distinct, independent branch of government.[15]

As the Court noted in its letter to the governor and legislative leaders, however, even though its rulemaking process could not constitutionally be subject to the Open Meeting Law, that process was relatively open and participatory.[16] Thus in 1978, the Court adopted Rule of Judicial Administration 103 to govern the rulemaking process. That rule requires that before any of the Court's rules committees recommends that the Court adopt or amend a rule of procedure, ordinarily it must first distribute the proposed rule (or rule amendment), together with any explanatory note or comment that will accompany the rule, to the *Pennsylvania Bulletin* for publication.[17] As published in the *Bulletin*, the rule proposal would include "a statement to the effect that comments regarding the proposed Rule are invited and should be sent directly to the proposing Rules Committee within a specified period of time." Any commentary received by the proposing committee must then be reviewed before it finalizes and submits the rule recommendation to the Court. Changes in the rule proposal that are based on the received commentary need not but may be again published in the *Bulletin* before the committee sends the recommendation to the Court. Thus even though it may not be subject to the legislative Open Meeting Law, the Court's rulemaking process solicits public input and is in fact open to public scrutiny.

In April 1978, the Criminal Rules Committee began to make public an extensive "Report" on each proposed rule, with supporting documentation and an invitation for comments from the bench, bar, and public. These detailed reports, published in the *Pennsylvania Bulletin* and in West's *Atlantic Advance Sheets*, are much more detailed than the "Comments" annotating the rules. They also provide a lasting public record of the committee's intention, and for the era discussed in this chapter, they also offer a handy and detailed historical reflection of the many issues facing the Court (and therefore the committee).

Even after the crest of the Due Process Revolution and its accompanying extensive rule changes, the work was substantial; for example, it will offer some measure of the pace of the Court's work that in the seven-year period from the 1978 start of the expanded published reports until 1985, approximately seventy reports were published about proposals to create, or in one way or another affect, some two hundred rules.[18]

C. Suspension of Procedural and Inconsistent Legislation

The Court has described Article V, Section 10(c) as containing two principles with respect to procedural legislation:[19] First, it grants the Court "exclusive power to enact procedural rules" with a declaration that "a law inconsistent with such a rule is suspended." Second, even in the absence of a specific, inconsistent Court-promulgated rule, it means that "[i]f . . . the legislature enacts a procedural statute, that statute is unconstitutional" because it would infringe on the Court's exclusive procedural rulemaking power under Article V, Section 10(c). Thus the Court has the power under the Pennsylvania Constitution to prevent legislative attempts to intrude on its exclusive constitutional authority over procedure.

The Court has resisted "temperately though firmly, any invasion of this Court's province, whether great or small," but it considers this "a matter of grave significance" and, therefore, has exercised its power to suspend statutes "only with great reluctance."[20] In this area, the Court has also been described as only utilizing "its powers in an attempt to 'assure that the judicial system is uniform and efficien[t],' while providing for 'the just determination of every judicial proceeding.'"[21]

The critical question in determining whether to suspend legislation is, of necessity, whether a matter covered by the statute is substantive or procedural, since the Court has exclusive power under Article V with respect to procedural matters, compared to the legislature's substantive role. The Court has acknowledged that an attempt to devise a universal principle for determining whether a matter is procedural or substantive has met with little success. However, it has stated that "as a general matter, substantive law creates, defines, and regulates rights; procedural law addresses the method by which those rights are enforced."[22]

Applying this substance-versus-procedure "definition," the Court has, for example, suspended statutes providing the Commonwealth with the right to a jury trial as a procedural right and inconsistent with then Pa. R. Crim. P. 1101,[23] the Capital Unitary Appeal Act provision prescribing detailed procedures for review of death penalty cases,[24] and legislation providing for local courts to establish and implement pretrial diversion programs.[25] On the other hand, the Court has rejected constitutional challenges to statutes argued to be procedural. For example, it held that a statute providing the requirements for stays of execution of death sentences pending petitions for collateral relief is substantive, setting forth the circumstances in which there is a right to a stay,[26] and it also upheld making victim impact statements admissible at death penalty hearings as substantive legislation.[27]

The General Assembly has itself acknowledged the Court's exclusive authority and need to promulgate rules governing procedural matters. Thus when the legislature enacted the Judicial Code to effectuate the unification of the judicial system,[28] it also passed the JARA to eliminate those statutory provisions that had dealt with matters of procedure and to refer the subjects of those provisions to the Court's rulemaking authority. Although many of these subjects were already covered by the Court's rules, in response to this legislation, the Court thoroughly reviewed the repealed statutes and amended its rules to more completely cover subjects previously covered by procedural statutes. Occasional proposals to curtail the Court's rulemaking authority—by requiring that rules adopted by the Court must be presented to the legislature or by altogether removing the Court's constitutional suspension power[29]—have not passed the General Assembly. Moreover, such critiques have largely subsided, as the Court's practices have demonstrated a careful approach to rulemaking, much of it in the area of criminal procedure during a challenging period.

V. CONCLUSION

The Supreme Court's work amid the exceptional developments of a challenging, unique, and defining period in criminal procedure was impressive. The period also proved to be one in which the Court refined its rulemaking process, a process that now accounts for so much of the judicial response to unifying and solving important procedural matters.

NOTES

James A. Shellenberger is a professor and faculty chair at Temple University Beasley School of Law and chief staff counsel to the Pennsylvania Supreme Court's Criminal Procedural Rules Committee, 1979–83. The late James A. Strazzella was a professor and faculty chair at Temple University Beasley School of Law and chair of the Pennsylvania Supreme Court's Criminal Procedural Rules Committee under five chief justices, 1972–85.

1. *See* James Strazzella (Reporter), *The Federalization of Criminal Law*, vol. 19 (Washington, D.C.: American Bar Association Criminal Justice Section, 1998) (containing data).

2. James Strazzella, "Ineffective Identification Counsel: Cognizability Under the Exclusionary Rule," *Temple Law Quarterly* 48 (1975): 241 (citing cases on growth of right to counsel into mid-1970s); James Strazzella, "Ineffective Assistance of Counsel Claims: New Uses, New

Problems," *Arizona Law Review* 19 (1978): 443 (collecting authorities on growth of ineffective counsel claim into late 1970s).

3. *See* Strazzella, "Ineffective Assistance," 443 (discussing expansion of procedural mechanisms for federal claim relief such as habeas, noting the seminal expansion cases and the effect of ineffectiveness claims as potentially neutralizing what would otherwise be forfeiture).

4. *See* Fay v. Noia, 372 U.S. 391 (1963) (setting federal habeas standard as "deliberate by-pass" by defendant, implying burden on prosecution to prove such election by knowing, intelligent, voluntary giving up of remedy in state proceeding; also indicating wide view of type of federal constitutional claims that could be raised on habeas); Townsend v. Sain, 372 U.S. 293 (1963) (expansive federal habeas court power to review facts); *cf.* Sanders v. United States, 373 U.S. 1 (1963) (in federal case, reflecting broad

view of ability of defendants to file successive posttrial relief claims).

5. Pa. Const. (1968), art. V, § 10 (with some limitations, giving the Supreme Court "general supervisory and administrative authority over all the courts"; power "to prescribe general rules governing practice, procedure and the conduct of all courts"; and declaring "[a]ll laws shall be suspended to the extent that they are inconsistent with rules prescribed under these provisions").

6. *See* Justice Thomas W. Pomeroy, foreword to "The Pennsylvania Supreme Court in Its First Decade Under the New Judiciary Article," *Temple Law Quarterly* 53 (1980): 613–36, 636nn17–18. Justice Pomeroy's article collects authorities and refers to the 1957 enabling statute (which preceded the 1968 Constitution; the constitutional provision mirrors that statute). That statute empowered the rules process and also dealt with suspension of legislation. The Criminal Procedure Rules Committee was originally formed in 1957 and the first Criminal Rules were adopted in 1964. *See* ibid., 618.

7. *E.g.*, Bruce Ledewitz, "What's Really Wrong with the Supreme Court of Pennsylvania," *Duquesne Law Review* 32 (1994): 409; Jason Bologna, "An Abuse of Power," *Temple Law Review* 71 (1998): 711.

8. A. Leo Levin and Anthony G. Amsterdam, "Legislative Control over Judicial Rule-Making: A Problem in Constitutional Revision," *University of Pennsylvania Law Review* 107 (1958): 9–14.

9. *See* Pomeroy, foreword to "Pennsylvania Supreme Court," 613–36, 636nn17–18.

10. For a discussion on the Federal Rules' capacity to act as a model, *see* Jerold Israel, "Federal Criminal Procedure as a Model for the States," *Annals of the American Academy of Political and Social Science* 543, no. 1 (1996), 130–43.

11. Act of April 28, 1978, P.L. 202, No. 53, § 10(19.1), 42 Pa.C.S. § 1703.

12. P.L. 486, No. 175, 65 P.S. § 262 *et seq.*

13. In re 42 Pa.C.S. § 1703, 394 A.2d 444 (Pa. 1978).

14. 394 A.2d at 446.

15. Ibid., 448–49.

16. Ibid., 450.

17. As far as the Criminal Procedure Rules were concerned, even before Rule 103 was adopted, the Criminal Rules Committee had prepublished some of its rule proposals in the *Atlantic Reporter* before the explanations that came to

be published as reports in the *Pa. Bulletin*.

18. *Pa. Bulletin*, Reports of the Criminal Procedure Rules Committee, vols. 8–15, 1978 (initial report 4-1-78) through 1985. *See also* "Pa. Supreme Court Reviews," *Temple Law Review Quarterly* vols. 47–57, 59–60 (1973–84) (providing some further detail on procedural changes in the period discussed here).

19. Commonwealth v. McMullen, 961 A.2d 842, 847–48 (Pa. 2008).

20. Payne v. Commonwealth Dept. of Corrs, 871 A.2d 795, 805, 801 (Pa. 2005).

21. Leonard Sosnov, "Criminal Procedure Rights Under the Pennsylvania Constitution: Examining the Present and Exploring the Future," *Widener Journal of Public Law* 3 (1993): 217, 223–24 (quoting Justice Samuel J. Roberts, foreword to "Pennsylvania Supreme Court Review, 1980," *Temple Law Quarterly* 54 [1981]: 403, and Pa. R. Crim. P. 2 [now Rule 101(A)]).

22. McMullen, 961 A.2d at 847 (Pa. 2008) (citing cases). *See also* Sosnov, "Criminal Procedure," 222–23 (first quoting Siddach v. Wilson & Co., 312 U.S. 1, 14 [1941], as to what is procedural—"the judicial process for enforcing rights and duties recognized by substantive law and for justly administering remedy and redress for disregard of them"—and then stating that substantive law is generally "limited to the designation of what conduct constitutes criminal offenses and to the provision for penalties for infractions, as well as to legislation, such as statutes dealing with privileges and privileged communications that directly affects the relations between people outside the criminal justice system. What is left to govern in the criminal justice system constitutes practice and procedure," the exclusive domain of the Pennsylvania Supreme Court).

23. Commonwealth v. Sorrell, 456 A.2d 1326 (Pa. 1982). Article I, Section 6 of the Pennsylvania Constitution was subsequently amended in 1998 to provide that "the Commonwealth shall have the same right to trial by jury as does the accused."

24. In re Suspension of Capital Unitary Act, 772 A.2d 676 (Pa. 1999).

25. Commonwealth v. Lutz, 495 A.2d 928 (Pa. 1985). *See also* Bergdoll v. Kane, 694 A.2d 1155 (Pa. Cmwlth. 1997) (Commonwealth Court held that amendment to Pennsylvania Constitution's Confrontation Clause for the purpose of allowing the Legislature to enact laws regarding how children my testify in

criminal cases would also require amendment of Article V, Section 10[c], because the manner in which testimony is received in court is procedural and therefore within the exclusive rule-making power of the Supreme Court).

26. Commonwealth v. Morris, 771 A.2d 721 (Pa. 2001).

27. Commonwealth v. Harris, 817 A.2d 1033 (Pa. 2002); Commonwealth v. Means, 773 A.2d 143 (Pa. 2001).

28. Act of July 9, 1976, P.L. 586, No. 142, § 2 *et seq.*, effective June 27, 1978.

29. S. Res. 779, 181st Leg. (Pa. 1997); H.B. 10, 179th Leg. (Pa. 1995).

CHAPTER 5

Supervising and Regulating the Practice of Law

THOMAS G. WILKINSON JR.

AND ROGER B. MEILTON

The history of the regulation of the legal profession in Pennsylvania is both unique and complicated, particularly when compared to the experiences of other states. Today, under Pennsylvania's Constitution, the Supreme Court regulates the practice of law and more than sixty-five thousand lawyers admitted to the practice of law in the Commonwealth. As noted in prior chapters, the Pennsylvania Constitution of 1968 established the Unified Judicial System (UJS), vesting in the Supreme Court general supervisory and administrative authority over all other courts.[1] Under Article V, Section 10(c), the Supreme Court is granted the power to prescribe general rules governing admission to the bar and the practice of law.[2]

From the colonial period through the late 1960s, the regulation of the practice of law in Pennsylvania was far more decentralized. During this time, the courts of Pennsylvania regarded the admission of lawyers to practice to be a judicial function. The power to control admission to the bar was exercised not only by the Supreme Court but also by the lower courts of the Commonwealth. This dual admission of attorneys to the bar of the Supreme Court set the stage for the "unique and complicated" Pennsylvania experience. The role of the Supreme Court in regulating the profession is, therefore, best described in three distinct periods: the colonial period until 1776, the postindependence period until 1968, and the modern era since 1968.

I. THE COLONIAL PERIOD

The early Dutch, Swedish, and English colonists brought with them their own legal traditions and customs. The most enduring traditions were those inherited from England, including the well-established view that lawyers and judges "possess a peculiar responsibility for the preparation and admission of recruits into their profession."[3] The long-established custom in England was that "admission to practice to the English lower courts was granted by judges. As soon, therefore, as our colonists abandoned the attempt—made in several colonies—to prohibit professional lawyers altogether, there was provided, by legislative process, the same method of admission to their local courts; for, from the point of view of the British Empire, all such courts, the highest as well as the lowest, were subordinate to those at Westminster."[4]

Robert MacCrate, a past president of the American Bar Association (ABA), noted in an address to the Pennsylvania Bar Association (PBA) in 1995 that William Penn planned "Pennsylvania law to be so plain and court procedures so simple that each person could plead his or her own case."[5] Early colonial Pennsylvania courts were relatively unsophisticated, local in nature, and under the control of the governor.[6] Penn's vision, however, of a court system free of the complexities of the English common law and legal customs was not to be realized. As the province grew and more lawyers educated in England arrived in Pennsylvania, the natural consequence was the continued attachment to English forms and practices.[7]

The 1722 act that formally created the Supreme Court also provided "that there may be a competent number of persons, of an honest disposition, and learned in the law admitted by the justices of the said respective courts, to practice as attorneys there, who shall behave themselves justly and faithfully in their practice."[8] The mode and time of studying the law were left to be regulated by the discretion of the different courts, which were the exclusive judges of their own rules.[9]

In eighteenth-century colonial Philadelphia, the preferred preparation for law was attendance at one of the Inns of Court in London. More than one hundred students from the American colonies studied law in the Inns of Court from 1760 until the Revolutionary War, eleven of whom were from Pennsylvania.[10] Like William Penn, who attended Lincoln's Inn,[11] lawyers trained in one of the four English Inns of Court. The other three inns were Gray's Inn, Inner Temple, and Middle Temple. Those who could not afford to study in England studied under the apprenticeship model.[12] In an apprenticeship, a student would associate with a lawyer who provided instruction in the legal theory and skills necessary to practice law. Thomas McKean, a signer of the Declaration of Independence and the first chief justice of the Supreme Court under the 1776 Pennsylvania Constitution, served an apprenticeship in New Castle, Delaware, before being admitted to the bar at the age of twenty-one. He later studied at Middle Temple.[13]

Apprenticeships remained the primary method of legal education until the emergence of law schools in the second half of the nineteenth century. Pennsylvania Supreme Court rules required attorneys to be examined before admission to the Court as early as 1759. By 1767, a more detailed rule of the Supreme Court required apprenticeship periods and practice experience prior to admission.[14] Supreme Court Rule 7 of 1767 required an apprenticeship for a four-year term and practice for one year in a county court or three years' apprenticeship and two years of practice. It also required a certificate of two examiners appointed by the Court affirming that such person is "well grounded in the principles of the law and acquainted with the practice."[15] Those who began study after the age of twenty-one were only required to apprentice for two years and practice for one year. "Gentlemen" in good standing, admitted to practice before courts in other colonies, or those having studied in the Inns of Court, were not subject to Rule 7 and were otherwise eligible for admission to the bar.[16] The Supreme Court's admission rules were amended in 1785 to require an "oath of allegiance and fidelity to the state" and establish residency requirements.[17] The Supreme Court Rule 24 of January 2, 1788, regulating admission to the bar, repeated the entire previous rule of 1785 and added new provisions.[18]

The Supreme Court and the other courts established by the Provincial Assembly in 1722 remained in session until the Revolutionary period. The Pennsylvania Constitution of 1776 established the Courts of Session, Common Pleas, and Orphans in each county.[19] A revised Pennsylvania State Constitution in 1790 vested executive power in the governor, legislative power in a bicameral legislature, and judicial power in the Supreme Court and "in courts of Oyer and Terminer and General Gaol Delivery, in a Court of Common Pleas, Orphans' Court, Register's Court, and a Court of Quarter Sessions of the Peace for each county, in Justices of the Peace and in such other Courts as the legislature may, from time to time, establish."[20] The Constitution of 1790 encouraged development of the Commonwealth's judicial system by grouping counties into judicial districts and placing president judges at the heads of the districts' Common Pleas Courts.[21]

II. THE POSTINDEPENDENCE PERIOD: 1776 TO 1968

At the close of the eighteenth century and continuing to the Civil War, public sentiment in the form of a "democratic movement" shifted in the direction of restricting the courts' power to set educational requirements for admission to the practice of law.[22] In his address to the PBA in 1995, Robert MacCrate noted,

> Despite the profession's progress in colonial America and the active participation by lawyers in the founding of the Republic, the legal profession in most parts of the new country following its birth entered a period of decline. At the center was the Jeffersonian hostility toward self-created elites, as represented by any profession. This hostility peaked during the presidency of Andrew Jackson, when various States threw the practice of law open to non-lawyers and provided only minimal qualifications for admission. Nevertheless, despite Pennsylvania's early reluctance to accept the professional lawyer and the general decline in much of America in the perception of the legal profession, this Commonwealth managed to maintain professional standards throughout the first half of the 19th Century.[23]

By the end of the eighteenth century, single lawyers or small groups of lawyers had begun giving lectures to individuals preparing to become lawyers through a number of proprietary law schools. These schools essentially provided the first law classes in the United States.[24] Associations of students preparing for the bar admission existed in Philadelphia at an early date.[25] The Law Academy, opened in Philadelphia in 1820, was loosely modeled after a 1790 lecture series by James Wilson, which itself proved to be short lived.[26] The school was founded by Peter S. Du Ponceau. It was intended "to be a 'national law school' both for students in law offices and for younger members of the bar—an avowed competitor with Harvard, in a city more accessible than Cambridge to the country at large. In 1832, however, the field of legal education was abandoned to the local university."[27] In Pittsburgh, there was an early initiative in the 1840s by a group of local practitioners to give lectures to aspiring law students. This ended by 1845, however, when a major fire destroyed the school's facilities. There was no immediate attempt to rebuild, partly due to the lack of enthusiasm of local practitioners, who benefitted financially from fees provided by the apprenticeship system.[28]

The firmly entrenched apprenticeship system inhibited to some extent the development of law schools in Pennsylvania.[29] Members of the profession were satisfied with a system under which they had trained, and to the extent that more was needed, it was envisioned that this could be provided by lectures offered by bar associations.[30] Early efforts to establish a law school at the University of Pennsylvania did not come to fruition until 1850. The Dickinson School of Law, founded in 1834 by Judge John Reed, is the oldest law school in Pennsylvania. The University of Pittsburgh School of Law was formally founded in 1895; however, legal studies were a part of the curriculum of the university as early as 1843, and its first law degrees were conferred in 1847. Temple Law School was founded in 1895.

University-based legal education, ultimately employing the case-study method in large classes, evolved as a substitute to the apprenticeship training system. Gradually, the majority of states that attempted to preserve a prescribed period of apprenticeship began to modify their rules in one way or another.[31] In Pennsylvania by 1870, it appears that the prescribed period of clerkship could be satisfied by attendance at a local law school.[32] By the 1890s, the University of Pennsylvania and Dickinson Law School offered law degrees that entitled their graduates to be directly admitted to the bar of the Pennsylvania Supreme Court. This "diploma privilege" was established in Pennsylvania in 1875,[33] abolished in 1881, and restored in 1889.[34] It permanently ended in 1902 with the establishment of State Board of Law Examiners Rules, including a requirement that practice applicants sit for the bar examination.[35]

In a comprehensive 1921 study entitled *Training for the Profession of Law in America*, Alfred Zantzinger Reed suggested that increased attendance at law schools evolved as a result of three causes. The first was the growing demand for lawyers as America transitioned from an agrarian to an industrial economy. Second, law schools began to be seen as the best source for legal education and preparation for the bar. And third, once the initial burden of establishing law schools was met, it was comparatively easy for the schools to build on their own success.[36]

The Civil War also saw the beginning of part-time law schools allowing for students engaged in other occupations to study law.[37] In 1860, the total number of law school students in the United States was 1,200. By 1890, that number had increased to more than 4,500. By the beginning of World War I, there were approximately 23,000 law students enrolled in law schools across the country.[38] By 2013, more than 139,000 students were enrolled in law schools approved by the ABA.

The emergence of local, state, and national bar associations in the nineteenth century also had a significant impact on the development of standards for admission to practice and the regulation of the bar. The Philadelphia Bar Association, the earliest county bar association and the nation's first chartered metropolitan bar association, was founded in 1802. There were roughly three hundred members of the bar in Allegheny County when its bar association was founded in 1870.[39] The Lancaster Bar Association began in 1880, and the Dauphin County Bar Association was founded in 1898. In 1895, there were thirty-nine separate and independent county bar associations established in Pennsylvania.[40] While bar associations were private organizations historically, admission to the bar of a county court was often intertwined with admission to membership in a county bar association. By 1860, Pennsylvania was the only state that required law students to register in their local counties before they commenced their legal studies.[41]

The ABA, formed in 1878,[42] was a leader in promoting law school education as a requirement for bar admission nationwide.[43] The organization formally recommended a graded, three-year law school course as a condition for bar admission starting in 1881.[44] This idea opposed the trend at the turn of the century to accept *either* a classroom education *or* an apprenticeship for bar admission purposes.[45] In 1891, only 20 percent of the nation's lawyers had graduated from law school. No state at that time required law school graduation as a prerequisite to licensing.[46]

The ABA had other goals as well. It supported the development of centralized examining boards for bar applicants in each state.[47] By 1892 and, more explicitly by 1908, the ABA asserted its disapproval of the "diploma privilege."[48] As law school education as a basis for bar admission began to be accepted in the twentieth century, the ABA's attention also turned to requiring a college or university degree for admission to law school.[49]

The year 1895 witnessed two major developments in Pennsylvania legal history. The first was the creation of the Superior Court by the Pennsylvania legislature. The second was the founding of the PBA by a group of prominent members of the legal profession from across the Commonwealth. Prior to the founding of the PBA, there was no single organization in a position to speak for all lawyers in Pennsylvania. Recounting the PBA's history in connection with its diamond anniversary in 1971, Henry Thomas Dolan described the nature of law practice in Pennsylvania at the close of the nineteenth century: "[T]he practice of law in Pennsylvania was Balkanized, in short. Sixty-seven little temporalities, like the multitudinous small states of Germany and Italy of a century previous, administered the mechanics of practice before their courts, and their standards of professional discipline, with more than a touch of vigorous independence. The attitudes were a holdover, undoubtedly, from a day not much earlier, when the mountain and forest barriers of Pennsylvania's rugged terrain were penetrable only to the determined traveller with an urgent errand impelling him."[50]

Beyond preserving local authority, it is clear that local bars sought to protect "county" lawyers from competing with other lawyers from outside the county.[51] In *Laffey v. Court of Common Pleas*,[52] a 1983 decision, the Pennsylvania Supreme Court observed the following in a footnote:

> Nearly a century ago, the practice of law in this Commonwealth was subject to a multitude of restrictions affecting a practitioner's admission to membership in the bar of each judicial district. For example, in the year 1896 there were fifty-four judicial districts and there were fifty-four sets of standards governing membership in the bars, as each district maintained its own requirements and these were applied in an independent fashion by each district's own Board of Examiners. Some required written examinations; others conducted oral ones. Some carefully scrutinized an applicant's background and qualifications; others were satisfied with a perfunctory inquiry. Even within any given county the requirements were subject to change as the whims of newly appointed Board members were implemented. It was an era when the internal combustion engine had not long been in existence, and the automobile was yet a rarity, but the peripatetic attorney who ventured to practice in a county other than his own encountered a web of rules restricting admission to the bar of each district to which he travelled.

Among the early objectives of the PBA were both the reform of the "balkanized" nature of the admission to practice and the adoption of statewide practice rules to address the proliferation and complexity of local rules of court. The PBA's effort to establish uniform rules for bar admission began in 1895, with the creation of a permanent Committee on Legal Education, and continued until the goal was reached in 1902.[53] The PBA's effort to promote the adoption of uniform statewide rules of practice, which has a history of its own, proved to be a much longer struggle, not coming to fruition until 1937 with the Supreme Court's adoption of statewide rules of practice.[54]

The PBA's initiative to establish uniform standards for bar admission came to a successful conclusion in 1902 with the Supreme Court's adoption of the PBA "memorial" recommending the creation of a State Board of Law Examiners.[55] By per curiam order of May 26, 1902, the Court established the board to oversee the registration and examination of law students.[56] While county courts retained authority over admission to practice in their respective courts, uniform educational requirements and examination for bar admission were to be established by the State Board of Law Examiners.

By an order of November 11, 1902, the Supreme Court adopted ten rules pertaining to the admission of attorneys by the State Board of Law Examiners. The rules provided that no person would be admitted to practice as an attorney except on recommendation of the state board. Prior to registration as a law student, an applicant had to show that "he was of good moral character and had to pass a preliminary examination on the English language and literature; outlines of universal history; history of England and United States; arithmetic, algebra through quadratics and plane geometry; modern geography; and the first four books of Caesar's Commentaries, the first six books of the Aeneid, and the first four orations of Cicero against Cataline."[57]

Law students completing three years of law school study or bona fide service of regular clerkship were required to advertise their intention to apply for admission, provide verification from three members of the bar known to the candidate who could certify as to his character, provide verification from the candidate's law school dean or preceptor attesting to attendance and diligent study, and pay a fee of $20.[58] Other rules listed the subjects of examination, the time and place of examination, the operation and duties of the State Board of Law Examiners, and the admission of attorneys previously admitted in other states.[59]

The State Board of Law Examiners Rules adopted in 1902 remained in effect with some amendment until they were substantially amended by the Supreme Court in 1923. These amendments provided for the investigation of the character and "moral qualifications" of applicants both prior to registration as law students and again on completion of the candidates' law studies. Under the rules, the determination of the "character and fitness" of candidates was to be determined by the board of the county in which the applicant resided or intended to practice. Applicants could appeal a local county board's negative determination to the state board and ultimately to the Supreme Court, but such appeals were seen as discretionary with the state board.[60]

There were other important features of the rules adopted in 1923. The revised rules no longer required preliminary examination of a candidate not holding a college degree prior to registration as a law student, instead substituting an examination conducted by the College Entrance Board. The College Entrance Board exam was viewed as rigorous, and thus registration as a law student by a candidate without a college degree was considered to be severely limited.[61] The new rules required each student to have a preceptor during the entire period of law study and to serve a six-month clerkship prior to admission to the bar. The rules retained the requirement for successful completion of a bar examination prior to admission.

Under the 1923 rules, a candidate seeking admission could still qualify to sit for the bar exam either through attendance at a three-year law school (four years in the case of part-time study), by "service of a *bona fide* clerkship in a law office for three years," or through a combination of law school and law clerkship. The clerkship method of law study was continued even though some started calling for its discontinuation. At least one commentator expressed the view that a law school education was a distinctly better method to prepare for the bar exam and law practice.[62] Over time, law school education became the preferred method; however, the option of "reading the law" remained until discontinued by order of the Supreme Court in 1971.[63]

An 1834 act provided that the "judges of the several courts of record of this Commonwealth shall respectively have the power to admit a competent number of persons of honest disposition and learned in the law to practice as attorneys in their respective courts."[64] Other legislative enactments in 1885, 1887, 1909, 1919, 1921, and 1923 expanded on the Act of 1834 by providing that admission of an attorney to practice before the Supreme Court operated as admission to practice in all courts of the Commonwealth. The Act of July 11, 1923, P.L. 151, limited the right to practice in all courts by providing that "admission . . . to practice in the Supreme Court shall *upon approval of the local examining board*, qualify such attorney to practice as an attorney-at-law in every other court of this Commonwealth."[65]

While the legislature was enacting laws to provide for uniform standards for admission to the practice of law, it is clear from a long series of cases that the Supreme Court was not prepared to relinquish its ultimate rulemaking authority providing for the admission of attorneys to the bar. The author of an article entitled "Pennsylvania Joins the Union," published in the *Pennsylvania Bar Quarterly* in 1966, observed that "while the Legislature was enacting and re-enacting statutes which, on their face called for a uniform standard of practice to be applied on a state-wide basis, the Courts of the Commonwealth and the local bar Associations were setting down their own rules and regulations. Like two ships in the night, the Legislature and the courts took little heed of one another."[66]

In *Splane Petition* in 1889, the Supreme Court upheld the decision of the Orphans' Court of Allegheny County, which refused to admit the petitioner, Splane, to practice before the Orphans' Court. In so doing, the Supreme Court found that the petitioner was not in compliance with admission rules then in effect and went further to suggest in dicta that the Act of 1887, under which the petitioner sought admission, was an unconstitutional encroachment on the Court's powers, stating, "The attorney is an officer of the court, and is brought into close and intimate relations with the court. Whether he shall be admitted, or whether he shall be disbarred, is a judicial and not a legislative question."[67]

In *Hoopes v. Bradshaw* in 1909, the Supreme Court upheld the validity of the Act of 1909 and directed the issuance of a mandamus to the prothonotary of Beaver County to file the appearance praecipe of a member of the bar of the Supreme Court. In so doing, the Court held that "all that the Act of 1909 does is to declare what effect is to be given to a purely judicial act of this court in directing the admission of an attorney at law to practice before it." Finding the act to be constitutional on this basis, the Court observed that there are certain functions of the lower courts with which the Act of 1909 does not interfere.

Among those is the right of courts to require practitioners to "establish an office in the county to whose courts he would be admitted."[68]

In *Olmsted's Case*, a 1928 decision, Chief Justice Moschzisker held that the Act of July 11, 1923, did not prevent county examining boards from requiring bar candidates to establish their principal place of practice within the county. In support of its decision, the Court said, "The true rule is as follows: Statutes dealing with admission to the bar will be judicially recognized as valid, so far as, but no further than, the legislation involved does not encroach on the right of the courts to say who shall be privileged to practice before them, and what circumstances persons shall be admitted to that privilege."[69]

The Principal Office Rule, requiring an attorney to maintain an office in a county as a prerequisite to admission to that county's bar, was firmly established by the holdings in *Hoopes* and *Olmsted*. As noted by the PBA Committee on Legal Education and Admission to the Bar in 1947, "In each of the 47 States . . . exclusive of Pennsylvania, a lawyer who has been admitted to the bar of its highest court has the privilege of practicing in any state Court within that State . . . He is free . . . to appear in its courts in several or all of its counties."[70] In contrast, "[w]ith the Principal Office rule intact, a Pennsylvania attorney could be denied the right to practice in any county other than that in which he maintained his principal office."[71]

Beyond the Principal Office Rule, many counties adopted rules postponing admission until after a period of residence in the county. A few also placed admissions on a quota basis, limiting the number of applicants admitted each year.[72] In 1947, under the direction of the PBA, the Committee on Legal Education and Admission to the Bar surveyed the rules of the various counties of Pennsylvania relating to limitations to local bar admission. The survey included principal office, residence, and any other rules that prevented an attorney admitted to the bar of the Supreme Court from appearing in a county court. The committee requested information from sixty-seven counties and received replies from fifty-nine.[73] In four counties, it was reported that judges annually or semiannually set the number of lawyers who could be admitted, but in two of those counties, the rule was not currently enforced.[74] In thirty counties, applicants for admission must have resided in the county for a certain period, from six months to five years, immediately prior to being admitted.[75] Lack of prior residence was also seen as an impediment to prompt admission in at least a few other counties.[76] Four counties required a clerkship to be served in that county, and at least twenty-six counties had a requirement relating to maintenance of an office in the county.[77] In a large part of the Commonwealth, under the rules in force at the time, a lawyer could not belong to the bar of more than one county and could, therefore, practice in only one of sixty-seven counties. As the PBA Committee on Legal Education and Admission to the Bar observed, "[T]here was no such thing as a statewide bar."[78]

While the PBA Committee on Legal Education and Admission to the Bar expressed its disapproval of the Principal Office Rule, the committee recognized that a lawyer could overcome this restriction by associating with local counsel when appearing in other county courts. The restriction of primary concern to the Legal Education and Bar Admission Committee was the residency requirement, which the committee believed severely limited a lawyer's mobility in terms of where he or she might choose to practice or live. The committee found the residency "requirements to be unworthy of Pennsylvania lawyers," stating, "[T]hey are vicious in their present effect and will be even more vicious in their future effects."[79] The committee was equally opposed to county rules establishing quotas for the number of attorneys admitted to any county court, viewing such rules as fundamentally unfair to bar applicants.[80]

The committee considered various means to accomplish its goal of abolishing residency requirements and quotas governing the number of lawyers admitted to practice. These options included litigation to determine the validity of the restrictions, legislation, and voluntary action by lawyers themselves. Choosing the course of voluntary compliance, the committee called on the PBA to approve its recommendations calling for the elimination of residency as a condition either for admission to the bar or for continued membership in a county bar and elimination of quotas for the admission to county bars.[81] The adoption in 1949 of Supreme Court Rule 12 1/2 ended the restrictive practice of quota systems and residency requirements for admission to county courts.[82]

In *Stewart v. Bechtel* in 1948,[83] the Supreme Court held that approval for admission to practice in the Philadelphia courts by the Philadelphia County Examining Board was not binding on the Montgomery County Examining Board. The Supreme Court, therefore, upheld the Montgomery County court's refusal to grant the appearance of a petitioner as an attorney in that court. It is interesting to note that in a concurring opinion, Justice Benjamin Jones observed,

> [T]he ultimate rule-making power in respect of admissions to practice law before the courts of this Commonwealth lies exclusively in this Court. It has never been disputed that the admission of attorneys to the practice of law involves the exercise of judicial power which, by Article V Section 1 of the Pennsylvania Constitution, is vested in the various courts of the Commonwealth; and, the paramount supervisory power over the courts of the Commonwealth is reposed in this Court by virtue of the Act of May 22, 1722, 1 Sm. L. 131, 140 Sec. XIII, which became constitutionally entrenched with the advent of our first State Constitution in 1776.[84]

Rule of Court 12 1/2 (later to become Rule 14) adopted by the Supreme Court in 1949 was an explicit recognition of the Principal Office Rule. *In re Christy Case* was a 1949 decision in which the Supreme Court held that the Principal Office Rule did not violate the Due Process Clause of the Fourteenth Amendment to the federal Constitution.[85] By denying certiorari, the US Supreme Court failed to disturb the Pennsylvania Supreme Court's finding of the constitutionality of the rule.[86]

In the May/June 2000 edition of *Pennsylvania Lawyer* magazine, an article by John D. Killian, a member of the Dauphin County Bar, recounts the challenges that faced lawyers seeking admission to practice in the 1950s.[87] Attorney Killian was first admitted to practice in New York State and worked in the office of the attorney general when he first came to Harrisburg. Among a number of obstacles he faced in seeking admission to the Pennsylvania Bar was a Dauphin County rule of court, then in force, providing that "[n]o person making application for admission to the Bar of Dauphin County shall be deemed able to qualify as to maintenance of a principal office in this county, as long as he or she is employed by the State or Federal Government on a full time basis."[88] Attorney Killian was ultimately successful in his quest for admission, but his account provides insight into bar admission requirements of the day.

In 1965, the Philadelphia Bar Association, with the support of other bar associations (including Allegheny, Crawford, Dauphin, Center, and Lycoming Counties), petitioned the Supreme Court to eliminate the Principal Office Rule. On November 19, 1965, the Court amended Rule 14 to provide that "[a]dmission to the Bar of this Court shall entitle such attorneys to admission to the Bar and to practice in all courts of this Commonwealth."[89] Resistance to full implementation of the new rule led to litigation, and on March 28, 1966, the Supreme Court amended Rule 14 to clarify the local rules suspended by Rule 14:

> Admission to the Bar of this Court shall entitle such attorney to practice in every Court of this Commonwealth, upon presentation to such Court of a certificate of the Supreme Court that the attorney is a member of the Bar of this Court in good standing. Any and all local rules governing the right to practice before any Court in any County or Judicial District of this Commonwealth, which require an office or a partner or associate or assistant within that County or District, or which prescribe length of residence therein as a prerequisite to practice in a local Court, or which limit the number of practicing attorneys upon a quota basis, or require advertising in a newspaper or a legal periodical, or prescribe other similar requirements, are hereby superseded.[90]

With this change, the Supreme Court asserted its ultimate authority to regulate the practice of law, and Pennsylvania lawyers were no longer restricted from practicing in any court in the Commonwealth.

Another significant hurdle for those seeking admission to the Pennsylvania Bar was the six-month clerkship requirement, first introduced in 1928. From the outset, law students experienced challenges in finding lawyers willing to assume the responsibility of serving as preceptors.[91] By the early 1950s, dissatisfaction with the requirement was on the rise. In an address to the Junior Bar Conference (now the Young Lawyers Division) of the PBA in Scranton on January 16, 1953, Brainerd Currie, dean of the School of Law at the University of Pittsburgh, expressed his view that the clerkship requirement should be abolished and characterized it as "an expression of nostalgia for the values that were lost when the law schools replaced law office study as the standard of preparation for the bar."[92] Dean Currie recognized, as did others, that the lack of standards, the lack of uniformity in the skills training received, and the practical limitations of the clerkship requirement had resulted in it becoming an unnecessary and perfunctory burden of limited educational value. By the mid-1960s, the Young Lawyers Section of the PBA was calling attention to the shortcomings of the requirement and actively calling for reform.[93] Concern with the effectiveness of the requirement notwithstanding, it remained in place until 1970. In that year, the requirement was addressed in a *University of Pennsylvania Law Review* comment examining and critiquing all the existing requirements for bar admission in Pennsylvania.[94] The authors of the comment recommended the substitution of a skills-and-methods course for the largely unpopular clerkship requirement. In January 1971, Rule 10 of the Supreme Court was amended so that the six-month period of clerkship under the guidance of a preceptor was no longer required.[95]

In the colonial period and well into the early twentieth century, law practice was exclusively a profession for white males. While the path to bar admission was challenging for those seeking admission, it was far more challenging, given the social attitudes and biases of the time, for women and minorities. This chapter cannot begin to do justice to the history, determination, and courage of the women, African Americans, and members of other minorities who first sought admission to the bar. For more, a reader may wish to consult online resources, including those cited in the endnotes that follow this chapter.

The first African American admitted to the Pennsylvania Bar was Jonathan Jasper Wright, born in 1840 in Luzerne County. He studied law with a firm in Montrose and in the chambers of a county judge in Wilkes Barre. Wright's initial attempt to be admitted to the Pennsylvania Bar was denied, but he persevered and sought admission again in 1866. On August 18, 1866, he was admitted to the bar and thereby became the first African American licensed to practice law in Pennsylvania. On February 1, 1870, Wright was elected to the South Carolina Supreme Court as an associate justice. He was the first African American elected to any appeals court in the nation.[96]

As noted in the introduction to this book, the first woman to be admitted to practice in Pennsylvania was Carrie Burnham Kilgore. After graduating from the University of Pennsylvania School of Law, she was admitted to the Orphans' Court of Philadelphia and to the Pennsylvania Supreme Court. Her admission to practice followed an act of the legislature (in 1885), a body she had addressed on the topic of admission of women a few years earlier.[97] Among the many highlights of her career, Kilgore argued before the Pennsylvania Supreme Court in favor of women's right to vote.[98]

The first woman admitted to practice in Pittsburgh was Agnes Fraser Watson. Born in Pittsburgh in 1866, she attended the University of Michigan Law School, returned to Pittsburgh, and applied to take the bar exam in the fall of 1895. On September 13, 1895, she passed the exam and became the first woman admitted to the Allegheny County Bar.

At her swearing-in, Judge Edwin Stowe said, "I want to say if the Supreme Court had not decided the question, I would not consent to any women practicing law in this court. But if women want to practice law and ride bicycles, I suppose it is none of my business. Let her be sworn."[99]

The first African American woman to be admitted to the Pennsylvania Bar was Sadie Tanner Mossell Alexander, born in Philadelphia in 1898. She earned both a master's degree and a doctorate at the University of Pennsylvania before enrolling at the University of Pennsylvania School of Law in 1924. The first African American woman to so enroll, Sadie Alexander graduated with honors and began her career in the legal profession in 1927.[100]

In May 2010, the Pennsylvania Supreme Court reversed a 163-year-old injustice by ordering the posthumous admission of George B. Vashon to the Pennsylvania Bar. First in 1847 and later in 1868, Vashon was denied admission to his hometown bar of Allegheny County because of his race. Ordering the posthumous admission, Chief Justice Castille said, "There is no question that denying George Vashon's admission to the Bar in 1847 and again in 1868 was blatantly discriminatory. By granting this petition, our Court recognizes, and is sensitive to the fact, that those prior practices in the Commonwealth's earlier history had a real effect on real people."[101]

Over the years, like all segments of society, the legal profession and the courts have made great progress in addressing issues of bias and discrimination. Today, admission to the bar is free from any qualifications relating to gender, race, or ethnicity. The legal profession is a diverse and vibrant profession very different from the times when lawyers like those noted previously first sought admission to the bar.

III. THE MODERN ERA: 1968 TO THE PRESENT

Like its federal counterpart, Pennsylvania's Constitution distributes power among three coequal branches of government: the legislature, the executive, and the courts. The Constitution of 1968 introduced historic changes to the nature and structure of Pennsylvania's judicial system. Article V, Section 10(c) of the Constitution expressly granted the Supreme Court the power to regulate lawyers and the practice of law throughout the Commonwealth.

A number of court-appointed boards assist the Court in regulating the profession, including the admission to practice in Pennsylvania courts, attorney conduct, continuing education, and other functions related to law practice in the Commonwealth. All such boards are appointed by the Court, and all operate under the general supervision of the Court.

The Pennsylvania Board of Law Examiners, first established in 1902, remains the Commonwealth's sole agency responsible for regulating admission to the practice of law in Pennsylvania. The board recommends to the Supreme Court educational standards for the licensing of attorneys. The board is empowered to recommend only those individuals who have "demonstrated the minimum competency and requisite character necessary to become a member of the bar."[102] The board oversees the registration of law students and conducts and administers the bar exam twice each year.

The Disciplinary Board was founded by the Supreme Court in March 1972, with the adoption of the Rules of Disciplinary Enforcement, effective November 1972.[103] The Rules of Disciplinary Enforcement give the board exclusive jurisdiction over attorney discipline, set forth the structure of the current system, and provide for full-time counsel and for the appointment of members of the Disciplinary Board and hearing committees.[104] The board assists the Supreme Court in maintaining the integrity of the profession, protecting the public, and safeguarding the reputation of the courts and the judicial system. The board enforces the Rules of Professional Conduct promulgated by the Supreme Court, effective April 1, 1988, and as amended on numerous occasions since then. The board is funded through an annual assessment of all licensed attorneys.

Prior to 1972, the process of lawyer discipline, much like the process of bar admission, was fragmented and the shared function of both state (the Board of Governance of the Pennsylvania Bar) and local county courts and agencies or tribunals established by the local courts or bar associations.[105] The Board of Governance was appointed in 1928 by the Supreme Court on the recommendation of the PBA.[106] The purpose of the Board of Governance was to provide some level of supervision over the local county disciplinary authorities.[107] The involvement of overlapping agencies, however, created confusion in the eyes of the public and "woeful inconsistency" in the sanctions imposed for comparable infractions.[108] There was no professional staff responsible for the administration of the disciplinary process or financing available to provide for such administration.[109] In the early 1970s, the Clark Commission of the ABA called for reform of bar discipline at a state level throughout the country.[110] At the same time, the PBA's Committee on Disciplinary Procedures was calling for reform.[111] The association recommended to the Supreme Court the establishment of a statewide system of disciplinary enforcement that, by March 1972, led to the Court's adoption of the Rules of Disciplinary Enforcement.[112]

The Disciplinary Board, established by the Rules of Disciplinary Enforcement, has exclusive jurisdiction over lawyer discipline and is responsible for administering private discipline to lawyers. The Office of Disciplinary Counsel (ODC), headed by the Chief Disciplinary Counsel, is also under the purview of the board.[113] The ODC is in charge of investigating potential misconduct, either after client or third-party complaints or as a result of their own investigation.[114] After investigating, the ODC has a number of options. It can dismiss the complaint, without any further action, with an educational letter or with a letter of concern.[115] It can also administer private discipline—either an informal admonition or a private reprimand—with or without conditions for the lawyer's compliance.[116] Only the Supreme Court is authorized to issue public discipline. Those penalties range from public censure to disbarment.[117] Lawyers may also consent to certain forms of discipline, pursuant to Pa. R.D.E. 215.[118]

Pennsylvania practitioners must be familiar with a substantial group of standards for lawyer professional conduct, including the Rules of Disciplinary Enforcement, the Rules of the Disciplinary Board, the Pennsylvania Bar Admission Rules, the Pennsylvania Continuing Education Rules, the Pennsylvania Interest on Lawyer Trust Account Board Rules, the Code of Civility, and the Rules of Professional Conduct (RPC).[119] Not all of these are enforced against current lawyers, as the Bar Admission Rules primarily concern preadmission behavior, and compliance with the Code of Civility is not mandatory. The RPC are arguably the most important of these rules, and they were codified in the Pennsylvania Code in 1988.[120] Prior to that time, these rules were part of the Code of Professional Responsibility.[121] They explain lawyers' duties and responsibilities and form the foundation for lawyer discipline in Pennsylvania and across the country.[122] These rules apply both to lawyers admitted in Pennsylvania and to those who offer any legal services in the state.[123] The Pennsylvania rules follow the structure of the ABA's Model Rules of Professional Conduct, which were adopted in 1983.[124]

The current rules are the third major iteration of the ABA's efforts to guide lawyers as to professional conduct. First, there was the 1908 Canons of Professional Ethics, a broad, aspirational set of guidelines. Next, the ABA adopted the 1969 Model Code of Professional Responsibility, which proved to be too confusing and underinclusive. The legal profession grew increasingly concerned about legal ethics in the 1970s, perhaps thanks to the number of lawyers involved in the Watergate scandal.[125] The ABA appointed the Kutak Commission in 1977 to form what is now the basis for today's Model Rules.[126] Forty-nine states and the District of Columbia have adopted the structure and the majority of the language of the Model Rules. Yet no state has adopted the rules verbatim, and the Model Rules are not binding on attorneys in any state.[127]

The process for amending the RPC is a multistep one. It often starts with the PBA, a voluntary bar recognized by the Supreme Court as the most representative of Pennsylvania lawyers.[128] As a voluntary bar,[129] the PBA cannot mandate adoption or revision of the ethical or disciplinary rules. The PBA has, however, played a major ongoing role in connection with the review of ABA Model Rules amendments and has occasionally issued recommendations to the Court for adoption of those amendments, frequently with minor state-specific revisions. These efforts have been undertaken in the first instance by the PBA's Legal Ethics and Professional Responsibility Committee.[130] The reports and recommendations of the committee are thereafter reviewed by the PBA's Board of Governors[131] and House of Delegates,[132] its policymaking body. At that point, the proposed rule amendments are submitted to the Supreme Court. The Court often seeks input from the Disciplinary Board and its rules committee in the process. The Court has no specific internal timetable for acting on such recommendations and on occasion chooses to take no action at all.

One such occasion was the proposed revision to Rule 8.4, "Misconduct." The PBA's Women in the Profession Committee and the PBA/Conference of State Trial Judges Joint Task Force to Ensure Gender Fairness in the Courts proposed an addition to the rule that would make sexual harassment in the practice of law explicitly prohibited by the Rules of Professional Conduct. The amendment was submitted to the Pennsylvania Supreme Court in 1996.[133] The Supreme Court, however, never acted on this amendment, and it therefore does not yet appear in the Pennsylvania Rules of Professional Conduct.

Pennsylvania is a "Model Rule state" but, like most states, has not adopted verbatim all the ABA Model Rules. For example, the ABA Model Rules require fee division among lawyers not of the same firm to be "in proportion" to the services performed by each lawyer.[134] The Pennsylvania rules have no such requirement. Instead, a lawyer may simply refer a matter to another lawyer outside the firm and still receive a portion of any fee.[135]

Among the other material differences is the provision concerning the scope of the duty of prosecutors once they discover "new, credible, and material evidence" that creates a "reasonable likelihood" that a previous conviction in their jurisdiction was erroneous. The Pennsylvania RPC and the ABA Model Rule 3.8, "Special Responsibilities of a Prosecutor," were virtually identical until February 2008, when the ABA added new subsections (g) and (h), which require a prosecutor in certain situations to disclose that evidence to the defense or take action to remedy a wrongful conviction.[136] The PBA recommended the change in 2009.[137] Groups such as the Pennsylvania Innocence Project urged support for the amendments.[138] The Disciplinary Board proposed the amendment in May 2010,[139] but to date, the Court has declined to approve the rule change.[140]

There have been two major ABA Model Rule overhauls in recent years that have also served to substantially update the Pennsylvania RPC: the Ethics 2000 and the Ethics 20/20 Commissions. In 1997, the ABA created the Ethics 2000 Commission under then president Jerome J. Shestak of Philadelphia as a systematic revision of the rules due to state-by-state disparities and a need to improve clarity and expand the scope of the guidance provided in the accompanying comments. The commission made significant changes in a number of areas, including providing more extensive guidance concerning the handling of conflicts of interest. The ABA adopted the vast majority of the Ethics 2000 Commission's proposals in 2001 and 2002 after soliciting public comment on the changes for four years around the country.[141] The Supreme Court adopted most of the Ethics 2000 rule amendments in August 2004, effective January 1, 2005.[142] Chief Justice Ralph J. Cappy described the decision to adopt as a balancing act between national practices and "values that are unique and important to Pennsylvania."

The ABA Ethics 20/20 Commission's objective was to review the Model Rules "in the context of advances in technology and global legal practice developments."[143] Again, after extensive groundwork by the PBA Legal Ethics and Professional Responsibility Committee, the PBA proposed amendments substantially consistent with the Model Rule amendments borne out of the ABA Ethics 20/20 Commission. These amendments addressed, among other things, the prevalence of electronic communication as well as a lawyer's ongoing duty to keep abreast of key technological developments as they impact the practice of law. The ABA House of Delegates formally approved these Model Rule amendments in August 2012,[144] and the Supreme Court did the same in October 2013.[145]

Some changes in the RPC emanate from the Supreme Court without any input from the organized bar. An example was the amendment of Rule 1.19, "Lawyers Acting as Lobbyists," which requires lawyers to abide by the statutes and regulations promulgated in the field to the extent consistent with the RPC. The process of implementing this change demonstrates the Supreme Court's reluctance to cede its authority to regulate Pennsylvania lawyers. In 2002, the Commonwealth Court struck down the existing Lobbying Disclosure Act as unconstitutional. The Supreme Court split three to three on appeal, leaving the law ineffectual.[146] The Court then approved Rule 1.19 in 2003, requiring compliance with registration and disclosure laws for lawyers functioning as lobbyists.[147] With these actions, the Court reconfirmed its role as the sole regulator of lawyer behavior while siding with those in the legislature and municipalities who sought to impose greater oversight on lobbying, including enhanced disclosure obligations.

The PBA's *Pennsylvania Ethics Handbook*, published by PBI Press, contains detailed information on disciplinary changes and explanations. This guide provides practical rule guidance, summaries of ethics opinions, and a number of other useful resources to locate relevant ethics provisions and guidance. The Disciplinary Board's website and RSS feeds also provide additional news, forms, and other information.[148] The PBA, the Philadelphia Bar Association, and the Allegheny County Bar Association also offer ethics guidance to members, upon written or telephone inquiry, concerning their prospective conduct and compliance with the rules.[149] While the courts and the Disciplinary Board are not required to follow that guidance, lawyers who adhere to the ethical guidance issued by these committees are seldom subject to discipline.

The Continuing Legal Education Board is charged with implementing and administering a program of required annual continuing education for all attorneys maintaining active licenses to practice. The educational requirement was introduced by order of the Supreme Court in 1992. Each attorney holding an active license to practice is required to attend a minimum of twelve hours of continuing legal education annually. At least two of the twelve hours of required instruction must be on the subject of legal ethics. The education requirement was further amended by the Court in 2003 to require that all newly admitted lawyers complete a four-hour "Bridge the Gap" course focusing on legal ethics and professional responsibility. The mission of the Continuing Legal Education Board is to assist the Court in ensuring that lawyers admitted to practice continue their education and maintain the requisite knowledge and skill necessary to fulfill their professional responsibilities.[150]

The Pennsylvania Client Security Fund was established by the Supreme Court in 1982 to reimburse clients who had suffered financial losses as a result of misappropriation of funds by Pennsylvania attorneys. The fund operates under the Pennsylvania Rules of

Disciplinary Enforcement and is sustained by a portion of the annual registration fee paid by each Pennsylvania lawyer. The fund's predecessors were established by the PBA and the Philadelphia Bar Association in 1960.[151] The PBA Client Security Fund was administered by a board of selected PBA members, and funding was provided through an annual contribution of $10,000 from the PBA.[152] The PBA encouraged county bar associations to establish similar funds, and thirteen had done so by 1976.[153] The PBA fund reimbursed county funds for 50 percent of their expenditures made in allowed claims.[154] The maximum amount available to a claimant was $15,000.[155] In 1975, the PBA first called for the creation of a statewide client security fund.[156] It proposed that it would be funded through an annual assessment of each member of the bar.[157] In 1982, the Supreme Court established the Client Security Fund as recommended by the PBA.[158]

The Interest on Lawyers Trust Account (IOLTA) Board, established in 1996 as a result of the Supreme Court's amended Rule 1.15 of the Pennsylvania Rules of Professional Conduct, creates a mandatory program in which lawyers pool nominal and short-term funds in interest-bearing accounts. The result is that funds that would otherwise earn no interest can be put to constructive use for the provision of civil legal services to the Commonwealth's poor and disadvantaged: "IOLTA is supervised by a nine member board appointed by the Supreme Court. It operates in a fashion similar to IOLTA programs established in every other state in the nation."[159]

The PBA Review and Certifying Board was established by the Supreme Court in 1992. Under the Rules of Professional Conduct, a lawyer may not designate himself or herself as a specialist in a particular field unless he or she has been certified as such by a Supreme Court–accredited organization. The Review and Certifying Board sets standards for and reviews applications from organizations seeking to certify a lawyer's expertise in a specific field of law practice. The board makes recommendations to the Court for accreditation or reaccreditation of certifying organizations.

The conduct of judges in the Commonwealth is overseen by the Judicial Conduct Board (JCB) and the CJD. The Constitution of 1968 established a specific mechanism for the discipline of judicial officers, independent of the legislature, governor, or trial court. Article V, Section 18 created the Judicial Inquiry and Review Board (JIRB), which had the power to investigate reports of judicial misconduct and prosecute and adjudicate them: "The flaw most obvious in the pre-1968 Constitutional system, and which provided a disincentive to implementing any of the earlier provisions, was the lack of any mechanism for imposing less serious disciplinary consequences than removal upon a judicial officer who had engaged in improper judicial conduct. The 1968 Constitution empowered the Judicial Inquiry and Review Board to impose sanctions less severe than removal from office."[160]

In 1993, the citizens of the Commonwealth approved the legislature's adoption of a constitutional amendment. The amendment, adopted on May 18 and effective August 11, abolished the JIRB and created the JCB, which is responsible for the investigation and prosecution of charges of judicial misconduct, and the CJD, which performs the adjudicatory function.[161]

IV. CONCLUSION

In the Commonwealth's early history, the regulation of lawyers by the Supreme Court, county courts, and the legislature was inconsistent and sometimes contradictory. Over time, as the Commonwealth emerged from its colonial roots and matured into a dominant center of commerce and industry, the existing patchwork of regulations proved to be untenable. Statewide transportation systems and technology overcame barriers with the result that parochial bar organizations were no longer sufficient to meet the needs of—or regulate—law practices that stretched beyond county borders. The growth of the bar itself was also a substantial factor in hastening the emergence of a statewide system of lawyer regulation. A 1920 census found 7,339 attorneys practicing in Pennsylvania. By 1972, that number had increased to more than 13,000. As of 2016, there were more than 65,000 attorneys[162] maintaining active licenses to practice in the Commonwealth. This dramatic growth of the statewide bar required the corresponding development of a uniform, statewide system to regulate it.

The Supreme Court maintains and superintends a uniform regulatory system as envisioned by the Constitution of 1968. In so doing, the Court calls on many practicing members of the bar to serve without compensation on the Court's various administrative boards and in other volunteer positions to support and facilitate the work of the Court in regulating the practice of law. By maintaining communications with the PBA and county bar associations, the Court is able to solicit feedback on existing regulations and proposed reforms. Through rigorous standards for the practice of law under a uniform system flexible enough to account for changing times, the Supreme Court protects both the public and the integrity of the legal profession in the Commonwealth.

NOTES

Thomas G. Wilkinson Jr. is a shareholder at Cozen O'Connor and a past president of the Pennsylvania Bar Association. Roger B. Meilton is the executive director emeritus of the Pennsylvania Bar Institute. The authors acknowledge with thanks the assistance of Kathryn Young, an associate in the Litigation Department of Cozen O'Connor, in the preparation of this chapter.

1. Pa. Cons. art. V, §§ 1–2.
2. Ibid., § 10(c).
3. Alfred Zantzinger Reed, *Training for the Public Profession of the Law: A Report to the Carnegie Foundation for the Advancement of Training*, vol. 11 (New York: Ayer Publishing, 1921) (hereafter *Reed Report*).
4. *See Reed Report*, 36.
5. Robert MacCrate, "The Educational Continuum in Pennsylvania," *Pennsylvania Bar Association Quarterly* 67 (November 9–10, 1995): 47.
6. For a detailed history of the courts of Pennsylvania in the Colonial Period, *see* William H. Loyd, *The Early Courts of Pennsylvania*, University of Pennsylvania Law School Series no. 2 (Boston: Boston Book Company, 1910).

7. Ibid., 46, 113.

8. Ibid., 71.

9. *See* Commonwealth ex rel. Brackenridge v. Judges, 1 S. & R. 187, 1814 Pa. LEXIS 77 (1814).

10. Loyd, *Early Courts*, 117.

11. Gerard J. St. John, "This Is Our Bar," *Philadelphia Lawyer* 64, no. 4 (Winter 2002), 1–3.

12. Loyd, *Early Courts*, 118.

13. Frank Marshall Eastman, *Courts and Lawyers of Pennsylvania 1623–1923*, vol. 2 (New York: American Historical Society, 1922), 285–86.

14. Joel Fishman, "The Establishment of the Pennsylvania State Board of Law Examiners, 1985–1902," *Pennsylvania Bar Association Quarterly* 76 (April 2005): 73n1.

15. Ibid., citing Pa. Supreme Court Rule 3 (April 10, 1759).

16. Fishman, "Establishment," 73n1.

17. Albert Smith Faught, "Early Rules of Court in Pennsylvania," *Dickinson Law Review* 44 (1940): 273, 280.

18. Ibid., 282.

19. The Pennsylvania Manual 3, 118 (5) (2007).

20. Pa. Const. art. V, § 1 (1790).

21. Ibid., § 4 (1790).

22. *Reed Report*, 85–90.

23. MacCrate, "Educational Continuum," 47.

24. Margaret Martin Barry, Jon C. Dubin, and Peter A. Joy, *Legal Education "Best Practices" Report, United States*, PIL Net, 1, http://www.google.com/url?sa=t&rct=j&q=&esrc=s&source=web&cd=1&ved=0ahUKEwi81YuN1aXVAhUh0IMKHUxNCMgQFggmMAA&url=http%3A%2F%2Fwww.pilnet.org%2Fcomponent%2Fdocman%2Fdoc_download%2F11-the-development-of-legal-education-in-the-united-states.html&usg=AFQjCNFwh-p-2yPdHPiZ_cf3NqZEFtSHZA.

25. *Reed Report*, 205.

26. St. John, "Our Bar."

27. *Reed Report*, 203. The Law Academy continued down to the mid-twentieth century.

28. Christina Martin, "Pittsburgh Celebrates Its 250th Year: A Look Back at the Legal Community over the Last Two-and-a-Half Centuries," *Juris Magazine*, 2009.

29. *Reed Report*, 126.

30. Ibid.

31. Ibid., 245.

32. Ibid., 247.

33. Ibid., 265.

34. Ibid., 267–68.

35. Fishman, "Establishment," 90–91.

36. *Reed Report*, 198–99.

37. Ibid., 193.

38. Ibid., 198.

39. Fishman, "Establishment," 75.

40. Henry Thomas Dolan, "The Diamond Anniversary History of the Pennsylvania Bar Association," *Pennsylvania Bar Association Quarterly* 62, no. 126 (1971): 131.

41. MacCrate, "Educational Continuum," 48.

42. "About the American Bar Association," *American Bar Association*, http://www.americanbar.org/about_the_aba.html.

43. Barry et al., *Legal Education "Best Practices" Report, United States*, 1.

44. Ibid., 172.

45. Ibid.

46. Hazel Weiser, "More History of the Regulation of Legal Education So That We Understand Where We Are Going and How We Got There," *Society of American Law Teachers* (blog), November 3, 2011, http://www.saltlaw.org.

47. Zantzinger, *Reed Report*, 103.

48. Ibid., 266.

49. Barry et al., *Legal Education "Best Practices" Report, United States*, 2.

50. Dolan, "Diamond Anniversary," 131.

51. "Report of the Committee on Legal Education and Admission to the Bar," *Annual Report of the Pennsylvania Bar Association* 53 (1947): 217.

52. 468 A.2d 1084, 1086n2 (Pa. 1983). For a review of the 1896 rules, *see* Alexander Simpson Jr., "Compilation of the Rules of the Courts of Common Pleas of the State of Pennsylvania," *Annual Report of the Pennsylvania Bar Association* 2 (1896): 281–690.

53. Dolan, "Diamond Anniversary," 133.

54. Ibid., 142.

55. *See* Fishman, "Establishment," 73–92, for a detailed history of the creation of the State Board of Law Examiners.

56. Ibid., 90.

57. Ibid.

58. Ibid.

59. *See* "History of the Board of Law Examiners," *Pennsylvania Board of Law Examiners*, http://www.pabarexam.org/board_information/history.htm, for a complete statement of the original ten rules.

60. Lon L. Fuller, "Legal Education and Admissions to the Bar in Pennsylvania," *Temple Law Quarterly* 25, no. 3 (1952): 274–76.

61. Walter C. Douglas Jr., "Pennsylvania's New Requirement for Bar Admission," *American Bar Association Journal* 14 (1928): 669, 672.

62. Ibid., 673.

63. Amendment to Rules 10, 12, and 15; Order of

the Pa. Sup. Ct. Jan. 25, 1971.

64. Olmsted's Case, 140 A. 634, 634 (Pa. 1928) (citing Act of April 14, 1834, P.L. 16).

65. *See* ibid. for the text of all of the applicable acts.

66. Sylvan M. Cohen, "Pennsylvania Joins the Union," *Pennsylvania Bar Association Quarterly* 38 (1966): 27, 28.

67. 16 A. 481, 483 (Pa. 1889).

68. 80 A. 1098, 1100 (Pa. 1911).

69. *See* Olmsted's Case, 140 A. 636.

70. "Report of the Committee," 211.

71. Charles Scarlata, "Pennsylvania Practice and Procedure—Principal Office Rule (Decisions)," *Duquesne University Law Review* 4 (1966): 483, 485.

72. Fuller, "Legal Education," 274.

73. "Report of the Committee," 210.

74. Ibid., 212.

75. Ibid.

76. Ibid.

77. Ibid.

78. Ibid., 214.

79. Ibid., 219.

80. Ibid., 223.

81. Ibid., 226–27.

82. Cohen, "Pennsylvania Joins," 29.

83. 61 A.2d 514 (Pa. 1948).

84. Ibid., 516.

85. 67 A.2d 85, 87 (Pa. 1949).

86. In re Christy Case, *cert. denied*, 338 U.S. 869 (1949).

87. John D. Killian, "The Old Way the Hard Way: A Lawyer's Reflections on His Struggle to Gain Admission to a County Bar at a Time When the Rules Were Tilted in Favor of the Establishment," *Pennsylvania Lawyer* 22 (May/June 2000): 50.

88. Ibid.

89. Cohen, "Pennsylvania Joins," 32.

90. Ibid., 32–34.

91. Fuller, "Legal Education," 290.

92. Brainerd Currie, "The Law Practice Clerkship," *Pennsylvania Bar Association Quarterly* 24 (1953): 223, 238.

93. Mercer D. Tate, "Is Pennsylvania's Legal Clerkship Obsolete?," *Pennsylvania Bar Association Quarterly* 36 (1965): 394.

94. Barry J. London, Geoffrey C. Lord, and Paul M. Schaeffer, "Admission to the Pennsylvania Bar: The Need for Sweeping Change," *University of Pennsylvania Law Review* 64 (1970): 118.

95. Amendment to Rules 10, 12, and 15; Order of the Pa. Sup. Ct. Jan. 25, 1971.

96. "Johnathan Jasper Wright Award," *University of South Carolina School of Law NBLSA*, http://

www.law.sc.edu/organizations/blsa/wright.shtml.

97. "Women and Penn: Distinguished Early Graduates, Faculty, and Benefactors of the University," *Penn University Archives and Records Center*, http://www.archives.upenn.edu/histy/features/women/biog.html.

98. "Carrie Sylvester Kilgore (Burnham)," *GENI*, http://www.geni.com/people/Carrie-Burnham-Kilgore/6000000018192728861.

99. "Women's History Month: Agnes Fraser Watson," *Allegheny County, Pennsylvania*, https://www.facebook.com/AlleghenyCounty/photos/p.806764762671576/806764762671576/?l=6310d659ad.

100. "Alexander, Sadie Tanner Mossell," *BlackPast*, http://www.blackpast.org/aah/alexander-sadie-tanner-mossell-1898-1989.

101. Tracy Carbasho, "Pa. Supreme Court Posthumously Admits Attorney to Pennsylvania Bar," *Lawyers Journal* 12, no. 18 (June 18, 2010): 4.

102. "Mission Statement," *Pennsylvania Board of Law Examiners*, http://www.pabarexam.org/board_information/mission.htm.

103. *See* "History," *Disciplinary Board of the Supreme Court of Pennsylvania*, http://www.padisciplinaryboard.org/about/history.php.

104. Ibid.

105. Gilbert Nurick, "The First Decade of the Disciplinary Board," *Pennsylvania Bar Association Quarterly* 54 (1983): 63, 64.

106. J. Paul MacElree, "The President's Message," *Pennsylvania Bar Association Quarterly* 16 (1945): 117, 133.

107. Justice Samuel J. Roberts, "Pennsylvania's Disciplinary Procedures for the Bar," *Pennsylvania Bar Association Quarterly* 39 (1968): 490, 493.

108. Nurick, "First Decade," 64.

109. Ibid.

110. Ibid., 63.

111. Ibid.

112. Ibid., 64.

113. "Structure of the Disciplinary System," *Disciplinary Board of the Supreme Court of Pennsylvania*, http://www.padisciplinaryboard.org/about/structure.php.

114. Edwin G. Frownfelter, "An Introduction to the Disciplinary Board," *Pennsylvania Ethics Handbook* 401 (2011): 406. *See also* "FAQs for Attorneys," *Disciplinary Board of the Supreme Court of Pennsylvania*, http://www.padisciplinaryboard.org/attorneys/faqs/.

115. Frownfelter, "Introduction," 409.

116. Ibid., 410.

117. Ibid., 411–12.

118. "Rules of Disciplinary Enforcement," *Disciplinary Board of the Supreme Court of Pennsylvania*, http://www.padisciplinaryboard.org/documents/PARDE-current.pdf.

119. Ibid.

120. Frownfelter, "Introduction," 403.

121. Ibid.

122. *See* Pa.R.P.C. 81.4 Pa. Code 1.0 *et seq.*, http://www.pacode.com/secure/data/204/chapter81/s81.4.html. The RPC were adopted by Order of the Supreme Court, dated October 16, 1987, effective April 1, 2008.

123. Pa.R.P.C. 8.5(a).

124. "About the Model Rules," *American Bar Association*, http://www.americanbar.org/groups/professional_responsibility/publications/model_rules_of_professional_conduct.html.

125. Stephen Gillers, *Regulation of Lawyers: Problems of Law and Ethics*, vol. 11 (New York: Wolters Kluwer, 2012).

126. Stephen Gillers, Roy D. Simon, and Andrew M. Perlman, *Regulation of Lawyers: Statutes and Standards*, vol. 4 (New York: Wolters Kluwer, 2013). The ABA also began requiring law school students to take a professional responsibility class in order to graduate. Ibid., 12.

127. Ibid., 3.

128. In re "Recognition of the Pennsylvania Bar Association as the Association Representing Members of the Bar of This Commonwealth," No. 198, Supreme Court Rules Docket No. 1 (June 29, 1998).

129. "State and Local Bar Associations," *American Bar Association*, http://www.americanbar.org/groups/bar_services/resources/state_local_bar_associations.html.

130. "About the Committee: Legal Ethics and Professional Responsibility Committee," last updated 2014, *Pennsylvania Bar Association*, http://www.pabar.org/public/committees/LEG01/about/mission.asp.

131. "About: Board of Governors," *Pennsylvania Bar Association*, last updated 2014, http://www.pabar.org/public/about/board.asp.

132. "About: House of Delegates," *Pennsylvania Bar Association*, http://www.pabar.org/public/about/house.asp.

133. *See* "Supporting Amendment to Rules of Professional Conduct to Prohibit Sexual Harassment in the Practice of Law," *Philadelphia Bar Association Board of Governors*, February 27, 1997, http://www.philadelphiabar.org/page/BoardResolution18532222000?appNum=2.

134. Model Rules of Prof'l. Conduct R. 1.5(e)(1), 2013, http://www.americanbar.org/groups/professional_responsibility/publications/model_rules_of_professional_conduct/rule_1_5_fees.html.

135. *See, e.g.*, Jeffrey L. Abrams, "Fees and Billing," *Pennsylvania Ethics Handbook* (2011): 167, 174.

136. Model Rules of Prof'l. Conduct R. 3.8(g).

137. Timothy W. Callahan, "The Lawyer as Advocate," *Pennsylvania Ethics Handbook* (2011): 187, 226.

138. David Richman, "David Richman, President of Pennsylvania Innocent Project, to the Disciplinary Board of the Supreme Court of Pennsylvania," July 2, 2010, http://www.innocenceprojectpa.org/newsandevents/docs/commentsonproposedamendment.pdf/.

139. "Disciplinary Board Proposes New Rules for Prosecutors: Question False Convictions," *Attorney E-Newsletter, Disciplinary Board of the Supreme Court of Pennsylvania*, May 2010, http://www.padisciplinaryboard.org/attorneys/newsletter/2010/may.php.

140. *See* "Variations of the ABA Model Rules of Professional Conduct Rule 3.8(g) and (h)," *American Bar Association CPR Policy Implementation Committee*, May 4, 2010, http://www.americanbar.org/content/dam/aba/administrative/professional_responsibility/mrpc_3_8_g_h.authcheckdam.pdf.

141. Gillers, Simon, and Perlman, *Regulation of Lawyers*, 5.

142. "Pennsylvania Supreme Court Approves Professional Conduct Rules Amendments," *News and Views, Pennsylvania Bar Association Government Lawyers Committee* 6 (Fall 2004), http://www.pabar.org/pdf/nvfall04hr.pdf.

143. "About Us: ABA Commission on Ethics 20/20," *American Bar Association*, http://www.americanbar.org/groups/professional_responsibility/aba_commission_on_ethics_20_20/about_us.html.

144. "Disciplinary Board Proposes Major Package of Rule Revisions; Comments Due 5/16/13," *Attorney E-Newsletter, Disciplinary Board of the Supreme Court of Pennsylvania*, April 2013, http://www.padisciplinaryboard.org/attorneys/newsletter/2013/april.php#story1.

145. "Supreme Court Approved Revisions to Rules of Professional Conduct," *Attorney E-Newsletter, Disciplinary Board of the Supreme Court of Pennsylvania*, October 2013, http://www.padisciplinaryboard.org/attorneys/newsletter/2013/october.php#story1.

146. *See* "State Supreme Court May Add to Fog over Pennsylvania Lobbyist Regulations," *Lehigh Valley Daily Call*, December 1, 2003, http://www.articles.mcall.com/2003-12-01/opinion/3503669_1_justices-legal-profession-state-supreme-court; "Lobbying and the Commission," *Pennsylvania State Ethics Commission*, http://www.ethics.state.pa.us/portal/server.pt/community/lobbying/9042.

147. "2003 Annual Report," *Disciplinary Board of the Supreme Court of Pennsylvania*, http://www.padisciplinaryboard.org/about/pdfs/2003-annual-report.pdf.

148. "Information for Attorneys," *Disciplinary Board of the Supreme Court of Pennsylvania*, http://www.padisciplinaryboard.org/attorneys/.

149. Pennsylvania: (800) 932-0311, ext. 2214; Philadelphia: (215) 238-6328, or e-mail pkazaras@philabar.org; Allegheny County: assigned by month, *see* http://www.acba.org/ACBA/Members/Ethics/OfficerAssignments.asp.

150. *See* "Home," *Supreme Court of Pennsylvania Continuing Legal Education Board*, http://www.pacle.org.

151. Robert B. Gigl Jr., "Pennsylvania's Clients' Security Fund: How Secure Is the Public?," *Villanova Law Review* 22, no. 2 (1976): 452, 455.

152. Ibid., 456.

153. Ibid.

154. Ibid., 456–57.

155. Ibid., 458.

156. Gigl, "Pennsylvania's Clients' Security," 452.

157. Ibid., 460.

158. "What Is the Pennsylvania Lawyers Fund for Client Security?," *Pennsylvania Lawyers Fund for Client Security*, http://www.palawfund.com/palaw/index.php/general-information/what-is-the-pennsylvania-lawyers-fund-for-client-security.

159. *See* "PA IOLTA Facts and Figures," *PA IOLTA Board*, http://www.paiolta.org/.

160. *See* "Commonwealth of Pennsylvania," *Court of Judicial Discipline*, http://www.cjdpa.org/.

161. Ibid.

162. "Annual Report 2016," *Disciplinary Board of the Supreme Court of Pennsylvania*, http://www.padisciplinaryboard.org/about/pdfs/2016-annual-report.pdf.

CHAPTER 6

Supervising and Regulating the Judiciary

ROGER B. MEILTON AND

THOMAS G. WILKINSON JR.

Similar to lawyer regulation, judicial regulation was a piecemeal, disjointed system until well into the twentieth century. Like its 1874 predecessor as amended, the Constitution of 1968 authorized other branches of government to remove jurists and permitted the automatic forfeiture of judicial office. The House of Representatives possesses the sole power of impeachment.[1] The 1968 Constitution contained amendments that created the Judicial Inquiry and Review Board (JIRB), the first independent judicial disciplinary body.[2] This remained in place until 1993, when the Judicial Conduct Board (JCB) and the Court of Judicial Discipline (CJD) were created in the JIRB's place. This separation was based on a recommendation by the Beck Commission to divide the prosecutorial and adjudicating arms of the disciplinary process.[3] This was designed to take the politics out of the judicial discipline system and lighten the load of the Pennsylvania Supreme Court, particularly since the Court at that time reviewed all recommendations de novo.[4]

The JCB investigates allegations of misconduct, and if it decides to launch a full investigation, it has a number of options. The JCB's staff typically investigates complaints by interviewing the complainants, attorneys, and witnesses and reviewing pertinent documents. The board analyzes the results of the investigation and determines what action, if any, will be taken.[5] It can dismiss the complaint, thereby ending the process; issue a letter of caution, indicating that the conduct was problematic but not a full rules violation; issue a letter of counsel, usually indicating an isolated or inadvertent violation; or file formal charges with the CJD, indicating that probable cause exists.[6] The JCB is composed of twelve members: an appellate judge, a Common Pleas judge, a Magisterial District Court judge, three attorneys, and six nonattorney citizens.[7] Responsibility for the members' appointment is split equally between the Supreme Court and the governor. Their political affiliation must be split evenly. Each member has a four-year term and serves without pay.[8]

The CJD can adjudicate the complaint once charges are filed by the JCB.[9] The CJD can decide on the sanctions, unlike its JIRB predecessor, which could only recommend sanctions. These include removal from the bench, suspension with or without pay, or probation.[10] The CJD is also a mix of lawyers and nonlawyers appointed by the governor and the Supreme Court. The Supreme Court appoints two Common Pleas, Superior, or Commonwealth Court judges; one Magisterial District judge; and one nonlawyer citizen. The governor appoints one Common Pleas, Superior, or Commonwealth Court judge; two lawyers; and one nonlawyer citizen.[11]

Respondent judges before the CJD are to be granted the constitutional rights afforded to criminal defendants.[12] The JCB must prove the charges at trial by clear and convincing evidence. However, unlike in criminal proceedings, the CJD may find that a respondent judge has violated a standard of conduct not charged by the JCB, so long as the conduct underlying the charged violation and the uncharged violation is the same, such that there is adequate notice and no compromise of due process.[13] In imposing sanctions, the CJD is guided by its mission as "protector of the integrity of the judiciary and the public's confidence in that branch of government."[14]

When the CJD determines that there has been a violation and imposes a sanction, either the respondent judge or the JCB may appeal the decision to the Supreme Court.[15] The Supreme Court's scope of review of appeals by respondent judges is set forth in Article V, Section 18(c)(2). The Pennsylvania Constitution, the Code of Judicial Conduct, and the Rules Governing the Standards of Conduct of Magisterial District Justices serve to codify the judicial ethics guidance in Pennsylvania. Under Article V, Section 18(d)(1) of the Constitution, a justice, judge, or justice of the peace will be subject to disciplinary action for any of the following: "[C]onviction of a felony; violation of section 17 of this article; misconduct in office; neglect or failure to perform the duties of office or conduct which prejudices the proper administration of justice or brings the judicial office into disrepute, whether or not the conduct occurred while acting in a judicial capacity or is prohibited by law; or conduct in violation of a canon or rule prescribed by the Supreme Court."

Significantly, the foregoing offenses are not limited to conduct in violation of the Code of Judicial Conduct, and, in particular, conduct that "prejudices the proper administration of justice" or that "brings the judicial office into disrepute" can be viewed as somewhat broad and vague. This raises concerns about whether the standard is adequately defined to support a finding of unethical conduct and sanction.[16]

In addition to the prosecutions involving the consequences of a criminal conviction or participation in criminal activity, the CJD's decisions imposing discipline have addressed misconduct ranging from failures to perform judicial duties diligently to judicial impartiality, disqualification, and recusal.[17] There is at least a perception that the JCB has recently focused more resources on pursuing discipline involving matters of judicial temperament, including judges' interactions with court employees, lawyers, and members of the public.[18]

The American Bar Association (ABA) and Pennsylvania Bar Association (PBA) also have played a part in crafting the ethical guidance for state court judges. The ABA has a Model Code of Judicial Conduct similar to its Model Rules of Professional Conduct. The code was first adopted in 1972, replacing the Canons of Judicial Ethics, which had been the suggested judicial conduct rules since 1924. The code underwent a systematic change in 2007.[19] The PBA's Judicial Administration Committee has the mission within the bar association to make recommendations concerning the court system in Pennsylvania.[20] In 2012, PBA president Thomas G. Wilkinson Jr. appointed a task force to examine and recommend adoption of a new judicial conduct code based on the ABA's model code updates. That task force report was delivered in early 2013, approved unanimously by the PBA House of Delegates in May 2013, and thereafter submitted to the Supreme Court for consideration. The Court also received a report with recommendations from an ad hoc committee chaired by Superior Court Judge Anne E. Lazarus. The report included the recommendation that all state judges complete an annual twelve-hour judicial education requirement. The Supreme Court recognized that the outdated canons were ripe for an overhaul and, in late 2013, adopted a substantially updated Code of Judicial Conduct drawing in large measure from the PBA and ad hoc committee recommendations.[21]

The updated code includes material changes, such as prohibiting nepotism in judicial hiring going forward and precluding judges from serving on for-profit boards, as well as more detailed standards for recusal and disqualification based on, among other things, judicial campaign contributions.[22] The Court in 2016 announced the adoption of a new judicial education requirement consisting of twelve credit hours annually, effective January 1, 2017.[23]

The Code of Judicial Conduct update gained impetus from high-profile criminal charges lodged against Supreme Court Justice Joan Orie Melvin in 2012 in Allegheny County. These charges arose from her alleged use of state resources—legislative and judicial staff—to perform campaign work. She was immediately suspended by the Supreme Court. Justice Orie Melvin was convicted on those charges in 2013 and subsequently resigned from the bench.[24]

One area giving rise to some constitutional debate is the Supreme Court's role in the judicial disciplinary process. The Court maintains that it has concurrent jurisdiction with the CJD.[25] The Court refers to this power as "the power of general superintendency over inferior tribunals."[26] As the highest court in the Commonwealth, the Supreme Court has the power to review the decisions of all other courts, including the CJD.[27] In practice, this means that the Supreme Court sometimes issues interim suspension orders to judges in the judicial disciplinary process, particularly where there is a perceived need for immediate action to protect and promote public confidence in the judicial system.[28] A problem then arises when both the CJD and the Supreme Court decide to issue interim relief suspending a trial judge, either with or without pay, and the orders of the two tribunals conflict.[29]

Such a conflict arose in the consolidated cases of Mark Bruno and Christine Solomon, two Pennsylvania judges accused of misconduct and subject to conflicting interim suspension orders. A ticket-fixing scandal resulting in the prosecution of nine judges elected, or assigned to, Philadelphia Traffic Court led to this important test of the Supreme Court's supervisory authority over judicial discipline. In *In re Magisterial Judge Bruno*,[30] the Court grappled with the question of whether it retained King's Bench jurisdiction to order the interim suspension of jurists, notwithstanding the judicial discipline scheme adapted by constitutional amendment in 1993.

The Court invited the JCB to participate in the briefing on the jurisdictional question, with the Administrative Office of Pennsylvania Courts (AOPC) maintaining that the CJD's discipline is concurrent with the jurisdiction of the Court. Both Judge Bruno and the JCB argued that the 1993 amendment establishing the two boards essentially removed the Court from participation in the judicial discipline system until an appeal from the JCB. The JCB, through Chief Counsel Robert A. Graci, also pointed out that the appellate power of the Supreme Court is different from that of superintendency over inferior courts and should be treated as such. Prior to the case, Chief Justice Ronald D. Castille made it clear that he disagreed: "We can act whenever we want to act," he said, "we're the Supreme Court."[31] In its amicus curiae brief submitted in the *Bruno* and *Solomon* appeals, the PBA made a series of suggested systemic improvements designed to avoid the issue of potentially conflicting authority while supporting the view that the Court reserved the supreme authority over inferior courts and coextensive power to address judicial misconduct, particularly where there was an immediate threat of harm to the public or litigants.[32] The Court resolved the conflict in an important unanimous opinion issued in October 2014.

Faced with a somewhat inconsistent series of decisions involving interim suspensions, the Court rejected the CJD's position that it was granted "exclusive" authority to discipline judges and instead concluded that the Court's King's Bench authority remained intact to "address extraordinary and emergent circumstances."[33]

The justices delivered five separate concurring opinions expressing a range of views on the interplay between the authority of the CJD and the Court to impose interim discipline. A common thread of these opinions was a desire to avoid conflicting directions and a general preference to permit the JCB and CJD to perform their assigned investigatory and adjudicatory functions in the first instance. The Court concluded that Article V, Section 18(a)(2) did not vest exclusive authority in the CJD to direct the interim suspension, with or without pay, of a jurist charged with a felony or against whom charges have been filed by the JCB with the CJD.

Drawing on an amicus brief submitted by the PBA, the Court explained that Article V, Section 18 simply delineates the CJD's authority within the disciplinary process and does not purport to limit the Court's authority to supervise the court system. The AOPC and PBA maintained, and the Court concluded, that both the Court and the CJD have constitutional authority to investigate a jurist and order sanctions, if warranted, but the Court has supreme and general authority over the Unified Judicial System (UJS).[34] While joining in a unanimous opinion authored by Chief Justice Castille, the five concurring opinions provided a range of views as to the circumstances where the Court should defer to the formal disciplinary process reposed in the JCB and CJD.[35]

Less than a month after announcing the *Bruno* decision, the Court again exercised its King's Bench power to address a scandal involving another justice, creating "[t]he compelling and immediate need to protect and preserve the integrity of the Unified Judicial System and the administration of justice for the citizens of this Commonwealth."[36] In a per curiam order, four justices suspended Justice Seamus McCaffery on an interim basis with pay pending an emergency determination by the JCB about whether there was probable cause to file formal misconduct charges.

The Court's order identified several bases for relieving Justice McCaffery of all judicial and administrative responsibilities. The suspension was precipitated by the disclosure by Attorney General Kathleen Kane that Justice McCaffery had exchanged numerous sexually explicit e-mails with at least one member of the office of the attorney general. The e-mails were uncovered as part of the attorney general's investigation of the office's handling of the high-profile Jerry Sandusky child abuse allegations involving Penn State University. The office reviewed thousands of e-mails in what the popular media dubbed the "porngate scandal," unearthing hundreds of sexually explicit e-mails found on state computers. In addition to ensnaring Justice McCaffery, the collateral fallout led to the dismissal or resignation of several other high-ranking state public officials. Another Supreme Court justice, Michael Eakin, reported himself to the JCB to investigate whether he had engaged in any misconduct in the same pornographic e-mail scandal. He also reported that Justice McCaffery had importuned him to urge Chief Justice Castille to retract his public statement that was critical of Justice McCaffery or face the public release of materials embarrassing to Justice Eakin.[37] In a concurring statement to the dismissal order, Chief Justice Castille stated that he would not refer the matter to the JCB due to its limited resources but instead would refer the investigation to a neutral fact finder.

The suspension and volley of charges between Chief Justice Castille and Justice McCaffery attracted nationwide media coverage[38] and dismay among leaders of the organized bar concerning the public perception of the integrity of the judiciary.[39] The latest series of high-profile judicial scandals also instigated renewed calls in the media and among reform advocates for structural enhancements in JCB processes and adoption of a constitutional amendment creating a hybrid appointment—an election system for choosing statewide appellate judges.[40]

Faced with an expedited JCB investigation, Justice McCaffery announced his resignation and permanent retirement from the bench on October 27, 2014, one week after his interim suspension. His resignation letter apologized for a "lapse in judgment" in transmitting such e-mails. The Court concurrently vacated its order issued a week earlier referring the matters concerning Justice McCaffery to the JCB, and the JCB announced the dismissal of its investigations into those matters.[41] While Justice McCaffery's resignation prompted a collective sigh of relief among the legal community, his departure also left the Court facing an unprecedented need to replace three justices, Chief Justice Castille through mandatory retirement and replacements for Justices Orie Melvin and McCaffery. Perhaps just as significant, Court watchers raised concerns that the dismissal of the JCB investigation into McCaffery's conduct without hearing was inappropriate and that the JCB lacks adequate resources and must be both more nimble and transparent to effectively fulfill its role and restore public confidence in the system.[42]

In January 2015, Thomas G. Saylor was inducted as the fifty-sixth chief justice of Pennsylvania. In the general election in November 2015, three new justices—Christine L. Donohue, Kevin M. Dougherty, and David N. Wecht—were elected to the Court. Following Justice McCaffery's assertion that Justice Eakin had also engaged in the exchange of offensive e-mails, the JCB launched an investigation in the fall of 2014. The Supreme Court also retained its own counsel to review Justice Eakin's e-mails as well as those of other justices. In December 2014, the JCB essentially concluded that Justice Eakin's receipt of offensive e-mails and failure to advise senders to desist from sending such material reflected a "lapse in judgment" that did not rise to the level of sanctionable misconduct.

Late in October 2015, after Attorney General Kathleen Kane publicly disclosed the contents of additional e-mails received and sent by Justice Eakin to friends and former colleagues via a private e-mail account, the JCB initiated a new investigation into Eakin's conduct pertaining to his e-mail communications. The JCB filed a complaint with the CJD on December 8, 2015. Following a hearing on December 23, 2015, the CJD suspended Justice Eakin from his judicial and administrative duties on the Supreme Court pending further orders from the Court. The CJD scheduled a trial of the charges pending against Justice Eakin for March 29, 2016. However, on March 16, 2016, he announced that he would resign from the Supreme Court. The CJD ultimately imposed a fine of $50,000 against Eakin and allowed him to retain his state pension.[43] In so doing, the CJD suggested that the sanction was mitigated by a number of factors, including the fact that the conduct was not criminal, credible witnesses for the justice testified that his judicial opinions were not reflective of any bias expressed in the e-mails, the justice's long-term service was otherwise exemplary, and he accepted responsibility and voluntarily resigned his commission on the Supreme Court.

Despite these recent developments, the vast majority of Pennsylvania judges serve the public with the high level of integrity and sense of fairness expected of members of the judiciary. In a 2014 interview, Robert A. Graci, the chief counsel of the JCB, expressed the view that "the greatest majority of the Commonwealth's judges are hard-working men and women doing difficult jobs under what are often trying circumstances. They may make mistakes . . . that can be corrected on appeal . . . but they are not engaging in misconduct."[44] While instances of judicial misconduct are infrequent, they do occur, and those in charge of monitoring the performance of those in judicial office take their roles seriously.[45] Maintaining the integrity of the judiciary is essential to preserving public confidence in the judicial system and the rule of law.

Roger B. Meilton is the executive director emeritus of the Pennsylvania Bar Institute. Thomas G. Wilkinson Jr. is a shareholder at Cozen O'Connor and a past president of the Pennsylvania Bar Association. The authors wish to thank Kathryn Young, an associate at Cozen O'Connor, for her research assistance.

1. *See* Pa. Const. art. VI, § 7 (1968). Moreover, Article V, Section 18 provides that "[a] justice, judge or justice of the peace convicted of misbehavior in office by a court, disbarred as a member of the bar of the Supreme Court or removed under this section shall forfeit automatically his judicial office and thereafter be ineligible for judicial office." Pa. Const. art. V, § 18(d)(3)(1968).

2. J. Summers and R. Melley, "The Court of Judicial Discipline: A Review of the First Twenty Years," *Pennsylvania Bar Association Quarterly* 84, no. 1 (January 2013): 1, 2. The JIRB consisted of nine members authorized to initiate complaints against judges and then make recommendations to the Supreme Court, which were reviewed de novo by the Court.

3. The Beck Commission, chaired by Superior Court judge Phyllis W. Beck, a coauthor of this book, was formed in 1987 by Governor Robert P. Casey. The 1993 amendment also was propelled by the adverse reaction of the public and the General Assembly to internal discord among Supreme Court justices, as well as a JIRB recommendation, after a two-year investigation that Supreme Court Justice Rolf Larsen not be disciplined, followed by a grand jury report concluding that he had engaged in misconduct while on the bench, including obtaining psychotropic drugs through improper means. Following his 1994 conviction in Allegheny County of two felony counts to violate the Controlled Substances Act, Justice Larsen was the first Supreme Court justice to be impeached by unanimous vote of the House and thereafter convicted and removed from the bench following a trial in the Senate. C. Geyh, "Highlighting a Low Point on a High Court: Some Thoughts on the Removal of Pennsylvania Supreme Court Justice Rolf Larsen and the Limits of Judicial Self-Regulation," *Temple Law Review* 68 (1995): 1041; *see also* In re Larsen, 532 Pa. 326, 616 A.2d 529 (1992).

4. "History of the Judicial Disciplinary Process in Pennsylvania," *Pennsylvania Court of Judicial Discipline*, http://www.pacourts.us/assets/files/setting-3514/file-3225.pdf?cb=8b7185.

5. *See* Judicial Conduct Board Rules of Procedure.

6. Summers and Melley, "Court of Judicial Discipline," 4.

7. Ibid.

8. "Current Board Members," *Pennsylvania Judicial Conduct Board*, 2014, http://judicialconductboardofpa.org/the-board/current-members/.

9. Summers and Melley, "Court of Judicial Discipline," 2.

10. Ibid., 8.

11. "History of the Judicial Disciplinary Process," 4.

12. In re Lokuta, 11 A.3d 427, 442 (Pa. 2011); In re Berkhimer, 930 A.2d 1255, 1258 (Pa. 2001). *See also* Pa. Const. art. V, § 18(b)(5) ("All hearings conducted by the [CJD] shall be public proceedings conducted pursuant to the rules adopted by the [CJD] and in accordance with the principles of due process and the law of evidence.").

13. In re Jaffe, 839 A.2d 487, 490 (Pa. Ct. Jud. Disc. 2003); In re Berry, 979 A.2d 991, 1003 (Pa. Ct. Jud. Disc. 2009).

14. In re Melograne, 812 A.2d 1164, 1168 (Pa. 2002).

15. On the law, the scope of review is plenary; on the facts, the scope of review is clearly erroneous; and as to sanctions, the scope of review is whether the sanctions imposed were lawful. Appeals by the JCB are limited to questions of law. *See* Ibid., § 18(c)(3).

16. Summers and Melley, "Court of Judicial Discipline," 11.

17. Ibid., 12–23.

18. *See, e.g.,* In re Lokuta, 964 A.2d at 988 (judge was "loud," "nasty," "out of control," "intimidating," and "oppressive" to her staff); Max Mitchell, "Conduct Board Increasingly Focusing on Demeanor Violations," *Legal Intelligencer*, July 15, 2014, http://www.thelegalintelligencer.com/id=1202662973464/Conduct-Board-Increasingly-Focusing-on-Demeanor-Violations.

19. Stephen Gillers, Roy D. Simon, Andrew M. Perlman, and John Steele, *Regulation of Lawyers: Statutes and Standards* (Philadelphia: Wolters Kluwer, 2013), 681–82.

20. "Judicial Administration Committee: About the Committee," *Pennsylvania Bar Association*, http://www.pabar.org/public/committees/judadmn/about/mission.asp.

21. In re Adoption of Rule 1910 of the Pennsylvania Rules of Judicial Administration, January 8, 2014 (per curiam). The majority of the new Code of Judicial Conduct became effective on July 1, 2014.

22. By order dated September 18, 2014, the Court ordered the adoption of new rules governing standards of conduct of Magisterial District judges, effective December 1, 2014. The new rules mirror many of the rules of conduct for trial and appellate jurists recently adopted as part of the overhaul of the Code of Judicial Conduct.

23. Per Curiam Order, December 9, 2016, No. 719, Supreme Court Rules Docket. The order served to established a twelve-member Continuing Judicial Education Board of Judges to guide development and delivery of continuing judicial education to judges serving in the UJS. In July 2017, Duquesne University School of Law announced the establishment of a new Thomas R. Kline Center for Judicial Education to offer a curriculum for trial judges to meet their CLE requirements in cooperation with the AOPC. The new center will draw on faculty from other area law schools.

24. Justice Orie Melvin's conviction on six criminal counts and certain aspects of her sentencing spawned several appeals and stays. In October 2014, Orie Melvin abandoned the appeal of her modified sentence and agreed to resume serving her sentence of three years of house arrest followed by two years of probation, volunteer service in a soup kitchen, and writing letters of apology to every judge in the Commonwealth. See Commonwealth v. Orie Melvin, No. 844 WDA 2013, 2014 WL 4100200 *105 (Pa. Super., Aug. 21, 2013).

25. Summers and Melley, "Court of Judicial Discipline," 3.

26. See Brief for Pennsylvania Bar Association as Amicus Curiae Supporting Administrative Office of Pennsylvania Courts, 3; In re Magisterial District Judge Mark A. Bruno, Magisterial District 15-1-01, No. 84 MM 2013 (Pa. 2013). See also In re Merlo, 17 A.3d 869, 871 (Pa. 2011).

27. See Brief for Pennsylvania Bar Association, 7–8.

28. See, e.g., In re Franciscus, 369 A.2d 1190, 1194–95 (Pa. 1977).

29. See Summers and Melley, "Court of Judicial Discipline," 3.

30. In re Magisterial District Judge Mark A. Bruno. The Judge Solomon matter also arose out of the traffic court investigation and involved, in part, Judge Solomon's alleged failure to cooperate with an administrative review undertaken of the traffic court operations as well as her challenge to the Court's authority either to issue an order to show cause why she should not be suspended for failure to cooperate with the Court-ordered administrative review of the traffic court or to appoint a special master in lieu of deferring the entire matter to the JCB. See In re Solomon, 66 A.3d 764 (Pa. 2013).

31. Zack Needles, "Supreme Court Mulls Its Power to Suspend Judges," Legal Intelligencer, September 11, 2013, http://www.thelegalintelligencer.com/id=1202618740545/Supreme+Court+Mulls+Its+Power+to+Suspend+Judges%3Fmcode=0&curindex=0&curpage=ALL.

32. Brief for Pennsylvania Bar Association, 23.

33. 101 A.3d 635, 682 (Pa. 2014). Therefore, "[w]here the orders of the Supreme Court and the CJD are dissonant . . . any order of this Court obviously is 'supreme.'" Ibid., 688.

34. Ibid., 665, citing Pa. Const. art. V, § 2(a); 42 Pa.C.S. §§ 502, 1723, 1724.

35. Max Mitchell, "Pa. Justices Win Turf Battle with CJD," Legal Intelligencer, October 7, 2014, http://www.thelegalintelligencer.com/id=1202672487563/Pa-Justices-Win-Turf-Battle-With-CJD?slreturn=20160015123532.

36. The Court also cited (1) media reports that Justice McCaffery might have contacted a Philadelphia traffic court official to secure favorable treatment of a traffic citation to his wife, (2) that he might have authorized his wife to accept substantial referral fees from plaintiffs while serving as his administrative assistant, and (3) that he might have improperly exerted influence over a judicial assignment on the Philadelphia Common Pleas bench.

37. Justice Eakin recused himself from the order.

38. See, e.g., Brad Blumstead, "Pa. Supreme Court in 'Sad State' as Scandals Tarnish Reputation," Pittsburgh Tribune, review, October 25, 2014, 1.

39. Intelligencer Editorial Board, "Post-McCaffery Suspension, Court Must Work on Rebuilding," Legal Intelligencer, October 22, 2014, http://www.thelegalintelligencer.com/id=1202674163943/PostMcCaffery-Suspension-Court-Must-Work-on-Rebuilding.

40. See, e.g., Inquirer Editorial Board, "Not Just Junk in Mail," Philadelphia Inquirer, November 10, 2014, A10; Lynn A. Marks and Suzanne Almeida, "How to Put Order into Pa.'s Courts," Philadelphia Inquirer, October 26, 2014, D1 (also urging mandatory annual ethics training); Jeff Blumenthal, "Does Electing State Judges

Work in Pa.?," *Philadelphia Business Journal*, October 24, 2014, http://www.bizjournals.com /philadelphia/print-edition/2014/10/24/does -electing-state-judges-work-in-pa.html.

41. Judicial Conduct Board, press release, October 27, 2014.

42. Peter Hall, "Experts Say Justices' Emails to AG's Office Warrant Review," *Morning Call*, November 2, 2014, A1; Chris Mondics, "Ouster Troubles Court Watchers," *Philadelphia Inquirer*, November 3, 2014, A3; Bruce Ledewitz, "Deal Leaves Court Issues Unresolved," *Philadelphia Inquirer*, October 30, 2014, A19; Hank Grezlak, "McCaffery's Departure Not the End of Pa. Judiciary's Woes," *Legal Intelligencer*, October 29, 2014, 3; *see also* Maida Milone, "Pa.'s Judicial Selection, Discipline Systems Must Be Strengthened," *Legal Intelligencer*, July 24, 2017 (urging greater fairness and predictability in the prosecution and adjudication of judicial discipline cases).

43. No. 13 JD 15 (Pa. Ct. Jud. Disc. March 24, 2016) (per curiam).

44. "Questions for the JCB Chief Counsel," *Pennsylvania Lawyer*, March/April 2014, 8–11.

45. A review of records of disciplinary actions taken by the JCB from 1993 to 2016 showed that two-thirds of all judicial discipline involved magisterial district justices, including the now disbanded Philadelphia Traffic Court and former district justices. According to the report, judges of the minor judiciary were the targets of fifty-seven of eighty-five disciplinary actions taken by the JCB since its founding. P. J. D'Annunzio, "Pennsylvania's Minor Judiciary Has an Ethics Problem," *Legal Intelligencer*, August 29, 2017.

CHAPTER 7

The Development and Improvement of Pennsylvania's Judicial Computer System

JOSEPH A. DEL SOLE, AMY CERASO,

AND THOMAS B. DARR

Although the Supreme Court's most prominent role is to serve as the highest legal authority on Pennsylvania law, it also performs other critical, but less visible, functions. Although Article V of the 1968 Pennsylvania Constitution gave the Commonwealth, for the first time, a Unified Judicial System (UJS),[1] it remained for the Court to implement the process of unification.

Computerization of the judicial branch was a key means of unification chosen by the Court. At the time of the adoption of Article V, there was no statewide automation at any level of the court system. Each county provided its own level of automation for the trial courts and district magistrates. There was no uniform appellate automated system and no vertical integration for information exchange.

In 1984, during the tenure of Chief Justice Robert N. C. Nix Jr., the Court began the task of evaluating the state of automation and determining how to improve its application. Justice Stephen A. Zappala was assigned the responsibility of developing a comprehensive plan for automation of the judiciary. The UJS Statewide Emergency Deployment Program Steering Committee was created. Its membership included representatives from the legislative branch, the business community, the bar association, and various courts, along with personnel from the Administrative Office of Pennsylvania Courts (AOPC).[2]

At the recommendation of the steering committee, in May 1986, the Court contracted with Maximus Inc., a prominent consulting firm in McLean, Virginia, to fully assess current judicial automation and develop a comprehensive information system master plan for the Commonwealth. In 1987, Maximus presented its final report in two volumes. In assessing the current status of automation, the report concluded, "Current court automation is fragmented across 67 counties comprising 60 judicial districts. Each judicial district, composed of a Court of Common Pleas and a number of District Justices, has approached automation unilaterally, resulting in different systems and different levels of automation. . . . Nearly twenty years after the inception of the Unified Judicial System, the District Justices remain virtually unautomated, the Courts of Common Pleas have followed divergent paths, and the Appellate Courts remain without full automation capabilities."[3]

The study recommended a long-term development plan, but the significant question was how the judiciary could obtain both capital and operating funds to fulfill the plan's promise.[4] That recurrent question came to define the judiciary's effort to develop and implement computerization almost as much as the planned systems themselves. Initially, given the possibility of limited federal funding, a State Justice Institute grant and Title IV-D[5] funds were considered as funding sources, but none was sufficient to implement the overall program.

In 1987, through the leadership of Justice Zappala and the court administrator of Pennsylvania, Nancy M. Sobolevitch,[6] the legislature passed Act 64, the first computer-funding bill for the Judicial Computer System (JCS).[7] This legislation adopted a mechanism to provide funding based on collections of fines, fees, and costs imposed within the court system. It provided that fines, fees, and costs in excess of those collected by the judiciary in fiscal year (FY) 1986–87 went to the newly created JCS Augmentation Account. This was accompanied by a $2 million appropriation in FY 1987–88 from the general fund in the form of a loan to be repaid from the JCS Augmentation Fund.[8]

Since the funding of judicial automation was based on increased collections of fines, fees, and costs, the automation project began in district magistrate offices. These offices had little, if any, automation, and what did exist was supplied by each county. The goal was to adopt and implement a uniform statewide plan of case management with a strong fiscal component to account for the payments of fines, fees, and costs collected at each of the approximately 550 district magistrate offices throughout the Commonwealth.[9]

The selection of senior staff at AOPC to supervise and coordinate development and implementation of this system was a vital first step. C. Sue Willoughby joined the court system in 1987 as director of fiscal operations and coordinator of the statewide automation project. Previously she had been the director of computer operations for the Democratic Caucus of the Pennsylvania House of Representatives. Working closely with Nancy Sobolevitch to guide early planning for judicial computerization, Ms. Willoughby soon relinquished her fiscal duties to focus exclusively on the JCS as director of judicial automation. She was the senior AOPC staff member responsible for project policy planning and administrative operations of the JCS in its first fifteen years. She retired in 2001.

John Davenport joined the AOPC in 1988 as director of information technology. A graduate of Lehigh University with a degree in engineering mechanics, Mr. Davenport worked in the private sector before joining the Pennsylvania court system, following service with the Army Corps of Engineers. Working in tandem with Sue Willoughby, he served as the technology architect for the JCS's initial projects and was a key participant in creating Pennsylvania's Justice Network (JNET), serving as its deputy architect from 2002 to 2009. He retired from the AOPC in 2002.

Director of Judicial Automation Amy Ceraso, Esq., began her duties in 2000 after working for the Pennsylvania judiciary in several roles. She began her work in judicial computerization as a staff attorney assisting with the development of the Statewide District Justice Automation System. As director, Ms. Ceraso has led planning for major statewide computer systems, notably the Common Pleas Court Management System (CPCMS), the system that provides case and financial management functions for all of Pennsylvania's trial courts and integrates with existing systems for Magisterial District and appellate courts. Ms. Ceraso's various experiences and skills combined to identify her as a second-generation leader of the JCS. She is a graduate of Simmons College and the University of Pittsburgh School of Law.

Ralph Hunsicker joined the AOPC in 1985 as a fiscal administrator and later as the judiciary's budget analyst. In 1989, he transferred to the Judicial Computer Project as district justice system project administrator and a year later became automation projects manager. He served in several leading management roles until 2012, when he was promoted to assistant director of judicial automation. Mr. Hunsicker played instrumental roles in developing every computer system presently used by Pennsylvania courts. He previously worked in computer-related positions at Lehigh University and private industry and graduated from Moravian College. Mr. Hunsicker retired from the AOPC in 2014.

The automation project began in earnest on June 15, 1988, when, at the direction of the steering committee, the AOPC issued a request for proposals seeking a comprehensive statewide district justice automation system, including hardware, software, training, support, and maintenance. The Supreme Court also appointed a working group composed of Magisterial District judges (MDJs) and AOPC staff to review the proposals and assist in developing software requirements based on the operations of their offices. The working group consisted of Judges James Russo (who was also a member of the steering committee), Stephen D. Mihalik, Nancy Longo, Mary Jane Fuller, Kevin Dwyer, Leo Armbruster, and Roger McCrae.

IBM was the successful bidder on the project and based its proposal on modifying an existing court case–management software package. A team of project managers, developers, and analysts was brought in to conduct intensive joint-application development sessions with the MDJ working group to review the software package and determine what needed to be changed to meet Pennsylvania's needs. At the same time, a comprehensive training package was developed and several trainers were brought on board to prepare for a two-and-a-half-year statewide rollout.

After successful pilots in three MDJ offices, the system was completed and deployed statewide in 1992 and has been in continuous use since that time. For the first time, MDJ offices used uniform case processing and fiscal procedures and forms. The Magisterial

District Justice System (MDJS) was updated significantly in 2010 to use new technology and to be able to interact more efficiently with other AOPC case-management systems, including the Court of Common Pleas system and the appellate court system.

Although automation itself progressed smoothly, funding remained an issue as the project moved forward. Consequently, the Supreme Court and the state court administrator in 1988 recruited a legislative and communications director, Thomas B. Darr, to assist in future efforts to stabilize computerization funding.[10] One means of funding the MDJS was a loan from IBM Credit Corporation. Interestingly, the option to finance was built into the original MDJS contract with IBM and exercised when funding for the project was inadequate. By 1990, it became clear that Act 64 alone could not provide sufficient funds to meet the cost of a modern computer system. Additionally, revenues from certain fines, fees, and costs were, over time, exempted from the funding base for judicial automation.

As a result, a second means to fund judicial automation was enacted by the legislature. Act 59-1990 assessed "user fees" on transactions at all court levels. A $1.50 fee for all criminal convictions and civil filings at the district magistrate level and a $5.00 fee on similar transactions at the trial and appellate level were imposed. In addition, $1 million already collected under Act 64 was refunded to certain exempted state agencies.

After implementation of the MDJS, automation staff began the process of determining software requirements for the different areas of the Courts of Common Pleas. Again using the "bottom up" approach to determine from local courts what software functionality they needed (rather than imposing a system from the "top down"), experts from each substantive court area—including judges, attorneys, rules committee staff, and filing office staff—were selected by the steering committee to participate in a series of joint application development sessions.

Unfortunately, funding remained an issue to the extent that, at one point, a lack of funding halted the Common Pleas project, necessitating the layoff of approximately twenty-five AOPC automation staff. Funding was again addressed by the legislature with Act 122-2002. This legislation increased the Act 59 filing fees to a uniform $10.00 and expanded those fees to apply to filings of deeds, mortgages, and property transfers. It also created the Access to Justice Account to fund civil legal services. Further, $2.00 of the $10.00 fee is earmarked for the Access to Justice Account. The funding method of JCS has remained unchanged since 2002.

As sufficient funding accumulated during the next several years in the JCS Augmentation Account, the decision was made to focus new work on a smaller project—automation of the three appellate courts—while the more expensive automation of Pennsylvania trial courts remained sidelined. Day-to-day operations of the MDJS continued with staff dedicated to that purpose while a small additional staff was assembled for the appellate work. Together with a team of appellate court users (again emphasizing the needs of users in planning), software was developed in-house and implemented in the three appellate courts. That software, the Pennsylvania Appellate Court Management System (PACMS), remains in use today, although it has been significantly enhanced over the past few years by the addition of document management and e-filing.

With completion of PACMS and the accumulation of additional funding, the critical decision was made to restart the Common Pleas Court project but to focus solely on those courts' criminal divisions. A somewhat unique request for proposal (RFP) was issued seeking vendors for four separate project "units"—Unit 1: project management, project analysis, and detailed design services; Unit 2: database design, conversion tasks, and database administrative services; Unit 3: programming services and notice, form, report, and document production services; and Unit 4: training services. The successful vendors—Deloitte, Sybase Inc., and the Davison Group Inc.—worked with AOPC to develop a criminal court module, the CPCMS. This system was installed in all counties by 2006 and continues to be used statewide. It has been the foundation for two additional Common Pleas Court modules—dependency court and delinquency court. The three remaining Common Pleas areas to be automated are Orphans' Court, Family Court, and Civil Court.

Of particular note is the Supreme Court's commitment to systematically improving and upgrading case-management systems over time. There are various reasons to do so. For instance, many enhancements have been made to the systems to accommodate changes in law, rules, and court practice. Several of the systems have been "refreshed" over the years to keep current with technology. For those reasons and to train new county court staff, AOPC maintains a staff that provides training to new and existing system users and help desks for each case-management system. Additionally, automation staff has developed and supports smaller applications used to manage the administrative functions of the courts (Administrative Support Application Project; ASAP) and assist the Pennsylvania Board of Law Examiners, which regulates admission to the Commonwealth's bar.

The proof of the Supreme Court's wisdom in automating Pennsylvania's judicial branch is today manifold. Initially the thought was simply that caseloads in a court system of Pennsylvania's size required the type of management systems that corporate America had long since adopted for its efficient operations. Hard as it might be to realize now, this thinking placed Pennsylvania's courts at the forefront of judicial administration nationally, a position the Pennsylvania judiciary continues to maintain.

Since the inception of the first MDJS and the completion of the CPCMS, many others in state government and the private sector (citizens and commercial entities alike) have seen ancillary benefits from the plans developed by the steering committee that first looked at automation. For instance, the MDJS has resulted in a more than 95 percent collection rate of adjudicated penalties as of July 2012. Overall collections of those penalties annually exceed the aggregate budget of the state court system, and increasing collection of adjudicated penalties is a judiciary priority.

Additionally, the data from Pennsylvania court computer systems have long been a keystone of the Commonwealth's JNET, of which the judiciary was a charter member, leading one Pennsylvania state trooper to note, "[T]he information [troopers] get off the computer can literally be a lifesaver for police officers performing their duties."[11] Similarly, those who fear domestic abuse can use online court system data to help ensure their personal safety. Finally, the expedited flow of information from Pennsylvania's JCS has benefitted groups as divergent as the media, which writes about trends in the justice system, and the General Assembly, which seeks court system data to craft new legislation. In all these respects, the Supreme Court's forward-thinking efforts to develop and improve judicial automation advanced the goal of a UJS and proved beneficial throughout the Commonwealth.

NOTES

Joseph A. Del Sole is a partner at Del Sole Cavanaugh Stroyd LLC, president judge emeritus of the Superior Court of Pennsylvania, and chair of the Common Pleas Court Automation Study Committee. Amy Ceraso is the director of judicial automation in the Administrative Office of Pennsylvania Courts. Thomas B. Darr is the court administrator of Pennsylvania. The authors acknowledge and thank Pennsylvania Supreme Court Chief Justice Emeritus Stephen A. Zappala for his assistance in preparing this chapter.

1. Pa. Const. art. V, § 1.
2. The membership of the UJS Statewide EDP Steering committee consisted of the following: Chief Justice Robert N. C. Nix Jr. and Justice Stephen A. Zappala* from the Supreme Court; Hon. Richard Snyder, State Senate designee; Judge David W. Craig* and Prothonotary G. Ronald Darlington from the Commonwealth Court; Hon. H. William DeWeese, State House designee; Judge James E. Rowley, Judge Phyllis Beck, and Charles A. Thrall, Esq., from the Superior Court; Raymond M. Seidel, Esq.,* Pennsylvania Bar Association designee; Francis J. Catania, president judge, Delaware County; Michael J. O'Malley,* president judge, Allegheny County; Edward J. Bradley, president judge, Philadelphia County; Magistrate Judge James E. Russo, president, Special Courts Association of Pennsylvania; David A Moore, senior vice president, Mellon Bank; Donna Holton, vice president, Penn Mutual Life Insurance Company; Nancy Sobolevitch,* state court administrator; C. Sue Willoughby,* director of fiscal operations, AOPC; Hon. Ted Simon, chair, Westmorland County Board of Commissioners; and Judge D. Brooks Smith, Blair County Court of Common Pleas. (*) designates Automation Subcommittee member.
3. Maximus Report Summary, Chapter II.
4. Maximus Report Summary, Exhibit IV.1.
5. 42 U.S.C. § 651, et seq.
6. Nancy M. Sobolevitch served as the fourth court administrator of Pennsylvania from 1986 until her retirement from the AOPC in 2000. A University of Pennsylvania graduate, Mrs. Sobolevitch was a former executive assistant to the speaker of the Pennsylvania House of Representatives and had been deputy director of the Pennsylvania Energy Council.
7. Act 64, 1987.
8. 42 Pa.C.S. § 3732(b). This loan was repaid in 1995.
9. As an example, fines for traffic violations and summary offenses were paid at the district magistrate offices.
10. Thomas B. Darr had been deputy legislative secretary to former governor Dick Thornburgh and, briefly, a journalist. He has graduate degrees from the University of Pittsburgh and Northwestern University.
11. Administrative Office of Pennsylvania Courts, "How the Judiciary Impacts Pennsylvanians," *Unified Judicial System of Pennsylvania*, 2014, http://www.pacourts.us/assets/files/page-255 /file-3531.pdf.

Image Gallery

FIG. 1 Supreme Court courtroom in Harrisburg, 2017. With kind permission of the Administrative Office of Pennsylvania Courts.

FIG. 2 Supreme Court courtroom in Philadelphia, 2017. With kind permission of the Administrative Office of Pennsylvania Courts.

FIG. 3 Supreme Court courtroom in Pittsburgh, 2017. With kind permission of the Administrative Office of Pennsylvania Courts.

FIG. 4 Portrait of Justice James Logan, 1731–39. With kind permission of the Administrative Office of Pennsylvania Courts.

FIG. 5 Portrait of Chief Justice William Allen, 1750–74. With kind permission of the Administrative Office of Pennsylvania Courts.

FIG. 6 Portrait of Chief Justice Benjamin Chew, 1774–77. With kind permission of the Administrative Office of Pennsylvania Courts.

FIG. 7 Portrait of Chief Justice Thomas McKean, 1777–99. Pennsylvania State Archives, MG-128.1 General Photo Collection, Political, Governor Collection of Portraits.

FIG. 8 Portrait of Justice Edward Shippen IV, 1791–99; Chief Justice, 1799–1805. Pennsylvania State Archives, MG-128.1 General Photo Collection, Political, Governor Collection of Portraits.

FIG. 9 Portrait of Justice John Bannister Gibson, 1816–27, 1851–53; Chief Justice, 1827–51. Source: William Draper Lewis, ed., *Great American Lawyers: The Lives and Influence of Judges and Lawyers Who Have Acquired Permanent National Reputation, and Have Developed the Jurisprudence of the United States* (Philadelphia: The John C. Winston Company, 1908), 3:351.

FIG. 10 Photograph of Justice John C. Bell Jr., 1950–61; Chief Justice, 1961–72. With kind permission of the Administrative Office of Pennsylvania Courts.

FIG. 11 Photograph of Justice John P. Flaherty, 1979–96; Chief Justice, 1996–2001. With kind permission of the Administrative Office of Pennsylvania Courts.

FIG. 12 Portrait of Justice Ralph J. Cappy, 1990–2001; Chief Justice, 2001–8. With kind permission of the Administrative Office of Pennsylvania Courts.

FIG. 13 Photograph of Justice Ronald D. Castille, 1994–2008; Chief Justice, 2008–14. With kind permission of the Administrative Office of Pennsylvania Courts.

FIG. 14 Photograph of Justice Thomas G. Saylor, 1998–2015; Chief Justice, 2015–present. With kind permission of the Administrative Office of Pennsylvania Courts.

FIG. 15 Supreme Court Justices, 1921. With kind permission of the Administrative Office of Pennsylvania Courts. L–R: Justice Sylvester B. Sadler, Justice Alex Simpson Jr., Justice Robert S. Frazer, Chief Justice Robert von Moschzisker, Justice Emory A. Walling, Justice John W. Kephart, Justice William I. Schaffer.

FIG. 16 Supreme Court Justices, 1927. With kind permission of the Administrative Office of Pennsylvania Courts. (1) Chief Justice Robert von Moschzisker, (2) Justice Robert S. Frazer, (3) Justice Emory A. Walling, (4) Justice Alex Simpson Jr., (5) Justice John W. Kephart, (6) Justice Sylvester B. Sadler, (7) Justice William I. Schaffer.

FIG. 17 Supreme Court Justices, 1937. With kind permission of the Administrative Office of Pennsylvania Courts. Top row, L–R: Justice Horace Stern, Justice James B. Drew, Justice William B. Linn, Justice H. Edgar Barns. Bottom row, L–R: Justice William I. Schaffer, Chief Justice John W. Kephart, Justice George W. Maxey.

FIG. 18 Supreme Court Justices, 1947. With kind permission of the Administrative Office of Pennsylvania Courts. Top row, L–R: Justice Allen M. Stearne, Justice Horace Stern, Justice Marion D. Patterson, Justice Charles Alvin Jones. Bottom row, L–R: Justice James B. Drew, Chief Justice George W. Maxey, Justice William B. Linn.

FIG. 19 Supreme Court Justices, 1951. With kind permission of the Administrative Office of Pennsylvania Courts. Top row, L–R: Justice T. McKeen Chidsey, Justice Charles Alvin Jones, Justice John C. Bell Jr., Justice Michael A. Musmanno. Bottom row, L–R: Justice Horace Stern, Chief Justice James B. Drew, Justice Allen M. Stearne.

FIG. 20 Supreme Court Justices, 1961. With kind permission of the Administrative Office of Pennsylvania Courts. Top row, L–R: Justice Michael J. Eagen, Justice Herbert B. Cohen, Justice Curtis Bok, Justice Henry X. O'Brien. Bottom row, L–R: Justice Michael A. Musmanno, Chief Justice John C. Bell Jr., Justice Benjamin R. Jones.

FIG. 21 Supreme Court Justices, 1971. With kind permission of the Administrative Office of Pennsylvania Courts. Top row, L–R: Justice Thomas W. Pomeroy Jr., Justice Henry X. O'Brien, Justice Samuel J. Roberts, Justice Alexander F. Barbieri. Bottom row, L-R: Justice Benjamin R. Jones, Chief Justice John C. Bell, Justice Michael J. Eagen.

FIG. 22 Supreme Court Justices, 1985. With kind permission of the Administrative Office of Pennsylvania Courts. Top row, L–R: Justice Stephen A. Zappala, Justice James Thomas McDermott, Justice William D. Hutchinson, Justice Nicholas P. Papadakos. Bottom row, L–R: Justice Rolf Larsen, Chief Justice Robert N. C. Nix Jr., Justice John P. Flaherty.

FIG. 23 Supreme Court Justices, 1995. With kind permission of the Administrative Office of Pennsylvania Courts. Top row, L–R: Justice Stephen A. Zappala, Justice Ralph J. Cappy, Justice Ronald D. Castille. Bottom row, L–R: Justice John P. Flaherty, Chief Justice Robert N. C. Nix Jr., Justice Frank J. Montemuro Jr.

FIG. 24 Supreme Court Justices, 2005. With kind permission of the Administrative Office of Pennsylvania Courts. Top row, L–R: Justice Max Baer, Justice J. Michael Eakin, Justice Thomas G. Saylor, Justice Sandra Schultz Newman. Bottom row, L–R: Justice Ronald D. Castille, Chief Justice Ralph J. Cappy, Justice Russell M. Nigro.

FIG. 25 Supreme Court Justices, 2017. With kind permission of the Administrative Office of Pennsylvania Courts. Top row, L–R: Justice David N. Wecht, Justice Christine L. Donohue, Justice Kevin M. Dougherty, Justice Sallie Updyke Mundy. Bottom row, L–R: Justice Max Baer, Chief Justice Thomas G. Saylor, Justice Debra McCloskey Todd.

PART 2

Decisional Law of the Supreme Court

Constitutional Law and Civil Rights

The Supreme Court and the Separation of Powers Under the Pennsylvania Constitution

HOWARD J. BASHMAN

Pennsylvania's Constitution has reflected a separation of powers among the executive, legislative, and judicial branches since the Commonwealth's original Constitution was ratified in 1776. Consequently, the separation of powers contained in Pennsylvania's Constitution predates the separation of powers reflected in the US Constitution, which took effect in 1789. Each of the four subsequently ratified versions of Pennsylvania's Constitution—in 1790, 1838, 1874, and 1968—continued to reflect the separation of powers among the three branches of Pennsylvania government.[1]

As commonly understood, the original intent of governmental separation of powers was to avoid the tyranny that colonists had experienced under the reign of the English monarchy due to the vast powers enjoyed by King George III. Under the structure of both the United States and the Pennsylvania governments, separating responsibility for enacting the laws, executing the laws, and adjudicating the meaning and constitutionality of the laws is viewed as serving an important structural guarantee to protect the rights and liberties of citizens.

When disagreements among the three branches of government arise, it often becomes the delicate responsibility of the judicial branch to address and resolve those disputes. Yet the judiciary possesses, at most, only the power of judgment. The legislative branch possesses the power to enact laws, to tax, and to appropriate the funds to be spent. The executive branch has the power to carry out the laws. The judiciary, by contrast, only has the power to announce what the law means, sometimes in the context of deciding whether the other two branches have acted in accordance with the law and within the confines of their constitutionally delegated powers. Because it must rely on the willingness of the other two branches of government to carry out or give effect to its rulings, the judiciary is sometimes characterized as the "least-dangerous branch" of government.

This chapter examines nine of the Pennsylvania Supreme Court's most significant separation-of-powers rulings issued over the past thirty-seven years. These rulings, the details of which are considered in the paragraphs that follow, present an accurate representation of the Court's current separation of powers jurisprudence. The disputes giving rise to these nine decisions often required the Court to safeguard the judiciary itself from impermissible encroachment from another branch. Other times, the judiciary has served as an impartial referee to adjudicate a dispute between the executive and legislative branches.

The cases examined herein reveal several recurring themes. One is that Pennsylvania's judiciary has not hesitated to preserve its own judicial turf from what the Supreme Court has perceived to be improper encroachment from the other two branches. Sometimes the Court's actions protecting its own powers have even come at the expense of the general public's perception of the Court itself. For example, a justice's loss of a retention election was attributed to the public's anger with the judiciary's active public support for preserving judicial pay raises. After a public outcry, all pay raises, both legislative and judicial, were repealed.

In *Stilp v. Commonwealth*,[2] the Supreme Court granted applications for extraordinary relief and assumed plenary jurisdiction to consider a lawsuit that several state court judges had initiated to challenge the constitutionality of the legislature's repeal of legislative and judicial pay raises to the extent that the pay raises lowered the pay of judicial officers. The General Assembly had approved the pay raises at 2 A.M. on July 7, 2005, without any floor debate, and Governor Ed Rendell signed the act into law later that day. After the pay raises took effect, Supreme Court Chief Justice Ralph J. Cappy wrote two opinion pieces for Pennsylvania legal publications defending the pay raises from his perspective as leader of the judicial branch.

The public's backlash was swift and vocal. On November 8, 2005, two Supreme Court justices—Russell M. Nigro and Sandra Schultz Newman—stood for retention elections. Previously, no Supreme Court justice had ever lost a retention election, at which the sole question is whether to allow the justice to serve another ten-year term in office. The voters in this typically low-turnout election defeated Nigro's retention bid and only narrowly approved Newman for retention.

On November 16, 2005, the General Assembly repealed the pay raise in its entirety, and Governor Rendell signed the repeal into law on that same day. Less than one year later, on September 14, 2006, Pennsylvania's highest court ruled by a vote of five to one that Pennsylvania's Constitution did not allow the salaries of current judges, who had received the pay raise during the period that the raise was in effect, to be diminished as the result of the pay raise repeal.[3] It is interesting to note that none of the justices serving on the Court when the *Stilp* decision issued lost his or her seat the next time he or she faced retention election. Thus it was the pay raise itself, rather than the judiciary's decision that

Pennsylvania's Constitution mandated that the judiciary retain the pay raise, that proved most politically controversial.

In 2012, the Supreme Court confronted an even more direct clash between the legislative and judicial branches concerning the legislature's power to enact laws and the judiciary's power to construe the meaning of Pennsylvania's Constitution. In *Mesivtah Eitz Chaim of Bobov, Inc. v. Pike County Board of Assessment Appeals*,[4] a religious summer camp sought to obtain an exemption from local real estate taxes, asserting that it satisfied the statutory definition of "purely public charity"—a term found in the Pennsylvania Constitution—that Pennsylvania's legislature had enacted into law in Act 55.

In 1985, the Supreme Court issued a ruling in *Hospital Utilization Project v. Commonwealth (HUP)*[5] setting forth a multipart test for determining whether an organization qualified as a "purely public charity" under Pennsylvania's Constitution. The *HUP* decision noted that the Constitution initially assigns to the legislature the duty to define the attributes of purely public charities but that the legislature had not acted to fill the void.

Dissatisfied in some respects with the Supreme Court's definition of "purely public charity" in the *HUP* ruling, Pennsylvania's General Assembly in 1997 enacted the Purely Public Charity Act. In that statute, the legislature preserved the essential considerations that the Supreme Court described in its *HUP* ruling but broadened the qualifications so that certain organizations that would not qualify as purely public charities under the *HUP* test nevertheless could qualify as such under Act 55.

The question presented in *Mesivtah Eitz Chaim of Bobov* was whether the judiciary would allow Act 55, which filled the legislative void that preceded the Supreme Court's ruling in *HUP*, to take precedence over the judicial criteria that the Supreme Court set forth in deciding the *HUP* case. By a vote of four to three, the Court held that because the Court's ruling in *HUP* purported to determine the meaning of a term found in Pennsylvania's Constitution, the legislature was powerless to relax the criteria for qualifying as a purely public charity in the absence of a constitutional amendment. After that ruling, supporters of Act 55's approach began the process of proposing a constitutional amendment that would allow the Act 55 test to supersede the *HUP* test for determining whether an organization is a purely public charity.[6]

One frequently recurring area of confrontation that has arisen between the legislative and judicial branches between 1978 and today involves efforts to legislate attorney conduct and the judiciary's own rulemaking and decisional practices. In a unanimous letter decision captioned *In re 42 Pa.C.S. §1703*,[7] the Supreme Court informed the governor and leaders of the General Assembly that the provisions of Pennsylvania's Public Agency Open Meeting Law purporting to apply to the Supreme Court, when acting in its rulemaking capacity, were unconstitutional in violation of the separation of powers. The letter ruling was unusual in that it anticipated, rather than responded to, a suit challenging application of the law to the judiciary.

In *Lloyd v. Fishinger*,[8] an evenly divided Supreme Court affirmed the ruling of the Superior Court that declared unconstitutional a Pennsylvania statute that prohibited attorneys from entering into a contingent-fee agreement with any hospitalized client within the first fifteen days of the client's hospitalization. The Court ruled that the statute violated the Pennsylvania Constitution's separation of powers. *Lloyd* stands as one of many Supreme Court rulings preserving the judiciary's own power to regulate attorney conduct in the event of improper legislative incursions.

For instance, a little more than five years later, in *Commonwealth v. Stern*,[9] a unanimous Supreme Court declared unconstitutional a Pennsylvania statute making it a crime for an attorney to pay a referral fee to a nonlawyer for referring a new client. The Court based its ruling on a provision contained in Pennsylvania's Constitution assigning the authority to regulate the conduct of attorneys to the judicial branch.[10]

The problem of drunk driving gave rise to the next turf battle between the judicial and legislative branches in *Commonwealth v. Mockaitis*.[11] In that case, the Supreme Court found unconstitutional, in violation of the separation of powers, a statute's "delegation to the judiciary of the executive functions necessary to effectuate issuance of an ignition interlock restricted license."[12] However, instead of striking down the entire law, the Court found the part that "delegate[s] to the courts the executive responsibility, more properly vested in the Department of Transportation" to be severable and simply excised the unconstitutional aspects of the law from the statute.[13]

In contrast with these decisions, the Supreme Court in 2014 rejected a separation-of-powers challenge to an alleged legislative encroachment on the judicial function. In *Zauflik v. Pennsbury School Dist.*,[14] a seriously injured minor challenged a $500,000 damages cap on tort claims against political subdivisions. The plaintiff's argument, in essence, was that the General Assembly usurped an exclusively judicial power by imposing a "statutory remittitur" on grounds wholly unrelated to the evidence but rather dependent solely on the identity of the tortfeasor.

The Court rejected this argument, concluding that the damages cap did not constitute a form of remittitur.[15] The Court also rejected the plaintiff's argument that the damages cap unconstitutionally infringed on her right to a jury trial under the Pennsylvania Constitution.[16] The *Zauflik* case demonstrates that Pennsylvania's highest court recognizes limits on the extent to which the judiciary will strike down laws alleged to infringe on the judicial function.

The Supreme Court's separation-of-powers jurisprudence also encompasses cases considering the boundaries between executive and legislative powers. In *Jubelirer v. Rendell*,[17] the Court considered the legislature's challenge to Governor Rendell's exercise of a line-item veto of an appropriation bill. The Court ruled that the relevant section of Pennsylvania's Constitution "prohibits the Governor from effectively vetoing portions of the language defining an appropriation without disapproving the funds with which the language is associated."[18]

The Court recognized that *Jubelirer* presented an unusual separation-of-powers challenge because "[t]he Governor's exercise of his veto power is unique in that it is essentially a limited legislative power, particularly in the appropriations context."[19] Nevertheless, the Court did not hesitate to curtail the governor from exercising the veto power more broadly than the Court understood the power to allow.

One year later, the Court considered an unusual separation-of-powers clash between local county government and Court of Common Pleas employees working in Jefferson County, Pennsylvania, in *Jefferson County Court Appointed Employees Ass'n v. Pa. Labor Relations Bd.*[20] Facing budgetary woes, Jefferson County determined that eleven salaried county positions had to be eliminated, including five employees of the Jefferson County Court of Common Pleas. The five employees filed labor union grievances, which resulted in a determination that they had been wrongly terminated and had to be rehired. Jefferson County, however, refused to abide by the grievance determinations that the employees had to be rehired.

The Supreme Court held that Jefferson County's determination that the Court of Common Pleas must terminate five employees violated the separation of powers. According to the Court's opinion, "As a co-equal and independent branch of government, the Judiciary has the right to decide how to square its operating needs within the budget allocated to it. Presumably, the Judiciary had options, other than eliminating five employee positions, which would have allowed it to operate within a reduced budget."[21] To be sure, ensuring that the judiciary receives proper funding on both statewide and local levels remains one of the most difficult balancing acts that the judiciary must pursue in interaction with the other two branches of government.

In 2015, in *Commonwealth v. Williams*,[22] the Supreme Court addressed a constitutional challenge to Governor Tom Wolf's decision to give at least a temporary reprieve from execution to death row inmates in Pennsylvania. *Williams* presented another unusual separation-of-powers issue because both the governor and the Commonwealth's prosecutorial power are considered to reside within the executive branch. In *Williams*, it was Philadelphia's district attorney's office that challenged the governor's grant of a death penalty reprieve to a particular death row inmate.

Even before any reprieve was issued, imposition of the death penalty in Pennsylvania was quite a rare occurrence. The last time that capital punishment was administered in the Commonwealth was in 1999. And Pennsylvania has only executed three death row inmates since the US Supreme Court allowed executions to resume in 1976. Thus it would not be statistically unusual if Governor Wolf's entire term concluded without any executions taking place. Some might wonder whether Governor Wolf's mistake, in the view of Philadelphia's lead prosecutor, was in affirmatively announcing his intention to preclude executions from occurring instead of merely allowing the current absence of executions to persist.

In *Williams*, the Court, consisting of only five justices, unanimously upheld the lawfulness of the governor's temporary death penalty reprieve.[23] Justice Correale F. Stevens issued a concurring opinion that, while agreeing with the outcome of the case, went on to observe that only the legislature, and not Pennsylvania's governor, had the power to abolish Pennsylvania's death penalty.[24]

The Supreme Court's decisions in the area of separation of powers jurisprudence represent by their very nature one of the most important and controversial subjects of the Court's jurisprudence. In cases that involve either actual or threatened infringements on the judiciary's own powers, it has shown a tendency to protect itself from transgressions from the other branches. Skeptics might view this as constituting an inappropriate tendency to expand the Court's own powers at the expense of the other two branches of government, but the Court's rulings in those areas do not seem to have precipitated any backlash from either of the other two branches. The Court has also displayed a praiseworthy willingness to referee disputes between the other two branches of government.

Looking ahead, it is difficult to predict what sort of separation-of-powers cases might confront the Supreme Court. What is clear from the Court's previous rulings is that it will carefully address such challenges on their merits and seek to arrive at the result that both the law and reason require. For a branch whose judgment is its only true power, that should keep the Supreme Court in good stead in the separation-of-powers area into the foreseeable future.

NOTES

Howard J. Bashman is the founder of Law Offices of Howard J. Bashman; founder of *How Appealing*, an appellate blog regularly visited by US Supreme Court justices and many other federal and state appellate judges, appellate lawyers, members of the news media, and other interested readers; and law clerk to the Honorable William D. Hutchinson, US Court of Appeals for the Third Circuit and formerly justice of the Supreme Court of Pennsylvania.

1. *See* Jubelirer v. Rendell, 953 A.2d 514, 529 (Pa. 2008).
2. 905 A.2d 918 (Pa. 2006).
3. Ibid., 981.
4. 44 A.3d 3 (Pa. 2012).
5. 487 A.2d 1306, 1317 (Pa. 1985).
6. The author of this chapter served as appellate counsel for Mesivtah Eitz Chaim of Bobov in the Supreme Court proceedings described previously but has attempted to describe the dispute impartially.
7. 394 A.2d 444 (Pa. 1978).
8. 605 A.2d 1193 (Pa. 1992).
9. 701 A.2d 568 (Pa. 1997).
10. Ibid., 570–73.
11. 834 A.2d 488 (Pa. 2003).
12. Ibid., 499.
13. Ibid., 503.
14. 104 A.3d 1096 (Pa. 2014).
15. Ibid., 1129–30.
16. Ibid., 1130–33.
17. 953 A.2d 514 (Pa. 2008).
18. Ibid., 537.
19. Ibid., 529.
20. 985 A.2d 697 (Pa. 2009).
21. Ibid., 708.
22. 129 A.3d 1199 (Pa. 2015).
23. Ibid., 1217–18.
24. Ibid., 1221 (Stevens, J., concurring).

CHAPTER 9

The Supreme Court and Religious Liberty

The Competing Visions of William Penn and Chief Justice John Bannister Gibson

GARY S. GILDIN

I. INTRODUCTION

The decisions of the Pennsylvania Supreme Court regarding the liberty of religious conscience present the clash of views of two titans of Pennsylvania history—William Penn, the founder of the colony, and John Bannister Gibson, a member of the Supreme Court for thirty-seven years (1816–53) and its chief justice for a quarter of a century (1827–51). The modern Supreme Court has yet to definitively rule which of the two visions prevails. The ultimate outcome will have profound consequences for religious freedom in general and for the rights of followers of nonmainstream faiths in particular.

To understand and assess the Supreme Court's opinions with respect to religion, one must be mindful of the time frame of these decisions. In 1940, the US Supreme Court in *Cantwell v. Connecticut*[1] first determined that the Free Exercise Clause of the First Amendment, by incorporation via the Fourteenth Amendment, limits state as well as federal governmental infringements on religious freedom. Before *Cantwell*, the principal source of law limiting state incursion on religious liberty was the state constitution. In this time period, then, the history of the Pennsylvania Supreme Court can be gleaned by examining its singular application of relevant provisions and values of the Pennsylvania Constitution.

Once the US Supreme Court ruled that the constraints of the Free Exercise Clause of the First Amendment applied to the states, the Pennsylvania Supreme Court became obliged to follow US Supreme Court interpretations of religious liberty in adjudging claimed violations of the federal Constitution. However, the Pennsylvania Supreme

Court retained the power to independently interpret the Pennsylvania Constitution to afford more generous shelter for religious liberty than the US Supreme Court deemed safeguarded by the First Amendment of the US Constitution. Analysis of the Pennsylvania Supreme Court's interpretation of the state Constitution after incorporation of the Free Exercise Clause, then, will be revelatory of both the Court's view of the proper scope of religious freedom and the Court's willingness to assert its autonomous role in our system of federalism.

II. THE PENNSYLVANIA CONSTITUTION

The significant history of the Supreme Court concerning religious liberty revolves around its interpretation of the unique text of the Pennsylvania Constitution. The state constitutional provisions regarding religious freedom are largely a reflection of William Penn's philosophy, which in turn had been codified in laws of the colony of Pennsylvania.

The principal protection of religious liberty lies in Article I, Section 3 of the Pennsylvania Constitution. The text of this provision is quite different from the Free Exercise Clause of the US Constitution. The first Pennsylvania Constitution was enacted fifteen years before the federal Bill of Rights[2] and was intended to reflect a view of religious freedom distinct from the collective vision of the thirteen states that ratified the First Amendment to the US Constitution.[3]

Article I, Section 3 sets forth two textual guarantees that, on their face, provide absolute security to the right of an individual to pursue his or her own religious convictions. The section prescribes that "all men have a natural *and indefeasible* right to worship Almighty God according to dictates of their own conscience."[4] The article further provides that "no human authority can, *in any case whatsoever*, control *or interfere* with the rights of conscience."[5]

The religious liberty clauses of the Pennsylvania Constitution embody William Penn's vision of religious tolerance.[6] Penn had suffered extreme persecution by the Anglican Church in England because of his Quaker beliefs. When he received the charter to Pennsylvania from King Charles II in 1861, Penn endeavored to conduct a "Holy Experiment," granting freedom of conscience to believers in God of all religious persuasions.[7] Rather than respond to his persecution by creating a colony vesting Quakers with official or preferred status, Penn recruited from a wide array of sects whose members had been oppressed in Europe.[8] Two tenets of William Penn's worldview were codified in colonial charters.[9] First, obligations to one's religious faith superseded the civil law so long as religious practices did not occasion a breach of the peace.[10] Second, liberty of conscience was guaranteed to mainstream and nonmainstream faiths alike. The seminal role of the Supreme Court, then, has been to interpret the distinctive text of Article I,

Section 3 and the two pillars of Penn's conception of the foundation and scope of liberty of conscience.

III. PREINCORPORATION CASES

The Pennsylvania Supreme Court's decisions in the era preceding the US Supreme Court's holding that the First Amendment limits state as well as federal invasions of religious liberty introduced competing visions. On the one hand, the Court announced a legal standard that extended generous security to religious belief that was largely, although not entirely, in keeping with William Penn's tenets. On the other hand, Chief Justice John Bannister Gibson proffered an institutional role for the Court that inverted Penn's hierarchy of fealty to God and state, significantly limiting the Court's power and willingness to protect liberty of conscience.

A. The Court's Adoption of a Legal Standard That Empowered Government to Limit Religious Liberty Only to Prevent a Breach of Peace

The Supreme Court's preincorporation interpretations of Article I, Section 3 announced a legal standard that, as Penn envisioned, afforded maximum protection to religious conscience. The Court insisted that government interests could interfere with the citizen's obligations to his religion only when necessary to protect the most substantial interests of society.[11] In *Commonwealth v. Wolf* (1817),[12] the Court held that Article I, Section 3 did not mandate a religious exception to Sunday closing laws; however, the Court agreed that only the most significant governmental interests would justify limitation of religion. The Court reasoned that it was "of the utmost moment" that all members of the public adhere to a day of rest "to invigorate their bodies for fresh exertions of activity."[13] The Supreme Court's demanding standard for justifying civil laws that clashed with an individual's religious belief reflected William Penn's vision of the primacy of the duty to the Creator.

While adopting a legal standard designed to afford abundant protection to religion, the Supreme Court approved the singular limitation on religious conduct accepted by William Penn and the colonial precursors to Article I, Section 3: government interests legitimately override an exercise of liberty of conscience that occasions a breach of the peace.[14] In *Updegraph v. Commonwealth* (1824),[15] the Court reviewed the conviction for blasphemy of a debating society member who had averred that the holy scriptures were a fable. Upholding the constitutionality of the prosecution,[16] the Court reasoned that Updegraph was not engaged in serious debate; rather, he was using insulting words that tended to "disturb the peace."[17] The *Updegraph* Court did not endorse a broad governmental power to cabin religious expression. To the contrary, in keeping with the limitation on conscience accepted by Penn and included in colonial charters, the Court viewed the state's interest to be "a *necessary* measure to preserve the tranquility of government."[18]

B. The Court's Interpretation of Article I, Section 3 Denied Religious Liberty to Non-Christian Faiths and Atheists

William Penn's "Holy Experiment" aspired to guarantee liberty of conscience to believers from all religious persuasions. While announcing a legal standard designed to afford generous protection to freedom of conscience, the Supreme Court departed from Penn's conceit by requiring members of minority religions (as well as nonbelievers)[19] to sacrifice their practices for the sake of followers of mainstream Christian religions.

The Supreme Court accepted that Christianity was the proper underpinning of secular laws. As just discussed, the Court in *Updegraph* upheld the blasphemy prosecution of the defendant, who, in the course of a weekly debating association discussion, stated that the holy scriptures were a mere fable and a contradiction that contained many lies. Reasoning that general Christianity "is and always has been a part of the common law of Pennsylvania,"[20] the Court endorsed the validity and importance of laws prohibiting profane speech against "Almighty God, Christ Jesus, the Holy Spirit or the Scripture of Truth."[21]

The Court rejected the defendant's argument that adoption of the Pennsylvania Constitution worked a repeal of Christianity as a constituent element of the common law. If it construed the state Constitution to overturn Christianity as a component of the common law, the Court reasoned, all laws founded on Christianity—such as "the act against cursing and swearing, and breach of the Lord's day; the act forbidding incestuous marriages, perjury by taking a false oath upon the book, fornication and adultery"—would be "carried away at one fell swoop."[22] Rather, the Court affirmed the prohibition of open, public denial of the popular religion as a legitimate means to preserve tranquility of government; it ruled that no benefit could be derived from allowing the subversion of a religion that enforced "the purest system of morality."[23]

By accepting Christianity as the basis of secular laws—and finding interference with those laws to be a breach of the peace justifying limitation of liberty of conscience—the Court sacrificed the freedom of religion of nonmainstream faiths. The *Updegraph* Court preferred the right of individuals of the "popular religion" to be free from words impugning their faith over the liberty of one of a different "conscientious religious feeling" to express his views in a debating society.[24]

The Court's affirmation of Sunday closing laws similarly required worshippers of minority faiths to conform their conduct to laws advancing moral tenets founded on Christianity. The Act of April 22, 1794, prohibited pursuing "any worldly employment or business whatsoever," except works of charity or necessity, on Sundays. In the Wolf case, Wolf, who was Jewish, believed he was to rest on the day of his Sabbath—Saturday—and, in turn, work on Sunday. The Court refused to exempt Wolf from the ban, reasoning that allowing him to work on Sunday would undermine the need for "the laboring part of the community [to] feel the institution of a day of rest as peculiarly adapted to invigorate their bodies for fresh exertion of activity."[25]

Just as the Court could not envision the defendant in *Updegraph* to be anything other than a "reviler of Christianity,"[26] the Court second-guessed Wolf's interpretation of his non-Christian faith. The Court asserted that the constitutional right to freedom of conscience was "never intended to shelter those persons who, out of mere caprice, would directly oppose their laws for the pleasure of showing their contempt and abhorrence of the religious opinions of the great mass of the citizens."[27] The Court ruled that the "true meaning" of the Fourth Commandment was "uniformly supposed to be" that people were to abstain from their usual labor one-seventh of the time to be devoted to worship and religious duties.[28]

While the Court's acceptance of Christianity as a component of the common law denied full protection of the right of conscience to members of minority faiths, an even more daunting challenge to Penn's vision was launched by the posture of Chief Justice Gibson.

C. Chief Justice Gibson's Competing Vision of Constitutional Protection of Religious Liberty

The opinions of Chief Justice John Bannister Gibson promote a point of view as to the contours of religious liberty under the Pennsylvania Constitution that is dramatically narrower than the aspiration of William Penn. Interestingly, Chief Justice Gibson's stingier interpretation of the scope of the right of conscience was not overtly animated by hostility to religion but reflects his strong and distinctive view of the respective roles of the judiciary and the legislature.

Chief Justice Gibson first expressed his view of liberty of conscience in his dissenting opinion in *Commonwealth v. Lesher* (1828).[29] The trial court had granted the Commonwealth's challenge for cause to a juror who asserted that the dictates of conscience would preclude finding any defendant guilty of murder, regardless of the law or the evidence. The Supreme Court affirmed the propriety of the challenge. In his dissenting opinion, Chief Justice Gibson first reasoned that seating the juror would not violate the juror's right to conscience under the Pennsylvania Constitution. Gibson circumscribed that right as follows: "But what are those rights? Simply a right to worship the Supreme Being according to the dictates of the heart, to adopt any creed or hold any opinion whatever on the subject of religion; and to do or forebear to do, any act, for conscience sake, the doing or forebearing of which *is not prejudicial to the public weal*."[30]

Chief Justice Gibson then espoused a broad perspective of when actions dictated by religion would prejudice the interests of society, in turn constricting constitutional shelter for religious conscience: "[W]here liberty of conscience would impinge upon the paramount right of the public, it ought to be restrained. Even Mr. Jefferson, than whom a more resolute champion of toleration, perhaps, never lived, claims no indulgence for anything that is detrimental to society, though it spring from a religious belief. . . . He denies the right of society to interfere, only where society is not a party of interest . . . but as far as the interests of society are involved, its right to interfere, on principles of self-preservation, is not disputed."[31]

The multiplicity of faiths spawned by Penn's "Holy Experiment" fortified Chief Justice Gibson's view that secular laws must take priority over individual conscience: "[W]ere the laws dispensed with, wherever they happen to be in collision with some supposed religious obligation, government would be perpetually falling short of its exigence. There are few things, however simple, that stand indifferent in the view of all the sects into which the Christian world is divided."[32] While Penn believed that one's religious obligations should supersede any duty to secular society, Chief Justice Gibson presumed that the juror in *Lesher* would, and should, set aside any religious scruples to reach a proper verdict based on the law and evidence.

Chief Justice Gibson reiterated the primacy of the citizen's obedience to the civil order in his majority opinion in *Philips v. Gratz*.[33] Gibson rejected a civil litigant's claim that because of his religion, the Court was obliged to exempt him from proceeding with trial on a Saturday: "[T]here are not duties half so sacred as those which the citizen owes to the laws. . . . That every other obligation shall yield to that of the laws, as a superior moral force, is a tacit condition of membership in every society."[34] Chief Justice Gibson's construction of the right of conscience was motivated by his view of the rightful institutional role of the judiciary relative to the province of the legislature. In his dissenting opinion in *Lesher*, Gibson agreed with the Commonwealth's policy argument that because the legislature had abolished peremptory challenges by the prosecution, disallowing a challenge for cause of the juror whose conscience precluded convicting anyone of murder afforded a clear advantage to the defendant. Nonetheless, he reasoned, greater harm would be caused were the courts, rather than the legislature, to remedy the wrong: "[F]eeling, as I do, a horror of judicial legislation, I would suffer any extremity of inconvenience, rather than step beyond the legitimate province of the court. . . . 'The discretion of a judge,' said one of the greatest constitutional lawyers that ever graced the English bench, 'is the law of tyrants: it is always unknown; it is different in different men; it is casual, and depends upon constitution, temper and passion. In the best, it is oftentimes caprice—in the worst, it is every vice, folly and passion to which human nature can be liable.'"[35]

In ruling in *Gratz* that the litigant's right to conscience did not justify a continuance to avoid proceeding with trial on Saturday, Chief Justice Gibson similarly opined that "consideration of policy adheres themselves with propriety to the legislature, and not to a magistrate whose course is prescribed not by discretion, but rules already established."[36] Gibson's advocacy of judicial restraint in *Lesher* and *Gratz* was not triggered by particular antipathy toward freedom of religion. In his earlier seminal dissenting opinion in *Eakin v. Raub*,[37] he offered a comprehensive and robust refutation of the power of the judiciary to void legislative acts that violate the state Constitution. Absent an express grant of the power of judicial review in the Constitution itself, he opined, "[I]t rests with the people, in whom full and absolute sovereign power resides to correct abuses in legislation, by instructing their representatives to repeal the obnoxious act."[38]

Others have recognized that deference to the legislature for protection of liberty of conscience leaves particularly vulnerable members of nonmainstream faiths who lack the clout to inform or impact legislation. As Justice Antonin Scalia of the US Supreme Court acknowledged approvingly in *Employment Division v. Smith*, "It may fairly be said that leaving accommodation to the political process will place at a relative disadvantage those religious practices that are not widely engaged in, but that unavoidable consequence of democratic government must be preferred to a system in which each conscience is a law unto itself or in which judges weigh the social importance of all laws against the centrality of all religious beliefs."[39] Justice Scalia has been called a "modern disciple" of Chief Justice Gibson.[40] As Gibson unabashedly proclaimed more than 150 years before Justice Scalia's opinion in *Smith*, "The sacrifice that ensues from an opposition of conscientious objection to the performance of a civil duty, ought, one would think, to be on the part of him whose moral or religious idiosyncrasy, makes it necessary."[41]

IV. POSTINCORPORATION CASES

The role of the Pennsylvania Supreme Court as a protectorate of religious liberty receded in 1940. That year, the US Supreme Court in *Cantwell v. Connecticut*[42] held that freedom of religion is one of the rights implicit in the concept of ordered liberty and thus guaranteed against infringement by state and local governments. In succeeding cases, the US Supreme Court interpreted the federal Constitution to afford sweeping shelter to religious faith. Religious followers would be exempted from laws that burdened the free exercise of their religion unless the government could prove (1) that the regulation promoted a "compelling" governmental interest and (2) that there were no alternative means of furthering that compelling interest that would be less restrictive of the citizen's religion.[43] As religious adherents sought security in the broad embrace of the Free Exercise Clause of the US Constitution, there was little need or opportunity for the Pennsylvania Supreme Court to interpret and apply the right to conscience under the Pennsylvania Constitution.[44]

The US Supreme Court's historic decision in *Employment Division v. Smith*[45] resurrected the vitality of state constitutions and state supreme courts as guardians of religious liberty. In *Smith*, the Court held that unless the government purposefully discriminated, the Court would no longer apply the compelling interest / no less restrictive alternatives test to laws that invaded religion. Instead, the Court would uphold laws of general applicability that had the effect (as opposed to the intent) of burdening an individual's faith whenever there was a rational basis for the law.[46]

The Supreme Court's *Smith* opinion returned state supreme courts to prominence as guarantors of religious liberty. While the Supremacy Clause of the US Constitution precludes state courts from refusing to enforce the floor of protection prescribed by decisions of the US Supreme Court, state courts are free to interpret their state constitutions to extend more generous liberties to the citizenry. In the wake of *Smith*, courts in at least eleven states have construed their state constitutions to require the government to satisfy the compelling interest / no less restrictive alternatives test to sustain regulations that, intentionally or inadvertently, burden religious exercise.[47]

Since *Smith*, the Pennsylvania Supreme Court has not taken up the issue of the standard of scrutiny that would be applied under the state Constitution to laws that have the effect of burdening liberty of conscience. However, sixteen years earlier, the Court in *Wiest v. Mt. Lebanon School District* concluded that "the protection of rights and freedoms secured in this section (Article I, Section 3) of our Constitution . . . does not transcend the protection of the First Amendment of the United States Constitution."[48]

V. THE FINAL, UNWRITTEN CHAPTER IN THE HISTORY OF THE SUPREME COURT REGARDING THE RIGHT TO CONSCIENCE

The definitive chapter in the Supreme Court's history regarding the right to conscience has yet to be written. In the future, the Court will likely be called on to reexamine whether Article I, Section 3 of the Pennsylvania Constitution extends greater protection than the US Constitution to citizens whose liberty of conscience has been infringed by laws of general applicability. The Court's ruling in *Wiest* did not conclusively resolve the question.[49] Among other things, the *Wiest* Court did not have the benefit of the litigants' analyses of the four criteria that the Court in *Commonwealth v. Edmunds*[50] subsequently mandated for construction of state constitutional claims. The briefs in *Wiest* did not assess the text of Article I, Section 3; the history of the provision, including Pennsylvania case law; related case law from other states; or policy considerations, including unique issues of state and local concern.[51]

When the modern Supreme Court is inevitably asked to consider an independent and more robust interpretation of the right of conscience under Article I, Section 3 of the Pennsylvania Constitution, it will be confronted with a choice between two historic visions—the "Holy Experiment" conducted by William Penn, founder of the colony, and the philosophy of judicial restraint and deference to the legislature vigorously fronted by Chief Justice Gibson. If the Court sides with Penn, it will affirm that (1) the citizen's duty to his or her Creator supersedes obligations to the secular, so long as respecting faith does not unavoidably undermine compelling societal interests, and (2) followers of nonmainstream faiths can obtain protection of their freedom from the courts where they have been unable to successfully inform or affect the legislative majority. If the Court sides with Chief Justice Gibson, it will proclaim that (1) the needs of the social order trump citizens' religious duties when the two conflict and (2) protection of nonmainstream faiths will be left primarily to the legislature. More generally, the Supreme Court's resolution of a plea for a construction of Article I, Section 3 that is more generous than the US Supreme Court's interpretation of the Free Exercise Clause will require the Court to determine whether the floor of rights established by decisions of the US Supreme Court is sufficient under, and consistent with, the unique history of the Pennsylvania Constitution.

NOTES

Gary S. Gildin is the dean and a professor of law at the Dickinson School of Law of the Pennsylvania State University. He is also the Hon. G. Thomas and Anne G. Miller Chair in Advocacy and the director of the Center for Public Interest Law and Advocacy. The author expresses his heartfelt thanks for the excellent research assistance of Dylan Woods, Erin Hayes, and Katherine Devanney.

1. 310 U.S. 296 (1940).
2. While modestly altered in 1790 and renumbered in 1874, Article I, Section 3 was part of the first Constitution of the Commonwealth of Pennsylvania that was adopted in 1776. *See* Gary S. Gildin, "Religious Freedom: Article I, Section 3," in *The Pennsylvania Constitution: A Treatise on Rights and Liberties*, ed. Kenneth G. Gormley, Jeffrey Bauman, Joel Fishman, and Leslie Kozler (Philadelphia: George T. Bisel, 2004), 130–32 (hereafter "Treatise").
3. The 1776 Pennsylvania Constitution also secured broader liberty than other state constitutions of the time, including the much-touted Virginia Declaration of Rights. Gildin, "Treatise," 127.
4. Pa. Const. art. I, § 3, emphasis added.
5. Ibid. Section 2 of the Declaration of Rights of the 1776 Constitution included multiple clauses barring governmental entanglement in matters of religion. The text provided that "no man ought or of right can be compelled to attend any religious worship, or erect or support any place of worship, or maintain any ministry contrary to, or against, his own free will or consent." Pa. Const. (1776), Declaration of Rights, cl. 2. Section 2 further provided that no person

"who acknowledges the being of God, [may] be justly deprived or abridged of any civil right of a citizen, on account of his religious sentiments or peculiar mode of religious worship." Ibid. Framers of the 1790 Constitution added the clause that "no preference shall ever be given by law to any religious establishments or modes of worship." Pa. Const. (1790), art. IX, § 3. The Framers of the 1874 Constitution added three provisions that prohibit diversion of public funds for sectarian purposes. Pa. Const. (1874) art. III, §§ 15, 29, 30. For an analysis of the separation of church and state provisions of the Pennsylvania Constitution, *see* Gildin, "Treatise," 153–99.
6. *See* Gildin, "Treatise," 118n29.
7. Ibid., 118nn31, 32.
8. Ibid., 118–19n34, 121n45.
9. Protection of religious freedom mirroring Penn's vision was prescribed in the following colonial precursors to the Pennsylvania Constitution: Chapter 16 of the West New Jersey Concessions; the first clause of the Fundamental Constitution (drafted by Penn but never enacted); the thirty-fifth provision of the "Laws Agreed Upon in England" (never approved by the settlers of the colony); the first chapter of "The Great Law"; and the first provision of the Charter of Liberties (or Privilege). *See* Gildin, "Treatise," 119–26.
10. *See* Gildin, "Treatise," 119n37.
11. Justice John Bannister Gibson's dissenting opinion in Commonwealth v. Lesher first articulated a test for measuring when government could rightfully limit religious exercise: "[W]here liberty of conscience would impinge

upon the *paramount* right of the public, it ought to be restrained." Commonwealth v. Lesher, 17 S. & R. 155, 160 (Pa. 1828) (Gibson, J., dissenting), emphasis added. While Justice Gibson did not demand a significant governmental justification to limit religious protection, *see* Section III (D), *infra*, Superior Court decisions construed the requirement that a governmental interest be "paramount" in order to sustain a restriction of religious liberty to be a "most substantial test," equivalent to the compelling interest test eventually adopted by the United States Supreme Court. Witoski v. Witoski, 513 A.2d 986, 989 (Pa. Super. 1986). *See also* Commonwealth v. Eubanks, 512 A.2d 619, 622 (Pa. 1985) (Religious freedom is a "fundamental" right, a designation that typically demands the highest governmental justification to sustain an infringement.).

12. Commonwealth v. Wolf, 3 S. & R. 48 (Pa. 1817).

13. Ibid., 51. In Specht v. Commonwealth, the Court similarly opined that "[a]ll agree that to the well-being of society, periods of rest are *absolutely necessary*." 8 Pa. 312, 323 (1948), emphasis added. While finding Sunday Closing Laws did not contravene Article I, Section 3, the Court subsequently held the law violated the prohibition against special laws regulating labor or trade set forth in Article III, Section 3 of the Pennsylvania Constitution. Kroger Co. v. O'Hara Twp., 392 A.2d 266 (Pa. 1978).

14. *See* "Laws Agreed Upon in England," provision XXXV (1682) reprinted in *A Collection of Charters and Other Publick Acts Relating to the Province of Pennsylvania* (Philadelphia: Franklin, 1740), 17 ("Obliged in conscience to live peaceably and justly in Civil Society."); "The Great Law," ch. 1, reprinted in *Charter to William Penn And Laws of the Province of Pennsylvania Passed Between the Years 1682 And 1700* (Harrisburg, Pa.: Hart, 1879), 108 ("Obliged in Conscience to live peaceably and quietly under civil government."); "Charter of Privileges," reprinted in *The Papers of Penn*, vol. 4, ed. Mary Maples Dunn and Richard S. Dunn (Philadelphia: University of Pennsylvania Press, 1981), 106 ("Obliged to live quietly under the Civil Government.").

15. Updegraph v. Commonwealth, 11 S. & R. 394 (Pa. 1824).

16. The Court did overturn the conviction on the ground that the language of the indictment was flawed.

17. 11 S. & R. 399.

18. Ibid., 405, emphasis added. The Court subsequently held that the prosecution of Jehovah's Witnesses who made incessant noise and repeated efforts to enter homes did not violate the Pennsylvania Constitution. The Court reasoned that the state Constitution does not extend protection to religious expression that is "inimical to the peace, good order and morals of society." Commonwealth v. Palms, 15 A.2d 481, 485 (Pa. 1940). *See also* Pittsburgh v. Raffner, 4 A.2d 224 (Pa. 1939) (upholding ordinance requiring Jehovah's Witnesses to obtain permit to peddle merchandise because ordinance was "designed to protect people in their homes and offices from being victimized by unscrupulous and unauthorized agents"). Confirming the justification required to sustain governmental incursions on religious liberty, the Court held that Article I, Section 3 guaranteed the right to attempt to convert members of the Roman Catholic faith absent evidence of "unrest" or "breach [of] the public peace." Application of Conversion Ctr., 130 A.2d 107, 109 (Pa. 1957).

19. In Epperson v. Ark., the US Supreme Court held that government may not prefer religion over nonreligion. *See* 393 U.S. 97, 103 (1968). *See also* Everson v. Bd. of Ewing Twp., 330 U.S. 1, 18 (1947).

20. Updegraph, 11 S. & R. at 400. The Court believed it was acting in accordance with the views of William Penn by endorsing "not Christianity founded on any particular religious tenets; not Christianity with an established church and tithes and spiritual courts; but Christianity with liberty of conscience to all men." *See also* Mohney v. Cook, 26 Pa. 342, 347 (1855) (even those who reject Christianity could not "get clear of its influence or reject those sentiments, customs and principles which it has spread among the people, so that, like the air we breathe, they have become the common stock of the whole country and essential elements of its life").

21. Updegraph, 11 S. & R. 398.

22. Ibid., 399.

23. Ibid., 405, quoting Chief Justice Zephania Swift, *System of Laws of the State of Connecticut*, 2 vols. (Windham, Conn.: John Byrne, 1795), 825.

24. Updegraph, 11 S. & R. at 405, 408. The Court took pains to point out that the law would continue to protect the right of Jews and Unitarians to worship free of punishment or persecution.

However, the state Constitution does not protect "the right publicly to vilify the religion of his neighbors and of the country." Ibid., 408.

25. Wolf, 3 S. & R. 50.

26. Updegraph, 11 S. & R. 408.

27. Ibid., 50. The Court subsequently ruled that prohibiting Sunday work was necessary in order to secure the rights of conscience of those who wanted to worship on Sunday. Johnston v. Commonwealth, 22 Pa. 102, 115 (1853).

28. Wolf, 3 S. & R. 50.

29. Commonwealth v. Lesher, 17 S. & R. 155 (Pa. 1828).

30. Ibid., 160 (Gibson, C.J., dissenting).

31. Ibid., 160–61.

32. Ibid., 161.

33. Philips v. Gratz, 2 Pen. & W. 412 (Pa. 1831).

34. Ibid., 417.

35. Ibid., 164–65.

36. Philips, 2 Pen. & W. at 417.

37. Eakin v. Raub, 12 S. & R. 330, 344 (Pa. 1825) (Gibson, J., dissenting).

38. Ibid., 355. *See also* Stanley I. Kutler, "John Bannister Gibson, Judicial Restraint and the 'Positive State,'" *Journal of Public Law* 14 (1965): 182.

39. Emp't Div. v. Smith, 494 U.S. 877, 890 (1990).

40. Walter J. Walsh, "The First Free Exercise Case," *George Washington Law Review* 73 (2004): 1, 44.

41. Philips, 2 Pen. & W. at 416–17.

42. Cantwell v. Conn., 310 U.S. 296 (1940).

43. Thomas v. Review Bd. of the Ind. Emp't Sec. Div., 450 U.S. 707, 718 (1981); Sherbert v. Verner, 374 U.S. 389, 406–7 (1963).

44. *See* In re Green, 292 A.2d 387 (Pa. 1972); Fitzgerald v. Philadelphia, 102 A.2d 887 (Pa. 1954) (adjudicating religious freedom claims under First Amendment to the US Constitution).

45. Emp't Div. v. Smith, 494 U.S. 872 (1990).

46. The Court subsequently struck down the US Congress's attempt to reinstate the compelling interest test through the Religious Freedom Restoration Act (RFRA), 42 U.S.C. § 2000bb-1 (1994), finding that legislation beyond Congress's power to enforce the provisions of the Fourteenth Amendment. *See* City of Boerne v. Flores, 521 U.S. 507 (1997) (striking down the RFRA as it applied to the states as an unconstitutional use by Congress of its enforcement powers under the Fourteenth Amendment; despite this decision, RFRA continues to be good law as applied in the federal arena).

47. *See* Gildin, "Treatise," 147–49.

48. Wiest v. Mt. Lebanon Sch. Dist., 320 A.2d 362, 366 (Pa. 1974). The Court reiterated this conclusion five years later in Springfield Sch. Dist. v. Dep't of Educ., 397 A.2d 1154, 1170 (Pa. 1979).

49. *See* Gildin, "Treatise," 144–46.

50. Commonwealth v. Edmunds, 586 A.2d 887 (Pa. 1990).

51. Ibid., 895.

CHAPTER 10

Free Expression Versus Reputation

The Supreme Court's Weighing of Interests

CARL A. SOLANO AND EDWARD J. SHOLINSKY

The Supreme Court of Pennsylvania has consistently touted the protections provided by the Commonwealth for freedoms of speech and press. As the Court explained in *Pap's A.M. v. City of Erie*, "Freedom of expression has a robust constitutional history and place in Pennsylvania. The very first Article of the Pennsylvania Constitution consists of the Pennsylvania Declaration of Rights, and the first section of that Article affirms, among other things, that all citizens 'have certain inherent and indefeasible rights.' Among those inherent rights are those delineated in § 7, which address 'Freedom of Press and Speech; Libels.'"[1]

The Court observed that Article I, Section 7 is broader than the federal Constitution's First Amendment in that it "affirms the 'invaluable right' to the 'free communication of thoughts and opinions,' and the right of 'every citizen' to 'speak freely' on 'any subject' so long as that liberty is not abused."[2] In the long history of the Commonwealth, however, the Court has struggled to match this broad expression of freedom with concerns about its "abuse." That tension is most clearly reflected in the Court's decisions on the law of defamation.

I. THE FOUNDATIONAL PERIOD

The Commonwealth's solicitude for freedom of expression has been traced to its founder, William Penn, and his prosecution in 1670 "for the 'crime' of preaching to an unlawful assembly."[3] As set forth in the preceding chapter, Penn's *Frame of Government of Pennsylvania* guaranteed freedom of conscience and religious worship.[4] While other forms of free expression were not formally guaranteed, the colony's Quaker-based tolerance influenced some early legal decisions. For example, when William Bradford, the first American printer south of Boston, was tried in 1682 for seditious libel because he criticized Pennsylvania officials for straying from Quaker values, he was allowed to defend himself by arguing that his statements were true and, therefore, not seditious—a startling break from the contemporary view that truth was irrelevant to the crime of libel.[5]

Four decades later, when Philadelphia lawyer Andrew Hamilton went to New York to defend a former Bradford apprentice, John Peter Zenger, in another libel prosecution, Hamilton echoed Bradford's argument and obtained an acquittal by the jury, despite the New York court's refusal to allow truth as a justification. Hamilton's ringing defense of the freedom to tell the truth was published throughout the colonies—particularly through Benjamin Franklin's widely read *Pennsylvania Gazette*—and helped shape a new public view of freedom of expression that again has been recognized by the Supreme Court as a foundational basis for Pennsylvania press freedoms.[6] Against this background, Pennsylvania in 1776 became the first state to protect "freedom of speech, and of writing, and publishing,"[7] making it "the flagship of free expression in the early Republic."[8]

The freedom was not unbounded, however, and scholars have contended that freedom of speech often did not extend to the views of those out of power.[9] The Supreme Court's 1788 decision in *Respublica v. Oswald*[10] illustrates the problem. Oswald, while on bail after being charged with libel, published an article accusing members of the Court of bias because of their political views. The Court cited Oswald for contempt because his article might prejudice the public and corrupt justice. Oswald argued that the Constitution gave him the freedom to speak freely and without restraint, but the Court, in an opinion by Chief Justice McKean, rejected that view, explaining, "The true liberty of the press is amply secured by permitting every man to publish his opinions; but it is due to the peace and dignity of society to enquire into the motives of such publications, and to distinguish between those which are meant for use and reformation, and with an eye solely to the public good, and those which are intended merely to delude and to defame."[11] The Constitution was not intended to make libel "sacred," and "good government" could punish abuse of the liberty of speech.[12]

Two years later, Chief Justice McKean chaired a committee of the whole during the framing of a new state Constitution.[13] The free speech provisions were redrafted to state that "no law shall ever be made to restrain the rights" of a free press, truth "may be given in evidence" in prosecutions for publications about public officials or conduct, "[t]he free communication of thoughts and opinions is one of the invaluable rights of man," and "every citizen may freely speak, write, and print on any subject"—but that those who do so are "responsible for the abuse of that liberty."[14] The new Constitution also recognized a right of "acquiring, possessing, and protecting property and reputation."[15]

In the years after the adoption of Pennsylvania's 1790 Constitution, the Supreme Court reiterated the view that libels are so destructive of society that they can readily be punished, both criminally and civilly.[16] In *Runkle v. Meyer*,[17] the Court considered whether the publisher of a third person's defamatory article could be sued for libel without violating press freedoms, and the Court had no hesitancy in answering affirmatively, comparing the publisher to one who "bespatters another's clothes with filth, as he passes the street, though at the instigation of a third person."[18]

Meanwhile, the turn of the nineteenth century found the Commonwealth embroiled in the heated political debates that accompanied the dawn of political parties at and following the end of President Washington's administration. Much of the controversy swirled around the caustic attacks made on President Adams and his fellow Federalists by a Philadelphia newspaper, the *Aurora*, which was published by Benjamin Franklin Bache (grandson of the famed publisher of the *Pennsylvania Gazette*) and his successor, William Duane. The attacks led to enactment of the federal Sedition Act of 1798,[19] which punished speech critical of the government. Duane was prosecuted under the act, but the statute expired after the election of the Federalists' opponents, led by Thomas Jefferson, and Duane was not tried.[20] Meanwhile, popular opposition to heavy-handed enforcement of the Sedition Act gave rise to the modern American theory that criticism of government actors is a fundamental aspect of the right of free expression.[21]

Although Pennsylvania played a major role in this critical evolution of the theory of free expression, its Supreme Court did not. As late as 1805, the Court continued to espouse a theory of seditious libel that was more in tune with the Sedition Act than its repeal. Thus in *Respublica v. Dennie*,[22] the Court addressed an action to punish Joseph Dennie, the editor of the Jeffersonian journal the *Port Folio*, for publishing views critical of certain forms of democracy. The Court held that the Constitution did not forbid prosecution of Dennie for seditious libel because his comments could be considered an "abuse" of the privilege of free speech. There is a difference, the Court explained, between publishing "temperate investigations of the nature and forms of government" and "those which are plainly accompanied with a *criminal intent*, deliberately designed to unloosen the social band of union, totally to unhinge the minds of the citizens and to produce popular discontent with the exercise of power."[23] The Court left it to the jury to determine whether Dennie had abused his privilege. The jury acquitted.[24]

II. THE NINETEENTH AND EARLY TWENTIETH CENTURIES

Throughout the rest of the nineteenth century and much of the twentieth, the right of free expression under the Pennsylvania Constitution played little role in Pennsylvania legal development in general and in the formulation of defamation law in particular. Scholars have observed that this generally was a period of state constitutional dormancy with respect to individual rights; indeed, when courts began to focus on constitutional rights in the twentieth century, they did so mainly with respect to the federal rights applicable to the states under the Fourteenth Amendment to the US Constitution, which was added in 1868.[25]

Rather than viewing defamation as an exception to the right of free speech that should be closely circumscribed, the Supreme Court focused mainly on protecting reputation interests and kept speech-based defenses relatively narrow. In 1984, the Court summarized this historical perspective in *Hepps v. Philadelphia Newspapers, Inc.*:[26]

> The underlying premise concerning the character of the defamed individual is the principle that any man accused of wrong-doing is presumed innocent until proven guilty. The decisions reasoned this principle transcended the criminal law and was equally applicable to the ordinary affairs of life. Based upon this premise we developed the rule that in actions for defamation, the general character or reputation of the plaintiff is presumed to be good. Since the gravamen of defamation is that the words uttered or written tend to harm the reputation, a consequence of the rule presuming the good reputation of the plaintiff was a presumption of the falsity of the defamatory words.[27]

Though the Court recognized that truth ("justification") was a complete defense,[28] it made clear that the mere fact that a defendant reasonably believed a statement to be true would not save him from liability.[29] Nor was proof of substantial truth sufficient. If the proof were to "extend not so broad as the allegation, or go beside it, or fall short of it, the defense will be held insufficient."[30] The burden of establishing that a statement was justified was placed squarely on the defendant as a matter of affirmative defense and, indeed, as late as 1971, the Court still authoritatively declared, "[A]lthough ordinarily in order to be actionable words must be false, falsity is not an element of a cause of action for libel in Pennsylvania."[31]

One area where the Court suggested a less restrictive attitude was its injection of the elusive concept of "malice" as a requirement for a defamatory statement to be actionable. An early leading case from 1806 is *M'Millan v. Birch*, which declared malice to be "an essential ingredient in slander."[32] Although the Court said malice would be implied, a defendant should be free to show that "there was no malice in my heart."[33] The Court held that the defendant's evidence that the speech at issue was made in a church presbytery while pleading a cause could rebut the presumption of malice and absolve him of liability. In *Sharff v. Commonwealth*,[34] the Court held that in a criminal prosecution for libel, malice had to be found by a jury.

Over time, however, the concept of "malice in my heart" blurred. Malice was implied, and little had to be shown to support the implication. As the Court explained in *Neeb v. Hope*, "Malice is said to be essential to an action for libel, but it is malice in a special and technical sense, which exists in the absence of lawful excuse, and where there may be no spite or ill will, or disposition to injure others. Every publication having the other qualities of a libel, if wilful and unprivileged, is in law malicious."[35] In *Summit Hotel Co. v. National Broadcasting Co.*,[36] the Court refused to call the resulting regime one of strict liability, but its distinction was narrow: "[O]ur rule is not one of absolute liability, but rather, of a very strict standard of care to ascertain the truth of the published matter," in which "[t]he fact of defamatory publication is evidentiary of such lack of due care." Several decades later, the Court explicitly acknowledged that this was a strict-liability regime.[37]

One brighter spot in this tapestry was the Court's development of the law of privilege, an issue in which the Court did recognize the importance of freedom of expression. In *Case of Austin*,[38] the Court recognized the privilege of a lawyer to make statements critical of a judge, explaining, "[C]onduct of a judge, like that of every other functionary, is a legitimate subject of scrutiny, and where the public good is the aim, such scrutiny is as open to an attorney of his court as to any other citizen." The Court reached a similar result in *Ex parte Steinman*,[39] relying in part on an 1874 amendment to Section 7 of the Declaration of Rights providing that "no conviction shall be had in any prosecution for the publication of papers relating to the official conduct of officers or men in public capacity, or to any other matter proper for public investigation or information where the fact that such publication was not maliciously or negligently made, shall be established to the satisfaction of the jury."

In *Briggs v. Garrett*,[40] the chair of a local civic committee read a letter by a city official that charged a judge seeking reelection with responsibility for a public works scandal. The Court held that there was a privilege to read the letter informing voters about the city official's charge because such an accusation against a candidate is "a matter for public information" and there was no "abuse" of free speech rights in disseminating it, even though the person reading the letter did not know whether the accusation was true: "If the voters may not speak, write or print anything but such facts as they can establish with judicial certainty, the right [of free speech] does not exist, unless in such form that a prudent man would be hesitant to exercise it."[41] Two years later, the Court held that this privilege to inform the public extended to press organizations.[42]

The theory of these cases ultimately evolved into a privilege of "fair report," under which a publisher could report defamatory information contained in government proceedings so long as the account was "fair, accurate and complete, and not published solely for the purpose of causing harm to the person defamed."[43] But the privilege was far from absolute. As the Court cautioned in *Conroy v. Pittsburgh Times*,[44] "The law, in cases of privilege, has been lenient to the claim, but it must not be allowed to become lax" and so must take care to reject such claims if a defendant could not prove the challenged statement to have been made on a proper occasion, from a proper motive, in a proper manner, and based on reasonable and proper cause.

In 1964, *New York Times Co. v. Sullivan* revolutionized defamation law by imposing new federal constitutional limitations on recovery as a means of securing greater "breathing space" for freedom of expression.[45] Suddenly there were new requirements for proof of fault by a plaintiff and new protections for a defendant who made innocent mistakes.[46] Similar protections might well have been grounded in the expansive language of Pennsylvania's constitutional protections for freedom of speech and press, but they were not. Indeed, in the face of the US Supreme Court's unveiling of a new era of solicitude for speech that previously might have been held actionable, the Pennsylvania Supreme Court showed little enthusiasm to join in. Rather than accepting the new federal decisions as a cue to engage in its own reinvigoration of state expression rights as they applied to defamation, the Court's decisions reflected a steadfast determination to protect the status quo or, at most, do no more than the federal courts held was required.

In *Corabi v. Curtis Pub. Co.*, for example, the Court engaged in an extensive review of defamation law to establish that the "constitutional privilege" established under *Sullivan* was fully consistent with traditional rules presuming that the defendant's statement was false and was conceded by the defendant to be false if the defendant failed to prove otherwise.[47] The Court also declined to interpret *Sullivan* to require proof of liability by clear and convincing evidence.[48] Each of these positions was later repudiated by the US Supreme Court.[49] In a decision difficult to square with *Sullivan* precepts, the Court upheld a verdict in favor of a murder suspect because, even though the article reported that she was not convicted, it also reported disputed facts that could suggest her guilt.[50]

In *Hepps*, the Court reiterated its view that Pennsylvania's traditional allocation to the defendant of the burden of proving truth was constitutionally justified. The Court reasoned that putting the burden of proof on the defendant met the constitutional floor set by *Sullivan* and its progeny because the plaintiff still had to show fault in the form of malice or negligence.[51] The US Supreme Court reversed, explaining that when the "scales are in such an uncertain balance" between putting the burden on the plaintiff or the defendant, "the Constitution requires us to tip them in favor of protecting true speech."[52]

As the US Supreme Court recognized greater protection of free expression, the Pennsylvania Supreme Court began to resist further advances, asserting a need to defend countervailing constitutional interests in reputation rights under the Pennsylvania Constitution. In *Hatchard v. Westinghouse Broadcasting Co.*,[53] the Court considered a Pennsylvania shield statute that it had construed in the 1960s to provide broad protections against compelled disclosure of reporters' sources.[54] The Court in *Hatchard* held that it needed to narrow that interpretation to protect only *confidential* sources because, under a broader interpretation, "serious questions would arise as to the constitutionality of the statute in light of the protection of fundamental rights [to reputation] provided for in the Pennsylvania Constitution."[55] As a result of the US Supreme Court's reversal in *Hepps*, some libel plaintiffs now would have to prove both falsity and actual malice, and the Court explained that a statute shielding discovery of information relevant to those issues would make it "virtually impossible" for the plaintiff to prove his or her case and leave the defamed individual without a meaningful remedy.[56] One year later, in *Sprague v. Walter*,[57] the Court reiterated that any broad interpretation of the state shield law would infringe the state constitutional interest in reputation, which had "been placed in the same category with life, liberty and property."[58]

These decisions are difficult to reconcile with the Court's oft-stated pronouncements[59] that the protection of free expression in the Pennsylvania Constitution is broader than that in the federal First Amendment. The Court had embraced that special nature of free expression in Pennsylvania even when balancing it against the right to acquire, possess, and protect property under Article I, Section 1 of the Pennsylvania Constitution, which the Court called "one of 'the Hallmarks of Western Civilization.'"[60] But cases like *Hepps*, *Hatchard*, and *Sprague* signaled that when reputation (an interest recognized in the same clause of Article I, Section 1 as property) was at issue, the Court favored striking a different balance. It did so even though reputation had never been characterized as "fundamental" in the federal cases to which the Court often looked in making such determinations,[61] and the Court had never accorded all rights under Article I, Section 1 such "fundamental" status.[62]

The Court made its revised weighing of interests explicit in *Norton v. Glenn*.[63] At issue was whether the Court should recognize a privilege of the press to neutrally report defamatory statements made by public officials. The privilege had not yet been recognized by the US Supreme Court under the First Amendment, though a number of lower courts had done so. The plaintiff sought recognition of the privilege as either a matter of First Amendment law or a protection under Article I, Section 7 of the Pennsylvania Constitution. The Court rejected both arguments. In so doing, the Court held that federal protections of expression already had been extended very far, and it could not imagine that the US Supreme Court would "tilt" further by adopting a privilege to neutrally report a public official's defamation.[64] The Court then held that it could "not interpret our state constitution as providing even broader free expression rights than does its federal counterpart" because doing so would "infringe on the protection granted by the Pennsylvania Constitution to reputation."[65] Henceforth, the Court declared, "[T]he protections accorded . . . by the US Supreme Court to the right of free expression in defamation actions would demarcate the outer boundaries of our Commonwealth's free expression provision."[66] The Court's rhetoric about the special role of free expression in Pennsylvania constitutional law was thus shunted aside, and the state provision was demoted to no more than a First Amendment redundancy insofar as defamation law was concerned.

In *American Future Sys., Inc. v. Better Bus. Bureau*,[67] decided in 2007, the Court carried the demotion of Pennsylvania free-expression rights further, noting that *Norton* had construed the state Constitution to "highly prioritize reputational interests" and thereby preclude any elevated role for interests of free expression.[68] At issue in the case was the notion of common-law privileges, which had been recognized as affording defenses to defamation for statements made in a proper manner or for a proper purpose, so long as a privilege was not "abused." Abuse of a privilege at common law could be shown by establishing that the defendant acted negligently, but under the new federal constitutional regime, all private-figure defamation plaintiffs had to prove negligence to recover.[69] Use of negligence as the standard to prove abuse of a privilege thus became superfluous if the plaintiff was a private figure. One solution would be to permit a defendant to maintain a privilege defense unless the plaintiff proved the privilege's abuse through conduct amounting to "actual malice"—a standard that was much higher than negligence and was inapplicable to defamation claims brought by private-figure plaintiffs. But the Court rejected that solution, stating, "[A]s a matter of common-law decisionmaking, Pennsylvania courts will not strengthen—for post-*Gertz* purposes—conditional privileges previously defined by reference to negligence principles so that, now, they may only be defeated by proving actual malice."[70] The Court also declined to require an actual malice standard if the speech at issue was about a matter of public concern.[71]

It is ironic that after the Supreme Court expressed a willingness to accord heightened protection to free expression under the Pennsylvania Constitution, it retreated from that position when it encountered such heightened protection actually being afforded under federal law. As a result, rather than recognizing free expression's primacy, the Court has afforded heightened protection to reputational interests, allowing them to trump advances in speech and press protections. Although these developments are disheartening to advocates of free expression, the Supreme Court has a long and venerable history, and there is still much time and opportunity to fine-tune this imbalance. Pennsylvania began its existence as a "flagship of free expression"; historians will watch to see whether it returns to that exalted role.

NOTES

Carl A. Solano authored this chapter when he was a partner at Schnader Harrison Segal & Lewis LLP. He later became a judge on the Superior Court of Pennsylvania. Edward J. Sholinsky is a partner at Schnader Harrison Segal & Lewis LLP.

1. 812 A.2d 591, 603 (Pa. 2002).
2. Ibid., 603.
3. Commonwealth v. Tate, 432 A.2d 1382, 1388 (Pa. 1981).
4. Frame of Government, "Laws Agreed Upon in England," § XXXV (1682).
5. *See* Proprietor v. Keith, Pa. Colonial Cas. 117 (Q.S. Phila. 1692) (S. W. Pennypacker, ed.);

T. R. White, *Commentaries on the Constitution of Pennsylvania*, vol. 95 (Philadelphia: T. & J. W. Johnson, 1907) (calling this "the earliest case on record" where proof of truth was allowed).
6. *See* In re Mack, 126 A.2d 679, 683–84 (Pa. 1956) (separate opinion of Bell, J.), *cert. denied*, 352 U.S. 1002 (1957); Kane v. Commonwealth, 89 Pa. 522, 526–27 (1879).
7. Pa. Const. (1776) § 12.
8. S. F. Kreimer, "The Pennsylvania Constitution's Protection of Free Expression," *University of Pennsylvania Journal of Constitutional Law* 5 (October 2002): 12, 15.

9. *See* L. W. Levy, *Legacy of Suppression: Freedom of Speech and Press in Early American History* (Cambridge, Mass.: Belknap Press of Harvard University Press, 1960), 19–21.

10. 1 Dall. 319 (Pa. 1788).

11. Ibid., 325.

12. Ibid., 325–26.

13. Robert Levere Brunhouse, *The Counter-Revolution in Pennsylvania, 1776–1790* (Harrisburg: Pennsylvania Historical Commission, 1942), 225.

14. Pa. Const. art. IX, § 7 (1790) (now art. I, the Declaration of Rights).

15. Ibid., § 1.

16. *See* Republica v. Cobbet, 3 Yeates 93, 101 (Pa. 1800) ("Libels are destructive both of public and private happiness, manifestly tend to breaches of the peace, and are good causes of forfeiture of a recognizance to keep the peace or of good behavior."); Republica v. Passmore, 3 Yeates 441, 442 (Pa. 1802) ("If the minds of the public can be prejudiced by such improper publications, before a cause is heard, justice cannot be administered.").

17. 3 Yeates 518 (Pa. 1803).

18. Ibid., 519.

19. 1 Stat. 596.

20. "Alien and Sedition Acts: 1798," *NET Industries*, 2014, http://www.law.jrank.org/pages/2396/AlienSeditionActs.html.

21. *See* New York Times Co. v. Sullivan, 376 U.S. 254, 276 (1964) ("the attack upon [the Sedition Act's] validity has carried the day in the court of history"); Tucker v. Philadelphia Daily News, 848 A.2d 113, 128–29 (Pa. 2004).

22. 4 Yeates 267 (Pa. 1805).

23. Ibid., 270, emphasis in original.

24. Ibid., 271.

25. *See* F. D. Rapone Jr., "Article I, Section 7 of the Pennsylvania Constitution and the Public Expression of Unpopular Ideas," *Temple Law Review* 74 (2001): 655, 667–79.

26. 485 A.2d 374 (Pa. 1984), *rev'd*, 475 U.S. 767 (1986).

27. Ibid., 378 (citations omitted).

28. *See, e.g.*, Steinman v. McWilliams, 6 Pa. 170 (1847).

29. Petrie v. Rose, 5 Watts & Serg. 364, 366 (Pa. 1843) ("[I]t is incompetent to a defendant in an action of slander to give evidence, in mitigation of damages, of facts and circumstances which induced him to suppose the charge true at the time it was made.").

30. Burford v. Wible, 32 Pa. 95, 96 (1858).

31. Corabi v. Curtis Pub. Co., 273 A.2d 899, 908 (Pa. 1971) (footnotes omitted).

32. 1 Binn. 178, 186 (Pa. 1806).

33. Ibid.

34. 2 Binn. 514 (Pa. 1810).

35. 2 A. 568, 570 (Pa. 1886).

36. 8 A.2d 302, 307 (Pa. 1939).

37. *See* American Future Sys., Inc. v. Better Bus. Bureau, 923 A.2d 389, 396 (Pa. 2007).

38. 5 Rawle 191, 205 (Pa. 1835).

39. 95 Pa. 220, 237 (1880).

40. 2 A. 513 (Pa. 1886).

41. Ibid., 523.

42. Press Co. v. Stewart, 14 A. 51, 53 (Pa. 1888).

43. *See* Sciandra v. Lynett, 187 A.2d 586, 588–89 (Pa. 1963).

44. 21 A. 154, 156 (Pa. 1891).

45. *See* 376 U.S. at 271–72.

46. *See, e.g.*, ibid.; Garrison v. La., 379 U.S. 64 (1964); St. Amant v. Thompson, 390 U.S. 727 (1968); and Gertz v. Robert Welch, Inc., 418 U.S. 323 (1974).

47. 273 A.2d at 907–11.

48. Ibid., 911–12.

49. *See* Phila. Newspapers v. Hepps, 475 U.S. 767 (1986); Anderson v. Liberty Lobby, Inc., 477 U.S. 242 (1986).

50. 273 A.2d at 915–18.

51. 485 A.2d 374, 385–86 (Pa. 1984).

52. 475 U.S. 776–77 (1986).

53. 532 A.2d 346, 350 (Pa. 1987).

54. *See* In re Taylor, 193 A.2d 181, 185 (Pa. 1963) (basing decision on the need of newsmen to be "able to *fully and completely* protect the sources of their information" and how it was "vitally important that this public shield against governmental inefficiency, corruption and crime be preserved against piercing and erosion"), emphasis in original.

55. 532 A.2d at 350–51.

56. Ibid., 349–51.

57. 543 A.2d 1078, 1084–85 (Pa. 1987).

58. *See also* Commonwealth v. Bowden, 838 A.2d 740 (Pa. 2003) (refusing to apply shield law to reporters' notes sought for a criminal proceeding); Castellani v. Scranton Times, L.P., 956 A.2d 937, 949–50 (Pa. 2008) (describing these decisions as limiting the shield law to its "core protections" of protecting confidential sources).

59. *See, e.g.*, DePaul v. Commonwealth, 969 A.2d 536, 546–47 (Pa. 2009); Pap's, 812 A.2d at 603; Ins. Adj. Bur. v. Ins. Comm'r., 542 A.2d 1317, 1324 (Pa. 1988); Tate, 432 A.2d at 1387–90; William Goldman Theatres, Inc. v. Dana, 173 A.2d 59, 61–62 (Pa. 1961), *cert. denied*, 368 U.S. 897 (1961).

60. Tate, 432 A.2d 1388–89.
61. *See* Paul v. Davis, 424 U.S. 693, 701–2 (1976).
62. *See* Nixon v. Commonwealth, Dep't of Publ. Welfare, 839 A.2d 277, 286–88 (Pa. 2003) (citing federal and state cases).
63. 860 A.2d 48 (Pa. 2004).
64. Ibid., 56–57.
65. Ibid., 57–59.
66. Ibid., 58; accord, Joseph v. Scranton Times, 129 A.3d 404, 428 (Pa. 2015).
67. 923 A.2d at 398.
68. *See also* ibid., 395 ("[R]eputational interests occupy an elevated position within our state Constitution's system of safeguards, and hence, in the context of defamation law the state Constitution's free speech guarantees are no more extensive than those of the First Amendment.").
69. *See* Gertz, 418 U.S. at 347.
70. 923 A.2d at 398.
71. Ibid., 398–400.

CHAPTER 11

Women on the Court and the Court on Women

DEBORAH L. BRAKE AND SUSAN FRIETSCHE

Our look at women and the Court begins with the underappreciated narrative of the first woman to serve on the Pennsylvania Supreme Court, Anne X. Alpern. Justice Alpern was appointed in 1961 by Governor David L. Lawrence to fill a vacancy on the Court. At the time, women were a rarity on the highest courts of their states. Ohio had earned the distinction of being the first US state to have a woman serving on its Supreme Court in 1923, a first that was not followed by any other state until thirty-six years later, when Hawaii's Supreme Court welcomed a female justice in 1959.[1] By the dawn of the 1970s, only four women were serving on their states' highest courts.[2]

Justice Alpern's accomplishment in becoming Pennsylvania's first female Supreme Court justice was short lived; she served for less than one year. When her term of appointment ended, she ran in the state's judicial elections for a full term but failed to win a seat. Analysts suggest that her defeat was at least partly attributable to the bitterness created by her role in conducting a voter fraud investigation targeting Philadelphia Democrats the previous year.[3]

Throughout her career, Justice Alpern was a pioneer for women in the legal profession. She graduated from the University of Pittsburgh School of Law in 1927 and, after a few years in private practice, began work as an assistant solicitor for the City of Pittsburgh in 1934 in what began as an unpaid role. She worked her way up to the position of city solicitor in 1942, becoming the first woman to serve as solicitor of a major American city. She next won a seat on the Allegheny County Court of Common Pleas and later rose to become the state's first female attorney general. Indeed, at the time, she was the first woman in any US state to hold that position. After her brief stint on the Supreme Court, she returned to the Court of Common Pleas, a seat she held until 1974. It was not until 1988, more than a quarter century after Justice Alpern broke the supreme judicial glass ceiling, that another woman would sit on the Commonwealth's highest court.

The story of Pennsylvania's short-lived gender integration on the Supreme Court is emblematic of the findings from political scientist Sally Kenney's study of "first" women justices, in which she found greater staying power for women on the bench when the "first" was the product of a movement to integrate an all-male bench and greater susceptibility to reversal when the first woman jurist on a high court "slipped in" more fortuitously.[4] In the entire history of the Pennsylvania Supreme Court, only nine women have worn justices' robes, and most of these trailblazers were interim appointments with a short tenure.

Twenty-seven years after Justice Alpern's abbreviated service on the Court, Justice Juanita Kidd Stout took office as an interim appointee and became the first African American woman to serve on the Supreme Court of any state. She was also the first African American woman to be elected to any court in the United States. Like Justice Alpern, Justice Stout served less than one year on the Supreme Court and retired when she reached the mandatory retirement age. Justice Sandra Schultz Newman, who served from 1996 to 2006, was the first woman to be elected to the Court. Justice Cynthia Baldwin was an interim appointee who served only two years, from 2006 to 2008. Justice Jane Cutler Greenspan, appointed to fill the vacancy created by the resignation of Chief Justice Ralph Cappy, served an abbreviated term from 2008 to 2009. Justice Joan Orie Melvin's judicial career ended abruptly on February 21, 2013, when she was found guilty of felony and misdemeanor offenses related to theft of services, conspiracy, and evidence tampering.

Justice Debra McCloskey Todd, who was elected in 2008, served as the sole female justice following Orie Melvin's removal from the bench until 2016, when as the result of a Democratic electoral sweep of three open Supreme Court seats, Justice Christine Donohue joined the Court. In June 2016, Governor Tom Wolf appointed Sallie Updyke Mundy to the Court to succeed Justice Michael Eakin, who resigned earlier that year in the wake of an e-mail scandal.

This chapter will explore two themes relating to women and the Court. First, it reflects on the Commonwealth's low representation of women on the Court and offers some thoughts on why this matters. Second, it reviews the Court's mixed record on cases involving what could loosely be called "women's issues"—cases with significant implications for gender equality. In this part, we contend that while the Court's record is very strong in eradicating sex-based classifications in the law, employing a strict version of what could be called formal equality in the law, its approach has faltered when confronted with cases that do not fit this paradigm. In cases involving issues where women are differently situated from men, as with respect to pregnancy and abortion and women's vulnerability to sex discrimination and sexual harassment at work, the Court's approach to gender equality has neither recognized nor remedied the full extent of gender-based harms women experience. In this latter class of cases, we critique the Court for failing to appreciate the gender equality stakes and for making an interpretive choice that leaves many gendered harms to women outside the law's reach.

While the relationship between a judge's background and her judicial perspective is complicated, a judge does bring her whole life experience with her to the bench. As now Associate Justice Sonia Sotomayor of the US Supreme Court remarked, "a wise Latina" judge brings a distinct set of experiences and perspectives to the art of judging; while she might not ultimately decide a case differently from her brethren, her life experiences will shape her understanding of, and appreciation for, the nuances of a case. We do not contend that the Pennsylvania Supreme Court would have reached a different result in any particular case if there had been more women jurists on its bench. Our claim, rather, is that the decisions in some of the Court's cases reveal an insufficient understanding of and attentiveness to gender-based harms and reflect a particular choice between competing interpretations—a choice that ultimately cuts short the law's responsiveness to gender-based harms. Even if greater gender diversity among the Court's justices would not change the result in a single case, a powerful female presence on the bench could provide female lawyers and female litigants with some reassurance that they will be treated fairly and with respect. The interests of women in the Commonwealth demand both a gender-diverse bench that reflects the gender diversity of the Commonwealth and a Court that is substantively committed to protecting the rights and interests of women while respecting the dignity of every person.

I. THE (UNDER)REPRESENTATION OF WOMEN ON THE SUPREME COURT

Despite Justice Alpern's groundbreaking legacy, Pennsylvania has not set any records for gender diversity on the High Court. In January 2016, the lone woman on the Court was joined by a second female elected justice. That addition put Pennsylvania on par with the national average for women jurists, who make up 27 percent of state supreme court justices. Pennsylvania's current 28.5 percent mark (two elected women out of seven seats) is higher than the low of Idaho's 11 percent but is well shy of Vermont's robust representation of women, at 40 percent of the bench.[5] As is the case in many other states, closed leadership networks and state electoral politics have not been kind to women jurists seeking a seat on Pennsylvania's highest court.[6] As noted, in June 2016, Justice Mundy was appointed to the Supreme Court, and she is running for election to her seat in the November 2017 general election, so it remains to be seen whether the Court will claim a third woman elected justice.

It would be naive to argue that having more women on the Court would have changed the result in any particular case heard by the Court, including any of those discussed later in this chapter. Certainly, the existing research on the impact of gender on the bench would not substantiate such sweeping claims. Assertions that women judges, as a group, have a "different voice" or distinctive methodology are controversial, even among women judges themselves. However, research on gender and judging has found a modest relationship between judges' gender and judicial decisions. Some research has found that women appellate judges are more likely to rule for plaintiffs in sex discrimination cases and more likely to convince their male colleagues to vote with them in such cases.[7] Relatedly, an empirical analysis of cases decided under state equal rights amendments (ERAs) found the percentage of women on the court to be one factor among several making it more likely that the court would decide in favor of the equality claim.[8] Another study found women judges to be more attentive to gender dynamics and more skeptical of gender stereotyping in cases involving rape and domestic violence.[9] A survey of women judges found that nearly three-quarters expressed a belief that women judges try to heighten their colleagues' sensitivity to gender bias, and one-third believed that they actually had made a difference in their male colleagues' appreciation of the gender impact of their decisions.[10]

Less controversial, and likely more supportable, are claims that women judges' life experiences influence their perspective and understanding of facts and issues in the cases, even if these experiences are not dispositive in determining the actual result they reach.[11] As Kenney, in her studies of women in the judiciary, points out, there are many ways women's life experiences shape their actions as judges apart from changing their actual judgments in cases. These kinds of effects include deterring sexist behaviors in the courtroom, hiring more women as law clerks, making or supporting calls for establishing gender bias judicial task forces, and moderating the behaviors of jurors, lawyers, and litigants.[12]

Importantly, however, even if having more women on the bench would not necessarily make for a more "feminist" court or body of case law, having a diverse judiciary is an important benchmark for a democratic society. Equal citizenship requires equal access to power, and courts no less than legislatures and executive officers wield great power. Kenney makes a persuasive case for increasing the numbers of both feminist judges and women judges irrespective of whether they are feminist.[13] Women who exercise judicial power, whatever their ideology or methodology, disrupt traditional understandings of gender that relegate women to domestic, passive, and subordinate roles. Feminist or not, women serving as judges challenge culturally ingrained assumptions about which citizens deserve to exercise power and are capable of rendering objective, competent judgments.

Changing the gender dynamics on a court is no small matter. Unfortunately, even judges and justices can engage in practices that contribute to a culture of male privilege and hostility toward women. In March 2016, Justice Michael Eakin followed the path of Justice Seamus McCaffery in resigning from the Supreme Court in the wake of a scandal exposing the e-mail exchange of racially insensitive, homophobic, and misogynist "jokes" and sexually explicit images among members of the judiciary, attorneys, and current and former government employees. The legitimacy of the Court depends on restoring public confidence and reassuring the people of Pennsylvania that such prejudice is not infecting the Court's judicial rulings. That will require a repudiation of the culture these e-mails evidenced.[14]

In calling for a more gender-diverse judiciary, we want to make clear that we do not expect women judges to speak with a distinctive "women's voice" any more than we expect men's judicial ideologies and methodologies to be defined by their gender. Recognizing the range of views and methods women bring to the bench will itself challenge dichotomous thinking about gender and the difference it makes. Ultimately, it is not only the presence of women on the Court that matters but the Court's ability to recognize gender-based harms and interpret the law in a way that is fair and equal for women. The remainder of this chapter examines the Court's case law on issues of particular significance for women.

II. THE COURT'S GENDER JURISPRUDENCE

Overall, the Court has taken a strong anticlassificatory, but ultimately limited, approach to gender equality rights. In short, the record is a mixed bag. We begin with a look at the Court's "strong" sex equality decisions and then turn to a group of cases where the Court has made interpretive choices that have cut short its commitment to ensuring that the law treats women as equals.

A. Tough on Stereotypes: Eradicating Sex-Based Classifications in the Law

As the women's movement gained strength in the 1970s, Pennsylvania's highest court was presented with a surge of challenges to sex-based classifications in a variety of laws. Sex discrimination law in the federal and state courts had begun to develop in earnest, and Pennsylvania's Constitution provided a ready source of authority for invalidating sex-based differential treatment. In addition to an equal protection guarantee similar to that of the federal Constitution, Pennsylvania's Constitution was amended in 1971 to add an ERA.[15] Indeed, as discussed more fully in the next chapter, Pennsylvania was among the first states to add a specific guarantee of equal rights for women to the state's Constitution.[16]

Like the cases brought in federal courts under the US Constitution during this era, these cases were often brought by male plaintiffs, and they were at least as likely to target a difference in treatment favorable to women as one that worked against women. For example, criminal laws incorporating sex-based classifications extending greater leniency to women failed to survive the Court's scrutiny. The Court struck down laws granting women earlier eligibility for parole[17] and reduced sentences[18] and rules mitigating the culpability of wives, who were presumed to be unwilling participants in crimes committed in the presence of their husbands.[19] Similarly, the Court struck down sex-based classifications granting women preferential treatment in family law, overruling a law permitting alimony for wives but not husbands,[20] the "tender years doctrine" favoring mothers in custody awards for young children,[21] and a statutory presumption that the father bears the financial burden of supporting minor children.[22] Male plaintiffs also succeeded in challenging the use of sex to calculate cheaper insurance premiums for female drivers.[23]

But women too won their cases before the Court when they challenged laws that classified and disadvantaged them because of sex. With the ERA as its guide, the Court ruled that the law could no longer presume a husband was the owner of all household goods used and possessed by both spouses[24] and that wives as well as husbands could recover damages for loss of consortium in personal injury lawsuits.[25] The Court applied its stringent approach to sex-based classifications evenhandedly, refusing to uphold sex-based generalizations and stereotypes.

In some cases, the Court embraced an even stronger liberal feminism in scrutinizing sex-based classifications than that taken by the federal courts interpreting the US Constitution. For example, in *Adoption of Walker*,[26] the Supreme Court relied on the ERA to strike down a section of the Adoption Act that required only the consent of the mother to effectuate adoption of a child born outside of marriage. The Court's reasoning—that any distinction between unwed mothers and unwed fathers is "patently invalid"—goes even further in the direction of strictly requiring equal treatment than the limit set by the US Supreme Court in such cases.[27] The federal Constitution, as interpreted by the US Supreme Court, permits some differential treatment of unwed mothers and fathers in circumstances where the father failed to take advantage of legally specified opportunities to confirm paternity or establish a meaningful relationship with a child.[28] More so than the US Supreme Court, its Pennsylvania counterpart has interpreted the sex equality guarantee to prohibit the stereotyping that underlies the use of gender as a proxy for gauging a parent's nurturing relationship with a child.

The Pennsylvania Supreme Court has also parted ways with the US Supreme Court in its approach to the degree of state action required to trigger its constitutional sex equality guarantee. To be fair, the US Constitution's Equal Protection Clause specifically signals state action as a predicate for such rights, beginning with the lead-in "No state shall," while the Pennsylvania ERA is more open-ended, guaranteeing equality of rights "under the law."[29] Still, the Pennsylvania Supreme Court exercised interpretive judgment—parting ways with some state courts that interpreted similar language more restrictively—to enable the ERA to reach the conduct of some private actors due to their connections to state and local government regulators, at least in some circumstances.[30] In the case adopting this approach, *Hartford Accident & Indemnity Co. v. Insurance Commissioner*,[31] the Supreme Court agreed with a male driver that the state's insurance commissioner violated the ERA by approving private insurance companies' use of sex-based differential rate tables that charged male drivers more for automobile insurance. The Court explicitly rejected the US Supreme Court's narrower approach to state action under the federal Equal Protection Clause as the controlling standard for Pennsylvania's ERA.[32] In doing so, the Court opened the door to broader applications of sex equality rights than would be permitted under the stricter federal approach to state action.[33]

Finally, the Court, in at least one instance, has taken a broader approach than the US Supreme Court to facially neutral rules that have the effect of disadvantaging women. At the same time that it struck down the state law's presumption that household goods acquired during marriage are the property of the husband in *DiFlorido v. DiFlorido*,[34] the

Court also invalidated the trial court's substituted rule that ownership resides in the actual purchaser of the goods. The Court explained in this 1975 decision that making ownership turn solely on which spouse paid for the goods would "fail to acknowledge the equally important and often substantial non-monetary contributions made by either spouse."[35] The Court backed up this result by explaining that the ERA disallowed imposing "different benefits or different burdens" on men and women, leading it to a rule presuming joint ownership of household goods acquired during marriage, absent specific proof rebutting the presumption.[36]

By applying the sex equality guarantee in the ERA to dislodge the law's imposition of unequal burdens on women, the Pennsylvania Supreme Court went beyond the narrower scope given by the US Supreme Court to the federal constitutional equal protection right. To the consternation of many critics, when reviewing the constitutionality of a law that is gender neutral on its face but has a disparate impact on women, the US Supreme Court requires proof of an invidious intent to discriminate against women—defined to mean that the burden was imposed precisely "because of" and not "in spite of" its harmful effect on women—in order to trigger the stringent equal protection review applicable to sex-based discrimination under the US Constitution.[37] The Pennsylvania Supreme Court's broader rule opened the door to potential applications of the ERA that extend beyond merely requiring facially identical treatment of men and women. For example, a 1999 federal district court decision applied the ERA to find that the Pennsylvania Interscholastic Athletic Association (PIAA) discriminated against a female basketball referee by refusing to assign her to boys' games, both in the regular season and in postseason play.[38] Because of a PIAA rule restricting postseason assignments to officials who had refereed in at least ten varsity games in the regular season, women were effectively barred from officiating in postseason play in the boys' games. The federal court rejected the PIAA's claim that the ERA did not reach facially neutral practices, explaining, "[W]hile a practice may purport to treat men and women equally, if it has the effect of perpetuating discriminatory practices, thus placing an unfair burden on women, it may violate the ERA."[39] While later decisions of the Pennsylvania Supreme Court have not always followed through on this insight, as discussed in the following sections, the Court nevertheless should be commended for recognizing, at least early on in its ERA jurisprudence, that restricting the ERA to reach only laws and practices that facially differentiate between men and women would not secure meaningful equality for women.

In the set of cases discussed previously, the Pennsylvania Supreme Court embraced a version of sex equality that insists on the treatment of men and women as individuals, regardless of sex. This approach to equality rights is liberal in orientation in the sense that it insists on treating persons as individuals and not as members of a social group. It is sometimes referred to as the "gender-blind" approach, since it insists that the law should not "see" the gender of the individuals subject to it, nor allot benefits or obligations based on a person's gender. In applying this model of sex equality rights, the Court has excelled.

But when presented with gender equality claims that go beyond targeting an explicit sex-based classification, the Court has had more difficulty grasping the gendered nature of the inequality and developing a theory of equal rights for addressing it. Ultimately, this latter set of cases, those involving more complex or subtle iterations of inequality, reveals the limits of the gender-blind approach to equal rights: in situations where men and women are differently situated, ensuring sex neutrality in the letter of the law does not go far enough in alleviating sex-based harms or gender inequality.

The discussion that follows highlights two areas of law in which these "harder" sex equality claims received an unreceptive audience on the Court and the justices' narrow approach to gender equality failed to grasp the issues and harms at the heart of the cases.

B. Discordant Notes: The Court's Vision of Sex Equality Reaches Its Limits

While helpful in addressing some forms of sex-based discrimination, the Supreme Court's gender-blind jurisprudence fell flat when confronted with what are sometimes termed "real differences" between the sexes that confound that model. This section discusses the Court's jurisprudence in two areas of the law that greatly affect women: access to medical care to terminate a pregnancy that poses a health risk to the woman and gender equality at work.

1. Equal Access to Abortion for Low-Income Women

The disconnect between the Court's approach to sex equality and the gender-based harms women actually experience is nowhere more pronounced than in the Court's treatment of abortion and, in particular, its response to state law barring public funds to pay for indigent women to terminate a pregnancy, even when continuing the pregnancy would jeopardize the woman's health. The Court not only rejected the argument that the state's abortion funding restriction—which denied Medicaid funding for abortion except in certain cases of rape or incest or unless necessary to avert the woman's death, discriminating against women on the basis of sex—but went so far as to express bewilderment that such an argument was even advocated. In *Fischer v. Department of Public Welfare*,[40] the Court unanimously upheld the Commonwealth's restrictions on funding abortions for indigent women, despite the law's full funding of medical expenses related to pregnancy and childbirth, against an equal protection and ERA challenge under the Pennsylvania Constitution. The statute challenged by the plaintiffs forbade the use of state Medicaid funds to pay for abortions unless necessary to avert the woman's death or the pregnancy was the result of reported rape or incest.[41] The Court began its opinion by blithely exclaiming, "This case does not concern the right to an abortion"[42]—seemingly unaware of the reality that, for those women who depended on Medicaid funds for access to health services, this was precisely what was at stake.

Decided after the US Supreme Court had issued similar rulings under the US Constitution, the Court's decision did not come as a total shock.[43] But it would be a mistake to view the Pennsylvania High Court's decision as foreordained by those US Supreme Court decisions. Unlike the federal Constitution, the Pennsylvania Constitution has the ERA, which specifically guarantees sex equality under the law. As the Court itself acknowledged, nothing bars the state Constitution's equal protection and equal rights guarantees from having a more expansive reach than that of the federal Constitution. Instead, the Pennsylvania Supreme Court made an interpretive choice, and that choice was to place abortion restrictions wholly outside the purview of sex discrimination law under the state Constitution.

The *Fischer* Court described abortion as "unique" and the sex-specific condition of pregnancy as the kind of "real difference" that separates women from men, making it effectively immune from sex discrimination law. "Abortion is inherently different from other medical procedures," the Court explained, describing it as "the purposeful termination of a potential life."[44] The Court's sympathy for the unborn was apparent throughout its opinion—in discussing the state's interest in protecting potential life ("to say that the Commonwealth's interest in attempting to preserve a potential life is not important, is to fly in the face of our own existence"[45]) and in approving of the fit between the law's objective and the furtherance of that objective (hailing "those unaborted new babies"[46] that the challenged law would save). The Court did not show the same sympathy for the indigent women whose pregnancies posed health risks, providing no data on the circumstances under which women sought Medicaid funding to terminate a pregnancy or the consequences to women of denying it. In the final analysis, the Court found it "obvious" that the statute does "not offend constitutional safeguards."[47]

In addressing the applicability of the ERA specifically, the Court's cabined view of sex equality was manifest throughout its opinion. The Court described the state's Medicaid restriction as distinguishing between two classes of pregnant women, those who choose to give birth and those who choose abortion, and expressed consternation that the plaintiffs "somehow" expected the Court to view this as sex discrimination.[48] The Court read the scope and thrust of the ERA narrowly "to eliminate sex as a basis for distinction."[49] Describing as "simplistic" the plaintiffs' argument that abortion-funding restrictions discriminate against women because only women have abortions, the Court saw little role for the ERA where sex-based inequalities stem from physical differences between the sexes, explaining, "[T]he ERA 'does not prohibit differential treatment among the sexes when, as here that treatment is reasonably and genuinely based on physical characteristics unique to one sex.'"[50] The Court then proceeded to lecture the plaintiffs on the facts of life: "In this world there are certain immutable facts of life which no amount of legislation may change. As a consequence there are certain laws which necessarily will only affect one sex."[51]

To the Court, the burdens on those women denied access to abortion were an artifact of nature, not of law. But of course, the "fact of life" that only women get pregnant does not determine the proper scope of the ERA when confronted with state laws that restrict how women can respond to the fact of pregnancy. For that linchpin in the analysis, the Court tracked a different Supreme Court opinion, one it did not cite in its own opinion: the notorious and now widely criticized case of *Geduldig v. Aiello*,[52] in which the US Supreme Court upheld, against an equal protection challenge, the exclusion of pregnancy from an otherwise comprehensive state disability wage-replacement law. Taking its cue from the Supreme Court's obtuse reasoning in that case, the *Fischer* Court opined, "[T]he statute does not accord varying benefits to men and women because of their sex."[53] In other words, men's abortions are excluded too—or would be, if they had them. Carrying the mantle of formal equality, the Court found the abortion-funding restriction, which did not provide different subsidies to one sex or the other, to fall outside the ERA's coverage because it did not involve "distinctions which 'rely on and perpetuate stereotypes' as to the responsibilities and capabilities of men and women."[54]

The formal equality model with which the Court saddled the ERA led it down a path that defanged the ERA in a class of cases where women needed its protection the most: where "real differences" between the sexes are invoked to justify laws that burden women. The Court's insistence that women's differential need for abortion is a real biological fact and not a gender stereotype misses the point. Precisely because pregnancy, or the potential for pregnancy, singularly differentiates women from men, it has played a central role in the law's subordination of women. Women's "unique" reproductive capacity has been used to keep women out of desirable jobs, deny them the vote, withhold the obligation of jury service, deny them athletic and other educational opportunities, and generally limit their involvement in public life. Gender ideologies about women and motherhood are central to the history of sex discrimination against women and its continuing legacies; the presence of "real differences" underlying a law should sharpen, not obscure, a court's inquiry into whether such a law discriminates against women. Had the Court looked deeper and been more receptive to a model of equality that goes beyond eliminating superficial sex distinctions from the face of the law, it might have perceived the presence of "social stereotypes connected with gender" after all.[55] State restrictions on abortion rest on an implicit value judgment that women's natural roles as mothers take precedence over other aspects of their lives, including their own health, and that women cannot be trusted to make the moral determination themselves of whether to carry a pregnancy to term.

The fact that the Medicaid restriction explicitly exempted pregnancies resulting from rape or incest itself reflects an implicit normative judgment about when women are morally responsible for their pregnancies and when they are not; it is a judgment that women can be fairly blamed for their sexuality and so must bear the consequences of motherhood unless they are the victims of a sex crime. The Court in *Fischer* made a point of describing abortion as a "voluntary choice made by women"—but of course, that assumes that sexuality is itself voluntary, so that women can be said to have chosen the condition necessitating a choice about how to respond to a pregnancy. This assumption disregards so much about the social conditions of sexuality, including power disparities between men and women in matters of sexuality, limited access to contraception, the realities of human sexual desire, and cultural pressures to have sex. The law's rape/incest exemption contains deeply ingrained messages about women's "fault" in all other sexual relationships.

In sum, the Court based its decision on a very narrow understanding of gender stereotyping, one not cognizant of the prescriptive stereotyping about motherhood embedded in such a law, which operates to channel women into compulsory motherhood and to fulfill societal expectations of maternal sacrifice for the well-being of "unborn babies."

While the Court in *Fischer* did closely track the development of federal constitutional law by the US Supreme Court—which, at the time it decided the *Geduldig* case, also had no sitting women justices—the result in *Fischer* was not inevitable. Other state supreme courts have found broader protection in their state constitutions of women's equality interests in reproductive healthcare, including in the context of Medicaid abortion coverage. The New Mexico Supreme Court, for example, struck down a similar Medicaid restriction under its similarly worded state ERA and, in doing so, noted that six other courts had also interpreted their state constitutions more expansively than the federal Constitution to reach the same result.[56] Rather than use the uniqueness of pregnancy to portray the abortion-funding restriction as sex neutral (on the theory that the law covered no conditions for men that were not also covered for women), the New Mexico court astutely observed that precisely because of its distinctiveness, pregnancy and the capacity to become pregnant have long been used to justify excluding women from public life and restricting women's roles. More states have sided with New Mexico on this score than with Pennsylvania when presented with state constitutional challenges to Medicaid restrictions denying women funding for medically necessary abortions.[57] The result reached by Pennsylvania's Supreme Court might have been different given a more fully developed factual record that informed the Court about the realities of low-income women's lives, the health implications for women of restricting access to medically necessary abortions, and the gender stereotyping inherent in a scheme that effectively forces many low-income women into compulsory motherhood.

Since *Fischer*, the Court has had scant opportunity to reconsider the legal rights of women seeking abortions, but there is reason to believe the Court's understanding of these issues might have evolved. In 2011, ruling in a case of first impression, the Court considered the appeal of a young woman who was denied judicial authorization for a confidential abortion when she was seventeen, just three months shy of her eighteenth birthday. In *In re Jane Doe*,[58] the trial court that denied her petition found that the young woman's decision not to consult her parents about her abortion constituted proof of her immaturity, rendering her incapable of giving valid consent to the medical procedure. This ruling was affirmed by the Pennsylvania Superior Court. A six-to-one majority of the Supreme Court reversed, holding that, as a matter of law, the failure to seek parental consent cannot serve as the basis for the denial of judicial authorization for an abortion. The Court reasoned that because the judicial bypass statute expressly provides for judicial authorization of confidential abortion care, allowing trial courts to deny minors' petitions because they availed themselves of the judicial bypass alternative would frustrate the purpose of the statute. The opinion's respectful tone is a far cry from the dismissive, almost sarcastic attitude of the *Fischer* Court. The lone dissenter—Justice Orie Melvin—would have upheld the denial of the young woman's bypass petition, thus illustrating our point that the mere presence of a female justice does not necessarily produce a more feminist bench.

2. Gender Equality at Work

A second area where the Court's gender discrimination jurisprudence has proven insufficient to address the full scope of gender-based inequality is in a subset of cases challenging sex inequality in the workplace. These cases involve challenges to discriminatory practices that do not quite fit the letter of the law's ban on the unequal treatment of men and women in employment.

The precise delineation of what it means to require equal employment opportunity has long been contested. Generally, such statutes have been interpreted to ban unfavorable differential treatment based on sex, race, and other prohibited criteria but not to unsettle the deep structures of bias that lead to occupational segregation or devaluation of the jobs predominantly held by women. A case in point is *Commonwealth ex rel. Human Relations Commission v. Beaver Falls City Council*,[59] in which the Supreme Court rejected the claims of two women hired to patrol parking meters, duties previously performed by police officers on the city's all-male police force. In a textbook display of the "gendering" of jobs, the city created the new position of "meter maid," advertised the position for only women to apply, developed the position to free (male) police officers from having to do this tedious (women's) work, and paid the women much less than what it had previously paid police officers to perform these duties. The women complained of pay discrimination in violation of the Pennsylvania Human Relations Act (PHRA), and the Pennsylvania Human Relations Commission (PHRC), which initially adjudicates complaints under the PHRA, agreed.

The Supreme Court saw it differently, however, and affirmed the lower court's rejection of the commission's finding. According to the Court, although it might have been discriminatory to limit the "meter maid" positions to women, the victims of that discrimination were any males who might have wanted these jobs and not the female "meter maid" complainants. As for their pay, the Court found the women's jobs to be unlike those of police officers, and therefore the women now in those jobs were not entitled to equal pay.

With the hindsight of nearly forty years of further development of employment discrimination law, this 1976 decision now seems fairly predictable. For the most part, employment discrimination law has not had much force in addressing occupational segregation or the devaluation of predominantly female-held jobs. However, once again, the Court's path was not foreordained. The dissenting opinions of Justices Roberts and Manderino reveal an alternative, and more substantive, vision of equal employment opportunity. They recognized that the job of meter maid was undervalued, despite the job's requirement of very similar duties to those previously performed by much higher-paid male police officers, precisely because it was structured as a "woman's job." Stereotypes and expectations about women—that they are not breadwinners, that they will accept low-wage, dead-end jobs because they have no ambition and lack real alternatives, and that they are fungible and replaceable if they leave—underlay the city's disparate pay structure. Had these two justices' visions of equal employment opportunity prevailed on the Court, Pennsylvania's gender-wage gap might have lessened considerably in the intervening decades.

A second example of the limits of the Supreme Court's gender-blind model of equal employment opportunity is a case decided three years later involving a school teacher who was fired after her request to extend her unpaid maternity leave, in order to breastfeed her allergic infant, was denied. In *Board of School Directors of Fox Chapel v. Rosetti*,[60] the Court held that it was not sex discrimination for the board to deny a discretionary leave that the teacher requested for these purposes, since the teacher was "treated no differently than any male teacher would be who had to remain at home to care for a physically or emotionally disabled newborn infant."[61] Accordingly, the case did not involve, as the majority saw it, "dissimilar treatment, on the basis of sex, of persons similarly situated."[62]

Once again, Justice Roberts, in dissent, saw the sex equality issue differently. He chastised the majority for ignoring "the obvious reality that only women can perform the breastfeeding function," such that the board's decision to deny a discretionary leave under these circumstances harmed new mothers in a way that would not harm new fathers.[63] While the majority's ruling is, alas, consistent with how most federal courts have perceived employers' refusals to accommodate lactating women, Justice Roberts's dissent shows that a broader interpretation of the state's ban on sex-based discrimination in employment was possible.

A final and more recent example of the limits of the Court's workplace sex equality jurisprudence comes from the 2009 case *Weaver v. Harpster*,[64] which involved the rights of employees who work for employers too small to be covered by the state's fair employment statute. The plaintiff, Mallissa Weaver, claimed that she was subjected to constant verbal and physical sexual harassment by her employer. But since only three persons, including Ms. Weaver, worked for the employer, it was too small to be covered by the PHRA, which bans sex discrimination and sexual harassment in employment but applies only to employers with four or more employees. After the PHRC rejected her claim for failure to meet the statutory threshold for the number of employees, Ms. Weaver brought a common-law tort action for wrongful discharge in violation of public policy, arguing that Pennsylvania's ERA and the state Human Relations Act reflected a strong public policy against sex discrimination and sexual harassment at work. A majority of the Court rejected her claim, interpreting the state's public policy, as reflected in those two sources, much more narrowly. In terms of the ERA, the Court explained, the public policy it established against sex discrimination did not encompass private employers acting with no authority or approval from the government. This aspect of the ruling cuts short the implications of the Court's earlier refusal to interpret the ERA to strictly require state action, an interpretation it eschewed in the *Hartford* case discussed previously. Viewing the *Hartford* ruling more narrowly, the *Weaver* Court explained that the ERA reaches only discrimination "under law," and in *Hartford*, that requirement was met by the insurance commissioner's extensive regulation of the insurance industry and its allowance of sex-based rate tables. In contrast, the *Weaver* Court viewed a private employer's sexual harassment of its workers as occurring without the imprimatur of the state.

The Court also declined to find any clear public policy against sexual harassment in the state's statutory employment discrimination law. Turning to the PHRA, the Court explained that the statute's public policy against sex discrimination was expressly limited to apply only to larger employers, leaving no state antidiscriminatory public policy that was applicable to small employers outside of the statutory framework. The Court's opinion adopts the tone of a neutral, if somewhat regretful, legalistic discourse on the formal limits of existing statutory law. Even so, the Court's own opinion revealed the malleability of the enterprise of determining whether the discharge of an employee under these circumstances violated an established public policy, as the Court finely parsed and distinguished its own precedents where it had found violations of public policy despite the absence of precisely analogous statutory authority.[65]

The upshot of the Court's reasoning was that it discerned no broad state public policy against sexual harassment in the workplace, leaving Ms. Weaver and other women in similar situations without a remedy for egregious sexual harassment at work. Once again, however, an alternative interpretation—one more sensitive to the substantive unfairness of the majority's approach—was evident in a dissenting opinion, this time written by one of the two (at the time) women on the Court. Justice Debra Todd, joined in her dissenting opinion by Chief Justice Castille, found Pennsylvania to have a more robust public policy against sex discrimination in employment, taking a broader view of the significance of the ERA and the state's statutory ban on sex discrimination. Justice Todd took the majority to task for failing to recognize the full scope of the state's fundamental public policy against gender discrimination and leaving the plaintiff, who was egregiously sexually harassed until she was forced out of her job, without a legal remedy.

Other state courts presented with similar disputes have sided with Justice Todd. For example, the California Supreme Court, ruling on a similar claim, held that female employees in that state could bring a wrongful discharge claim against a private employer for sexual harassment that resulted in their constructive discharge by relying on the public policy against sex discrimination reflected in California's constitution.[66] While there is no unanimity among state courts on this question, the split in authority once again shows room for interpretation.[67]

To be fair, the Pennsylvania Supreme Court later backtracked somewhat from its refusal to recognize a broad public policy against sex discrimination in a more recent case, *Philadelphia Housing Authority v. American Federation of State, County and Municipal Employees*.[68] In that case, a male warehouse worker was discharged after an internal investigation for sexually harassing a female coworker. He then filed a grievance under a collective bargaining agreement between the union and the employer, which permitted termination of employees only for "just cause," and convinced an arbitrator that he should be reinstated with back pay. The Philadelphia Housing Authority challenged the arbitration award, and the Supreme Court agreed, ruling that the award violated a clear public policy against sexual harassment in employment. While the Court's appreciation of such a broad public policy against sexual harassment was welcome, its holding does not overrule or undo the damage of *Weaver*'s failure to recognize a public policy sufficient to support the wrongful discharge claim in that case.[69]

III. CONCLUSION

As this discussion suggests, gender equality in the workplace requires moving beyond the elimination of sex-based rules or practices that on their face treat male and female employees differently. In the aforementioned cases, the Court made interpretive choices that left broader promises of equal employment opportunity unfulfilled. While the Court has proceeded partway down a path of eradicating gender stereotypes in law, it faithfully followed this course only insofar as men's and women's similarities inscrutably cohered. The result is that the Court has succeeded in removing stereotypical and facially sex-based classifications from law but left undisturbed the deeper structures of gender bias. Its commitment to gender equality in law has faltered in those areas where formal equality is not enough to address gender-based harms and inequality.

In the final analysis, Pennsylvania's highest court should be more open to women jurists so that it better reflects the diversity of the people of Pennsylvania, *and* it should interpret the law in a way that is attentive to gender injustice and fully responsive to the injuries and rights of women. Only when both of these goals have been reached will the Court's legacy on gender justice live up to the ideals of the Commonwealth.

NOTES

Deborah L. Brake is a professor of law and John E. Murray Faculty Scholar at the University of Pittsburgh School of Law. Susan Frietsche is a senior staff attorney at the Western Pennsylvania Office of the Women's Law Project.

1. Sally J. Kenney, *Gender and Justice: Why Women in the Judiciary Really Matter* (New York: Routledge, 2012), 46–47.
2. Ibid.
3. Anne X. Alpern, Papers of Anne X. Alpern, 1918–74, University of Pennsylvania ArchiveGrid, http://www.beta.worldcat.org/archivegrid/collection/data/77080041.
4. Kenney, *Gender and Justice*, 49.
5. Ibid., 197n4 (using statistics from 2011).
6. For commentary on the hurdles faced by women seeking judicial election or appointment, *see* ibid., 3, 25–27.
7. Ibid., 3, 19, 30–31, 36.

8. Lisa Baldez, Lee Epstein, and Andrew D. Martin, "Does the U.S. Constitution Need an Equal Rights Amendment?," *Journal of Legal Studies* 35 (2006): 243, 268–72. Other factors correlating with success on state ERA claims included selection of the standard of scrutiny and the political ideology of the judges.

9. Kenney, *Gender and Justice*, 30.

10. Ibid., 5–6.

11. Ibid., 6.

12. Ibid., 40.

13. Ibid., 9.

14. *See* Debra Todd, "Press Statement by Madame Justice Debra Todd," http://www.pacourts .us/assets/files/setting-4370/file-4750.pdf ?cb=ef5cef (deploring the "email exchanges contain[ing] offensive images, comments, and 'jokes,' some of which are sexually explicit and demeaning to women," along with "the derogatory stereotyping and mocking of racial, ethnic, and religious groups, as well as gays and lesbians," and calling for a "complete and thorough investigation by the Judicial Conduct Board").

15. The ERA states, "Equality of rights under the law shall not be abridged in the Commonwealth of Pennsylvania because of the sex of the individual."

16. *See* Linda J. Wharton, "State Equal Rights Amendments Revisited: Evaluating Their Effectiveness in Advancing Protection Against Sex Discrimination," *Rutgers Law Journal* 36, no. 1 (2005): 1201–56. In fact, not counting the few states that had originally included sex-based rights in their constitutions, Pennsylvania was *the* first. *See also* Weaver v. Harpster, 975 A.2d 555, 574 (Pa. 2009) (Todd, J., dissenting) (noting that Pennsylvania was the first state to pass an ERA to its constitution).

17. Commonwealth v. Butler, 328 A.2d 851 (Pa. 1974).

18. Commonwealth v. Staub, 337 A.2d 258 (Pa. 1975).

19. Commonwealth v. Santiago, 340 A.2d 440 (Pa. 1975).

20. Henderson v. Henderson, 327 A.2d 60 (Pa. 1974).

21. Commonwealth ex rel. Spriggs v. Carson, 368 A.2d 635 (Pa. 1977).

22. Conway v. Dana, 318 A.2d 324 (Pa. 1974).

23. Hartford Accident & Indemnity v. Ins. Comm'r, 482 A.2d 542 (Pa. 1984); *see also* Bartholomew v. Foster, 541 A.2d 393 (Pa. Comwlth. 1998), *aff'd* per curiam 563 A.2d 1390 (1989).

24. DiFlorido v. DiFlorido, 331 A.2d 174 (Pa. 1974).

25. Hopkins v. Blanco, 320 A.2d 139 (Pa. 1974).

26. 360 A.2d 603 (Pa. 1976).

27. Ibid., 605.

28. *See* Lehr v. Robertson, 463 U.S. 248 (1983) (upholding New York law requiring an unwed father to register paternal rights in "putative father registry" or satisfy other statutory criteria, such as listing his name on the birth certificate or living with the child, in order to establish his right to notice of, and deny consent to, adoption of an infant child). *See also* Nguyen v. INS, 533 U.S. 53 (2001) (upholding federal immigration statute conferring automatic US citizenship on nonmarital children born overseas to US citizen mothers but denying requiring US citizen fathers to meet certain statutory requirements in order to confer US citizenship on their nonmarital children born overseas); Parham v. Hughes, 441 U.S. 347 (1979) (upholding Georgia statute denying the father but not the mother the right to sue for wrongful death of child born outside of marriage, unless the father had formally legitimated the child).

29. Pa. Const. art. I, § 28.

30. For discussion of other state courts taking a stricter approach to state action, *see* Wharton, "State Equal Rights," 1234–37.

31. 482 A.2d 542 (Pa. 1984).

32. Ibid., 549.

33. *See, e.g.*, Welsch v. Aetna Ins. Co., 494 A.2d 409 (Pa. Super. 1985) (in suit by male drivers against private insurance companies charging sex-differential rates, finding denial of equal rights "under law" because state law compelled drivers to obtain insurance coverage).

34. 331 A.2d 174 (Pa. 1975).

35. Ibid., 179.

36. Ibid., 179–80.

37. Personnel Admin. v. Feeney, 442 U.S. 256 (1979).

38. Kemether v. Pennsylvania Interscholastic Athletic Assoc., Inc., 1999 WL 1012957 (E.D. Pa. November 8, 1999).

39. Ibid., *20.

40. 502 A.2d 114 (Pa. 1985).

41. The statute had strictly required that a victim report rape to the law enforcement authorities with jurisdiction over the rape within seventy-two hours of the assault and that incest victims report to law enforcement or public health authorities within seventy-two hours of notice of the pregnancy. In both circumstances, the

victim was required to report the name of the offender, if known. The prompt reporting portions of these reporting provisions were struck down as a violation of privacy by the Commonwealth Court, a ruling that the Commonwealth did not appeal to the Pennsylvania Supreme Court. Later, in a challenge brought under the US Constitution's Supremacy Clause, the US Court of Appeals for the Third Circuit ruled that the lack of a process by which the reporting requirements could be waived for those women who were physically or psychologically incapable of reporting frustrated Congress's intent to make abortion care available for all sexual assault survivors. Elizabeth Blackwell Health Center for Women v. Knoll, 61 F.3d 170 (3d Cir. 1995).

42. 502 A.2d at 116.
43. Maher v. Roe, 432 U.S. 464 (1976) (upholding state ban on Medicaid funding for nontherapeutic abortions, despite the state's payment of childbirth expenses); Harris v. McRae, 448 U.S. 297 (1980) (upholding federal ban on use of federal Medicaid funds for abortion unless necessary to save the life of the woman or if the pregnancy resulted from rape or incest).
44. 502 A.2d at 120.
45. Ibid., 122.
46. Ibid., 122–23.
47. Ibid., 120.
48. Ibid., 124.
49. Ibid. (quoting Henderson v. Henderson, 327 A.2d 60 [Pa. 1974]).
50. Ibid., 125 (citations omitted).
51. Ibid., 125. See also ibid., 126 ("[T]he decision whether or not to carry a fetus to term is so unique as to have no concomitance in the male of the species.").
52. 417 U.S. 484 (1974).
53. 502 A.2d at 126.

54. Ibid., 125. See also ibid., 126 ("Thus, this statute, which is solely directed to that unique facet is in no way analogous to those situations where the distinctions were 'based exclusively on the circumstance of sex, social stereotypes connected with gender, [or] culturally induced dissimilarities.'").
55. Ibid., 126.
56. N.M. Right to Choose v. Johnson, 126 N.M. 788, 797 (1998) (citing opinions of courts in California, Connecticut, Massachusetts, Minnesota, New Jersey, and Virginia).
57. See Wharton, "State Equal Rights," 1248–54 (discussing the case law).
58. 33 A.3d 615 (Pa. 2011).
59. 366 A.2d 911 (Pa. 1976).
60. 411 A.2d 486 (Pa. 1979).
61. 502 A.2d at 131.
62. Ibid.
63. Ibid., 133 (Roberts, J., dissenting).
64. 975 A.2d 555 (Pa. 2009).
65. Ibid., 502–3 (discussing cases where the Court has found wrongful discharge against public policy in a variety of situations not clearly governed by state statutory prohibitions).
66. Rojo v. Kliger, 801 P.2d 373 (Cal. 1990); see also Badih v. Myers, 43 Cal. Rptr. 2d 229 (Cal. App. 1995) (permitting claim for wrongful discharge based on pregnancy discrimination, despite employer's exemption from the state's employment discrimination statute because it had fewer than five employees).
67. 975 A.2d at 575 (Todd, J., dissenting) (citing authority from other states).
68. Pennsylvania State Ass'n of Cty. Comm'rs v. Commonwealth, 52 A.3d 1117 (Pa. 2012).
69. In fact, the Court's reasoning was much narrower: upholding the arbitration award and reinstating the employee would place the employer in violation of both Title VII and the PHRA for failing to remedy a severe sexually hostile environment.

CHAPTER 12

Article I, Section 28 of the Pennsylvania Constitution

Prohibiting the Denial or Abridgment of Equality of Rights Because of Sex

PHYLLIS W. BECK AND

MICHELE HUDZICKI-GRIMMIG

I. INTRODUCTION

On May 18, 1971, Pennsylvania became one of the first states in the twentieth century to enact an equal rights amendment (ERA). The Commonwealth's ERA, set forth in Article I, Section 28 of the Constitution, commands, "Equality of rights under the law shall not be denied or abridged in the Commonwealth of Pennsylvania because of the sex of the individual."[1] Although broad, the amendment clearly intends that men and women be treated equally under the law. Soon after its passage, many sexual discrimination claims were brought before the courts under the newly enacted amendment.

In applying a constitutional amendment, courts review the amendment's language to ensure that it is properly interpreted and that a proper scope and standard are applied. However, the text of the ERA is broad and tells the courts little about the manner in which it should be interpreted. Moreover, the legislative intent of the amendment is unknown because the official record of its passage is not available, leaving the courts little guidance in interpreting its very broad language.

Lower courts and federal courts interpreting the ERA have looked for clarity from the Pennsylvania Supreme Court. However, an analysis of the Supreme Court's case law reveals that it has provided little guidance. Both lower courts and the federal courts have opined that they cannot, with certainty, predict how the Pennsylvania Supreme Court will decide key issues. For example, what level of scrutiny applies to alleged violations of the ERA? Does a private cause of action lie under the ERA? In addition to discussing these unanswered questions, this chapter will demonstrate two resulting trends: One, the Supreme Court has often applied the ERA's goal of gender equality to diminish protections of women that preexisted the ERA, with the result that its decisions have actually benefited males more than females. Two, it appears that the ERA is a fading tool in championing women's rights.

II. HISTORY

A. Passage of the Amendment

The ERA was enacted in 1971 to recognize societal developments, ensuring equality of rights and eliminating gender bias. Historically, the law reflected a paternalistic view that women were, both intellectually and financially, in need of male protection. Arguably, the ERA, and subsequent legislation that codified it,[2] was enacted to ensure that women would no longer be treated as subservient and in need of extra protection.

B. Relevant Legislative and Executive Actions

Fervor was high after the ERA's enactment in 1971. The state government made great strides in adopting some laws and repealing others to implement the ERA's mandate of equality of the sexes. Indeed, the governor appointed a commission to review the laws for gender bias.[3] Moreover, the attorney general published numerous opinions on a variety of issues that equalized the rights of women with the rights of men. Although many laws were amended or repealed, there were still many issues that made their way through the courts on claims of gender-based discrimination filed by both females and males.

III. PENNSYLVANIA CASE LAW: PRELIMINARY CONSIDERATIONS

Although some of the cases addressed in the following sections were noted in the preceding chapter on gender equality, our focus here is narrower—namely, the extent to which these cases have left unanswered fundamental questions concerning application of the ERA.

A. Applicable Standard

The level of scrutiny that courts apply to a constitutional issue is often dispositive of the issue. Over time, both federal and state courts have developed three basic levels of scrutiny:

strict scrutiny, intermediate scrutiny, and rational basis review. The higher the level of scrutiny, the more likely it is that the challenged legislation or action will be found to offend the Constitution. More than four decades after the ERA was promulgated, it remains uncertain exactly which level of scrutiny applies to alleged violations of the amendment. Although an early Supreme Court decision suggested that a more rigid scrutiny would apply, later decisions have seemingly diluted that standard.[4] To date, the issue has not been squarely decided.

In 1974, in *Henderson v. Henderson*,[5] the Supreme Court suggested that alleged violations of the ERA would be strictly scrutinized because the ERA condemned virtually all classifications on the basis of gender. The *Henderson* Court stated, "The thrust of the Equal Rights Amendment is to insure the equality of rights under the law and to eliminate sex as a basis for distinction. The sex of citizens of this Commonwealth is no longer a permissible factor in the designation of the legal rights and legal responsibilities. The law will not impose different benefits or different burdens upon the members of a society based on the fact that they may be man or woman."[6]

The *Henderson* Court was asked to determine whether, under the ERA, a husband could seek alimony *pendent lite* (APL), counsel fees, and expenses from his wife in a divorce action. Answering this question in the affirmative, the Court emphasized that different treatment of women and men would no longer be recognized under the law. The *Henderson* Court's strong recognition of the ERA's goal—the end of gender-based distinctions—suggested that such distinctions would henceforth be strictly scrutinized. That proved not to be the case.

In 1985, the Court chose to recognize different legal rights for men and women in a case involving women's reproductive rights. In *Fischer v. Department of Public Welfare*,[7] the plaintiffs challenged Pennsylvania's Abortion Control Act of 1982, which prohibited federal Medicaid funds to be used for indigent women's abortions except to preserve their lives or in cases of rape or incest. Plaintiffs alleged an ERA violation in the fact that "all medically necessary services for men are reimbursable, while a medically necessary abortion, which by its nature can only affect women, is not reimbursable."[8]

The Court, however, saw no issue of disparate treatment of men and women for medically necessary services. Instead, the Court found that "the basis for the distinction here is not sex but abortion, and the statute does not accord varying benefits to men and women because of their sex, but accords varying benefits to one class of women, as distinct from another, based on a voluntary choice made by the women."[9] The Court then looked to and agreed with decisions from other states "that the E.R.A. 'does not prohibit differential treatment among the sexes when, as here that treatment is reasonably and genuinely based on physical characteristics unique to one sex.'"[10] Carrying or aborting a child, the Court explained, is so unique to women that it has "no concomitance in the male of the species."[11] Ultimately, the Court held that women can be treated differently where their reproductive rights are concerned. The Court maintained that its decision comported with the US Supreme Court's holding in *Harris v. McRae*,[12] which provided that the Commonwealth was not required to use public funds for an indigent woman's abortion except when her life is in jeopardy due to the pregnancy or in cases of rape or incest. This decision left in doubt the degree to which gender distinctions would be scrutinized in Pennsylvania.

In 1993, the Third Circuit, relying on *Fischer*, decided *Williams v. The School District of Bethlehem*,[13] which investigated whether the ERA and federal constitutional law invalidated a school policy that prevented a boy from playing on the high school girls' field hockey team. The district court had granted a permanent injunction of the school policy, finding that it violated the ERA and the Equal Protection Clause of the federal Constitution. However, the district court had been unable to determine which level of scrutiny should be applied to the school policy.

Reviewing this decision, the Third Circuit examined the school district's policy to determine "whether there are genuine physical differences between boys and girls or whether, instead, the policy is based on unwarranted and stereotyped assumptions about the sexes."[14] With regard to the appropriate level of scrutiny, the Third Circuit noted that a heightened scrutiny test for gender-based classifications should be commended. However, like the district court, the Third Circuit was "hesitant to decide this uniquely state law matter" because, "[u]nfortunately, the Supreme Court of Pennsylvania has not yet addressed the proper level of scrutiny under the ERA."[15] The Third Circuit ultimately found it unnecessary to predict the appropriate level of scrutiny because a remand for "fact finding" was necessary to determine whether there are any real physical differences between boys and girls to warrant different treatment and whether, as argued, boys are likely to dominate the girls' teams if admitted.[16]

Some commentators have claimed that Pennsylvania's ERA is one of the "most forceful" state ERAs protecting equality interests, not only protecting civil and political rights but also prohibiting discrimination and applying the strictest scrutiny among the states.[17] Based on Pennsylvania case law, that belief is not supportable.[18]

B. Whether State Action Is Required

With regard to the ERA's mandate of equality of the sexes "under the law,"[19] the question becomes whether the ERA prohibits discrimination only by or at the behest of the Commonwealth (so-called state action) or whether it also prohibits discrimination that is exclusively private. Like the appropriate level of scrutiny for ERA claims, this fundamental question remains unresolved.

In *Hartford Accident and Indemnity Company v. Insurance Commissioner of the Commonwealth*,[20] the question was whether the ERA was violated by automobile insurance rates that charged young men more than young women. The state insurance commissioner had determined as a matter of public policy that the gender-based rates were discriminatory and therefore invalid pursuant to the ERA. On appeal to the Supreme Court, the insurance company argued, in part, that the commissioner was not justified in looking to the ERA because the commissioner's decision was not state action but a mere private action, "an unauthorized attempt to impose his personal theories and perceptions of social policy upon the insurance industry."[21] The Supreme Court rejected the insurance company's argument:

> [T]he notion that the interpretation of this insurance statute involves the concept of "state action" is incorrect in this context. The state action test is applied by courts in determining whether, in a given case, a state's involvement in private activity is sufficient to justify the application of a federal constitutional prohibition of state action to that conduct. The rationale underlying the "state action" doctrine is irrelevant to the interpretation of the scope of the Pennsylvania Equal Rights Amendment, a state constitutional amendment adopted by the Commonwealth as part of its own organic law. The language of that enactment, not a test used to measure the extent of federal constitutional protections, is controlling.[22]

In light of this differentiation, the Court made clear that the ERA is triggered if the conduct at issue is "under the law," meaning created by some governmental body. The Court went on to define "under the law" as "the conduct of state and local government entities and officials of all levels in their formulation, interpretation and enforcement of statutes, regulations, ordinances and other legislation as well as decisional law."[23] Consequently, the actions of the state insurance commissioner in setting insurance rates are clearly "under the law."[24] Based on this analysis, the Court held that different automobile insurance rates for men and women constituted impermissible gender discrimination under the ERA.[25] However, while it had ruled that the commissioner's actions had arisen "under the law," the Court did not squarely decide whether a private cause of action exists under the ERA.

Attempting to answer this question, the Third Circuit in 1990 stated the following in dicta, citing lower Pennsylvania courts: "We are of the view that a private right of action is available for cases of gender discrimination under the Pennsylvania ERA."[26] However, eighteen years later, the Superior Court in *Dillon v. Homeowner's Select, Affinity Insurance Services, Inc.* held that no private right of action for monetary damages exists against a private employer for gender discrimination under the ERA.[27] In support of this ruling, the Superior Court explained that the Supreme Court in *Hartford* had "defined the scope of application of the Equal Rights Amendment to gender-based discrimination *by state or local entities or officials*, including through statutes, official policies and the rulings of its courts and administrative agencies. This position accords with our state constitutional jurisprudence generally, a basic tenet of which is that the provisions of Article I of the Pennsylvania Constitution are intended to govern only the action of the state government."[28]

The Superior Court, again relying on *Hartford*, concluded that "the scope of the provisions of the Pennsylvania Constitution is measured exclusively by 'the language of the enactment.' Nothing in the text of the ERA suggests that it is intended to regulate the private conduct of the citizens of the Commonwealth."[29] In the absence of clear guidance from our Supreme Court, federal courts have cited the Superior Court's *Dillon* decision as the law of Pennsylvania.[30]

IV. PENNSYLVANIA CASE LAW: SUBSTANTIVE LAW

In its effort to equalize the sexes pursuant to the ERA, the Supreme Court has, in a number of circumstances, invalidated protections for women that existed prior to the ERA. The result has been that gender equality has been achieved at the expense of women.

A. Spousal Rights/Responsibilities

Proponents of the ERA were initially gratified by Supreme Court decisions that elevated the rights of women to equal those of men, especially in the marital realm. For instance, in 1974, the Supreme Court decided the case of *Hopkins v. Blanco*, holding that a wife can seek to recover for loss of her husband's consortium.[31] Previously, the common-law doctrine viewed a wife as a husband's property, or chattel. As a result of this early view, a husband had an interest in his wife's services; conversely, a wife had no such right or interest in her husband's services. The *Hopkins* Court noted that the passage of the ERA changed the common-law view of a wife as chattel.[32]

However, as the preceding chapter concludes with regard to gender equality decisions in general, the Supreme Court's application of the ERA to spousal support cases bene-fited men more than women. Equalizing the sexes theoretically meant that women were no longer seen as the weaker sex financially. Indeed, prior to the ERA, the divorce code provided that only a wife could file for APL, counsel fees, and expenses in a divorce action. The common-law theory was based on the notion that women, as the weaker sex financially, could not properly support themselves during the pendency of a divorce action. As a result of the ERA's passage and the need to equalize the laws, the Supreme Court in *Henderson* opined, "Thus, as it is appropriate for the law where necessary to force the man to provide for the needs of a dependent wife, it must also provide a remedy for the man where circum-stances justify an entry of support against the wife. In short, the right of support depends not upon the sex of the petitioner but rather upon need in view of the relative financial circumstances of the parties."[33] The Court found support for its decision in the recently enacted amendment to the divorce code allowing for *either* spouse to file for APL, counsel fees, and expense pursuant to an action in divorce.[34]

In applying the ERA to the distribution of marital estates as well, the Court reached "a classification that was neutral on its face but disproportionately disadvantaged women."[35] In the 1975 case of *Butler v. Butler*,[36] a wife claimed she did not understand the financial ramifications of her husband's instructions that she contribute her money to the marital estate.[37] Since women were no longer considered inferior, intellectually or financially, the Court overturned prior case law that created a constructive trust for a wife when her husband obtained her property without adequate consideration unless he could prove that he acted in good faith and did not take undue advantage of his wife.[38] The Court held that this one-sided view benefiting women as the weaker gender cannot withstand the ERA.[39] Indeed, the Court determined, based on the specific facts in *Butler*, that a wife was equal to her husband in financial knowledge, and therefore the husband could not have taken undue advantage of his wife.[40]

The ERA also affected the structure of child support cases. In 1979, the Supreme Court in *Commonwealth ex rel. Stein v. Stein* held that it was the responsibility not of the husband but rather of both parties to support children in a divorce.[41] The *Stein* Court noted the holding in *Henderson* that a right of support depends not on the parties' gender but on the parties' financial circumstances.[42] In the same year, the Court went on to decide *George v. George*,[43] in which a wife sued for "bed and board" (spousal support) due to her husband's marital misconduct. The trial court found the support statute unconstitutional because husbands were unable to obtain the same relief.[44] On appeal, the Supreme Court found, as it had in *Stein*, that the statute for bed and board should not be abolished; instead, a husband should be permitted to obtain the same relief as a wife, thereby equalizing the law.[45]

With the Court determining that wives clearly have the same rights and responsibilities as their husbands, it decided *Simeone v. Simeone*[46] in 1990. There, the Court posited that a paternalistic approach did not comport with the ERA, and therefore judicial standards governing marital agreements could no longer consider only the fairness of the prenuptial agreement; instead, the agreement would be reviewed under general contract principles.[47] The Court noted that "the law has advanced to recognize the equal status of men and women in our society" and the paternalistic presumptions of sheltering women have been discarded.[48] *Simeone* did, however, retain the duty of full and fair disclosure in fashioning marital agreements, and it rejected earlier case law upholding prenuptial agreements that *either* made a reasonable provision for the spouse *or* were entered after a full and fair disclosure of the general financial positions of the parties and the statutory rights being relinquished.[49] Indeed, prenuptials were no longer to be seen as contracts of adhesion where the man had greater power and influence due to economic superiority.[50] The *Simeone* Court determined that the ERA ostensibly equalized the parties economically.[51]

B. Support/Custody

The Court's equalization of the sexes to the detriment of women also occurred in cases involving child and spousal support and custody. In the 1974 case of *Conway v. Dana*,[52] a father argued that a mother's earnings should be considered in calculating child support pursuant to the ERA. The Court agreed that the presumption that the father is the primary supporter of the minor children must be discarded in light of the ERA's equalization of the sexes.[53] The Court held that, pursuant to the ERA, both parents would henceforth be responsible for the support of their children.[54] This decision equalized the rights and burdens between the sexes, once again to the advantage of men. The Supreme Court also determined that the ERA equalized the rights of men in cases of adoption. In 1976, the Court decided *Adoption of Walker*, which held that the ERA prohibited a distinction between unwed mothers and unwed fathers simply based on their gender and that both parents would be provided the same rights and privileges under the Adoption Act.[55] The Court held that unwed fathers must be given notice and provide consent to the adoption of their biological child, thereby striking down a provision of the Adoption Act that only unwed mothers had the rights of notice and consent.[56]

The Supreme Court also applied the ERA to cases arising under the Custody Act. In *Commonwealth ex rel. Spriggs v. Carson*, the Court abolished the "Tender Years Doctrine," which presumed that custody of young children should remain with their mothers. According to the Court, this doctrine was infirm under the ERA because it was "predicated upon traditional or stereotypic roles of men and women" and "requires the male parent to overcome its effect by presenting compelling contrary evidence of a particular nature."[57]

C. Criminal Law

This pattern—equalizing the sexes by rejecting pre-ERA protections of women—continued in the criminal law. In 1974, the Supreme Court in *Commonwealth v. Butler* held that the criminal sentencing statute that prohibited minimum sentences for women while allowing them for men violated the ERA.[58] The following year, in *Commonwealth v. Santiago*, the Court invalidated the common-law doctrine of coverture, which presumed that a wife who commits a crime in the presence of her husband was coerced into the act by the husband.[59] The Court noted that such a presumption could not be reconciled with the ERA.[60]

D. Insurance Rates

In other notable cases, the Supreme Court applied the ERA to gender-based insurance rates. These cases continued to differentiate between state and private action to determine if the ERA could be applied to the alleged discriminatory policy.

In *Hartford*, discussed earlier, the Court found that the state insurance commissioner's disapproval of higher insurance rates for young men was proper, given that the ERA prohibited such distinctions.[61] *Hartford* has been invoked by lower courts considering the same issue. For instance, based on the Court's holding in *Hartford*, male plaintiffs filed a complaint alleging similar discrimination in the gender-based rates of another insurance company in a Superior Court case, *Welsch v. Aetna Insurance Company*.[62] Although the Superior Court ultimately dismissed the plaintiffs' claims on jurisdictional grounds, it opined that, pursuant to

Hartford, the test to determine if the ERA is triggered is not whether the policy was based on "state action"; rather, the test was whether the policy enacted "comported with the E.R.A. and was an appropriate exercise of [the insurance commissioner's] statutory authority."[63]

The Commonwealth Court also relied on *Hartford* to address the insurance rate issue in two cases in 1988. The first, *Bartholomew v. Foster*,[64] involved a petition alleging that the insurance commissioner should be enjoined from enforcing a regulatory provision allowing insurance companies to base rates in part on gender-based factors that are supported by sound actuarial principles. The Commonwealth Court, citing *Hartford*, noted, "[T]he presence or absence of state action does not preclude this Court from resolving the matter."[65] Instead, the Court looked to the alleged discriminatory policy pursuant to the ERA and concluded that even if the actuarial data are sound, a rate differential perpetuates stereotypes that are no longer permitted under the ERA.[66] The Court determined that the ability to operate a motor vehicle is not based on a physical characteristic uniquely related to one's gender.[67]

In contrast, in *NOW v. Commonwealth*, the National Organization for Women filed suit arguing that the insurance commissioner's decision to charge women and men the same insurance rates violated the ERA.[68] NOW posited that insurance rates should be based on sound actuarial data of mileage rather than overcharging women to subsidize men's rates.[69] The Court, however, found that NOW failed to provide substantial evidence to support its claim; thus the practice of charging identical rates to men and women did not violate the ERA.[70]

These cases make clear that "significant changes in insurance rates wrought by the ERA have thus had the unexpected effect of benefitting men more than women."[71]

V. CONCLUSION

This analysis of Pennsylvania case law demonstrates that the level of scrutiny and types of actions available under the ERA remain unclear, that the amendment has actually benefited males more than females, and that it is a fading tool in championing women's rights. What has been said of another state's experience with an ERA statute applies equally to Pennsylvania: "The ultimate irony in the adoption of the equal rights provision is that women *have* given up 'privileges' they have always enjoyed in return for 'rights' that were never in jeopardy."[72]

NOTES

Phyllis W. Beck is chair and CFO of the Independence Foundation; a retired judge of the Superior Court of Pennsylvania, 1981–2005; and former vice dean of the University of Pennsylvania Law School, 1977–81. Michele Hudzicki-Grimmig is a staff attorney at the Superior Court of Pennsylvania.

1. Pa. Const. art. I, § 28 (prohibiting denial or abridgement of equality of rights because of sex).

2. The ERA was later codified in 1 Pa.C.S. § 2301 (equality of rights based on sex provides). That statute provides the following:
   (a) General rule.
   In recognition of the adoption of section 28 of Article I of the Constitution of Pennsylvania, it is hereby declared to be the intent of the General Assembly that where in any statute heretofore enacted there is a designation restricted to a single sex, the designation shall be deemed to refer to both sexes unless the designation does not operate to deny or abridge equality of rights under the law of this Commonwealth because of the sex of the individual.

3. "Impact of the Pennsylvania State Equal Rights Amendment: A Report on the Impact of the State Equal Rights Amendment in Pennsylvania Since 1971," *Pennsylvania Commission for Women* (Harrisburg, Pa.: The Commission, 1980), 11–16.

4. Jennifer Friesen, *State Constitutional Law: Litigating Individual Rights, Claims and Defenses*, LexisNexis, vol. 1, sec. 3-2(e)(1), 4th ed. (Wilmington, Del.: Matthew Bender, 2006), 3–23.

5. Henderson v. Henderson, 327 A.2d 60 (Pa. 1974).

6. Ibid., 62.

7. 502 A.2d 114 (Pa. Super. 1985).

8. Ibid., 124.

9. Ibid., 125.

10. Ibid. (citations omitted).

11. 502 A.2d at 126.

12. 448 U.S. 297, 311 (1980). In a dissenting opinion, Justice Stevens opined, "[I]n *Roe v. Wade* the Court held that even after fetal viability, a State may 'regulate, and even proscribe, abortion *except where it is necessary, in appropriate medical judgment, for the preservation of the life or health of the mother.*'" Ibid., citing Roe v. Wade, 410 U.S. 113, 165 (1973), emphasis in original. Justice Stevens further stated that Roe squarely held that states may not protect the interest of the fetus when there is a conflict of interest with a pregnant woman's health. As in McRae, the Court in Fischer did not focus on the disparate treatment of Medicaid funding for all medically necessary male procedures but not all female medically necessary procedures but instead focused on women's reproductive rights, arguably overturning a portion of Wade.

As Justice Stevens concluded, "It is thus perfectly clear that neither the Federal Government nor the States may exclude a woman from medical benefits to which she would otherwise be entitled solely to further an interest in potential life when a physician, 'in appropriate medical judgment,' certifies that an abortion is necessary 'for the preservation of the life or health of the mother.'" Ibid., citing 410 U.S. at 165.

13. 998 F.2d 168 (3d Cir. 1993).

14. Ibid., 178.

15. Ibid., 179.

16. Ibid.

17. Friesen, *State Constitutional Law*, vol. 1, sec. 3.01(2) and sec. 3.02(5)(a).

18. In addition to the Williams court's inability to discern the appropriate level of scrutiny, a Philadelphia trial court in 1983 expressed it frustration that the high level of scrutiny suggested in Henderson had been diluted. Rejecting a party's request for a lower form of intermediate scrutiny, known as "substantial relationship," the trial court stated,
   Nine years ago, in Henderson v. Henderson, *supra*, our Pennsylvania Supreme Court had declared that the "thrust" of the Pennsylvania ERA was "to eliminate sex as a basis for distinction." To equate this "thrust" of the Pennsylvania ERA with the standard of "substantial relationship" is to suggest that our legislature and the citizens of this Commonwealth engaged in an empty act, notwithstanding the sober and deliberate process involved in adding a provision to our State Constitution. We are not prepared to adopt such trumpery.
   Newburg v. Bd. of Public Ed., 26 Pa. D. & C. 3d 682, 710 (Pa. Com. Pl. 1983).

19. Pa. Const. art. I, § 28; 1 Pa.C.S. § 2301.

20. Hartford Accident & Indemnity v. Ins. Comm'r, 482 A.2d 542 (Pa. 1984).

21. Ibid., 581.

22. Ibid., 586.

23. Ibid.

24. Ibid.

25. Ibid., 586. The Pennsylvania Legislature amended the relevant legislation after the decision in Hartford.

26. Pfeiffer v. Marion Center Area Sch. Dist., 917 F.2d 779, 789 (3d Cir. 1990), overruled in part on other grounds; Fitzgerald v. Barnstable Sch. Comm'n, 555 U.S. 246 (2009) (citations omitted).

27. 957 A.2d 772, 779 (Pa. Super. 2008), emphasis added.

28. Ibid., 776, emphasis in original.

29. Ibid., 779.

30. *See, e.g.,* Donnelly v. O'Malley & Langan, PC, 370 Fed. Appx. 347, 349 (3d Cir. 2010), citing Dillon and stating that the provisions of Article I, Section 1 of the Pennsylvania Constitution "govern only the actions of the state government."

31. 320 A.2d 139 (Pa. 1974).

32. Ibid., 141.

33. 327 A.2d at 62.

34. Ibid.

35. *See* Linda J. Wharton, "State Equal Rights Amendments Revisited: Evaluating Their Effectiveness in Advancing Protection Against Sex Discrimination," *Rutgers Law Journal* 36, no. 1 (2005): 1201–56.

36. 347 A.2d 477 (Pa. 1975).

37. Ibid.

38. Ibid.

39. Ibid., 480.

40. Ibid., 481.

41. 406 A.2d 1381 (Pa. 1979).

42. Ibid., 1385.

43. 409 A.2d 1 (Pa. 1979).

44. Ibid.

45. Ibid., 2.

46. 581 A.2d 162 (Pa. 1990).

47. Ibid., 165.

48. Ibid.

49. As an example of such case law, *see* In re Estate of Geyer, 533 A.2d 423 (Pa. 1987).

50. Simeone, 581 A.2d at 165.

51. Ibid.

52. 318 A.2d 324 (Pa. 1974).

53. Ibid., 326.

54. Ibid.

55. 360 A.2d 603, 605 (Pa. 1976).

56. Ibid., 606.

57. Commonwealth ex rel. Spriggs v. Carson, 368 A.2d 635, 639 (Pa. 1977).

58. 328 A.2d 851, 859 (Pa. 1974).

59. 340 A.2d 440, 445 (Pa. 1975).

60. Ibid., 446.

61. Hartford, 482 A.2d at 549.

62. 494 A.2d 409 (Pa. Super. 1985).

63. Ibid., 412.

64. 541 A.2d 393, 395 (Pa. Cmwlth. 1988).

65. Ibid., 397.

66. Ibid.

67. Ibid.

68. 551 A.2d 1162 (Pa. Cmwlth. 1988). NOW's argument was that since women drove less, they should not have to pay the same insurance rates as their male counterparts, who spent more time on the road and thus were more apt to get into an accident. Ibid., 1164.

69. Ibid., 1164–66.

70. Ibid., 1167.

71. Phyllis W. Beck and Patricia A. Daly, "Prohibition Against Denial or Abridgment of Equality of Rights Because of Sex," in *The Pennsylvania Constitution: A Treatise on Rights and Liberties*, ed. Kenneth G. Gormley, Jeffrey Bauman, Joel Fishman, and Leslie Kozler (Philadelphia: George T. Bisel, 2004), 707, 726.

72. Paul Benjamin Linton and Ryan S. Joslin, "The Illinois Equal Rights Provision at Twenty-Five: Has It Made a Difference?," *Southern Illinois University Law Journal* 21 (1997): 275, 284.

CHAPTER 13

The Supreme Court's Enforcement of Antidiscrimination Laws

TERESA FICKEN SACHS

> The arc of the moral universe is long,
> but it bends towards justice.
>
> —Dr. Martin Luther King Jr.[1]

Pennsylvania has been ahead of other states, and the federal government, in enacting laws that protect against many forms of discrimination. Under Pennsylvania's Public Accommodations Act, passed in 1935 and amended in 1939, it was a misdemeanor offense for any place of public accommodation to withhold services based on race, creed, or color.[2] In 1955, the Pennsylvania Fair Employment Practices Act was passed, prohibiting employment discrimination.[3] That act was amended in 1961 to broaden its scope to prohibit discrimination in housing and public accommodations and, consistent with its broader purpose, its name was changed to the Pennsylvania Human Relations Act (PHRA).[4] In 1974, the PHRA was further expanded to prohibit discrimination based on disability or handicap.[5] These statutory provisions significantly predated their federal counterparts—the Civil Rights Act of 1964,[6] the Fair Housing Act of 1968,[7] and the Americans with Disabilities Act of 1990.[8]

While prior chapters focused on the Supreme Court's gender equality jurisprudence, this chapter addresses the Court's application of antidiscrimination laws in the areas of school and housing desegregation, public accommodations, and housing, employment, and age discrimination. In these areas, the Court has often been a leader nationally, but the development of its jurisprudence has also illustrated Dr. King's principle that the bend toward justice can have a longer arc.

The Supreme Court's first opportunity to interpret the PHRA in the school context came in the 1967 case of *Pennsylvania Human Relations Commission v. Chester School Dist.*[9] In a decision that remains a landmark in school desegregation jurisprudence, the Supreme Court upheld the authority of the Pennsylvania Human Relations Commission (PHRC) to order school desegregation.

To fully appreciate the Court's *Chester School District* decision, however, it is useful to consider how far antidiscrimination law progressed in the middle part of the twentieth century. Only a decade earlier, in 1956, the Supreme Court had rejected efforts to desegregate Girard College. In *Girard Will Case*,[10] the Court was faced with the question of whether the school's discriminatory admissions requirements violated the Fourteenth Amendment. The "college"[11] was created by the 1830 will and bequests of Stephen Girard ("merchant, mariner, banker and philanthropist") to be a residential and instructional institution for "poor male white orphan children."[12] To that end, Girard bequeathed his entire residuary estate to "[t]he Mayor, Aldermen and Citizens of Philadelphia" in trust; the school was created and operated, beginning in 1848, in accordance with the stipulations of Girard's will.[13] In 1954, two African American applicants who had been denied admission, joined by the mayor and the City of Philadelphia's Commission on Human Relations, filed petitions against the Board of Directors of City Trusts (the trustee of the college), alleging that the restriction to white children had been rendered unconstitutional by the Fourteenth Amendment. The lower court denied the petitions, and the Supreme Court affirmed, ruling that the Fourteenth Amendment did not apply because the operation of the college by the board of trusts was not "state action": "It would seem entirely clear, viewed from any and all angles, that the administration of the Girard Trust by the Board of Directors of City Trusts does not in the slightest degree represent 'State action' which would bring the present situation within the ambit of the Fourteenth Amendment."[14] The majority opinion by Chief Justice Stern and the concurring opinion by Justice Bell cited the right of a private individual to dispose of his property as he sees fit ("[I]n this country a man's prejudices are part of his liberty");[15] opined that the college was a private, not public, institution ("The college has been supported and maintained for now over a century by Girard's estate; not a penny of State or city money has ever gone into it");[16] and described the city's trustee duties as "completely divorced from that of its ordinary government functions."[17] Justice Musmanno disagreed in a lengthy dissent, saying, "It is difficult to imagine a testamentary disposition more completely interwoven with the public's welfare and responsibilities than the Girard will."[18] The dissent detailed the actions of the Commonwealth and city governments in the creation and management of the college, including five statutes enacted by the General Assembly, forty-eight city ordinances enacted by the city, and ongoing direct supervision by the city and the Commonwealth legislature.[19] Justice Musmanno also took issue with the majority's reliance on the "unambiguous" language of the will, pointing out that the will's terms had been altered in other respects—most drastically, the change in admission requirements to admit "orphans" who had lost only fathers, not both parents.[20]

The US Supreme Court granted certiorari and reversed in a four-paragraph per curiam opinion, stating, in relevant part, "The Board which operates Girard College is an agency of the State of Pennsylvania. Therefore, even though the Board was acting as a trustee, its refusal to admit [these applicants] to the college because they were Negroes was discrimination by the State. Such discrimination is forbidden by the Fourteenth Amendment."[21]

The US Supreme Court remanded "for further proceedings not inconsistent with this opinion,"[22] and the case was returned to the Philadelphia Orphans' Court. The following year, however, the case was again before the Pennsylvania Supreme Court.[23] The Orphans' Court had entered decrees removing the board as trustee and substituting thirteen private citizens who could comply with the terms of the will without violating the Fourteenth Amendment.[24] The Pennsylvania Supreme Court affirmed the Orphans' Court's decrees as "not inconsistent" with the US Supreme Court's opinion: "Had the [US] Supreme Court so intended [that these applicants be admitted], it would have said so."[25] Justice Musmanno again dissented from what he termed the "manifest illegality" of the Orphans' Court's decision, asserting that the US Supreme Court's reversal clearly directed that the applicants be admitted to the college ("There was nothing else pending. The admittance or rejection of the applicants was the only issue in the entire litigation"); that the Orphans' Court could not properly remove the city as trustee unless the city was incapable, incompetent, or unwilling to act (which it was not); and that even such a substitution of trustees would not make the college a private institution so as to remove its administration from the reach of the Fourteenth Amendment.[26] The US Supreme Court denied further review.[27]

Subsequently, in *Girard Clarification Petition*,[28] the Pennsylvania Supreme Court denied a request to clarify its opinions. The majority deferred to a pending federal court proceeding, *Commonwealth v. Brown*,[29] but this time, both Justices Bell and Musmanno authored dissents stating that the Court should specifically address the applicants' arguments that Girard's admission policies violated Pennsylvania's Public Accommodations Act,[30] a statute that the Court's earlier opinions had not discussed.[31] The federal court ultimately ruled in *Commonwealth v. Brown* that denying admission to African American students violated the students' rights to equal protection under the Fourteenth Amendment.[32]

Ten years after narrowly construing the concept of "public" in upholding Girard's admission restrictions, however, the Supreme Court broadly construed the phrase "directly or indirectly" in enforcing a desegregation order in the *Chester School District* case. In contrast to the *Girard Will* opinions, the Court's analysis in *Chester School District* not only was forward-looking at the time but remains compelling today. The *Chester School District* case arose after protesters in Chester asserted that the school district's system of public school "zones" resulted in de facto segregation of schools based on race, with schools of different racial composition being treated differently by the school district.[33] The PHRA provides that it is an "unlawful discriminatory practice" for any "place of public accommodation" to "deny to any person because of his race ... either directly or indirectly, any of the accommodations, advantages, facilities or privileges" that are required.[34] The school district denied that it was directly or indirectly discriminating; rather, the district contended, the composition of its schools was due to residential patterns for which it was not responsible.[35] The PHRC directed the school district to cease and desist from its practices and to take immediate corrective measures.[36]

The district appealed, arguing that unless it had intentionally fostered or maintained segregation in its schools, it was not "directly or indirectly" engaging in discrimination, and the PHRC did not have authority to order it to take affirmative steps to relieve racial imbalance.[37] The intermediate courts (the Dauphin County Court of Common Pleas, sitting as the Commonwealth Court, and the Superior Court) agreed with the school district's position.[38] However, the Supreme Court granted allowance of appeal and reversed.

In particular, the Court rejected the lower courts' interpretation that "directly or indirectly" in this context contemplated intentional or affirmative acts. In rejecting that narrow view, the Court looked to both the plain language of the statute and the circumstances of its passage. With respect to language, Section 12 of the PHRA specifies that "the provisions of this Act shall be construed liberally for the accomplishment of the purposes thereof."[39] The Supreme Court held that the more reasonable construction of when accommodations are being "directly or indirectly" withheld would be "where, as here, the responsible party has the power to take corrective measures ... its failure to act amounts to the continued withholding" of the benefits of an integrated education.[40]

The Supreme Court also looked to the circumstances of the PHRA's passage, which removed any "latent ambiguity" in the language.[41] As part of the 1961 amendments to the PHRA, the statute's declaration of policy was amended to specifically refer to discrimination in housing and public accommodation resulting in racially segregated schools as one of the evils "threatening the peace, health, safety and general welfare of the Commonwealth and its inhabitants."[42] These pronouncements would have been unnecessary if the legislature had intended to address only de jure segregation by acts of public officials—which was already unconstitutional under *Brown v. Board of Education*.[43]

Having concluded that the PHRA prohibited de facto segregation, the Supreme Court next addressed whether the legislature intended to grant the PHRC jurisdiction over problems of racial imbalance. Again, the Court applied an expansive interpretation of the PHRA and, in doing so, rejected the lower courts' narrower interpretation that racial segregation was the result of discrimination in housing and employment and could be "largely overcome" by enforcement in those areas or through "the recognition by man of the inherent worth of his neighbor regardless of race, creed or color."[44] In a passage that continues to resonate nearly fifty years later, the Supreme Court rejected that view as a "vast oversimplification":

There are many social and economic causes for the rigidified residential patterns which dominate our communities, and despite anti-discrimination laws the barriers to integrated housing are often difficult to breach. Indeed the way to attack discrimination in housing and employment may be to begin with a program of quality integrated education. The best way to demonstrate the "inherent worth of [one's] neighbor" is to place individuals in a situation where they are exposed to their neighbor. This is especially true if a child can become aware of his neighbors' capabilities before his prejudices have had a chance to develop, but inter-racial cooperation may also have a beneficial effect on the thinking of adults. Thus, participation in such school activities as the P.T.A. may promote a better understanding which is the crucial first step toward the achievement of a truly integrated society. To paraphrase Mr. Justice Holmes, one such experience may be worth several volumes of sociology.[45]

The Supreme Court also rejected the school district's arguments that allowing the PHRC to have jurisdiction over racial imbalances would usurp the school district's functions under the school code and destroy the neighborhood school system. Even if those fears were justified (which the Court questioned), they would not warrant usurping the PHRA's legislative goal.[46] The Court pointed out that in light of increasing population density in urban areas, resultant shrinking neighborhoods, and racial and socioeconomic stratifications, the "traditional" neighborhood schools serving heterogeneous communities were being replaced by homogeneous public schools that are "the very antithesis of the common school heritage."[47]

The Supreme Court's opinion in *Chester School District* was significant in two other respects. First, it affirmed that the procedure followed by the PHRC—in which the PHRC itself, rather than an aggrieved individual, was the complainant—was proper.[48] Second, the Court rejected the school district's argument that because "racial imbalance" was not defined in the PHRA, the legislature failed to provide adequate standards such that the PHRA was an unconstitutional delegation of legislative authority. In this regard, the Court held that the legislature could properly delegate the power to determine facts on which the law depends and that the racial disparity existing in the district (with certain schools from 87 percent to virtually 100 percent segregated) would "satisfy any definition of de facto segregation."[49]

Five years later, in *Balsbaugh v. Rowland*,[50] the Supreme Court issued another significant school desegregation decision, holding that race-conscious corrective measures, including pupil assignment and busing, were constitutionally permissible means of overcoming segregation. The Court held that the PHRC acted "well within its rights in ordering that steps be taken to eliminate racial segregation" and that the school district's plan in response was not a product of "duress" but rather a "salutary endeavor by the Board to improve the quality of education within the District while at the same time complying with the instruction of the [PHRC]."[51] The Court "emphatically disagree[d]" that the school district's adoption of the plan, which included busing of students, violated taxpayers' rights to equal protection by altering the existing "neighborhood school structure." In so holding, the Court referred back to its *Chester School District* opinion and noted the "meticulous care" taken by the district to "render the assignment and busing of pupils fair and equitable."[52]

The issue before the Court in *Balsbaugh* was whether the chosen method of addressing racial imbalance was permissible, not whether an "imbalance" existed. However, the Court addressed the definition of racial imbalance the following year in *Uniontown Area School District, Appellant, v. PHRC.*[53] The Court in *Uniontown* upheld the PHRC's definition, which deemed a school "racially imbalanced" if the percentage of minority students was 30 percent greater or less than the percentage of such minority students in the same grade span of the district.[54] Although the PHRC's definition was not mandated by the statute (which, as noted, did not define "racial imbalance"), the Court held that the PHRC acted within its legislative rulemaking power in adopting that definition, and the definition was not arbitrary or unreasonable.[55] The Court accordingly also upheld the PHRC's order directing five school districts to remedy the de facto segregation found to exist in those districts.[56]

The following year, in *Pennsylvania Human Relations Commission v. Norristown Area School Dist.,*[57] the Supreme Court rejected another challenge to the PHRC's authority: the school district's argument that the PHRC's definition of a segregated school was a "regulation" that was invalid because it had not been filed with the Department of State pursuant to the Administrative Agency Law.[58] In 1968, the PHRC, together with the Pennsylvania Department of Public Instruction, developed and disseminated "Desegregation Guidelines for Public Schools" and "Recommended Elements of a School Desegregation Plan" to assist in eliminating racial imbalance in the public schools of the Commonwealth.[59] The school district argued that the PHRC was engaged in rulemaking and that the PHRC's administrative regulations were subject to the requirements of the Administrative Agency Law, including filing.[60] The PHRC asserted that it did not treat the guidelines as binding regulations and did not claim that they had the force of law; rather, they were statements of policy useful for guidance in the PHRC's case-by-case adjudications.[61] The Supreme Court upheld the PHRC's position, holding that the guidelines were "statements of policy and not regulations subject to the filing and publication requirements of the Administrative Agency Law."[62] Accordingly, the Court affirmed the PHRC's order requiring the school district to develop and submit a plan to eliminate racial segregation in its racially imbalanced schools.[63]

In *Pennsylvania Human Relations Commission v. School Dist. of Philadelphia,*[64] the Court upheld the authority of the PHRC to require school districts to submit plans to eliminate racial imbalances, and the authority of the Commonwealth Court to enforce such orders, but also upheld the Commonwealth Court's enforcement of a plan the PHRC had rejected. The opinion involved the Pittsburgh and Philadelphia school districts; Pittsburgh appealed from an order enforcing a desegregation plan, and the PHRC appealed from an order approving Philadelphia's voluntary desegregation plan—a plan the PHRC had rejected as inadequate.[65] In the Pittsburgh appeal, the Supreme Court rejected the city's arguments challenging the PHRC's power to order a plan and the Commonwealth Court's power to enforce it, noting that those issues were "settled."[66] The Court did clarify, consistent with its holding in *Norristown*, that the PHRC's guidelines are not "regulations" and that the Commonwealth Court erred in mandating that Pittsburgh strictly adhere to those guidelines.[67] In the Philadelphia appeal, the Supreme Court upheld the Commonwealth Court's approval, over the PHRC's objection, of Philadelphia's voluntary plan, finding that the Commonwealth Court did not err or abuse its discretion in doing so.[68]

However, Justice Nix issued a vigorous dissent that hearkened back to, and quoted from, the Supreme Court's landmark *Chester School District* opinion. Justice Nix opined that the PHRC's determinations were supported by substantial evidence and should have been upheld in both cases; instead, the Commonwealth Court impermissibly substituted its own judgment in place of the PHRC's.[69] Justice Nix asserted that this result reduced the agency's role to an "advisory" one and frustrated the legislature's intent to create an agency that would have expertise in the area and the power to carry out the purposes of the act.[70] Justice Nix pointed out that in the Philadelphia situation, "a decade has passed without a resolution of this urgent problem," and he chastised the majority for accepting a voluntary desegregation plan "in this setting of procrastination and delay."[71]

II. DEFINING "PUBLIC" ACCOMMODATIONS

As described earlier, the Supreme Court in *Girard Will* employed a restrictive interpretation of what constituted a "public" accommodation for purposes of the constitutional arguments being advanced in that case. However, in cases specifically addressing the statutory elements, the Court has interpreted the "public" element broadly. In the 1955 opinion in *Everett v. Harron*,[72] the Court not only applied an inclusive interpretation of "public" but also affirmed the right of individuals to pursue civil remedies. The provision at issue in *Everett* was the Public Accommodations Act, the PHRA's predecessor statute; the defendant argued that the act did not apply to swimming pools because the act did not list them. The Court pointed out that the list in the statute did not purport to be exclusive: "Defendants contend that their establishment does not fall within the range of this statutory enactment because the section in question goes on to provide that 'A place of public accommodation, resort or amusement, within the meaning of this section shall be deemed to include' some enumerated forty-odd places but does not specifically name 'swimming pools.' However, this does not imply that only the places thus mentioned are within the purview of the statute for the list does not purport to be exclusive of all places other than those specifically named."[73] Significantly, the Court in *Everett* also held that although the Public Accommodations Act appeared as part of the Penal Code and specified criminal sanctions for violations, claimants were entitled to enforce the law:

Does not the statute confer upon persons against whom illegal discrimination is practiced a right of action to redress the grievance thereby suffered? The answer to this question must undoubtedly be in the affirmative. It will be noted that section 654 begins by stating that "All persons within the jurisdiction of this Commonwealth shall be entitled to the full and equal accommodations . . . of any places of public accommodation, resort or amusement." *If, therefore, they are "entitled" to such privileges they are likewise entitled to enforce them, since wherever there is a right there is a remedy.* Indeed, the section refers, in another connection, to "presumptive evidence in any civil or criminal action," thus indicating that civil relief was contemplated by the legislature. Nor does the fact that a criminal penalty is provided for in the enactment render such remedy exclusive or supersede the right of action for damages in a civil proceeding, it being generally held that where a statute imposes upon any person a specific duty for the benefit of others, if he neglects or refuses to perform such duty he is liable for any injury caused by such neglect or refusal if such injury is of the kind which the statute was intended to prevent.[74]

In *PHRC v. Alto-Reste Park Cemetery Association*,[75] a 1973 case, the Supreme Court again interpreted "public accommodation" broadly, holding that the PHRA applied to cemeteries even before the statute was amended to specifically refer to them. The cemetery in *Alto-Reste* refused burial to non-Caucasians; the cemetery denied that it was a place of public accommodation at the time of the events in question because, at that time, the PHRA had not yet been amended to specifically mention cemeteries.[76] The Court held that a cemetery is clearly a "place of public accommodation," which the act defines as a "place which is open to, accepts or solicits the patronage of the general public" and "includes *but is not limited to* the enumerated specific accommodations."[77] The Court accordingly held that a cemetery "falls squarely within the broad scope of" the statute.[78] In so holding, the Court cited its *Chester School District* opinion recognizing that the provisions of the PHRA are to be "construed liberally for the accomplishment of the purposes thereof."[79]

In its 1972 opinion in *PHRC v. Loyal Order of Moose, Lodge No. 107*,[80] the Supreme Court had interpreted the "public" component even more broadly, holding that although the PHRA does not reach organizations that are "distinctly private," where a fraternal organization allowed members to bring nonmembers into its dining room and bar, the organization is a place of "public accommodation" as to guests and is therefore subject to the antidiscrimination provisions of the PHRA.[81]

III. DISCRIMINATION IN HOUSING

Another of the Supreme Court's most significant cases addressing discrimination arose in the context of public housing shortly after the Court's first significant school desegregation case. In *PHRC v. Chester Housing Authority*,[82] the Court upheld a PHRC order that required the housing authority to take affirmative steps to remedy racial segregation in four public housing projects administered by the authority. The Court cited its decisions relating to desegregating schools and observed that "the statutory scheme does not treat housing differently from schooling for purposes of ending racial discriminations."[83] On the contrary, "[r]emoval of racial discrimination and assurance of equal opportunity in housing are strong and fundamental policies of this Commonwealth."[84] The Court opined, "In our view, racial imbalance means substantial statistical disparity."[85] The racial composition figures of the four housing projects, which were almost 100 percent segregated, constituted "substantial evidence" supporting the PHRC's adjudication, and the commission's finding that racial imbalance in the four projects increased segregation in Chester's public schools was likewise supported by substantial evidence.[86] Finally, the Court reviewed each challenged aspect of the PHRC's order and concluded that the order was not "a patent attempt to achieve ends other than those which can fairly be said to effectuate the policies of the Human Relations Act" (the test for ruling that the agency's order was invalid).[87] In fact, the Supreme Court reinstated several aspects of the PHRC's order that had been vacated by the Commonwealth Court; in all other respects, the Supreme Court affirmed the Commonwealth Court and, in so doing, affirmed the actions ordered by the PHRC to remedy the discriminatory housing practices.

IV. EMPLOYMENT DISCRIMINATION

In *General Electric Corp. v. PHRC*,[88] the Supreme Court, in a case of first impression, analyzed the burden of proof under Section 5(a) of the act, which prohibits an employer from discriminating against any individual based on any protected classification (race, gender, etc.) "if the individual is the best able and most competent to perform the services required."[89] The complainants in *General Electric* were female employees of a department that was phased out; they asserted that female employees were not given the same opportunities to be placed in other positions within the company as male employees with less seniority.[90] The issue was whether, to prove discrimination, the female employees had the burden to prove that they were "the best able and most competent to perform the services required" under Section 5(a).[91]

The Supreme Court held that, on the contrary, the burden is on the employer to demonstrate that the complainant was *not* "best able and most competent to perform the services required."[92] The Court found that the "best able and most competent" clause of Section 5(a) of the PHRA "is best read as an expression of the business necessity doctrine"—a doctrine recognized by the US Supreme Court in which "the unintended discriminatory impact of an employment policy may be justified" if it is "necessary for the safe and efficient operation of the enterprise."[93] Under that doctrine, a complainant must establish that he or she is a member of a protected minority, that he or she applied for a job for which he or she was qualified, that his or her application was rejected, and that the employer continued to seek other applicants of equal qualification; the "burden then shifts to the employer to justify his employee selections on the basis of job-related criteria which are necessary for the safety and efficiency of the enterprise."[94] The Supreme Court held that imposing the same shifting burden in employment discrimination claims was most consistent with the Pennsylvania statute:

> The purpose of the [best able and most competent] clause is to protect employers from having to select employees who do not meet their qualification standards. In essence, it serves as a limitation upon the right to equal employment broadly bestowed upon the citizens of this Commonwealth by the PHRA. We believe that notions of fairness and common sense dictate that the burden of establishing such a limitation should fall upon the party in whose favor the limitation is designed to operate. Such a conclusion is in accord with the developments in fair employment law in the federal courts and we have been presented with no reasons which persuade us that the language of Section 5(a) should be read otherwise.[95]

Placing the burden on the employer was further justified by pragmatic considerations: "Where employment decisions have been based upon the employer's subjective assessments, it is the employer alone who can articulate the rationale behind his decisions."[96] The Court reiterated in *Allegheny Housing Authority v. Human Relations Commission*[97] that the burden does not shift to the defendant until after the plaintiff has made a prima facie showing; the defendant must then provide evidence of a "legitimate, non-discriminatory reason" for the decision.[98] Once the defendant satisfies its burden of production, the claimant retains the burden of persuasion on the evidence as a whole, and the PHRC decides, based on all the evidence, whether the plaintiff has shown that the employer intentionally discriminated.[99] Where, however, the plaintiff's evidence indicates that the plaintiff could not perform some aspects of the job, the plaintiff has not produced sufficient evidence of discrimination to make out a prima facie case.[100] Likewise, the claimant did not make out a prima facie case that his employer discriminated against him based on his non-job-related handicap, obesity, where the claimant's own evidence was that obesity was not a handicap: "A person who attempts to make a *prima facie* case on the basis that he is regarded as having a physical or mental impairment . . . must show that he is regarded as having a physiological disorder, cosmetic disfigurement or anatomical loss which affects the body systems."[101]

The *General Electric* Court rendered another important ruling: evidence of conduct that occurred *before* the specific conduct at issue in the case was nevertheless relevant and admissible to prove the substance of the complaint.[102] As the Court explained, a current facially neutral policy could incorporate employment criteria that a claimant had been precluded from attaining because of an abandoned discriminatory policy, so that "the impact of the past discriminatory practice is perpetuated and the former victim is deprived of equal employment opportunity just as surely as if she were the current object of an overt discriminatory practice."[103] Accordingly, the Court held that "if an employer has in fact engaged in past discriminatory actions, and if the impact of these actions is perpetuated by the employer's otherwise neutral present employment policy, then that employer's present policy may be found to be in violation of Section 5(a) of PHRA."[104]

However, in a decision that limited the scope of the PHRA, a majority of the Court in *Commonwealth v. Pittsburgh Press Co.*[105] held that Section 5(g) of the statute[106] was unconstitutional. Section 5(g) made it unlawful for an advertiser seeking employment to specify the job seeker's "race, color, religious creed, ancestry, age or national origin" or to specify such a preference as to a prospective employer.[107] Section 5(e) made it unlawful for any person to aid in a discriminatory act. The PHRC found that by accepting "situation wanted" advertisements that violated Section 5(g), the *Pittsburgh Press* violated Section 5(e).[108] The Commonwealth Court reversed, and the Supreme Court affirmed the Commonwealth Court, holding that the restriction imposed by Section 5(g) infringed on an advertiser's First Amendment rights because the restriction "goes directly to the advertiser's right to freely express his or her job qualifications, abilities, personal experience, or educational history."[109] The Court distinguished *Press I*, in which the US Supreme Court ruled that placing "help-wanted" ads with sex-preference designations constituted abetting illegal sex discrimination by employers.[110] The Court in *Press II* opined that prospective employees' uses of prohibited employment criteria was not itself illegal and could not reasonably be said to aid an employer who might be predisposed to use forbidden criteria (which were readily obtainable by the prospective employer in the interview process); thus enforcing Section 5(g) did not justify its restriction on the advertiser's freedom of expression.[111]

Justice Nix dissented, expressing his "most vehement disagreement" with the majority's decision, which he termed a "startling result" that "totally ignores this Commonwealth's strong commitment to an egalitarian society."[112] Justice Nix asserted that "the qualifications sought to be communicated are not legitimate concerns in the employment decision and are solely for the purpose of encouraging discriminatory employment practices. It is not simply a request to be hired as the majority contends, rather it seeks to pollute the hiring decision by introducing the prohibited considerations."[113] Justice Nix rejected any distinction between the pending case and *Press I*, asserting that both cases involved the same type of discriminatory, and prohibited, employment activity:

> The majority perceives a distinction in the nature of the transactions here and that encountered in *Press I*. I confess that I am unable to comprehend that distinction. In both instances the illegal activity condemned was discriminatory employment. In *Press I*, the regulation was directed to the conduct of the prospective employer. In this appeal, the conduct of the prospective employe

is being regulated. Both regulations were directed to the same end, i.e. discriminatory hiring. Further, both regulations did not impinge upon the free flow of commercial information necessary to make the employment decision. The only information restrained was information not lawfully relevant to the proposed commercial transaction.

Finally, in both *Press I* and the instant appeal, we are concerned with the right of the newspaper to publish the information. There is obviously no greater right derived by the newspaper to communicate the expressions of a potential employe than its right to disseminate the needs of a potential employer. I am therefore of the view that the employe's rights of freedom of expression under the first amendment have not been abridged by the state's legitimate exercise of its police power in an attempt to eradicate one of the most pervasive and elusive evils in our society today.[114]

The following year, however, the Supreme Court issued a groundbreaking decision in *Chmill v. City of Pittsburgh*.[115] The issue before the Court in *Chmill* was whether a municipal employer found guilty of racial discrimination by a federal court could voluntarily institute temporary remedial race-conscious hiring; the Court held that it could.[116] The *Chmill* case arose from a federal court's determination, six years earlier, that the Pittsburgh Bureau of Fire and the Pittsburgh Civil Service Commission had been discriminating against African American applicants in violation of federal law.[117] After modifications to testing procedures failed to remedy the makeup of the fire department, the commission certified equal numbers of white and minority applicants for new positions.[118] A group of white applicants, asserting that they would have been hired but for the quotas, filed suit and alleged that the hiring violated, inter alia, the PHRA.[119] The complainants did not dispute that a court could order race-conscious relief but argued that an employer could not voluntarily adopt racial preferences in hiring.[120]

The Supreme Court declined to interpret the act so narrowly, instead holding that the voluntary remedial hiring was a necessary practical response to the existing federal mandate to correct racial discrimination and did not violate the PHRA: "[T]he legislative history of the Act, the time of its enactment and our prior construction of it all demonstrate without the slightest doubt that the Act's prohibitions against the use of race in employment and against quota hiring are not a bar to race-conscious voluntary remedial action."[121]

V. ANTIDISCRIMINATION REGULATIONS

The year after the *Chmill* decision, the Supreme Court in *Hospital Association of Pennsylvania v. Commonwealth of Pennsylvania, Department of Public Welfare*[122] upheld antidiscrimination regulations enacted by the PHRC. *Hospital Association* arose as a result of "Contract

Compliance Regulations" enacted by the PHRC in 1974 and 1975.[123] Unlike the guidelines related to school desegregation, the regulations at issue in *Hospital Association* were promulgated pursuant to the PHRC's rulemaking authority and were mandatory; they required every contract with or agency of the Commonwealth to contain a nondiscrimination clause "barring discrimination in employment because of race, color, religious creed, national origin, ancestry, sex or age."[124] The regulations specified the language and scope of the clause, including requirements that contractors furnish records for compliance investigations, actively recruit minority subcontractors, and include the nondiscrimination clause in the contractors' own subcontracts.[125] The hospital complainants objected to including the nondiscrimination clause in their contracts with the Department of Public Welfare, asserting that the clause, particularly its "subcontractor" requirement, would involve extensive administrative costs in procurement operations that were conducted based on oral communications.[126]

The Commonwealth Court granted a temporary injunction staying that requirement and related requirements (as to furnishing records, recruitment of minority contractors, and defining contract terms by reference to the regulations).[127] The Supreme Court vacated the injunction, holding that the record did not establish that the hospitals would be required to reduce oral agreements to writing or would otherwise sustain any immediate and irreparable harm from complying with the requirements.[128] Thus the Court upheld the PHRC's antidiscrimination regulation.

VI. AGE DISCRIMINATION

The Supreme Court has addressed age discrimination claims in the context of the PHRA and the Pennsylvania Constitution. For instance, in *McIlvaine v. Pennsylvania State Police*,[129] the limitation at issue was the portion of the administrative code requiring state police officers to retire at age sixty.[130] The Court, after resolving a procedural issue, affirmed on the basis of the Commonwealth Court's opinion; the Commonwealth Court's conclusion was that age limitations did not violate either the PHRA or the Constitution.[131] Justice Roberts dissented, opining that a mandatory retirement provision based solely on age violated both the PHRA and Article 26, that the Commonwealth Court erred in relying on cases that predated the amendment of Article 26, and that the Commonwealth Court also erred by improperly shifting the burden of proving the bona fide occupational qualification exception to the employee rather than the employer.[132]

In *Gondelman v. Commonwealth*,[133] the Supreme Court rejected a claim that a provision of the Pennsylvania Constitution itself instituted unconstitutional age discrimination. The provision required judges to retire at age seventy. The challengers in *Gondelman* argued that the "retirement" section of the Constitution, Article V, Section 16(b), conflicted with two other sections of the Constitution, specifically Article I, Section 1 ("Inherent rights of mankind"), which stated that certain rights are "indefeasible," and Article I, Section 26 ("No discrimination by the Commonwealth or its subdivisions"), which prohibits the Commonwealth or any of its subdivisions from denying or discriminating as to any civil right.[134] The Court ruled that the Constitutional argument "would be convincing if its focus was directed at a legislative enactment, an executive regulation, or a judicial decision. Here, however the challenge relates to a pronouncement of the people."[135] In other words, no governmental classification was at issue; instead, the people retained the power to use classifications such as age to structure their government and had chosen to do so. The Court therefore dismissed the Constitutional challenges.[136]

However, the Article V, Section 16(b) retirement provision that the Supreme Court upheld in *Gondelman* was back before the Court some fourteen years later in *Driscoll v. Corbett*.[137] The petitioners in *Driscoll* (judges who would be required to retire before their elected terms expired) argued (as in *Gondelman*) that Section 16(b)'s retirement provision deprived them of inherent rights guaranteed by Article I and, in doing so, violated their rights to equal protection and substantive due process under the Pennsylvania Constitution.[138] The petitioners' equal protection argument was that Section 16(b) was an age-based classification that did not withstand either intermediate scrutiny (i.e., it was not substantially related to an important government interest) or even the lowest level of rational basis review.[139] They cited intervening societal and demographic changes (including increasing longevity and a decline in cognitive impairment among older individuals), budgetary and judicial staffing concerns that could be ameliorated by allowing judges to delay retirement rather than drawing pensions from the Commonwealth, and existing procedures for removing incapacitated judges (in Article V, Section 18) that rendered the mandatory retirement age unnecessary.[140] For the same reasons, the petitioners argued that Section 16(b) violated their substantive due process rights by impinging on their property rights in retaining judgeships to which they had been elected for ten-year terms without meeting the required due process standard.[141]

The Supreme Court reached the same conclusion in *Driscoll* that it had reached in *Gondelman*. With respect to the equal protection argument, the Court concluded that the "rational basis" test applied and that there was no compelling reason to depart from it or to find that the legislatively imposed age limit was irrational.[142] The Court further explained that a constitutional amendment that was valid at the outset did not become unconstitutional due to changed circumstances; the proper response to changed circumstances would be to direct any appeal to the legislature.[143] With respect to the substantive due process challenge, the Court opined that an "amendment to the organic law of the Commonwealth will only be deemed to violate the constitution that it amends (if at all) where the challenger has shown—clearly, palpably, and plainly—that the amendment is so unreasonable as to be considered 'irrational.'"[144] The Court's determination in *Gondelman*—that the constitutional amendment in Section 16(b) was not "irrational"—remained binding.[145] The Court reiterated this holding shortly after *Driscoll*, in *Friedman v. Corbett*,[146] and also rejected the *Friedman* petitioners' additional arguments, holding that voters do not have a constitutionally protected entitlement to enjoy the "full service" of the judge they elected and holding that the 2001 amendment to Article V, Section 16(b)—in which the retirement date was changed from the day the judge attains the age of seventy to December 31 of the year in which the judge attains that age—was not "irrational."[147]

VII. CASES DEFINING SCOPE AND PROCEDURE UNDER THE PHRA

The Supreme Court's significant opinions in this area are not limited to addressing specific areas of claimed discrimination. Other opinions of the Court warrant mention because they have defined the PHRC's authority, clarified the appropriate procedure to be followed in pursuing relief under the PHRA, and delineated the scope of judicial review of PHRC determinations.

For example, in *Driscoll v. Carpenters District Council of Western Pennsylvania*,[148] the Court held that the National Labor Relations Act (NLRA)[149] does not preempt the PHRA. Accordingly, the claimants were entitled to the remedies provided by the PHRA for alleged discriminatory practices in the operation of a labor union hiring hall.[150]

Moreover, the Court has repeatedly enforced the mandatory nature of PHRC proceedings. In *Clay v. Advanced Computer Applications*[151] and *Mercy Hospital of Pittsburgh v. PHRC*,[152] the Supreme Court held that when the PHRA applies, aggrieved parties must first exhaust their administrative remedies with the PHRC, and if they fail to do so, they may not pursue other legal remedies against their employers. The Court further clarified this rule in *Fye v. Central Transportation, Inc.*,[153] holding that where the PHRC's investigation was closed at the claimant's request, the claimant could not later seek relief in the trial court. Similarly, the Court held in *Erie Human Relations Commission v. Erie Ins. Exchange*[154] that an employer who failed to appeal from the Erie HRC's adjudication could not contest the merits of the HRC's adjudication in subsequent enforcement proceedings.[155] However, the Court held in *First Judicial District of Pennsylvania v. PHRC*[156] and *Court of Common Pleas of Erie County v. PHRC*[157] that the separation of powers doctrine prevents the PHRC from investigating or adjudicating complaints regarding employment policy or discipline within the judicial branch. Instead, "[t]he [S]upreme [C]ourt has the sole power and the responsibility to supervise the 'practice, procedure, and the conduct of all courts.'"[158]

The Supreme Court has also upheld the PHRC's right to determine, when a new complaint arises, whether the complaint falls within the commission's jurisdiction. In *PHRC v. Lansdowne Swim Club*,[159] the commission previously concluded that it did not have jurisdiction over a complaint against a swim club because its investigation at that time concluded that the club was not a place of public accommodation.[160] However, when another complaint arose three years later, the PHRC was not bound by its prior determination; on the contrary, it retained authority to conduct another investigation, including issuing subpoenas to investigate whether it had jurisdiction: "We emphasize here that the Commission's authority in this regard is not limited to its first investigation of an organization, but exists each time it conducts an investigation pursuant to the Act. To hold otherwise would undermine the broad discretion of the Commission and impede its ability to develop a clear body of law on discriminatory practices."[161]

With respect to the scope of the PHRC's authority, the Supreme Court has affirmed the broad scope of relief the commission can order to address a determination of discrimination. In *Pennsylvania Human Relations Commission v. Freeport Area School Dist.*,[162] the issue before the Court was whether the PHRC could order affirmative relief for all victims of the discriminatory practice (as the PHRC asserted) or could only order such relief with respect to the particular named complainants (as the defendant asserted). The Court took an expansive and practical view of the PHRC's authority, holding that it had the power to order relief applicable to all persons in an affected class, not merely to the complainants:

> Nothing in the Act limits PHRC's power to investigate, conciliate or adjudicate depending upon the source of the complaint. Nothing in the Act limits the remedy which PHRC may order depending upon the source of the complaint.
>
> Moreover, relief, when granted, is class relief. The respondent is ordered to cease and desist from the unlawful discriminatory practice with regard to all persons in the affected class. The act draws no distinction between the scope of "injunctive" relief and the scope of affirmative relief. Affirmative relief may be ordered "as, in the judgment of the Commission will effectuate the purpose of [the] act."[163]

In so holding, the Court rejected the school district's argument that extending relief to the other claimants would violate the district's due process rights. While due process problems could theoretically arise ("[A] failure to inform a respondent concerning the scope of investigation and possible relief might vitiate an otherwise lawful exercise of PHRC's authority"),[164] the evidence before the Court disproved any such claim in the *Freeport* case: "Freeport had ample notice not only that the investigation was to go beyond its discrimination against the named complainant, but itself supplied the names of persons who had been affected by the policy which was alleged to be discriminatory."[165] The Court therefore held that the "PHRC may order affirmative relief for persons other than the named complaint when (1) the complainant alleges that such other persons have been affected by the alleged discriminatory practice and (2) such other persons entitled to relief may be described with specificity."[166]

In fact, the Supreme Court has upheld the PHRC's authority to impose a penalty for employment discrimination against an entity that was not the claimant's employer. In *PHRC v. Transit Casualty Insurance Company*,[167] a claimant lost her job as a delivery driver because Transit Casualty, the insurer for the delivery company, refused to continue insuring her. The Court held that the PHRC had the power, under Sections 5(e) and 9 of the act,[168] to order Transit Casualty to pay lost earnings to a victim of discrimination, even though Transit Casualty was not the victim's employer, where Transit Casualty engaged in an unlawful discriminatory employment practice that caused the loss suffered by the victim.[169]

Although the Supreme Court has enforced, and deferred to, the PHRC's authority when the statute applies, the Court has also carefully defined the limits of the PHRC's powers, and available remedies, in accordance with the statute. Thus the Court held in *Hoy v. Angelone*[170] that a plaintiff in a lawsuit alleging a PHRA violation was not entitled to assert a claim for punitive damages because the PHRA does not provide that right. In *PHRC v. Zamantakis*,[171] the Court held, in a plurality decision, that the PHRC was not authorized to award damages for mental anguish and humiliation under the act. In *Wertz v. Chapman Township*,[172] the Court held that a plaintiff in a lawsuit alleging a PHRA violation was not entitled to a jury trial because the PHRA does not provide that right. In *Pennsylvania State Police v. PHRC*,[173] the Court held that the PHRC could not order a candidate who had been discriminated against in the application process to be reinstated to the process with back pay. The PHRC had required the employer to prove that the candidate would not have been hired even in the absence of discrimination. Because the application process had not yet been completed, the PHRC placed an improper burden on the employer.

The Supreme Court has similarly held that the PHRC is not entitled to employ investigatory tools beyond those specified in its own statute or in the agency law. In *Pennsylvania Human Relations Commission v. St. Joe Minerals Corp., Zinc Smelting Div.*,[174] the PHRC sought to compel answers to written interrogatories from the respondents as part of its investigatory powers under Section 7(g) of the PHRA. Section 7(g) empowers the PHRC to "hold hearings, subpoena witnesses, compel their attendance, administer oaths, take testimony of any person under oath or affirmation and, in connection therewith, to require the production for examination of any books and papers relating to any matter under investigation."[175] The Court concluded that the act did not authorize written interrogatories under either Section 7(g) or Section 6 (which gives the PHRC all powers conferred on administrative agencies generally by the Administrative Code of 1929).[176] The power and authority of an agency must be conferred by clear legislative language: "A doubtful power does not exist." The Court declined to find that such power was "necessarily implied" in the statute.[177] In concluding that the PHRC did not have the power to compel answers to written interrogatories, the Court balanced the commission's needs against the burden placed on responding parties. Even though interrogatories would facilitate investigations, they would also place the investigative burden on a respondent to prove the case against it.[178]

With respect to PHRA procedure, the Supreme Court in *Pennsylvania Human Relations Commission v. United States Steel Corp.*[179] and *Pennsylvania Human Relations Commission v. St. Joe Minerals Corp., Zinc Smelting Div.*[180] clarified the requirements for a valid complaint by the PHRC. In *US Steel*, the Court held that a complaint was deficient because it did not "set forth the particulars" of the alleged discriminatory practice as required by Section 9 of the PHRA.[181] In *St. Joe*, the Court explained the "particulars" that are required for the complaint to pass muster. The PHRC had amended its complaint in *St. Joe* to comport with *US Steel*; the question for the Supreme Court was whether the amended complaint was sufficient. The Court held that it was: the complaint sufficiently set forth "particulars" where it identified the discriminatory practice (that the respondent "discriminates in its hiring of Blacks and females and fails or refuses to utilize recruitment sources which will, or may reasonably be expected to, provide it with Black and female applicants"), and it supported the assertion of discriminatory practice with statistics, such as the percentages of African Americans and females in the respondent's work force compared to the percentages in the surrounding county and the number of minorities in managerial positions:

> The statistics demonstrate substantial employment imbalances at respondent's place of business. The complaint demonstrates the fact that respondent hires fewer women than men, has a disproportionate number of Caucasian employes in managerial positions, employs a smaller percentage of Blacks than the percentage residing in the surrounding county. The complaint does more than give respondent notice that a complaint has been filed against it; it informs it of the facts giving rise to the Commission's reason to believe that respondent is engaging in unlawful employment practices. Hence, the complaint comports with Pennsylvania Rule of Civil Procedure 1019, which this Court has suggested guides us in assaying the sufficiency of a complaint under § 9 of the PHRA.[182]

The Supreme Court has also supported the PHRC's broad authority by narrowly construing the ability of courts to alter PHRC's determinations. In *PHRC v. Alto-Reste Park Cemetery Association*,[183] the Court adopted the following standard for judicial review of the PHRC's decisions: "The (Commission's) order will not be disturbed 'unless it can be shown that the order is a patent attempt to achieve ends other than can fairly be said to effectuate the policies of the Act.'"[184] Moreover, the Court stated these policies broadly: the commission's charge is "to not only fashion an effective remedy for the individual aggrieved, but also to guard against and deter the same discriminatory action from recurring, to the detriment of others within the same class."[185] Applying that analysis, the Court in *Alto-Reste* affirmed the actions ordered by the PHRC against a cemetery that had refused to bury non-Caucasians. Specifically, the PHRC acted within its authority in ordering the cemetery to maintain written records to indicate whether any person was refused burial and, if so, the reasons and also in ordering the cemetery to advertise that it does not discriminate on the basis of race in the sale of its plots.[186] The PHRC had exceeded its authority in only one respect—it was not authorized to require the cemetery to write a public apology to a decedent's widow; such action was an "[a]ttempt to achieve ends other than those which can fairly be said to effectuate the policies of the Act."[187]

Despite the narrow scope of review, however, the Court has held that Pennsylvania courts may vacate a labor arbitration award if the award was contrary to public policy as set forth in, inter alia, the PHRA. In *Philadelphia Housing Authority v. American Federation of State, County & Municipal Employees, Dist. Council 33, Local 934 (AFSCME)*,[188] a labor arbitrator reinstated an employee discharged for acts constituting sexual harassment.[189] The Supreme Court vacated the ruling, explaining that even though a court ordinarily may not vacate an arbitrator's award on an issue that falls within a collective bargaining agreement, a court may do so if the award violates a well-defined and dominant public policy; in *AFSCME*, the Court held that the arbitrator's award forcing the employer to reinstate the harasser with full back pay, and without any sanction, violated a well-defined and dominant public policy against sexual harassment in the workplace, a public policy "grounded in both federal and state law against sex discrimination in employment, including Title VII, the regulations of the EEOC [Equal Employment Opportunity Commission], and this Commonwealth's own PHRA."[190]

VIII. CONCLUSION

As the Supreme Court stated in *Chester School District*, "Pennsylvanians are justly proud of this Commonwealth's leadership in promoting equal opportunities for all its citizens."[191] The "arc" in Pennsylvania has not been geometrically perfect, but the Supreme Court's decisions have steadily and surely bent toward justice.

NOTES

Teresa Ficken Sachs is a shareholder at Marshall Dennehey Warner Coleman & Goggin.

1. Shelby County, Alabama v. Holder, 133 S. Ct. 2612, 2645, 186 L. Ed. 2d 651, 688, 2013 US LEXIS 4917 (2013) (Ginsburg, J., dissenting), quoting Gary May, *Bending Toward Justice: The Voting Rights Act and the Transformation of American Democracy* (New York: Basic Books, 2013), 144. These words, frequently cited by Dr. King, were drawn from nineteenth-century minister and abolitionist Theodore Parker: "I do not pretend to understand the moral universe; the arc is a long one, my eye reaches but little ways; I cannot calculate the curve and complete the figure by the experience of sight, I can divine it by conscience. And from what I see I am sure it bends towards justice." Theodore Parker, "The Present Aspect of Slavery in America and the Immediate Duty of the North" (speech delivered in the hall of the State house, Massachusetts Anti-slavery Convention, January 29, 1858).

2. Act of June 11, 1935, P.L. 297, amended by the Act of June 24, 1939, P.L. 872, § 654, 18 P.S. §

4654. An offense was punishable by a fine of up to one hundred dollars and/or imprisonment for up to ninety days.

3. Pennsylvania Fair Employment Practice Act, No. 222, 1955 Pa. Laws 744 (passed October 27, 1955).

4. Pennsylvania Human Relations Act, No. 19, secs. 1–2, §§ 2, 5(h), (i), 1961 Pa. Laws 47, 48, 52–53 (43 P.S. §§ 951–52, 955[h]–[i]).

5. Act of December 19, 1974, No. 318, secs. 1–4, 7 §§ 2–5, 11–12.2, 1974 Pa. Laws 966, 966, 968–972.

6. The Civil Rights Act of 1964, Pub. L. No. 88–352, 78 Stat. 241 (codified as amended at 42 U.S.C. §§ 1981–2000h–6 [1970]).

7. The Fair Housing Act of 1968, P.L. No. 90-284, 82 Stat. 81 (codified as amended at 42 U.S.C. §§ 3601–31 [1970]).

8. Americans with Disabilities Act of 1990, P.L. No. 101-336, 104 Stat. 327 (codified as amended at 42 U.S.C. §§ 12101–300 [1994]).

9. 233 A.2d 290 (Pa. 1967).

10. 127 A.2d 287 (Pa. 1956).

11. The students were to be admitted between the ages of six and ten years. Ibid., 288.
12. Ibid.
13. Ibid., 288, 289.
14. Ibid., 295.
15. Ibid., 290, 291, quoting Dulles Estate, 218 Pa. 162, 163, 67 A. 49.
16. 127 A.2d at 293–94.
17. Ibid., 294.
18. Ibid., 321.
19. Ibid., 321–23.
20. Ibid., 328–29.
21. Pennsylvania v. Board of Directors of City Trusts of the City of Philadelphia, 353 U.S. 230, 77 S. Ct. 806, 1 L. Ed. 2d 792 (1957), citing Brown v. Board of Education, 347 U.S. 483 (1954).
22. 353 U.S. at 231.
23. Girard College Trusteeship, 138 A.2d 844 (Pa. 1958).
24. Ibid., 846–47.
25. Ibid., 846.
26. Ibid., 861, 865–67.
27. 357 U.S. 570 (1958).
28. 224 A.2d 761 (Pa. 1966).
29. 270 F. Supp. 782 (E.D. Pa. 1967).
30. Act of June 24, 1939, P.L. 872, § 654, 18 P.S. § 4654.
31. 224 A.2d at 762–69.
32. 270 F. Supp. 782 (E.D. Pa. 1967). The US Court of Appeals for the Third Circuit affirmed, 392 F.2d 120 (3d Cir. 1968), and the US Supreme Court denied certiorari, 391 U.S. 921, 88 S. Ct. 1811, 20 L. (Ed. 2d 657) (1968). Three days later, the trustees voted to admit African American students.
33. 233 A.2d 290, 292–94 (Pa. 1967).
34. 43 P.S. § 955(i)(1).
35. 233 A.2d at 294.
36. Ibid., 293.
37. Ibid., 294.
38. Ibid., 292.
39. Ibid., 294, citing 43 P.S. § 962(a).
40. 233 A.2d at 294–95.
41. Ibid., 295.
42. Ibid., 296.
43. Ibid., 295–96, discussing Brown, 347 U.S. 483.
44. 233 A.2d at 296–97.
45. Ibid., 297 (internal footnote omitted).
46. Ibid., 298.
47. Ibid., 299, quoting Robert L. Carter, "De Facto School Segregation: An Examination of the Legal and Constitutional Questions Presented," *Case Western Reserve Law Review* 16, no. 3 (1965): 502, 507.
48. 233 A.2d at 294.
49. Ibid., 301.
50. 290 A.2d 85 (Pa. 1972)
51. Ibid., 91.
52. Ibid., 92.
53. 313 A.2d 156 (Pa. 1973).
54. Ibid., 159.
55. Ibid., 170.
56. Ibid., 171.
57. 374 A.2d 671 (Pa. 1977).
58. Administrative Agency Law, Act of June 4, 1945, P.L. 1388, as amended, formerly codified in 71 P.S. § 1710.21, superseded by the Commonwealth Documents Law, Act of July 31, 1968, P.L. 769, No. 240, as amended, 45 P.S. § 1101 *et seq.*
59. 374 A.2d 674.
60. Ibid., 675.
61. Ibid., 678.
62. Ibid., 673.
63. Ibid., 680–81.
64. 390 A.2d 1238 (Pa. 1978).
65. Ibid., 1245.
66. Ibid., 1246.
67. Ibid., 1248.
68. Ibid., 1250–53.
69. Ibid., 1257 (Nix, J., dissenting).
70. Ibid., 1255–56 (Nix, J., dissenting).
71. Ibid., 1260 (Nix, J., dissenting).
72. 110 A.2d 383 (1955).
73. Ibid., 385.
74. Ibid., 385–86, emphasis added.
75. 306 A.2d 881 (Pa. 1973).
76. Ibid., 884–85.
77. Ibid., 885.
78. Ibid., 886.
79. Ibid., citing Chester School District, 233 A.2d 294, and Pennsylvania Human Relations Act, *supra* § 12(a), 43 P.S. § 962(a).
80. 294 A.2d 594 (Pa. 1972).
81. Ibid., 598.
82. 327 A.2d 335 (Pa. 1974).
83. Ibid., 340.
84. Ibid.
85. Ibid., 338n14.
86. Ibid., 345.
87. Ibid., 346, citing Pennsylvania Human Relations Commission v. Alto-Reste Park Cemetery Association, 306 A.2d 881, 887 (Pa. 1973).
88. 365 A.2d 649 (Pa. 1976).
89. Ibid., citing Pennsylvania Human Relations Act, Act of October 27, 1955, P.L. 744, Section 5(a), as amended, 43 P.S. § 955(a) (Supp. 1974–75).

90. 365 A.2d at 653.

91. Ibid., 654.

92. Ibid.

93. Ibid., citing Griggs v. Duke Power Company, 401 U.S. 424, 430–31 (1971).

94. Ibid., citing McDonnell-Douglas Corp. v. Green, 411 U.S. 792, 800 (1973).

95. Ibid., citing 365 A.2d at 656–57.

96. Ibid., 657.

97. 532 A.2d 315 (Pa. 1987).

98. Ibid., 318.

99. Ibid.

100. Fairfield Township Vol. Fire Co. No. 1 v. Pennsylvania Human Relations Commission, 609 A.2d 804 (Pa. 1992).

101. Civil Service Commission of City of Pittsburgh v. PHRC, 591 A.2d 281 (Pa. 1991).

102. Ibid., 657–58.

103. Ibid., 658.

104. Ibid., 659–60.

105. 396 A.2d 1187 (Pa. 1979).

106. 43 P.S. § 955(g).

107. Ibid.

108. 396 A.2d at 1189.

109. Ibid., 1190.

110. Ibid., citing Pittsburgh Press Co. v. Pittsburgh Commission on Human Relations, 413 U.S. 376 (1973).

111. 396 A.2d at 1190.

112. Ibid., 1191–92 (Nix, J., dissenting).

113. Ibid., 1193.

114. Ibid.

115. 412 A.2d 860 (Pa. 1980).

116. Ibid., 862.

117. Ibid., citing Commonwealth of Pennsylvania v. Glickman, 370 F. Supp. 724 (W.D. Pa. 1974).

118. 412 A.2d at 864.

119. Ibid., 865.

120. Ibid., 867.

121. Ibid., 872.

122. 433 A.2d 450 (Pa. 1981).

123. Ibid., 451–52.

124. Ibid., citing 16 Pa. Code. §49.101(a).

125. 433 A.2d at 451–52, citing 16 Pa. Code. §49.101(d).

126. 433 A.2d at 453.

127. Ibid.

128. Ibid., 454–55.

129. 309 A.2d 801 (Pa. 1973).

130. Ibid., 802, citing Section 205 of the Administrative Code of 1929, Act of April 9, 1929, P.L. 177, 71 P.S. § 65(d).

131. Article I, Section 26 of the Pennsylvania Constitution prohibits the Commonwealth and its political subdivisions from discriminating against any person in the exercise of any civil right.

132. 309 A.2d at 806.

133. 554 A.2d 896 (Pa. 1989).

134. Pa. Const. art. I, § 26.

135. 554 A.2d at 904.

136. Ibid., 905.

137. 69 A.3d 197 (Pa. 2013).

138. Ibid., 204. The Court did not determine whether Section 16(b) violated the PHRA, noting that the PHRA, like its federal counterpart, was subject to material exclusions that the petitioners had not addressed.

139. Ibid., 203.

140. Ibid.

141. Ibid., 204.

142. Ibid., 210–11.

143. Ibid., 212.

144. Ibid., 214, citing Gregory v. Ashcroft, 501 U.S. 452, 471 (1991).

145. 69 A.3d at 214.

146. 72 A.3d 255 (Pa. 2013).

147. Ibid., 259–60. A ballot referendum scheduled to be submitted to voters in the November 2016 general election will, if passed, raise the retirement age of the Commonwealth's judges and justices from seventy to seventy-five.

148. 579 A.2d 863 (Pa. 1990).

149. Act of July 5, 1935, C. 372, § 1, 49 Stat. 449, as amended by the Labor Management Relations Act of June 23, 1947, C. 120, § 1, 61 Stat. 136.29 U.S.C. § 141, et seq.

150. 579 A.2d at 868.

151. 559 A.2d 917 (Pa. 1989).

152. 451 A.2d 1357 (Pa. 1982).

153. 409 A.2d 2 (Pa. 1979).

154. 348 A.2d 742 (Pa. 1975).

155. Ibid., 745.

156. 727 A.2d 1110 (Pa. 1999).

157. 682 A.2d 1246 (Pa. 1996).

158. 727 A.2d at 1112, citing Pa. Const. art. V, § 10(c).

159. 526 A.2d 758 (Pa. 1987).

160. Ibid., 759.

161. Ibid., 763.

162. 359 A.2d 724 (Pa. 1976).

163. Ibid., 727, quoting from 43 P.S. § 959.

164. 359 A.2d at 727–28.

165. Ibid., 728.

166. Ibid.

167. 387 A.2d 58 (Pa. 1978).

168. 43 P.S. § 955(e), 959.

169. 387 A.2d at 62–63.

170. 720 A.2d 745 (Pa. 1998).
171. 387 A.2d 70 (Pa. 1978).
172. 741 A.2d 1272 (Pa. 1999).
173. 517 A.2d 1253 (Pa. 1986).
174. 382 A.2d 731 (Pa. 1978).
175. Ibid.
176. 43 P.S. § 956, citing 71 P.S. §§ 51–732 (1962 & Supp. 1977–78).
177. 382 A.2d at 736.
178. Ibid.
179. 325 A.2d 910 (Pa. 1974).
180. 382 A.2d 731 (Pa. 1978).
181. 325 A.2d 910, 912–13 (Pa. 1974), citing 43 P.S. § 959 (1964).
182. 382 A.2d 731, 735–36.
183. 306 A.2d 881 (Pa. 1973).
184. Ibid., 887.
185. Ibid., 888.
186. Ibid., 888–89.
187. Ibid., 889.
188. 52 A.3d 1117 (Pa. 2012).
189. Ibid., 1120.
190. Ibid., 1123.
191. 293 A.2d 298.

CHAPTER 14

The Supreme Court and the Contours of State and Federal Power in Revolutionary Pennsylvania

JOHN J. HARE

I. INTRODUCTION

In a celebrated series of cases known collectively as the Olmsted Affair, the relationship between state and federal authority was contested in Pennsylvania against the backdrop of the American Revolution. When the Affair began in 1778, state sovereignty was a core political principle and modern notions of federal power were inconceivable. By 1809, when the Affair ended, federal supremacy had emerged as a central tenet of American constitutional law. In the intervening decades, the Pennsylvania Supreme Court and the US Supreme Court rendered decisions in the Affair that played a key but underappreciated role in defining America's novel form of government.

II. FEDERAL POWER IN THE REVOLUTION AND EARLY REPUBLIC

Having declared independence and chosen revolution in 1776, the thirteen American colonies needed a government to replace the British system they were attempting to overthrow. Given the choice between a strong national government that reminded them of the Crown and a decentralized confederation of sovereign states, it is not surprising that the Founding Fathers initially chose the latter. Ratified in 1781, the Articles of Confederation opened with a greeting from "we the undersigned Delegates of the States," and it envisioned no more than "a firm league of friendship" between the states.[1] The Articles left no doubt where power resided: "Each *state* retains its sovereignty, freedom, and independence, and every power, jurisdiction, and right, which is not by this Confederation expressly delegated to the United States, in Congress assembled."[2] By design, the first Revolutionary government flatly rejected broad federal power.

When the Revolution ended, however, it quickly became apparent that the Articles were inadequate to govern the fledgling nation. While Congress was empowered to declare war, it could not raise an army and was instead dependent on the willingness and availability of state militias. This left the national government unable to defend Americans as Britain began to violate the 1783 Treaty of Paris, which ended the Revolution, by impressing American sailors into forced conscription and infringing on American fishing rights. The lack of a true national defense threatened American tranquility, but the economic disorganization spawned by the weak federal government was even more problematic. As the 1780s wore on, America struggled to compete economically, and Congress, prohibited by the Articles from imposing taxes or raising revenue, became increasingly unable to pay off the debts it accumulated during the fight for independence. Nor could Congress effectively regulate trade, with the result that each state developed a body of regulations that benefitted itself and targeted its neighbors to the detriment of all.[3]

In a letter to Thomas Jefferson in 1786, James Madison described the situation: "The States are every day giving proofs that separate regulations are more likely to set them by the ears than to attain the common object. When Massachusetts set on foot a retaliation of the policy of Great Britain, Connecticut declared her ports free. New Jersey served New York in the same way. And Delaware I am told has lately followed the example in opposition to the commercial plans of Pennsylvania. A miscarriage of [an] attempt to unite the states in some effectual plan will have another effect of a serious nature. . . . I almost despair of success."[4]

The lack of an "effectual plan," and especially the lack of federal courts with broad jurisdiction, prevented the resolution of conflicts among the states when they inevitably arose. The Articles of Confederation never mentioned, much less created, a federal judiciary. Instead, they provided that "[f]ull faith and credit shall be given in each of these States to the records, acts, and judicial proceedings of the courts and magistrates of every other State."[5] The Articles thus recognized no forum to resolve disputes among the states, and while they were bound to respect each other's actions, they were free to ignore the actions or laws of the national government.

In six short years, these and other deficiencies in the Articles of Confederation exposed the urgent need for stronger federal authority. The result was the constitutional convention of 1787, which met in Philadelphia to simply revise the Articles but ultimately created a new Constitution that erected an unprecedented form of government. While the Articles had been introduced by "we the undersigned Delegates of the States," the Constitution began emphatically with "WE THE PEOPLE of the United States."[6] This seemingly minor change was nothing less than the culmination of the Revolution, which transitioned sovereignty from a distant king to the states and ultimately to the people of the new nation.

To be sure, much remained to be done, and the proper relationship between state and federal power would be contested through the ratification fight, in amendments to the Constitution, in a Civil War that claimed more than six hundred thousand American lives, and in the century and a half since. But the Constitution's vesting of sovereignty in the new national citizenry allowed federal authority to flourish in a way that was previously inconceivable. In the two short decades that followed the Constitution's ratification in 1790, that federal authority was consolidated and enshrined as a guiding principle of American constitutional law. The rapid rise of federal power, and the corresponding decline of state power, generated tremendous controversy, and it was left to courts to resolve the controversy in real cases that presented profound questions about the form of government that the new Constitution had created.

III. ORIGINS OF THE OLMSTED AFFAIR

In early September 1778, in the midst of the Revolution, four Connecticut fishermen—Gideon Olmsted, Artemus White, Aquila Rumsdale, and David Clark—were captured by the British while fishing off the coast of Cape Charles, Maryland. They were transported to Jamaica and impressed into the crew of the *Active*, a single-masted British sailing vessel known as a sloop. They were then forced to assist in her delivery of arms and supplies to the British army in New York.[7]

While under way, Olmsted and his associates forcibly took control of the *Active*, after a fierce battle against fourteen members of her crew, and steered her toward Little Egg Harbor in New Jersey. Within sight of shore, however, the *Active* was pursued and seized by an armed Pennsylvania brig named the *Convention*, acting in concert with an American privateer named the *Gerard*. On September 8, 1778, the *Convention* and the *Gerard* forced the *Active* to port in Philadelphia and claimed her as a prize for themselves, their crews, and Pennsylvania. Olmsted countered that the *Active* was his prize because he had already seized the sloop by the time it was overtaken by the *Convention* and the *Gerard*.[8] These competing claims to the *Active* would be litigated for more than thirty years.

IV. THE LITIGATION

News of the *Active*'s dramatic capture on the high seas spread quickly, and newspapers widely reported the competing claims to the prize. However, Pennsylvania officials soon realized that there was no forum in which to try the claims because the traditional forum, British vice-admiralty courts that operated throughout the colonies, had not survived the Revolution and the dissolution of Pennsylvania's colonial government.[9] On September 9, 1778, only one day after the *Active* docked in Philadelphia, the Pennsylvania legislature established a new admiralty court. Because admiralty disputes frequently implicate the interests of more than one state, the legislation creating the new court provided that any appeals from its rulings, like the appeals from admiralty courts in other states, would be heard by a federal court known as the Court of Appeals. This court, the first federal court, was created by the Continental Congress in 1777 and had jurisdiction over "appeals in all cases of capture."[10]

However, the Pennsylvania legislation that authorized review by the Court of Appeals also provided that such appeals could challenge only rulings of law by the state admiralty court: "[F]indings of the facts by the jury shall be without re-examination or appeal."[11] The legislature selected prominent Lancaster lawyer George Ross to serve as the judge of the new admiralty court.[12] Ross was the last signer of the Declaration of Independence among the Pennsylvania delegation. Having begun his career as a loyal Tory and Crown prosecutor, Ross became a strong advocate for the rebel cause, serving in the Pennsylvania militia and the Continental Congress.[13]

On November 4, 1778, the competing claims to the *Active* proceeded to trial before Judge Ross and a jury. Because the jury consisted entirely of Pennsylvanians, it is not surprising that the verdict favored the local interests and undervalued the heroic actions of Olmsted and his associates in seizing control of the *Active* from the British. The four men collectively received one-fourth of the prize, as did the State of Pennsylvania, the *Convention* and her crew, and the *Gerard* and her crew. Judge Ross expressed his view that the award to Olmsted and his associates was too little, but he recognized that such fact-finding was not subject to review and, therefore, he felt "coerced by the express language of the law into confirmation of the verdict."[14]

Olmsted at once appealed to the federal Court of Appeals, purporting to challenge the legal rulings of the state court.[15] The Court of Appeals consisted of five leading legal scholars from different states. Its president was Thomas McKean, the chief justice of Pennsylvania, who (as Ken Gormley notes in his introduction to this book) has been described as the father of Pennsylvania's judicial system. McKean had a remarkable career. Born in New London Township, Chester County, he held degrees from Princeton, Dartmouth, and the University of Pennsylvania and was a delegate to the First and Second Continental Congresses, a signer of the Declaration of Independence and the Articles of Confederation, a veteran of the Revolution who participated in George Washington's defense of New York City, the president of Congress, the president of Delaware, and Pennsylvania governor.[16] As an early and fierce advocate of independence, McKean was described by John Adams as "one of the three men in the Continental Congress who appeared to me to see more clearly to the end of the business than any others in the body."[17]

McKean left his most lasting impression during his term as chief justice of Pennsylvania, which began in 1777 and lasted for twenty-two years, making him the Court's longest-serving leader. In that capacity, he played a key role in establishing judicial independence as a centerpiece of American democracy. While such independence is often traced to the 1803 opinion of John Marshall, chief justice of the US Supreme Court, in *Marbury v. Madison*, McKean's rulings on the subject predated *Marbury* by more than a decade. As one scholar has concluded, "[O]nly the historiographical difficulty of reviewing court records and other scattered documents prevents recognition that McKean, rather than John Marshall, did more than anyone else to establish an independent judiciary in the United States. As chief justice under a Pennsylvania constitution he considered flawed, he assumed it the right of the court to strike down legislative acts it deemed unconstitutional, preceding by ten years the US Supreme Court's establishment of the doctrine of judicial review."[18]

In addition to fostering judicial independence, McKean strongly believed that the appearance of judicial bias undermined the credibility of the court system. This latter concern became apparent when Olmsted's case arrived at the Court of Appeals. Although McKean was the Court's president, he disqualified himself from hearing the case because of "his connection with Pennsylvania as Chief Justice and otherwise."[19] The case then proceeded before the remaining four judges.[20] On December 15, 1778, the Court of Appeals reversed the state admiralty court verdict and awarded the entire prize to Olmsted and his associates. The Court also ordered the federal marshal in Pennsylvania to sell the *Active* and her cargo and to deliver the full proceeds (minus expenses) to Olmsted.[21]

The direct conflict between state and federal authorities then began. On December 28, 1778, having received the Court of Appeals' ruling, Judge Ross refused to alter the state jury's verdict. To justify his conclusion, Judge Ross characterized the verdict as the product of fact-finding, which the Court of Appeals was prohibited from reversing. Judge Ross then ordered the sale of the *Active*, which occurred in January 1779, for the sum of 47,981 pounds, 2 shillings, and five pence (about $7.3 million today). Ross delivered the proceeds to the Pennsylvania treasurer, David Rittenhouse.[22] Rittenhouse invested the funds in certificates of federal debt and gave Ross a bond requiring Rittenhouse to indemnify Ross if the latter was ever compelled to pay the proceeds to Olmsted as required by the Court of Appeals' ruling in 1778. In the face of this defiance by state officials, the Court of Appeals took no action to enforce its decrees, "lest consequences might ensue . . . dangerous to the public peace of the United States."[23]

The impasse between Pennsylvania and the national government remained unbroken for the next eleven years. In 1790, two events occurred that spurred Olmsted to renewed action to collect his judgment. First, the states ratified the Constitution, Article III of which specifically extended the jurisdiction of the federal courts to maritime and admiralty cases. Second, Judge Ross died. Because the new Constitution had reaffirmed the Court of Appeals' authority to rule in his favor, and because he wanted to act before Judge Ross's estate was closed, Olmsted sued Ross's executors in the Lancaster County trial court, seeking to enforce the Court of Appeals' 1778 ruling that Olmsted and his companions were entitled to the proceeds of the *Active*'s sale. When Ross's executors failed to defend the case, the Lancaster court ruled for Olmsted. However, Ross's executors then sued

Rittenhouse, the former state treasurer, on the indemnity bond he had given Ross when the latter had paid the *Active*'s proceeds into the treasury in 1779. In April 1792, that case, captioned *Ross v. Rittenhouse*,[24] came before the Pennsylvania Supreme Court, which then sat as both a trial and an appellate court.

V. THE PENNSYLVANIA SUPREME COURT'S FIRST RULING

Joining Chief Justice McKean in deciding the case were Justices Edward Shippen IV and Jasper Yeates. Shippen was the scion of a prominent Philadelphia family of merchants, judges, and politicians, and his daughter, Peggy, was married to Benedict Arnold. His grandfather had been appointed by William Penn as Philadelphia mayor, and he also served as chief justice of Pennsylvania (1699–1701). His father, Edward Shippen III, the namesake of Shippensburg, was also a Philadelphia mayor, a longtime county judge, one of the founders of the College of New Jersey (now Princeton University), a subscriber to the College of Philadelphia (now the University of Pennsylvania), and a founder of the Pennsylvania Hospital and the American Philosophical Society. In 1799, Justice Shippen succeeded Thomas McKean as chief justice of Pennsylvania.[25]

Justice Yeates served on the Supreme Court from 1791 to until his death in 1817. A prominent Lancaster lawyer, Yeates was an early advocate of the Revolution and later served as a delegate to the Pennsylvania convention that ratified the US Constitution. In 1791, while serving on the Pennsylvania Supreme Court, he was appointed by President George Washington to serve on a commission sent to negotiate an end to the Whiskey Rebellion, a violent tax protest by farmers in western Pennsylvania that was suppressed by a force of thirteen thousand militia personally led by Washington.[26]

Just as he had believed that a conflict of interest prevented him from deciding Olmsted's claims while serving as president of the Court of Appeals in 1778, Chief Justice McKean believed it was inappropriate for Pennsylvania jurists and jurors to decide *Ross v. Rittenhouse* because of the state's financial interest in the *Active*'s proceeds. As a result, he called on the US Supreme Court to decide the case. However, as McKean explained at the beginning of the *Ross* opinion, his request was refused and his Court was left to resolve the case:

> [W]hen the business was before the Court of Appeals of the United States, in December, 1778, I had the honor to be President of that Court; but declined sitting on account of my connection with this State as Chief Justice, and otherwise; and that the same reason still subsisted. That the next thing to giving a righteous judgment, was to endeavor to give general satisfaction; which circumstance might not probably be attained by our decision of the present controversy, both Court and Jury being in some measure interested, as they were all citizens of Pennsylvania. For these reasons, I expressed a wish, that some mode might be adopted for trying

the cause in the Supreme Court of the United States. . . . [O]ur expectations have been disappointed, and we are obliged, at last, to decide the controversy.[27]

Justice Yeates also felt the conflict of interest: "I have only to add, that it would also have afforded me much pleasure, if this argument had been conducted before the Judges of the Supreme Court of the United States. We formerly indulged ourselves with hopes of it. . . . We may be considered, in some remote degree, as parties in the present suit, and the decision of the Federal judges would probably have given more general satisfaction. But the parties have insisted on our opinion; and we are bound to give it."[28]

Having reluctantly agreed to decide the case, McKean's Court unanimously ruled that the Lancaster County court, not being an admiralty court, had no jurisdiction to rule for Olmsted in his claims against Judge Ross's executors. However, on the more fundamental question of whether the federal Court of Appeals had authority to overrule the state jury verdict dividing the *Active* prize, the Court split. The main point of contention was whether the Pennsylvania statute limiting appeals to the Court of Appeals to questions of law but not fact improperly restrained the federal court's authority. To Justice Shippen, the federal Court of Appeals could not be restrained by the Pennsylvania statute because it needed broad authority to offer other nations a uniform interpretation of American admiralty law. As Shippen explained,

> I own I am not convinced, that the sovereign power of the nation, vested by the joint and common consent of the people and States of the Union, with the exclusive rights of war and peace, and with the consequent, and necessary powers, of judging in the last resort of the legality of captures on the ocean, can, either in reason or sound law, be precluded from deciding an appeal, both of facts and law, arising in cases of prize. . . . Because, otherwise, no steady and uniform rules of decision could be established, and foreign nations could never know, or confide in, the grounds of our decisions.[29]

Justice Yeates found it unnecessary to address the Court of Appeals' authority in light of the unanimous agreement that the state court lacked jurisdiction to enforce the decree for Olmsted. Nonetheless, he suggested agreement with Justice Shippen that the Court of Appeals had authority to reverse the state jury verdict because admiralty cases fell within the authority of Congress to act in the interests of the nation as a whole. "I am, however, compelled to say," wrote Yeates, "that the powers of Congress must necessarily be supposed to have been co-extensive with the great objects which America then had in view, and competent to protect and advance the united interests of the whole."[30] Clearly, Yeates felt that a state statute could not frustrate the obligation of Congress to act in the nation's interests.

But to Chief Justice McKean, the Court of Appeals must yield to the Pennsylvania statute because that legislation merely incorporated the well-settled principle of the English common law that appeals were proper on issues of law but not fact. As McKean explained,

The genius and spirit of the Common Law of England, which is law in Pennsylvania, will not suffer a sentence or judgment of the lowest Court, founded on a general verdict, to be controuled or reversed by the highest jurisdiction; unless for error in matter of law, apparent upon the face of the record. This is enforced by the act of Assembly of the 9th of September, 1778, in clear and express words, in the very case under consideration; which . . . allows an appeal in all cases, unless from the verdict of a Jury; having a reference to the subject matter, and meaning that the facts should not be re-examined, or appealed from; but that an appeal might be made notwithstanding, with respect to any error in matter of law.[31]

The justices' conflicting opinions reveal a great deal about the changing relationship between state and federal authority only nine years after the Revolution and less than two years after ratification of the Constitution. While the federal authority contemplated in the Constitution was far greater than it had been in the Articles of Confederation, it was left to the judiciary to define the scope of the authority and its relationship to the states. Chief Justice McKean, the original revolutionary long opposed to distant centralized power, believed that a state statute reflecting an ancient common-law principle was a viable brake on the jurisdiction of a federal court. But his colleagues' recognition of the "sovereign power of the nation" reflected an emerging view of federal supremacy that would ultimately prevail, although it was unthinkable when the *Active* ported in Philadelphia only fourteen years earlier. The Olmsted Affair would continue for another seventeen years, and in that time, its importance in American constitutional law would grow further still.

VI. THE UNITED STATES SUPREME COURT AND THE CONSOLIDATION OF FEDERAL SUPREMACY

After the ruling in *Ross*, which again delayed his recovery of the *Active* prize, Olmsted took no further action until 1803, when he was eighty-two years old. In that year, he filed suit in federal court against Elizabeth Sergeant and Esther Waters, the daughters and heirs of David Rittenhouse, to recover the proceeds of the *Active*'s sale that were paid to Rittenhouse in 1779. The suit was heard by Richard Peters, the federal judge presiding in the Pennsylvania district. Judge Peters ruled in Olmsted's favor and directed Sergeant and Waters to turn the proceeds of the *Active*'s sale over to Olmsted.[32] Still refusing to recognize federal authority over the matter, the Pennsylvania legislature enacted a statute directing Sergeant and Waters to pay the certificates into the Pennsylvania treasury and further authorizing Governor McKean to protect the women's persons and property against any effort by federal officers to enforce Judge Peters's ruling.[33]

Remarkably, for four more years, the federal court took no action to enforce its decree for fear of bringing the governments of the United States and Pennsylvania into direct, and perhaps armed, conflict. In 1807, tired of waiting, Olmsted asked the US Supreme Court to break the stalemate by requiring Judge Peters to enforce his federal decree. The action, captioned *United States v. Peters*, was decided by the US Supreme Court on February 20, 1809.[34]

Writing for the Court, Chief Justice John Marshall emphasized that the case presented a fundamental constitutional issue: Can a state defy a federal court order? Although Marshall was deeply troubled by the direct conflict between the state and federal governments, and therefore proceeded "[w]ith great attention, and with serious concern,"[35] he had no doubt that Pennsylvania must yield: "If the legislatures of the several states may, at will, annul the judgments of the courts of the United States, and destroy the rights acquired under those judgments, the constitution itself becomes a solemn mockery; and the nation is deprived of the means of enforcing its laws by the instrumentality of its own tribunals. So fatal a result must be deprecated by all; and the people of Pennsylvania, not less than the citizens of every other state, must feel a deep interest in resisting principles so destructive of the union, and in averting consequences so fatal to themselves."[36]

Peters was a truly historic decision for two reasons. It was the first time the US Supreme Court struck down a state statute, as indicated by the fact that Chief Justice Marshall cited no legal authority and instead appealed to the citizenry's "deep interest" in avoiding conflict between the state and federal governments. For this reason, scholars have suggested that *Peters* is more important than even *Marbury v. Madison* in establishing independent judicial power.[37] Second, Chief Justice Marshall's declaration that a state's defiance of a federal court ruling would make a "solemn mockery" of the Constitution is the most strongly worded assertion of federal supremacy in our early constitutional history. For this reason, *Peters* remains a leading precedent for the now settled principle "that states must bend to the dictates of the federal courts."[38]

VII. FORT RITTENHOUSE

When he received the US Supreme Court's ruling, Judge Peters moved to enforce his decree that David Rittenhouse's daughters and heirs must pay the proceeds from the *Active*'s sale to Olmsted. In March 1809, Judge Peters directed US Marshal John Smith to arrest the heirs for violating the federal decree. When Marshal Smith arrived at the heirs' home at the corner of Seventh and Arch Streets in Philadelphia, he discovered the house, which the local press dubbed "Fort Rittenhouse," surrounded by the Pennsylvania militia commanded by General Michael Bright. In the only instance of armed conflict between state and federal officials in our nation's history, bayonets were drawn and the marshal was prevented from entering the house.[39]

The incident was reported throughout the United States. One newspaper noted the stark choice presented to the militiamen when they were given conflicting orders by

Marshal Smith and General Bright: "In the name and by the authority of the United States, said the Marshal addressing the soldiers, I command you to lay down your arms and permit me to proceed. In the name and by the authority of the Commonwealth of Pennsylvania, I command you to resist him, replied Gen. Bright, in which he was obeyed."[40]

The marshal withdrew and announced plans to return in three weeks with a force of two thousand men. Rumors of civil war spread quickly, the Pennsylvania legislature passed new resolutions condemning the federal courts' exercise of jurisdiction, and Pennsylvania's new governor, Simon Snyder, unsuccessfully requested intervention by President James Madison.[41]

In the end, with no option other than firing on the marshal, Pennsylvania officials relented. On April 13, 1809, three days before the federal force was scheduled to assemble, Marshal Smith returned to Fort Rittenhouse and was permitted to enter the back door. Although one of Rittenhouse's daughters was away, another was at home, and she was taken into custody.[42] This retreat by Pennsylvania officials was a key event in the ascendency of federal power, and especially federal judicial power. As scholars have aptly noted, "Pennsylvania caved. Vertical supremacy began to take hold."[43]

VIII. THE PENNSYLVANIA SUPREME COURT'S SECOND RULING

Elizabeth Sergeant, the Rittenhouse daughter who had been arrested, petitioned the Pennsylvania Supreme Court for a ruling, known as a writ of habeas corpus, that would release her from federal custody. While it now sounds odd for a prisoner to apply to a state court for release from federal custody, this was common practice until the latter half of the nineteenth century because early Americans looked to the states, not the federal government, as the sovereign protectors of their freedom.[44]

Sergeant's petition, captioned as *Olmsted's Case*,[45] was heard by Chief Justice William Tilghman and his colleagues in the summer of 1809. Tilghman, who succeeded to Justice Shippen's seat on the Court, served as chief justice from 1806 until 1827. In 1801, he had been appointed by President John Adams to a newly created federal court, the Third Circuit Court of Appeals, and he served as chief judge of the circuit until its abolition in 1802. Prior to his ascension to the Pennsylvania Supreme Court, he served as president judge of the Court of Common Pleas of Philadelphia and a judge of the Pennsylvania High Court of Errors and Appeals.[46] Although his personal views on the governor's decision to forcibly oppose the federal marshal at Fort Rittenhouse are not known, Chief Justice Tilghman reported the public's sentiments in a private letter to Justice Yeates: "It is generally thought that the Governor was wrong in calling out the militia."[47]

The key question presented by Elizabeth Sergeant's petition was whether the federal Court of Appeals had jurisdiction in 1778 to reverse the state jury verdict and award the entire *Active* prize to Olmsted and his companions. If the Court of Appeals had such authority, Sergeant should have complied with Judge Peters's directive to relinquish the share of the prize that was entrusted to her father as Pennsylvania's treasurer pursuant to the jury's verdict. Rejecting the view of the Pennsylvania legislature and others who sought to enforce the jury verdict, Chief Justice Tilghman, writing for a unanimous Court, held that the Court of Appeals had the power to reverse the verdict. The chief justice concluded his opinion by expressing his wish "that this long continued controversy will be brought to a termination without any material interruption of that harmony between this state and the United States."[48]

The Supreme Court's vindication of federal authority meant that Sergeant had improperly defied the federal decree and should remain in federal custody until the share of the *Active* proceeds that she retained was paid to Olmsted and his companions, whose rights had been vindicated at long last. Nonetheless, Chief Justice Tilghman left no doubt that, in a proper case, a state court had the power to free a citizen improperly imprisoned by federal authorities because, he explained, states were the final bulwark against excesses by the federal government. When such excesses occur, Tilghman reasoned, "it is in vain to expect that the states will submit to manifest and flagrant usurpations of power by the United States, if (which God forbid) they should ever attempt them."[49]

This confirmation of a state court's power to grant habeas corpus relief to federal prisoners is perhaps the earliest enunciation of that principle by any court. It also remained the prevailing view of American law for more than a half century, until 1872, when the US Supreme Court conclusively prohibited state court jurisdiction over habeas corpus claims by federal prisoners.[50]

IX. CONCLUSION

The Olmsted Affair reflected and significantly influenced the debate that created the form of government that we now take for granted. When the Affair began in 1778, citizens looked primarily to their states for governance and protection. Their fear and mistrust of distant, centralized power spawned both the Revolution and the Articles of Confederation that subordinated Congress to the states. In that context, it is not surprising that Pennsylvania authorities favored their own jurors' verdict over the contrary decision of the federal Court of Appeals. However, as the inadequacies of the Articles were revealed in the wake of the Revolution, the need for a stronger national government became apparent. The result was the Constitution, and the courts were left to define what it meant.

When the Affair first arrived in the Pennsylvania Supreme Court in 1792, the debate over the breadth of federal authority was raging. The majority view of Justices Shippen and Yeates reflected an emerging deference to federal authority that ultimately prevailed but was inconceivable only a decade earlier. Chief Justice McKean, on the other hand, embraced a view of state sovereignty that seems alien today but was well within the mainstream in

1792. Even as he embraced the past, however, McKean ushered in a groundbreaking new power—judicial review—that would become as fundamental to our constitutional law as federal supremacy itself.

In 1809, when the Pennsylvania Supreme Court decided *Olmsted's Case*, its second vindication of federal power in the Affair, the debate was largely over and federal supremacy had prevailed. To be sure, strains of state sovereignty remained, as with Chief Justice Tilghman's seminal announcement of a state's power to grant habeas corpus relief to federal prisoners, and the concept has resurfaced in various debates over the past two centuries. Indeed, the defeat of states' rights in the Olmsted Affair has been identified as a contributing cause of the Civil War.[51] But the rapid rise of federal power was essentially complete when the Affair ended in 1809, and the Pennsylvania Supreme Court's rulings did much to hasten and explain that rise.

NOTES

John J. Hare is a shareholder at Marshall Dennehey Warner Coleman & Goggin. The author thanks Shane Haselbarth, Esq., and Meredith L. Lussier, Esq., for their reviews of this chapter and the book's manuscript.

1. "Articles of Confederation, Preamble," *United States Government Printing Office*, http://www.gpo.gov/fdsys/pkg/SMAN-107/pdf/SMAN-107-pg935.pdf.

2. Ibid., art. II.

3. Congressional weakness was manifested in many ways, but it was especially evident during Shay's Rebellion, an insurgency primarily of war veterans frustrated by a prevailing economic depression. With Congress unable to raise an army, the rebellion spread throughout western and central Massachusetts in 1786, destabilizing large segments of the population before it was suppressed by mercenaries hired by wealthy merchants. *See generally* Eric Foner, *Give Me Liberty! An American History* (New York: W. W. Norton, 2006), 118–21.

4. "To Thomas Jefferson from James Madison, 18 March 1786," *Founders Online*, http://www.founders.archives.gov/documents/Jefferson/01-09-02-0301.

5. "Articles of Confederation, Art. IV," *United States Government Printing Office*, http://www.gpo.gov/fdsys/pkg/SMAN-107/pdf/SMAN-107-pg935.pdf.

6. "Constitution of the United States, Preamble," *United States Government Printing Office*, http://www.gpo.gov/fdsys/pkg/CDOC/pdf/CDOC-110hdoc50.pf.

7. For excellent accounts of the Affair, *see* Gary D. Rowe, "Constitutionalism in the Streets," *Southern California Law Review* 78 (2005): 401–57; Hampton L. Carson, "The Case of the Sloop 'Active,'" *Pennsylvania Magazine of History and Biography* 16, no. 4 (January 1893): 385–98; and M. Ruth Kelly, *The Olmsted Case: Privateers, Property, and Politics in Pennsylvania, 1778–1810* (Selinsgrove: Susquehanna University Press, 2005).

8. Rowe, "Constitutionalism," 412–13; Carson, "Case of the Sloop," 393–98.

9. *See generally* Charles S. Andrews, "Vice-Admiralty Courts in the Colonies," in *Records of the Vice-Admiralty Court of Rhode Island 1716–1752*, ed. Dorothy S. Towle (Washington, D.C.: American Historical Association, 1936), 1–79; and C. Ubbelohde, *The Vice-Admiralty Courts and the American Revolution* (Chapel Hill: University of North Carolina Press, 1960).

10. "Articles of Confederation, Art. IV, § I," *United States Government Printing Office*, http://www.gpo.gov/fdsys/pkg/SMAN-107/pdf/SMAN-107-pg935.pdf; *see also* H. Bourguignon, *The First Federal Court: The Federal Appellate Prize Court of the American Revolution, 1775–1787* (Philadelphia: American Philosophical Society, 1977).

11. The relevant legislation and subsequent proceedings are set forth in Thomas Lloyd, *The*

Report of the Trial of Gen. Michael Bright Before Washington and Peters, in the Circuit Court of the United States in and for the District of Pennsylvania, in the Third Circuit (Philadelphia: P. Byrne, 1809), 137, available in the Stanford University Law Library, #AP-ABT-ZKr.

12. Richard Peters, ed., *The Whole Proceedings in the Case of Olmsted and Others Versus Rittenhouse's Executrices* (Philadelphia: William P. Farrand, 1809), 51.

13. Denise Kiernan and Joseph D'Agnese, *Signing Their Lives Away: The Fame and Misfortune of the Men Who Signed the Declaration of Independence* (Philadelphia: Quirk Books, 2009), 64–67.

14. Rowe, "Constitutionalism," 412; Lloyd, *Report of the Trial*, 154–57.

15. The Court of Appeals required litigants to post security before it would hear appeals. Because Olmsted lacked the necessary means to post security without his share of the prize, he solicited assistance from speculators, who were promised a share of the prize in exchange for posting the security. The successful suitor was Benedict Arnold, then military commander of Philadelphia, who had embarked on a campaign of risky business ventures to support an extravagant lifestyle with his new bride, Peggy Shippen, one of Philadelphia's leading socialites. Still two years away from his treason at West Point, Arnold, along with a partner, was assigned a sizable piece of Olmsted's share of the Active prize in exchange for posting the security necessary to support Olmsted's appeal. *See* Rowe, "Constitutionalism," 414.

16. This biographical information is taken from G. S. Rowe, "A Valuable Acquisition in Congress: Thomas McKean, Delegate from Delaware to the Continental Congress, 1774–1783," *Pennsylvania History: A Journal of Mid-Atlantic Studies* 38, no. 3 (July 1971): 225–64.

17. Charles F. Adams, "Letter from John Adams to John Jackson, December 30, 1787," in *The Works of John Adams, Second President of the United States*, vol. 10 (Boston: Little Brown, 1850–56), x, 269.

18. John M. Coleman, *Thomas McKean, Forgotten Leader of the Revolution* (Rockaway, N.Y.: American Faculty Press, 1975).

19. National Archives, Founders Archives, Publication No. M-162, "The Revolutionary War Prize Cases: Records of the Court of Appeals in Cases of Capture, 1776–1787" (1954); *see also* Ross v. Rittenhouse, 2 U.S. 160, 161–62 (Pa. 1792).

20. With Benedict Arnold's assistance, Olmsted retained James Wilson to represent him in the Court of Appeals. Wilson, a leading legal theorist of the Revolutionary generation, had signed the Declaration of Independence and would go on to play a major role in drafting the US Constitution. He was one of the six original justices appointed by George Washington to the US Supreme Court. *See* Rowe, "Constitutionalism," 414.

21. Peters, *Whole Proceedings*, 75–77.

22. Rittenhouse is better known as an astronomer, inventor, and, later, the first director of the US Mint.

23. *See* Rowe, "Constitutionalism," 415.

24. 2 U.S. (2 Dall.) 160; *see also* Lloyd, *Report of the Trial*, 65–67.

25. This biographical information is taken from Randolph Shipley Klein, *Portrait of an Early American Family: The Shippens of Pennsylvania Across Five Generations* (Philadelphia: University of Pennsylvania Press, 1975), 233–42.

26. This biographical information is taken from Philip S. Klein and Ari Hoogenboom, *A History of Pennsylvania* (University Park: Pennsylvania State University Press, 1980), 117, 250.

27. 2 U.S. 160, 161–62 (quotation omitted).

28. Ibid., 169–70.

29. Ibid., 165.

30. Ibid., 169.

31. Ibid., 163.

32. Lloyd, *Report of the Trial*, 203–7.

33. Ibid., 209–11.

34. 9 U.S. 115 (1809).

35. Ibid., 135.

36. Ibid., 136.

37. *See, e.g.*, Mark A. Graber, "Establishing Judicial Review? Schooner Peggy and the Early Marshall Court," *Political Research Quarterly* 51, no. 7 (1998): 221, 224 (identifying Peters as the "real test for a more independent judicial power"); Rowe, "Constitutionalism," 408 ("Peters deserves our attention, then, partly because of the role it played, and continues to play, in the construction of judicial supremacy over the last half century. It is a source for modern myth making, yet has not been subject to anything like the obsessive visions and revisions that Marbury has endured.").

38. Ibid., 407.

39. Lloyd, *Report of the Trial*, 211–13.

40. Rowe, "Constitutionalism," 426–27. Professor Rowe indicates that this account is based on a report attributed to the *Philadelphia True American*.

41. Lloyd, *Report of the Trial*, 215–16.

42. Ibid., 220.

43. Barry Friedman and Erin F. Delaney, "Becoming Supreme: The Federal Foundation of Judicial Supremacy," *Columbia Law Review* 100, no. 2 (2011): 1154.

44. Todd E. Pettys, "State Habeas Relief for Federal Extrajudicial Detainees," *Minnesota Law Review* 92, no. 2 (2007): 271–72 ("When suffering restraints at the hands of federal authorities, therefore, citizens often turned not to the courts of the new and unfamiliar sovereign—a sovereign that many feared would abuse its power in oppressive ways—but rather to the courts of the sovereign that had already earned the people's confidence and loyalty.") (citation omitted).

45. Frederick C. Brightly, *Brightly's Reports of Cases Decided by the Judges of the Supreme Court of Pennsylvania, the Court of Nisi Prius, at Philadelphia, and also in the Supreme Court, with Notes and References to Recent Decisions* (Philadelphia: J. Kay, Jun & Brother, 1851), 9.

46. This biographical information is taken from John Golder, *Life of the Honourable William Tilghman, Late Chief Justice of the State of Pennsylvania* (Philadelphia: Thomas Town, 1829), 18–33.

47. Letter of William Tilghman to Jasper Yeates, April 11, 1809, discussed in Rowe, "Constitutionalism," 429.

48. Brightly, *Brightly's Reports*, 9, 15.

49. Ibid.

50. *See* Tarble's Case, 80 U.S. (13 Wall.) 397, 402 (1872).

51. *See* Rowe, "Constitutionalism," 410 ("In the last analysis, the Olmsted Affair changed the shape of Pennsylvania politics and spurred the development of two highly divergent visions of nationalism and federalism. Although the case took place in the North and involved a Revolutionary War-era dispute, and although Chief Justice Marshall's brand of nationalism won the day in *Peters*, . . . the case also generated a fierce backlash in which was forged a retooled states' rights creed that would resonate in the South in the decades leading up to the Civil War.").

SECTION 2

Tort Law

CHAPTER 15

The Floodgates of Strict Liability

The Johnstown Flood of 1889, the Supreme Court, and the Rise of Modern American Tort Law

JED H. SHUGERMAN

Pennsylvania was the turning point in one of the most contested questions in the common law: Is there a place for strict liability in tort law? The received wisdom is that American judges rejected strict liability for dangerous activities through the nineteenth and early twentieth centuries. Historians, legal scholars, and treatise writers had cited the American rejection of the English strict liability precedent, *Fletcher v. Rylands*, as the definitive proof of the American commitment to the fault rule. This apparent fact was used to demonstrate the clarity and coherence of the fault rule or, conversely, the proindustry, procorporate bias of American judges.[1]

The Pennsylvania Supreme Court first answered no, but in the wake of one of the biggest disasters in American history—pitting rich tycoons against thousands of poor victims—the Supreme Court reversed course, and most American courts followed. This story suggests some surprising twists in ideas about law, politics, economics, and morality.

I. *RYLANDS*: REJECTION AND ADOPTION

John Rylands was the leading textile manufacturer and probably the wealthiest industrialist in England.[2] In 1860, to provide an additional source of water for a massive steam-powered textile mill, he hired a contractor to dig a large ditch and create a reservoir. The reservoir collapsed into an abandoned coal-mining shaft, and that shaft ultimately connected with Thomas Fletcher's active coal mines,[3] which the reservoir flood destroyed.[4]

An initial arbitration proceeding framed one issue for the English courts: Could Rylands be held liable without fault?[5] The Court of Exchequer ruled against Fletcher's case because it fit none of the traditional causes of action of trespass, negligence, and nuisance.[6] Trespass required a more direct harm; nuisance required a more continuous, ongoing harm; and negligence required negligence, of course. Fletcher then appealed to the Exchequer chamber, where Justice Blackburn announced a broad statement of liability without fault for risky uses of land: "[T]he person who for his own purposes brings on his lands and collects and keeps there anything likely to do mischief if it escapes, must keep it in at his peril, and, if he does not do so, is *prima facie* answerable for all the damage which is the natural consequence of its escape."[7] Blackburn then qualified this sweeping doctrine of strict liability by focusing on what is "naturally there" in an apparent defense of traditional uses of land, such as agriculture and mining.[8]

The House of Lords affirmed the Exchequer chamber and its strict liability rule in 1868. Lord Cairns emphasized the difference between natural use and unnatural use: such a "non-natural use" must be "likely to do mischief," rather than a use that would be expected "in the ordinary course of the enjoyment of the land."[9] The decision shifted the burden from the plaintiff, who would otherwise have to prove that the defendant was negligent, to the defendant, who would now have to prove either that the plaintiff had "defaulted" or that the accident was an "act of God." The effect was liability without fault. English courts would tightly cabin *Rylands* thereafter so that strict liability was only a narrow area of English tort law.

In America, the initial reception was mixed. Massachusetts and Minnesota immediately adopted *Rylands*[10] and consistently expanded their application of its doctrine.[11] One expansion was a notable opinion by Judge Oliver Wendell Holmes.[12] Then the tide turned against *Rylands*. The New York Court of Appeals rejected *Rylands*,[13] followed by New Hampshire and New Jersey.[14] Then in 1886, Pennsylvania rejected *Rylands* in *Pennsylvania Coal Co. v. Sanderson*, producing the last of the major rejections of the nineteenth century.[15]

One striking feature of these decisions is their explicit use of economic arguments in favor of the fault rule as a support for industrial growth.[16] New York's highest court, unanimously holding that liability for such damage required proof of negligence, offered its industrialist social contract theory—namely, that civilization requires individuals to sacrifice some rights for demands of economic and industrial development:

> By becoming a member of civilized society, I am compelled to give up many of my natural rights, but I receive more than a compensation from the surrender by every other man of the same rights, and the security, advantage and protection which the laws give me. So, too, the general rules that I may have the exclusive and undisturbed use and possession of my real estate, and that I must so use my real estate as not to injure my neighbor, are much modified by the exigencies of the social state. We must have factories, machinery, dams, canals and railroads.

They are demanded by the manifold wants of mankind, and lay at the basis of all
our civilization. If I have any of these upon my lands, and they are not a nuisance,
. . . I am not responsible for any damage they accidentally and unavoidably do my
neighbor. He receives his compensation for such damage by the general good, in
which he shares, and the right which he has to place the same things on his land.[17]

This broad principle reflects a laissez-faire policy preference for industrial development
over protection of personal property rights and, accordingly, a style of utilitarian efficiency.
Rather than arguing that individuals have a natural right to use their land as they so choose, the
New York court's rationale emphasized the overall economic benefits, which justified
the curtailing of natural rights.

Later that same year, the New Jersey Supreme Court criticized *Rylands*'s distinction
of natural and unnatural uses as a framework better suited for a "primitive condition of
mankind, whatever that may have been."[18] Such a rule, the judges argued, would be an
impediment to economic growth: the imperative in *Rylands* "would impose a penalty on
the efforts, made in reasonable, skilful, and careful manner, to rise above a condition of
barbarism. It is impossible that legal principle can throw so serious an obstacle in the way
of progress and improvement."[19] For these judges, strict liability was a vestige of a primitive
time, inconsistent with modern industrial growth:

> [T]he rules of [strict] liability for damage done by brutes or by fire. . . . were
> certainly introduced in England at an immature stage of English jurisprudence,
> and an undeveloped state of agriculture, manufacturers and commerce, when
> the nation had not settled down to those modern, progressive, industrial pur-
> suits which the spirit of the common law, adapted to all conditions of society,
> encourages and defends. They were introduced when the development of many
> of the rational rules now universally recognized as principles of the common
> law had not been demanded by the growth of intelligence, trade, and productive
> enterprise,—when the common law had not been set forth in the precedents,
> as a coherent and logical system on many subjects other than the tenures of real
> estate . . . [W]hatever may be said of the origins of those rules, to extend them, as
> they were extended in *Rylands v. Fletcher*, seems to us contrary to the analogies
> and the general principles of the common law, as now established. To extend
> them to the current case would be contrary to American authority, as well as to
> our understanding of legal principles.[20]

This New Jersey decision emphasizes "productive enterprise," the necessities of modern
industrial society, and legal science's core principle of negligence.

Pennsylvania swung back and forth during the long *Sanderson* litigation, but it wound
up in favor of the Pennsylvania Coal Company and the trickle-down economics of the fault

rule. In 1878 and 1880, in two initial rulings in *Sanderson*,[21] the Supreme Court approved of *Rylands*, but it reversed itself in an 1886 appeal in the same case, producing, as noted, the last of the major *Rylands* rejections of the nineteenth century.[22] The Sanderson family had purchased land and a residence outside Scranton, induced in part by a "perfectly pure"[23] stream running through the tract. After the Sandersons built a dam and cistern to use the stream for fishing, washing, and drinking water, the Pennsylvania Coal Company began mining coal along the stream above the Sandersons' land. The mine water, both pumped and trickling naturally out of the shafts, ran to the stream, "corrupt[ing] the water of the stream, and . . . render[ing] it worse than worthless for any domestic or household use."[24]

In the first appeal in 1878, the Supreme Court voted six to one to reverse the trial court's holding that the Sandersons must show the coal company's negligence to recover. Relying on the language of natural versus unnatural use in *Rylands*,[25] the Court held that the coal company defendants had created "an *artificial* watercourse from their mine to Meadow Brook"[26] and that the jury should be the one to decide if it damaged the Sandersons' land. While the Court was clear that in cases of "material and appreciable injury," the plaintiffs have a right to recover, it also emphasized that "[t]he proprietors of large and useful interests should not be hampered or hindered for frivolous or trifling causes."[27] The Court specified that anthracite coal mining was an "immense public and private interest" that required pumping of water and "should not be crippled and endangered by adopting a rule that would make colliers answerable in damages for corrupting a stream into which mine-water would naturally run."[28] Two years later, in 1880, the Court upheld the same ruling in *Sanderson I* by a vote of four to two.[29] The Court recognized that "all lawful industries result in the general good" but noted that they are still "instituted and conducted for private gain, and are used and enjoyed as private rights" and cannot "justly claim the right to take and use the property of [other] citizens without compensation."[30]

The case was sent back for a new trial, and this time a jury found for the Sandersons. But then the Supreme Court flipped the other way. The coal company won its appeal in 1886, four to three.[31] Justice Woodward, the author of the 1878 opinion, had died, and a new member of the Court, Justice Silas Clark, authored a complete reversal. Taking up the moralist debate, his opinion primarily emphasized that coal mining and its resulting water leakage were natural uses of land. Justice Clark's opinion referred to mine-water runoff or mining in general as "natural" an unmistakable twenty-six times.

The Court then distinguished the Pennsylvania Coal Company's natural use of the land from the unnatural use that resulted in liability in *Rylands*.[32] In its repeated discussions of "natural" flow of water and the "mere force of gravity,"[33] the Court ignored its own statement of the facts: "The water which percolated into the shaft was by *powerful engines* pumped therefrom, and as it was brought to the surface, it passed . . . by an *artificial* water-course."[34] The opinion was thus inconsistent about how natural the mine-water damage was.

Justice Clark moved on to his most significant argument, the economic importance of mining to the state. He noted early in his opinion that Pennsylvania annually produced thirty million tons of anthracite and seventy million tons of bituminous coal,[35] of vast importance to the state economy and "the entire community."[36] Justice Clark then turned to the reasoning in the Court's 1878 decision that trifling damages should not impede important industries, but he now characterized the Sandersons' case as "trifling": "The plaintiff's grievance is for a mere personal inconvenience; and we are of the opinion that mere private personal inconveniences, arising in this way and under such circumstances, must yield to the necessities of a great public industry, which, although in the hands of a private corporation, subserves a great public interest. To encourage the development of the great natural resources of a country trifling inconveniences to particular persons must sometimes give way to the necessities of a great community."[37] Clark concluded his opinion with a quotation raising the consequentialist stakes: "The population, wealth, and improvements are the result of mining, and of that alone."[38] His take-home message was that imposing liability on basic mining activities would risk too much harm to the community and its economy.

With New York, New Hampshire, and New Jersey rejecting *Rylands*, and with Pennsylvania reversing course to reject it too, America's treatise writers wrote off *Rylands*.[39] The academics' dismissal of *Rylands* fit into a larger historical interpretation of American tort law: proindustry fault liability dominated the nineteenth and early twentieth centuries,[40] and the mid-twentieth century marked the gradual rise of strict liability.[41] Many prominent torts casebooks and legal historians have featured this supposed rejection of *Rylands* as a centerpiece for their historical claims about the dominance of the fault rule.

It is true that *Rylands* had a mixed reception in America for about two decades, and it is true that federal courts almost completely ignored it well into the twentieth century.[42] However, contrary to the received historical wisdom, by the turn of the twentieth century, a majority of states had adopted *Rylands* explicitly or had adopted a general strict liability rule for unnatural activities, hazardous activities, or *Rylands*-like storage of large amounts of water (and these cases do not include the separate line of strict liability cases for fire or blasting). While three prominent states—New York, New Hampshire, and New Jersey—had rejected *Rylands* with strong warnings about its effect on industry and social welfare, only two states through 1883 had adopted *Rylands* explicitly. As of 1889, a mere six states had. But then the 1890s were the turning point. By 1900, eighteen states adopted *Rylands*, with seven more leaning toward it.[43]

What accounts for this dramatic reversal in the late 1880s and 1890s? Broad social, economic, and political forces had set the table for the adoption of strict liability: increasingly heavy industries developing side by side with urban or residential areas, business cycles (bust in the 1870s, boom in the 1880s, and bust in the 1890s), and the rise of the Populists as critics of industry's excess in the 1890s. While these factors contributed to the small bump toward *Rylands* in the 1880s,[44] they were not sufficient to explain the enormous spike in the 1890s. The trigger for this wave of adoptions was an unprecedented disaster that put reservoirs in a horrifying new light.

II. THE JOHNSTOWN FLOOD AND THE
AMERICAN ADOPTION OF *RYLANDS*

In the mountains east of Pittsburgh, the South Fork Fishing and Hunting Club owned a 450-acre artificial recreational lake, one of the largest reservoirs in the world.[45] The club was known as "The Bosses Club" because of its titans-of-industry membership, including Andrew Carnegie, Andrew Mellon, and Henry Clay Frick. Despite the dam's history of instability, and despite multiple warnings of structural problems, the club's owners and employees disregarded the dam's leaks and crumbling foundation.[46]

On the stormy night of May 31, 1889, the dam in the mountains collapsed, unleashing twenty million tons of water into the valley below.[47] One of the most deadly disasters in American history, the flood completely destroyed Johnstown, killing two thousand people.[48] According to historian David McCullough, a western Pennsylvania native, the flood turned into "the biggest news story since the murder of Abraham Lincoln"[49] and sparked "the greatest outpouring of popular charity the country had ever seen."[50] The Johnstown Flood was the Hurricane Katrina of the nineteenth century, and it was by far the most fatal flood in American history. Storms and dams no longer looked so innocent to a generation of Americans. The flood devastated a corner of Pennsylvania and, less dramatically, wreaked havoc in a corner of American tort law: the liability standard for unnatural or hazardous activities.

As the cause of the dam collapse above Johnstown became clearer, the public focused its anger on the South Fork Club and its wealthy members,[51] and the media called on those members to compensate the Johnstown victims.[52] The club made a modest donation, but some of its incredibly wealthy members donated only trivial amounts to the town, and some tactlessly denied any responsibility to the newspapers. This series of incidents provoked a violent mob's attack on the club.[53] A county commission quickly investigated the dam and, on June 7, announced that the owners were "culpable in not making [the dam] as secure as it should have been, especially in view of the fact that a population of many thousands were in the valley below; and we hold that the owners are responsible for the fearful loss of life and property."[54] Newspapers around the country condemned the club for being "negligent," criminally negligent, or even guilty of manslaughter.[55] However, not one victim recovered a penny through the legal system. Several families and entrepreneurs sued the club, but two torts claims failed to produce any damage verdicts and were never appealed.[56] Although the barrier to recovery was more likely a combination of the club's lack of assets and the difficulty of piercing the corporate veil to claim the members' enormous assets, McCullough's account suggests that the public and the media perceived that the negligence rule had prevented recovery.[57]

Just two months after the Johnstown Flood, a note in the *American Law Review* described the horrors of the flood and called for courts to adopt *Rylands*.[58] After several pages describing the terrifying power of collected waters, the note author observed that the flood had transformed a vibrant town into a pile of "a great mass of earth, stones, trees, houses, railway locomotives, cars, human bodies, and what not ... very deep and ... very solid."[59] The author then offered *Rylands* as "[t]he best answer which has ever yet been given," which had been "adopted by several American courts, though denied by some."[60] He explained how *Rylands* placed the burden on the defendant and shifted the question more to causation:

> It is good enough for the practical purpose of charging with damages a company of gentlemen who have maintained a vast reservoir of water behind a rotten dam, for the mere pleasure of using it for a fishing pond, to the peril of thousands of honest people dwelling in the valley below. It is enough that they are *prima facie* answerable. That takes the question to the jury. The jury will do the rest. They can be safely trusted to say whether or not it was the plaintiff's default, that is the fault of some poor widow in Johnstown, whose husband and children were drowned while she was cast ashore and suffered to live.[61]

We have no record of a Pennsylvania court applying *Rylands* against the South Fork Fishing Club. However, courts in Pennsylvania and around the United States began applying *Rylands* to a wide range of other cases.[62]

The Johnstown Flood swept in a new attitude toward big industry and liability. In *Robb v. Carnegie Bros.*,[63] an 1891 case involving Andrew Carnegie, the most prominent figure connected to the flood, the Pennsylvania Supreme Court applied strict liability to a basic and necessary function in the manufacturing of coal. The plaintiff's counsel cited *Rylands* and argued that this damage, unlike the mine water in *Sanderson*, was not from a "natural product" but rather "brought" to the defendants' property.[64] The case was first argued on October 5, 1889, just five months after the Johnstown Flood.

The Court applied strict liability in a unanimous decision, with three of the *Sanderson* justices changing their preflood stances.[65] One of these was Justice Silas Clark, the author of *Sanderson*, who had been so solicitous of industry.[66] The *Robb* ruling limited "natural activities" to the natural "develop[ment of] the resources of his property," which sharply distinguished *Sanderson*.[67] The key distinction between *Sanderson* and *Robb* rested on the natural/unnatural dichotomy: coal mining itself was natural, but any further development or manufacturing of the coal was not natural.[68] Again, this dispute over naturalness and nonnaturalness was an implicit reference to *Rylands*.

Robb further eviscerated *Sanderson* by squarely rejecting its reasoning about the supreme importance of industrial development. *Robb* first asserted, "It is a fundamental principle of our system of government that the interest of the public is higher than that of the individual."[69] Then the opinion moved on to the point that industry is private, not public, like roads, rails, highways, and canals:

> [T]he production of iron or steel or glass or coke, while of great public importance, stands on no different ground from any other

branch of manufacturing, or from the cultivation of agricultural products. They are needed for use and consumption by the public, but they are the results of private enterprise, conducted for private profit and under the absolute control of the producer. He may increase his business at will, or diminish it. He may transfer it to another person, or place, or state, or abandon it. He may sell to whom he pleases, at such price as he pleases, or he may hoard his productions, and refuse to sell to any person or at any price. He is serving himself in his own way, and has no right to claim exemption from the natural consequences of his own act. The interests in conflict in this case are therefore not those of the public and of an individual, but those of two private owners who stand on equal ground as engaged in their own private business.[70]

The language here emphasizes the private and self-interested choices of the industrialist. The most apparent cause for the sudden change in the justices' suppositions about industry and the individual homeowner was the Johnstown Flood.

Three months later, in *Lentz v. Carnegie Bros.*,[71] the Supreme Court again ruled unanimously against the Carnegie Company, holding it liable without fault for damages caused by the same coke works. In 1893, in *Hauck v. Tide Water Pipe-Line Co.*,[72] the Court similarly distinguished *Sanderson* by unanimously finding the storage of oil unnatural and subject to strict liability. The author of this opinion, Chief Justice Paxson, had been one of the *Sanderson* majority, but now he sharply limited *Sanderson* to the "necessary" and "essential" development of "the land itself."[73] Throughout the next three decades, Pennsylvania courts in more than a dozen cases continued to expand strict liability for more activities, based primarily on the natural versus unnatural use distinction.[74]

A majority of state courts adopted *Rylands* only a few years after the flood—after most courts had ignored the English strict liability precedent for about two decades. For a list of states and their cases for and against *Rylands*, see Appendix A. The chart on the following page shows the pattern of adoptions.

The line marked by diamonds demonstrates state courts' explicit adoptions of *Rylands*. The line marked by squares tracks the total number of states adopting *Rylands*, plus states leaning toward it (meaning the adopting of a rule similar to *Rylands* in applying strict liability to unnatural or dangerous activities; otherwise favorable language on *Rylands*; or on balance favoring *Rylands*, even if the precedents are mixed). The Johnstown Flood was May 31, 1889. Note the rapid rise of adoptions from 1889 to 1900, especially the line marked by diamonds for explicit adoptions.

The pattern of adoption starting in the mid-1880s, before the Johnstown Flood, is attributable to a couple factors. First, disastrous California floods in the early 1880s led to that state's adoption of *Rylands* in 1886. Some of those floods related to hydraulic mining, and two other states adopting *Rylands* in the 1880s were mining states (Nevada in 1885,

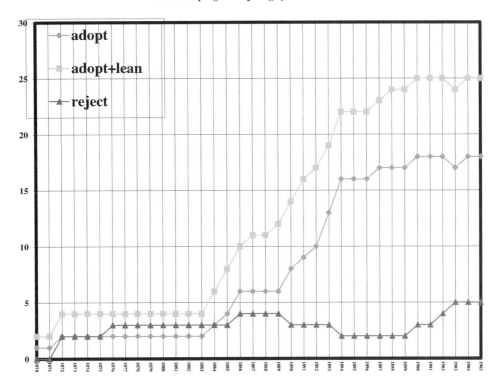

Colorado in 1887). Second, upper Midwestern states were the majority of the other states in the 1880s (Michigan in 1884, Illinois in 1885–87, and Iowa in 1886). In the 1880s, this region's population and industry were growing rapidly, often side by side with increased risk. The Midwest's political balance had recently shifted toward Grangerism and agrarian populism and against industry.[75]

Pennsylvania's switch against *Sanderson* and toward *Rylands* provides a good example of the role of moral argument in the adoption of strict liability. In *Robb*, decided a little more than a year after the flood, the Pennsylvania Supreme Court emphasized the private and self-interested choices of the industrialist. Before the flood, judges celebrated the public benefits of industry; afterward, judges derided the privateness and the selfish orientation of the industrialist. As private and self-interested, industry deserved no privileges for its services. Instead, it owed heightened duties because of the moral accountability for its choices. The Supreme Court's depiction of the industrialist as tremendously powerful, capricious, and manipulative—and deserving of no special protection from the law—stands in remarkable contrast to the Court's dicta in *Sanderson* extolling the public service of the capitalists. The *Robb* Court easily could have applied the "assumption of risk" defense against the plaintiff, who had knowingly bought land adjacent to the Carnegie coke ovens (albeit before they were expanded significantly). He had even helped construct some of the ovens as a paid contractor.[76] Surely, then, the Supreme Court could have condemned him for turning around a few years later and suing the Carnegie Company for pollution he not only was aware of but also helped create. The most apparent cause for the sudden change in the justices' suppositions about industry and the individual homeowner was the Johnstown Flood.

The Supreme Court mixed utilitarian arguments with a moral approach in *Commonwealth ex rel. Attorney General v. Russell*, in which oil producers had polluted a borough's water supply by pouring salt water into a creek that fed the borough reservoir. The Court repeatedly emphasized the importance of clean water to the whole community and argued from consequences that the public good limited the property rights of the few. But at the end of the opinion, Justice Williams, writing for a unanimous Court, drove home his conclusion with a distinct moral argument about duty and the social contract:

> It [would] seem that civil liberty required that other interests than those of the individual should be reckoned with, and that each person must be held to have surrendered such of his natural rights upon coming into society as could not be asserted consistently with a due respect for the rights of others and for the public good. For myself I can see no reason why our duty towards others ought not to place limits upon our rights of property similar to those which it has put upon our natural rights of person. "*Sic utere tuo non alienum laedas*" expresses a moral obligation that grows out of the mere fact of membership in civil society. In many instances it has been applied as a measure of civil obligation, enforceable at law among those whose interests are conflicting.[77]

This passage turned the tables on the proindustry social contract arguments of the anti-*Rylands* cases, *Losee, Brown v. Collins*, and *Sanderson*. Those cases conceived of the social contract as a bargain by all individuals to accept the benefits and costs of industrialization, but after the Johnstown Flood, the Supreme Court rewrote that social contract. The new compact was that all individuals surrendered their right to develop their property in ways hazardous to others. This argument was premised not on a utilitarian calculus but rather on a sense of "moral obligation."

Throughout the 1890s and the first two decades of the 1900s, courts in more than a dozen cases continued to carve away at *Sanderson* and applied strict liability to more and more hazardous industries, based almost entirely on the natural versus nonnatural use distinction.[78] During this period, the Pennsylvania Supreme Court declared and repeated that *Sanderson* "has never been and never ought to be extended beyond the limitations put upon it by its own facts."[79] Later decisions relied on *Robb's* moralistic denigration of "private enterprise conducted for private profit" and repeated *Robb's* rejection of industry's claim that it was serving the public interest.[80] In 1898, in *Gavigan v. Atlantic Refining Co.*,[81] the Supreme Court turned up the moral rhetoric, calling a defendant "selfish" while conceding that his storage of gas and oil was legal. Rather than focusing on particular actions, whether in terms of legality, due care, or social utility, the Court instead turned to general moral condemnation.[82] This moment suggests that the Court no longer categorized public and private interests in terms of economic benefits but instead did so based on moral judgments. The key struggle over the categories of natural and unnatural should be seen in a similar light, as they also took on a moral judgment of what activities were appropriate in which communities.

Many other courts embraced Pennsylvania's turn to moral distinctions and arguments. The Vermont Supreme Court upheld a jury verdict against a canal company for diverting a stream and consequently flooding a marble quarry. The court emphasized the "wrongful[ness]" of the stream diversion (even though it recognized that the flooding was not foreseeable) and praised the *Rylands* decision in broad moral terms: "[T]he [*Rylands*] doctrine is founded in good sense; for where one, in managing his own affairs, causes, however innocently, damage to another, it is obviously only just that he should be the party to suffer; that he is bound so to use his own as not to injure another."[83]

The Ohio Supreme Court continued the theme of questioning the privileges and motivations of private industry. While conceding that these companies produce, "along with many evils . . . valuable services . . . to the public," the Ohio court observed that "they are not, in the eye of the law, public enterprises, but, on the contrary, are organized and maintained wholly and entirely for private gain; and so soon as gain ceases to follow their operation, just so soon do the operations themselves cease."[84]

Maryland's highest court explicitly held that property rights trumped social utility. While this decision dealt with a nuisance case, the court wrote broadly about liability in addition to adopting *Rylands*: "No principle is better settled than that where a trade or business is carried on in such a manner as to interfere with the reasonable and comfortable enjoyment by another of his property, . . . a wrong is done to the neighbor, for which an action will lie, . . . although the business may be a lawful business, and one *useful to the public*, and although the best and most approved appliances may be used in the conduct and management of the business."[85] This passage is a fairly clear articulation of strict liability from a rights perspective and a rejection of the instrumental perspective. Again, the court might have framed this passage (anachronistically) in terms of internalizing negative externalities or some more contemporary economic argument, but instead, the court put the harm in terms of "wrongs" trumping "usefulness." Other courts around the country approvingly cited this particular passage from the Maryland Supreme Court.[86] The Maryland court continued with the questioning of industrial self-interest and linked private interests and public duties: "Having brought this water upon its premises to be used by it *for [the defendant's] own purposes*, the defendant was *bound* to provide proper drains or means for its escape without injury to the property of others."[87] When New York switched from opposing to adopting *Rylands* after the flood, it abandoned its economic arguments from *Losee* and emphasized the language of naturalness versus unnaturalness, a more moralist theme.

Federal judges and appointed state judges generally ignored or rejected *Rylands*, while elected state judges overwhelmingly adopted *Rylands* or a similar strict liability rule. Moreover, it was the elected judges who shifted from economic arguments to moralistic arguments as they adopted strict liability. It makes sense that elected judges were more likely than appointed judges to respond to disastrous events and adopt strict liability, an intuitive conclusion. However, counterintuitively, judges elected to relatively long terms were far more likely to adopt strict liability in the wake of these disasters and public fears than judges elected to shorter terms. Some of these judges never expected to face another election, but even without direct political pressure, they were the most responsive group of judges in adopting *Rylands* after the flood. To put it simply, elected judges were more populist, and judges elected to long terms were superpopulist.[88]

Pennsylvania was a striking example of this pattern because it had extended the terms of Supreme Court justices to remarkably long twenty-one-year terms as a reaction to corruption in the 1870s. Pennsylvania elites had become increasingly exasperated by corruption and party machines. These leaders called for a new constitutional convention in 1873.[89] Across the spectrum, debate at the 1873 convention focused on insulating the judiciary from the rank partisanship that infected the political branches of Pennsylvania government.[90] In the 1870s, urban machine politics led to "the tyranny of local political bosses of the majority party."[91] Pennsylvania's leaders listed "the conferring of political patronage upon the courts" among the issues that should be addressed at the convention.[92] In an editorial, a prominent civic affairs leader laid out three broad aims that would need to be accomplished, one of which was achieving "prompt judicial protection against municipal corruption."[93]

The 1873 convention reached a compromise to extend the terms of Supreme Court justices from an already lengthy fifteen-year term to the quasi-life term of twenty-one years. Longer terms were intended not to insulate judges from the people but rather to insulate judges from corruption so that they could better serve the people that had elected them in the first place. It is not surprising that these judges generally would respond to the Johnstown Flood by siding with public perceptions rather than industry. Even if the public did not know anything about *Rylands* or tort doctrine, these judges were able to translate a more general concern about modern hazards into a specific doctrinal change, regardless of industry's preferences.

One interpretation of these patterns is that the state bench was less influenced by the pressures of upcoming elections and more by the selection effect of past elections. Shorthand for these effects are filtering, role fidelity, and fear and favor. First, these elections created a populist filter: some elite professional jurists were filtered out of the partisan political process, while local lawyer politicians were filtered in. Second, elected judges then conceived of their legitimacy as being democratically accountable—even if they never faced another election. I suggest their role fidelity as elected judges led them to perceive public opinion as an important factor in their decisions. After winning popular elections, these judges were more likely to have embraced their democratic legitimacy (whether it was more fact or fiction). In his 1975 work *Justice Accused*, Robert Cover explains that mid-nineteenth-century judges who opposed slavery often ruled against fugitive slaves because they set aside their conscience and constituency in favor of formalistic rule of law. His term for this adherence to formalism was "role fidelity," and in his case, appointed judges were faithful to a professional role that led them to detach from their own personal views, from public opinion, and even from morality.

In the case of late nineteenth-century tort law, I suggest the mirror image: elected judges had a role fidelity more similar to legislators than to appointed judges in that they were entrusted and empowered to shape the law in light of recent events, public opinion, and their own moral views. The change to judicial elections was a shift from a formalistic approach based on professional training and elite selection to a more democratic approach that elevated the importance of both constituency and conscience. This different self-conception would lead judges to respond to events and regard public opinion as a legitimate influence on their rulings. Even if some of these initial elections were the product of machine politics, partisanship, and even an unfair vote, I speculate that judges were able to "filter" out those experiences (a second, more internal filtering process) and imagine that their election was the legitimate will of the public.

Even if elections had a populist filtering effect and altered the judges' mental approaches to law to make them more populist, almost all state judges served for a term of years and would have to face the political process—whether appointment or election—to retain their seats. The evidence suggests that special interests and party politics were powerful influences in that political process and would counterbalance the populist impulse generated by elections. Elected judges with more job security could be more faithful to their role (hence, role fidelity) and public opinion. Thus the counterintuitive historical pattern demonstrated by the evidence—that judges elected to long terms were the most responsive—actually makes sense when we consider the countervailing pressures of populism versus special interests in elections. The courts and the literature on judicial independence often refer to these forces and remark that judges must be able to interpret and apply the law "without fear or favor."[94] With regard to *Rylands*'s adoptions, appointed judges generally were unresponsive, elected judges were responsive, and judges elected to long terms were the most responsive.[95] Viewing the Johnstown Flood in the broader history of American tort law, it is apparent that the Pennsylvania Supreme Court was both a follower—in being responsive to the disaster and changing public perceptions of risk—and a national leader in adopting modern tort doctrine.

NOTES

Jed H. Shugerman is a professor of law at Fordham University.

1. *See* Jed Shugerman, "The Floodgates of Strict Liability: Bursting Reservoirs and the

Adoption of Fletcher v. Rylands in the Gilded Age," *Yale Law Journal* 110 (2000): 333, 341.

2. A. W. B. Simpson, "Legal Liability for Bursting Reservoirs: The Historical Context of Rylands v. Fletcher," *Journal of Legal Studies* 13 (1984): 239n117.

3. Fletcher v. Rylands, 159 Eng. Rep. 737, 740 (Ex. 1865).

4. Simpson, "Legal Liability," 241–42.

5. Kenneth Abraham, "Rylands v. Fletcher: Tort Law's Conscience," in *Torts Stories*, ed. R. Rabin and S. Sugarman (New York: Foundation Press, 2003), 211.

6. Rylands, 159 Eng. Rep. 744–47. At the time of the accident, the doctrine of *respondeat superior* did not make an employer legally responsible for independent contractors. *See* William L. Prosser, *Handbook on the Law of Torts* (St. Paul, Minn.: West Publishing, 1964), 480, § 70. This rule applies today, although there are many exceptions, including one for "inherently dangerous activities." Ibid.; *see also* John W. Wade, *Prosser, Wade and Schwartz's Cases and Materials on Torts*, 10th ed. (New York: Foundation Press, 2000), 666.

7. Fletcher v. Rylands, 1 L.R.-Ex. 265, 279 (Ex. Ch. 1866).

8. Ibid., 280.

9. Rylands v. Fletcher, 3 L.R.-E. & I. App. 330, 338–39 (H.L. 1868).

10. Ball v. Nye, 99 Mass. 582 (1868); Cahill v. Eastman, 18 Minn. 324, 334–37, 344–46 (1872).

11. Shipley v. Fifty Assocs., 101 Mass. 251 (1869), *aff'd*, 106 Mass. 194 (1870). *See infra* for other Massachusetts cases.

12. Davis v. Rich, 62 N.E. 375 (Mass. 1902).

13. Losee v. Buchanan, 51 N.Y. 476 (1873).

14. Brown v. Collins, 53 N.H. 442 (1873); Marshall v. Welwood, 38 N.J.L. 339 (1876).

15. 6 A. 453 (Pa. 1886) (hereafter Sanderson III).

16. Francis Bohlen, "The Rule in *Fletcher v. Rylands* (pt. 1)," *University of Pennsylvania Law Review* 59 (1911): 304.

17. Losee, 51 N.Y. at 485.

18. Ibid., 448.

19. Ibid.

20. Brown, 53 N.H. at 449–50.

21. 86 Pa. 401 (1878) (hereafter Sanderson I), *aff'd*; 94 Pa. 302 (1880) (hereafter Sanderson II).

22. Sanderson III.

23. Ibid., 401.

24. Ibid.

25. Ibid., 406.

26. Ibid., emphasis added.

27. Ibid., 408.

28. Ibid.

29. *See* Sanderson v. Pennsylvania Coal Co., 94 Pa. 302 (1880). Justice Woodward, the author of the 1878 opinion, had died. The 1880 opinion emphasized that the coal company's public benefits did not exempt them from liability for damage to private property.

30. Sanderson II, 94 Pa. 302, 307.

31. Pennsylvania Coal Co. v. Sanderson, 6 A. 453 (Pa. 1886).

32. Ibid., 460 ("The distinction is obvious; and we cannot see how Rylands v. Fletcher can be supposed to have any application in the consideration of this case.").

33. *See, e.g.*, ibid., 457.

34. Ibid., 454.

35. Ibid., 455.

36. Ibid., 457.

37. Ibid., 459.

38. Ibid., 464. This decision also added moralistic anti-Rylands language by arguing that the law should not obligate an "innocent person" to be an insurer against accidents.

39. *See* Shugerman, "Floodgates," for a discussion of these treatises.

40. *See, e.g.*, Lawrence M. Friedman, *A History of American Law* (New York: Simon and Schuster, 1973), 409–27; Morton Horwitz, *The Transformation of American Law, 1780–1860* (Cambridge, Mass.: Harvard University Press, 1977), 85–108; Bernard Schwartz, *The Law in America* (New York: McGraw-Hill, 1974), 55–59; G. Edward White, *Tort Law in America* (Oxford: Oxford University Press, 1980), 3–19; Guido Calabresi, "Some Thoughts on Risk Distribution and the Law of Torts," *Yale Law Journal* 70 (1961): 499, 515–17; Albert A. Ehrenzweig, "Negligence Without Fault," *California Law Review* 54 (1966): 1422, 1425–43; Charles O. Gregory, "Trespass to Negligence to Absolute Liability," *Virginia Law Review* 37 (1951): 359; Simpson, "Legal Liability," 209, 214–16; *cf.* Richard A. Posner, "A Theory of Negligence," *Journal of Legal Studies* 1 (1972): 29 (examining the era of fault and arguing that fault prevailed as the most economically efficient doctrine). *Contra* Robert L. Rabin, "The Historical Development of the Fault Principle: A Reinterpretation," *Georgia Law Review* 15 (1981): 925, 927; and Gary T. Schwartz, "Tort Law and the Economy in Nineteenth-Century America: A Reinterpretation," *Yale Law Review* 90 (1981): 1717, 1720.

41. *See* Gregory, "Trespass to Negligence"; William K. Jones, "Strict Liability for Hazardous Enterprise," *Columbia Law Review* 92 (1992): 1705, 1706–11; Virginia E. Nolan and Edmund Ursin, "The Revitalization of Hazardous Activity Strict Liability," *North Carolina Law Review* 62 (1987): 257; Rabin, "Historical Development," 961.

42. *See* Shugerman, "Floodgates."

43. *See* the graph at the end of this article for the patterns of adopting. "Leaning" means that the state had adopted a very similar rule without relying on Rylands, or that they had relied on Rylands, but with some recognition that it was controversial.

44. In the mid-1880s, Michigan, Illinois, and Iowa adopted or leaned toward Rylands. This trend before the Johnstown Flood might be attributable to the factor discussed in Shugerman, "Floodgates," as a background factor: urban growth and residential expansion near industrial activity. Chicago and other areas of the Midwest were experiencing rapid urban and industrial growth in the 1880s. *See* John T. Cumbler, *Northeast and Midwest United States: An Environmental History* (Santa Barbara, Calif.: ABC-CLIO, 2005), 138–41.

45. Douglas Newton, ed., *Disaster, Disaster, Disaster: Catastrophes Which Changed Laws* (New York: Watts, 1961), 17.

46. David McCullough, *The Johnstown Flood* (New York: Simon and Schuster, 1968).

47. *See* Newton, *Disaster*, 18.

48. Ibid., 36; McCullough, *Johnstown Flood*, 264.

49. McCullough, *Johnstown Flood*, 203.

50. Ibid., 224–25. The donations from numerous states and other countries totaled almost $4 million in cash, plus food and other necessities.

51. Ibid., 237.

52. *See* ibid., 241.

53. Ibid., 241–43, 255.

54. Ibid., 246.

55. *See* Shugerman, "Floodgates," for a survey of the media's outrage. *See also* "The Club Is Guilty," *N.Y. World*, June 7, 1889; "The Broken Dam," *Pittsburgh Commercial Gazette*, June 4, 1889; "The Dam Defective," *Pittsburgh Commercial Gazette*, June 5, 1889; "That Fatal Dam: An Expert Engineer Says It Was in Every Respect of Very Inferior Construction," *Pittsburgh Commercial Gazette*, June 8, 1889; "From the St. Louis Republic," *Pittsburgh Commercial Gazette*, June 5, 1889.

56. According to David McCullough's account, one claim was brought by Nancy Little against the club and another by James and Ann Jenkins against the members. However, while McCullough is one of the most talented historians of his generation, he is not a lawyer, and his descriptions of the cases are very short and vague, the procedural history is ambiguous, and it is even unclear who the defendants were. McCullough, *Johnstown Flood*, 258. McCullough does explain that the club was insolvent and had no assets and that "there is no account of how things went in court, as it was not the practice to record the proceedings of damage suits."

57. *See* ibid., 258–59 (noting how the victims' lawyers and the media stressed the difficulty of proving individual negligence).

58. The *American Law Review* was a bimonthly publication regarded as "the most influential legal periodical of the nineteenth century." Thomas A. Woxland and Patti J. Ogden, *Landmarks in American Legal Publishing* (St. Paul, Minn.: West Publishing, 1989), 48. Its notes were not student pieces but legal comments written by perhaps the most "distinguished . . . group of working editors" in the history of legal publishing. Erwin C. Surrency, *A History of American Law Publishing* (Dobbs Ferry, N.Y.: Oceana, 1990), 192. In the *Review*'s early years, its editorial staff resembled an all-star team of legal scholars and practitioners, including Oliver Wendell Holmes, Arthur Sedgwick, John C. Ropes, and John C. Gray. "American Law Periodicals," *Albany Law Journal* 2 (1870): 445, 449. For a discussion of the significance of these editors, *see* Surrency, *History*, 2. Another publication described this group as "illustrious." The *American Law Review* "earned . . . a large measure of influence, and its value to lawyers as an organ worthy to represent them, can hardly be over-estimated." Woxland and Ogden, *Landmarks*, 48.

59. McCullough, *Johnstown Flood*, 646.

60. Ibid., 647.

61. Ibid.

62. *See* R. M. M., "The Absolute Nuisance Theory in Pennsylvania," *University of Pennsylvania Law Review* 95 (1947): 783–85.

63. Robb v. Carnegie Bros. & Co., 22 A. 649 (Pa. 1891).

64. Ibid.

65. Ibid. The reversing Justices were Clark, Green, and Paxson.

66. *See* Thomas B. Cochran, ed., *Smull's Legislative Handbook* (Harrisburg, Pa.: Lane S. Hart, 1887), 351.

67. Robb, 22 A. at 650–51.

68. Ibid. ("But the defendants are not developing the minerals in their land or cultivating its surface. . . . The injury, if any, resulting from the manufacture of coke at this site, is in no sense the natural and necessary consequence of the exercise of the legal rights of the owner to develop the resources of his property.").

69. Ibid., 651.

70. Ibid.

71. 23 A. 219 (Pa. 1892).

72. 26 A. 644, 644–45 (Pa. 1893); *see also* Gavigan v. Atl. Ref. Co., 40 A. 834, 835 (Pa. 1898).

73. 26 A. at 645.

74. *See* Evans v. Reading Chem. Fertilizing Co., 28 A. 702 (Pa. 1894) (per curiam); Good v. City of Altoona, 29 A. 741 (Pa. 1894); Hindson v. Markle, 33 A. 74, 76 (Pa. 1895); Commonwealth v. Russell, 33 A. 709 (Pa. 1896); Robertson v. Youghiogheny River Coal Co., 33 A. 706 (Pa. 1896); Gavigan, 40 A. 834; Keppel v. Lehigh Coal & Navigation Co., 50 A. 302 (Pa. 1901); Campbell v. Bessemer Coke Co., 23 Pa. Super. 374, 380 (1903); Sullivan v. Jones & Laughlin Steel Co., 57 A. 1065 (Pa. 1904); Green v. Sun Co., 32 Pa. Super. 521 (1907); Vautier v. Atl. Ref. Co., 79 A. 814 (Pa. 1911); Welsh v. Kerr Coal Co., 82 A. 495 (Pa. 1912); Mulchanock v. Whitehall Cement Mfg., 98 A. 554 (Pa. 1916).

75. *See* Shugerman, "Floodgates"; for a list of cases, *see* Appendix A.

76. *See* Robb, 145 Pa. at 324.

77. 33 A. 709, 711 (Pa. 1896).

78. *See* Evans v. Reading Chem. Fertilizing Co., 28 A. 702 (Pa. 1894) (per curiam); Good v. City of Altoona, 29 A. 741 (Pa. 1894); Hindson v. Markle, 33 A. 74, 76 (Pa. 1895); Commonwealth v. Russell, 33 A. 709 (Pa. 1896); Robertson v. Youghiogheny River Coal Co., 33 A. 706 (Pa. 1896); Gavigan v. Atlantic Refining Co., 40 A. 834, 835 (Pa. 1898); Keppel v. Lehigh Coal & Navigation Co., 50 A. 302 (Pa. 1901); Campbell v. Bessemer Coke Co., 23 Pa. Super. 374, 380 (Pa. Super. 1903); Sullivan v. Jones & Laughlin Steel Co., 57 A. 1065 (Pa. 1904); Green v. Sun Co., 32 Pa. Super. 521 (1907); Vautier v. Atl. Ref. Co., 79 A. 814 (Pa. 1911); Welsh v. Kerr Coal Co., 82 A. 495 (Pa. 1912); and Mulchanock v. Whitehall Cement Mfg., 98 A. 554 (Pa. 1916).

79. Sullivan, 57 A. 1068. *Contra* Harvey v. Susquehanna Co., 50 A. 770 (Pa. 1902). Pennsylvania eventually distanced itself from Rylands and reembraced Sanderson during World War I and the conservative 1920s. *See* Alexander v.

Wilkes-Barre Anthracite Coal Co., 98 A. 794, 795–96 (Pa. 1916); and Householder v. Quemahoning Coal Co., 116 A. 40, 41 (Pa. 1922).

80. Campbell v. Bessemer Coke Co., 23 Pa. Super. 374, 380 (Pa. Super. 1903).

81. 40 A. 834, 835 (Pa. 1898).

82. Ibid., 835–36.

83. Gilson v. Delaware & H. Canal Co., 26 A. 70 (Vt. 1890).

84. Columbus & H. Coal & Iron Co. v. Tucker, 26 N.E. 630, 632 (Ohio 1891).

85. Susquehanna v. Malone, 20 A. 900 (Md. 1890).

86. The cases citing this passage at length are Frost v. Berkeley Phosphate Co., 20 S.E. 280, 283 (S.C. 1894); Susquehanna Fertilizer Co. v. Spangler, 39 A. 270, 271 (Md. 1898); Shelby Iron Co. v. Greenleaf, 63 So. 470, 471 (Ala. 1913); and United States v. Luce 141 F. 385, 417 (Del. 1905). This passage even found its way into Cooley's treatise on torts. However, Cooley defended the fault rule and applied this passage to nuisance law, rather than torts in general. Thomas Cooley, *A Treatise on the Law of Torts* (Chicago: Callaghan, 1907), 2, 1243–45. This case has been cited approvingly by the Tenth Circuit and the supreme courts of Arizona, California, Indiana, Iowa, New York, North Carolina, North Dakota, Oklahoma, Pennsylvania, Tennessee, Utah, and Washington.

87. Baltimore Breweries Co. v. Ranstead, 28 A. 273, 274 (Md. 1894), emphasis added.

88. Jed Shugerman, "The Twist of Long Terms: Judicial Elections, Role Fidelity, and American Tort Law," *Georgetown Law Journal* 98 (2010): 1349.

89. *Debates of the Convention to Amend the Constitution of Pennsylvania*, vol. 4 (Harrisburg, Pa.: Benjamin Singerly, 1873), 486.

90. Mahlon H. Hellerich, "The Origin of the Pennsylvania Constitutional Convention of 1873," *Pennsylvania History* 34 (1967): 158.

91. Ibid., 162.

92. Ibid., 66.

93. Ibid., 185.

94. *See, e.g.,* Judicial Code of Conduct, Canon 1 comment; Republican Party of Minn. v. Kelly, 63 F. Supp. 2d 967 (D. Minn. 1999); Hans A. Linde, "The Judge as Political Candidate," *Cleveland State Law Review* 40 (1992): 1.

95. For more on the history of elected judges, *see* Jed Shugerman, *The People's Courts: Pursuing Judicial Independence in America* (Cambridge, Mass.: Harvard University Press, 2012).

CHAPTER 16

The Supreme Court and Medical Malpractice Law

CHARLES L. BECKER, SHANIN SPECTER,

AND THOMAS R. KLINE

I. INTRODUCTION

Calling physicians to account for errors is nothing new. More than four thousand years ago, the Code of Hammurabi decreed, "If the doctor has treated a gentleman with a lancet of bronze and has caused the gentleman to die, or has opened an abscess of the eye for a gentleman with a bronze lancet, and has caused the loss of the gentleman's eye, one shall cut off his hands." Although Roman law replaced such retribution with compensation, it had long recognized claims for mala praxis, or "bad practice," and this theory of liability was carried forward into the English common law, which resolved the first known negligence suit against a physician in 1374.[1] The term *malpractice* can be traced to Sir William Blackstone's seminal 1768 text *Commentaries on the Laws of England*, which defines the term as a "great misdemeanor and offence at common law."[2]

In the United States, claims for medical malpractice began appearing with some regularity in the early 1800s. By midcentury, such claims had dramatically increased due to a number of factors, including an increase in all types of litigation that accompanied America's rapid industrialization, an increased focus on personal responsibility that slowly replaced notions of religious fatalism, and antielite sentiments against physicians and other professionals that marked the populism of Jacksonian democracy.[3] Whatever the cause, the effect was clear: the number of medical malpractice cases on appeals courts' dockets grew a remarkable 950 percent between 1840 and 1860.[4] One scholar noted in 1860 that most of the oldest physicians in almost every part of the country had by then been either sued or threatened with suit.[5]

Pennsylvania was at the leading edge of the rising tide of medical malpractice litigation. By 1850, perhaps only New York saw more malpractice suits.[6] This trend continued for approximately a century, until the 1960s, when a wholesale expansion of tort law spurred a further increase in the volume of such suits. Consequently, for more than a century and a half, the Pennsylvania Supreme Court has been called on to adopt and apply traditional tort concepts to medical malpractice litigation, often in novel circumstances. This chapter recounts the Court's important work in this regard. It begins with a discussion of how the common-law elements of negligence—duty, breach, causation, and damages—have been defined and applied in suits against healthcare providers to develop the unique body of medical malpractice law we recognize today. It next addresses the Court's review of statutes governing medical malpractice litigation and the promulgation of procedural rules specifically governing such litigation. Finally, the chapter reviews the Court's ongoing efforts to track medical malpractice filings and verdicts and to inform the public about the evolution of the litigation by publishing detailed statistics on its official website. As a whole, the chapter assesses the Court operating in four distinct capacities—as a common-law court, constitutional- and statutory-review court, rulemaking body, and research and public information bureau.

II. THE COURT'S COMMON-LAW DECISIONS ON MEDICAL MALPRACTICE

The Court has demonstrated a sophisticated approach to medical malpractice issues when acting as a common-law court, with its first such decision dating before the Civil War. While the common-law negligence elements of duty, breach, causation, and damages are commonly understood in tort litigation generally, they raise complicated issues when applied to the unusual circumstances of medical malpractice cases.

A. Duty

The Supreme Court's frequent and most important malpractice cases have defined the scope of a healthcare provider's duty of care to a patient. The earliest of these decisions, *McCandless v. McWha* in 1853,[7] addressed the fundamental question of whether a physician who has not acted negligently can be liable for a bad outcome experienced by a patient. On the one hand, an ancient strain of legal theory held physicians liable for any untoward result (a patient's death or the loss of an eye, punishable in the Code of Hammurabi), regardless of whether the physician did anything wrong. On the other hand, the common law largely supplanted this concept of strict liability with the fault-based precept that because bad results happen even when due care is provided, physicians should not be held liable in the absence of negligence. *McCandless*, the first Pennsylvania decision to use the term *malpractice*, involved a claim "for malpractice in setting a broken leg of the plaintiff."[8] Reflecting the older concept of strict liability, the trial court charged the jury that the physician could be held liable if the broken leg failed to heal straight and equal with the uninjured leg. The jury found for the plaintiff and the defendant appealed.

The Supreme Court vacated the verdict on the basis that the trial court had allowed the defendant to be found liable regardless of fault. According to the Court, a contract for medical services did not include a warranty of cure, a mere bad outcome without corresponding negligence does not constitute malpractice, and a surgeon's duty is only to provide reasonable skill and diligence "such as thoroughly educated surgeons ordinarily employ."[9] To be sure, the Court explained, "the law has no allowance for quackery," but it simply "demands *qualification* in the profession practiced—not extraordinary skill such as belongs only to a few men of rare genius and endowments, but that degree which ordinarily characterizes the profession."[10] A physician "is bound to be up to the improvements of the day" and "must apply himself with all diligence to the most accredited sources of knowledge" because the patient "is entitled to the benefit of these increased lights."[11] But liability can attach only if the physician is negligent.[12] This foundational statement of a physician's duty of care remains the law today.

The Court also spent considerable effort addressing whether a physician's standard of care is defined by local custom and practice, known as the "locality rule," or by the broader standards of the medical profession as a whole. The "locality rule" had taken hold in the eighteenth century and endured well into the following century as courts recognized that many physicians practiced in rural communities without ready access to cutting-edge medical advancements, and it was therefore unfair to subject them to a standard of care that reflected the more sophisticated practice in large cities.[13] At first, the Supreme Court embraced the "locality rule." In its 1959 decision in *Donaldson v. Maffucci*, the Court explained that a physician who is not a specialist "is required to possess and employ in the treatment of a patient the skill and knowledge usually possessed by physicians *in the same or similar locality*."[14]

Twelve years later, however, in its 1971 decision in *Incollingo v. Ewing*,[15] the Court rejected local custom as a valid component of a physician's duty to patients. In *Incollingo*, the defendant physician invoked the locality rule and argued that he was not negligent because his failure to pay attention to written warnings associated with a drug and his prescribing the drug over the telephone without having seen the patient was an accepted practice among local physicians. The Court rejected the argument that the medical profession may set its own standard of conduct by establishing a local custom of practice. Quoting Justice Oliver Wendell Holmes of the US Supreme Court, the Court stated, "What usually is done may be evidence of what ought to be done, but what ought to be done is fixed by a standard of reasonable prudence, whether it is usually complied with or not."[16]

Instead, henceforth, the standard of care of physicians in Pennsylvania would be an objective one—that is, "the statement that 'A physician is required to exercise only such reasonable skill and diligence as is ordinarily exercised in his profession' . . . is not to be taken in isolation, and in disregard of the admonition to give due regard to the advanced state of the profession and to exercise the care and judgment of a reasonable man in the exercise of medical skill and knowledge."[17] In a concurring opinion, Justice Samuel J.

Roberts voiced his agreement that in light of the modern state of medicine and the national dissemination of medical information, the locality rule was no longer sound:

> During the period of its original formulation in the middle and late nineteenth century the "locality rule" was plausibly expedient. The law was arguably wise in indulging in the assumption that medical knowledge, skill and care varied considerably from community to community. . . .
>
> Present day conditions, however, cast much doubt upon the rule. Modern systems of transportation and communication, the proliferation and widespread dissemination of medical literature, and the prevalence and availability of seminars and postgraduate courses make it both possible and desirable for *all* practitioners to be reasonably familiar with current medical advances. Furthermore, the major source of a physician's professional expertise is not the particular locality in which he practices but initially the institutions in which he received his education and professional training.
>
> In light of the foregoing, the locality rule is an anachronism. . . . The standard of care required of a specialist or general practitioner should be that of a reasonable specialist or general practitioner in similar circumstances practicing medicine in light of present day scientific knowledge.[18]

In 1981, ten years after *Incollingo*, the Supreme Court's application of an objective, "reasonable man" standard of care was incorporated into Pennsylvania's standard jury instructions. That basic instruction remains in effect today: "A physician must have the same knowledge and skill and use the same care normally used in the medical profession. A physician whose conduct falls below this standard of care is negligent."[19]

In addition to defining physicians' duties in the negligence context, the Court began to develop and enunciate the physician's duty to obtain a patient's informed consent. In its 1966 decision in *Gray v. Grunnagel*, the Court stated that in "the absence of an emergency, the consent of the patient is 'a prerequisite to a surgical operation by his physician' and an operation without the patient's consent is a technical assault."[20] The Court explained further that "it will be no defense for a surgeon to prove that the patient had given his consent, if the consent was not given with a true understanding of the nature of the operation to be performed, the seriousness of it, the organs of the body involved, the disease or incapacity sought to be cured, and the possible results."[21] More recently, in its 2008 decision in *Fitzpatrick v. Natter*, the Court expanded the ability to sue for lack of informed consent by holding that a patient "need not show that she would have chosen differently had she possessed the missing information, but only that the missing information would have been a substantial factor in this decision."[22]

In addition to recognizing this new duty to obtain informed consent, the Court also expanded traditional tort duties by imposing liability on surgeons for the acts of others under their supervision in the operating room and requiring hospitals to be responsible for malpractice that occurs within their walls. First, in its 1949 decision in *McConnell v. Williams*, the Court ruled that surgeons can be vicariously liable for the negligent actions of nurses or interns in the operating room.[23] *McConnell* involved a hospital intern who improperly introduced silver nitrate into the eye of a young child in the operating room, rendering her blind.[24] Finding that the surgeon could be held liable, the Court explained, "It can readily be understood that in the course of an operation in the operating room of a hospital, and until the surgeon leaves that room at the conclusion of the operation . . . he is in the same complete charge of those who are present and assisting him as is the captain of a ship over all on board."[25] Ever since, the "captain of the ship" doctrine has been a recognized basis on which surgeons can be liable for the acts of others in the operating room. In two subsequent decisions, *Shull v. Schwartz* and *Scacchi v. Montgomery*, both decided in 1950, the Court clarified that the "captain of the ship" doctrine is limited to events that occur *inside* the operating room and during the course of an ongoing operation.[26]

The Court also expanded the liability of hospitals. Traditionally, hospitals were nonprofit endeavors that were run by religious or other charitable organizations. Because they were charitable, hospitals were generally protected from civil liability under the theory that recovery of a judgment by one patient would deplete resources that could be used to treat other patients. This protection was known as "charitable immunity." However, by the mid-twentieth century, medicine was increasingly seen as a business, and for-profit interests began to acquire and operate hospitals. As this occurred, the traditional rationale for protecting charitable resources gave way to the recognition that hospitals, even ones that remained affiliated with religious or other charitable groups, were professionally managed, multi-million-dollar enterprises that should be subject to the same rules and liabilities as other such enterprises.

In 1965, in *Flagiello v. Pennsylvania Hospital*, the Court considered whether the time had come to abolish charitable immunity and subject hospitals to civil liability.[27] While the Court was divided on whether the public policy considerations for and against continuing immunity should be balanced by the legislature rather than the judiciary, the Court finally concluded that the issue involved a legal question that it was duty bound to resolve. "[W]e have a duty to perform," the Court reasoned, "and that is to see that justice, within the framework of law, is done."[28] Having resolved to decide the question, the Court had little doubt that charitable immunity as "an instrument of injustice . . . long ago outlived its purpose if, indeed, it ever had a purpose consonant with sound law."[29] *Flagiello*, which presaged the widespread abolition of charitable immunity in the United States in the decade that followed, enabled plaintiffs to bring suits against not only individual medical professionals but also the nonprofit institutions that employed them.

The duties of hospitals were further expanded in 1991, when the Court rendered its landmark decision in *Thompson v. Nason Hospital*.[30] Even after the abolition of charitable immunity in *Flagiello*, hospitals were not themselves viewed as healthcare providers that could be subject to medical malpractice liability. Instead, such liability could be asserted only against physicians, nurses, and other professionals. Hospitals could be subjected to liability only on agency principles like *respondeat superior*. They could not be sued directly in negligence for deficient or nonexistent policies and procedures governing medical practice within their walls. This changed with *Thompson*'s recognition of a cause of action for "corporate negligence," which provided that hospitals owe duties directly to patients to (1) use reasonable care in the maintenance of safe and adequate facilities and equipment, (2) select and retain only competent physicians, (3) oversee all persons who practice medicine within its walls as to patient care, and (4) formulate, adopt, and enforce adequate rules and policies to ensure quality care for the patients.[31] In 2012, in *Scampone v. Highland Park Care Ctr., LLC*, the Court extended *Thompson*'s theory of corporate negligence to nursing homes as well.[32]

Finally, during the 1990s, the Court confronted complicated issues regarding whether healthcare providers owe duties to people other than their patients, including the public at large. In *Goryeb v. Commonwealth Department of Public Welfare*, the Court imposed a duty of care on mental health professionals to victims who were shot by a discharged mental patient because the victims "could foreseeably be affected" if the discharge of the patient was improper.[33] The Court further extended this duty in *Sherk v. County of Dauphin*, holding that under the logic of *Goryeb*, a police officer shot by a released mental patient could recover from the hospital for its negligent release of the patient.[34]

The Court limited this duty to third parties in *Estate of Witthoeft v. Kiskaddon*. In that case, an ophthalmologist knew through an examination that his patient's corrected eyesight did not meet the 20/70 standard required for a driver's license in Pennsylvania.[35] The ophthalmologist failed to report the patient's deficient eyesight to state authorities, and the patient later struck and killed a bicyclist while driving. The Court declined to create a private cause of action against the defendant, explaining, "[I]t is an unreasonable extension of the concepts of duty and foreseeability to broaden a physician's duty to a patient and hold a physician liable to the public at large within the factual scenario of this case."[36]

The Court's reluctance to impose additional duties on healthcare professionals was further seen in *Althaus v. Cohen*, in which a psychiatrist diagnosed and treated a child for sexual abuse by her parents. The child was removed from the family home and the parents were arrested and prosecuted by the local police. All charges were dropped when it was determined that the child had fabricated the accusations and was unable to distinguish fact from fantasy. The parents sued the psychiatrist, alleging negligence in diagnosing and treating the child and exacerbating the child's condition. After a jury returned a verdict in the plaintiff's favor, the Supreme Court considered whether the psychiatrist owed a duty of care to the parents as a threshold matter. Recognizing that the parents were third parties to the counseling relationship, the Court declined to "impos[e] a duty of care to non-patients upon a therapist who treats sexually abused children."[37]

B. Breach

In addition to defining the duties owed to patients, the Court has rendered a number of important decisions addressing the circumstances in which a duty is breached. The earliest such cases involved the question of whether a physician who makes an error of judgment breaches the standard of care if the error itself does not constitute negligence. This "error of judgment" doctrine holds that medical practice is complicated and that an error that would have been made by a reasonable physician cannot be a basis for liability. Therefore, a plaintiff must show that the physician's decision breached the standard of care, not merely that it was erroneous. Applying the doctrine in a physician's favor, the Court's 1891 decision in *Williams v. Le Bar* explained that where "the most that a case discloses is an error of judgment on the surgeon's part, there is no liability."[38] In 1939, the Court again addressed the doctrine in *Hodgson v. Bigelow*, holding that liability does not attach for a physician's error of judgment "unless it is so gross as to be inconsistent with the degree of skill which it is the duty of every physician to possess."[39] Finally, in its 1935 decision in *Duckworth v. Bennett*, the Court again ratified the "error of judgment" doctrine.[40]

In 2014, the Court revisited the "error of judgment" doctrine and, in a sharply divided vote, ruled that its inclusion in a jury charge required a new trial because it unnecessarily confused the question of negligence before the jury. Specifically, in *Passarello v. Grumbine*, the Court concluded that the instruction was confusing because it asked the jury to not only determine whether a physician was negligent because of a failure to adhere to an objective standard of care but also consider whether the physician's "error" in the exercise of his or her "judgment" concerning an objective standard of care is not negligence.[41]

While *Duckworth*'s reliance on the "error of judgment" doctrine is no longer viable, the case remains notable for its articulation of the "two schools of thought" doctrine, which holds that a physician does not breach a duty of care by choosing, in the exercise of his or her professional judgment, one of two or more accepted courses of treatment.[42] The doctrine remains a viable defense under Pennsylvania law, though it was limited under certain circumstances by three cases decided within a year of each other in the early 1990s. In its 1992 decision in *Jones v. Chidester*, the Court noted that the doctrine operates as "a complete defense to malpractice" but stated that a "school of thought should be adopted not only by 'reputable and respected physicians' in order to insure quality but also by a 'considerable number' of medical practitioners."[43] In *Levine v. Rosen*, also in 1992, the Court held that the doctrine does not apply in cases claiming failure to diagnose.[44] Finally, in *Sinclair by*

Sinclair v. Block, decided in 1993, the Court held that the doctrine does not apply where a physician improperly performed a medical procedure.[45]

C. Causation

Although not as frequent as cases involving duty, the Court's causation cases have had a lasting impact on Pennsylvania medical malpractice law. First, in its 1966 decision in *Dornon v. Johnson*, the Court held that a physician's breach of duty must be a "substantial factual cause" of the injury for which damages are sought.[46] This concept, later referred to as "substantial factor," or "factual cause," continues to be the benchmark for proving causation in medical malpractice cases.

The Court's 1978 decision in *Hamil v. Bashline*, one of the most important medical malpractice rulings ever handed down in Pennsylvania, further refined the standard for causation.[47] That case involved whether and how a plaintiff can meet the traditional "substantial factor" standard of proving causation in a case where the harm might have occurred regardless of what the defendant did (or did not do) to prevent it.

The facts of *Hamil* were straightforward. The plaintiff and her husband presented to the emergency room at a hospital with her husband complaining of severe chest pains. As the hospital did not have working electrocardiogram equipment, the plaintiff was forced to transport her husband to a private physician's office for further evaluation. Her husband died at that office during the electrocardiogram. The plaintiff filed a wrongful death action.[48] At trial, her expert could not testify with the usual reasonable degree of medical certainty that the hospital's failure to have working electrocardiogram equipment caused the decedent's death because he might well have died of a heart attack even if the hospital had working equipment. Recognizing that any greater certainty was impossible, the plaintiff's expert testified that the negligence "probably" caused the decedent's death and that there was a 75 percent chance that the decedent would have survived had the hospital possessed working electrocardiogram equipment. The plaintiff lost the verdict, and on appeal, the Supreme Court discussed the burden of proving causation in a case where the harm might have occurred even if the defendant was not negligent.

The Court began its analysis by explaining that the plaintiff's negligence claim amounted to a claim for negligent performance of an undertaking to render services as described in the Restatement (Second) of Torts, Section 323. This provision encompasses situations where a defendant failed in a duty to protect the plaintiff against harm from another source, necessitating an inquiry into (1) what happened and (2) whether the harm might have been avoided had the defendant acted in a nonnegligent manner.[49] The Court went on to explain that "such cases by their very nature elude the degree of certainty one would prefer and upon which the law normally insists before a person may be held liable. Nevertheless, so that an actor is not completely insulated because of uncertainties as to the consequences of his negligent conduct, Section 323(a) tacitly acknowledges this difficulty and permits the issue to go to the jury upon a less than normal threshold of proof."[50]

Applying this standard, the Court held that once a plaintiff has demonstrated that the defendant's acts or omissions "have increased the risk of harm to another, such evidence furnishes a basis for the fact-finder to go further and find that such increased risk was in turn a substantial factor in bringing about the resultant harm; the necessary proximate cause will have been made out if the jury sees fit to find cause in fact."[51] *Hamil* thus established the process for proving causation under the rubric of increased risk of harm in medical malpractice cases.

Although *Hamil* arose in the context of a claim for negligent treatment, the Court extended this precedent to cases involving a physician's misdiagnosis, such that evidence that the misdiagnosis increased the risk of harm is sufficient to create a jury question on causation.[52] The Court has also made clear that an evidentiary showing through expert medical testimony, made with a reasonable degree of medical certainty[53] that a defendant increased the risk of harm sustained by the plaintiff, suffices to make out a prima facie case of liability.[54] The Court has subsequently explained that *Hamil* and its progeny require a twofold analysis on causation: (1) whether the expert could testify to a reasonable degree of certainty that the defendant's action could cause the harm sustained by the plaintiff and then (2) whether the acts complained of caused the actual harm suffered by the plaintiff.[55]

In 1981, three years after *Hamil*, the Court rendered another landmark causation decision that considered whether expert testimony is required to establish causation in all medical malpractice cases or whether an inference of negligence might arise, without expert testimony, where direct proof of causation is absent but the circumstances indicate that the defendant must have been negligent. This inference of negligence is known as "*res ipsa loquitur*," which allows a jury to find negligence without expert testimony where the defendant's conduct is the only plausible explanation for a plaintiff's harm. In previous cases, the Court precluded *res ipsa loquitur* in the medical malpractice context,[56] but it considered the question anew in 1981 in *Jones v. Harrisburg Polyclinic Hospital*.[57]

In *Jones*, the plaintiff suffered nerve pain in her neck, back, and arms as a result of abdominal surgery. Because the plaintiff was unconscious during the surgery, she had no direct evidence of what caused the injury. As a result, she invoked *res ipsa loquitur* and argued that the only plausible explanation for her nerve pain was malpositioning during surgery. The jury returned a verdict in the plaintiff's favor. After the Superior Court reversed, the Supreme Court reinstated the verdict on grounds that the plaintiff was permitted to rely on *res ipsa loquitur* in a medical malpractice case. The Court acknowledged its prior reticence to recognize *res ipsa loquitur* in the medical malpractice setting[58] and explained that "[t]here is no longer a need to be reluctant to permit circumstantial proof in medical malpractice cases where the nature of the evidence provides the requisite reliability of the inference sought to be drawn."[59] It concluded that the inference of negligence should be permitted in those medical malpractice cases where the evidence is such that "it can be established from expert medical testimony that such an event would not ordinarily occur absent negligence."[60]

In its 2003 *Toogood v. Owen* decision, the Court confirmed that *res ipsa loquitur* is a "procedural bypass to at least an inference, if not a direct proof, of negligence" for plaintiffs in medical malpractice suits.[61] At the same time, the Court cautioned that the doctrine "must be carefully limited" and "the realm of reasonable choice is best defined by those engaged in the practice."[62]

D. Damages

Although the Court's decisions regarding damages in medical malpractice cases have not been as prominent as rulings on duty, breach, and causation, a notable exception is the 1980 decision in *Kaczkowski v. Bolubasz*, which involved the calculation of a plaintiff's future lost earning capacity.[63] Prior to 1980, calculation of such lost earning capacity required a reduction to present value without accounting for inflation or increases in productivity. This resulted in insufficient awards for future lost earnings.[64] In *Kaczkowski*, the Court agreed that this approach "sacrifices accuracy to the prejudice of the victim by failing to compensate the victim to the full extent of the injury sustained."[65] The Court explained that it had a "responsibility to the citizenry to keep abreast of changes in our society"[66] and that the evolution of modern economics means that "the courts of this Commonwealth can no longer maintain their ostrich-like stance and deny the admissibility and relevancy of reliable economic data concerning the impact of productivity and inflation on lost future earnings."[67] To achieve a fairer approach, the Court adopted the "total offset method" for projecting an award of future lost earnings. This method specifically considers inflation and productivity increases and assumes that such factors will offset interest rates over time. Because these factors offset, there is no need to reduce an award of future wages to present value. As the Court explained, the total offset method "assumes that the effect of the future inflation rate will completely offset the interest rate, thereby eliminating any need to discount the award to its present value."[68]

III. THE COURT'S HANDLING OF STATUTES GOVERNING MEDICAL MALPRACTICE LITIGATION

In addition to applying common-law principles to the peculiarities of medical malpractice litigation, the Supreme Court has been frequently called on to interpret statutes governing aspects of that litigation. These statutes first surfaced in the 1960s and have presented important issues of statutory construction and constitutional law.

In the area of mental health law, the legislature enacted the Mental Health and Mental Retardation Act (MHMRA)[69] in 1966 and the Mental Health Procedures Act (MHPA)[70] in 1976. The Court has been required to interpret both statutes in response to medical negligence claims. In *Rhines v. Herzel*, a patient in a mental hospital was killed by another patient with known homicidal tendencies who was allowed to associate with other patients without supervision.[71] The hospital argued that it was statutorily immune from suit under the MHMRA.[72] The Court rejected this argument, holding that the statutory immunity provision did not apply to claims of gross negligence and that gross negligence had been pled by allegations that the hospital allowed the patient to kill another and "conceal her body in the hospital grounds for several weeks thereafter."[73]

In 1989, the Court faced a similar question under the MHPA in *Farago v. Sacred Heart General Hospital*.[74] There, a patient in a co-ed inpatient psychiatric unit reported that she had been raped in a bathroom by a male patient.[75] After reviewing the circumstances and the statute, the Court found that the hospital had not been negligent in treating the patient in the "least restrictive environment" possible and that the hospital had not acted in a grossly negligent manner that would be required to withhold their statutory immunity.[76]

In 1974, the legislature enacted the Peer Review Protection Act (PRPA).[77] This important statute was intended to help hospitals self-regulate by evaluating physicians to determine if they should have privileges at a hospital and to provide immunity from liability for doing so.[78] However, in *Cooper v. Delaware Valley Med. Ctr.*, the plaintiff alleged that the hospital was using its review board maliciously to discriminate against physicians in receiving new patients in favor of the controlling member of the board. The Court found that although the act was intended to protect hospitals in many respects, it did not protect hospitals from a malicious abuse of the peer review process.[79]

The PRPA's confidentiality provision also has been subjected to judicial scrutiny. In *Hayes v. Mercy Health Corp.*, a physician sought discovery of an audiotape recording of the board's peer review session that addressed his performance.[80] In deciding that the physician was entitled to the tape, the Court held that the confidentiality provision was intended to protect the peer review process from litigation by patients but did not apply to participants or subjects seeking to determine if the peer review process had been misused.[81]

In 1975, the legislature enacted the Health Care Services Malpractice Act (HCSMA),[82] which sought to directly regulate medical malpractice claims by, inter alia, requiring such claims to be submitted to mandatory arbitration. The Court's initial review of the HCSMA occurred in its 1978 decision in *Parker v. Children's Hospital of Philadelphia*, which challenged the constitutionality of the mandatory arbitration requirement.[83] The Court allowed the legislature's experiment with mandatory arbitration for medical malpractice claims to continue, finding that "deference to [the] coequal branch" required an allowance of a "reasonable period of . . . time to test the effectiveness of the legislation."[84]

Revisiting the same challenge two years later in *Mattos v. Thompson*, the Court found that while a reasonable and short delay to allow for arbitration would be constitutional, the provision had left six cases unresolved for four years, and 73 percent of all cases filed had not been resolved since the statute was enacted.[85] Having provided time to test the effectiveness of the act, the Court struck down the section enabling original jurisdiction to the arbitration panel, holding that it impermissibly interfered with the right to a jury trial guaranteed by Article I, Section 6 of the Pennsylvania Constitution.[86]

Lower courts initially read *Mattos* narrowly, requiring the Court to elaborate on the decision in a string of subsequent cases. First in *Chiesa v. Fetchko*, the Court held that all provisions of the arbitration process of the act had been declared unconstitutional; therefore, the courts did not have to consider collateral sources in their damage awards.[87] Then in *Heller v. Frankston*, the Court corrected the Commonwealth's mistaken belief that the decision in *Mattos* allowed concurrent jurisdiction between the courts and arbitration panels in a case regarding a dispute over the contingency fees allowed under the act.[88] There the Court again expressed that all provisions regarding the arbitration process were unconstitutional under the right-to-trial provision of the Pennsylvania Constitution and that the attorney's contingency fees were both "ancillary to and a component of that arbitration scheme."[89] The Court also reiterated that *Mattos* completely nullified Articles III, IV, V, and VI of the act.[90]

In the 1990s, the Court had occasion to address several issues related to the Catastrophic Loss (CAT) Fund, a state-affiliated entity that provided additional coverage to qualified healthcare providers beyond their primary insurance.[91] In *American Casualty v. Phico Ins. Co.*, the Court held that while hospitals are statutorily eligible to draw on the CAT Fund for the actions of their employees, a nurse was not eligible to participate in the fund on an individual basis.[92] In *King v. Boetther*, the Court held that the fund was required to pay postjudgment interest on a medical malpractice verdict.[93] It thereafter held in *Legal Capital, LLC v. Medical Prof'l Liab. Catastrophic Loss Fund* that a plaintiff could assign its right to payment from the CAT Fund to a third party.[94]

The Court also addressed the activities the fund was required to insure. First, in *Physicians Ins. Co. v. Pistone*, the Court decided that a physician's sexual acts toward his patient were not covered "professional act[s]."[95] Later, the Court also held that a daily bath administered in a nursing home by a nurse's aide that was prescribed by a physician was a "professional act," and therefore the home was entitled to draw on the CAT Fund in a claim against the aide for the patient's burns when placed into a scalding bath.[96]

Lastly, in *Dellenbaugh v. Commonwealth Med. Prof'l Liab. Catastrophic Loss Fund*, the Court addressed the state's liability for claims made against healthcare providers who had not made their required premium payment, even when the fund had not reported the provider's noncompliance to the board, which allowed them to continue practice.[97] The Court reviewed the purpose of the act, which was to "make available professional liability insurance at a reasonable cost," and held that it would be "inherently contrary" to this purpose to pay claims for providers who had not paid their annual surcharge.[98]

In *Lloyd v. Commonwealth Med. Prof'l Liab. Catastrophic Loss Fund*, the Court revisited the question of whether the CAT Fund properly denied a claim based on a hospital's failure to pay a surcharge fee.[99] There, a hospital failed to pay the fund's required premiums for a physician as part of the hospital-physician employment agreement. On filing a claim with the fund, the hospital was notified that it would be denied, at which point it belatedly paid the surcharge.[100] After a large verdict for the plaintiff, the physician tendered the primary insurance along with "any and all rights" against the fund or hospital. The plaintiff then pursued the fund, challenging it on three separate grounds: (1) the plaintiff challenged the validity of the regulation that allowed the CAT Fund to exclude those who did not pay the surcharge, (2) the plaintiff argued that the fund did not suffer prejudice for the delayed payment of the surcharge, and (3) the plaintiff argued that the fund should be compelled to produce discovery on the times that it previously might have paid a claim for a provider who had not made timely payment.[101] The Court disregarded all three arguments, holding that the fund could not be compelled to pay claims for noncompliant providers and that, even if it had paid claims in the past, the Court could not compel it to violate the law again simply because it might have done so in the past.[102]

The Court also addressed a novel attempt to minimize self-insurance costs in *Milton S. Hershey Med. Ctr. v. Pa. Med. Prof'l Liab. Catastrophic Loss Fund*.[103] There, a hospital attempted to draw twice on the fund to pay a settlement: after tendering both the physician's and hospital's primary insurance along with the fund's million dollars in excess coverage for the physician, the hospital then attempted to claim a second million under a vicarious liability theory, primarily to avoid implicating the hospital's own self-funded excess insurance.[104] The Court rejected the hospital's claim. Although the justices agreed that the statute was ambiguous and could be read in that manner, the Court characterized the idea of paying twice for every claim as contrary to the fund's purpose, providing liability insurance "at reasonable cost."[105]

In 2002, the legislature enacted the Medical Care Availability and Reduction of Error (MCARE) Act[106] as a successor to the Health Care Services Malpractice Act. Among the MCARE Act's numerous salient provisions is a section defining the qualifications for expert testimony in medical malpractice actions.[107] The Court has rendered two significant decisions interpreting this aspect of the act. In its 2009 decision in *Freed v. Geisinger*, the Court held that an otherwise competent and properly qualified nurse was permitted to testify under the MCARE Act on medical causation about the cause of pressure sores, a subject well within a nurse's knowledge, and was not prohibited by the Professional Nursing Law from giving such expert opinion testimony.[108] In reaching its conclusion, the Court overturned its previous decision in *Flanagan v. Labe*, which had disallowed nurses from giving expert causation testimony.[109] In 2010, in *Vicari v. Spiegel*, the Court again addressed expert qualifications under the MCARE Act, making clear that a physician can give a standard-of-care opinion if, though he practiced in a different specialty than the defendant, he practiced in a specialty that had a substantially similar standard of care for the specific care at issue.[110]

IV. THE COURT'S PROMULGATION OF RULES RELATING TO MEDICAL MALPRACTICE AND EFFORTS TO TRACK MEDICAL MALPRACTICE FILINGS AND OUTCOMES

The HCSMA and the MCARE Act were promulgated partly in response to concerns about the volume and impact of medical malpractice litigation in Pennsylvania. In January 2003, the Supreme Court itself waded into the fray by promulgating two sets of rules specifically governing medical malpractice litigation. First, the Court promulgated Rules 1042.1 through 1042.12 governing professional liability actions (including actions arising out of alleged negligent medical care), which required any attorney filing a new professional liability action to file a "Certificate of Merit" warranting that an appropriate licensed professional had supplied to the attorney a written statement that there existed a reasonable probability that the defendant's actions were negligent and that such conduct was a cause in bringing about harm to the plaintiff.[111] Second, the Court promulgated Rule 1006(a.1), which created a new venue rule specific to medical malpractice actions.[112] This new rule made the venue for a medical malpractice action proper only where the cause of action arose, regardless of the location of the physician's office or any hospital affiliation.

In 2011, the Supreme Court amended Rule 1006(a.1) to fix a problem that arose from its original formulation. The original version of the rule provided that the venue was limited to the county where care was rendered. Several courts interpreted this provision as effectively precluding a plaintiff from bringing a medical malpractice action in Pennsylvania based on negligence that occurred in another state, even when jurisdiction existed in Pennsylvania, because there was no Pennsylvania county in which the negligence occurred.[113] The Court remedied this problem by further amending Rule 1006(a.1) to provide that the provision did not apply to causes of action that arose outside the Commonwealth; the general venue rules applied instead.[114]

The Court accompanied its promulgation of these rules with extensive follow-up research on medical malpractice litigation in Pennsylvania. Since 2003, the Court has maintained and published extensive statistics, broken down by county, case filings, jury verdicts, and nonjury verdicts in medical malpractice cases. These statistics are currently available on the "Research and Statistics" section of the Unified Judicial System's website (https://www.ujsportal.pacourts.us/). They show a dramatic reduction in medical malpractice filings since the Court promulgated these rules. From 2000 to 2003, an average of 2,733 new medical malpractice cases was filed per year in Pennsylvania. In 2010, that number had dropped to 1,490. In 2015, the most recent year for which statistics are available, the number had risen slightly to 1,530—still a reduction of more than 44 percent from the 2000–2003 average. The Supreme Court's diligence in collecting, maintaining, and publishing these statistics has helped demonstrate that the conditions that existed in the early 2000s no longer exist with respect to medical malpractice filings, and the Court continues to provide valuable information to Pennsylvanians about the operations of their judicial system.

V. CONCLUSION

Medical malpractice has become a major area of law and practice in Pennsylvania, fostered and managed by the Supreme Court over many decades through virtually every way that the Supreme Court acts—through its common-law decisions, its review of statutes under principles of statutory construction and under the Pennsylvania Constitution, its promulgation of procedural rules specific to medical malpractice litigation, and its research and publication of statistics on medical malpractice filings and results. This continues to be a dynamic area of law, and the Court will doubtless continue to play a vital role in defining and developing it.

NOTES

Charles L. Becker is a partner at Kline & Specter, PC, and a lecturer in law at the University of Pennsylvania Law School. Shanin Specter is a founding partner of Kline & Specter, PC, and an adjunct professor of law at the University of Pennsylvania Law School. Thomas R. Kline is a founding partner of Kline & Specter, PC; a chairman of the Drexel University Thomas R. Kline School of Law; and a lecturer in law at the University of Pennsylvania Law School. The authors thank the following 2014 summer associates at Kline & Specter, PC, for their invaluable assistance in producing this chapter: Andrew Austin, Ben Fabens-Lassen, Stephen Pederson, and Elia Robertson. The authors also thank John Hare for his encouragement and review of this chapter and for his essential leadership and oversight in the development of this book.

1. Stratton v. Swanlond, Y. B. 48 Edw. 3, fol. 6, pl. 2 (1375) (Eng.) (decided in 1374 but published in 1375), reprinted in Carlton B. Chapman, "Stratton vs. Swanlond: The Fourteenth-Century Ancestor of the Law of Malpractice," Pharos 45 (1982): 20–22.
2. See Robert I. Field, "The Malpractice Crisis Turns 175: What Lessons Does History Hold for Reform?," Drexel Law Review 4 (2011): 7, 10–11, discussing Sir William Blackstone, Commentaries on the Laws of England (Oxford: Clarendon Press, 1765–69), 122 (additional citations omitted).
3. Field, "Malpractice Crisis," 14–16.
4. James C. Mohr, "American Medical Malpractice Litigation in Historical Perspective," Journal of the American Medical Association 283 (2000): 1731–32.
5. Kenneth Allen De Ville, Medical Malpractice in Nineteenth-Century America: Origins and Legacy (New York: New York University Press, 1990), 2.
6. Field, "Malpractice Crisis," 12, citing De Ville, Medical Malpractice, 28–30 ("The proliferation of malpractice cases spread from state to state. It first appeared in western New York State. By 1850, it had reached Pennsylvania and Ohio and, by the mid-1850s, Vermont, New Hampshire, and Massachusetts.").
7. 22 Pa. 261 (1853).
8. Ibid., 267.
9. Ibid.
10. Ibid., emphasis in original.
11. Ibid.
12. Ibid.
13. See Small v. Howard, 128 Mass. 131, 132 (1880) (explaining that the locality rule protected rural and small-town practitioners by holding that that they were "not bound to possess that high degree of art and skill possessed by eminent surgeons practicing in large cities").
14. 156 A.2d 835, 838 (Pa. 1959), emphasis added.
15. 282 A.2d 206 (Pa. 1971).
16. Ibid. (quoting Texas & Pacific Railway Co. v. Behymer, 189 U.S. 468, 470 [1935]).
17. Ibid., 283.
18. Ibid., 298–99 (citations omitted).
19. Pennsylvania Supreme Court, Committee for Proposed Standard Jury Instructions, Civil Instructions Subcommittee, Pennsylvania

Suggested Standard Civil Jury Instructions, 4th ed. (Mechanicsburg, Pa.: Pennsylvania Bar Institute, 2011), § 14.10.

20. 223 A.3d 663, 669 (Pa. 1966) (citing Dicenzo v. Berg, 340 Pa. 305, 307 [1940]); *see also* Valles v. Albert Einstein Med. Ctr., 805 A.2d 1232, 1237 (Pa. 2002) (holding that informed consent requires a physician to "advise the patient of those material facts, risks, complications and alternatives to surgery that a reasonable person in the patient's situation would consider significant in deciding whether to have the operation").

21. 223 A.3d at 166. *See also* Morgan v. MacPhail, 704 A.2d 617, 620 (Pa. 1997) (refusing to apply the doctrine of informed consent to non-surgical procedures, such as therapeutic or intravenous administration of drugs).

22. 961 A.2d 1229 (Pa. 2008). The Court analyzed the informed consent issues in Fitzpatrick under the rubric of the Medical Care Availability and Reduction of Error (MCARE) Act, 40 P.S. §§ 1303.101, *et seq.*, which was enacted in 2002. Section 504 of the MCARE Act replaced the common law of informed consent, adding the concept that a plaintiff need only show that the missing information would have been a substantial factor in the patient's decision. The concept of "substantial factor" had not been present in the common-law rubric.

23. 65 A.2d 243 (Pa. 1949). Prior to this, the duty was far more restricted. *See, e.g.*, Stewart v. Manasses, 90 A. 574, 575 (Pa. 1914) ("The injury was caused by the negligence of a hospital nurse, for whose service the plaintiff paid the hospital, and whose work the defendant was under no duty to supervise, and would not have been permitted to supervise, and for whose negligence he was not responsible.").

24. McConnell, 65 A.2d at 244.

25. Ibid., 246 (citations omitted).

26. Shull v. Schwartz, 73 A.2d 402, 403 (Pa. 1950) ("Even though the intern had been negligent in post-operative treatment, where the surgeon did not personally participate therein, the surgeon cannot be held liable."); Scacchi v. Montgomery, 75 A.2d 535, 537 (Pa. 1950) ("There was no evidence that the hospital intern or nurse were negligent in their post-operative care of the patient, but even if they had been, the defendant, under the facts in this case, would not have been liable.").

27. 208 A.2d 192 (Pa. 1965).

28. Ibid., 202.

29. Ibid., 202; *see also* ibid., 197 ("If a hospital functions as a business institution, by charging and receiving money for what it offers, it must be a business establishment also in meeting obligations. . . . One of those inescapable obligations is that it must exercise a proper degree of care for its patients, and, to the extent that it fails in that care, it should be liable in damages as any other commercial firm would be liable.").

30. 591 A.2d 703 (Pa. 1991).

31. Ibid., 707.

32. 57 A.3d 582 (Pa. 2012).

33. 575 A.2d 545, 549 (Pa. 1990).

34. 614 A.2d 226, 229 (Pa. 1992) (construing both the Sovereign Immunity Act and the Mental Health Procedures Act [MHPA] to reach this holding).

35. 733 A.2d 623 (Pa. 1999).

36. Ibid., 630.

37. 756 A.2d 1166, 1170 (Pa. 2000) (balancing the social utility of treatment for the child against the foreseeability of the harm).

38. 21 A. 525, 525 (Pa. 1891).

39. 7 A.2d 338, 342 (Pa. 1939); *see also* Ward v. Garvin, 195 A. 885 (Pa. 1938).

40. 181 A. 558, 559 (Pa. 1935) ("Where competent medical authority is divided, a physician will not be held responsible if, in the exercise of his judgment, he followed a course of treatment advocated by a considerable number of his professional brethren in good standing in his community.").

41. 87 A.3d 285, 305–6 (Pa. 2014).

42. Duckworth, 181 A. at 559 (quoted previously).

43. 610 A.2d 964, 969 (Pa. 1992); *see also* ibid., 967 ("Where competent medical authority is divided, a physician will not be held responsible if in the exercise of his judgment he followed a course of treatment advocated by a considerable number of recognized and respected professionals in his given area of expertise.").

44. 616 A.2d 623, 628 (Pa. 1992) ("The two schools of thought doctrine does not relieve a doctor from liability for failure to recognize symptoms of an illness.").

45. 633 A.2d 1137, 1141–42 (Pa. 1993) (holding the trial court erred by failing to instruct the jury that the two schools of thought doctrine was inapplicable to plaintiff's claim that the doctor failed to properly apply forceps during delivery).

46. 218 A.2d 808, 809 (Pa. 1966).

47. 392 A.2d 1280 (Pa. 1978).

48. Ibid., 1282–84.
49. Ibid., 1286–87.
50. Ibid., 1288.
51. Ibid.
52. Gradel v. Inouye, 421 A.2d 674 (Pa. 1980); Jones v. Montefiore Hosp., 431 A.2d 920 (Pa. 1981).
53. Hamil, 392 A.2d at 1285; *see also* Gradel, 421 A.2d at 679 (1980) ("Expert medical opinion on causation need not be unqualified and absolute, i.e., stated in 'categorical terms'; ordinarily, it must establish that the injury was, to a 'reasonable degree of medical certainty,' caused by the alleged negligence.").
54. Hamil, 392 A.2d at 1288; *see also* Gradel, 421 A.2d at 679 ("Medical opinion need only demonstrate, with a reasonable degree of medical certainty, that a defendant's conduct increased the risk that the harm sustained by plaintiff would occur. The jury, not the medical expert, then has the duty to balance probabilities and decide whether defendant's negligence was a substantial factor in bringing about the harm.").
55. Mitzelfelt v. Kamrin, 584 A.2d 888, 894 (1990).
56. *See, e.g.,* Donaldson v. Maffucci, 156 A.2d 835, 838 (Pa. 1959) ("No presumption or inference of negligence arises merely because the medical care or surgical operation terminated in an unfortunate result which might have occurred even though proper care and skill had been exercised, and where the common knowledge or experience of laymen is not sufficient to warrant their passing of judgment. In such cases the doctrine of res ipsa loquitur or of exclusive control may not be invoked, and *expert testimony in support of the plaintiff's claim is an indispensable requisite to establish a right of action.*") (internal citations omitted); *see also* Smith v. Yohe, 194 A.2d 167, 170 (Pa. 1963) (noting that generally *res ipsa loquitur* is not applicable in medical malpractice suits, and "the *only* exception to the requirement that expert testimony must be produced is 'where the matter under investigation is so simple, and the lack of skill or want of care so obvious, as to be within the range of the ordinary experience and comprehension of even non-professional persons'"), emphasis in original.
57. 437 A.2d 1134 (Pa. 1981).
58. Ibid., 1137.
59. Ibid., 1138.
60. Ibid.
61. Toogood v. Owen J. Rogal, D.D.S., P.C., 824 A.2d 1140, 1147 (Pa. 2003).
62. Ibid., 1149; *see also* Quinby v. Plumsteadville Family Practice, Inc., 907 A.2d 1061 (Pa. 2006) (applying a three part test to invoke the doctrine of *res ipsa loquitur*).
63. 421 A.2d 1027 (Pa. 1980).
64. Ibid.
65. Ibid., 1032.
66. Ibid., 1033.
67. Ibid.
68. Ibid., 1034. In the MCARE Act, the General Assembly enacted a provision that requires future damages for loss of future earning capacity in a medical malpractice action to be reduced to present value "based upon the return that the claimant can earn on a reasonably secure fixed income investment." 40 P.S. § 1303.510. Under this approach, such damages are presented to the jury with evidence of the effect of inflation and productivity increases over time. Based on this information, the jury determines the appropriate discount rate to be applied to the present value calculation. *See* ibid. This approach may produce a larger or smaller lump-sum award for loss of future earnings capacity depending on whether the jury decides the interest will outpace inflation and productivity increases or vice versa. The jury also may decide that these factors will offset, resulting in an award consistent with the rationale of Kaczkowski.
69. 50 P.S. § 4603.
70. Ibid., §§ 7101, *et seq.*
71. 392 A.2d 298, 299 (Pa. 1978).
72. Ibid., 300 (discussing the MHMRA).
73. Ibid.
74. 562 A.2d 300 (Pa. 1989).
75. The patient was discovered in the bathroom with the patient by a staff member but only reported the attack two weeks later. Ibid., 301.
76. Ibid., 302 (discussing the MHPA, 50 P.S. §§ 7102, 7144).
77. 63 Pa.C.S. § 425.
78. 654 A.2d 547 (Pa. 1995).
79. Ibid., 554.
80. 739 A.2d 114, 115 (Pa. 1999).
81. Ibid., 118.
82. 40 P.S. § 1303.701(d).
83. 394 A.2d 932 (Pa. 1978).
84. Ibid., 940.
85. 421 A.2d 190, 194–95 (Pa. 1980).
86. Ibid., 195.
87. 475 A.2d 740 (Pa. 1984).
88. 475 A.2d 1291, 1296 (Pa. 1984).
89. Ibid., 1294.

90. Ibid., 1295.
91. 40 P.S. §§ 1301.101, *et seq.*
92. 643 A.2d 91 (Pa. 1994).
93. 645 A.2d 219 (Pa. 1994).
94. 750 A.2d 299 (Pa. 2000).
95. 726 A.2d 339 (Pa. 1999).
96. Strine v. Commonwealth Med. Care Availability & Reduction of Error Fund, 894 A.2d 733, 742 (Pa. 2006).
97. 756 A.2d 1172, 1173 (Pa. 2000).
98. Ibid., 1174.
99. 821 A.2d 1230 (Pa. 2003).
100. Ibid., 1231–32.
101. Ibid., 1232.
102. Ibid., 1235–37.
103. 821 A.2d 1205 (Pa. 2003).
104. Ibid., 1206–7.
105. Ibid., 1207, 1211.
106. 40 P.S. §§ 1303.101, *et seq.*
107. 971 A.2d 1201, 1210 (Pa. 2009) (discussing the MCARE Act).
108. Ibid., 1211.
109. Ibid., 1205, 1210–11 (discussing Flanagan v. Labe, 690 A.2d 183 [Pa. 1997]).
110. Vicari v. Spiegel, 989 A.2d 1277, 1280–81 (Pa. 2010).
111. Pa.R.C.P. 1042.1.
112. Pa.R.C.P. 1006.
113. *See, e.g.,* Searles v. Estrada, 856 A.2d 85 (Pa. Super. 2004).
114. The Official Note to Pa.R.C.P. 1006(a.1) states, "This provision does not apply to a cause of action that arises outside of this Commonwealth." The amendment, dated June 15, 2011, became effective August 1, 2011.
115. 104 A.3d 338 (Pa., November 19, 2014).

CHAPTER 17

The Ebb and Flow of the Law

The Supreme Court's Product Liability Jurisprudence

JAMES M. BECK

[**Editor's Note:** Pennsylvania product liability law was substantially altered by the Supreme Court's 2014 decision in *Tincher v. Omega Flex*.[115] That decision created a new hybrid standard for the determination of liability and recognized that "prior decisional law" might be considered anew in its wake. Because the Commonwealth's product liability law has begun a new era, we thought it useful to include two chapters assessing the history and present state of the law from two very different perspectives. These perspectives are offered by leadings practitioners from the defense and plaintiffs' bars, James M. Beck and Clifford A. Rieders, respectively. Their chapters illustrate that informed observers can look at the same body of case law and reach very different conclusions, which suggests that ultimate judgments about a court's work are often difficult to reach because they lie in the eye of the beholder.

—J. J. H.]

What follows is a short history of about 170 years of Pennsylvania Supreme Court product liability jurisprudence. I considered, but discarded, an alternative title, "What a Long, Strange Trip It's Been," because, beyond the number of years, the trajectory of Pennsylvania law in this area has not been particularly "long." A burst of change occurred between 1966 and 1977, bookended by *Webb v. Zern*[1] and *Azzarello v. Black Brothers Co.*[2] and driven by what the Court later described as a view of strict liability as a "hoped for panacea."[3] Before that time, Pennsylvania law was rather unremarkable. Afterward, until late 2014, the law was largely mired in expansive "panacea" rhetoric, while its centerpiece, the strict dichotomy between "negligence" and "strict liability" concepts, slowly devolved into contradiction and confusion. That dichotomy might have qualified post-*Azzarello* Pennsylvania law as "strange," at least in the sense of being—admittedly—idiosyncratic.[4] That, however, is no longer true.

This past, as they say, is prologue. For a decade, the Court commented on the short-comings of its product liability precedent. In late 2014, the Court finally overruled *Azzarello* and adopted a "composite" defect standard for design cases, incorporating elements of both "consumer expectation" and "risk-utility" tests.[5]

I. THE EARLY YEARS

The year 2015 marked the Supreme Court's 170th year of grappling with product liability issues. Its first decision was *Spencer v. Campbell*,[6] a premises liability product liability case in current jargon, addressing product-related injuries to a customer's property. The suit was against the owner of the product because, as the Court pointed out, the remote seller of the product was not in privity (i.e., in a direct transactional relationship) with the plaintiff and therefore not amenable to suit.[7] Thus privity was present at the creation of product liability law in Pennsylvania. The Court's first product liability decision involving an actual manufacturer, *Elkins, Bly & Co. v. McKean*,[8] dealt with an exception to privity for "guilty knowledge" amounting to a "crime against society."[9] Such knowledge was not proven—largely because of the "number of hands through which the [product] had passed"—and the verdict was set aside.[10]

These cases make clear that the early battles concerning product liability largely cemented privity.[11] In product liability tort cases, however, the tide started turning early. Pennsylvania departed from the requirement of privity where the product was intended for human consumption in *Catani v. Swift & Co* (1915).[12] Privity was outright abolished in tort-based (negligence) product liability cases in *Foley v. Pittsburgh–Des Moines Co.* (1949).[13]

Negligence, however, was not the plaintiffs' favored theory in early product liability cases, although plaintiffs did at times prevail, particularly on warning claims.[14] During this time, a plaintiff's contributory negligence, however small, was a complete defense, and in many cases involving the use of products, plaintiffs were to some degree contributorily negligent.[15] Thus plaintiffs preferred to bring actions involving allegedly defective products under warranty theories rather than negligence, and a notable change in the law assisted this transition.

By the mid-twentieth century, numerous commercial transactions, such as sales of goods, increasingly crossed state lines. State laws governing such transactions, dating to before the emergence of a truly national economy, varied significantly. Efforts to harmonize disparate state laws culminated in 1952 in the promulgation of a model act, the Uniform Commercial Code (UCC). On April 6, 1953, Pennsylvania became the first state to adopt the UCC.[16] Plaintiffs increasingly invoked the new warranties in the UCC to avoid the strictures of negligence, chiefly the defense of contributory negligence. Such contractual theories probably extended the reign of privity by shifting the underlying law from tort to contract, where a privity requirement was legislatively enacted in the UCC.[17] In warranty-based product liability actions, privity defeated implied warranty claims as late as 1963, in

Hochgertel v. Canada Dry Corp.,[18] and remained the law through 1966, in *Miller v. Preitz*,[19] where the Court deferred to the legislature.[20] That deference was ephemeral.

II. THE GREAT SHIFT: *WEBB* TO *AZZARELLO*

On the same day as *Miller*, the Court decided *Webb v. Zern*[21] and, in what might be the most portentous single page of text in the history of Pennsylvania tort law, discarded all prior Pennsylvania product liability precedent. To replace it, the Court "adopt[ed] a new basis of liability," the "modern attitude" of Restatement (Second) of Torts, Section 402A (1965).[22] Unlike the UCC, the Restatement (Second) was not a model act. Rather, it was a four-volume treatise published by a prestigious private group, the American Law Institute (ALI). Although it purported merely to "restate" existing common law, in reality, Restatement (Second), Section 402A, the treatise's most controversial section, revolutionized product liability law.

Under Section 402A, "strict liability" attached where (1) the defendant was a product "seller" and (2) the product at the time of sale (a) was in a "defective condition unreasonably dangerous to the user," (b) reached the user "without substantial change," and (c) caused "physical harm" to the user or the user's property.[23] *Webb* gave no reason for this dramatic shift beyond broadly incorporating the dissenting opinions in *Miller*.[24] Those dissents contain the first of many cost-shifting policy justifications for the then novel concept of "strict liability" regarding products: "The underlying purpose of Section 402A is to insure that the costs of injuries resulting from defective products are borne by the manufacturers that put such products on the market rather than by the injured persons who are powerless to protect themselves. . . . [T]he burden of injuries caused by defects in such products should fall upon those who make and market the products and the consuming public is entitled to the maximum of protection. Only through the imposition of liability under the provisions of Section 402A can this be accomplished."[25]

The terse manner in which the Supreme Court adopted Section 402A left many blank spaces in the law, some of which were filled in quickly, while others never were. In 1966, the same year that *Miller* and *Webb* were decided, the Court in *Ferraro v. Ford Motor Co.*[26] recognized assumption of the risk as a defense to strict liability.[27] Two years later, in *Bialek v. Pittsburgh Brewing Co.*,[28] the Court had its first encounter with the all-too-frequent argument that "negligence" evidence should be excluded from strict liability cases—in that instance, the defendant's manufacturing process. While such evidence was relevant to "due care," a negligence concept, it also "tend[ed] to show" that the product "was not defective or unreasonably dangerous."[29] The Court held in favor of admissibility: "It is elementary that evidence admissible for one purpose is not rendered inadmissible because it would be inadmissible for another purpose and because the jury might improperly consider it for that other purpose."[30] In a third case, *Bartkewich v. Billinger*,[31] the Court recognized the defenses of abnormal use and obvious danger. Neither a guard nor a warning was necessary where the plaintiff deliberately placed his hand in an operating glass crusher.[32] No grand statements of public policy accompanied any of these decisions, which favored the defense.

Such statements occurred where strict liability was invoked to expand liability. In *Kassab v. Central Soya Co.*,[33] the Court invoked "policy reasons" to abolish vertical privity[34] in contract-based warranty actions so that, "coextensive[ly]" with Section 402A, "large, financially responsible manufacturers who place their wares in the stream of commerce" could not escape contractual liability.[35] Judicial notions of social policy were even more evident in *Salvador v. Atlantic Steel Boiler Co.*,[36] which abolished horizontal privity as well.[37] All injured product users were granted standing to sue. Public policy considerations drove the Court to surmount statutory limits to liability: "[A] manufacturer by virtue of section 402A is effectively the guarantor of his products' safety. Our courts have determined that a manufacturer by marketing and advertising his product impliedly represents that it is safe for its intended use. We have decided that no current societal interest is served by permitting the manufacturer to place a defective article in the stream of commerce and then to avoid responsibility for damages caused by the defect."[38] The terms "guarantor" and "intended use" thus entered the product liability lexicon.

The strict liability ax fell on contributory negligence in 1975, in *McCown v. International Harvester Co.*,[39] where the plaintiff's negligence caused an accident, and he was injured when he violently struck his vehicle's interior. In a *Webb*-like four paragraphs, the Court abandoned more than a century of contributory negligence doctrine. Applied to strict liability, contributory negligence "would defeat one theoretical basis for" strict liability—namely, that the manufacturer "impliedly represents that [its product] is safe for its intended use."[40] Contributory negligence "would contradict this normal [consumer] expectation of product safety."[41]

Two years later, public policy was explicitly invoked in *Francioni v. Gibsonia Truck Corp.*[42] to extend strict liability to leased, rather than sold, products: "[P]ublic policy demands that responsibility be fixed wherever it will most effectively reduce the hazards to life and health inherent in defective products."[43] For all practical purposes, the lease in *Francioni* was the equivalent of a sale, so the Court's "policy statement" warranted "extending [Section 402A's] application to anyone who enters into the business of supplying human beings with products. Where the fundamental principles are applicable, the imposition of artificial distinctions will only frustrate the intended purpose."[44]

A significant theoretical leap in the development of Pennsylvania's unique approach to product liability occurred in *Berkebile v. Brantly Helicopter Corp.*[45] Although a mere plurality opinion by two justices (with three others concurring in the result), *Berkebile* introduced key elements that found their way into decades of product liability jurisprudence. The *Berkebile* plurality held that "the 'reasonable man' standard in any form has no place in a strict liability case."[46] In this respect, the plurality followed California law, which it characterized as "the vanguard of product liability," to find it "improper to charge the jury on 'reasonableness'" in a strict liability case.[47] The *Berkebile* plurality grounded its decision in "policy": "To charge the jury or permit argument concerning the reasonableness of a consumer's or seller's actions and knowledge, even if merely to define 'defective condition,' undermines the policy considerations that have led us to hold in *Salvador* that the manufacturer is effectively the guarantor of his product's safety."[48]

Another aspect of *Berkebile*'s rejection of the "reasonable man" negligence standard was the plurality's disapproval of liability based on foreseeability. "Foreseeability," the plurality stated, "is a test of negligence" and is therefore "irrelevant" to strict product liability.[49] Regardless of reasonableness or foreseeability, "[t]he seller must provide with the product every element necessary to make it safe for use."[50] Defect "is not to be governed by the reasonable man standard."[51] In sum, "In the strict liability context we reject standards based upon what the 'reasonable' consumer could be expected to know or what the 'reasonable' manufacturer could be expected to 'foresee' about the consumers who use his product."[52] The California law that *Berkebile* followed, however, actually rejected Restatement (Second), Section 402A.[53] Since *Berkebile*, and at least until 2014, to say that Pennsylvania law "follows" Section 402A would be incorrect.

Berkebile set the stage for *Azzarello v. Black Brothers Co.*,[54] a 1978 decision that became the centerpiece of Pennsylvania product liability jurisprudence for more than thirty-five years. *Azzarello* erected a doctrinal wall separating "strict liability" and "negligence," justifying this result "principally because [manufacturers] are in a position to absorb the loss by distributing it as a cost of doing business."[55] The Court pronounced the public policy of Pennsylvania:

> The development of a sophisticated and complex industrial society with its proliferation of new products and vast change in the private enterprise system has inspired a change in legal philosophy from the principle of caveat emptor which prevailed in the early nineteenth century market place to the view that a supplier of products should be deemed to be "the guarantor of his products' safety." The realities of our economic society as it exists today forces the conclusion that the risk of loss for injury resulting from defective products should be borne by the suppliers, principally because they are in a position to absorb the loss by distributing it as a cost of doing business. In an era of giant corporate structures, utilizing the national media to sell their wares, the original concern for an emerging manufacturing industry has given way to the view that it is now the consumer who must be protected. Courts have increasingly adopted the position that the risk of loss must be placed upon the supplier of the defective product without regard to fault or privity of contract.[56]

Building on *Salvador*, the Court declared, "[T]his expansion of the supplier's responsibility for injuries resulting from defects in his product has placed the supplier in the role of a guarantor of his product's safety," but it is "not intended to make him an insurer of all injuries caused by the product."[57]

Seizing upon the same California precedent, *Azzarello* disapproved Section 402A's "unreasonably dangerous" formulation of product defect because it "rings of negligence."[58] Defining product defects in terms of unreasonable danger "tend[ed] to suggest considerations which are usually identified with the law of negligence."[59] The strict liability terminology modeled in *Azzarello* for charging the jury focused on "whether the product is safe for its intended use"[60]—that is, "the supplier must at least provide a product which is designed to make it safe for the intended use. Under this standard, in this type case, the jury may find a defect where the product left the supplier's control lacking any element necessary to make it safe for its intended use or possessing any feature that renders it unsafe for the intended use."[61]

Unlike *Berkebile*, the *Azzarello* decision did not completely exclude "reasonableness." Rather, the Court repurposed the Restatement's "unreasonably dangerous" element, demoting it to a preliminary "question of law" for courts to decide before strict liability claims are submitted to juries.[62] For the jury's benefit, the Court devised a unique jury instruction that combined *Salvador*'s "guarantor" and "intended use" language with the "any element" terminology from *Berkebile*: "The (supplier) of a product is the guarantor of its safety. The product must, therefore, be provided with every element necessary to make it safe for (its intended) use, and without any condition that makes it unsafe for (its intended) use. If you find that the product, at the time it left the defendant's control, lacked any element necessary to make it safe for (its intended) use or contained any condition that made it unsafe for (its intended) use, then the product was defective, and the defendant is liable for all harm caused by such defect."[63]

III. THE LONG, GRADUAL DECAY OF STRICT LIABILITY

The policy-driven approach to strict liability, previewed in *Salvador* and *Berkebile* and crystallized in *Azzarello*, created a dichotomy between strict liability and "negligence concepts" that persisted, at least in name, until late 2014. The Court's next encounter with strict liability after *Azzarello* involved causation rather than defect. In *Sherk v. Daisy-Heddon*,[64] decided in 1982, the plaintiff was a bystander deliberately shot with the defendant's air rifle by an actor fully aware of its "lethal" potential who disobeyed instructions not to use it.[65] Given such facts, no warning by the defendant could have changed the actor's conduct and thus prevented the plaintiff's injuries. The Court held that strict liability did not relax the standards of causation that had previously justified the defense of abnormal use/misuse of a product in negligence cases: "There appears to be no reason to doubt that strict liability has made no change in the rule, well settled in the negligence cases, that the seller of the product is not to be held liable when the consumer makes an abnormal use of it. Sometimes this has been put on the ground that the manufacturer has assumed responsibility only for normal uses; sometimes it has gone off on 'proximate cause.'"[66] In strict liability as well as negligence, an actor "with sufficient appreciation of the nature of the risk of his misuse of the [product] is exclusively responsible for the consequences of his misuse."[67]

In 1987, however, the dichotomy between negligence and strict liability returned in full force in *Lewis v. Coffing Hoist Division*.[68] Faced with whether evidence of compliance with industry standards was admissible in strict liability, the majority of a bitterly divided Court reiterated that "negligence concepts" such as reasonableness and foreseeability "have no role in . . . strict liability."[69] The Court emphasized that in *Azzarello*, it had taken "another approach," different from either the "consumer expectations" or the risk/utility theories in other states.[70]

Although industry standards could influence defectiveness or feasibility of alternative designs,[71] the Court dispensed with the more relaxed dual-relevancy position it had taken in *Bialek*. It prohibited juries from learning about a product's conformity to industry standards because such evidence also concerned negligence and therefore would be a "distract[ion]": "Having reached the conclusion that evidence of industry standards relating to the design of the [product] involved in this case, and evidence of its widespread use in the industry, go to the reasonableness of the [defendant's] conduct in making its design choice, we further conclude that such evidence would have improperly brought into the case concepts of negligence law."[72] Dissenting Justices Hutchinson and Flaherty lamented that strict liability was becoming "madness."[73] Although not apparent until much later, *Lewis* was the high-water mark of *Azzarello*'s wall of separation between negligence and strict liability.

In *McCormick v. Columbus Conveyer Co.*,[74] the Court issued the first of several decisions involving the intersection of product liability with the statute of repose for improvements to real property. The Court held that something could be both a "product" for Restatement Section 402A purposes and an "improvement" under the statute.[75] The policy argument—that subjecting products to the statute of repose "would eviscerate much of product liability law"—was unsuccessful.[76] Because the product was custom designed and not "mass-produced," the defendant's role brought it within scope of the statute of repose.[77]

In 1990, *Azzarello*'s holding that defect was a question of law for the court, rather than a question of fact for the jury, was extended to warning claims in *Mackowick v. Westinghouse Electric Corp*.[78] That did not help the plaintiff, a skilled professional whose lapse had caused the accident. The Supreme Court held that product warnings (and by implication, design) need not be directed to the least-experienced or least-responsible potential user but rather "to the understanding of the intended user."[79] The law "does not require the manufacturer to educate a neophyte in the principles of the product."[80] Where a product's "intended users" are sophisticated, its warnings may be commensurate with the expected degree of user expertise: "A warning of inherent dangers is sufficient if it adequately notifies the intended user of the *unobvious* dangers inherent in the product.... A seller or manufacturer should be able to presume mastery of basic operations by experts or skilled professionals in an industry, and should not owe a duty to warn or instruct such persons on how to perform basic operations in their industry."[81] Thus in *Mackowick*, the Court merged the *Azzarello* element of a product's "intended use" with a plaintiff's corresponding status as an "intended user." This aspect of *Mackowick* represented the Court's first meaningful limitation on the scope of strict liability post-*Azzarello*.

Walton v. Avco Corp.,[82] decided in 1992, involved a novel issue—whether Pennsylvania should recognize a postsale duty to warn in strict liability, despite Section 402A's measuring defectiveness from the date of sale. *Walton* stated that the "Court has continually fortified the theoretical dam between the notions of negligence and strict 'no fault' liability"[83] and recited that in strict liability, "[t]he duty to provide a non-defective product is non-delegable."[84] The postsale nature of duty, however, pushed the Court toward a negligence formulation. A trigger for a postsale duty to warn could not be fashioned without considering what it is "reasonable" for a manufacturer to do: "Because of the likelihood that a purchaser will have a product serviced by its own technicians or by an unaffiliated service center, or possibly not serviced at all, sellers must make reasonable efforts to warn the user or consumer directly."[85] A postsale warning obligation could not be universal. Rather, this duty was limited to what was reasonable, given the "peculiarities of the industry," and did not apply at all to "mass-produced or mass-marketed products" that "becom[e] impossible to track or difficult to locate."[86] *Walton*'s reasonableness analysis was the first crack in the "theoretical dam" between negligence and strict liability. It would not be the last.

That "dam" looked healthy in 1993, when the Supreme Court decided *Kimco Development Corp. v. Michael D's Carpet Outlets*,[87] which extended *McCown*'s preclusion of contributory negligence to the comparative fault replacement that the legislature crafted in 1978.[88] The Court repeated that "we have been adamant that negligence concepts have no place in a strict liability action."[89] Beyond "the conceptual confusion that would ensue should negligence and strict liability concepts be commingled," the Court held that comparative fault would undermine the "purpose" of strict liability: "[T]he underlying purpose of strict product liability is undermined by introducing negligence concepts into it. Strict product liability is premised on the concept of enterprise liability for casting a defective product into the stream of commerce.... The deterrent effect of imposing strict product liability standards would be weakened were we to allow actions based upon it to be defeated, or recoveries reduced by negligence concepts."[90]

The "dam" weakened significantly four years later in *Davis v. Berwind Corp.*,[91] when the Court adopted a test for evaluating whether a product was "substantially changed" prior to an accident that came straight out of negligence—"reasonable foreseeability": "The seller is not liable if a safe product is made unsafe by subsequent changes. Where the product reached the user or consumer with substantial change, the question becomes whether the manufacturer could reasonably have expected or foreseen such an alteration of its product."[92] Using that test, the Court affirmed entry of judgment n.o.v. (*non obstante veredicto*, meaning "notwithstanding the verdict") where the plaintiff's employer removed a safety device that the defendant manufacturer had specifically warned should be in place whenever its product was operating.[93] Addressing the role of foreseeability in a design defect claim, the Court held that as a matter of law, a warning against doing something could not establish the "foreseeability" of such conduct: "Such conclusion defies common sense. It also renders warnings of any nature meaningless since the manufacturer must anticipate that the user will engage in the precise conduct which the warning cautions against."[94] Thus a product user cannot establish a defect predicated on the user's own disregard of the warnings.

On evidentiary issues, in *Spino v. John S. Tilley Ladder Co.*,[95] the Court retreated from the absolutist position taken in *Lewis*. Returning to the ordinary rule that "while evidence can be found inadmissible for one purpose, it may be admissible for another,"[96] the Court held that, notwithstanding *Lewis*, evidence of the absence of similar accidents, probative of causation in both negligence and strict liability, "may be admitted in a design defect product liability action if relevant to a contested issue."[97]

Schroeder v. Commonwealth, DOT,[98] a 1998 case, was mostly about spoliation of critical evidence—namely, the product. The Court held that in a design defect case, a plaintiff's loss of the product at issue did not necessarily require judgment for the defendant because the design alleged would be a "common defect" present in any other unit of the same product, thereby allowing testing of other units.[99] Of greater importance to the development of Pennsylvania product liability law, the *Schroeder* Court for the first time stated the elements of crashworthiness: "Under this [crashworthiness] theory, [plaintiff] must prove (1) that the design of the vehicle was defective and that when the design was made, an alternative, safer, practicable design existed; (2) what injuries, if any, the plaintiff would have received had the alternative safer design been used; and (3) what injuries were attributable to the defective design."[100] The *Schroeder* formulation of crashworthiness remains that used in Pennsylvania to this day.[101]

The distinction between negligence and strict liability took another serious hit in *Duchess v. Langston Corp.*[102] Resolving a muddle of conflicting lower court opinions, the Court unanimously held that evidence of subsequent remedial measures is excludable in both negligence and strict liability.[103] As to policy, the Court stated, "More fundamentally, we are unable to meaningfully distinguish claims asserting negligent design from those asserting a design defect in terms of their effect on the implementation of remedial measures and/or design improvements. . . . [T]he prospect of our rules inhibiting such policy and, correspondingly, the continual process of improvement and innovation in the marketplace, favors the broader application of the evidentiary exclusion. . . . [T]here are analytical similarities between strict liability and negligence in relation to claims of defective design, and we agree with those courts that have concluded that no distinction between the two justifies differential treatment [of subsequent remedial measures]."[104]

Such doctrinal differences were "marginal" because both theories employ "similar" forms of risk/utility balancing and because, in either case, the threat of damages acts as a "deterrent."[105] Instead, the Court "emphasized the precept of strict liability theory that a product's safety be adjudged as of the time that it left the manufacturer's hands."[106]

As just quoted, *Duchess* recognized the "analytical similarities between strict liability and negligence in relation to claims of defective design" and "agree[d] with those courts that have concluded that no distinction between the two [theories of liability] justifies differential treatment" of subsequent remedial measures evidence.[107] The *Duchess* Court was also unimpressed with previously enunciated social policy bases for separating strict liability and negligence—that "recovery without proof of fault" was intended "in part, to alleviate the burden on injured plaintiffs and to provide a mechanism to achieve loss spreading."[108] The Court responded, "Such policies, however, have not been, and cannot be, applied to remove all forms of restriction imposed upon plaintiffs' proofs in product liability actions. . . . [P]laintiffs will generally remain free to present expert testimony to support the theory that a design change was necessary to render the product safe."[109]

Duchess set the stage for *Phillips v. Cricket Lighters*,[110] which in 2003 brought the fissures in the *Azzarello* public policy edifice into plain view. *Phillips* concerned whether a defendant had an obligation, enforceable by strict liability, to childproof a cigarette lighter. The claim was problematic under existing law because a child was not an "intended user" of such a product but only an allegedly "foreseeable," albeit unintended, user—foreseeability being a negligence concept ruled out of bounds in strict liability by the *Azzarello* line of cases.[111]

The lead opinion followed *Mackowick* and found strict liability inapplicable because the accident had been caused by an unintended user.[112] The Court rejected, first, the proposition that "intended use" was somehow equivalent to privity of contract[113] and, second, that intended use was too "narrow" and should be widened through use of foreseeability:

> There is some visceral appeal to [this] argument. . . . This visceral response has been memorialized in our tort law as a negligence cause of action.
>
> Yet, the cause of action presently being examined is not a negligence claim; rather, it sounds in strict liability. And strict liability affords no latitude for the utilization of foreseeability concepts such as those proposed by Appellee. We have bluntly stated that negligence concepts have no place in a case based on strict liability.[114]

The majority admitted, however, that prior opinions had "muddied the waters" with "careless use of negligence terms in the strict liability arena," citing, in particular, *Davis*.[115] Recognizing that it would be "imprudent of us to wholesale reverse all strict liability decisions which utilize negligence terms," the majority nonetheless "reaffirm[ed] that in this jurisdiction, negligence concepts have no place in strict liability law," this dichotomy being "the very underpinning of the strict liability cause of action."[116]

Only Chief Justice Cappy and Justice Zappala, however, joined the opinion. Justices Saylor, Castille, and Eakin—more justices than joined any other opinion in *Phillips*—concurred, recognizing that the *Azzarello* negligence/strict liability divide was beset by "pervasive ambiguities and inconsistencies."[117] These justices concluded that *Azzarello*'s negligence/strict liability dichotomy "cannot be justly sustained in theory in relation to strict product liability cases predicated on defective design" and was "demonstrably incongruent with design-defect strict liability doctrine as it is currently implemented in Pennsylvania."[118] They conceded that negligence and strict liability cannot be coherently separated.

The concurring justices also urged the Court to move "candidly" to the unitary reasonableness-based product liability standard of the ALI's new Restatement (Third) of Torts, Product Liability, Section 2, which was published in 1998 and departs from the Restatement (Second) in significant ways, including abolishing "consumer expectation" as a separate test in favor of risk/utility balancing and requiring plaintiffs alleging a design defect to prove the existence of a reasonable alternative design. Justice (now chief justice) Saylor, writing for the concurring justices, stated, "I believe that the time has come for this Court, in the manner of so many other jurisdictions, to expressly recognize the essential role of risk-utility balancing, a concept derived from negligence doctrine, in design defect litigation. In doing so, the Court should candidly address the ramifications, in particular, the overt, necessary, and proper incorporation of aspects of negligence theory into the equation. This Commonwealth's product liability jurisprudence is far too confusing for another opinion to be laid down that rhetorically eschews negligence concepts in the strict liability arena."[119]

In the decade after *Phillips*, the Restatement (Second) versus Restatement (Third) issue posed by the three concurring justices loomed over the law of product liability in Pennsylvania. The *Phillips* case itself made a rare second appearance before the Court.[120] Under the UCC's definition of *merchantability* as "goods being fit for ordinary purposes," the Court extended its "intended user" analysis to implied warranty.[121] Given the Court's prior disposition of the strict liability issue, the Court had no opportunity to revisit that issue.[122]

In 2005, *Harsh v. Petroll*[123] did not directly address the Restatement issue,[124] but it nonetheless tore down another piece of the wall between negligence and strict liability. In particular, the Court rejected the plaintiff's argument that the negligence of other drivers in a crashworthiness case could not be apportioned against the strict liability of the vehicle manufacturer through joint and several liability: "[A]lthough crashworthiness theory establishes a basis to support manufacturer liability for enhanced injury, it does not require that a manufacturer be the exclusive cause of such injury, nor does it diminish the causal link that exists between an initial collision and all resultant harm. Since [the driver's] negligence and the automobile design defect discerned by the jury were both determined to have been substantial factors in causing the deaths of the Harsh family members, the trial court did not err in assessing liability jointly and severally."[125]

The Restatement issue resurfaced the next year in *Pennsylvania Dep't of General Services v. United States Mineral Products Co.*,[126] a property damage case involving what might be described as "fireworthiness"—whether "foreseeable" destruction by fire constituted an "intended use" of a product so that strict liability would apply. The Court, following the strict liability rationale from *Phillips*, held as a matter of law that "reasonably foreseeable events" such as accidental fires were not "intended uses" of products.[127] Thus the scope of "intended use" cannot be expanded by reliance on foreseeability.

The Court elected to maintain, for the time being, the *Azzarello* negligence/strict liability dichotomy. However, the Court addressed the unsettled nature of strict liability generally. Conceding the "substantial deficiencies" in "current" law, the Court imposed a moratorium on any additional strict liability, pending a reevaluation of whether, and on what terms, strict liability of any sort should be retained as Pennsylvania law: "As directed to the strict liability arena, however, such an argument contravenes the strong admonition . . . in *Phillips* . . . that there are substantial deficiencies in present strict liability doctrine, [and] it should be closely limited pending an overhaul by the Court."[128]

In other words, "the prevailing consensus in *Phillips* was that there would be no further expansions under existing strict liability doctrine."[129] *General Services* acknowledged that a plurality of the Court in *Phillips* desired a thoroughgoing overhaul of strict liability: "[I]n *Phillips*, a plurality of the Court, viewing the condition of Pennsylvania strict liability doctrine as impaired, advocated reform. . . . The rationale of this concurrence was . . . that such clear precedent [that negligence concepts have no place in strict liability] was in tension with other aspects of Pennsylvania strict liability doctrine."[130]

The Court appeared poised to carry out precisely this overhaul in *Bugosh v. I.U. North America, Inc.*[131] However, *Bugosh*, a 2009 asbestos case, did not involve claims against actual manufacturers—only against intermediate sellers. The liability of "nonmanufacturing sellers" is assessed under different standards.[132] Shortly after oral argument on the Restatement issue, the Court dismissed the appeal as improvidently granted over the dissent of two of the concurring justices in *Phillips*.

In *Schmidt v. Boardman Co.*,[133] the Court sought to decide two questions but was unable to resolve either definitively. The unsettled state of Pennsylvania product liability law had surfaced several times since *General Services*, but until *Schmidt*, the existential question addressed by the *Phillips* concurrence and mentioned by the majority in *General Services* had not returned to the Court. In *Schmidt*,[134] the Court criticized the "no-negligence-in-strict-liability rubric" for "resulting in material ambiguities and inconsistency in Pennsylvania's procedure."[135] The *Azzarello* negligence/strict liability dichotomy is faulty for applying "risk-utility balancing . . . on facts most favorable to the plaintiff" and for "yield[ing] minimalistic jury instructions . . . which lack essential guidance concerning the key conception of product defect."[136] Most importantly, it is fundamentally unfair to utilize negligence concepts as a one-way street devoted to expanding liability: "[We] commented on the fundamental imbalance, dissymmetry, and injustice of utilizing the no-negligence-in-strict-liability rubric to stifle manufacturer defenses, while at the same time relying on negligence concepts to expand the scope of manufacturer liability."[137] Nonetheless, *Schmidt* was "not selected to address the foundational concerns."[138]

In 2012, *Beard v. Johnson & Johnson, Inc.*[139] was the Court's first encounter with the "threshold risk-utility analysis" process that the lower courts had created in the wake of *Azzarello*.[140] Although it would have been more straightforward to address the Restatement question first, the appeal was not presented in that fashion but rather involved "subsidiary issues": "[W]e again recognize the continuing state of disrepair in the arena of Pennsylvania strict-liability design defect law.... [S]everal Justices have favored review of the foundational questions[, but] a majority consensus has not yet been attained in any case. . . . [O]bviously, all Justices are not of a like mind on this subject, as this appeal involves subsidiary issues."[141]

Leaving the "foundational question" for another day, the Court observed in *Beard* that "[f]or better or worse, this Court's decisions have relegated our trial courts in the unenviable position of 'social philosopher' and 'risk-utility economic analyst.'"[142] Taking the broader view of this "assignment," the Court held that in determining whether a product's design was "unreasonably dangerous" and thus warranted submission to the jury on a strict liability theory, it was imperative to take into consideration all uses to which the product could be put and not merely the use allegedly causing a particular plaintiff's injury. A "wider-ranging assessment . . . was obviously intended from the outset," given "the open-ended factors" that are "the basis for risk-utility review."[143] Nonetheless, the Court found *Azzarello*'s insistence that this function be carried out by courts rather than juries rather puzzling: "It may be cogently argued that risk-utility balancing is more legitimately assigned to a jury, acting in its role as a voice for the community and with the power to decide facts, rather than to a trial judge acting on a summary record. Indeed, such is the approach of the Restatement Third."[144]

In *Reott v. Asia Trend, Inc.*,[145] the Court revisited causation issues in strict liability—whether, with comparative fault and contributory negligence ruled inapplicable to strict liability,[146] a plaintiff's role in bringing about his or her own injuries was admissible evidence. *Reott* held that it was, as long as a jury could conclude that the plaintiff had acted in a "highly reckless" fashion that "was the sole or superseding cause of the injuries sustained."[147] Analogizing to previously recognized defenses of assumption of the risk and abnormal use, the Court designated such evidence as an affirmative defense on which the defendant had the burden of proof.[148] Such limitations were seen as necessary to avoid "eviscerat[ing]" strict liability "by demonstrating a plaintiff's comparative or contributory negligence."[149] Once again, the foundational question of which Restatement to follow was not presented, as *Reott* involved a manufacturing defect, which is subject to true strict liability even under the Third Restatement.[150]

After a decade of uncertainty, the Supreme Court addressed the foundational questions of the Second versus the Third Restatements and the extent to which negligence and strict liability concepts could be separated in *Tincher v. Omega Flex, Inc.*[151] In that 2014 decision, the Court unanimously overruled *Azzarello*, decisively rejecting the concept of a wall between negligence and strict liability concepts. Rather than adopting the Third Restatement, a majority elected to retain a "properly calibrated" form of strict liability under Section 402A.[152]

According to the *Tincher* Court, *Azzarello* "articulate[d] governing legal concepts which fail to reflect the realities of strict liability practice and to serve the interests of justice."[153] The *Azzarello* decision "compounded the problem . . . [by] approving jury instructions in strict liability cases generally." The instruction that a manufacturer was a "guarantor" of product safety proved "impractical" and employed legal "terms of art" that the charge failed to explain.[154] The "every element" test for defect was also erroneous, having been taken "out of context by the majority in *Azzarello* as the standard of proof in a strict liability action."[155] As a whole, that instruction "perpetuated jury confusion . . . rather than dissipating it,"[156] and "the 'approval' of such jury instructions . . . stunted the development of the common law in this area from proceeding in a more logical, experience-based and reason-bound fashion."[157]

In addition, *Tincher* repudiated the negligence/strict liability dichotomy on which exclusion of evidence in cases such as *Lewis* was predicated. Far from being separate, "the theory of strict liability as it evolved overlaps in effect with the theories of negligence and breach of warranty":[158]

> [A] strict reading of *Azzarello* is undesirable. . . . Subsequent application of *Azzarello* elevated the notion that negligence concepts create confusion in strict liability cases to a doctrinal imperative, whose merits were not examined to determine whether such a bright-line rule was consistent with reason. . . . [T]he effect of the *per se* rule that negligence rhetoric and concepts were to be eliminated from strict liability law was to validate the suggestion that the cause of action, so shaped, was not viable.[159]

> [T]hose decisions essentially led to puzzling trial directives that the bench and bar understandably have had difficulty following in practice.[160]

Tincher also removed the task of conducting the risk-benefit calculus in design defect cases from the judiciary and returned it to the jury. In this respect, *Azzarello*'s "directives" had been "problematic on their face":[161] "[T]rial courts simply do not necessarily have the expertise to conduct the social policy inquiry into the risks and utilities of a plethora of products and to decide, as a matter of law, whether a product is unreasonably dangerous except perhaps in the most obvious of cases."[162] *Azzarello*'s approach only "encourage[d] trial courts to make either uninformed or unfounded decisions of social policy."[163]

Chastened by the errors it perceived in *Azzarello*—and, indeed, in the entire "first decade" of strict liability[164]—*Tincher* professed "modesty" in its approach to replacing existing law.[165] The Court first implored the legislature to enact "comprehensive legislative reform" that "address[ed] this arena of substantive law."[166] Failing that, the Court was loath to replace the failed body of broad product liability principles enunciated in *Azzarello* with another set of "principles of broad application" represented by the Third Restatement:[167] "[O]ur reticence respecting broad approval of the Third Restatement is separately explainable by looking no further than to the aftermath of Azzarello, whose negligence rhetoric-related doctrinal proscription arising from a peculiar set of circumstances had long-term deleterious effects on the development of strict liability law in Pennsylvania."[168] Alternative designs were "relevant and even highly probative" and, in the "typical case . . . evidence of an alternative product design is the most persuasive and efficient means of convincing the trier of fact."[169] But not all cases were "typical," so the Court was unwilling to adopt the Third Restatement's position that an alternative design was an essential element of all design defect cases: "The Third Restatement approach presumes too much certainty about the range of circumstances, factual or otherwise, to which the 'general rule' articulated should apply."[170] Thus "the area of strict liability law remains complex and our decision here does not purport to foresee and account for the myriad implications or potential pitfalls as yet unarticulated or unappreciated. . . . [B]right lines and broad rules always offer a superficially enticing option. However, we cannot elevate the lull of simplicity over the balancing of interests embodied by the principles underpinning . . . the relevant area of law."[171]

Instead of the Third Restatement, *Tincher* adopted what it called a "composite" approach to strict liability, incorporating both the risk/utility test from the Third Restatement and the consumer expectation test from Section 402A, Comment *i*: "The combined standard, which states consumer expectations and risk-utility tests in the alternative, retains the features of each test, in practice, offering the parties a composite of the most workable features of both tests."[172] *Tincher* discussed both standards, recognizing the strengths and drawbacks of each.

The consumer expectation standard is that "the product is in a defective condition if the danger is unknowable and unacceptable to the average or ordinary consumer"[173] and "[t]he nature of the product, the identity of the user, the product's intended use and intended user, and any express or implied representations by a manufacturer or other seller are among considerations."[174] Limitations of the consumer expectation test are that (1) "obvious dangers" exempt poorly designed products from liability and that (2) the test becomes "arbitrary" if applied to "complex" products "whose danger is vague or outside the ordinary consumer's contemplation."[175]

The "risk/utility" standard is "a test balancing risks and utilities or, stated in economic terms, a cost-benefit analysis."[176] This means that "[t]he risk-utility test offers courts an opportunity to analyze post hoc whether a manufacturer's conduct in manufacturing or designing a product was reasonable, which obviously reflects the negligence roots of strict liability."[177] Limitations of the risk/utility test are that (1) it is not "immediately responsive in the (typical) case implicating allegations relating to a particular design feature" and that (2) "in some respects, it conflicts with bedrock moral intuitions regarding justice in determining proper compensation."[178]

Initially, the plaintiff selects the test as "master of the claim in the first instance."[179] Defendants may challenge any "overreaching by the plaintiff."[180] In choosing the correct test, the Court recognized that "the theory of strict liability as it evolved overlaps in effect with the theories of negligence *and* breach of warranty."[181] The composite test thus reflects a "duality of purpose."[182] Manufacturers typically "engage in a risk-utility calculus" typical of negligence, whereas intermediate sellers "implicitly represent" their products' nondefectiveness analogously to a warranty.[183]

As the Court emphasized in *Tincher*, the "typical" design defect case (at least against a manufacturer) involves foreseeable risks, akin to negligence, and thus approximates the "alternative design" approach of the Third Restatement: "[This] claim was essentially premised upon the allegation that the risk of harm related to [the product's design] was both foreseeable and avoidable. . . . These allegations, at least, *bear the indicia of negligence.* Indeed, in some respects this is the 'typical' case, which explains both the insight that in design cases, the character of the product and the conduct of the manufacturer are largely inseparable, and the Third Restatement's approach of requiring an alternative design as part of the standard of proof."[184] The Court's reluctance to adopt the Third Restatement was therefore primarily because "courts do not try the 'typical' products case exclusively."[185]

Thus emphasizing that "judicial pronouncements should employ due modesty,"[186] the *Tincher* Court retrenched, inviting legislation and embracing a modest view of itself as the arbitrator of tort social policy. The social policy declarations that accompanied the adoption of strict liability in the early cases were therefore muted, although still present. The "salient public policy" remained "that those who sell a product are held responsible for damage caused to a consumer despite the reasonable use of the product."[187] "Policy" became as much a matter of limitation as it was of expansion:

> [A]s a matter of policy, articulating categorical exemptions from strict liability is not a viable or desirable alternative. Courts, which address evidence and arguments in individual cases, are neither positioned, nor resourced, to make the kind of policy judgments required to arrive at an a priori decision as to which individual products, or categories and types of products, should be exempt.[188]

> The principal point is that a jurisdiction is free to adopt a policy that reduces a supplier's exposure to strict liability for a product. . . . [P]ublic policy also adjusts

expectations of efficiency and intuitions of justice considerations in the context of product liability.[189]

While it is too early to tell how future cases will be decided, the Court's emphasis on "modesty" is not unusual. In *Conway v. The Cutler Group, Inc.*,[190] a few months before *Tincher*, the Court sounded similar themes by invoking privity to limit the implied warranty of habitability to initial home buyers only.[191] The Court declined to expand liability for reasons of "public policy," relying on precedent that predated the strict liability efflorescence that began in *Webb*: "[T]he courts' authority to declare public policy is limited. In our judicial system, the power of courts to formulate pronouncements of public policy is sharply restricted; otherwise they would become judicial legislatures.... If, in the domain of economic and social controversies, a court were, under the guise of the application of the doctrine of public policy, in effect to enact provisions which it might consider expedient and desirable, such action would be nothing short of judicial legislation."[192]

V. THE EXCEPTIONAL CASE: PRESCRIPTION MEDICAL PRODUCTS

The Supreme Court's precedent has always treated product liability in the medical context—chiefly involving prescription drugs—differently from that of other products. This divergence began in 1942 with *Henderson v. National Drug Co.*,[193] long before the concept of strict liability. In *Henderson*, the Court held that negligence, not warranty, was the only viable theory.[194] Drug companies are held "to a high degree of responsibility under both the criminal and the civil law for any failure to exercise vigilance commensurate with the harm"; however, lowering the negligence standard of proof would "ill-serve" the public: "If those who make and compound drugs and medicines in packages or bottles, under the strict conditions prescribed by the [forerunner of the Food, Drug & Cosmetics Act], can be mulcted in damages every time some person uses such drugs or medicines with harmful results, the making and selling of such products would be a most peculiarly hazardous enterprise."[195] A second early shoe dropped in *DiBelardino v. Lemmon Pharmacal Co.*, where the Court likewise barred implied warranty claims that sought to impose strict liability.[196]

Modern prescription medical product liability in Pennsylvania began in 1971 with *Incollingo v. Ewing*.[197] That case was critical to the development of pharmaceutical product liability in Pennsylvania in at least four respects. Most importantly, the Court adopted the learned intermediary rule: "Since the drug was available only upon prescription of a duly licensed physician, the warning required is not to the general public or to the patient, but to the prescribing doctor. The question, therefore, in this case is whether the warning that was given to the prescribing doctors was proper and adequate."[198]

Second, in light of the policies expressed by Restatement (Second) of Torts, Section 402A, Comment *k* (1965), the Court reaffirmed *Henderson*'s holding that negligence was the only viable cause of action: "Since the strict liability rule of § 402A is not applicable, the standard of care required is that set forth in § 388 of the Restatement dealing with the liability of a supplier of a chattel known to be dangerous for its intended use. Under this section, the supplier has a duty to exercise reasonable care to inform those for whose use the article is supplied of the facts which make it likely to be dangerous."[199]

Third, the Court recognized the principle of warning causation—that is, unless an adequate warning to the physician would have made a difference in the ultimate outcome, the plaintiff has not established the element of causation. Where nothing a pharmaceutical defendant "did or failed to do had a material influence on [a doctor's] prescription of the drug," a claim based on that doctor's actions was not made out.[200]

Finally, the Court recognized a claim in negligence for overpromotion of a drug sufficient to overcome an otherwise adequate product warning: "[W]hether or not the printed words of warning were in effect cancelled out and rendered meaningless in the light of the sales effort made by the detail men" was a "question properly for the jury."[201]

Subsequent cases consolidated the Court's rulings in *Incollingo*. *Baldino v. Castagna* reiterated the holdings about the learned intermediary rule and negligence as the proper theory in pharmaceutical cases.[202] *Coyle v. Richardson-Merrell, Inc.* extended the learned intermediary rule to pharmacists.[203] *Coyle* also touched on more general issues, rejecting the same cost-shifting rationale for liability that the Court had earlier credited in strict liability cases: "Reliance on cost-shifting as the only factor to be considered in whether a given party should be exposed to liability" is unjustified because it "would result in absolute liability rather than strict liability."[204] *Hahn v. Richter*[205] reaffirmed the Court's long-standing preference for negligence, rather than strict liability, in this area: "[W]here the adequacy of warnings associated with prescription drugs is at issue, the failure of the manufacturer to exercise reasonable care to warn of dangers, *i.e.*, the manufacturer's negligence, is the only recognized basis of liability."[206]

Cafazzo v. Central Medical Health Services, Inc.[207] rejected the cost-shifting basis for strict liability even more pointedly in rejecting an effort to hold healthcare providers strictly liable as intermediate suppliers of medical products. Cost shifting did not justify converting malpractice liability to strict liability: "To assign liability for no reason other than the ability to pay damages is inconsistent with our jurisprudence." *Cafazzo* voiced significant second thoughts about strict liability: "[B]efore a change in the law is made, a court, if it is to act responsibly must be able to see with reasonable clarity the results of its decision and to say with reasonable certainty that the change will serve the best interests of society. . . . It is . . . not clear enough that strict liability has afforded the hoped for panacea in the conventional products area that it should be extended so cavalierly in cases such as the present one."[208]

More recently, in its 2014 decision in *Lance v. Wyeth*, the Court again reiterated both the learned intermediary rule and the negligence standard.[209] Borrowing from the Third Restatement, the Court recognized a novel design-based negligence claim allowing liability—even in the absence of an alternative design—for not removing a drug that is "too dangerous to be used by anyone" from the market before the Food and Drug Administration (FDA) recalled it:[210] "[W]e have . . . found no such viable rule grounded in any precedent of this Court concerning negligence doctrine which would insulate pharmaceutical companies from civil liability for manufacturing and/or disseminating products which they know or should have known are simply too dangerous to be used."[211] The exact scope of the negligence liability theory recognized in *Lance* remains unclear.[212]

VI. OTHER PRODUCT-SPECIFIC PRODUCT LIABILITY ISSUES

The Supreme Court's product liability jurisprudence has also addressed a number of other salient issues.

A. Product Identification

The Court has refused to extend product liability beyond the manufacturer of the product that injured the plaintiff. In *Skipworth v. Lead Industries Association*,[213] decided in 1997, the Court refused to apply "market share liability," which would have extended liability to manufacturers of competing products with similar attributes. The Court applied a "negligence" principle to all theories of liability: "Pennsylvania . . . follows the general rule that a plaintiff, in order to recover, must establish that a particular defendant's negligence was the proximate cause of her injuries. Adoption of the market share liability theory would result in a significant departure from this rule . . . [and] would lead to a distortion of liability which would be so gross as to make determinations of culpability arbitrary and unfair."[214]

Product identification issues have also arisen in asbestos litigation. In its 2007 decision in *Gregg v. V-J Auto Parts Co.*,[215] the Court applied a "frequency, regularity, proximity analysis" to enforce product identification and to confine liability to defendants whose products "substantially contributed" to a plaintiff's injury.[216] This point was reiterated six years later in *Howard v. A.W. Chesterton Co.*[217]

B. Reliability of Expert Testimony

Product liability litigation has been at the forefront of the Court's decisions regarding the admissibility of expert testimony. In *Blum v. Merrell Dow Pharmaceuticals, Inc.*,[218] decided in 2000, the opinions of an expert who ignored extensive human epidemiology in favor of animal data were "so flawed as to render his conclusions unreliable and therefore inadmissible under either *Frye* or *Daubert*, so a choice between the two standards is unnecessary to the resolution of this appeal."[219]

Three years later, another product liability case, *Grady v. Frito-Lay, Inc.*,[220] answered the question left open in *Blum*—namely, whether Pennsylvania remains a "*Frye* state": "After careful consideration, we conclude that the *Frye* rule will continue to be applied in Pennsylvania. In our view, *Frye*'s 'general acceptance' test is a proven and workable rule, which when faithfully followed, fairly serves its purpose of assisting the courts in determining when scientific evidence is reliable and should be admitted."[221]

The Court also addressed the *Frye* standard in 2012 in *Betz v. Pneumo Abex LLC*,[222] an asbestos case that rejected a narrow interpretation of *Frye*: "[A] *Frye* hearing is warranted when a trial judge has articulable grounds to believe that an expert witness has not applied accepted scientific methodology in a conventional fashion in reaching his or her conclusions. We believe a narrower approach would unduly constrain trial courts in the appropriate exercise of their discretion in determining the admissibility of evidence."[223] The Court held that "any exposure" theories of causation are inadmissible as in "irreconcilable conflict" with scientific principles of dose response.[224]

C. Circumstantial Proof of Defect

The Court has allowed a "malfunction theory," whereby an unexplained product malfunction—one occurring in the absence of other causes—is circumstantial evidence from which a jury may infer defect. A plurality of the Court recognized this theory in *Kuisis v. Baldwin-Lima-Hamilton Corp.*[225] but held that it could not apply because, as a matter of law, the age of the product at the time of the accident made "normal-wear-and-tear" such an alternative cause.[226]

In 1989, a majority of the Court endorsed the "malfunction theory" in *Rogers v. Johnson & Johnson Products, Inc.*:[227] "This theory encompasses nothing more than circumstantial evidence of product malfunction. It permits a plaintiff to prove a defect in a product with evidence of the occurrence of a malfunction and with evidence eliminating abnormal use or reasonable, secondary causes for the malfunction."[228] The Court fine-tuned the theory two decades later in *Barnish v. KWI Building Co.*,[229] holding that plaintiffs may not simultaneously advance theories incompatible with a circumstantial case: "[I]f the plaintiff's theory of the case includes another cause for the malfunction . . . a reasonable jury could not conclude that the product was defective" under the malfunction theory.[230] Therefore, "prior successful use" of a product "undermines the inference that the product was defective when it left the manufacturer's control."[231]

D. Component Part Defense

The Court recognized the existence of issues peculiar to component part manufacturers in *Burbage v. Boiler Engineering & Supply Co.*,[232] holding that such a manufacturer is liable where "the jury found no substantial change" in a component that was incorporated into a larger product.[233]

In *Wenrick v. Schloemann-Siemag Aktiengesellschaft*,[234] the Court held that judgment as a matter of law was appropriate where the claimed defect resided not in the component but rather in how another party installed it. To impose a duty to warn on the manufacturer of a nondefective component was too much for the Court to accept: "We are not prepared to accept such a radical restructuring of social obligations."[235]

Another variant of the component part defense arose in *Jacobini v. V. & O. Press Co.*[236] In that 1991 case, the Court held that the manufacturer of a component part had no duty to warn about a defect not in its component but rather in other parts of the completed assemblage for which the manufacturer was not responsible: "[L]imits on a manufacturer's duty to warn come into play where . . . the manufacturer supplies a mere component of a final product that is assembled by another party and dangers are associated with the use of the finished product. This is particularly true where the component itself is not dangerous, and where the danger arises from the manner in which the component is utilized by the assembler of the final product, this being a matter over which the component manufacturer has no control."[237]

E. Medical Monitoring

The Court first approved of recovery for medical monitoring—the costs of prophylactic medical tests of an otherwise uninjured person—as "appropriate and just" in a 1996 asbestos case.[238] The Court recognized medical monitoring as a generally applicable form of recovery in *Redland Soccer Club Inc. v. Department of the Army*:[239] "It was the nonspeculative nature of a claim for medical monitoring . . . that prompted our recognition of a claim for [such] monitoring."[240] In another rejection of strict liability, in defining the elements of an actionable medical monitoring claim, the Court required a showing of negligence:

> [A] plaintiff must prove the following elements to prevail on a common law claim for medical monitoring: (1) exposure greater than normal background levels; (2) to a proven hazardous substance; (3) *caused by the defendant's negligence*; (4) as a proximate result of the exposure, plaintiff has a significantly increased risk of contracting a serious latent disease; (5) a monitoring procedure exists that makes the early detection of the disease possible; (6) the prescribed monitoring regime is different from that normally recommended in the absence of the exposure; and (7) the prescribed monitoring regime is reasonably necessary according to contemporary scientific principles.[241]

VII. CONCLUSION

After 170 years of product liability decisions, the old has become new again in the jurisprudence of the Pennsylvania Supreme Court. After an extended detour through an admittedly idiosyncratic "any element" test for strict liability that sought to divorce such liability from its antecedents in negligence and warranty law, the Court in *Tincher* returned product liability to its roots. How the new "composite" standard will develop, of course, remains to be seen and will only become apparent in the fullness of time as the common law continues to evolve under the Supreme Court's guidance.

NOTES

James M. Beck is a senior life sciences policy analyst at Reed Smith LLP.

1. 220 A.2d 853 (Pa. 1966).
2. 391 A.2d 1020 (Pa. 1978).
3. Cafazzo v. Central Medical Health Services, Inc., 668 A.2d 521, 527 (Pa. 1995).
4. *See* Lewis v. Coffing Hoist Div., 528 A.2d 590, 593 (Pa. 1987) (noting that Azzarello is "another approach" different from either "consumer expectations" or risk/utility balancing).
5. Tincher v. Omega Flex, Inc., 104 A.3d 328, 401 (Pa. Nov. 19, 2014); *see* Arthur L. Bugay, "*Tincher v. Omega Flex, Inc.*: A Lightning Strike on Pennsylvania Product Liability Law," *Pennsylvania Bar Association Quarterly* 85 (2014): 39–46.
6. 9 Watts & Serg. 32 (Pa. 1845).
7. Ibid., 35.
8. 79 Pa. 493 (1876).
9. Ibid., 502–3.
10. Ibid.
11. *See, e.g.*, Smith v. Pennsylvania R.R. Co., 50 A. 829, 830 (Pa. 1902) (rejecting "liability to the public"); First Presbyterian Congregation v. Smith, 30 A. 279, 282 (Pa. 1894) (rejecting duties owed to "third parties"); Fitzmaurice v. Fabian, 23 A. 444, 444 (Pa. 1892) (rejecting "dut[ies] to a stranger"); Curtin v. Somerset, 21 A. 244, 245 (Pa. 1891) (rejecting duties owed "to the whole world").
12. 95 A. 931, 933–34 (Pa 1915).
13. 68 A.2d 517, 530–32 (Pa. 1949) (adopting Restatement of Torts, § 388 [1939]).
14. *See* Maize v. Atlantic Refining Co., 41 A.2d 850, 853 (Pa. 1945) (holding that adequacy of warnings is an issue for the jury and that evidence of industry practice is not conclusive of liability).
15. *See* Hummel v. Womeldorf, 233 A.2d 215, 217 (Pa. 1967); Notarianni v. Ross, 119 A.2d 792, 793 (Pa. 1956); Ralston v. Baldwin Locomotive Works, 87 A. 299, 299 (Pa. 1913).
16. Act of April 6, 1953, P.L. 3, 12A P.S. §§ 10–102.
17. *See* §§ 2–318.
18. 187 A.2d 575 (Pa. 1963).
19. 221 A.2d 320, 324–25 (Pa. 1966).
20. Ibid., 325 (pointing out that "strict liability in assumpsit" is "circumscribed by the limitations" of the UCC).
21. 220 A.2d 853 (Pa. 1966).
22. Ibid., 854.
23. Ibid. (quoting Restatement [Second] of Torts, § 402A [1965]).
24. Ibid., 854.
25. 221 A.2d at 334–35 (Jones, J., dissenting in pertinent part) (footnote and citations omitted); *accord* ibid., 220 A.2d at 338 (citing "public interest in affording the maximum protection . . . to human life, health and safety"; "inability of the consumer to protect himself"; a "seller's implied assurance of the safety of [its] product"; and "the superior ability of the manufacturer or seller to distribute the risk of loss") (Roberts, J., dissenting in pertinent part) (footnotes omitted).
26. 223 A.2d 746 (Pa. 1966).
27. Ibid., 748.
28. 242 A.2d 231 (Pa. 1968).
29. Ibid., 235.
30. Ibid.
31. 247 A.2d 603 (Pa 1968).
32. Ibid., 606 ("[W]e hardly believe it is any more necessary to tell an experienced factory worker that he should not put his hand into a machine

that is at that moment breaking glass than it would be necessary to tell a zoo-keeper to keep his head out of a hippopotamus' mouth.").

33. 246 A.2d 848 (Pa. 1968).

34. "Vertical privity" involved who in the chain of product distribution could be sued. *See* Salvador v. Atlantic Steel Boiler Co., 319 A.2d 903, 904n1 (Pa. 1974).

35. Ibid., 853–54.

36. 319 A.2d 903 (Pa. 1974).

37. Unlike "vertical privity," which involved who in the chain of product distribution could be sued, "horizontal privity" involved which product users, beyond the actual product purchaser, could bring suit. *See* Salvador, 319 A.2d at 904n1.

38. Ibid., 907 (citations omitted).

39. 342 A.2d 381 (Pa. 1975).

40. Ibid., 382 (quoting Salvador).

41. Ibid., 382.

42. 372 A.2d 736 (Pa. 1977).

43. Ibid., 738 (citation and quotation marks omitted).

44. Ibid., 739 (citation and quotation marks omitted). The Court would revisit similar nonseller strict liability issues twice more, holding in Nath v. National Equip. Leasing Corp., 439 A.2d 633, 636 (Pa. 1981) (financier) and Musser v. Vilsmeir Auction Co., 562 A.2d 279, 281–82 (Pa. 1989) (auctioneer) that entities with only "tangential participation" and "no control over [product] manufacture" are not subject to strict liability.

45. 337 A.2d 893 (Pa. 1975), *abrogated by* Reott v. Asia Trend, Inc., 55 A.3d 1088 (Pa. 2012).

46. 337 A.2d at 900.

47. Ibid., 899–900 (following Cronin v. J.B.E. Olson Corp., 501 P.2d 1153 [Cal. 1972]).

48. Ibid., 900.

49. Ibid. (citation omitted).

50. Ibid., 902 (discussing warning claims).

51. Ibid.

52. Ibid. (citation omitted).

53. Rather than apply § 402A, the California precedent that Berkebile relied on rejected it. Cronin, 501 P.2d at 1160 ("We have not hesitated to reach conclusions contrary to those set forth in Restatement [§] 402A."). Eventually the California Supreme Court retreated from Cronin's absolutist view of strict liability: "[T]he claim that a particular component 'rings of' or 'sounds in' negligence has not precluded its acceptance in the context of strict liability." Anderson v. Owens-Corning Fiberglas Corp., 810 P.2d 549, 556 (Cal. 1991).

54. 391 A.2d 1020 (Pa. 1978).

55. Ibid., 1023.

56. Ibid., 1023–24 (quoting Salvador, 319 A.2d 903).

57. Ibid., 1024.

58. Ibid., 1025.

59. Ibid.

60. Ibid., 1026–27 (footnote omitted).

61. Ibid., 1027–28.

62. Ibid., 1026.

63. Ibid., 1027n12 (citation and quotation marks omitted).

64. 450 A.2d 615 (Pa. 1982).

65. Ibid., 617–18.

66. Ibid., 618 (citation and quotation marks omitted).

67. Ibid. The Court followed Sherk in Phillips v. A-Best Products Co., 665 A.2d 1167 (Pa. 1995), holding that considering the plaintiff's employer's safety training program and admissions of prior knowledge by plaintiff, causation from an inadequate warning had not been proven. Ibid., 1171. Phillips is discussed more fully later.

68. 528 A.2d 590 (Pa. 1987).

69. Ibid., 591.

70. Ibid., 593. Chief Justice Robert N. C. Nix Jr. authored both Azzarello and Lewis.

71. Ibid., 593–94.

72. Ibid., 594.

73. "I am compelled, in the words of a popular song, to 'speak out against the madness.' The instant madness is a creeping consensus among us judges and lawyers that we are more capable of designing products than engineers. A courtroom is a poor substitute for a design office." Ibid., 596 (Hutchinson and Flaherty, J.J., dissenting).

74. 564 A.2d 907 (Pa. 1989).

75. Ibid., 909.

76. Ibid., 910.

77. Ibid., 910–11. McCormick still sets the framework for cases involving both product liability and the statute of repose for improvements to real property. Products not physically affixed to real estate are not within the statute. Vargo v. Koppers Co., 715 A.2d 423, 426 (Pa. 1998) (applying revised statute). Products lacking customized design have not been protected by the statute of repose, even if physically attached to real estate, McConnaughey v. Building Components, Inc., 637 A.2d 1331, 1334 (Pa. 1994), whereas individually designed products involving the defendant's "individualized expertise" are protected. Noll v. Harrisburg Area YMCA, 643 A.2d 81, 86 (Pa. 1994).

78. 575 A.2d 100, 102–3 (Pa. 1990).
79. Ibid., 102.
80. Ibid.
81. Ibid., 102–3 (citations and quotation marks omitted), emphasis original.
82. 610 A.2d 454 (Pa. 1992).
83. Ibid., 462.
84. Ibid., 459 (quoting Berkebile, 337 A.2d at 903).
85. Ibid., 459 (citations omitted).
86. Ibid.
87. 637 A.2d 603 (Pa. 1993).
88. *See* 42 Pa.C.S. § 7102.
89. 637 A.2d at 606 (citations omitted).
90. Ibid., 606–7 (quotation from Azzarello omitted).
91. 690 A.2d 186 (Pa. 1997).
92. Ibid., 190 (citations omitted).
93. Ibid., 188.
94. Ibid., 190–91 (footnote omitted), emphasis original.
95. 696 A.2d 1169 (Pa. 1997).
96. Ibid., 1172 (following Bialek, 337 A.2d at 903).
97. Ibid., 1173.
98. 710 A.2d 23 (Pa. 1998).
99. Ibid., 27–28.
100. Ibid., 28n8.
101. In Stecher v. Ford Motor Co., 812 A.2d 553 (Pa. 2002), the Superior Court had attempted to shift the burden of proof as to apportionment of injury (crashworthiness elements two and three) from the plaintiff to the defendant. This Supreme Court, chastising the lower court for deciding an unnecessary issue, reversed and vacated that ruling. Ibid., 557–58.
102. 769 A.2d 1131 (Pa. 2001).
103. Ibid., 1145.
104. Ibid., 1143–44 (citations and footnote omitted). Instead of relying on California law, as it had in Azzarello and Berkebile, the Court rejected a California rule that held subsequent remedial measures admissible in strict liability. Ibid. (disagreeing with Ault v. International Harvester Co., 528 P.2d 1148 [Cal. 1974]).
105. 769 A.2d at 1141.
106. Ibid., 1140.
107. Ibid., 1144.
108. Ibid., 1145.
109. Ibid.
110. 841 A.2d 1000 (Pa. 2003).
111. Ibid., 1005.
112. Ibid. (noting "the standard that the product need be made safe only for the intended user appears to be equally applicable").
113. Ibid., 1006.
114. Ibid. (footnote omitted).
115. 841 A.2d at 1006–7.
116. Ibid., 1007.
117. Ibid., 1012 (concurring opinion). Justice Sandra Schultz Newman concurred and dissented, largely with respect to the negligence claim, which was allowed. Justice Russell M. Nigro concurred in the result without opinion.
118. Ibid., 1014.
119. Ibid., 1015–16.
120. 883 A.2d 439 (Pa. 2005).
121. Ibid., 444–45 (the product's "ordinary purpose certainly was not to be a two-year-old child's plaything").
122. Ibid., 442n2.
123. 887 A.2d 209 (Pa. 2005).
124. Ibid., 218n16.
125. Ibid., 219.
126. 898 A.2d 590 (Pa. 2006).
127. Ibid., 600–601.
128. Ibid., 601 (citation and footnote omitted), emphasis added.
129. Ibid., 601n10.
130. Ibid., 602n15.
131. 971 A.2d 1228 (Pa. 2009).
132. *See* Restatement (Third) of Torts, Product Liability, § 2, comment *o* (1998).
133. 11 A.3d 924 (Pa. 2011).
134. 11 A.3d 924.
135. Ibid., 940.
136. Ibid.
137. Ibid.
138. Ibid.
139. 41 A.3d 823 (Pa. 2012).
140. *See, e.g.*, Riley v. Warren Mfg., Inc., 688 A.2d 221, 225 (Pa. Super. 1997); Fitzpatrick v. Madonna, 623 A.2d 322, 324–26 (Pa. Super. 1993); Dambacher v. Mallis, 485 A.2d 408, 423n5 (Pa. Super. 1984) (en banc), *appeal dismissed*, 500 A.2d 428 (Pa. 1985).
141. Beard, 41 A.3d at 836 (citations and quotation marks omitted).
142. Ibid.
143. Ibid., 837.
144. Ibid., 838n18.
145. 55 A.3d 1088 (Pa. 2012).
146. *See* Kimco, 637 A.2d 603 (Pa. 1993); McCown, 342 A.2d 381 (Pa. 1975).
147. Reott, 55 A.3d at 1101.
148. Ibid., 1100–1101.
149. Ibid., 1098.
150. Ibid., 1101–2 (Saylor, J., concurring).
151. 104 A.3d 328 (Pa. 2014).

152. Ibid., 399.

153. Ibid., 376.

154. Ibid., 379.

155. Ibid., 365.

156. Ibid., 377.

157. Ibid., 379.

158. Ibid., 401.

159. Ibid., 381.

160. Ibid., 375.

161. Ibid., 380.

162. Ibid., 395.

163. Ibid.

164. Ibid., 365. The Court characterized the development of strict liability from Webb through Azzarello as "a series of missed opportunities to develop a vibrant and coherent body of common law."

165. 104 A.3d at 377–78.

166. Ibid., 381.

167. Ibid., 396.

168. Ibid., 399.

169. Ibid., 397.

170. Ibid., 398.

171. Ibid., 406 (quoting Scampone v. Highland Park Care Center, LLC, 57 A.3d 582, 598 [Pa. 2012]).

172. 104 A.3d at 391.

173. Ibid., 387.

174. Ibid. (citing, inter alia, Restatement § 402A, comment *i*).

175. 104 A.3d at 388.

176. Ibid., 389.

177. Ibid.

178. Ibid., 390.

179. Ibid., 406.

180. 104 A.3d at 406.

181. Ibid., 401, emphasis original.

182. Ibid.

183. Ibid., 403.

184. Ibid., 405 (case-specific facts omitted), emphasis added.

185. Ibid.

186. Ibid., 378.

187. Ibid., 389.

188. Ibid., 396.

189. Ibid., 398–99, 402.

190. 99 A.3d 67 (Pa. 2014).

191. Ibid., 72.

192. Ibid. (quoting Mamlin v. Genoe, 17 A.2d 407, 409 [Pa. 1941]) (citations omitted).

193. 23 A.2d 743 (Pa. 1942).

194. Ibid., 749 (holding that "[a]n action against a druggist to recover for personal injuries should be *ex delicto* and not *ex contractu*").

195. Ibid., 748 (citations omitted).

196. 208 A.2d 283, 285–86 (Pa. 1965).

197. 282 A.2d 206 (Pa. 1971).

198. Ibid., 220.

199. Ibid., 220n8.

200. Ibid., 219.

201. Ibid., 220.

202. 478 A.2d 807, 810, 812 (Pa. 1984).

203. 584 A.2d 1383, 1386–88 (Pa. 1991).

204. Ibid., 1387.

205. 673 A.2d 888 (Pa. 1996).

206. Ibid., 891 (citation omitted).

207. 668 A.2d 521 (Pa. 1995).

208. Ibid., 527 (citation and quotation marks omitted).

209. 85 A.3d 434, 457–58n6 (Pa. 2014).

210. Ibid., 458–60 (following Restatement [Third] of Torts—Product Liability, § 6[c] [1998]).

211. Ibid., 461.

212. It is unclear whether this theory of liability extends beyond products that, as in Lance, had already been removed from the market. Compare ibid., 458 (holding that "tendering into the market a drug which it knows or should know is so dangerous that it should not be taken by anyone" can "violate" the "duty of care") with ibid., 457n33 (noting this "theory of liability would present more difficult questions," where the drug "maintained its FDA approval, it remained on the market, and U.S. doctors continued to prescribe it"). Given that the broader view would likely result in preemption, *see* Mutual Pharmaceutical Co. v. Bartlett, 570, 133 S. Ct. 2466, 2477–78 (2013) (state-law duty to "stop selling" drug held preempted as in conflict with drug's FDA approval), Lance should probably be construed in accordance with its facts to avoid raising constitutional questions.

213. 690 A.2d 169 (Pa. 1997).

214. Ibid., 173 (citation and footnote omitted). The Court left the door ajar for "a situation which would compel us to depart from our time-tested general rule." Ibid., 232, presumably referring to litigation involving diethylstilbestrol, which was the first synthetic estrogen—indeed, the first widely prescribed generic drug—that spawned market-share liability. No such situation has since arisen.

215. 943 A.2d 216 (Pa. 2007).

216. Ibid., 224.

217. 78 A.3d 605, 608 (Pa. 2013) ("Bare proof of some de minimus exposure to a defendant's product is insufficient to establish substantial-factor causation.").

218. 764 A.2d 1 (Pa. 2000).

219. Ibid., 4. The Court was referring to the competing tests to assess scientific testimony enunciated in Frye v. United States, 293 F. 1013 (D.C. Cir. 1923); and Daubert v. Merrell Dow Pharms., Inc., 509 U.S. 579 (1993). The expert's "selective review of the [epidemiologic] data" failed under either test. 764 A.2d at 4n5.

220. 839 A.2d 1038 (Pa. 2003).

221. Ibid., 1044.

222. 44 A.3d 27 (Pa. 2012).

223. Ibid., 53 (citation omitted).

224. Ibid., 55–57.

225. 319 A.2d 914, 920 (Pa. 1974) (holding that "in the absence of other identifiable causes, the malfunction itself is evidence of a 'defective condition'").

226. Ibid., 922–23.

227. 565 A.2d 751 (Pa. 1989).

228. Ibid., 754 (citations omitted).

229. 980 A.2d 535 (Pa. 2009).

230. Ibid., 542.

231. Ibid., 547.

232. 249 A.2d 563 (Pa. 1969).

233. Ibid., 566 (following Restatement [Second] of Torts § 402A, comment g [1965]).

234. 564 A.2d 1244 (Pa. 1989).

235. Ibid., 1248.

236. 588 A.2d 476 (Pa. 1991).

237. Ibid., 479 (citation omitted).

238. Simmons v. Pacor, Inc., 674 A.2d 232, 239–40 (Pa. 1996).

239. 696 A.2d 137 (Pa. 1997).

240. Ibid., 145.

241. Ibid., 145–46 (footnote omitted), emphasis added.

CHAPTER 18

Clash of Titans

The Supreme Court and Product Liability

CLIFFORD A. RIEDERS AND

PAMELA L. SHIPMAN

The history of the Pennsylvania Supreme Court's consideration of liability for defective products and the doctrine of the Restatement (Second) of Torts, Section 402A was an outgrowth of the national trend to recognize the difficulty of proof of a product defectively designed or manufactured. Since the dawn of the modern age of manufacturing, the courts have attempted to ameliorate the difficulty of proving negligence in design and manufacture. Doctrines developed based on specific objects and events, such as dams breaking. With the passage of time, this ad hoc analysis gave way to a more comprehensive approach. The automobile age heralded a new attitude toward product liability as recognized by the seminal case of *MacPherson v. Buick Motor Co.*[1]

Restatement (Second), Section 402A was promulgated by the American Law Institute (ALI) in 1965[2] during a period when the courts nationwide were struggling with the issue of adequate consumer protection.[3] Strict liability in tort evolved during a time when three people were killed every hour of every day from household hazards.[4] In 1970, the President's Commission on Product Safety reported that some twenty million Americans were injured each year as a result of incidents connected with consumer products.[5] An additional seven million injuries were reportedly connected to industrial products.[6] The legal community recognized that there was a need for a coherent statement of manufacturers' liability for defective products.[7]

About a decade after its promulgation, thirty-two states had adopted Restatement (Second), Section 402A or a rule substantially modeled after it.[8] Pennsylvania was an early adherent, adopting Section 402A in *Webb v. Zern* in 1966.[9] The case was heard by Chief Justice John C. Bell and Justices Musmanno, Jones, Cohen, Eagen, O'Brien, and Roberts. The *Webb* Court was clearly a progressive one. In fact, Chief Justice Bell,[10] in his dissent in *Webb*, complained, "In the last few years, the Supreme Court of Pennsylvania has radically changed the law in 30 different branches or fields which, prior thereto, had been firmly established. They have done this either by expressly overruling our prior decisions, or sometimes by evasion and necessary implication. Today, no one knows from month to month or whenever the Supreme Court of Pennsylvania . . . meets, what the law will be tomorrow—or, by retrospectively, what the Court will now say it always should have been—or what anyone's rights, privileges, liabilities and duties are."[11]

Chief Justice Bell was obviously the conservative voice on the Court and often dissented when he felt the Court's decisions were too liberal.[12] Prominent in Pennsylvania Republican politics, in the 1930s, Bell opposed the New Deal policies of President Franklin D. Roosevelt and wrote booklets attacking the New Deal that were widely distributed in Pennsylvania.[13] Elected lieutenant governor in 1942, he served just nineteen days as Pennsylvania's governor in January 1947[14] prior to his appointment as a justice of the Pennsylvania Supreme Court.

The majority opinion in *Webb v. Zern* was authored by Justice Herbert B. Cohen.[15] A well-known attorney and Democratic politician from York, Pennsylvania,[16] Justice Cohen had no judicial experience prior to his ascension to the Supreme Court in 1957,[17] and it is clear that the real leaders in the move toward adoption of strict liability for defective products were Justices Benjamin Rowland Jones and Samuel Roberts.

A Republican from Luzerne County, Justice Jones served as an Orphans' Court judge for five years in Luzerne County prior to his election to the Pennsylvania Supreme Court in 1957.[18] Justice Roberts's legal practice included service as assistant district attorney of Erie County and special deputy attorney general of Pennsylvania, as well as a ten-year term as president judge of the Erie County Orphans' Court.[19] He was elected to the Supreme Court of Pennsylvania in 1962.[20]

Daryl Fair, in his "Collective Biography" of the Court, lists Justice Roberts among the Republicans on the Court at that time.[21] Justice Roberts, in particular, has been acknowledged as a leader in the "modernization" of the jurisprudence of the Commonwealth:[22] "His opinions . . . recognize[d] the need to have a balance between respect for the past and the need for progressive justice. He believed that law, by its very nature is dynamic and that law existed to serve people and must adapt to changing views and needs."[23]

Webb was little more than an announcement of a fait accompli, as the adoption of Section 402A had been presaged by earlier opinions. The emerging trend was evident both nationally and in Pennsylvania. As early as 1963, the Pennsylvania Supreme Court noted that "nearly a third of the American jurisdictions, including Pennsylvania, have broken away from the rule of 'privity of contract' in cases involving food, beverages and like goods for human consumption."[24] In a case decided the same day as *Webb*, *Miller v. Preitz*,[25] the movement to expand liability for defective products was acknowledged: "Since 1958, almost every court that has considered the question has expanded the doctrine of strict liability to cover all defective products, regardless of lack of proof of negligence."[26] In his opinion in *Webb*, Justice Cohen pointed to the legal reasoning of Justices Jones and Roberts in *Miller* as providing the foundation for the Court's decision: "The development of the law in that area [liability in trespass for defective products] is chronicled in the Concurring and Dissenting Opinions of Justices Jones and Roberts to the decision of this Court in *Miller v. Preitz*, Pa. 221 A.2d 320 (1966). One will also find there citations to modern case law and commentaries which extend and recommend the extension of the law of strict liability in tort for defective products. The new Restatement of Torts reflects this modern attitude."[27]

Miller was an action *in assumpsit* brought by the estate of a deceased minor against the seller and manufacturer of a defective vaporizer-humidifier for alleged breaches of implied warranties of merchantability. The minor was a nephew of the purchaser of the vaporizer, which was being used for this minor in accordance with its ordinary purpose—to relieve nasal congestion—when it suddenly shot boiling water on the child's body, causing injuries that resulted in his death three days later.

The majority opinion in *Miller* was again authored by Justice Cohen. He construed the language of the Pennsylvania Commercial Code to extend a warranty remedy to the estate of the deceased child because the term *family* under Section 2-318 of the code was interpreted to include a nephew; but Justice Cohen did not find a warranty claim available against the remote sellers (the distributor and manufacturer) because there was no privity of contract with them. Noting that the "privity" requirement had long been abandoned in Pennsylvania in actions in trespass for negligently caused injuries, and recognizing the social policy considerations behind imposing strict liability in tort on all those who make or market any kind of defective product—notwithstanding an absence of negligence on their part—the majority felt constrained by the fact that no claim had been brought in trespass. While clearly sympathetic to the policy arguments underlying Section 402A, Justice Cohen and the majority in *Miller* nevertheless declined to overlook the procedural distinctions between the forms of action: "As a result, a determination of law as to strict liability for defective products in a trespass action must await an appropriate case."[28]

Justice Roberts, in his concurring and dissenting opinion, felt no such compunction. He stated that the majority's "application of the privity doctrine to bar a direct action against [defendants], stems from a desire to maintain doctrinal purity and to compel adherence to strict forms of pleading." In his view, the majority's "concern with form, while possibly justified under certain circumstances, is not appropriate in the instant case and merely delays action on the part of this Court which is long overdue."[29]

Justice Jones likewise concurred in the allowance of a claim against the retailer but dissented with respect to the dismissal of the claim against the remote sellers. In a lengthy opinion, he reviewed the jurisprudence relating to vertical and horizontal privity:

> The instant litigation poses for us the question whether we shall continue to require the establishment of privity in an assumpsit action. . . . Many of the leading scholars in the field as well as courts in other jurisdictions have with great logic

and persuasion illustrated the unsoundness and illogic of retaining the concept of privity in the field of product liability. Dissatisfaction with the requirement of privity stems from the recognition that it is completely unrealistic to limit a manufacturer's breach of warranty liability to his immediate vendee, who is most often himself a vendor who intends not to use, but merely to serve as a commercial conduit for the product, or to limit a retailer's breach of warranty liability to his immediate vendee when both the retailer and his vendee are well aware at the time of the sale of the product that others than the vendee will use or come in contact with it.[30]

Justice Jones urged the abolishment of horizontal privity: "[I]f we are to retain the requirement of privity, then I . . . would hold that the warranties extend to any person or persons whom the seller could have reasonably foreseen would use, consume or be affected by the product."[31] He also favored the abolition of vertical privity. He argued for the adoption of Restatement (Second), Section 402A and the confinement of assumpsit actions to those cases where the damages are solely commercial.[32] Citing the landmark California case of *Escola v. Coca Cola Bottling*,[33] Justice Jones noted the underlying purpose of Section 402A as ensuring "that the costs of injuries resulting from defective products are borne by the manufacturers that put such products on the market rather than by the injured persons who are powerless to protect themselves."[34] He further espoused the rationale often advanced at the time by the leading advocates for strict liability in tort:

> Those who make and market products which are to be used and consumed by the public must be held to a special responsibility to any member of the using or consuming public who may be injured by the use and consumption of the product. The public, with justification, expects that, in the case of products of which it has a need and for which it must rely upon those who make and market the product, such manufacturers and sellers, be they proximate or remote, will stand behind the products; the burden of injuries caused by defects in such products should fall upon those who make and market the products.[35]

It was these policy rationales that formed the underpinning for *Webb v. Zern*.

Once *Webb v. Zern* was decided, the defense of privity would soon fall, despite the procedural distinctions between trespass and assumpsit. Strict liability has often entered through the barnyard door of privity: "privity" represented an artificial defense, the abolishment of which created an environment for the introduction of strict liability concepts.

Only two years later, in *Kassab v. Soya*,[36] the Supreme Court overruled *Miller*. Justice Roberts was once again in the forefront, authoring the opinion that held that a purchaser of a product may maintain an action *in assumpsit* against a remote manufacturer for injury to commercial breed cattle caused by a breach of an implied warranty for cattle feed. Justice Roberts noted,

Courts and scholars alike have recognized that the typical consumer does not deal at arm's length with the party whose product he buys. Rather, he buys from a retail merchant who is usually little more than an economic conduit. It is not the merchant who has defectively manufactured the product. Nor is it usually the merchant who advertises the product on such a large scale as to attract consumers. We have in our society literally scores of large, financially responsible manufacturers who place their wares in the stream of commerce not only with the realization, but with the avowed purpose, that these goods will find their way into the hands of the consumer.[37]

Kassab abolished vertical privity *in assumpsit* cases brought under the commercial code and indicated that the code should be construed as coextensive with Section 402A.[38]

Justice Cohen continued to insist that the Court should proceed more cautiously. He did not view the issue of privity as properly before the Court in *Kassab* and therefore contended that the majority should have awaited a better opportunity "to completely change the traditional doctrine of privity of contract in the breach of warranty area."[39]

The onslaught of "reform" was not to be denied, however. By 1974, the last vestige of privity was disposed of in *Salvador v. Atlantic Steel Boiler Company*.[40] By that time, both Chief Justice Bell and Justice Cohen had left the Court. Once again, it was Justice Roberts who announced the decision in *Salvador*: "We have decided that no current societal interest is served by permitting the manufacturer to place a defective article in the stream of commerce and then to avoid responsibility for damages caused by the defect. He may not preclude an injured plaintiff's recovery by forcing him to prove negligence in the manufacturing process. *Webb v. Zern*. Neither may the manufacturer defeat the claim by arguing that the purchaser has no contractual relation to him. *Kassab v. Central Soya*. Why then should the mere fact that the injured party is not himself the purchaser deny recovery?"[41]

The next significant step for Pennsylvania product liability law occurred in the *Berkebile v. Brantly Helicopter* case,[42] decided in 1975. Chief Justice Jones again took the lead. Although some have said that "Section 402(A)'s greatest strength is its ambiguity and breadth," which allowed for "the expansion of the concept of strict liability and protection for the consumer,"[43] that very ambiguity caused the courts to struggle with how to define the parameters of a strict liability products action. In *Berkebile*, Chief Justice Jones noted the difficulties trial courts had labored under while trying to articulate the appropriate standards in such cases. He found that the use of the phrase "unreasonably dangerous" in defining "defective condition" for the jury improperly injected negligence principles into strict liability theory and urged the purging of any form of "reasonable man" standard from strict liability cases. He wrote,

The salutary purpose of the "unreasonably dangerous" qualification is to preclude the seller's liability where it cannot be said that the product is defective;

this purpose can be met by requiring proof of a defect. To charge the jury or permit argument concerning the reasonableness of a consumer's or seller's actions and knowledge, even if merely to define "defective condition" undermines the policy considerations that have led us to hold in *Salvador* that the manufacturer is effectively the guarantor of his product's safety. The plaintiff must still prove that there was a defect in the product and that the defect caused his injury; but if he sustains this burden, he will have proved that as to him the product was unreasonably dangerous. It is therefore unnecessary and improper to charge the jury on "reasonableness."[44]

Only one other justice, however, concurred in Chief Justice Jones's opinion;[45] the other five justices who heard the case concurred in the result only. For a time, the federal courts applying Pennsylvania law reasoned that the views expressed in Chief Justice Jones's opinion in *Berkebile* were not the law of Pennsylvania and that it was proper to instruct a jury that it must find that a defective condition is unreasonably dangerous to the user or consumer.[46] Indeed, US District Judge Daniel H. Huyett III opined that the "unreasonably dangerous" language is an integral part of Section 402A. He felt that to read Chief Justice Jones's opinion as striking the phrase "unreasonably dangerous to the user or consumer" from Section 402A in Pennsylvania, which would otherwise remain fully applicable, would be to "disembowel" Section 402A without replacing it with a clear standard by which the scope of a seller's liability for defects can be measured.[47]

Defining the role of the jury as opposed to that of the judge appears always to have been something of a compromise. *Berkebile* began that process. The Supreme Court had to do something with the "unreasonably dangerous" language in 402A and ensure that it had a function distinct from a determination as to whether a product was to be found dangerous by the finder of fact.

In *Azzarello v. Black Bros. Co.*,[48] the Supreme Court in 1978 confirmed that the "unreasonably dangerous" terminology of Section 402A was not appropriate as a jury instruction. Chief Justice Jones was by this time gone from the Court. The opinion was authored by Justice Robert Nix, who had joined with Jones in *Berkebile*. In *Azzarello*, however, no dissenting views were expressed and the decision was unanimous.[49]

The grandson of a slave who rose to become dean of South Carolina State College and the son of a powerful Pennsylvania congressman, Justice Nix was the first African American to serve on the Supreme Court and later ascended to the post of chief justice.[50] After serving as a deputy attorney general in Pennsylvania, he practiced criminal defense law at his father's law firm, Nix, Rhodes and Nix.[51] Active in Democratic politics,[52] he was later elected to the Philadelphia Court of Common Pleas in 1967. He was elected to the Supreme Court in 1971 in a landslide decision.[53]

Justice Nix was generally regarded as a champion of individual rights and social justice,[54] which undoubtedly translated into a judicial philosophy that supported consumer protection. In *Azzarello*, he wrote eloquently of the inequity of the marketplace as a justification for strict liability in tort:

> The development of a sophisticated and complex industrial society with its proliferation of new products and vast change in the private enterprise system has inspired a change in legal philosophy from the principle of caveat emptor which prevailed in the early nineteenth century marketplace to a view that a supplier of products should be deemed to be "the guarantor of his products' safety." *Salvador v. Atlantic Steel Boiler Co.* 457 Pa. 24, 32, 319 A.2d 903, 907 (1974). The realities of our economic society as it exists today forces the conclusion that the risk of loss or injury resulting from defective products should be borne by the suppliers, principally because they are in a position to absorb the loss by distributing it as a cost of doing business. In an era of giant corporate structures, utilizing the national media to sell their wares, the original concern for an emerging manufacturing industry has given way to the view that it is now the consumer who must be protected. Courts have increasingly adopted the position that the risk of loss must be placed upon the supplier of the defective product without regard to fault or privity of contract.[55]

The rationale for excising "unreasonably dangerous" from Section 402A for purposes of instructing the jury rested on a recognition that the term "unreasonably dangerous" was a means of identifying products for which it is justifiable to place the risk of loss on the manufacturer or supplier.[56] Justice Nix reasoned that the question of whether the utility of a product outweighed the unavoidable danger it might pose was a question of social policy, and formulation of social policy is a judicial function: "Restated, the phrases 'defective condition' and 'unreasonably dangerous' as used in the Restatement formulation are terms of art invoked when strict liability is appropriate. It is a judicial function to decide whether, under plaintiff's averment of the facts, recovery would be justified; and only after this judicial determination is made is the cause submitted to the jury to determine whether the facts of the case support the averments of the complaint."[57]

Therefore, the *concept* of "unreasonably dangerous" under the Restatement (Second), Section 402A was not abandoned; it was simply restricted to consideration by the Court, while the *term itself* was deleted from jury instructions because of its tendency "to suggest considerations which are usually identified with the law of negligence."[58] In its place, the *Azzarello* Court formulated the standard that "the jury may find a defect where the product left the supplier's control lacking any element necessary to make it safe for its intended use or possessing any feature that renders it unsafe for the intended use."[59]

Justice Nix was also responsible for writing the opinion that established another significant tenet of Pennsylvania product liability law under Section 402A—the doctrine that evidence of industry standards is not admissible in a strict liability products case. In *Lewis v. Coffing Hoist Div., Duff-Norton Co., Inc.*, decided in 1987, Justice Nix noted that the clear implication of the *Azzarello* decision was not simply that certain language was deleted from jury instructions but also that "negligence concepts have no place in a case based on strict liability."[60] It logically followed that evidence of industry standards relating to the design of an allegedly defective product, and evidence of its widespread use in the industry, goes to the reasonableness of the manufacturer's conduct in making its design choice, and therefore the majority concluded that such evidence is inadmissible as improperly introducing concepts of negligence law.[61] In his concurring opinion, Justice Rolf Larsen added, "[A] manufacturer cannot avoid liability to its consumers that it injures or maims through its defective designs by showing that 'the other guys do it too.'"[62] Justices William D. Hutchinson and John P. Flaherty Jr., however, took the opposite view, writing in their separate dissents that such evidence, while not conclusive, was indeed relevant and probative, not necessarily of the reasonableness of the manufacturer's use of the particular design, but rather of its safety.[63] Justice Hutchinson, in particular, a Republican from Pottsville who spent ten years in the Pennsylvania legislature before his election to the Supreme Court in 1981,[64] took a more business-friendly view, arguing that it was "madness" to believe that "judges and lawyers . . . are more capable of designing products than engineers."[65] He opined, "Industry standards are written by individuals considered by their peers in industry, academia and research to be especially knowledgeable in a particular technical specialty. These standards contain their collective expert wisdom. . . . Their collective opinion is at least as valuable as any individual expert witness's."[66]

Difficulties with the application of a rigid boundary between negligence concepts and strict liability surfaced early in the jurisprudence following *Azzarello*, however, particularly in failure-to-warn and product misuse cases. Whether there was actually a difficulty in the application of the boundary, as opposed to pushback from the industrial community, is a question beyond the scope of this chapter. *Berkebile* and *Azzarello* created a hybrid system between negligence (the judge's job in determining whether a product was sufficiently unreasonable to be adjudicated by a jury) and strict liability (the function of the jury to state whether the product lacked an element necessary to make it safe). Subsequent justices picked up on this dichotomy of functions to claim a systemic inconsistency in Pennsylvania's product liability jurisprudence.

The case of *Sherk v. Daisy-Heddon, a Div. of Victor Comptometer Corp.*[67] in 1982 was a harbinger of the struggles and confusion to come. The *Sherk* case involved a product liability action against the manufacturer of an air rifle, the "Daisy Power King," for the death of fourteen-year-old James Sherk as a result of a BB shot to the head accidentally inflicted by his friend Robert Saenz. At trial, the plaintiff proceeded against the manufacturer of the air rifle on the theory that the manufacturer had failed to provide an adequate warning of the rifle's lethal propensity and that the alleged failure to warn had caused James Sherk's death.[68] The jury returned a verdict in favor of the manufacturer, but on appeal, a panel of the Superior Court reversed the judgment entered on the verdict and remanded for a new trial. The Superior Court deemed a new trial to be necessary because, in its view, the trial court had improperly refused to charge the jury on negligence and had erroneously excluded evidence of the "community's perception" that BB guns previously marketed by the appellant were nonlethal.[69] The Supreme Court, however, reversed, finding that the plaintiff's own evidence demonstrated that "[t]he Power King air rifle was misused by Robert Saenz in a manner that Robert Saenz knew could cause serious bodily injury. Despite his knowledge that BBs fired from the Power King could kill animals and blind a person, Robert Saenz directed the Power King from close range at James Sherk's head."[70]

The majority concluded, therefore, that the alleged "defect" in the warnings accompanying the Power King air rifle did not cause James Sherk's death, quoting Dean Prosser's observation that strict liability "made no change in the rule, well settled in the negligence cases, that the seller of the product is not to be held liable when the consumer makes an abnormal use of it."[71]

Interestingly, the majority opinion in *Sherk* was authored by Chief Justice Roberts, one of the principal leaders in the Supreme Court's move to recognize the principles of Section 402A and adopt strict liability in tort. The more liberal viewpoint in *Sherk* was expressed in the vigorous dissent of Justice Rolf Larsen.[72] Another reading of *Sherk* is that it was an anomaly because it involved the use of a weapon, and Pennsylvania is a strong hunting state, where the use of guns cannot be impaired in an effective way by the judiciary.

A Democrat from Allegheny County, Justice Larsen was elected to the Supreme Court in 1977. As a jurist,[73] he is probably best known for his landmark 1979 opinion in *Pugh v. Hughes*,[74] in which the Court held that residential leases contain an implied warranty of habitability. Eccentric and outspoken, he was considered a "free-thinker"[75] whose progressive leanings are apparent in his opinions. In personal injury cases, he was regarded as "perhaps the most consistently pro-plaintiff justice."[76]

The key for Justice Larsen in *Sherk* was the fact that the conduct of Robert Saenz, conduct he viewed as a "subsequent act of negligence," was *eminently foreseeable and was to be expected.*[77] In his lengthy and heavily researched dissenting opinion, Justice Larsen reviewed significant product liability decisions in both Pennsylvania and other jurisdictions and recounted the legal arguments of notable scholars in the field. He remarked on the difficulty of applying the *Azzarello* formulation to the warning context: "*Azzarello* left open, however, the question 'what is a defect?' in situations wherein a defect is asserted because warnings are absent or inadequate."[78] Foreshadowing the future struggles in the Supreme Court's jurisprudence, he noted, "The problem of devising a workable standard of 'defect' which accomplishes the twin objectives of limiting a supplier's liability to injuries caused by identifiable 'defects' (including those caused by lack of adequate warnings), while still preventing negligence concepts from slipping back into the strict liability arena, is undoubtedly the most troublesome and controversial problem in product liability law today."[79]

It was as if Justice Larsen had read opinions authored by his successors on the bench decades later and was addressing the debate over intended use, intended user, and foreseeable misuse when he argued,

Despite the language of "intended use" in the *Azzarello* definition of "defect," "intended use" cannot be construed to be a ceiling on the manufacturer's liability since, as occurred here, the product might well invite other non-"intended" uses. The rationale of *Azzarello* was to *relieve* the plaintiff of added burdens of proving elements that ring of negligence, yet the elevation of "intended use" to a supplier's defense, as the lower court rulings and the majority have done in effect, would impose the ultimate burden upon the consumer—the burden of proving the manufacturer/seller's subjective intent. The negligence concepts of a supplier's fault or lack of fault have been interjected into the dispute, contrary to the admonitions of *Azzarello* and of *Berkebile*. *Berkebile* stated "[b]ecause the seller is liable in strict liability regardless of any negligence, whether he could have foreseen a particular injury is irrelevant in a strict liability case." If a supplier's foreseeability is irrelevant, it goes without saying that the supplier's *intent* is irrelevant. Accordingly, the language "lacking any element necessary to make it safe for its *intended use* or possessing any feature that renders it unsafe for the *intended use*" . . . must be read merely to establish the supplier's *minimum* duty, i.e., the product must *at least* be safe for its intended use.[80]

The argument over intended use and foreseeability and where to draw the line between negligence concepts and strict liability continued over the next two decades. Lower courts continued to employ foreseeability considerations in addressing the notion of "intended use" in product liability claims. The theory was that when the Supreme Court in *Berkebile v. Brantly Helicopter Corp.* stated that "foreseeability" has no place in a strict liability action, "it did so in order to *relax* the plaintiff's burden of proof," but "intended use" nevertheless encompassed "foreseeability" because "[t]he proper limits of responsibility for the defendant-seller . . . is whether the use to which the product was put was *intended or foreseeable (objectively reasonable)* by the defendant."[81] In *Burch v. Sears Roebuck & Co.*, for example, the Superior Court found that abnormal use of a product will negate liability "only if it was not reasonably foreseeable by the seller."[82]

In *Riley v. Warren Manufacturing*,[83] on the other hand, the Superior Court ruled as a matter of law that the manufacturer of a bulk feed trailer was not liable for injuries sustained by the operator's grandson, who was accompanying him while he delivered feed, when the grandson put his hand inside the discharge tube, making contact with the blades of the airlock device used to expel the feed. The panel found that the trailer was not intended to be used by or around children, and despite arguments by the plaintiff that it was "foreseeable" that someone might place his or her hand inside the discharge tube and come in contact with the blades, "it is inappropriate to discuss foreseeability, a negligence principle, when analyzing a product liability theory."[84]

Yet one month later, the Supreme Court in *Davis v. Berwind Corp.*[85] confirmed the view that foreseeability could be examined in the context of substantial change to the product: "The seller is not liable if a safe product is made unsafe by subsequent changes.... Where the product has reached the user or consumer with substantial change, the question becomes whether the manufacturer could have *reasonably expected or foreseen* such an alteration of its product."[86]

In the area of strict liability for failure to warn of product dangers, the blending of negligence and strict liability principles was particularly acute. As some commentators have noted,[87] confusion existed in the lower courts about whether strict liability for failure to warn even constitutes a theory of recovery separate and distinct from negligence: "One decision from the superior court has suggested that strict liability for failure to warn is identical to liability grounded in negligence, and another decision has suggested that there is such substantial overlap between the two theories that it is difficult to distinguish between them. Although there are similarities between the two doctrines, a close reading of the decided cases demonstrates that strict liability has been treated as a separate theory of liability."[88]

Meanwhile, the shifting perspective on product liability and questions regarding its underlying policy justifications occurring nationally began to find their way into discussions of Pennsylvania law as well. Following the adoption of Section 402A, nationally there were approximately fifteen years of expansion in strict liability and victims' access to the courts. Then the pendulum began to swing back.[89]

In the 1990s, the ALI began to revise its treatment of product liability law. The perception on the part of industry that liberalization of product liability law had opened the door to increased litigation and higher insurance costs led "tort reformers" in favor of restricting product liability laws to campaign in the late 1980s and early 1990s for revisions in tort law as a part of a project under the auspices of the ALI. Known as the Enterprise Responsibility Project, the movement ultimately evolved, undoubtedly as a result of intense lobbying by its proponents, into a component of the more general revisions to the Restatement (Second) of Torts.[90]

The result—the Restatement (Third) of Torts, Product Liability, published in 1998—departs significantly from its previous approach to this area of the law. Indeed, the introduction characterizes the Restatement (Third) as "an almost total overhaul of Restatement (Second) as it concerns the liability of commercial sellers of products."[91] The Restatement (Third) approach essentially abandons strict liability for design defects and warning cases in favor of a "foreseeability test" and proof of design alternatives.[92] Some commentators and courts have pointed out that the use of "foreseeability" effectively eradicates the distinction between strict liability and negligence.[93] Unlike the broad acceptance Section 402A received, the Restatement (Third) of Torts, Product Liability has become a battleground, engendering criticism from both academia and the nation's courtrooms.

Proponents of the Restatement (Third) argue that Section 402A was designed to address manufacturing defects and, therefore, is an imperfect vehicle for dealing with defective design and failure-to-warn cases. Some of the impetus for the change to a negligence standard has come from the notion that embracing negligence concepts—that is, "reasonableness"—is merely making explicit criteria that are implicitly utilized in the tests for design and failure-to-warn cases. The Restatement (Third) and its proponents also argue that the deterrence effect of strict liability results in "excessively sacrificing product features" and that a negligence-based regime would be "fair" because it would cause "consumers to engage in safe use and consumption of products."[94]

Critics of the new Restatement approach, on the other hand, view it as a regression and abandonment of the consumer protection policies that gave birth to strict liability for defective products under Section 402A. Many commentators have charged that the Restatement (Third) was heavily influenced by, if it was not the product of, insurance, business, and manufacturing interests.[95] Such commentators characterize the Restatement (Third) as "representing an unwanted ascendancy of corporate interests under the guise of tort reform."[96]

To date, approximately fifteen years after its publication, the Restatement (Third) remains a subject of debate, and its provisions have not been universally accepted. Some jurisdictions have adopted the Restatement (Third) approach, while others have explicitly rejected it. Some courts have recognized portions of the Restatement (Third) as consistent with their state's jurisprudence but have adopted only certain selected sections. In yet other jurisdictions, Section 402A continues to control.

This unsettled state of affairs is mirrored by the Pennsylvania experience, magnified by the fact that the US Court of Appeals for the Third Circuit undertook to decide Pennsylvania's position on the Restatement (Third) before the justices of the Pennsylvania Supreme Court were themselves ready to undertake that task. Consideration of the Restatement (Second) / Restatement (Third) controversy surfaced in the 2003 case of *Phillips v. Cricket Lighters*.[97] A deeply divided Supreme Court held that strict liability principles did not apply against the manufacturer of a cigarette lighter in a case where it was alleged that the product was defective because it was not childproof. In a plurality opinion,[98] authored by Chief Justice Ralph Cappy, a Democrat and former Allegheny County Common Pleas Court judge elected to the Supreme Court in 1989,[99] the Court held that Section 402A did not apply because the manufacturer of the lighter did not intend it to be used by children. In response to arguments that the use was "foreseeable," Chief Justice Cappy reasoned that it would be improper under Pennsylvania law to import principles of negligence into a strict liability claim, concluding that the doctrine must be reserved for situations where the use being made of the product was in keeping with what the supplier intended.[100] Justice Cappy then went on to rule that the plaintiffs should nonetheless have been permitted to make a claim for negligence.[101]

Justice Saylor concurred in *Phillips* in the disposition of the strict liability and negligence claims "under present law" but identified the Restatement (Third) as the most viable approach for the assessment of the plaintiff's claims, under which the claim would have survived.[102] Widely regarded as an intellectual leader on the Court on product liability issues, Justice Saylor used his concurring opinion in *Phillips* to expound "at length on the inherent tensions in Pennsylvania law between strict liability and negligence principles, arguing that the Third Restatement properly reconciles that conflict."[103] The opinion began as follows:

> As a pillar of their reasoning concerning the character of strict product liability doctrine in Pennsylvania, the lead Justices retrench the Court's periodic admonishment to the effect that negligence concepts have no place in a strict liability action. A decided majority of courts and commentators, however, have come to recognize that this proposition cannot be justly sustained in theory in relation to strict product liability cases predicated on defective design; moreover, it is demonstrably incongruent with design-defect strict liability doctrine as it is currently implemented in Pennsylvania trial courts and in federal district courts applying Pennsylvania law. Furthermore, while the parties to the litigation underlying this appeal may not have expressly developed the approach of the product liability segment of the Third Restatement as such in their submissions, the Restatement position represents a synthesis of law derived from reasoned, mainstream, modern consensus. Particularly in light of pervasive ambiguities and inconsistencies in prevailing Pennsylvania jurisprudence in this area, I view this appeal as an opportunity to examine the range of readily accessible, corrective measures. In my judgment, the [Third] Restatement's considered approach illuminates the most viable route to providing essential clarification and remediation, at least on a prospective basis.[104]

Additionally, in *Duchess v. Langston Corporation* (2001),[105] Justice Saylor wrote the majority opinion, holding that the "subsequent remedial measures doctrine," usually applied in negligence cases, would also apply to strict liability cases.[106] His opinion in *Duchess* contained numerous references to similarities between negligence and product liability actions.[107]

A member of the Republican Party,[108] Justice Saylor was elected to the Supreme Court in 1997. He served on the Superior Court of Pennsylvania from 1993 to 1997. Prior to that, he was first deputy attorney general for Pennsylvania from 1983 to 1987, the director of the Pennsylvania Bureau of Consumer Protection from 1982 to 1983, and a first assistant district attorney for Somerset County from 1973 to 1976.[109] Justice Saylor became chief justice of Pennsylvania in January 2015.[110]

Justice Saylor was joined in *Phillips* by Justices J. Michael Eakin and Ronald D. Castille. Prior to his judicial career, Justice Castille served for nearly twenty years in the Philadelphia district attorney's office, including four years as district attorney.[111] Born in Miami, he came to Philadelphia as a young US marine lieutenant for treatment at the nearby naval hospital after he was hit by machine-gun fire in South Vietnam on his twenty-third birthday, which cost him his right leg. For his actions, he received a Bronze Star and two Purple Hearts. Justice Castille developed an attachment to the Philadelphia area and returned there after graduating from the University of Virginia Law School.[112] As the Republican candidate for the Supreme Court,[113] he was elected in 1993 and became chief justice in 2008.[114]

Also a Republican, Justice J. Michael Eakin is a former Cumberland County district attorney. He was elected to the Superior Court in 1995 and served there for six years before his election to the Supreme Court in 2001.[115] He is known as the "Rhyming Justice" for occasionally incorporating verse into his opinions.[116] He resigned from the bench in March 2016.[117]

Three years after *Phillips*, in *Pennsylvania Department of General Services v. US Mineral Products Co.*,[118] Justice Saylor again authored an opinion, this time in the majority, with significant ramifications for Pennsylvania product liability law. The majority opinion in the case refused to "extend" strict liability to cover foreseeable conditions that are no fault of the intended user. This conclusion should not be read, however, as suggesting that Justice Saylor was committed to the traditional law of strict liability. In fact, he mentioned several times that this reticence to extend the doctrine was appropriate because the doctrine needed a complete overhaul, not tweaking.[119] Focusing on "intended user" and "intended use" and rejecting Superior Court precedents that had recognized foreseeability as an element in determining the existence of a legal duty to a party—that is, whether a party can be considered an intended user or whether the occurrence at issue represented an "intended use"—the Supreme Court's pronouncements in the *Phillips* and *Department of General Services* cases advanced concerns about whether the firm line between negligence and strict liability under the *Azzarello* case should remain and raised the possibility of an alternate approach, perhaps through the Restatement (Third). Whether *Phillips* and *General Services* clarified or confused Pennsylvania law is debatable, but the debate itself was clearly joined by these cases.

Following these developments, in 2009, a panel of the US Court of Appeals for the Third Circuit, in *Berrier v. Simplicity Mfg., Inc.*,[120] predicted that the Pennsylvania Supreme Court would adopt Section 1 of the Restatement (Third) of Torts to provide a cause of action for bystanders in a product liability case. *Berrier* involved an injury to a minor who was run over by her grandfather while he was making a turn with his riding lawn mower in reverse. The mower did not have a "No Mow in Reverse" system to deactivate the mower blades. The plaintiff argued that she should be protected as an innocent bystander under Section 402A, but the district court disagreed and dismissed the plaintiff's case. On appeal, the Third Circuit reversed, applying the "foreseeable risk of harm" standard under the Restatement (Third) of Torts, Product Liability to provide the plaintiff with an opportunity for recovery.[121] At that time, the panel observed, the Pennsylvania Supreme Court had recently granted allocatur in *Bugosh v. I.U. North America, Inc.* to determine "[w]hether this Court should apply § 2 of the Restatement (Third) of Torts in place of § 402A of the Restatement (Second) of Torts."[122] Relying heavily on Justice Saylor's endorsement of the Third Restatement in his concurring opinion in *Phillips*, which was joined by Justices

Castille and Eakin, the federal court speculated that there were enough votes on the Court to adopt Section 2 of the Third Restatement as the law of Pennsylvania and "that the Justices who would adopt section 2 would adopt as well . . . section 1, rather than trying to parse the applicable provisions of the Third Restatement and thereby supplant some of the Second Restatement and not others."[123]

The Third Circuit's prediction proved incorrect, however. The Pennsylvania Supreme Court dismissed the appeal in *Bugosh* as improvidently granted.[124] Subsequent courts, commentators, and litigants debated the meaning of the *Bugosh* dismissal, but clearly a majority of the Court at that time was not willing to address whether to throw out Section 402A of the Restatement (Second), adopt all or part of the Restatement (Third), or even modify existing Pennsylvania law. In dissent, Justice Saylor, joined again by Chief Justice Castille, stated that the Court should have taken the opportunity to engage in such an overhaul, urging the prospective adoption of the Restatement (Third).[125]

Justice Saylor's dissent in *Bugosh* revealed that the majority apparently refused to adopt adopt "the whole of Section 2" of the Restatement (Third), as he would have voted to do, let alone the Restatement (Third) of Torts in its entirety. He acknowledged that if the majority were to do anything, it would be to "devise a replacement scheme" of its own,[126] which presumably would be more in line with established Pennsylvania jurisprudence than the Restatement (Third).

As noted in the excellent commentary by Arthur Bugay and Craig Bazarsky,[127] the combination of the *Berrier* prediction and the *Bugosh* dismissal created turmoil in the federal district courts: "Some applied the Restatement (Third), reasoning that the *Berrier* opinion remained binding precedent. Others applied the Restatement (Second), reasoning that the *Bugosh* dismissal invalidated the *Berrier* prediction."[128] Meanwhile, the Pennsylvania appellate courts continued to apply the Restatement (Second) in product liability matters heard after the *Bugosh* and *Berrier* decisions.[129]

Nevertheless, in the 2011 case of *Covell v. Bell*,[130] the Third Circuit reaffirmed *Berrier* and applied the Restatement (Third). The court refused to reexamine the *Berrier* analysis; instead, the court stated that these issues were "resolved only two years ago."[131] The court reasoned that the dismissal in *Bugosh* was on procedural grounds only, without any substantive effect, and therefore, "*Bugosh* [was] of no consequence"[132] to their original prediction, such that the *Berrier* decision was binding precedent.

As a result, after *Berrier* and *Covell*, the law applicable to a product liability action depended on whether the case was filed in state or federal court and, if in federal court, what judge was assigned to the case. Certainly it would be an understatement to say that "the proper approach to the foundational elements of a strict liability claim [was] a subject in current controversy" in the Pennsylvania Supreme Court at that time, as Justice Saylor observed in a concurring opinion in *Barnish v. KWI Building Company*.[133]

Of the justices who participated in *Bugosh*, in addition to Justice Saylor, Chief Justice Castille and Justice Eakin were seen as favoring the Restatement (Third)—at least in part. Justices Debra McCloskey Todd, Max Baer, and Seamus McCaffery were generally thought to be resistant to the Restatement (Third) approach. It is noteworthy that the divide appeared to be drawn along political lines, with the Republican members of the court (Justices Saylor, Castille, and Eakin) supporting what can be seen as the "tort reform" approach of the Restatement (Third), while the Democratic members (Justices Todd, Baer, and McCaffery) were generally thought to be opposed to implementing the new Restatement.

Chief Justice Castille joined Justice Saylor's opinion in every case that discussed the Restatement (Third), with the exception of *Lance v. Wyeth*.[134] *Wyeth*, however, did not entail a consideration of whether Pennsylvania's strict liability and negligence theories could be "reconciled" through the application of the Restatement (Third).[135] Castille's dissent in that case appears to involve a disagreement over the procedural posture of the case and was not a substantive one.

Like Chief Justice Castille, Justice Eakin also joined Justice Saylor's opinions in every case that discussed the Restatement (Third), with the exception of *Bugosh*. The *Bugosh* departure, however, might have simply reflected a disagreement regarding whether that case was appropriate for addressing the substantive issues and not any difference in legal philosophy. Considering that he also dissented in *Lance* on the grounds that the issue was not properly preserved and presented, this is a likely interpretation of his position in *Bugosh*. In addition to Justice Eakin, voting with the majority to dismiss the *Bugosh* appeal as improvidently granted were Justices Todd, McCaffery, and Baer.

A Democrat who formerly served on the Superior Court before assuming her place on the Supreme Court in 2008, Justice Todd apparently staked out a position in support of the Section 402A theory. She stated in her dissent in *Reott v. Asia Trend, Inc.*, "I . . . *presently* consider *Berkebile* to be an authoritative statement of Pennsylvania law."[136] In *Reott*, her dissent centered on her concern that the majority improperly equated a defense that the plaintiff's highly reckless conduct was the "sole cause" with the defense of superseding cause, the former in her view negating cause-in-fact, while the latter served as an affirmative defense.[137] Thus she would appear to be something of a purist—and perhaps, a traditionalist—bent on the application of tort theory.

In opinions she authored on the Superior Court, Justice Todd appeared quite comfortable with a risk-allocation, public policy argument. For example, in *Stecher v. Ford*, she stated, "If we were to impose upon an injured party the necessity of proving which impact in a chain collision did which harm, we would actually be expressing a judicial policy that it is better that a plaintiff, injured through no fault of his own, take nothing, than that a wrongdoer pay more than his theoretical share of the damages arising out of a situation which his wrong has helped to create."[138] At one point in *Ettinger v. Triangle-Pacific Corp.*,[139] in an opinion she wrote applying Section 402A to the question of whether a partially assembled industrial oven was a "product in the stream of commerce," she quoted *Davis v. Berwind Corp.*: "Section 402A reflects the social policy that a seller or manufacturer is best able to shoulder the costs and to administer the risks involved when a product is released into the stream of commerce."[140]

Justice Seamus P. McCaffery, like Justice Todd, is a member of the Democratic Party who was elevated to the Supreme Court from the Superior Court in the 2007 election.[141] Born in Belfast, Northern Ireland, he was formerly a US marine, an air force reserve officer, and a Philadelphia city policeman who put himself through law school while serving as a police officer.[142] Product liability cases from his tenure on the Superior Court seem to indicate a willingness to accept the social policy considerations underlying the Restatement (Second) of Torts. In *Donoughe v. Lincoln Elec. Co.*, McCaffery specifically confirmed his view that a trial judge is to perform a risk-utility analysis, acting as a sort of "social philosopher and a risk-utility economic analyst," although he acknowledged that the risk-utility analysis is not particularly well suited to a warnings case.[143] Ultimately, however, Justice McCaffery had no impact on the resolution of the Restatement (Second) / Restatement (Third) controversy. He resigned in the fall of 2014[144] and did not participate in the decision that finally brought the debate to a conclusion.

Justice Max Baer's record on product liability issues was perhaps the most intriguing of the justices who sat on the *Bugosh* Court. A Democrat and Pittsburgh native,[145] Justice Baer is a former deputy attorney general and Allegheny Common Pleas Court judge. He was elected to the Supreme Court in 2003.[146] In the first post-*Bugosh*, post-*Berrier* product case in front of the Court, *Barnish v. KWI Bldg. Co.*,[147] Justice Baer wrote the majority opinion and did not mention *Berrier* or the Restatement (Third). It was unclear whether this suggested a continued adherence to Section 402A or simply that the Court was waiting for an appropriate vehicle to address the issue.

In two previous cases, he sided with Justice Saylor and then against him. In *Harsh v. Petroll*,[148] Baer joined the unanimous opinion that contained Justice Saylor's dicta about the desirability of "additional clarification" in product liability law. The actual holding in that case, however, concerned the application of apportionment or joint and several liability among defendants in an enhanced-injury crashworthiness case. As a result, Justice Saylor's dicta regarding the Restatement was not necessarily an indication of Baer's position.

In *Pennsylvania Department of General Services v. US Mineral Products Co.*,[149] Justice Baer joined the dissent authored by Justice Sandra Schultz Newman, who left the Court in 2006.[150] In Justice Newman's opinion, when an intended user utilizes a product in the intended way, foreseeable conditions can be part of determining whether a product is defective. Specifically, building materials that release dangerous compounds when ignited are defective because a fire is a foreseeable condition even if the intended user uses the building in the intended fashion.[151] Baer joined Newman's opinion rather than Saylor's.

That Justice Baer sided with Justice Newman was considered by some as a sign that he was not irrevocably committed to Justice Saylor's point of view. The Third Circuit in *Berrier*, however, saw Justice Baer's joinder in Newman's dissent in *Department of General Services* as evidence that he was favorable to an adoption of the Restatement (Third) because Justice Newman, while basing her opinion on an application of Section 402A, stated, "I recognize the apparent and possible appeal in the more progressive approach adopted by the Third Restatement."[152]

In 2012, in *Beard v. Johnson & Johnson*,[153] the Supreme Court "again chose not to adopt the Restatement (Third) as had been repeatedly predicted by the Pennsylvania federal appellate court."[154] In the *Beard* decision, Justice Baer filed a concurring opinion, which Justices McCloskey, Todd, and McCaffery joined, in which he expressly stated that "the current law of Pennsylvania . . . is § 402A of the Restatement (Second) of Torts."[155] Justice Baer attempted to "distance" himself from language in the majority opinion that could be read as approval of the Restatement (Third)[156]—in particular, Justice Saylor's footnote supportive of assigning the risk-utility analysis to the jury.[157]

Justice Baer then directly addressed the Third Circuit's interpretation of his joining Justice Newman in *Department of General Services*:

> I recognize that the United States Court of Appeals for the Third Circuit utilized my joinder of similar language in a footnote of a concurring and dissenting opinion of former Justice Newman to predict that I would support the adoption of the Restatement Third. . . . In that footnote, Justice Newman merely "recognize[d] the apparent and possible appeal" of the Restatement Third, in the process of concluding that the argument [concerning its adoption] . . . was not before the Court in that case. . . . Respectfully, the Third Circuit misconstrued my joinder . . . as an inclination on my part to adopt the Restatement Third. Until such time as this Court is presented with a case to resolve this difficult issue, I express no opinion on the merits of the adoption of the Restatement Third.[158]

Thereafter, the appointment of Justice Correale F. Stevens sparked speculation that he would break the perceived deadlock and hold the key to the future of Pennsylvania product liability law. Appointed to the Supreme Court in July 2013 by Governor Tom Corbett to fill the unexpired term of Justice Orie Melvin, Stevens is a Republican with considerable judicial experience. He served on the Superior Court from 1997 to 2013, presiding as its president judge from 2011. Before becoming a Superior Court judge, he sat on the Luzerne County Court of Common Pleas from 1991 to 1996. Before that, he was also elected to four terms in the state House of Representatives, beginning in 1980, and was a former Luzerne County district attorney and Hazleton city solicitor.[159]

Despite his rather lengthy term on the Superior Court, Justice Stevens's reported appellate decisions involving defective products gave few clues to his position on the controversy surrounding the future of Pennsylvania product liability law. He did, however, seem comfortable with negligence concepts inserting themselves into the strict liability context. In *Putt v. Yates-Am. Mach. Co.*,[160] his opinion followed the traditional rule that "if there has been a substantial modification made to the product, *which was not reasonably foreseen by the manufacturer*, and if the modification is a superseding cause of the user's injury, the manufacturer is relieved of liability even if there was a design defect existing at the time the product was delivered to the purchaser."[161] In *Coffey v. Minwax Co., Inc.*,[162] a 2000 case involving a woodwork refinishing product that allegedly burst into flames, expert testimony that the most likely cause was the customer's insertion or withdrawal of a plug from an electrical outlet in the near vicinity was not inadmissible on the ground that it introduced negligence concepts into a strict liability action. Rather, the expert's testimony was ruled admissible to rebut the customer's claim as to either defect or proximate causation. Nevertheless, it is unclear whether these opinions represented a predisposition on Justice Stevens's part to favor the Third Restatement's incorporation of reasonable foreseeability into the design defect cases or simply reflected an application of what he viewed as existing Pennsylvania precedent.

Resolution of the controversy seemed almost certain when the Supreme Court granted a petition for allowance of appeal in the case of *Tincher v. Omega Flex*. The issue accepted for review was "[w]hether this Court should replace the strict liability analysis of Section 402A of the Second Restatement with the analysis of the Third Restatement."[163] *Tincher* was a property damage case arising out of a fire that occurred when lightning struck the plaintiffs' home and ignited the defendant's "TracPipe" corrugated stainless-steel tubing, which had been used in its construction, destroying the home. The plaintiffs' contention at trial, on which they prevailed, was that the design of the piping made it susceptible to igniting from lightning strikes.[164] During trial, the lower court denied the defendant's motion in limine seeking application of the Restatement (Third) of Torts, Product Liability.[165] On appeal, the Superior Court affirmed.[166]

The action was actually brought by an insurance company as a subrogation case.[167] At argument, counsel for appellees for the first time argued that *Azzarello* should be overruled while retaining the Restatement (Second) of Torts, Section 402A.[168] Given the concession by the appellees' counsel, it was almost certain that some change would be forthcoming. How far that change would go toward altering the landscape of Pennsylvania product liability law was a question that scholars and practitioners debated as they awaited the outcome of the *Tincher* appeal. On November 19, 2014, the Supreme Court issued its decision in *Tincher*,[169] ending the speculation and ushering in a new era in Pennsylvania product liability law.

In an opinion authored by Chief Justice Castille, the majority[170] essentially "split the baby," overruling *Azzarello*[171] but rejecting the Restatement (Third) of Torts[172] and reconfirming that Section 402A of the Restatement (Second) of Torts remained the law of Pennsylvania.[173] Justice Saylor, joined again by Justice Eakin, continued to advocate for the adoption of the Restatement (Third) in his concurring and dissenting opinions.

In many ways, the solution crafted by Chief Justice Castille and the majority is indeed Solomon-like. The opinion carefully reviews the history and development of strict liability, including its social policy underpinnings, and returns to an examination of "foundational principles" in order to reach its rather elegant, if less than comprehensive, result. The Court noted that the strict liability cause of action is based in tort, which implicates duties "imposed by law as a matter of social policy"[174] rather than in contract, which involves duties imposed by mutual agreement between particular individuals.[175] The policies embodied in Pennsylvania's approach to product liability—specifically, that the risk of loss should be placed on those who profit from making and putting a product in the stream of commerce, as articulated in *Miller v. Preitz*[176] and relied on by *Webb v. Zern*— were in turn derived from the Restatement (Second) approach.[177] The Court held that those policies remain, regardless of the overruling of *Azzarello*, and therefore concluded that a departure from the approach of the Second Restatement, which focuses on the nature of the product and the consumer's reasonable expectations with respect to the product rather than on the conduct of either the manufacturer or the person injured,[178] was not warranted. In a telling footnote, Chief Justice Castille declared, "While the Second Restatement formulation of the principles governing the strict liability cause of action in tort may have proven substantially less than clear, the policy that formulation embodies has not been challenged here and has largely remained uncontroverted."[179]

The Court also stated, "Unlike the Third Restatement, we believe that the Second Restatement already adopted, and properly calibrated, permits the plaintiffs to tailor their factual allegations and legal argumentation to the circumstances as they present themselves in the real-world crucible of litigation, rather than relying upon an evidence-bound standard of proof."[180]

The most immediately recognizable effect of overruling *Azzarello* will be to shift the "gatekeeping" analysis of the risk-utility calculus from the authority of the judge to the province of the jury. Another of the principal effects is its abolishment of the artificial separation between negligence concepts and strict liability that had arisen in recent years, ostensibly as a result of the dictates of *Azzarello*.[181] Nevertheless, while the "bright line" demarcation between negligence concepts and strict liability theory has been removed from Pennsylvania law, the majority opinion in *Tincher* made it clear that the law of strict liability for defective products in Pennsylvania is directed at "tortious conduct . . . not the same as that found in traditional claims of negligence and commonly associated with the more colloquial notion of 'fault.'"[182] The Court explained, "Essentially, strict liability is a theory that effectuates a further shift of the risk of harm onto the supplier than either negligence or breach of warranty theory."[183] The law in Pennsylvania will continue to require that a plaintiff prove that the seller, manufacturer, or distributor placed on the market a product in a "defective condition" and will not require proof of conduct under a fault-based rubric.

In the view of some commentators, the majority in *Tincher* effectively returned Pennsylvania law to the day before the decision in *Azzarello* in 1978.[184] Certainly, the opinion contemplates that absent action by the state legislature, product liability will develop on a case-by-case basis under the common law.[185] In the view of the authors, however, the principles of *Azzarello* were not changed by *Tincher*; *Tincher* simply altered the way *Azzarello* is applied. Instead of a bifurcation of functions between the judge and the jury, the courts will exercise their traditional role of determining issues of law by ruling on dispositive motions and articulating the law through jury instructions. The jury, as fact finder, will determine the credibility of witnesses and testimony offered, the weight of evidence relevant to the risk-utility calculus, and whether a party has met the burden to prove the elements of the strict liability cause of action.[186]

Although the Court swept away years of jurisprudence in overruling *Azzarello*, it exercised judicial restraint in not designing a comprehensive system of product liability. This approach has left many questions unanswered. The Court declined to outline what evidence is admissible under the Restatement (Second) approach in a post-*Tincher* world. The cases that prohibited evidence of compliance with industry and government standards based their decisions on *Azzarello*.[187] With *Azzarello* and the negligence/strict liability dichotomy overruled, and without specific guidance on evidentiary matters from the *Tincher* Court, defense attorneys will undoubtedly attempt to introduce evidence that was previously inadmissible, such as federal regulatory standards, industry standards, and technological feasibility, as well as comparative fault and reckless conduct on the part of plaintiffs.[188] The plaintiffs' bar, in contrast, will argue that *Tincher* did not overrule the cases that barred industry and government standards from being introduced and that the "core principles" reaffirmed by the *Tincher* majority dictate that the rule against their admission be retained.

The Court did provide certain guidelines with respect to the test for a defective product. The majority adopted the view that a plaintiff may prove a violation either of the consumer expectation standard or of a risk-utility analysis in demonstrating the defectiveness of the design of a product.[189] The nature of the product, the identity of the user, the product's intended use and intended user, and any express or implied representations by a manufacturer or other seller are among the considerations relevant in assessing the reasonable consumer's expectations.[190] However, Chief Justice Castille wrote that the consumer expectations test alone would not be sufficient to vindicate basic public policy undergirding strict liability.[191] With new and technologically complex products, "ordinary consumer expectations" might not exist. *Tincher* therefore offered an alternative test. The risk-utility standard offers another perspective on what a "reasonable person" would conclude with respect to the probability and seriousness of harm caused by a product as opposed to the burden or costs of taking precautions: "Stated otherwise, a seller's precautions to advert the danger should anticipate and reflect the type and magnitude of the risk posed by the sale and use of the product."[192]

The risk-utility test has its own theoretical and practical shortcomings. In the prescription drug arena, for example, there might be no alternative design available. Therefore, declaring the plaintiff the "master of the claim" in the first instance,[193] the Court decreed that a plaintiff will have the option of premising the case on either "consumer expectations" or "risk-utility" theory or both. The Court further suggested that in certain circumstances where the risk-utility theory is utilized, the burden may be shifted to the defendant to demonstrate that an injury-producing product is not defective.[194] Depending on the manner in which future cases develop this aspect of the *Tincher* decision, burden shifting could prove an enormous boon to personal injury plaintiffs.

In a certain sense, the decision in *Tincher* brought to a close one chapter in the history of Pennsylvania product liability law: Pennsylvania's unique status based on the division of duties between judge and jury established as a result of *Azzarello* is no more. Going forward, however, as litigants, attorneys, and the judiciary strive to fill the gaps in Pennsylvania's jurisprudence left by the *Tincher* decision, the evolving nature of product liability law will undoubtedly lead to yet more titanic struggles.

NOTES

Clifford A. Rieders is a founding partner at Rieders, Travis, Humphrey, Waters & Dohrmann. Pamela L. Shipman is a senior associate at Rieders, Travis, Humphrey, Waters & Dohrmann. In addressing the serious and detailed topic of the Restatement (Second), § 402A, in contradistinction to the Restatement (Third), we have relied on much information garnered from litigation briefs we have written. An important thank you goes to Roz Kaplan, Jeffrey White, Irwin Aronson, and Barbara Axelrod. Prior associates in this office, including Joel McDermott, have also been of assistance.

1. 111 N.E. 1050 (N.Y. 1916).
2. Introduction to Restatement (Second) of Torts (Philadelphia: American Law Institute, 1965). Section 402A was authorized for publication in 1964. *See* American Law Institute, *41st Annual Meeting Proceedings* (Philadelphia: American Law Institute, 1964), 349–375.
3. Oscar S. Gray, "Reflections on the Historical Context of Section 402," *Touro Law Review* 10 (1993): 85–86.
4. Sandra F. Gavin, "Stealth Tort Reform," *Valparaiso University Law Review* 42 (2008): 433n11 (citing US Consumer Product Safety Commission, 1990 Annual Report, 9–34).
5. Ibid., 433n12 (citing US National Commission on Product Safety, *Final Report Presented to the President and Congress* [Washington, D.C.: US Government Printing Office, 1970]).
6. Ibid., 433n13 (citing US President Nixon [1969–74], *The President's Report on Occupational Safety and Health: Including Reports on Occupations Safety and Health by the US Dept. of Labor (page 1), Occupational Safety and Health Review Commission (page 87) [and] US Dept. of Health, Education, and Welfare (page 97)* [Washington, D.C.: US Government Printing Office, 1972]).
7. Gray, "Reflections," 85–86.
8. West v. Caterpillar Tractor Co., Inc., 336 So.2d 80, 87n1 (Fla. 1976). Compare *American Law of Product Liability*, §§ 16.9, 16.20 (citing decisions in thirty jurisdictions through 1976 and seven jurisdictions adopting Section 402A subsequently).
9. 220 A.2d 853 (Pa. 1966) (Cohen, J., majority coauthor) (Eagan, J., concurring) (Bell, C.J., dissenting).
10. Chief Justice Bell sat on the Supreme Court from 1950 to his retirement in January 1972. He became chief justice of Pennsylvania in 1961. "Governor John Cromwell Bell Jr.," *Pennsylvania Historical and Museum Commission*, http://www.phmc.state.pa.us/portal/communities/governors/1876-1951/john-bell.html.
11. 220 A.2d at 855–56 (Bell, C.J., dissenting) (footnote omitted).
12. "Governor Bell."
13. Those booklets included such titles as *Can We Think and Dare We Speak* (1934), *What Do You Know About the New Deal?* (1935), and *New Deal Fairy Tales* (1936), ibid.
14. When Governor Edward Martin was elected to the US Senate in 1946, he resigned his office to avoid losing seniority with the new session of Congress, leaving Bell to succeed him for the remaining nineteen days and act

as a "placeholder" for the incoming Governor James H. Duff. It was Duff who appointed Bell to the Supreme Court in 1950.

15. Born in York, Pennsylvania, in 1900 to Russian immigrant parents, Herbert B. Cohen achieved notoriety as a young attorney when he defended John Blymire in 1928 in the sensational "Hex" witchcraft trial. Cohen argued the insanity defense, but the jury convicted Blymire of first-degree murder. Jim McClure, "Noted York Family—the Cohens—Produced Pa. Supreme Court Justice," *York Town Square* (blog), December 27, 2007, http://www.yorkblog.com/yorktownsquare/2007/12/27/cohen-etc/. *See also* Joseph David Cress, *Murder and Mayhem in York County* (Charleston, S.C.: History Press, 2011), 84.

16. He rose to the post of Democratic majority floor leader of the state House, later becoming minority floor leader. He served as attorney general for Governor George Leader from 1954 to 1956. McClure, "Noted York Family."

17. Daryl L. Fair, "Pennsylvania Supreme Court Justices: A Collective Biography, 1933–1963," *Pennsylvania History* 35, no. 3 (July 1968): 273.

18. Ibid., 245n6. He was chief justice of Pennsylvania from 1972 to 1977.

19. Samuel J. Roberts was born in Brooklyn, but his family moved to Erie, Pennsylvania, when he was a child. "Chief Justice Samuel J. Roberts Scholarship," *Erie County Bar Association, 2015*, https://www.eriebar.com/public-roberts-scholarship.

20. "Samuel J. Roberts," *Erie Hall of Fame*, http://www.eriehalloffame.com/nominees/Roberts.asp. Following twenty years of service as a justice, he was elevated to chief justice of Pennsylvania on January 3, 1983.

21. Fair, "Collective Biography," 245n6. In addition to Justices Roberts and Jones, Chief Justice Bell and Justice O'Brien were also Republicans. Justices Musmanno, Eagen, and Cohen were affiliated with the Democratic Party.

22. "Samuel J. Roberts."

23. Ibid. *See also* Justice Roberts's opinion in Hack v. Hack, 433 A.2d 859 (Pa. 1981) (Abolition of interspousal tort immunity) ("One of the great virtues of the common law is its dynamic nature that makes it adaptable to the requirements of society at the time of its application in court. . . . Law must be stable, and yet it cannot stand still.") (citation omitted).

24. Hochgertal v. Canada Dry Corp., 187 A.2d 575, 578 (Pa. 1963).

25. 221 A.2d 320 (Pa. 1966).

26. Ibid., 334n17.

27. Webb, 220 A.2d at 854, emphasis added.

28. Miller, 221 A.2d at 325. That case was, of course, Webb.

29. Ibid., 336.

30. Ibid., 332–33.

31. Ibid., 333.

32. Ibid., 334.

33. 150 P.2d 436 (Cal. 1944) (Traynor, J., concurring).

34. Miller, 221 A.2d at 334.

35. Ibid., 334.

36. 246 A.2d 848 (Pa. 1968).

37. Ibid., 853.

38. According to Kassab,

> The majority opinion in *Miller* candidly admits that the policy considerations underlying the imposition of strict liability in tort are precisely the same as those which dictate the abolition of privity in contract actions for breach of warranty. Yet, the Court in *Miller* nevertheless retreated from the modern view because of a belief that section 2–318 of the Uniform Commercial Code requires privity in suits against a remote manufacturer. We no longer adhere to such a belief for we are convinced that, on this issue, the code must be coextensive with Restatement section 402A in the case of product liability.
>
> Ibid., 854.

39. Ibid., 859 (Cohen, J., concurring in result).

40. 319 A.2d 903 (Pa. 1974).

41. Ibid., 907.

42. 337 A.2d 893 (Pa. 1975).

43. Frank J. Vandall, "Constricting Product Liability: Reforms in Theory and Procedure," *Villanova Law Review* 48 (2003): 850.

44. Berkebile, 337 A.2d at 900.

45. Justice Robert N. C. Nix Jr. In a later case that year, however, a unanimous Court adopted comment *n* of the Restatement to hold that contributory negligence is not a defense in a Section 402A action. The opinion was again authored by Chief Justice Jones. *See* McCown v. Int'l Harvester Co., 342 A.2d 381 (Pa. 1975).

46. Bair v. Am. Motors Corp., 535 F.2d 249, 250 (3d Cir. 1976); Beron v. Kramer Trenton Co., 402 F. Supp. 1268, 1277 (E.D. Pa. 1975).

47. Beron, 402 F. Supp. at 1273–76.

48. 391 A.2d 1020 (Pa. 1978).

49. In addition to Nix, the appeal was heard by Chief Justice Eagen and Justices O'Brien, Roberts, Pomeroy, Manderino, and Packel.

50. Larry Teitelbaum, "In Memoriam—Robert C. Nix, Jr.," *Penn Law Journal* (Spring 2004): https://www.law.upenn.edu/alumni/alumnijournal/Spring2004/in_memoriam/nix.html.

51. Ibid.

52. Gajutra Bahadur, Sam Wood, and Jeff Gelles, "Ex-Justice Nix Dead at 75," *Philly.com*, August 24, 2003, http://www.articles.philly.com/2003-08-24/news/25454050_1_justice-nix-chief-justice-color-barrier.

53. Teitelbaum, "In Memoriam."

54. Ibid. *See also* Bahadur, Wood, and Gelles, "Ex-Justice Nix." One of his most important opinions protected the rights of defendants to challenge unlawful police tactics, and he pushed for application of broader rights accorded by the state Constitution than were dictated by the US Supreme Court.

55. Azzarello, 391 A.2d at 1023–24.

56. Ibid., 1025.

57. Ibid., 1026.

58. Ibid., 1025.

59. Ibid., 1027.

60. 528 A.2d 590, 593 (Pa. 1987).

61. Ibid., 594.

62. Ibid., 595.

63. Ibid., 595–96 (Flaherty, J., dissenting).

64. "William D. Hutchinson, 63, Appellate Judge, Ex-legislator," *Morning Call*, October 10, 1995 (obituary). Justice Hutchinson was appointed to the Third Circuit by President Ronald Reagan in 1987.

65. Lewis, 528 A.2d at 596 (Hutchinson, J., dissenting).

66. Ibid.

67. 450 A.2d 615 (Pa. 1982). The result in Sherk might also have been influenced by that fact that the case involved the use of a gun at a time when the debate over gun control and gun violence was only beginning to emerge following the assassination attempt on President Reagan in March 1981.

68. Ibid., 616.

69. Ibid., 617.

70. Ibid., 618.

71. Ibid. (quoting William Prosser, "The Fall of the Citadel," *Minnesota Law Review* 50 [1966]: 824).

72. He was joined by Chief Justice O'Brien.

73. Unfortunately, Justice Larsen achieved considerable notoriety for his public feud with several of the other justices and for the fact that he was ultimately removed from the bench after his conviction for criminal conspiracy to illegally obtain prescription drugs. For a full accounting of the sad story, *see* Charles G. Geyh, "Highlighting a Low Point on a High Court: Some Thoughts on the Removal of Pennsylvania Supreme Court Justice Rolf Larsen and the Limits of Judicial Self-Regulation," *Temple Law Review* 68 (1995):1041–77, http://www.repository.law.indiana.edu/facpub/602. *See also* Michael DeCourcy Hinds, "Convicted Pennsylvania Justice Is Facing Impeachment," *New York Times*, May 13, 1994, http://www.nytimes.com/1994/05/13/us/convicted-pennsylvania-justice-is-facing-impeachment.html.

74. 405 A.2d 897 (Pa. 1979).

75. Emilie Lousberry, "He Stood Alone Now He Stands Accused," *Philly.com*, October 29, 1993, http://www.articles.philly.com/1993-10-29/news/25938574_1_rolf-larsen-fellow-justices-ralph-j-cappy.

76. Ibid. Despite his personal failings, "in terms of decisions and the quality of his opinions and things [many lawyers acknowledge] . . . that he has been quite good."

77. Sherk, 450 A.2d at 622 (Larsen, J., dissenting), emphasis in original.

78. Ibid., 629 (citing Azzarello, 391 A.2d at 1027n11).

79. Ibid., 630–31.

80. Ibid., 634, emphasis in original.

81. Brief of *Amicus Curiae*, Pennsylvania Trial Lawyers Association on Behalf of Appellees, Phillips v. Cricket Lighters, 2002 WL 32178112, *17 (Pa.) (quoting Eshbach v. W.T. Grant Co., 481 F.2d 940 [3d Cir. 1973]).

82. 467 A.2d 615, 619 (Pa. Super. 1983).

83. 688 A.2d 221 (Pa. Super. 1997).

84. Ibid., 227.

85. 690 A.2d 186 (Pa. 1997).

86. Ibid., 190, emphasis added (citing Eck v. Powermatic Houdaille, 527 A.2d 1012 [Pa. Super. 1987]).

87. *See* S. Gerald Litvin and Gerald Austin McHugh Jr., "Strict Liability for Failure to Warn of Product Hazards," in *Pennsylvania Torts: Law and Advocacy*, West's Pennsylvania Practice Series (St. Paul, Minn.: Thomson Reuters, 2013), §9.43.

88. Ibid. (citing, respectively, Remy v. Michael D's Carpet Outlets, 571 A.2d 446 [Pa. Super. 1990]; and Harford Mutual Ins. Co. v. Moorhead, 578 A.2d 492 [Pa. Super. 1990]).

89. Vandall, "Constricting Product Liability," 850. Vandall maintains that the retrenchment began

in the early 1980s, when state legislatures began passing statutes of repose holding that a product's cause of action could die before the injury even occurred. Ibid., 850–51.

90. Clifford A. Rieders and Nicholas F. Lorenzo Jr., "The Restatement Third of Torts: A Deliberate Step Backward for Product Liability?," *The Barrister* 29 (Summer 1998): 21–23.

91. Introduction to Restatement (Third) of Torts, Product Liability (Philadelphia: American Law Institute, 1998).

92. *See* Restatement (Third) of Torts, Product Liability, § 2(b), (c).

93. Green v. Smith & Nephew AHP, Inc., 629 N.W.2d 727, 751 (Wis. 2001) (holding that § 2[b] incorporates an element of foreseeability of risk of harm, blurs the distinction between strict product liability claims and negligence claims, and is fundamentally at odds with current Wisconsin product liability law); David G. Owen, "Defectiveness Restated: Exploding the 'Strict' Product Liability Myth," *University of Illinois Law Review* 743(1996): 760 (concluding that by limiting consideration of risks to those that are foreseeable, § 2[b] establishes a negligence principle); Rebecca Tustin Rutherford, "Changes in the Landscape of Product Liability Law: An Analysis of the Restatement (Third) of Torts," *Journal of Air Law and Commerce* 63 (1997): 233 (opining that the test "is nearly identical to the traditional negligence standard").

94. Restatement (Third) of Torts, Product Liability, § 2, comment *a*.

95. *See, e.g.*, Patrick Lavelle, "Crashing into Proof of a Reasonable Alternative Design: The Fallacy of the Restatement (Third) of Torts, Product Liability," *Duquesne Law Review* 38 (2000): 1067 ("[T]his project, infected as it was with reporter bias and improper influence, has produced nothing more than a position paper reflecting the views of special interests groups with whom the selected reporters are aligned."); Note, "Just What You'd Expect: Professor Henderson's Redesign of Product Liability," *Harvard Law Review* 111 (1998): 2366–67 (tort reform campaign launched by manufacturers and insurers moved in the 1990s to use ALI to promote their agenda through reporters who had written extensively in favor of limiting manufacturers' liability); Rieders and Lorenzo, "Restatement Third," 24 ("[I]t became obvious that much of the American Law Institute was made up of corporate

lawyers and law professors who supported tort reform. . . . The new restatement of product liability . . . evolved from a very small cadre of Thornburg Justice Department officials, insurance funding groups and professors."); John F. Vargo, "The Emperor's New Clothes: The American Law Institute Adorns a 'New Cloth' for Section 402A Product Liability Design Defects—a Survey of the States Reveals a Different Weave," *University of Memphis Law Review* 26 (1996): 509–15 (recounting "ALI's Pro-Manufacturer Movement").

96. Halliday v. Sturm, Ruger & Co., 792 A.2d 1145, 1154–55 (Md. 2002).

97. 841 A.2d 1000 (Pa. 2003).

98. Justice Sandra Schultz Newman concurred in the affirmance of summary judgment with respect to the strict liability claim but dissented in part, as she would not have allowed the negligence action to proceed. Justice Russell M. Nigro concurred in the result, and Chief Justice Stephen Zappala did not participate in the decision. (By this time, Zappala was no longer the chief justice.)

99. "Ralph Cappy," *Ballotpedia*, https://www.ballotpedia.org/Ralph_Cappy. Justice Cappy became chief justice of Pennsylvania in 2003 and served until his retirement in 2007. One of his first significant actions on becoming chief justice was to shepherd through to enactment new rules regarding medical malpractice requiring certificates of merit before the case could proceed. *See also* "Ralph J. Cappy, Former Pennsylvania Supreme Court Chief Justice, Dead at 65," *Daily Report*, May 4, 2009, http://www.dailyreportonline.com/PubArticleDRO.jsp?id=1202551797134&slreturn=20131019170008.

100. Phillips, 841 A.2d at 1006–7.

101. Ibid., 1008–10.

102. Ibid., 1012–23 (Saylor, J., concurring).

103. S. Gerald Litvin and Gerald Austin McHugh Jr., "Defenses—the Intended Use Doctrine," in *Pennsylvania Torts: Law and Advocacy*, West's Pennsylvania Practice Series (St. Paul, Minn.: Thomson Reuters, 2013), § 9.66.

104. Phillips, 841 A.2d at 1012.

105. 769 A.2d 1131 (Pa. 2001).

106. An exception was that evidence of subsequent design changes may be admissible if the defense opens the door to the issue of feasibility. Ibid., 1159.

107. Language in Duchess has often been cited by proponents of the Restatement (Third) for

the proposition that Pennsylvania law already requires proof of an alternative design as part of the plaintiff's prima facie case. Justice Saylor himself debunked this notion in Lance v. Wyeth, 85 A.3d 434, 443n12, 458n36 (Pa. 2014) (noting that Duchess did not require proof of an alternative safer design as an absolute prerequisite to a claim of a design defect).

108. Jan Murphy, "Profile: Pennsylvania Supreme Court Justice Thomas G. Saylor," *PennLive.com*, August 18, 2012, http://www.pennlive.com/specialprojects/index.ssf/2012/08/profile_pennsylvania_supreme_c_1.html.

109. "Chief Justice Thomas G. Saylor," *Unified Judicial System of Pennsylvania*, http://www.pacourts.us/courts/supreme-court/supreme-court-justices/justice-thomas-g-saylor.

110. Mark Scolforo, "Pennsylvania's New Chief Justice Scholarly, Collegial," *Morning Call*, December 30, 2014, http://www.mcall.com/news/nationworld/pennsylvania/mc-pa-supreme-court-chief-justice-saylor-20141230-story.html.

111. "Lawmakers, Lawyers and Law Schools Praise Ongoing Chief's Reign" *AOPConnected: Newsletter of the Administrative Office of PA Courts*, no. 4 (2014): 4, http://www.pacourts.us/assets/files/setting-3710/file-4215.pdf?cb=941179.

112. Larry Eichel, "Chief Justice Seat Awaits Castille," *Philly.com*, September 12, 2007, http://www.articles.philly.com/2007-09-12/news/25223279_1_ronald-d-castille-chief-justice-retirement-age. *See also* Zygmont Pines, "Adios, Dear Chief," *AOPConnected: Newsletter of the Administrative Office of PA Courts*, no. 4 (2014): 2, http://www.pacourts.us/assets/files/setting-3710/file-4215.pdf?cb=941179.

113. Eichel, "Chief Justice."

114. Ibid.

115. "Justice J. Michael Eakin," *Unified Judicial System of Pennsylvania*, http://www.pacourts.us/courts/supreme-court/supreme-court-justices/justice-j-michael-eakin.

116. Justin Geldzahler, "Late Night Court: The Lyrical Comedy of Justice J. Michael Eakin," *Splitsider.com*, October 3, 2012, http://www.splitsider.com/2012/10/late-night-court-the-lyrical-comedy-of-justice-j-michael-eakin/.

117. "Suspended Pa. Supreme Court Justice J. Michael Eakin Resigns from Bench in Email Scandal," *PennLive.com*, March 15, 2016, http://www.pennlive.com/news/2016/03/suspended_pa_supreme_court_jus.html.

118. 898 A.2d 590 (Pa. 2006).

119. Ibid., 601 ("[T]here are substantial deficiencies in present strict liability doctrine, [and] it should be closely limited pending an overhaul by the Court.").

120. 563 F.3d 38 (3d Cir. 2009).

121. Ibid. Webb v. Zern was itself essentially a bystander case, as the Third Circuit acknowledged in its opinion. Berrier, 563 F.3d at 47 ("*Webb* was a bystander who simply had the misfortune of being in the same room as the keg when it exploded.").

122. 596 Pa. 265, 942 A.2d 897 (2008).

123. Berrier, 563 F.3d at 63.

124. Bugosh v. I.U. N. Am., Inc., 971 A.2d 1228, 1229 (Pa. 2009).

125. Ibid., 1241–44 (Saylor, J., dissenting).

126. Ibid., 1241.

127. Arthur L. Bugay and Craig L. Bazarsky, "The Future of Pennsylvania Product Liability as Applied by Federal and State Courts: *Covell v. Bell Sports, Inc.*," *Pennsylvania Bar Association Quarterly* 83 (2012): 139.

128. Ibid., 148 (citing Hoffman v. Paper Converting Mach., 694 F. Supp. 2d 359, 365 [E.D. Pa. 2010]) (reasoning Bugosh dismissal was irrelevant and applying Berrier precedent); Richetta v. Stanley Fastening Sys., 661 F. Supp. 2d 500, 506–7 (E.D. Pa. 2009) (holding that court is bound by Berrier precedent); Durkot v. Tesco Equip., 654 F. Supp. 2d 295, 299 (E.D. Pa. 2009) ("While it is true that the reasoning behind the Pennsylvania Supreme Court's decision in *Bugosh* cannot be known, it is evident that the justices were not in agreement to adopt the Third Restatement in that case."); Milesco v. Norfolk Southern Corp., 2010 WL 55331 (M.D. Pa. 2010) ("[D]ismissal of *Bugosh* was a clear indication that [the Supreme Court of Pennsylvania] intend[ed] for the Second [Restatement] to apply in the Commonwealth for the time being.").

129. *See* Barnish v. KWI Bldg. Co., 980 A.2d 535, 541 (Pa. 2009) (quoting § 402A of the Restatement [Second] and discussing the factors a plaintiff must prove "[t]o bring a Section 402A claim"); Reott v. Asia Trend, Inc., 7 A.3d 830 (Pa. Super. 2010) (reviewing "the relevant law" on what is required "to state a product liability cause of action under section 402A of the Restatement [Second] of Torts in Pennsylvania"), *aff'd* 55 A.3d 1088 (Pa. 2012); Lance v. Wyeth, 4 A.3d 160, 169 (Pa. Super. 2010) (noting that "[o]ur Supreme Court has never adopted [the Restatement (Third)], and it runs contrary to

law as stated in . . . Restatement [Second] of Torts, § 402A"); Estate of Hicks v. Dana Co., 984 A.2d 943, 976 (Pa. Super. 2009) (holding that "§ 402A has remained the law in Pennsylvania since its adoption by our Supreme Court in *Webb v. Zern*" and "[c]onsequently the trial court did not err when it denied Appellant's request to have this matter proceed pursuant to the Restatement [Third] of Torts—Product Liability, § 2 [1997]"); French v. Commonwealth Assoc., 980 A.2d 623, 632 (Pa. Super. 2009) (quoting Restatement [Second] of Torts § 402A as the law of Pennsylvania).

130. 651 F.3d 357 (3d Cir. 2011).

131. Ibid., 363.

132. Ibid., 364.

133. 980 A.2d 535 (Pa. 2009) (Baer, J., joined by Eakin, Todd, McCaffery, and Greenspan, J.J.) (Saylor, J., concurring, joined by Castille, C.J.).

134. 85 A.3d 434 (Pa. 2014). Lance v. Wyeth is a prescription drug case.

135. Ibid., 434n23. The Supreme Court previously decided that strict liability has no application in the field of prescription drugs. *See* Hahn v. Richter, 673 A.2d 888, 889–90 (Pa. 1996).

136. 55 A.3d 1088, 1107n7 (Pa. 2012) (Todd, J., dissenting), emphasis added.

137. Ibid., 1102.

138. 779 A.2d 491, 496 (Pa. Super. 2001) (quoting Mitchell v. Volkswagenwerk, AG, 669 F.2d 1199 [8th Cir. 1982]).

139. 799 A.2d 95 (Pa. Super. 2002).

140. Ettinger, 799 A.2d at 105 (quoting Davis v. Berwind Corp., 690 A.2d 186 [Pa. 1997]).

141. "Seamus P. McCaffery," *Ballotpedia*, http://www.judgepedia.org/Seamus_P._McCaffery.

142. James N. Katsaounis, "Seamus P. McCaffery: The Mason, Judge, Military Man, Police Officer, Husband, and Father," *Pennsylvania Freemason*, http://www.pagrandlodge.org/freemason/1104/seamus.html.

143. 936 A.2d 52, 66 (Pa. Super. 2007). The Donoughe decision held in favor of the plaintiff.

144. "Seamus P. McCaffery."

145. "Max Baer's Biography," *VoteSmart*, http://www.votesmart.org/candidate/biography/59058/max-baer#.WZ8GtPiG05s.

146. "Justice Max Baer," *Unified Judicial System of Pennsylvania*, http://www.pacourts.us/courts/supreme-court/supreme-court-justices/justice-max-baer.

147. 980 A.2d 535 (Pa. 2009).

148. 887 A.2d 209 (Pa. 2005).

149. 898 A.2d 590 (Pa. 2006).

150. "The Hon. Sandra Schultz Newman," *Drexel University Thomas R. Kline School of Law Board*, http://www.drexel.edu/law/about/board/BoardMembers/The%20Hon%20Sandra%20Schultz%20Newman/.

151. Dep't of General Services, 898 A.2d at 615–19 (Newman, J., dissenting).

152. Ibid., 616n2 (quoted in Berrier, 563 F.3d at 57).

153. 41 A.3d 823 (Pa. 2012).

154. Daniel Cummins, "A Maze of Uncertainty: PA Product Liability Law Remains in a Confusing State of Flux," *Westlaw Journal: Automotive* 32, no. 17 (2013): 5.

155. Beard, 41 A.3d at 839 (Baer, J., concurring).

156. Ibid.

157. "In footnote 18, the Majority could be interpreted to favor the adoption of the Restatement Third, by stating 'It may be cogently argued that risk-utility balancing is more legitimately assigned to a jury. . . . Indeed, such is the approach of the Restatement Third.'" Ibid.

158. Ibid.

159. Tom Fontaine, "New Justice to Assume Melvin's Former Supreme Court Seat," *TribLIVE.com*, July 27, 2013, http://www.triblive.com/news/allegheny/4413706-74/stevens-court-justice#ixzz2v10NM5vP.

160. 722 A.2d 217 (Pa. Super. 1998).

161. Ibid., 22, emphasis added.

162. 764 A.2d 616 (Pa. Super. 2000).

163. 64 A.3d 626 (Pa. 2013) (order granting allowance of appeal on that issue only).

164. *See* Tincher v. Omega-Flex, Inc., Civ. No. 1472 EDA 2011, 2011 WL 9527303 (Chester Co. C.C.P. August 5, 2011).

165. Ibid.

166. Tincher v. Omega-Flex, Inc., 60 A.3d 860 (Pa. Super. 2012) (Table).

167. *See* Brief for Defendant-Appellant Omega Flex, Inc., filed July 17, 2012, in Tincher v. Omega-Flex, Inc., Civ. No. 1472 EDA 2011, 2012 WL 4942008 (Pa. Super.), 1 (referencing "Plaintiffs Terrence and Judith Tincher, represented by their insurer USAA Property & Casualty Insurance Company").

168. Arthur Bugay, "*Tincher v. Omega Flex, Inc.*: A Lightning Strike on Pennsylvania Product Liability Law," *Pennsylvania Bar Association Quarterly* 85 (2014): 40n11.

169. 104 A.3d 328 (Pa. 2014).

170. Chief Justice Castille was joined by Justices Todd, Baer, and Stevens. Justices Saylor and Eakin concurred in part and dissented in part.

Justice McCaffery did not participate in the decision.

171. Tincher states, "We agree that reconsideration of *Azzarello* is necessary and appropriate, and to the extent that the pronouncements in *Azzarello* are in tension with the principles articulated in this Opinion, the decision in *Azzarello* is overruled." Tincher, 104 A.3d at 376.

172. While recognizing the calls for adoption of the Restatement (Third) in the name of "reform" and the prediction of the Third Circuit that the Pennsylvania Supreme Court "would simply adopt the Third Restatement approach," the Court expressly declined to do so, stating, "[T]his Court has not taken that decisional leap." Ibid., at 381.

173. Ibid., 335, 399.

174. Ibid., 399 (internal quotations omitted).

175. Ibid.

176. 221 A.2d 320 (Pa. 1966).

177. Tincher, 104 A.3d at 381–82; *see also* ibid., 383 ("Incorporating the strict liability cause of action into Pennsylvania common law, the *Webb* court expressly relied upon the Second Restatement and relevant scholarly commentary to supply its justification.").

178. Ibid., 369.

179. Ibid., 400n25.

180. Ibid., 399. The majority also recognized the criticism of the Restatement (Third) raised by the plaintiffs' bar because its drafts were "largely composed by those who represent[ed] corporate interests" who "fail[ed] to leave the client at the door." Ibid., 355n7.

181. Tincher, 104 A.3d at 376–78, esp. 376 ("Subsequent decisional law has applied *Azzarello* broadly, to the point of directing that negligence concepts have no place in Pennsylvania strict liability doctrines; and . . . . those decisions essentially led to puzzling trial directives that the bench and bar understandably have had difficulty following in practice.").

182. Ibid., 400.

183. Ibid., 402.

184. Arthur L. Bugay, "A New Era in Pennsylvania Product Liability Law—*Tincher v. Omega Flex Inc.*: The Death of *Azzarello*," *Pennsylvania Bar Association Quarterly* 86, no. 1 (January 2015): 12.

185. "The principal point is that judicial modesty counsels that we be content to permit the common law to develop incrementally, as we provide reasoned explications of principles pertinent to factual circumstances of the cases that come before the Court." Tincher, 104 A.3d at 406.

186. Ibid., 406–7. "A question of whether the party has met its burden of proof is properly 'removed'—for example, via adjudication of a dispositive motion—'from the jury's consideration only where it is clear that reasonable minds [cannot] differ on the issue.' . . . Thus, the strict liability construct we articulate today comfortably accommodates the gate-keeping role ordinarily relegated to the trial court in tort actions." Ibid., 407 (internal citations omitted).

187. *See* Lewis v. Coffing Hoist Div., 528 A.2d 590, 594 (Pa. 1987); Estate of Hicks v. Dana Co., 984 A.2d 943, 965 (Pa. Super. 2009); Carrecter v. Colson Equip. Co., 499 A.2d 326, 330 (Pa. Super. 1985).

188. *See, e.g.,* James M. Beck, "Tincher Opens Door to Previously Excluded Negligence Evidence," *Legal Intelligencer*, February 3, 2015, http://www.thelegalintelligencer.com/id=1202716633012/Tincher-Opens-Door-to-Previously-Excluded-Negligence-Evidence.

189. Tincher, 104 A.3d at 401.

190. Ibid., 387.

191. Ibid., 388–89.

192. Ibid., 389.

193. Ibid., 406.

194. Ibid., 408–9.

Criminal Law

CHAPTER 19

The 1778–1779 Chester and Philadelphia Treason Trials

The Supreme Court as Trial Court

CARLTON F. W. LARSON

Trial and appellate judges are clearly separated under modern American law. But in eighteenth-century Pennsylvania, as in many other colonies, justices of the Commonwealth's highest court presided over criminal trials in addition to handling appellate work. During the American Revolution, the three justices of the Pennsylvania Supreme Court (Chief Justice Thomas McKean, Justice John Evans, and Justice William Augustus Atlee) followed colonial practice in sitting as a trial court to hear felony cases. Under what was known as the "commission of oyer and terminer and general jail delivery," the justices would travel from county to county and collectively preside over criminal trials. There was no risk of conflict of interest in subsequent appellate proceedings; the judgments entered by the court of oyer and terminer could not be appealed to the Pennsylvania Supreme Court (or to any other court). The justices thus had both the first and the last words with respect to the law applied at felony trials.

Between 1778 and 1780, the justices presided over approximately four dozen trials for high treason, cases in which the Commonwealth of Pennsylvania alleged that one of its citizens had betrayed the state by aiding the armed forces of Great Britain. The bulk of these cases arose from the British occupation of Philadelphia between September 1777 and June 1778. The subsequent trials were the subject of intense public interest and vituperative controversy. Radicals complained that too many defendants were being acquitted, while others, primarily Quakers, viewed the trials as politically vindictive. As late as 1857, a Philadelphian would claim that the execution of two Quakers convicted of treason in 1778 had "created a feeling in the community that is not yet worn out."[1]

The ultimate decision to convict or acquit rested with the juries. In a prior work, I have argued that jury selection mattered in these cases; defense counsel appear to have used peremptory challenges along religious, economic, and political lines to shape the jury in ways favorable to the defense.[2] Nonetheless, the justices played an important role in at least three respects. First, they charged the grand jury. Second, during the trials, they issued rulings on evidentiary matters and on the interpretation of Pennsylvania's treason statute and delivered charges to the trial juries that conveyed their impressions of the quality of the evidence. Third, in the rare cases in which juries convicted defendants, the justices petitioned the state's Supreme Executive Council (SEC), the state's plural executive, for leniency, arguing that the death penalty was an inappropriate punishment. This chapter explores these issues by focusing on a series of trials in Chester and Philadelphia Counties beginning in the fall of 1778 and concluding in the spring of 1779.

I. GRAND JURY CHARGES

The charge to the grand jury was a critical component of eighteenth-century criminal law. Judges used the opportunity to opine expansively on the nature of society and the justifications for criminal punishments. They also discussed in considerable detail the offenses that were subject to the grand jury's jurisdiction.

Chief Justice McKean appears to have taken the lead in charging the grand juries. His first charge was delivered in Lancaster in April 1778, followed by a similar charge in York a few weeks later. The charge to the York grand jury was subsequently published at the grand jury's request.[3] The Lancaster and York charges were similar to the ones McKean later delivered in Philadelphia.[4]

McKean spent the bulk of his charge describing the events leading to the Revolution, arguing that the British had repeatedly violated the guarantees of the English constitution and the rights of American colonists. The argument was a careful constitutional justification for the legality of the Revolution and, by extension, for the legitimacy of his Court. Although historians have long debated the varied social, political, and economic causes of the Revolution, for McKean, a signer of the Declaration of Independence, the cause could not have been clearer—a series of unlawful, unconstitutional acts by the British government.[5]

Only after setting forth this constitutional justification for revolution did McKean turn to the specifics of felony law, which would be the immediate subject of the grand jurors' attention. The details of Pennsylvania's new statute against treason consumed most of his discussion, although he did briefly describe murder and manslaughter. McKean concluded the charge by advising the grand jurors in "all doubtful cases to incline rather to acquittal than to crimination; for it is safer to err in acquitting than in punishing, on the side of mercy than on the side of justice."[6]

Throughout the treason trials, the Supreme Court justices were called on to decide issues of procedure, determine the admissibility of evidence, and interpret the state's criminal statutes. They also resolved legal challenges to indictments and issued charges to the petit juries. Regrettably, source materials survive for only a handful of the trials.

A. Procedure

The justices confronted their first full-blown treason case in Chester County in September 1778, a week before they began hearing cases in Philadelphia.[7] In the case of wheelwright Joseph Malin, defense attorneys James Wilson and George Ross, both of whom had signed the Declaration of Independence, moved that defendants in treason cases be provided a copy of the indictment, a list of the prosecution witnesses, and the names of the panel from whom the jury would be drawn at least five days before trial.[8]

This motion invoked a long history. The famous Treason Trials Act of 1696, enacted in the wake of Stuart excesses in treason cases, had entitled a treason defendant to a copy of the indictment five days before trial and a copy of the jury panel two days before trial. A statute from the reign of Queen Anne, effective upon the death of the pretender, extended these protections by providing the defendant with a list of the prosecution witnesses, including their professions and places of abode, along with the jury panel and the indictment ten days prior to trial. Michael Foster's influential treatise on the law of treason had expressed doubts about this statute, arguing that "furnishing the prisoner with the names, professions, and places of abode of the witnesses and jury so long before the trial may serve many bad purposes which are too obvious to be mentioned." At minimum, Foster felt, the Crown should be entitled to the same opportunity "of sifting the character of the prisoner's witnesses."[9] According to Court prothonotary Edward Burd, Wilson and Ross had "insisted" on the benefit of this Statute of Anne, even though they requested a shorter time frame than the act required.[10]

The motion raised the important question of whether provisions of English treason law, intended to be beneficial to the defendant, were applicable in Pennsylvania. The justices concluded that the Pennsylvania Assembly had specifically repealed all provisions of English law respecting high treason, including the Treason Trials Act and the Statute of Anne. But the assembly had not passed new legislation governing procedure in treason trials. The Court was thus left to fashion a rule on its own. It concluded that the defendant could have the indictment and the panel list one day before trial but was not entitled to the witness list at all.[11]

This was not an especially generous decision. Indeed, Pennsylvania treason defendants in 1778 would have fewer protections than English defendants in 1696. Nonetheless, it is possible that the Court routinely provided this information earlier than the absolute minimum of one day. When sentencing Abijah Wright to death later that winter, for example, Chief Justice McKean stated, "A copy of your indictment, and of the panel of the jury who were to try you, was delivered to you many days before your trial, that you might be prepared in the best manner for your defence and challenges."[12]

B. Evidentiary Issues

Evidentiary issues must have arisen quite frequently, not only in treason trials, but in all the criminal trials presided over by the justices. Unfortunately, witness testimony and objections survive for only a few trials. Two significant evidentiary issues arose in the Joseph Malin trial in Chester County. The first arose out of Malin's own incompetence. He had gone over to what he thought were British troops but that were actually American. He had thus attempted to join the British army but had failed. Pennsylvania law did not criminalize attempted treason, and at the time of the Malin trial, there was no generalized law of criminal attempt; the subject first appears in legal treatises in the nineteenth century.[13] Accordingly, erroneously going to American troops could not legally amount to treason. Pennsylvania Attorney General Jonathan Dickinson Sergeant sought to introduce words spoken by Malin to indicate his true intent. Wilson and Ross objected, arguing that as "words did not amount to treason, no general evidence could be given of a man's sentiments; but that the intention expressed by any words offered in evidence, must relate immediately to the overt act laid and proved on the indictment." Since adherence to American troops, "even under the supposition that they were British," did not amount to treason, no words relating to this evidence could be introduced. The attorney general agreed that "words alone do not amount to treason" but argued that the evidence could be admitted to show the defendant's intent.[14]

The justices agreed with Wilson and Ross in part, ruling that "no evidence of words relative to the mistake of the American troops can be admitted; for any adherence to them, though contrary to the design of the party, cannot possibly come within the idea of treason." Nonetheless, since there was evidence that the defendant was "actually with the enemy at another time, words indicating his intention to join them, are proper testimony to explain the motives, upon which that intention was afterwards carried into effect." In other words, the overt act of treason could not be going to the American corps but the subsequent act of being present with British troops. With respect to that overt act, the evidence was admissible.[15]

The second issue arose when Attorney General Sergeant sought to call a witness to testify that the defendant "had been seen parading with the enemy's light horse in the city of Philadelphia." According to Alexander Dallas's *Pennsylvania Reports*, Wilson and Ross objected that the evidence could not be introduced, since overt acts of treason must be tried in the county where the act occurred. Sergeant replied that once an overt act had been proved in Chester County, "corroborative evidence may be given of overt acts committed in any other county." The Court agreed with the attorney general, holding that "evidence might be given of an overt act, committed in another county, after an overt act was proved to have been committed in the county where the indictment was laid and tried."[16]

After the Chester County sitting, the justices moved on to Philadelphia. The first trial was that of Abraham Carlisle, accused of accepting a commission as gatekeeper for the City of Philadelphia under the British occupation. Carlisle's attorneys—James Wilson, George Ross, and William Lewis—objected to the prosecution's first witness, who proposed to testify that Carlisle had taken salt from persons at the city gate and had the power of granting passes. This testimony, the defense attorneys argued, was inadmissible because it did not speak to the overt act of accepting a commission. Until such an overt act was proved, no other testimony could be admitted. Chief Justice McKean, speaking for the Court, ruled that the testimony did not support the charge of accepting a commission, but it could support the indictment's further allegation that Carlisle had joined the British army.[17] With respect to a different prosecution witness, however, the justices agreed with the defense that the evidence supported only the lesser charge of misprision of treason and was therefore inadmissible.[18]

The trial of John Roberts raised two contested evidentiary issues.[19] The first involved a witness who was called to prove that Roberts had unsuccessfully attempted to convince him to join the British army. The act of the assembly had declared that "persuading others to enlist" in the armies of an enemy was an act of high treason. Attorneys Wilson and Ross argued that "persuading" requires success. The Latin *suadeo* meant only "advising"; *per-suadeo* meant an "advising through"—that is, a success. The justices agreed and ruled that the act applied only to those cases resulting in an actual enlistment. The evidence could be admitted, however, for the different purpose of showing that the defendant had joined the armies of the enemy.[20]

The second issue concerned the admissibility of the defendant's confession that he had gone to Head of Elk to communicate information to Joseph Galloway, the former speaker of the Pennsylvania Assembly who was acting as superintendent of police in British-occupied Philadelphia. Roberts's attorneys argued that the evidence was inadmissible, as no other evidence to this act had been offered. A confession, they claimed, could be used to corroborate what two witnesses had already established, but it could not be used as proof of the overt act itself. The justices ruled that in the absence of other testimony, evidence of a confession could not support the charges of giving intelligence to the enemy; nevertheless, it was good for corroboration and could be introduced to support other charges in the indictment. After the defendant's conviction, Wilson and Ross moved for a new trial, arguing that the "evidence given respecting his declarations, or confessions, was altogether illegal, and ought not to have been allowed." The justices rejected this motion.[21]

Given the rudimentary state of evidence law in the 1770s, it is hard to argue that the justices consistently erred in favor of the prosecution or the defense. The inclination to allow prosecution evidence to be admitted, but only for limited purposes, arguably struck a reasonable balance between the prosecution and the defense positions.

C. Challenge to an Indictment

Following Carlisle's conviction, his attorneys filed a motion in arrest of judgment, arguing that the indictment was legally defective because it was "vague and uncertain" and that the defendant "could not be apprized of the particulars urged against him." The justices heard oral arguments on this motion the week after Carlisle's conviction but ultimately overruled all defense objections.[22]

D. Jury Charges

At the close of the evidence in each trial, the justices delivered a charge to the jury. It is possible that each justice delivered a separate charge, although Chief Justice McKean might have delivered the charge for the Court as a whole. Regrettably, none of the charges in the treason cases have survived, so we only have indirect evidence of their content. A contemporary described Justice McKean's charge in the Abraham Carlisle case as "favorable" to the defense.[23] The chief prosecutor, Joseph Reed, stated on October 23, 1778, that "[t]he Court began to think its charges give too much countenance to acquittals—I have thought so from the beginning, tho it is an error on the favorable side."[24] In close cases, these charges might well have made a difference.

III. THE DEATH PENALTY AND POSTCONVICTION PROCEEDINGS

The death penalty loomed over all the treason trials. Pennsylvania law made treason a capital offense, and if a jury convicted, the justices had no choice but to impose a death sentence. They did have a choice, however, with respect to the ferocity with which they announced it. In the case of John Roberts, convicted of serving as a guide to the British, Chief Justice McKean's death sentence was scathing. Roberts, McKean claimed, had "endeavoured the total destruction of the lives, liberties, and property of all his fellow citizens" and supported a cause that "has been complicated with the horrid and crying sin of murdering thousands, who were not only innocent, but meritorious; and aggravated by burning some of them alive and starving others to death." Roberts's acts of kindness to Americans, although well documented, could "by no means compensate for treason."[25]

Yet a day after delivering this sentence, McKean did a curious thing. He transmitted a petition from the jury to the state's SEC arguing for clemency. Under the state Constitution, the SEC had the power "in cases of treason and murder . . . to grant reprieves, but not to pardon till after the next session of the Assembly."[26] McKean and his colleague

Justice Evans recommended the petition for "favorable acceptance." The petition, signed by ten of the twelve jurors who had voted to convict Roberts, argued that "it appears to us . . . Roberts was under the influence of fear, when he took the imprudent step of leaving his family and coming to reside among the enemy, while they had possession of the city." Although the jurors were obliged by their oath "to pronounce him guilty," they knew that "juries are but fallible men," and the evidence "was of a very complicated nature, and some parts of it not reconcileable with his general conduct."[27]

Chief Justice McKean and Justice Evans acted similarly in the case of Abraham Carlisle, mentioned previously. Both justices favorably endorsed the unanimous petition of Carlisle's jury that stated, "[B]y the oath we had taken, and upon the whole of the evidence before us, we were constrained to give our verdict against him, agreeable to the laws of our country, yet from the knowledge we have of his former blameless character, the consideration of his advanced age, and our sympathy with his distressed family and reputable connexions, our sentiments of humanity lead us to wish that the rigor of the law may be abated in his case."[28] Prosecutor Joseph Reed stated that he had "always expected" such a petition from the jurors in both cases, but he was surprised by the actions of the justices.[29]

The pattern repeated itself with the April 1779 conviction of George Hardy. The entire jury petitioned the SEC for clemency, stating that it had "heard the testimony with candor, weighed it without partiality, and decided on it without prejudice."[30] Although the jurors were constrained to convict by the law and by the evidence, "they did unanimously at the time of agreeing on the verdict, and still do think, the said George Hardy a fit object of Mercy" and thus "with humility, but with fervor" recommended a pardon.[31] All three Supreme Court justices endorsed the petitions. They observed that Hardy's character was good, his prospects for reformation high, and "his death (being a man of small note or consideration) would afford little benefit by the example." They also stated, "[M]ore than one, at least equally criminal with this man, has been tried before us, and acquitted by the extreme lenity and tenderness of the Juries."[32]

The justices' appeals for clemency proceeded from a more general discomfort with the death penalty in treason cases that might have animated the very high acquittal rates by the juries. In a convulsive civil war, it was easy to imagine a friend or a neighbor who might have chosen the other side. Such persons were not incorrigible criminals but had the possibility of redemption. The SEC, however, took a sterner view and granted clemency only to George Hardy. Abraham Carlisle and John Roberts were executed.

Chief Justice McKean's death sentence in the Roberts case received far more attention than his subsequent petition for mercy, and he was widely reviled as a hanging judge. In January 1779, the British captain John André, who a year later would be hanged as a spy for his role in the Benedict Arnold plot, delighted his audience with an elaborate account of a dream about the rebels. André imagined himself in Hades, watching souls being tried:

> The first person to be called upon was the famous chief-justice McKean,
> who I found had been animated by the same spirit which formerly possessed the

memorable [Justice George] Jeffries [of England]. I could not but observe a flash of indignation in the eyes of the judges upon the approach of this culprit. His more than savage cruelty, his horrid disregard to the many oaths of allegiance he had taken, and the vile sacrifices he had made of justice to the rebellion, were openly rehearsed.... He was condemned to assume the shape of a blood-hound, and the souls of Roberts and Carlisle were ordered to scourge him through the infernal regions.[33]

In the same vein, a Philadelphia poet wrote, "Who guards McKean and Joseph Reed the vile / Help'd he not murder Roberts and Carlisle?"[34]

These depictions were grossly exaggerated, although plausible if one was only familiar with McKean's death sentence. Once the jury had voted to convict, McKean and his fellow justices were obligated to impose the death penalty. The justices, however, did have discretion as to whether to urge the SEC for clemency. By doing so, they implicitly agreed that the success of Revolution did not hinge on the scaffold as an *in terrorem* example to their fellow citizens.

IV. CONCLUSION

The overall performance of the Pennsylvania Supreme Court justices in the treason cases stands up well to historical scrutiny. Some rulings favored the prosecution, others the defense. Even if some of these rulings were questionable, there does not seem to be any pattern of consistent unfairness. Perhaps the most apt summary is this: the justices were doing their best to judge evenhandedly while applying unfamiliar law in the midst of a chaotic war and widespread popular resentment against those persons who were suspected of having aided the enemy.

The trial function of the Supreme Court justices also gave them an intimate knowledge of trial courts, a knowledge that was almost certainly beneficial when they returned to their appellate function. Although few would argue that appellate judges today should routinely preside over criminal trials, the change to an all-appellate system was not without its costs. The justices of the eighteenth-century Pennsylvania Supreme Court could not have imagined that one day their successors would no longer look defendants, witnesses, and jurors in the eye and would instead engage the hurly-burly world of trial courts solely through the rarified atmosphere of appellate proceedings.

NOTES

Carlton F. W. Larson is a professor of law at the University of California Davis School of Law.

1. Winthrop Sergeant, *Loyalist Poetry of the Revolution* (Philadelphia: Collins, 1857), 164.

2. Carlton F. W. Larson, "The Revolutionary American Jury: A Case Study of the 1778–1779 Philadelphia Treason Trials," *Southern Methodist University Law Review* 61, no. 4 (2008):

1441–1524.

3. Thomas McKean, *Charge Delivered to the Grand-Jury, by the Honourable Thomas McKean, Esquire, Chief Justice of Pennsylvania, at a Court of Oyer and Terminer, and General Goal Delivery, Held at York, on the 21st Day of April, 1778; and Published at the Special Request of the Said Grand-Jury* (Lancaster, Pa.: Francis Bailey, 1778).

4. *Notes of Charges Delivered to Grand Juries by Chief Justice Thomas McKean, in His Own Writing, 1777–1779* (Philadelphia: Historical Society of Pennsylvania, 1778). The title is inexact, as no charges were delivered until 1778.

5. The best modern defense of the constitutional argument for revolution is John Philip Reid, *Constitutional History of the American Revolution*, 4 vols. (Madison: University of Wisconsin Press, 1986–93).

6. McKean, *Charge Delivered*, 18.

7. The Chester trials have posed difficulties for scholars because of peculiarities in the source material. The records for the Chester sitting of the Court have not been preserved, and thus details of the trial must be gleaned from other sources. Historians have generally relied on Alexander Dallas, who included the Malin trial in his first volume of *Pennsylvania Reports*, published in the 1790s. Dallas, however, erroneously placed the trial in Philadelphia County, even though this was directly contradicted by the jurisdictional arguments raised in the case. Dallas similarly reported a motion made in the cases of Joshua Molder and John Taylor and erroneously attributed them to Philadelphia County. The most reliable sources for the Chester sitting are a September 19, 1778, letter by Court prothonotary Edward Burd to Jasper Yeates, preserved in the Jasper Yeates Papers at the Historical Society of Pennsylvania, and an account in the September 22, 1778, issue of the *Pennsylvania Packet* (hereafter *Pa. Packet*).

8. "Edward Burd to Jasper Yeates, Sept. 19, 1778," Jasper Yeates Papers, Historical Society of Pennsylvania (hereafter HSP), http://www2.hsp.org/collections/manuscripts/y/Yeates0740.html. Alexander Dallas provides an account of this motion under the caption "Respublica v. Molder et al." Edward Burd's contemporary letter, however, indicates that this motion was made as part of the Malin trial. Burd describes it as a "general motion," so it is possible that the motion was made on behalf of all treason defendants and was later attributed

by Dallas to the Molder defendants. It is also possible that the same motion was later made on behalf of the Molder defendants and the Court simply reiterated its previous ruling.

9. Michael Foster, *A Report of Some Proceedings on the Commission of Oyer and Terminer and Goal Delivery for the Trial of the Rebels in the Year 1746 in the County of Surrey, and of Other Crown Cases: To Which Are Added Discourses upon a Few Branches of the Crown Law* (Oxford: Clarendon Press, 1762), 250.

10. "Edward Burd to Jasper Yeates, Sept. 19, 1778."

11. Ibid.

12. *Pa. Packet*, December 8, 1778.

13. Francis Bowes Sayre, "Criminal Attempts," *Harvard Law Review* 41 (1928): 821–59.

14. Respublica v. Malin, 1 U.S. 33, 33–34 (Ct. Oyer & Term., at Phila. 1778).

15. Ibid.

16. Ibid., 34–35.

17. Respublica v. Carlisle, 1 U.S. 35, 36–38 (Ct. Oyer & Term., at Phila. 1778).

18. Samuel Hazard, ed., "Notes of C.J. McKean in Case of Ab'm Carlisle," in *Pennsylvania Archives*, vol. 7 (Philadelphia: Joseph Severns, 1853), 44, 47–48.

19. For a comprehensive analysis of the John Roberts trial, *see* David W. Maxey, *Treason on Trial in Revolutionary Pennsylvania: The Case of John Roberts, Miller* (Philadelphia: American Philosophical Society, 2011).

20. Respublica v. Roberts, 1 U.S. 39 (Ct. Oyer & Term., at Phila. 1778). The Dallas volume states, "In support of the prosecution, it was urged, that the attempt to prevail, constituted the crime; and that it was like a case of a man's sending intelligence to the enemy, which was an act equally criminal in the sender, whether the intelligence was received, or not." Chief Justice McKean's notes on the trial, however, do not include this argument on behalf of the prosecution. In fact, he notes that the state conceded that "persuading to enlist without actually enlisting may not be treason, but it may show *quo animo* that the prisoner joined the British army." These notes suggest that the prosecution arguments were not as strong as the Dallas reports, which were reconstructed at a much later date, made them out to be. Notes of Thomas McKean in the Roberts trial, Morristown National Historical Park, Morristown, NJ.

21. Roberts, 1 U.S. at 39–40.

22. Carlisle, 1 U.S. at 38.

23. "Thomas Franklin to Elias Boudinot, Oct. 4, 1778," Elias Boudinot Papers, HSP.

24. "Joseph Reed Letter, Oct. 23, 1778," Joseph Reed Papers, Reel 2, New York Historical Society.

25. *Pa. Packet*, November 7, 1778.

26. Pa. Const. (1776), § 20.

27. Samuel Hazard, ed., "Petition of the Jury in Case of John Roberts," in *Pennsylvania Archives*, vol. 7 (Philadelphia: Joseph Severns, 1853), 25.

28. Don Corbly, "Memorial of Jurors and Judges in Favor of Abra'm Carlisle," in *Pennsylvania Traitors and Criminals during the Revolutionary War*, by Don Corbly (Raleigh, N.C.: Lulu Press, 2013), 234.

29. "Joseph Reed Letter, Oct. 23, 1778," Joseph Reed Papers, Reel 2, New York Historical Society.

30. Petition of Jurors re George Hardy, Clemency File, RG-27, Pennsylvania State Archives.

31. Ibid.

32. Samuel Hazard, ed., "Petition of Judges in Case of George Hardy," in *Pennsylvania Archives*, vol. 7 (Philadelphia, Joseph Severns, 1853), 326–27.

33. Quoted in Frank Moore, *Diary of the American Revolution* (New York: Charles Scribner, 1860), 122.

34. Jonathan Odell, *The American Times: A Satire*, in Sergeant, *Loyalist Poetry*, 11.

CHAPTER 20

Slavery and the Supreme Court

High Court Justices and the Problem of Fundamental Justice

PAUL FINKELMAN

We think of Pennsylvania as a free state and an antislavery state. Yet between 1786 and 1861, the Pennsylvania Supreme Court heard more than one hundred cases involving slavery and blacks.[1] Many of these were routine, run-of-the-mill cases in which slavery or race was incidental to the facts and the jurisprudence, such as a contested will in which the legacy included a "servant boy Harry,"[2] a suit against the African Methodist Episcopal Church by a man who wished to be restored to his membership and role as a trustee,[3] and a suit over a $5,000 bequest to educate the natives of Africa.[4] But many of the Court's cases were central to the important issues of slavery, emancipation, and race in Pennsylvania. For example, in the state's first reported slavery case, *Pirate, alias Belt v. Dalby*,[5] the Supreme Court ruled that someone born of a slave mother was a slave, even though his complexion was nearly white. On the other hand, three years later, the same Court ruled that three children born of a slave mother in Pennsylvania were free because their master had failed to properly register them under the state Gradual Emancipation Act of 1780.[6]

These cases illustrate that Pennsylvania's experience with slavery was deeply complicated. Slavery was present in Pennsylvania in the 1680s, and most elite and wealthy Pennsylvanians owned slaves. But Pennsylvania was also the home of the first antislavery society in the new nation, and the Pennsylvania legislature was the first in the history of the world to pass a law to end slavery. In the 1780s, Pennsylvania moved toward equal rights, but in the 1830s, the Supreme Court supported the disfranchisement of African American voters. An understanding of the Court's jurisprudence on slavery and race begins in the colonial period and continues through the statutes passed during and immediately after the Revolution.

I. EARLY ANTISLAVERY IN PENNSYLVANIA

Pennsylvania's antislavery legacy is strong. The first protest against slavery in American history came from Germantown in 1688. This famous document, written by a group of German immigrants affiliated with the local Quaker meeting, succinctly challenged the fundamental morality of slavery: "[T]ho they are black we cannot conceive there is more liberty to have them slaves, as it is to have other white ones. There is a saying that we shall doe to all men like as we will be done ourselves; making no difference of what generation, descent or colour they are. And those who steal or rob men, and those who buy or purchase them, are they not alike?" Refugees from religious oppression in their homeland, these recent arrivals in Penn's colony made the obvious comparison of their situation to that of slaves: "In Europe there are many oppressed for conscience sake; and here there are those oppressed who are of a black colour." They also noted that slavery led to fundamental violations of biblical law: "And we who know that men must not commit adultery—some do commit adultery, in others, separating wives from their husbands and giving them to others; and some sell the children of these poor creatures to other men. Ah! doe consider well this thing, you who doe it, if you would be done at this manner? and if it is done according to Christianity?" As pacifists, they warned that slavery would inevitably lead to violence, and they asked if blacks have "as much right to fight for their freedom, as you have to keep them slaves." Their conclusion was that slavery "offended public morality, threatened the peace of the community, and violated Christian values."[7]

This protest illustrated tension in Pennsylvania over slavery that would exist for more than a century and a half. On one hand, many Pennsylvanians were deeply offended by the immorality and oppression of slavery. This was especially true among Quakers, Mennonites, and members of other pietistic faiths, and later among Baptists and Methodists. On the other hand, other Pennsylvanians, especially High Church Protestants and a significant number of wealthy Quakers, saw nothing wrong with slavery, which was profitable, common in the Atlantic world, and sanctioned by both the law of man and the law of God. It was also extremely convenient for the many elite citizens whose slaves worked as servants in about 20 percent of the homes in Philadelphia. Whether reading about Old Testament slave owners, like Abraham, Jacob, and Job, or reading St. Paul's letter to Philemon, religious Pennsylvanians found scriptural justification for buying and selling human beings. Like almost all other Americans, Pennsylvanians had a strong respect for private property, which included slaves. Finally, the race of the slaves *did* matter to white Pennsylvanians, who were willing to "do unto others" things they would not want done to themselves precisely because Africans were so different from them.

Thus from the 1680s until the Revolution, Pennsylvanians debated slavery more than residents of any other colony. From the 1730s to the eve of the Revolution, the relentless agitation of antislavery Quakers caused enormous turmoil in the Philadelphia yearly meeting. Starting about 1735, Benjamin Lay publicly attacked slaveholding among his fellow

Quakers. By 1737, some Quaker meetings in New Jersey and Pennsylvania had banned him as a "frequent Disturber" and a "disorderly person" for his relentless and sometimes outrageous condemnations of slavery. That year, he wrote *All Slave-Keepers That Keep the Innocent in Bondage, Apostates Pretending to Lay Claim to the Pure & Holy Christian Religion*. Benjamin Franklin printed this tract but did not identify himself as the printer because he wanted to avoid an open breach with the wealthy and powerful Quaker leadership in Philadelphia. The fierce denunciations of slavery in Lay's book led to his expulsion from the Society of Friends, which had prohibited members from publishing antislavery tracts. However, in 1758, a year before Lay's death, the Philadelphia Quaker meeting finally condemned trafficking in slaves.[8]

Although Lay scandalized his fellow Quakers, and his often intemperate language alienated many in the community, he set the stage for John Woolman's profoundly important *Some Considerations on the Keeping of Negroes* (1754) and the writings and preaching of Anthony Benezet. In the 1760s, there were still many Quaker slave owners in the colonies, and in Rhode Island, many were still actively involved in the African slave trade. But by the beginning of the American Revolution, most Pennsylvania Quaker meetings had condemned slavery and many Quakers were committed to manumitting their own slaves. In 1775, Benezet helped organize the Society for the Relief of Free Negroes Unlawfully Held in Bondage, the first antislavery organization in the United States. However, the organization only met four times that year before the Revolution diverted attention away from striving for slaves' freedom to fighting to preserve American liberty.[9] Two-thirds of the members were Quakers whose pacifism left them politically vulnerable when the Revolution began.

II. ENDING SLAVERY AND THE REVOLUTION

Even though Benezet's organization ceased to function, the Revolution put new pressure on supporters of slavery in Pennsylvania. The ideology of the Revolution as set out in the Declaration of Independence—"All men are created equal" and are entitled to the rights of "life, liberty, and the pursuit of happiness"—implied that slavery was wrong. The author of this language, Thomas Jefferson, owned at least 150 slaves at the time and never imagined his flowery language applied to his human property or black people in general.[10] However, throughout the North, patriots argued that slavery violated the spirit of the new nation. Furthermore, thousands of blacks joined the Continental Army, providing manpower for the Revolution while disproving racist assumptions about their worthiness to be free.

This set the stage for passage of Pennsylvania's Act for the Gradual Abolition of Slavery on March 1, 1780.[11] This was the first law in history for the purpose of abolishing slavery. Some places had seen slavery disappear over time. Chief Justice Lord Mansfield of the Court of King's Bench in England had ruled, in *Somerset v. Stewart* (1772),[12] that slaves could not be held against their will in Great Britain, but he emphatically asserted that his decision applied *only* to the mother country and did not affect the status of slavery in any British colonies or the status of slaves transported from Africa to the New World. French courts and local legislatures had reached similar decisions, although the French parliament and crown modified this theory of law to allow French owners to bring their slaves from the New World or Africa for limited periods of time.[13]

But the action of the Pennsylvania legislature was emphatically different and ground-breaking. Most importantly, it ended slavery in a place where it was legal and supported by positive law dating from 1706. *Somerset* merely denied masters the right to bring their slaves into a jurisdiction, Great Britain, where there were no statutes supporting slavery. The elaborate 1780 statute provided that the children of all slave women would be born free and that no new slaves could be brought into the state. Thus as the existing slaves passed away, slavery in Pennsylvania would quite literally die out.

From a modern perspective, the 1780 law was hardly perfect or even just. The children of slave women were required to serve the masters of their mothers until they turned twenty-eight. This provision was designed to compensate masters for raising the children of their slaves and also educating them in preparation for a life of freedom. The legislators also feared that if the children of slaves were born free, with no indenture, masters would abandon them, perhaps forcing mothers to give up their children at birth and at the same time requiring that the state build orphanages or other facilities to raise these children. Modern economists argue that this scheme compensated the masters far more than the cost of raising these children and denied the children of slaves the fruits of their labor during some of their most productive years.[14] But the members of the Pennsylvania legislature did not have the benefit of modern economic analysis or data-crunching computers. They were trying to solve a problem that no other legislature in the history of the world had ever tried to solve.

A more pressing critique is that this law, while gradually ending slavery, did not actually free any slaves. Any child of a slave woman born in Pennsylvania before March 1, 1780, would be a slave for life. One can imagine families in which older children born in 1778, 1779, or early 1780 would be slaves for life, as would their parents, while younger children born on or after March 1, 1780, would eventually become free. The inherent unfairness of these rules was balanced, in the minds of the legislators, with the need to respect private property. An immediate end to slavery probably would have led to a backlash from the many influential and wealthy slave owners living in Philadelphia, where almost every elite family, and many less wealthy residents of the city, owned slaves who were used as household servants. It is also likely that a more sweeping law could not have been passed because of opposition from defenders of private property. Slavery, after all, had been legal in Pennsylvania for a century, and to suddenly take slave property from owners seemed to violate a fundamental tenant of the Revolution, which was opposed to arbitrary government and the seizure of private property by the state. During the Revolution, many states were willing to confiscate the property of loyalists, but taking property from patriots was another matter.

The new law was thus an attempt to balance the Revolution's respect for property with the Revolution's aspirations for liberty. However, the law made clear that the long-term goal of the newly independent Commonwealth was liberty. It began with a remarkable two-paragraph preamble that explained this novel act and the motivation for it.

First, the statute noted that the "arms and tyranny of Great Britain" had been used to oppress the people of Pennsylvania and that the people of the state had "a grateful sense of the manifold blessings" of being delivered "from that state of thraldom, to which we ourselves were tyrannically doomed."[15] Thus the representatives of the Commonwealth declared they could now "rejoice that it is in our power to extend a portion of freedom to others." In essence, the white revolutionaries of Pennsylvania recognized that if it was wrong for the British government to politically "enslave" them, then it was equally wrong for Pennsylvanians to enslave others directly.

Having established the moral obligation to end slavery, the legislature turned to the vexing question of race in American society. The response here reflected a mixture of the state's Quaker heritage and the Enlightenment science and deism of some of its leading citizens, including Benjamin Franklin, Benjamin Rush, and one of the state's newest immigrants, the radical pamphleteer Tom Paine. The preamble continued,

> It is not for us to enquire why, in the creation of mankind, the inhabitants of the several parts of the earth were distinguished by a difference in feature or complexion. It is sufficient to know, that all are the work of an Almighty hand. We find, in the distribution of the human species, that the most fertile as well as the most barren parts of the earth are inhabited by men of complexions different from ours, and from each other; from whence we may reasonably, as well as religiously, infer, that He, who placed them in their various situations, hath extended equally his care and protection to all, and that it becometh not us to counteract his mercies.

The legislature then used this wartime legislation to point out that emancipation was only possible because of the Revolution and the separation from England: "We esteem it a peculiar blessing granted to us, that we are enabled this day to add one more step to universal civilization, by removing, as much as possible, the sorrows of those, who have lived in undeserved bondage, and from which, by the assumed authority of the Kings of Great-Britain, no effectual, legal relief could be obtained." This was not an attempt, like Thomas Jefferson's disingenuous paragraph in the draft of the Declaration of Independence, to blame the whole problem of slavery and the slave trade on King George. The Continental Congress had wisely deleted Jefferson's self-serving and dishonest language.[16] Rather, this was a correct observation that under British rule, emancipation was not possible without the king's consent, which was unlikely to be forthcoming.

The second preamble, Section 2 of the new law, focused on one of the greatest injustices of slavery: the destruction of black families. The lawmakers noted that bondage "not only deprived" slaves "of the common blessings that they were by nature entitled to, but has cast them into the deepest afflictions, by an unnatural separation and sale of husband and wife from each other and from their children, an injury, the greatness of which can only be conceived by supposing that we were in the same unhappy case."[17] This was the first time that any government in the Western world asked whites to see blacks as people just like themselves and to officially take the position that the law should treat all people with some measure of equality. Thus "in grateful commemoration of our own happy deliverance from that state of unconditional submission, to which we were doomed by the tyranny of Britain,"[18] Pennsylvania became the first jurisdiction in history to take steps to formally and legally end slavery.

The rest of the law set out how slavery would be dismantled. As already noted, the children of all slave women would be born free, subject to an indenture. After the indenture expired, these now fully free people would be given "freedom dues" just like the money or property given to free white indentured servants at the end of their service. The law required that every slave owner register his or her slaves with the county clerk by November 1, 1780, and pay a $2.00 registration fee for each slave, which was a considerable sum at the time. Any slaves not properly registered in a timely manner would be free.[19] Masters of children born to their slaves would be held liable to the Overseers of the Poor if these free people were, in the future, unable to support themselves, *unless* the master freed the servants before the end of their indenture. This provision created a great incentive for masters to educate the children of their slaves and prepare them for life after bondage. In a remarkable innovation—unheard of in any other slave society—the law provided that slaves charged with crimes "shall be enquired of, adjudged, corrected and punished, in like manner as the offences and crimes of the other inhabitants of this state are and shall be enquired of," with the sole caveat that slaves could not testify against free people.[20] However, this meant that free blacks and indentured blacks could testify against whites. While no Pennsylvanian could import any new slaves, the legislation allowed visiting masters to bring slaves into the state for up to six months, after which they would be free. In addition, recognizing that Philadelphia was the national capital, the law allowed "delegates in congress from the other American states, foreign ministers and consuls" to keep their "domestic slaves attending upon" them for an indefinite period of time.[21]

This was a remarkable law, and it would be copied in part by most of the other Northern states when they passed their own gradual abolition acts, although the subsequent state laws reduced the indenture periods for the children of slave women. In 1782, the legislature passed a supplementary act giving residents of two western counties extra time to register their slaves, because in 1780, it was unclear if they were actually living in Pennsylvania or Virginia.[22] In 1788, a new law closed various loopholes in the 1780 act. This law required registration of the children of slave women within six months after their birth, with provision for their freedom if they were not properly registered. The law prohibited masters from selling spouses away from each other or removing pregnant slaves to slave states so their children would be born as slaves. The law also strictly prohibited Pennsylvanians from participating in the African slave trade.[23]

III. SLAVERY BEFORE THE COURTS

In the wake of the Revolution and the passage of the 1780 act, opponents of slavery rejuvenated Benezet's virtually defunct organization in 1784 as the Pennsylvania Society for Promoting the Abolition of Slavery, and for the Relief of Free Negroes Unlawfully Held in Bondage. In April 1787, the society was reorganized as the Pennsylvania Society for Promoting the Abolition of Slavery, and for the Relief of Free Negroes Unlawfully Held in Bondage, and for Improving the Condition of the African Race. However, it was almost always called the Pennsylvania Abolition Society (PAS). The new leadership represented the political, social, and economic elite of Philadelphia and included Dr. Benjamin Rush, Hilary Baker (soon to be the mayor of Philadelphia), James Pemberton, Jonathan Penrose, Thomas Paine, Richard Peters, and Tenche Coxe.[24] The crowning jewel of this rejuvenated leadership was the new president of the PAS, Benjamin Franklin, who was the most famous American in the world and the living embodiment of the ideals of the Revolution. The members, like the new leaders, were a glittering group of merchants, lawyers, entrepreneurs, and civic and political leaders. The newly rejuvenated PAS worked hard to protect the freedom of blacks in the state and to implement new laws passed to gradually end slavery in the Commonwealth. The PAS became the first civil rights organization in the nation to use the courts as a vehicle for implementing social change. The PAS was able to operate in this manner because, during and after the Revolution, the legislature had passed laws, in 1780, 1782, and 1788, that were designed to dismantle and eventually end slavery in the Commonwealth. Not surprisingly, the PAS quickly used the law—and its many attorney members—to fight against slavery and for the rights of free blacks. The PAS, led by the most important men in Pennsylvania, became the model for future public interest litigation-based organization, such as the NAACP Legal Defense and Education Fund, the Anti-defamation League, and the American Civil Liberties Union. The PAS, and others, brought numerous cases to the Pennsylvania courts, which led the Supreme Court to interpret and apply the laws of 1780, 1782, and 1788. In these cases, the Court tended to follow a strict adherence to the statutes, although in some cases, the Court might have been more creative in furthering liberty.

IV. REGISTRATION CASES

The first reported case to interpret the 1780 law was *Respublica v. Negro Betsey*,[25] which involved three children of a slave mother, all of whom were born before the 1780 act. As such, they could have been held as slaves for life. But their owner neglected to register the three children or their parents. The parents had already won their freedom, and the children now asked to be reunited "under the care . . . of those parents."[26]

Chief Justice Thomas McKean, who would soon become an ally of Jefferson and his proslavery Democratic-Republican Party, would have condemned the children to bondage until age twenty-eight, arguing that the 1780 law did not specifically declare that unregistered children of slaves were unconditionally free. He conceded that the children could not be slaves for life because they were never properly registered but argued that even though they were born before 1780, the children should be treated as indentured servants and have to serve their master until age twenty-eight. In what can only be seen as a racist analysis (even for the period), McKean argued that the child—Betsey—would be worse off if free because "[w]ere she discharged from her master, she would be incapable to take care of herself, and her parents are unable to educate her." Showing little appreciation for the family interests of blacks or the horrors of slavery, McKean concluded, "She cannot suffer so much by living with a good master, as being with poor and ignorant parents. By a contrary judgment, she, as I have just hinted, would be little benefited, and her master, who hitherto has derived no advantage from her services, and has been subjected to considerable expences for her food, clothing, and lodging would be a great sufferer."[27] The opportunity of the master to recoup his expenses was far more important to McKean than the liberty of a young girl or her right to be raised by her parents.

McKean's argument gained no support from the rest of the Court. Justice William A. Atlee succinctly noted that the 1780 law provided that "no negro or mulatto then within the State, shall, from and after the said first day of November, be deemed a slave, or servant for life . . . unless his, or her name, shall be entered as aforesaid" with the county clerk. This had not been done, and so the plaintiffs could not be slaves. Atlee further noted that the law clearly stated "that no man or woman of any nation or colour, except the negroes and mulatoes, who shall be registered as aforesaid, shall be deemed, adjudged, or holden, within the territories of this Commonwealth, as slaves, or servants for life; but as freemen and free-women."[28] Atlee also focused on the family issues, pointing out that the preamble to the 1780 law had noted that "among the unhappy circumstances formerly attending these people" was the "unnatural separation and sale of husband and wife, from each other, and from their children." Atlee noted that "in the present case, it is attempted to separate these children from their parents, by a construction which appears to me to clash with the intention of the makers of the law; while such a construction as will secure freedom to them, and restore them to their parents, will I think, agree best with the design of the Legislature."[29]

The other justices agreed with Atlee in separate opinions, and the three black children gained their liberty and the right to live with their parents. The importance of this case—the first to interpret the 1780 law—is illustrated by its length. The report of the case covered eleven pages of the first volume of Alexander Dallas's *Pennsylvania Reports*. Only two cases, at twelve pages each, were longer, and the vast majority of the cases reported in that volume were dispatched with fewer than three full pages.

After this case, the Court heard numerous other registration cases, almost always reading the statute strictly, which usually favored black plaintiffs. For example, in 1794, the Court released "negro Robert" because he had not been properly registered in 1780.[30] Similarly, Aberilla Blackmore lost her slaves in 1797 because they had been brought into the state too late to be registered under a supplemental law for slaves owned by people in Westmoreland County. In 1780, there was no clear boundary between Virginia and Pennsylvania in the southwestern corner of Pennsylvania, in what was then Westmoreland County. In 1781, part of Westmoreland became Washington County.[31] Many slave owners in this area did not comply with the 1780 law because they believed they were actually living in Virginia. In 1782, the legislature passed a special act allowing masters of slaves who had lived in the area before September 23, 1780, to register their slaves. The legislature chose that date because that was when Pennsylvania agreed to accept the boundary, even though the border was not finalized until the following year. The Blackmores had bought land there in March 1780, intending to move with their slaves. They finally moved there with their slaves in December 1780. After the passage of the 1782 supplemental law, they immediately complied with all the registration requirements. But this was insufficient to preserve their claim to these slaves because, as Justice Jasper Yeates noted, Blackmore's slaves had not been living in Pennsylvania on September 23, 1780, and the fact that Blackmore owned land in the state at the time had no effect on the status of the people who she claimed as slaves but were in fact now free.[32] Other slaves in these two counties also gained their freedom from faulty registrations,[33] but properly registered slaves, who had been living there before September 23, 1780, remained in bondage.[34]

The Court was usually strict about interpreting the registration requirements because otherwise, "fraud and perjury" by masters would "make slaves of Negroes really free."[35] In one case, the Court held that only an owner could register slaves, and the slave Elson went free because someone other than the owner had registered him.[36] But the Court refused to release slaves for meaningless technicalities. For instance, Hannah did not gain her freedom because her master had registered her as "a slave" but did not write on the registration form that she was a "slave for life." The Court ruled that "slave . . . signifies a perpetual servant."[37] In another case in 1815, Chief Justice William Tilghman acknowledged that "freedom is to be favoured, but we have no right to favour freedom at the expense of property." Here Tilghman reversed a lower court's decision to free the slave Peggy because he believed the registration had been made in a timely manner.[38] This was a close case, and a different appellate judge might have interpreted all ambiguous facts in favor of liberty, as the trial judge had. But Tilghman, who was himself a slave owner, clearly sympathized with his fellow master. In this case, he suggested that the state purchase all remaining slaves and free them, which would have ended the issue (and of course enriched him personally).[39]

But in other cases where important requirements of the registration procedures were not fulfilled, Chief Justice Tilghman and the other justices ordered blacks released from their bondage. The children of slaves had to be registered within six months of their birth. The reason was clear: if masters could wait longer, they could lie about when a slave woman gave birth and squeeze a few more months or years of labor out of a slave. Thus Jesse gained his freedom when the Court concluded that his master had not registered him on time.[40]

Perhaps the most bizarre case involving the technical requirements of registration was *Wilson v. Belinda*, decided in 1817. In 1780, when Belinda was less than two years old, her owner registered her, and seven other slaves, with authorities in Cumberland County, as required by the gradual abolition act. Her owner, John Montgomery, provided most of the registration information required by the law but failed to indicate his occupation, the county of his residence, and the sex of Belinda and two other slaves. A trial court held that Belinda was free because she was not properly registered. Chief Justice Tilghman, speaking for a unanimous Court, rejected Belinda's arguments that she was free because Montgomery failed to note his occupation. Tilghman argued that Montgomery might not have actually had an occupation, although this seems unlikely. Tilghman also refused to free Belinda because Montgomery had failed to indicate his county of residence when registering the slaves because, Tilghman said, he actually lived in the county where he registered Belinda.[41] In refusing to free Belinda because of this failure to comply with the law, Tilghman ignored the possibility that such faulty registrations would have allowed for the illegal enslavement of one who was either free or illegally imported into the state.

Despite his flexible application of the requirements of the 1780 law, Tilghman was persuaded that the failure to indicate Belinda's gender required that she be set free. The purpose of the registration was to prevent fraud and protect the liberty of black people who might otherwise be illegally claimed as slaves. Wilson, who now claimed to own Belinda, argued that "*the sex is implied in the name*, and therefore there was no occasion to be more explicit." But Tilghman rejected this claim, noting that "[i]t may be very true, that every one who hears the name of *Belinda*, would suppose at once, that the person was a female. The name, however, is not a certain criterion of sex; for men are sometimes called by the names generally given to women, and *vice versa*."[42] Tilghman further asserted that the statute required the sex of the slave be put into the registration and that failure to do so, for whatever reason, voided the registration.

Justice John Bannister Gibson emphatically agreed, suggesting that without the sex of the slaves, it would be possible for a master to commit fraud and keep a free person in servitude: "We cannot recognize the name *Belinda* as being exclusively that of a female, or as sufficiently indicating a particular sex; for the act requires the age and sex to be '*severally* and *respectively* set forth.'"[43]

When Pennsylvania passed the 1780 act, slavery was legal in every one of the thirteen newly independent states. Philadelphia was America's largest city and the capital of the new nation. Given this status, the legislature accommodated visitors who brought slaves with them. The law did this in two ways. First, it allowed visitors to bring a slave into Pennsylvania for up to six months. Second, the law gave members of Congress, diplomats, and other government officials the right to keep slaves in the state for an unlimited period. However, to reduce the fraudulent use of slaves by people moving to the state, the 1788 amendment to the law provided that slaves would be immediately free if their master "intended" to permanently reside in Pennsylvania. A number of slaves won their freedom through the six-months rule.[44] The PAS was particularly vigilant in trying to free slaves whose masters had overstayed their welcome. Both the Court of Common Pleas and the Supreme Court heard cases on what constituted a six-month stay.

In 1794, the Supreme Court ruled against the claim of two slaves owned by Madame Chambrè, a refugee from the French colony of Santo Domingo (Haiti). Chambrè lived in Philadelphia for five months and three weeks and then moved with her slaves to New Jersey, where slavery was still completely legal. The slaves then ran back to Philadelphia, and when captured, lawyers for the PAS argued they were free because Chambrè had left the state only "to avoid the operation of the [gradual abolition] act."[45] The implication here was that she "intended" to move to Pennsylvania, and thus the slaves became free under the 1788 law because of her intention. However, the lawyers for the slaves presented "no proof . . . that she had ever intended to settle in Pennsylvania." The PAS lawyers also tried to argue that the slaves had been there for six lunar months and thus were free. The lawyers understood this claim was unusual but argued that "even if the computation by calendar months were more usual at common law, a different construction would be adopted in favour of liberty, and to prevent an evasion of the most honourable statute in the Pennsylvania code." This was a plea for the Court to adopt any construction of the law that would favor liberty. The justices of the Court in the 1790s were probably reasonably sympathetic to these sentiments, but they were unimpressed by the argument. When Madame Chambrè's lawyer tried to speak to this issue, the Court stopped him, declaring that the justices "were, unanimously, of opinion, that the legislature intended calendar months," and the blacks were remanded to Madame Chambrè.[46]

Although Madame Chambrè's slaves remained in bondage, the logic of this case worked to the benefit of another slave, whose master brought his slaves back and forth from Trenton in order to avoid keeping him in the state for six continuous months. The Court found that this proved the owner's intention to reside in Pennsylvania, and the slave went free.[47]

The last case on this issue involved a slave named Charity Butler, who as a young child was taken in and out of Pennsylvania a number of times over a two-year period.[48] Each visit only lasted a short time. Many years later, Butler and her children escaped from Maryland and claimed to be free because, as a child, Butler had gained her freedom under the six-months rule. In rejecting Butler's freedom claim, the Supreme Court accepted a jury's verdict that Butler was never in the state for six consecutive months. The Court said that it would have reached a different result if there had been a "fraudulent shuffling backward and forwards in *Pennsylvania*, and then into *Maryland*, and then back to *Pennsylvania*." But here there was no evidence of this, and so Butler and her children were returned to Maryland.[49] In his opinion, Justice Thomas Duncan noted that the Commonwealth had resorts at York and Bedford, and Southerners often summered at these places. If the six months was cumulative, these visitors would not be able to return each year with their servants.[50]

Both the Pennsylvania Supreme Court and the US Circuit Court also heard cases involving congressmen. The federal case was a collateral attack on an abolitionist after a Southern master, Pierce Butler, lost his slave because he kept the slave in Philadelphia longer than six months. Butler was no ordinary visitor to Philadelphia. He was a signer of the Constitution and then a US senator. From 1787 to 1804, he spent most of his time in Philadelphia and kept his slave Ben there. For most of this time, he was in the constitutional convention or the Congress. But for a two-year period, when Butler was not a member of Congress, he lived in Philadelphia with Ben in his house. With the help of the PAS and the Quaker abolitionist Isaac T. Hopper, Ben gained his freedom in the Philadelphia trial court under the six-months rule. Butler then sued Hopper in federal court under the Fugitive Slave Law of 1793 for helping his slave escape. Butler claimed that Ben was worth at least $2,000. US Supreme Court Justice Bushrod Washington, while riding circuit, ruled that when Butler was not in Congress, he had no right to keep a slave in the state more than six months. Ben thus went free and Butler lost his civil suit against Hopper.[51]

A decade later, a case involving an actual member of Congress reached the Supreme Court. During the War of 1812, Representative Langdon Cheves of South Carolina remained in the state with his slave Lewis for more than six months. Lawyers for the PAS tried to prevent Lewis's return to slavery, claiming he was free under the six-months rule. Lewis's attorneys argued that the exemption for members of Congress was no longer applicable because Philadelphia was no longer the nation's seat of government. But the Court disagreed. The statute was clear and represented an effort by Pennsylvania to get along with the slave states of the South, and the exemption for members of Congress existed even if Congress no longer met in Philadelphia. This argument was particularly compelling because Representative Cheves had fled Washington when the British army invaded the city during the War of 1812 and remained in Philadelphia because it was virtually impossible for him to return home. As a result, he kept his slave.[52]

The interstate comity expressed in favor of Representative Cheves extended to fugitive slaves as well. In 1819, for example, the Court quashed a writ of habeas corpus designed to release a fugitive slave from jail. Chief Justice Tilghman held that he was obligated to enforce the fugitive slave law of 1793 and not interfere with the return of those slaves who escaped from the South.[53] However, the Court also supported the state's attempt to protect its free blacks from kidnapping. In 1826, Pennsylvania required that no one could remove an alleged fugitive slave from the state without first receiving a certificate of removal from a state judge.[54] In 1837, four Maryland men, including Edward Prigg, brought Margaret Morgan and her children before Thomas Henderson, a York County justice of the peace, to obtain a certificate of removal under the law.[55] Henderson refused to issue the writ because he believed that Morgan was actually free under Maryland law and at least one (and maybe more) of Morgan's children had been born in Pennsylvania and were certainly free under the 1780 law. Prigg and his cohorts then took Morgan and her children to Maryland in violation of the 1826 law, and she and her children were soon sold in the South. After extensive negotiations, authorities in Maryland agreed to cooperate with Pennsylvania's extradition requisition for Prigg so he could be tried for kidnapping. A jury in York County convicted Prigg, and the Supreme Court affirmed his conviction in 1841. A year later, the US Supreme Court reversed this outcome. In an intensely proslavery decision, Justice Joseph Story held that the Pennsylvania Act of 1826 was unconstitutional and that the states had no power to interfere in the return of fugitive slaves, even to prevent the kidnapping of their own citizens.[56]

After *Prigg*, Pennsylvania courts were less supportive of the enforcement of the fugitive slave laws. This was in part because of the rise of antislavery politics in the Keystone State, but it was also a reaction to the US Supreme Court's overwhelmingly proslavery decision, which made it impossible for the free states to protect their citizens from Southern kidnappers. Thus in 1848, the Court released thirteen abolitionists from prison, rejecting the three-year sentence at hard labor or solitary confinement for rioting, after they helped rescue a fugitive slave. The Court offered a short history of the abuses of the criminal justice system in England, including a denunciation of the Star Chamber and "burning in the hand, cutting off the ears, placing in the pillory, whipping, or imprisonment for life." The Court declared that all such punishments, as well as "the pillory, tumbril, and ducking-stool," belonged to a "barbarous age" and were no longer acceptable in Pennsylvania.[57] The sentence of these opponents of slavery smacked of the same sort of barbarism, and the Court would have none of it. All the defendants were released after spending about nine months in the state penitentiary.

However, when the abolitionist Passmore Williamson was incarcerated by federal authorities for allegedly helping a slave escape, the Supreme Court refused to issue a writ of habeas corpus.[58] The opinion was written by Justice Jeremiah Black, a proslavery Democrat who had no sympathy for abolitionists. That the Court declined to try to release an abolitionist from federal custody was not surprising; courts in Massachusetts and Ohio acted in a similar fashion. But the *Williamson* case offered the opportunity for the Court to take a more forceful stand against slavery. In 1847, Pennsylvania had repealed its six-months rule, which meant that slaves brought to Pennsylvania by their masters were now instantly free. Williamson had not in fact helped a slave who escaped into Pennsylvania, and thus he should not have been prosecuted by the federal government for violating the fugitive slave law of 1793. Instead, Williamson had helped a slave leave her master *after* the master had brought her to Philadelphia. Thus this was not a fugitive slave case, and the federal courts should have had no jurisdiction over the issue. Williamson's case offered the Pennsylvania Supreme Court an opportunity to affirm Pennsylvania's right to prevent slaves from being brought into the state and protect the liberty of free blacks in the state. But Justice Black had no interest in the rights or liberty of slaves, free blacks, or abolitionists, and so he refused to assert Pennsylvania's liberty interest in the case.

VI. A COURT CAUGHT BETWEEN SLAVERY AND FREEDOM

The *Williamson* case illustrates the complexity of slavery and freedom in Pennsylvania. In 1780, Pennsylvania was on the cutting edge of ending slavery in the North, even as the state tried to balance the issues of slavery, freedom, liberty, property, and interstate harmony in the new nation. By the 1850s, Pennsylvania symbolized the tensions in the North between the emerging antislavery Republican Party and the proslavery Democratic Party, symbolized by Pennsylvania's only successful presidential candidate, the doughfaced, pro-slavery Democrat James Buchanan.[59]

The state no longer tolerated slavery, and after 1847, all people in the state (except actual fugitive slaves) were free and visitors were no longer allowed to bring slaves into the state. But despite a clear statute that freed any slave voluntarily brought into the state, the Supreme Court in the *Williamson* case would not help challenge the proslavery arro-gance of the Polk administration. This contrasts with New York, where the courts and the state government fought hard to protect the right of the state to emancipate slaves brought into New York by their masters.[60] In 1860, the New York Court of Appeals emphatically held that any slave brought into the state was immediately free. But Justice Black in Penn-sylvania had no interest in siding with freedom, even when the statutes were clear and not in doubt. James Buchanan would reward Black for his proslavery loyalty by making him the attorney general of the United States and then his secretary of state. The decision in *Williamson* also contrasts with the actions of the state courts in *Prigg* in 1841 and a half century earlier, when the slave of Pierce Butler gained his freedom in the state.

The Supreme Court over the years also vacillated in its support of the rights of free blacks. Under the state's first two Constitutions, free blacks were allowed to vote. But in *Hobbs v. Fogg* in 1837, the Court upheld the right of an election official to refuse to allow a black to vote.[61] This helped set the stage for the new state Constitution of 1838, which limited the vote to "white freemen" of the state.[62] This change was a result of Jacksonian democracy, which expanded access to the ballot for white men while taking voting rights away from blacks. At this time, Jeremiah Black was a young attorney and an ardent Jacksonian. The leader of the Jacksonians in Pennsylvania was James Buchanan.

Thus the connection between the Court's failure to protect black freedom in the 1850s was tied to the long-standing opposition to black rights in the Pennsylvania Democratic Party.

In 1853, the Court considered the relationships among landownership, race, and political rights. The case involved the right of a black man to claim vacant land owned by the Commonwealth under the state's preemption law. The Court was emphatic that "[t]he question has no relation to the political rights of the colored population." Two decades after *Hobbs v. Fogg*, Jacksonians in Pennsylvania happily reiterated the racist doctrine of that case and the legitimacy of the 1838 Constitution, which limited voting to "white freemen." Justice Ellis Lewis, another power in the state Democratic Party and an ardent Jacksonian, reaffirmed the reasonableness of denying blacks the right to vote. The Court declared that until the "white population, who settled this Commonwealth" decided to enfranchise nonwhites, "the negro and the Indian must be content with the privileges extended to them, without aspiring to the exercise of the elective franchise, or to the right to become our legislators, judges and governors."[63]

But Justice Lewis saw a huge distinction between political rights and economic rights. This illustrates, to some extent, the difference between Northern and Southern Jacksonians. Slaveholding Jacksonians, like Chief Justice Roger B. Taney of the US Supreme Court, were ready to deny blacks *any* rights.[64] But at least in Pennsylvania, the Jacksonians were willing to concede that blacks were entitled to some property rights. Consequently, Lewis asserted there was "nothing in the principles of the common law, or in the former condition of the colored population, which excludes them from acquiring, in like manner, freedom and the right to purchase property, by the consent, either express or implied, of those who had heretofore held them in bondage."[65] The Court found that "the effect" of the state's abolition of slavery was "to give to the colored man the right to acquire, possess and dispose of lands and goods, as fully as the white man enjoys these rights. Having no one to look to for support but himself, it would be a mockery to tell him he is a 'free man,' if he be not allowed the necessary means of sustaining life. The right to the fruits of his industry and to invest them in lands or goods, or in such manner as he may deem most conducive to his comfort, is an incident to the grant of his freedom."[66]

Thus by the eve of the Civil War, all blacks in Pennsylvania were free and entitled to many basic common-law rights. The Supreme Court supported these two principles. But the Court did not aggressively defend freedom or prefer freedom to slavery. And the Democratic majority on the Court emphatically supported the idea that blacks had no role to play in the Commonwealth's political process. All that would change in the next decade as new egalitarian leaders such as Simon Cameron, William Kelley, and most of all, Thaddeus Stevens gained political power and the United States followed Pennsylvania's lead from 1780 in finally ending slavery at the national level.

Paul Finkelman is the John E. Murray Visiting Professor of Law at the University of Pittsburgh School of Law and currently holds the Fulbright Chair in human rights and social justice at the University of Ottawa College of Law.

1. We do not have an exact count of all slave cases before the Pennsylvania Supreme Court. In her groundbreaking compilation of reported cases involving slavery and blacks, Helen T. Catterall found 102 state cases and 35 federal cases in Pennsylvania. Helen T. Catterall, *Judicial Cases Concerning Slavery and the Negro*, 5 vols. (Washington, D.C.: Carnegie Institution, 1926), 4:243–318. However, not all cases at this time were reported. For example, in 1840, the Supreme Court affirmed the kidnapping conviction of Edward Prigg but did not issue an opinion in the case; the outcome is thus unreported. The US Supreme Court reversed this decision in Prigg v. Pennsylvania, 41 U.S. (16 Pet.) 539 (1842). For a history of that case, *see* Paul Finkelman, "Storytelling on the Supreme Court: *Prigg v. Pennsylvania* and Justice Joseph Story's Judicial Nationalism," *Supreme Court Review* (1995): 247–94. Similarly, the case of Commonwealth ex rel. Annette, a mulatto Girl v. John Irvine is mentioned in the opinion of the Court in Commonwealth ex rel. Cribs v. Vance, 15 S. & R. 36, 38 (Pa. 1825) as "not yet reported" and apparently never was reported.

2. Huston's Appeal, 9 Watts 472, 473 (Pa. 1820).

3. Green v. African Methodist Episcopal Soc'y, 1 S. & R. 254 (Pa. 1815). The Court ordered that Green be restored to his position in the Church.

4. Missionary Soc'y's Appeal, 30 Pa. 425 (Pa. 1858). The Court upheld the bequest.

5. 1 Dall. 167 (Pa. 1786).

6. Respublica v. Negro Betsey, 1 Dall. 469 (Pa. 1789).

7. The full document is found in Kermit L. Hall, Paul Finkelman, and James W. Ely Jr., *American Legal History: Case and Materials*, 54th ed. (Oxford: Oxford University Press, 2011), 58–59.

8. David Brion Davis, *The Problem of Slavery in Western Culture* (Ithaca: Cornell University Press, 1966), 320–26.

9. Gary B. Nash and Jean R. Soderlund, *Freedom by Degrees: Emancipation in Pennsylvania and Its Aftermath* (Oxford: Oxford University Press, 1991), 80.

10. *See generally* Paul Finkelman, *Slavery and the Founders: Race and Liberty in the Age of Jefferson*, 3rd ed. (New York: Routledge, 2014).

11. An Act for the Gradual Abolition of Slavery, Act of March 1, 1780. The full text is available online through the "Avalon Project" at Yale Law School, http://www.avalon.law.yale.edu/18th_century/pennst01.asp.

12. 1 Lofft 1 (1772) (12 Geo. 3); 9 Eng. Rep. 499 (KB, 1772). For a discussion of this case, *see* Paul Finkelman, *An Imperfect Union: Slavery, Federalism, and Comity* (Chapel Hill: University of North Carolina Press, 1981); and William M. Wiecek, *The Sources of Anti-slavery Constitutionalism in America, 1760–1848* (Ithaca: Cornell University Press, 1977).

13. Sue Peabody, *There Are No Slaves in France: The Political Culture of Race and Slavery in the Ancient Regime* (Oxford: Oxford University Press, 1996).

14. Robert W. Fogel and Stanley L. Engerman, "Philanthropy at Bargain Prices," *Journal of Legal Studies* 3, no. 2 (1974): 377.

15. All quotations in this paragraph and the next come from Section I of An Act for the Gradual Abolition of Slavery, Act of March 1, 1780.

16. Finkelman, *Slavery and the Founders*, 203–5.

17. An Act for the Gradual Abolition of Slavery, Act of March 1, 1780, Section II.

18. Ibid.

19. For example, in Commonwealth ex rel. Jesse v. Craig, 1 S. & R. 23 (Pa. 1814), Jesse (a black man) was released from bondage because his owner had failed to register him within six months of his birth as servant.

20. Act of 1780, sec. VII.

21. Ibid., sec. X.

22. An Act to Address Certain Grievances Within the Counties of Westmoreland and Washington, Act of April 13, 1782.

23. An Act to Explain and Amend an Act, Entitled "An Act for the Gradual Abolition of Slavery," Act of March 29, 1788.

24. Nash and Soderlund, *Freedom by Degrees*, 124–25.

25. 1 U.S. 469 (Pa. 1789).

26. Ibid.

27. Ibid., 471–72.

28. Ibid., 472–73.

29. Ibid., 474.

30. Respublica v. Gaoler, 1 Yeates 368 (Pa. 1794).

31. Today this area includes Westmoreland, Washington, Greene, and Fayette Counties.

32. Pennsylvania v. Blackmore, Addison 284 (Pa. 1797).

33. Lucy v. Pumfrey, Addison 380 (Pa. 1799); John v. Dawson, 2 Yeates 449 (Pa. 1799).

34. Giles v. Meeks, Addison 384 (Pa. 1799); Campbell v. Wallace, 3 Yeates 572 (Pa. 1803).

35. Lucy, at 381.

36. Elson (a negro) v. M'Colloch, 4 Yeates 115 (Pa. 1804).

37. Respublica v. Findlay, 3 Yeates 261 (Pa. 1801).

38. Marchand v. Negro Peggy, 2 S. & R. 18 (Pa. 1815).

39. Ibid., 19.

40. Commonwealth ex rel. Jesse v. Craig, 1 S. & R. 23 (Pa. 1814).

41. However, in other cases, the Court was more concerned about the owner's occupation being listed on the registration. In Commonwealth v. Barker, 11 S. & R. 360 (Pa. 1824), for instance, the court freed a young man named Frank because the owner (Baker) had failed to put down his occupation on the registration form. Baker claimed he had "no occupation," but the Court held "it was incumbent on the master to remove all doubt," and Baker's "evidence" was not "sufficient for the purpose" because it appeared from other evidence that he "was a partner of a manufacturing company." Ibid., 361. Also, in Commonwealth ex rel. Cribs v. Vance, 15 S. & R. 36 (Pa. 1825), a decision authored by Justice Duncan upheld the registration of Pompey Cribs, a servant for twenty-eight years, on the basis that "Esq." was sufficient to identify the owner, who at the time was a sitting judge on a county court. Two of the five members of the Court dissented in this case and would have freed Cribs. In another (unreported) case, "yeoman was a sufficient description" of the owner's occupation. Ibid., 38.

42. Wilson v. Belinda, 3 S. & R. 396, 398 (1817). Tilghman reached this result without knowing about the future popular Johnny Cash song, "A Boy Named Sue." Shel Silverstein, "A Boy Named Sue," recorded by Johnny Cash (1969).

43. Belinda, 3 S. & R. at 401–2.

44. For an extensive discussion of this law and the jurisprudence surrounding it, *see* Finkelman, *Imperfect Union*, 46–63.

45. Commonwealth v. Chambrè, 4 Dall. 143, 144 (Pa. 1794).

46. Ibid.

47. Commonwealth v. Smyth, 1 Browne 113 (Pa. 1809).

48. Butler v. Delaplaine, 7 S. & R. 378 (Pa. 1821).

49. Ibid., 379–80.

50. Ibid., 383–85.

51. Butler v. Hopper, 4 F. Cas. 904 (C.C.D. Pa. 1806). For more on this case, see Lydia Maria Child, *Isaac T. Hopper: A True Life* (Boston: John P. Jewett, 1853) 98–103; Nash and Soderland, *Freedom by Degrees*, 136.

52. Commonwealth ex rel. Lewis v. Holloway, 6 Binney 213 (Pa. 1814).

53. Wight, alias Hall, v. Deacon, 5 S. & R. 62 (Pa. 1819).

54. "An Act to give effect to the provisions of the constitution of the United States relative to fugitives from labor, for the protection of free people of color, and to prevent Kidnapping," ch. L, Pennsylvania Session Law, 1826 150 (1826).

55. The details of this case are found in Finkelman, "Storytelling," 247–94.

56. Prigg v. Pennsylvania, 41 U.S. 539 (1842).

57. Clellans v. Commonwealth, 8 Pa. 223, 228–29 (1848).

58. Passmore Williamson's Case, 26 Pa. 9 (1855).

59. For a superb collection of essays on Buchanan, *see* John W. Quist and Michael. J. Birkner, eds., *James Buchanan and the Coming of the Civil War* (Tallahassee: University of Florida Press, 2013). For a discussion of Buchanan's proslavery views, *see* Paul Finkelman, "James Buchanan, *Dred Scott*, and the Whisper of Conspiracy," in *James Buchanan and the Coming of the Civil War*, ed. John W. Quist and Michael J. Birkner (Tallahassee: University of Florida Press, 2013), 20–45.

60. *See* Lemmon v. The People, 20 N.Y. 562 (1860); and Finkelman, *Imperfect Union*, 284–312.

61. 6 Watts 553 (Pa. 1837).

62. Pa. Const. art. V, § 7.

63. Formans v. Tamm, 1 Grant 23 (Pa. 1853).

64. *See* Dred Scott v. Sandford, 60 U.S. 393 (1857), and Paul Finkelman, "Coming to Terms with *Dred Scott*: A Response to Daniel A. Farber," *Pepperdine Law Review* 39 (2012): 49–74; Paul Finkelman, "Was *Dred Scott* Correctly Decided? An 'Expert Report' for the Defendant," *Lewis and Clark Law Review* 12 (2008): 1219–52; and Paul Finkelman, "*Scott v. Sandford*: The Court's Most Dreadful Case and How It Changed History," *Chicago-Kent Law Review* 82 (2007): 3–48.

65. Foremans v. Tamm, 1 Grant 23 (Pa. 1853).

66. Ibid., 25.

CHAPTER 21

When Felons Don't Kill

The Felony Murder Rule in Pennsylvania

ARTHUR G. LEFRANCOIS

Courts of last resort react. They react to legislation, decisions of other courts, and their own prior cases. Further, justices come and go and social realities change, as do legal and moral norms. In a line of influential murder cases spanning four decades, the Pennsylvania Supreme Court zigged before it zagged and did so against a backdrop of war, civil unrest, student protests, and rising crime rates. And it did so in cases in which defendants committing felonies were charged with murder for killings committed by those resisting them. Justice Henry O'Brien would later say, without overstatement, that the litigation generated by the first of these cases had proved "vexing to the courts" and had "perplexed a generation of law students, both within and without the Commonwealth."[1] The entire line of cases, he said, had "spawned reams of critical commentary" that were "virtually impossible to catalogue."[2]

I. GUN-CRAZY DUO

"Manhunt Is Staged for 'Gun Crazy' Duo," sang the headline of the 1947 *Associated Press* story, which quoted Detective Inspector George Richardson as having broadcast a charge to "[t]ake them dead or alive for murder!" Richardson cautioned law enforcement officers to be careful in dealing with the "wanton killers."[3] Readers of this story surely assumed that one of the duo—David Almeida or James Smith—had killed off-duty patrolman Cecil Ingling as they were escaping from a Philadelphia robbery. Or maybe the killer was their partner, Edward Hough, who was arrested at the scene. Hough later pled guilty to first-degree murder and was sentenced to death (a sentence later reduced to life imprisonment). Almeida and Smith were apprehended some months after the robbery and were tried separately and convicted of first-degree murder. Smith received a life sentence, Almeida a death sentence (later reduced to a life sentence). Almeida appealed.

As for the men being "wanton killers," it was never clear who fired the shot that killed Officer Ingling. The best evidence ultimately suggested that one of the policemen responding to the robbery was the (accidental) killer, but the Commonwealth contended that the shooter's identity made no difference. Indeed, the trial judge in David Almeida's case said that he would instruct the jury (he didn't) that it would have made no difference had the fatal shot been fired by the patrolman's wife.[4] This must have surprised Almeida. How could he face the death penalty for a killing neither he nor his accomplices committed?

II. BUT IS IT MURDER?

The Commonwealth had a theory at its disposal: the felony murder doctrine. Under this common-law principle, a person can be convicted of murder for an accidental death that occurs during the commission of a felony. The intention to commit the felony suffices for the malice aforethought necessary for murder, even absent any intention to kill or recklessness about whether death might occur.

There are American statutory versions of the doctrine as well. Pennsylvania's legislature was the first to establish degrees of murder, doing so at the end of the eighteenth century. Influenced by Quaker thought, the idea was to distinguish between murders that warranted the death penalty and murders that did not. The legislature determined that murders that were willful, deliberate, and premeditated deserved the death penalty. So did murders occurring during the course of specified felonies. So "felony murder" came to mean two things in Pennsylvania. The first (the common-law meaning) was that a killing during a felony could be murder, regardless of the lack of any intention to kill or to do serious bodily harm or recklessness about whether one's actions might risk death. The second (the statutory meaning) was that a murder that occurred during certain felonies (like burglary and robbery) was murder in the first degree and so qualified for the death penalty.

Supporters of the felony murder rule liked the idea that it provided a disincentive to commit a felony—or at least to do so in a manner risking death. Detractors were disturbed that accidental deaths could be murders, even in the absence of any "real" malice aforethought. Academics roundly criticized the doctrine, and England abandoned it by statute in 1957. Some criticisms of the doctrine were pragmatic, including the argument that it had no meaningful deterrent effect. Other criticisms were based on notions of justice or morality. The felony murder rule, it was said, made bad luck more important than criminal intention. This was thought to be especially objectionable, given the seriousness of the crime of murder and its resultant punishment (sometimes death). Notwithstanding the criticisms, American states, including Pennsylvania, retained the rule, although courts and legislatures imposed a good number of restrictions on its application.

A. *Almeida*: A Police Officer Kills a Police Officer, and the Court Gets Tough on Crime

The question before the Supreme Court in the case of the "wanton killers" who likely didn't kill was whether the felony murder rule ought to apply in a case where the killing was done not by one of the robbers but by a police officer opposing them. The symbolic—to say nothing of the personal—stakes were high. In a case decided in 1947, just two years before *Almeida* (and just six years after the attack on Pearl Harbor), the Court used the language of patriotism and national defense to describe robbery victim Earl Shank's resistance. Shank's firing a gun to repel armed—and shooting—robbers was "as proper and as inevitable as it was for the American forces at Pearl Harbor . . . to return the fire of the Japanese invaders." And if Earl Shank had accidentally killed one of his coworkers in the process, the defendants would be liable for first-degree murder.[5] Feelings could run high about felons who used deadly weapons.

Chief Justice Maxey's unusually long majority opinion in Almeida's case upheld his conviction of first-degree murder and death sentence on the theory that, so long as the robbery was the cause of the death, the felons were responsible, even if they didn't do the killing. Maxey cited the case involving Earl Shank, decisions by other state courts and courts in other countries, and treatise writers in support of this "proximate cause" view of felony murder. He sought as well to ground the opinion in notions of "justice" and "utility."[6] The opinion thus stood for the proposition that a felon could be held responsible for the murder of a police officer killed by a police officer. Felons bore such risks as a cost of doing business.

B. *Thomas*: A Victim Kills a Felon, and the Court Gets Tougher on Crime

Several years later, in the case of *Commonwealth v. Thomas*,[7] District Attorney (and soon Philadelphia mayor) Richardson Dilworth and First Assistant District Attorney (and later chief counsel for the Senate Watergate Committee) Sam Dash teamed up for the prosecution. The question in *Thomas* was whether the felony murder doctrine applied to a robber whose victim killed the robber's accomplice. Justice John Arnold's short majority opinion (*Almeida* had already done most of the heavy lifting) reversed an earlier decision for the defendant. Justice Arnold invoked cases where the Court had determined that felons could be responsible for killings they did not directly commit (get-away drivers, defendants already in police custody, defendants whose accomplices caused their own deaths). There was some pragmatic moralizing here as well, as Justice Arnold said that applying the rule in this case was "consistent with reason and sound public policy, and is essential to the protection of human life." He also invoked the "primal human instinct" to defend one's self, family, and property, and the duty (of "individuals and nations") to oppose unlawful aggression.[8] World War II and the Korean War were still very much with the United States.

Justice John Bell, concurring in *Thomas*, was at pains to defend the majority opinion in *Almeida*, seeing that case as convincing and controlling. His concurrence focused also on the dissenting opinions of Justices Charles Jones, who had resigned from the federal bench to join the Court and who was to become chief justice the following year, and Michael Musmanno, a record-setting dissenter who had joined the Court three years after the *Almeida* decision.

Justice Jones, an unsuccessful Democratic gubernatorial candidate in 1938, had been the lone dissenter in *Almeida*, although that dissent was not a direct assault on the essence of *Almeida*'s holding. His *Thomas* dissent was different. Joined by Justice Thomas Chidsey (who, like Musmanno, had joined the Court after the *Almeida* decision), Jones argued that a *justifiable* homicide (a victim killing a robber) could not at the same time be a *criminal* homicide by a surviving robber.[9] He also appealed to the common law, the law of other jurisdictions, and Pennsylvania precedent in rejecting the application of the felony murder rule to facts like those in *Thomas*. More important, he sought to position *Almeida* as a sort of judicial aberration, calling it unique and unworthy of broader application. He took note of the trend to restrict rather than to expand the felony murder doctrine. Finally, he argued that *Almeida* was the first Pennsylvania case to impose felony murder liability for a killing by a third party resisting the felony.[10] All these themes would prove important in the ultimate unraveling of *Almeida*'s "proximate cause" theory of felony murder.

In Justice Musmanno's dissent, the killing of the robber by the victim was not only *justified* but *compelled* (by self-defense and to apprehend the fleeing felon). Musmanno thus co-opted Justice Arnold's duty theme and his wartime metaphor as well. And where Jones had sought to highlight the paradox of the felony murder rule applying in cases where a victim *justifiably* killed a robber, Musmanno hyperbolized the paradox into one where an act (a victim killing a felon) that the law "*demanded*" and "*required*" was simultaneously murder by the surviving felon.[11] Musmanno also made a linguistic argument: under the terms of the Pennsylvania statute, felony murder applied to "murder" in the course of certain felonies, not mere "killing." The majority had "torture[d] the word 'murder' into the word 'killing.'" Musmanno excoriated the majority opinion as "an arbitrary exercise of power rising out of a zeal to combat criminals."[12] There was considerable merit to the linguistic argument—that the felony murder statute fixes the degree of an independently established murder but does not establish murder itself. The argument based on the justifiability of the killing (an argument made by Justice Jones as well) was more of a contrivance than anything else, exploiting the idea that felons' lives were expendable. It would, nevertheless, feature importantly in the demise of the proximate cause theory of felony murder.

Justice Bell seemed to sense that the kind of broad application of the felony murder doctrine seen in *Almeida* was in jeopardy, perhaps because of shifting personnel on the Court, perhaps because of the fragility inherent in the proximate cause theory. He argued that Justice Musmanno found the identity of the victim central to felony murder liability (so that the killing *of a felon* would not be murder), while Justice Jones found the identity of the killer critical (so that a killing *by someone other than one of the felons* would not be murder). Presaging the more urgent, defiant tone he would adopt three years later, he concluded with a jeremiad against "turn[ing] back the clock," "hair-splitting technicalities . . . to absolve murderous robbers," "coddling criminals," and the "terrible brutal crime wave which is sweeping our State and Country." Extending the felony murder doctrine had become, for him, necessary to the "protection and welfare of the people."[13] Given that robbers, or other felons, could be punished with lengthy prison terms for the felonies they committed, it was not obvious just why such murder convictions were necessary to protect the people.

C. Reacting to *Almeida* and *Thomas*

Almeida and *Thomas*, along with other Pennsylvania cases that extended the felony murder doctrine, garnered a good bit of judicial and scholarly attention. While a handful of state courts outside Pennsylvania exploited the *Almeida* rationale, commentators questioned the propriety of using the felony murder doctrine to impose first-degree murder liability where one resisting the felony accidentally killed an innocent person or intentionally killed one of the felons. Writing in the *University of Pennsylvania Law Review* in 1956, the famous criminal law scholar (then relatively early in his academic career) Norval Morris argued against the Court's "extension of the felony-murder rule."[14] Morris canvassed extensive legal territory in repudiating *Almeida* and *Thomas*. He also distinguished between heat and light in the battle over the appropriate contours of the felony murder rule, observing that it is "much easier to seek to justify one's prejudices by an emotional appeal than it is to support them with socially meaningful and methodologically defensible propositions."[15] Morris pointed to the novel nature of the Court's extension of the felony murder doctrine, the failure of deterrence theory to justify the Court's holdings (if we're trying to deter dangerous felonies, we'd be better off increasing the punishments for those felonies—not imposing murder liability for even unintended results caused by resisters), the lack of a retributive (just deserts) rationale for the holdings, and the legislative (not judicial) responsibility for such lawmaking in the service of justice and utility.[16]

Other commentators weighed in as well, suggesting that the Court's extensions of the felony murder rule were unfair,[17] that they diluted the idea of proximate cause,[18] and that the rule itself was untenable.[19]

D. *Redline*: A Police Officer Kills a Felon, and the Court Thinks Again

By 1958, another felony murder case was before the Court. *Almeida* had involved a robber's criminal liability for the accidental killing of a policeman by another policeman. *Thomas* had been about a robber's responsibility for the killing of his accomplice by the victim. The new case, *Redline*, was about a robber whose accomplice was killed by a police officer during flight from the felony.[20] The larger issue was whether the Court would continue its aggressive application of the felony murder doctrine, pressed so fervently by Justice Bell in his *Thomas* concurrence. In a stark rebuke of the Court's recent felony murder jurisprudence, Chief Justice Jones, who had dissented in *Almeida* and *Thomas*, wrote the majority opinion reversing *Redline's* first-degree murder conviction. His opinion characterized *Almeida* as a "radical departure" from the common law and unworthy of extension.[21] It also overturned *Thomas*.[22]

In a dramatic turn of events, Justice Bell stood alone in his dissent. Of the five *Redline* justices who had served on the *Thomas* Court, three continued in their opposition to the *Thomas* rule, and Justice Arnold, who had authored the *Thomas* opinion, apparently changed his view. Justice Herbert Cohen, who had served as state attorney general before joining the Court only a year earlier, concurred in the majority opinion, but only to indicate that he wouldn't have split hairs—he'd have overturned *Almeida* as well as *Thomas*. The Commonwealth's former chief lawyer called *Almeida* "judicial *ex post facto* law-making."[23]

The Court seemed to roundly repudiate the proximate cause theory of felony murder and reestablish the agency theory. If so, it wasn't enough to show that a shoot-out with police or victims somehow caused a death; it was now necessary to show that a felon had done the actual killing. Except if that were true, why hadn't the Court overruled *Almeida*? The agency theory, after all, rested on a powerful moral intuition—whatever first-degree murder was, it wasn't made out under the felony murder doctrine unless a felon did the killing and not someone resisting the felony. The agency theory rested as well on strong statutory and historical grounds. So just what did *Redline* do, since it overruled *Thomas* (where a victim killed a felon) but not *Almeida* (where a police officer killed a police officer)? Rejecting *Thomas* was consistent with rejecting the proximate cause theory in favor of the agency theory, but preserving *Almeida* was not.

Chief Justice Jones's lengthy majority opinion (an ironist might note that it was more than half as long as Justice Bell's dissent) sought to return homicide law to something like its pre-*Almeida* state. He canvassed older cases in an effort to show that the agency theory of felony murder had prevailed outside of Pennsylvania for years and had done so within Pennsylvania until *Almeida*. He cited scholarly commentary supporting the agency theory. He noted the Pennsylvania legislature's cautioning against excessive punishment. He distinguished—not even to his satisfaction—*Almeida* from *Redline*. In the former case, an innocent person (Officer Ingling) had been killed. In the latter, one of the felons had been killed. While the former killing might have been excusable, the latter was justifiable, and it was inconceivable that one could be criminally responsible for the justifiable act of another. Justice Jones disarmingly found this distinction (based in important part on the status of the victim) of little legal significance. He was right in doing so, since neither justifiable nor excusable killings are criminal. But the excusable/justifiable distinction was of *some* utility, he said, in that it helped constrain the rule of *Almeida*. And the distinction had been used before—at least in his and Justice Musmanno's dissenting opinions in the

Thomas case. He concluded with a suggestion that *Almeida* could always be overruled if the Court were ever asked to decide a case having similar facts (a case where a resister killed an innocent).[24]

Justice Bell wrote an angry dissent. Harking back to his *Thomas* concurrence, his opening salvo lamented the "coddling" and "freeing" of "murderers, communists and criminals on technicalities made of straw." He suggested that criminals were better protected by law than were "law-abiding citizens."[25] He appealed to the old ("legal principles which are several hundred years old") and the new ("the law is not static—it is progressive").[26] Having earlier extolled the virtues of dynamism in law (if law were static, its domain "would be as large and extensive as the principality of Monaco"),[27] Bell concluded with a generalized lament against American judges whom he thought had recently begun to undercut the law's certainty.[28] The only case he cited in this regard was a 1944 US Supreme Court decision[29] outlawing a particular method of disenfranchising African American primary voters. That Court had upheld the practice nine years earlier, much as Justice Bell's Court had extolled the virtues of the proximate cause theory of felony murder nine years prior to *Redline*. Even though the Warren Court's "revolution" in criminal procedural rights had yet to occur, Bell complained that "the highest Courts in the land are constantly weakening or eliminating the few safeguards which remain to protect law-abiding communities against dangerous criminals."[30]

The evisceration of the *Almeida/Thomas* theory of felony murder was pragmatically, if not formally, complete. *Almeida* had been marginalized as an aberration, and *Thomas* was overruled altogether. The Court was so displeased with what it had wrought in the latter case that it took the unusual step of pointing out that Mr. Thomas had suffered no undue penalty, as the district attorney's office had since dropped the murder prosecution and Thomas had pled guilty to armed robbery.[31] Responding to this, Justice Bell suggested that the responsible assistant district attorney "should have been held 'in contempt' and *severely* punished."[32] This wasn't the first time state officials had had second thoughts about the rule's application. Professor Morris had written of a Pennsylvania trial judge who instructed a jury in a pre-*Redline* first-degree murder case with *Redline*-like facts (officer kills escaping accomplice) that the charge against the surviving felon was made out even if the evidence established that the police officer did the killing. Professor Morris reported that the judge (the immensely talented Curtis Bok, who would later serve on the state's Supreme Court) afterward explained his hope that if the jury had convicted the defendant (it didn't), the Court would take that occasion to limit the reach of *Almeida*.[33]

E. Reacting to *Redline*

Given the reception that the *Almeida/Thomas* line of cases had had among judges and scholars, it was hardly surprising that *Redline* was more warmly greeted. Indeed, criticism seemed limited, for the most part, to the idea that the Court did not go so far as to overrule

Almeida. A commentator in the *Harvard Law Review* wrote in favor of the case's limitation of the proximate cause theory and argued that *Almeida* should have been swept away altogether by *Redline*, since the law offers protections even to felons.[34] Seeking to undercut *Redline*'s distinction between the not-overruled *Almeida* (where the homicide victim was an innocent) and the overruled *Thomas* (where the homicide victim was an accomplice), the author pointed to the unhelpfulness of the justifiable/excusable distinction (neither kind of killing is punished), the irrelevance of a resister's marksmanship (first-degree murder liability should not hinge on whether a resister shoots a felon or an innocent), the nonportability of the tort theory of assumption of risk, and the inadequacy of public anger as a justification for the imposition of first-degree murder liability in cases where felons don't kill.[35] A writer in the *University of Pennsylvania Law Review* was of a similar mind but added that it was possible to see *Redline* as repudiating the proximate cause theory, the failure to overrule *Almeida* notwithstanding.[36] Justice Bell, dissenting in *Redline*, had made a similar point, though more poetically. He likened *Almeida* to Mohammed's coffin, in seeming equipoise between heaven and earth. But unlike Mohammed's coffin, said Bell, *Almeida* was poised for a "speedy flight into the bowels of the earth."[37]

Ambiguity about *Redline*'s meaning remains. Did it impose the agency limitation on felony murder doctrine, requiring that a felon do the killing? Or did it focus instead on the identity of the victim, requiring that the victim be an innocent? Professor David Crump, writing in 2009, treated *Redline*'s rule as a restriction on felony murder based on the identity of the victim (a cofelon).[38] Two years earlier, Professor Leonard Birdsong cited *Redline* as the signal case on agency theory, the theory that what matters is not who dies but who kills.[39] The University of Pennsylvania's Paul Robinson, then at Rutgers-Camden, wrote quite rightly in 1984 that it was unclear whether *Redline* was based on the identity of the killer, the killed, or the combination.[40]

F. *Smith v. Myers*: Undoing *Almeida*

Eventually the Supreme Court weighed in on the mystery that was *Redline*. In 1970, twenty-one years after the decision in *Almeida*, which *Redline* had failed to overrule, James Smith—who along with David Almeida had formed the "Gun-Crazy Duo" the newspapers had warned of—won an order for a new trial in a case before the state's highest court. Justice Henry O'Brien's majority opinion acknowledged that the *Almeida* line of cases had proved troublesome to courts, law students, and commentators.[41]

The majority opinion was simultaneously a primer on and a critique of the felony murder rule. Reiterating Justice Musmanno's dissent in *Thomas*, O'Brien wrote that statutory felony murder does not establish murder; it simply fixes its degree.[42] That is, once murder has been established, it becomes first-degree murder if it was committed in the course of particular felonies the statute lists. So statutory felony murder *requires* murder; it doesn't *establish* it. O'Brien next moved to the common law on felony murder, the doctrine that *does* establish murder by treating the intention to do a felony as the malice required by murder. He noted the many ("thoroughly warranted") moral and practical criticisms of the common-law doctrine. His point was not to abolish the doctrine but to undermine it so as to avoid the kind of broad application of it witnessed in *Almeida* and *Thomas*. He underscored *Redline*'s claim that until *Almeida*, the agency doctrine had prevailed in Pennsylvania. But where *Redline* had refused to overturn *Almeida*, the majority opinion here did so unequivocally. The majority claimed that the "case law of centuries and the force of reason" required as much.[43] Taking a page from Justice Bell's angry and mournful dissent in *Redline*, the majority opinion concluded, "We thus give *Almeida* burial, taking it out of its limbo and plunging it downward into the bowels of the earth."[44]

After *Smith v. Myers*, felony murder had not been entirely repudiated, but the proximate cause theory had been rejected in favor of the agency theory. For felony murder liability, it would not be enough that one had started a gunfight that ended in death. Instead, to bear culpability for murder, a felon or an accomplice would have to do the killing act. The decision reflected the moral intuition underlying the agency theory and simultaneously jettisoned the convenient, but unpersuasive, claim that a justifiable killing by X could not be a criminal killing by Y.

Predictably, now Chief Justice Bell dissented. How could he not, with his Mohammed's coffin simile being used as the trope that symbolized *Almeida*'s passing? To make things worse, as in *Redline*, he stood alone. And as with his *Redline* dissent, his first line gave a good sense of his views: "This is the age of Crime and Criminals, and the peace-loving citizen is the forgotten man."[45] His opinion was of a piece with the "law and order" rhetoric that helped sweep Richard Nixon to the presidency two years earlier and Ronald Reagan to his first gubernatorial term two years before that (Reagan was reelected the year *Redline* was decided).

America faced a "tidal wave of ruthless crime," largely attributable to "pro-criminal decisions of the highest Courts in our State and Country."[46] As for the crime wave, "gangs terrorize with impunity" and the "desecration of churches" and "forcible seizure of buildings and college campuses" go unpunished because of the "timidity" of public officials and the "mollycoddling" and "ultra-lenient sentences of many lower Court Judges."[47] Higher courts were complicit. Justice Bell's Court had been thought to be "one of the two or three best Courts in our Country," and yet *Smith v. Myers* was unaccountably a "pro-criminal Opinion" that was "disastrous to the safety and protection of Society."[48] The majority opinion had no "legal or moral justification" and would "produce the most harmful damage to law-abiding citizens ever inflicted" by Bell's Court.[49] In a footnote qualifying this proposition, Bell suggested that his Court might have inflicted more damage to the law abiders in Pennsylvania in other cases, but in those cases, unlike *Smith*, the Court was dutifully obeying dictates laid down by the US Supreme Court.[50] The country's highest courts were "completely oblivious of the rights, the security, the safety and the welfare of the law-abiding public."[51]

At the beginning of the 1960s, the US Supreme Court had determined that unconstitutionally obtained evidence should be excluded in state criminal trials (overruling its contrary decision from only twelve years earlier).[52] In the last half of the decade, that Court required the now familiar *Miranda* warnings in custodial interrogations[53] and expanded the reach of the Fourth Amendment's protections against government intrusions.[54] In the middle of the decade, Philadelphia had rioted, and syndicated writer Jim Bishop had written a sympathetic four-column series detailing Edward Hough's (the third member of the *Almeida* trio) harrowing experiences with Pennsylvania's criminal justice system.[55] Times were changing.

And so by the new decade's dawn, Justice Bell had lost his battle. The proximate cause theory's practical rejection in *Redline* and formal demise in *Smith* was, for him, surely a kind of agonizing symbolic death of older values, all the worse because it was both quick (*Redline*) and drawn out (*Smith*). In Bell's view, civil unrest, student protests, and increases in violent crime rates over the decade preceding *Smith* were exacerbated, perhaps even caused, by a kind of indiscriminate tolerance of the sort to which he objected even in the 1950s. As his dissenting opinions show, he was disconsolate that his Court, and the world, seemed to be moving on. His "law and order" claims for the proximate cause variant of the felony murder doctrine were trumped by more nuanced claims regarding law's nature, purpose, and effects. Criminal law could at least aspire to protect, and treat rationally, all people—even felons. How far it came from doing so was quite another question.

NOTES

Arthur G. LeFrancois is a professor at the Oklahoma City University School of Law. The author would like to thank Riane Fern for her thoughtful research assistance.

1. Commonwealth ex rel. Smith v. Myers, 261 A.2d 550, 551 (Pa. 1970).
2. Ibid., 551n3.
3. Richard Miller, "Manhunt Is Staged for 'Gun Crazy' Duo," *Pottstown Mercury*, February 1, 1947, 2.
4. Commonwealth v. Almeida, 68 A.2d 595, 598 (Pa. 1949).
5. Commonwealth v. Moyer, 53 A.2d 736, 742 (Pa. 1947).
6. Almeida, 68 A.2d at 611–12.
7. 117 A.2d 204 (1955).
8. Ibid., 205.
9. Ibid., 213 (Jones, J., dissenting).
10. Ibid., 213–16.
11. Ibid., 225 (Musmanno, J., dissenting), emphasis added.
12. Ibid., 222.
13. Ibid., 213 (Bell, J., concurring).
14. Norval Morris, "The Felon's Responsibility for the Lethal Acts of Others," *University of Pennsylvania Law Review* 50 (1956): 105.
15. Ibid., 66.
16. Ibid., 57, 68.
17. William F. Schulz Jr., "Criminal Law and Procedure," *University of Pittsburgh Law Review* 18 (1957): 221.
18. Frederick J. Ludwig, "Foreseeable Death in Felony Murder," *University of Pittsburgh Law Review* 18 (1956): 59.
19. Note, "Felony Murder as a First Degree Offense: An Anachronism Retained," *Yale Law Review* 66 (January 1957): 433.
20. Commonwealth v. Redline, 137 A.2d 472 (Pa. 1958).
21. Ibid., 473.
22. Ibid., 482.
23. Ibid., 502 (Cohen, J., concurring).
24. Ibid., 474–83 (majority opinion).
25. Ibid., 483 (Bell, J., dissenting).

26. Ibid., 483, 486.

27. Ibid., 486.

28. Ibid., 486, 499–500.

29. Smith v. Allwright, 321 U.S. 649 (1944).

30. Redline, 137 A.2d at 500n15 (Bell, J., dissenting).

31. Ibid., 482 (majority opinion).

32. Ibid., 499n13 (Bell, J., dissenting).

33. Morris, "Felon's Responsibility," 54–55, 55n28.

34. "Recent Cases," *Harvard Law Review* 71 (1958): 1567.

35. Ibid., 1566–67.

36. "Recent Cases," *University of Pennsylvania Law Review* 106 (1958): 1178–79.

37. Redline, 137 A.2d at 499n14 (Bell, J., dissenting).

38. David Crump, "Reconsidering the Felony Murder Rule in Light of Modern Criticisms: Doesn't the Conclusion Depend upon the Particular Rule at Issue?," *Harvard Journal of Law and Public Policy* 32 (2009): 1182–83.

39. Leonard Birdsong, "The Felony Murder Doctrine Revisited: A Proposal for Calibrating Punishment That Reaffirms the Sanctity of Human Life of Co-felons Who Are Victims," *Ohio Northern University Law Review* 33 (2007): 505.

40. Paul H. Robinson, "Imputed Criminal Liability," *Yale Law Review* 93 (1984): 644n129.

41. *See* William Blackstone, *Commentaries on the Laws of England*, vol. 3, 1st ed. (Oxford: Clarendon Press, 1765), 41.

42. Commonwealth ex rel. Smith v. Myers, 261 A.2d 550, 553 (Pa. 1970).

43. Ibid., 553–58.

44. Ibid., 559–60.

45. Ibid., 560 (Bell, J., dissenting).

46. Ibid.

47. Ibid., 560n1.

48. Ibid., 560. Dissenting in Redline, Bell had characterized the majority's argument there as one pressed "continuously and vigorously . . . for the last ten years by convicted murderers." 137 A.2d 498 (Bell, J., dissenting).

49. Smith, 261 A.2d at 561.

50. Ibid., 561n2.

51. Ibid., 560.

52. Mapp v. Ohio, 367 U.S. 643 (1961).

53. Miranda v. Arizona, 384 U.S. 436 (1966).

54. Katz v. United States, 389 U.S. 347 (1967).

55. Jim Bishop, "Two Letters for Your Son," *Indiana Evening Gazette*, March 2, 1966, 6; "A Convict Named Eddie: Crime and Vengeance—Part One," *Indiana Evening Gazette*, March 23, 1966, 6; "A Convict Named Eddie: Crime and Vengeance—Part Two," *Indiana Evening Gazette*, March 24, 1966, 6; "A Convict Named Eddie: Conclusion," *Indiana Evening Gazette*, March 25, 1966, 6.

Labor Law and Economic Rights

CHAPTER 22

The Supreme Court and the Labor Movement

JEFFREY P. BAUMAN

Over the last three centuries in Pennsylvania, the interactions between workers, unions, and capital and the laws that govern those relationships in many ways mirrored the experience of the labor movement across the nation; yet, in certain ways, our Commonwealth's experience with working people and their attempts to gain greater prosperity and safer working conditions is uniquely Pennsylvanian. The study of the legal relationships between Pennsylvania workers and their representatives and their employers is set against an uncommonly robust, and at times violent, history of the labor movement in our Commonwealth, including watershed events such as the Great Railroad Strike of 1877 and the battle at Carnegie Steel's Homestead Works in 1892. This chapter traces the trajectory of labor's struggle for greater rights and protections in the workplace by viewing three distinct eras and considering discrete aspects of the laws impacting the labor movement during those times, as influenced by the Pennsylvania Supreme Court.

Examination of the various legal tools used to address "the labor question" begins with post-Revolution attempts to thwart collective action by workers through the common-law criminal charge of conspiracy. Next, large-scale disruption of the economy by workers at the turn of the twentieth century that led to the widespread and effective use of the civil injunction to quash mass strikes, picketing, boycotts, and violence is considered. Finally, more recent developments in Pennsylvania labor law are contemplated, including the enactment of the 1970s-era labor statutes giving public-sector employees the right to collectively bargain and, specifically, decisions regarding the evolving relationship between the judiciary and the arbitration process. In each of these periods, and with each of these legal tools, a common theme emerges—an initial resistance by the judiciary to labor's actions, followed by decisions according workers greater rights and liberties supportive of their attempts for better living conditions and a participation in workplace governance, ultimately reflecting acceptance and acknowledgement of the societal and economic realities of the employee-employer relationship and emblematic, perhaps, of more mature and positive relationships between labor and capital and the law.

I. LABOR LAW IN POST-REVOLUTION PENNSYLVANIA: THE CRIMINAL CONSPIRACY

In Pennsylvania in the late 1700s and early 1800s, the emerging law in response to the nascent labor movement and, more specifically, workers' efforts to combine for economic improvements, can be best understood against the backdrop of a rapidly changing economy in a society still attempting to understand the import of the recently fought Revolution. This early period was marked by the use of the crime of conspiracy as a legal way to combat the rise of labor unrest that challenged the hierarchical craft system.

In colonial times, the economy was structured with artisans, or masters, being independent sole proprietors, producing small quantities of goods from their homes or small shops. The master trained apprentices who often lived with the master and his family and generally transitioned from apprentice to journeyman to independent master. After the Revolution, however, the United States, and Pennsylvania in particular, became a significant exporter of shoes, increasing production to meet demands. Master cordwainers established prices for their product and wages for themselves but also set the wages for the increasing number of journeymen—those wage workers between apprentice and master who were attempting to accumulate enough capital to become independent. While the wages of master cordwainers rose due to the increased demand for shoes, the earnings of the journeymen, the new class of wage laborers, did not. This prompted the journeymen to attempt to create associations and act in combination to control their labor to increase wages.

While work stoppages were not totally foreign to the colonies, notions of solidarity and combinations by journeymen associations were distrusted and their actions met with resistance.[1] Indeed, workers who combined in an effort to obtain greater wages and prevent others from working were viewed by many as criminals engaged in oppressive behavior, injurious not only to the particular business subjected to the strike but also to others who would work for lower wages. Combinations were believed to act as a restraint on individual bargaining and be repressive to the regional society as a whole, hindering competitiveness with rival eastern cities.[2] Indeed, journeymen combinations were perceived as a form of self-government, contrary to notions of individual choice and freedoms, ideals over which many had just fought and that were fresh in the minds of labor and capital. Such collective action was initially met with judicial responses based on the English common law and, in particular, criminal conspiracy prosecutions.[3]

The first labor-related prosecution for criminal conspiracy in America arose from the Philadelphia journeymen shoemakers strike to protest low wages. George Pullis and others, acting as members of a journeymen cordwainers association, were indicted for engaging in the strike and threatening strikebreakers. Accused of attempting to regulate the trade of the city, the journeymen's combination was argued to be injurious to the public good and threatening to the public interest and well-being of the community. Relying on the common-law theory of conspiracy, the presiding judge, Recorder Moses Levy, condemned the combination as both selfish and in conflict with the recently created constitutional government and found the journeymen's concerted actions to raise wages to be criminal in *Commonwealth v. Pullis*.[4] Thus was established the far-reaching rule that labor's attempts to regulate wages through collective action were illegal.[5]

Jurisprudentially, the conspiracy trial also brought to the fore the significant question concerning the new nation's recognition of and reliance on English common law, expressed by the political conflict between the radical republicans espousing the largely exclusive nature of legislative law and the continued power of the law of the courts—the common law.[6] The trial also raised profound questions regarding what constituted freedom and democracy in this newly created nation, as only thirty years after the Declaration of Independence and twenty years after the adoption of the Constitution, both sides accused the other of oppression, insurrection, and acting as their own government, essentially analogizing their respective conduct to that of the Crown from which the young nation had just gained independence.[7] The trial of the journeymen cordwainers, which implicated the wider campaign against the common law, resulted in the Court embracing the power of the common law over assertions of exclusive lawmaking authority residing in the legislature, as well as the strength of capital over labor, and a reaffirmation of individual bargaining over collective action.

While *Pullis* served as arguably the strictest prohibition on combinations in the new republic, the Pennsylvania Supreme Court's later decisions served as catalysts for the ultimate demise of the conspiracy model by the mid-nineteenth century. The defining decision in *Pullis* did not ascend to the Supreme Court; however, the Court's later decision in *Commonwealth v. Carlisle*[8] became the most authoritative statement of the law on conspiracies in the labor area and significantly softened the per se illegality of labor combinations.

This modified version of the law of criminal conspiracy was born from a motion to discharge a group of employers—master ladies' shoemakers—for conspiring to deny employment to journeymen except at a reduced wage. Justice John Bannister Gibson, writing for the Court, rejected the previously stated broad approach to conspiracy and thus avoided labeling certain desirable associations as criminal; instead, he looked to the motive for the combination—the nature of the object to be obtained—as determinative of legality.[9] Under this approach, combinations of individuals (or businesses) acting in concert would no longer in and of themselves be the basis for a criminal indictment, and indeed, the Court appeared to view artisan combinations as not necessarily harmful. Thus a finding of a lack of intention to injure or lack of injury, or where injury was not a necessary consequence of the combination, now led to acquittal.[10]

While not involving a combination of workers, *Carlisle* no doubt later served as an influential basis for arguably the most important labor combination decision of the early 1800s—the Massachusetts Supreme Judicial Court's decision in *Commonwealth v. Hunt*.[11] In that decision, members of the Boston Journeymen Bootmaker's Society refused to work for a master who employed workers who were not members of the society and gave their master notice to discharge the nonmembers working for him. The members were charged with conspiracy. In an opinion by Chief Justice Lemuel Shaw, the Massachusetts Supreme Judicial Court, like the Pennsylvania Supreme Court, found that it was not inherently illegal for workers to attempt to organize a union, compel recognition of the union, or obtain concessions from the employer as long as the means employed by the union were legal, leading to the acceptance of strikes for higher wages and better working conditions.[12] As the society used fair and lawful methods, the court held the charge of conspiracy could not stand. By the mid-1800s, in the aftermath of *Hunt*, charges of criminal conspiracy to quell actions by labor gradually fell into disuse.

Thus the Pennsylvania Supreme Court's decision in *Carlisle* liberalized the seemingly absolutist law against combinations of workers announced in *Pullis* and allowed for the possibility that organizing and simple strikes could be lawful. While marking an incremental shift in favor of workers, and at least an emerging recognition of the realities of the societal and economic power differential between labor and capital, the practical impact of the demise of the criminal conspiracy was questionable, and the continued use of the means/ends analysis by courts in granting injunctive relief against collective action remained a challenge. This period also signaled, however, that labor would not necessarily adhere to traditional limitations but would continue to defy social and economic norms through the exercise of collective action for fairer wages and better working conditions.

II. LABOR LAW IN THE LATE NINETEENTH TO EARLY TWENTIETH CENTURIES: THE LABOR INJUNCTION

The period after the Civil War was a time of rapid economic growth for the nation and opportunity for labor. The evolution of manufacturing, including wholesale changes in the scale of enterprises and corporate structure, resulted in unprecedented industrial progress, a surge in productivity, and the accumulation of vast amounts of wealth. With industrialization and a newfound prosperity came a rapid increase in the need for semi-skilled and unskilled labor, resulting in workers—including large numbers of newly arrived immigrants—being given the chance for a fresh start in the New World. Indeed, numerous individuals, such as Pittsburgh steelmaker Andrew Carnegie, president of the Pennsylvania Railroad Thomas Scott, founder of Pittsburgh Plate Glass John Pitcairn, and Philadelphia transportation magnate Peter Widener, rose from humble beginnings to acquire a degree of wealth not seen before in America.

Yet the shift from an agrarian to an industrialized economy, including its change in the means of manufacturing, increased mechanization, the use of a large supply of unskilled laborers, and frequent boom-bust economic cycles, led to societal and labor unrest. Vast numbers of employees were brought together under common supervision and subjected to extremely difficult and dangerous working conditions. The sea change in the means of production displaced the belief that workers enjoyed a property interest in their employment. Antagonisms arose between skilled and unskilled labor and between existing American employees and the influx of unskilled ethnic workers. Workers in steel, rail, and coal labored long hours, six to seven days a week, in brutal and dangerous conditions. Workplace accidents were common, exemplified by the Darr Mine explosion of 1907 in Westmoreland County, Pennsylvania, which killed 239 miners and constituted the worst mine disaster in Pennsylvania history. Laborers often lived in company housing, purchased their necessities in company stores, and were kept in line by company detectives and police. In many ways, these workers were nothing more than indentured servants.[13] Frequent employer callousness to subsistence wages, skill-based and racial and ethnic antagonisms, difficult living conditions, and oppressive and unsafe work environments sparked a quest for a voice in the workplace. These dire circumstances, fueled by desperation brought on by frequent economic depressions, resulted in unprecedented mass strikes, picketing, boycotts—and often violence. Indeed, it is argued that the workers' greatest power to effect change came not through formal organization into unions but through their ability to disrupt the economy.[14]

Nowhere were these tumultuous times more prevalent, and the suffering due to the shift in the labor-capital paradigm more felt, than in Pennsylvania, typified by the Great Railroad Strike of 1877 and the Homestead Strike of 1892. While full treatment of these watershed events is beyond the scope of this chapter, these turning points in the labor movement are instructive as to the power of workers' collective action, as well as use of the state's police power to quell labor unrest. In July 1877, just one year after the celebration of the country's centennial, the impact of four previous years of severe depression—which led to repeated wage cuts and layoffs, leaving millions of workers unemployed—resulted in a spontaneous uprising of trainmen of the Baltimore and Ohio Railroad and then the Pennsylvania Railroad, who conducted strikes at certain rail centers, including Pittsburgh (at that time the nation's largest industrial center) and Philadelphia. The largely leaderless strike spread, crippling transportation in the east, resulting in violence and the burning of railroad and city property and millions of dollars in damage. After Pittsburgh militia refused to move against the strikers, militia from Philadelphia were imported to restore order, and in the aftermath, twenty-six lay dead in Pittsburgh and thirteen lay dead in Reading, Pennsylvania.[15] It was the first labor insurrection to spread into a national civil disorder.

Fifteen years later, the 1892 lockout of workers at Carnegie Steel's Homestead Works outside of Pittsburgh resulted in one of the bloodiest and most infamous battles between labor and capital in American history. In an attempt to rid the works of the Amalgamated Association of Iron and Steel Workers, and after failed negotiations, Henry Clay Frick, then chairman of Carnegie Steel, on orders from Andrew Carnegie, locked out the employees, declared that the mill was to be operated nonunion, and sent for Pinkerton detectives to secure the plant, allowing replacement workers to continue production. The Pinkertons were met on the grounds by hundreds of armed workers, with the resulting battle leading to the surrender of the Pinkertons, and ultimately thirty-five lives were lost. With the strikers in firm control of the mill, the workers won the battle but lost the war: the Pennsylvania National Guard was summoned and martial law imposed. With this show of force by the state, order was quickly restored and the strike ultimately broken. Homestead constituted a resounding defeat for organized labor, setting back unionism in the steel industry for the next four decades and, perhaps more important, permanently disabusing workers of the notion of holding a property interest in their jobs.[16]

These and other similar scenarios of large-scale economic disruption, in Pennsylvania and all over the country, were repeated throughout the turn of the twentieth century. Large groups of workers, often aided by strike agitators, not only withdrew their labor through the strike but, through verbal intimidation, leafleting, and often physical violence, stopped others from working in the strikers' positions. This prevented capital from using strikebreakers and continuing production. Bitter and protracted strikes occurred in the anthracite coal regions of eastern Pennsylvania in the early 1900s, in Pittsburgh during the Great Steel Strike of 1919, and in the bituminous coal areas of central and southern Pennsylvania in the 1920s. Union organizers such as Mary Harris "Mother" Jones traversed the state in support of textile workers in Philadelphia, mine workers in the east, and steelworkers in the west, fighting against child labor and working for improved wages and unionization.

To combat this increasingly common, large-scale, and violent labor unrest, capital turned to use of the labor injunction. Much more desirable than the charge of criminal conspiracy, with its accompanying procedural protections for the accused, injunction proceedings were initiated by an ex parte hearing before an often friendly tribunal and not a jury of peers. An injunction could be quickly secured that was broad in scope, even including lawful speech; subject to a lengthy appeal process; and backed by the court's power to punish a violation of the injunction by contempt proceedings, including possible citation and imprisonment. While the means and ends of the strike were considered, any goals that a judge considered to be inappropriate, or actions that were objectionable, were deemed impermissible and thus enjoinable, rendering the labor injunction a highly effective mechanism in ending concerted activities by workers.[17]

While recognizing the workers' ability to organize into associations, to strike, and to lawfully attempt to induce others to refuse to work for an employer, early Pennsylvania Supreme Court decisions upheld injunctive relief for even peaceful actions if accompanied by some unpleasantness or discomfort to strikebreakers or customers, leading to significant restraints on labor.[18] Injunctions were routinely upheld for acts constituting a nuisance, including where striking printers and pressmen followed strikebreakers to and from their boarding houses, interfered with them in the streets, and engaged in "all manner of threats, menaces, intimidation, opprobrious epithets, ridicule and annoyance."[19] Similarly, a unanimous Supreme Court, in an opinion by Justice James Mitchell, rejected the notion that strikers could take any action short of physical violence to obtain their ends and overturned a master's determination denying an injunction where striking miners followed workers to and from their lodging and used intimidation, including calling the strikebreakers "scabs" and "blacklegs," to dissuade them from working.[20] Enticement by members of a glassworker's union to break a covenant not to join a union—the famed "yellow dog" contract in which an employee pledged not to become a union member or engage in union activities—was deemed to be interference with management prerogatives and the right to contract and served as a basis for injunctive relief, which was upheld on appeal in an opinion by Justice J. Hay Brown, writing for a unanimous Court in *Flaccus v. Smith*.[21] Likewise, in a unanimous decision written by Justice John Kephart, the Court found that while workers may organize for bettering their working conditions, intimidating conduct—including marches and parades with music bands—amounted to prohibited means of stopping strikebreakers from taking miners' positions; indeed, "[t]he very fact of parading at the time and place constituted intimidation and was properly enjoined . . . Persuasion, too long and persistently continued, becomes a nuisance and an unlawful form of coercion."[22] Finally, during the early years of the labor injunction, conduct by a union against another union was found to be subject to enjoinment for using mental and moral coercion to intimidate plumbers belonging to one union into joining its rival union in a decision authored by Justice John Dean.[23]

With the onset of the Great Depression, however, economic, political, and social forces combined in the 1930s to force a marked transformation in the relationship among labor, capital, and the state and the laws governing collective bargaining and collective action. With catastrophic unemployment, and those holding jobs facing the repeated and sharp slashing of wages, unprecedented numbers of workers, joined by the unemployed, engaged in strikes and sit-ins in the automobile, shipping, textile, coal, and steel industries. A collapsing economy brought change to electoral politics as well, resulting in the political tide turning to support labor as a way out of the Depression. While in previous times, company police or the federal or state militia quickly and sometimes violently ended such strikes, now the state conceded to labor's power, becoming largely neutral in labor disputes in light of the labor movement's newfound political muscle.

While the injunction proved to be a powerful tool against labor, quickly ending strikes and, as a result, requiring workers to cease employing their most effective weapon to achieve their goals, it did nothing to remedy the underlying issues that caused workers to act in the first place and was increasingly criticized as a regressive tool against labor.[24] The federal government's passage of the 1932 Norris–La Guardia Act, followed by the Pennsylvania General Assembly's enactment of the 1937 Labor Anti-injunction Act, severely restricted the use of injunctions in labor disputes. Ultimately the government that had effectively put down labor insurrection not only remained neutral but conceded to labor's main demand—the right to organize—and, in essence, sponsored unions through the passage of the federal National Labor Relations Act (NLRA) in 1936, followed by the Pennsylvania Labor Relations Act in 1937.

Labor's struggle, resulting in newfound power, unbridled by the injunction, and coupled with the state's support, translated to the liberation of the movement and an unprecedented ability to organize workers. By the mid-twentieth century, the Pennsylvania Supreme Court found it had no jurisdiction to enjoin the union message in the absence of disorder, intimidation, threats, or violence. In the landmark decision in *Kirmse v. Adler*, union members, by circulars, placards, and music played on automobile loudspeakers, requested that customers boycott a theater in support of the union's demand for wages for its workers.[25] The Court, in a decision authored by Justice Kephart, over a lone dissent, made clear that picketing, if peaceful and unaccompanied by disorder, coercion, or related activities, was lawful. The Court thus adopted a just cause approach, permitting some remedy when justified, based on public policy standards favoring unions. Here the Court found that the primary goal of the picketers was the protection of their employment at union wage rates, while the means involved an injury to the employer through loss of patronage; yet such a loss, in light of the right of the union to express its views to the public, was without remedy. The Court, emblematic of the new era in labor relations, explained that except in rare circumstances, Pennsylvania courts would not intervene in labor disputes and would maintain a policy of neutrality.

Nevertheless, it was not shy to uphold injunctive relief when overriding policies of protection and safety became paramount.[26] As earlier expressed by Chief Justice George W. Maxey in *Carnegie-Illinois Steel Corp. v. United Steelworkers*, where in 1946, hundreds of picketers amassed to deny maintenance personnel entrance to the Homestead Steel Works, made threats of violence, and physically restrained employees from entering the grounds, the Court retains the clear authority to uphold the invocation of police power in cases of lawlessness where appropriate,[27] a middle-ground trend that continues today.[28]

Finally, forcefully protecting the rights of free expression, the Supreme Court found speech in the labor context to be of constitutional dimension, contrary to its earlier decisions in this area.[29] As early as 1931, the Supreme Court in *Kraemer Hosiery Co. v. Am. Fed. of Full Fashioned Hosiery Workers*[30] recognized a union's right under Article I, Section 7 of the Pennsylvania Constitution to persuade employees of an "unwise" contract and to leave their employment. This decision was reaffirmed two years later, when the *Kirmse* Court recognized labor's right of freedom of expression to induce employees to withdraw their labor and join a union under the Pennsylvania Constitution, predating the federal constitutional guarantee by almost ten years.[31] In a subsequent opinion in *Airbrake Shoe Co. v. District Lodge 9 Int'l Assoc. of Machinists*,[32] Justice Thomas McKeen Chidsey recognized peaceful picketing as a form of assembly and free speech under the federal and Pennsylvania Constitutions. Later, in *West Penn Township School Dist. v. International Brotherhood of Electrical Workers*, the venerable former governor and later chief justice John Bell reaffirmed that peaceful picketing for organizational or other lawful reason was protected by the Pennsylvania Constitution but susceptible to injunction "if conducted in an unlawful manner or for an unlawful purpose."[33]

Ultimately, the Supreme Court's experience with the labor injunction reflects a similar evolution to that of the criminal conspiracy, with early experience routinely upholding injunctive relief and significantly impairing the power of labor but later decisions severely limiting its power, permitting greater worker expression—even to the point of being constitutional in nature—and allowing labor to make significant gains.

III. LABOR LAW IN THE LATE TWENTIETH AND EARLY TWENTY-FIRST CENTURIES: JUDICIAL REVIEW OF PUBLIC-SECTOR GRIEVANCE ARBITRATION AWARDS

Maturation of the relationship between labor and management through the effects of federal and state legislation governing private-sector employees, as well as a limited acceptance of unionization, resulted in a certain degree of overall industrial peace. As a result of such increased harmonious relations, and to a large extent the federalization of labor relation law, the state judiciary's involvement in labor issues diminished. Yet as a national trend in the late 1960s and early 1970s allowed for collective bargaining in the public sector, perhaps due to a newfound confidence in collective bargaining to address labor strife, various states enacted statutes permitting certain public employees a greater say in their workplaces. The Commonwealth followed suit with the passage of legislation allowing public-sector employees to organize and collectively bargain, and the Supreme Court's role in labor relations, as well as that of the newly created Commonwealth Court, was reinvigorated.[34]

In 1968, the legislature passed the Policemen and Firemen Collective Bargaining Act (Act 111), which permitted police and fire employees the right to collectively bargain and, when agreement could not be reached, mandated interest arbitration to forge a collective bargaining agreement in lieu of the right to strike. Two years later, the General Assembly passed the Public Employee Relations Act (PERA), which extended collective bargaining rights to virtually all state and local governmental employees and included the right to strike. Early on, the Supreme Court gave full support to the statutes and the administrative body charged with their implementation—the Pennsylvania Labor Relations Board. Over the following forty years, the Supreme Court weighed in on all aspects of labor relations under these statutes, including appropriate bargaining unit determinations,[35] permitted subjects of collective bargaining,[36] and the proper resolution of unfair labor practices.[37]

Perhaps the greatest area of controversy and significant change in the law under these public-sector statutes, however, has concerned the judicial review of grievance arbitration awards. Disputes often arise in the interpretation of a contract, and a collective bargaining agreement is no exception. While contractual disagreements are often resolved in courts, grievance arbitration, when conducted by specialized tribunals versed in labor relations and chosen by the parties themselves, has proven to be an effective and inexpensive means of serving the unique ongoing relationship between labor and management and the desirable policy of minimizing work disputes and production stoppages.[38] Indeed, a grievance arbitration provision in a collective bargaining agreement is typically the quid pro quo for a no-strike clause, by which workers agree to waive the use of their most powerful weapon—the strike. Lastly, and perhaps most importantly, an arbitration award is meant to be final and binding, avoiding a lengthy and expensive appeals process with the specter of the vacatur of the award. The frequent vacating of an arbitrator's award would incentivize appeals and undermine the admirable qualities of arbitration; thus an appropriate standard of review for an appellate court reviewing an arbitration award is essential to vindication of the arbitral process.[39]

Due in great part to police and fire employees' inability to strike, the Supreme Court has consistently embraced a highly deferential standard of review of an arbitrator's award under Act 111. Indeed, shortly after the passage of Act 111, the Court in the *Washington Arbitration Case* determined that although there existed no statutory right to appeal an interest arbitration award under Act 111, in order to ensure the constitutional rights of the parties, a party could appeal an arbitration award in the limited nature of "narrow certiorari."[40] More than a quarter century later, in *Pennsylvania State Police v. Pennsylvania State Troopers' Assoc. (Betancourt)*,[41] the Court was faced with the issue of whether the federal essence test, used to review arbitration awards under PERA, as discussed in the following sections, or the Act 111 interest arbitration standard of narrow certiorari would apply to Act 111 grievance arbitration awards. After reviewing the history of Act 111 and stressing the prohibition on police and fire personnel from striking and the legislative intent against protracted litigation, and desirous of a quick resolution to labor disputes, Justice Ralph Cappy found the proper standard of review was narrow certiorari. Under that standard, an appellate court reviewing an arbitrator's award could only overturn an arbitrator's award based on (1) the arbitrator's jurisdiction, (2) the regularity of the proceedings, (3) whether the arbitrator exceeded his or her powers in rendering the award, or (4) whether the award resulted in a deprivation of constitutional rights. While not without its critics on the Commonwealth Court[42] and in scholarship,[43] the narrow certiorari standard has been consistently upheld and applied by the Supreme Court.

The same consistency cannot be said for the Court's articulation of the applicable standard of review regarding arbitration awards under PERA. Indeed, the appropriate standard of review of arbitration awards rendered under PERA has changed in breadth and framework multiple times in the past twenty-five years and remains, to a large degree, unresolved.

Consistent with the general policy favoring arbitration and deference to an arbitrator's award, in 1977, the Supreme Court, in its seminal decision in *Community College of Beaver Co. v. Community College of Beaver Co., Society of the Faculty*, penned by Justice Thomas Pomeroy, set forth the proper standard of review to be used by a reviewing court in assessing an arbitrator's award.[44] Specifically, in that decision, the Court articulated a standard consistent with the federal standard expressed in the famed *Steelworkers Trilogy*,[45] determining that judicial review of an arbitration award rendered under PERA was limited to a determination of whether the award "draws its essence" from the underlying collective bargaining agreement, hence giving it the moniker "the essence test."[46] This embrace of a deferential review of arbitration awards by the judiciary made clear that the alternative dispute resolution procedures created by the legislature under PERA to resolve labor disagreements would largely occur without court intervention.

Shortly after the adoption of the essence test, however, the Supreme Court, in certain decisions rendered in the mid-1980s, permitted reviewing courts to consider whether the arbitrator's award was "manifestly unreasonable" or a "reasonable interpretation" of the collective bargaining agreement in discerning its legitimacy.[47] This relaxed standard gave the courts a greater ability to vacate an arbitrator's award when they disagreed with the decision and often arose in the context of a court reversing an arbitrator's reinstatement of an employee who was terminated for misconduct.

Faced with various iterations of the essence test, the Court in *State System of Higher Education (Cheyney University) v. State College and University Professional Association (PSEA-NEA)*[48] sought to clarify the proper standard of review. Justice Cappy rejected a reasonableness inquiry and instead set forth a two-part test for review of an arbitration award. First, the reviewing court was to determine if the issue was properly within the terms of the collective bargaining agreement. Second, the reviewing court was to uphold the award if the arbitrator's interpretation could rationally be derived from the agreement.[49] Emphasizing the deferential nature of the review, Justice Cappy emphasized that a court should vacate an arbitrator's award only where it "indisputably and genuinely is without foundation in, or fails to logically flow from, the collective bargaining agreement."[50] Yet less than a year later, the meaning of the essence test was seriously questioned in *City of Easton v. AFSCME*,[51] which was announced in an opinion written by Justice Russell Nigro for a slim majority of the Court over a vigorous dissent by Justice Cappy joined by two other justices. The case involved an employee who engaged in dishonesty by filing multiple time sheets and was then terminated for willful misconduct, only to be reinstated by an arbitrator. A majority of the Supreme Court embraced the notion that a governmental entity cannot bargain away powers that are essential to the completion of its function—that is, a "core functions" exception to the essence test whereby an entity could not bargain away the right to discharge an employee for certain conduct related to the heart of the agency's services. In creating this exception, the majority again relied on its prior recently discounted decisions embracing a reasonableness or rationality standard of review.

While two interim decisions attempted to regain consensus and offer clarification to the appropriate standard of review and, in doing so, distinguished and cabined the core functions exception to the essence test,[52] it was not until *Westmoreland Intermediate Unit #7 v. Westmoreland Intermediate Unit #7 Classroom Assistants Educational Support Personnel Association*[53] that the Court, again through Chief Justice Cappy at the end of his tenure, rejected the core functions exception as lacking the proper deference and potentially swallowing the essence test. Specifically, after tracing the history of the decisional evolution of the appropriate standard of review, the Court reoriented the focus of appellate review by reaffirming the essence test as articulated by the two-prong analysis set forth in *Cheyney University*. In doing so, it offered and embraced the adoption of the federal public policy exception to the otherwise deferential review to be given to an arbitrator's award, where such policy is well defined, dominant, and ascertained by reference to laws, not general considerations of public interest.[54] Acknowledging that the parties did not have the opportunity to consider applicability of the public policy exception, the Court remanded the matter to the Commonwealth Court for consideration of the newly adopted exception.

Finally, in 2012, the Supreme Court in its most recent decision in this area, in *Philadelphia Housing Authority v. AFSCME, District Council 33, Local 934*,[55] considered an arbitrator's award reinstating an employee discharged by his employer for sexual harassment and applied for the first time the public policy exception. Tracing the federal treatment of the public policy exception and the narrow nature of the exception and noting the strong public policy against sexual harassment in the workplace, the Court, in an opinion penned by Chief Justice Ronald Castille, vacated the arbitrator's award. Justice Thomas Saylor joined the majority opinion but, astutely discerning a return to the core functions test by the majority, offered the prospect that areas of managerial prerogatives could play a role in proper appellate court review of an arbitrator's award, suggesting future evolution in this area of the law.[56]

Thus while expressed as a straightforward standard of review, the meaning of the degree of deference to be given to an arbitrator's award under the essence test is one that has, for more than a quarter century, vexed and continues to challenge the Supreme Court. Consistent with similar areas of the law, however, the Court once again exhibited over time an ongoing change in terms of an applicable standard, first embracing a reasonableness-based test largely favoring an employer's ability to vacate an adverse arbitration award and then maturing into a more deferential analysis, with an unsurprising retention of an overarching public policy safety valve.

IV. CONCLUSION

The change in economic, social, and legal norms that produced the greatest industrial expansion known to the nation came with significant conflicts in the relationship among labor, capital, and the law. In various areas confronting labor relations, the Supreme Court has contributed to the rich history of the labor movement in the Commonwealth, often initially adopting an antilabor position only to soften its stance and recognize greater rights for workers. The Court's influence on the labor movement, over time, has had a profoundly positive impact on working people and their struggles for a better way of life, safer working conditions, a degree of industrial democracy, and ultimately, dignity in the workplace.

There is no question that the Supreme Court's jurisprudence will play a significant role in the continued evolution of labor relations in Pennsylvania.

NOTES

Jeffrey P. Bauman is the deputy chief staff attorney to Justice Debra Todd of the Pennsylvania Supreme Court, a former staff attorney to Chief Justice Ralph J. Cappy of the Pennsylvania Supreme Court, and an adjunct professor of law at Duquesne University School of Law. Thanks to Justice Todd for her unceasing support, John Hare for his guidance and patience, and Leslie Kozler and Kim Collins for their helpful comments and insights. This chapter is dedicated to my parents, Guy and Pat Bauman.

1. *See generally* Thomas Kohler, "The Notion of Solidarity and the Secret History of American Labor Law," *Buffalo Law Review* 53 (2005): 883; William E. Forbath, "The Shaping of the American Labor Movement," *Harvard Law Review* 102 (1989): 1111; Herbert Hovenkamp, "Labor Conspiracies in American Law, 1880–1930," *Texas Law Review* 66 (1988): 919.

2. *See generally* Christopher Tomlins, *Law, Labor, and Ideology in the Early American Republic* (Cambridge: Cambridge University Press, 1993), 109–14.

3. Ibid., 114–27.

4. Philadelphia Mayor's Court, 1806. The case is reprinted in John R. Commons, Ulrich B. Phillips, Eugene A. Gilmore, Helen L. Sumner, and John B. Andrews, *A Documentary History of American Industrial Society*, vol. 3 (Cleveland: Arthur H. Clark, 1910), 59–248.

5. *See also* Commonwealth v. Wood, 3 Binn. 414, 415 (Pa. 1811) (discussing trial of journeyman hatters for conspiracy).

6. Tomlins, *Law, Labor, and Ideology*, 136–37.

7. *See* Duane Rudolph, "How Violence Killed an American Labor Union," *Rutgers Law Review* 67 (2015): 1407 (offering a detailed analysis of Pullis and conceptualizing labor violence).

8. Frederick C. Brightly, *Brightly's Reports of Cases Decided by the Judges of the Supreme Court of Pennsylvania, the Court of Nisi Prius, at Philadelphia, and also in the Supreme Court, with Notes and References to Recent Decisions* (Philadelphia: J. Kay, Jun & Brother, 1851), 9 (reported earlier in *Hall's Journal of Jurisprudence*, 1 [1821]).

9. Ibid., 39–40; *see generally* Tomlins, *Law, Labor, and Ideology*, 145–47.

10. Tomlins, *Law, Labor, and Ideology*, 145–47.

11. 45 Mass. (4 Met.) 111 (1842).

12. Ibid., 129–34.

13. Frances Fox Piven and Richard A. Cloward, *Poor People's Movements: Why They Succeed, and How They Fail* (New York: Vintage Books, 1979), 97–100.

14. Ibid., 172–73.

15. Ibid., 103.

16. *See* William Serrin, *Homestead: The Glory and Tragedy of an American Steel Town* (New York: Vintage Books, 1993); Les Standiford, *Meet You in Hell: Andrew Carnegie, Henry Clay Frick, and the Bitter Partnership That Transformed America* (New York: Crown, 2005).

17. *See generally* Herman Stern, "Two Decades of Pennsylvania Law on Picketing in Industrial Disputes (1933–1954)," *Temple Law Quarterly* 28 (1954): 50, 51–52.

18. *See generally* Seth F. Kreimer, "The Pennsylvania Constitution's Protection of Free Expression," *University of Pennsylvania Journal of Constitutional Law* 5 (2002): 12, 32–33.

19. Murdock, Kerr & Co. v. Walker, 25 A. 492, 493 (Pa. 1893).

20. O'Neill v. Behanna, 37 A. 843, 844 (Pa. 1897).

21. 48 A. 894, 894–95 (Pa. 1901).

22. *Jefferson & Indiana Coal Co. v. Marks*, 134 A. 430, 432–33 (Pa. 1926).

23. Erdman v. Mitchell, 56 A. 327, 331–32 (Pa. 1903).

24. *See* Felix Frankfurter and Nathan Green, *The Labor Injunction* (New York: Macmillan, 1930); Thomas R. Haggard, "Private Injunctive Relief Against Labor Union Violence," *Kentucky Law Journal* 71 (1983): 509, 513.

25. 166 A. 566, 569–70 (Pa. 1933).

26. *See* Wortex Mills, Inc. v. Textile Workers Union of Am, 85 A.2d 851, 855–56 (Pa. 1952) (upholding enjoining of textile workers engaged in a general strike from picketing entrance of plant of employer who had no relationship with textile unions); *see generally* Nicholas Unkovic, "Mass Picketing Law in Pennsylvania," *Dickinson Law Review* 64 (1960): 111.

27. 45 A.2d 857, 861–62 (Pa. 1946) ("When any individual or organization under whatsoever name attempts to use force to gain his or its ends they are attempting to usurp governmental functions. This attempt unless promptly and effectively restrained by legally constituted authority leads to lawlessness, disorder, and anarchy which is the very negation of all government. The law cannot temporize with lawlessness.").

28. *See, e.g.,* Giant Eagle Markets Co. v. United Food and Commercial Workers Union, Local Union No. 23, 652 A.2d 1286, 1291 (Pa. 1995) (upholding injunctive relief in light of mass picketing, blocking of entrances, swarming customers and "other acts of terror and intimidation").

29. *See* City of Duquesne v. Fincke, 112 A. 130, 132–33 (Pa. 1920) (finding rights under Pennsylvania Constitution to mirror those of the federal constitution and neither charter granted the right to assemble with others, undermining the notion of independent rights under state constitutions); Fredrick D. Rapone Jr., "Article I, Section 7 of the Pennsylvania Constitution and the Public Expression of Unpopular Ideas," *Temple Law Review* 74 (2001): 655, 670–76 (providing in-depth analysis of Fincke and independent rights of free speech jurisprudence under the Pennsylvania Constitution); *see also* Kreimer, "Pennsylvania Constitution's Protection," 53–54; *see generally* Kenneth G. Gormley, *The Pennsylvania Constitution: A Treatise on Rights and Liberties* (Philadelphia: George T. Bisel, 2004).

30. 157 A. 588, 591 (Pa. 1931).

31. 166 A. at 569; *see* Thornhill v. Alabama, 310 U.S. 88 (1940).

32. 94 A.2d 884, 887–88 (Pa. 1953).

33. 145 A.2d 258, 261 (Pa. 1958).

34. James Crawford and Anne E. Covey, "Contribution of the Commonwealth Court to Public Employee Labor Law: The First Forty Years," *Widener Law Journal* 20 (2010): 143, 154–56.

35. *See, e.g.,* Lancaster Co. v. PLRB, 94 A.3d 979 (Pa. 2014); PLRB v. Altoona Area School Dist., 389 A.2d 553 (Pa. 1978).

36. City of Erie v. PLRB, 32 A.3d 625 (Pa. 2011); PLRB v. State College Area School Dist., 337 A.2d 262 (Pa. 1975).

37. Lancaster Co. v. PLRB, 124 A.3d 1269 (Pa. 2015); PLRB v. Mars Area School Dist., 389 A.2d 1073 (Pa. 1978).

38. *See generally* Frank Elkouri and Edna Asper Elkouri, *How Arbitration Works,* 4th ed. (Washington, D.C.: BNA Books, 1988).

39. The standard of review refers to the manner of examination by an appellate court of the lower tribunal's decision. Morrison v. Dep't of Pub. Welfare, 646 A.2d 565, 570 (Pa. 1994); Lu-in Wang, "The Pennsylvania Issue: Honoring Chief Justice Ralph J. Cappy: *Morrison v. Department of Public Welfare* and the Pennsylvania Revolution in Scope and Standard of Review," *Duquesne Law Review* 47 (2009): 609; *see also* Jeffrey P. Bauman, "Standards of Review and Scopes of Review in Pennsylvania—Primer and Proposal," *Duquesne Law Review* 39 (2001): 513, 515 (offering standard of review "describes the degree of deference given by the reviewing court to the action or decision of the lower tribunal").

40. 259 A.2d 437, 441 (Pa. 1969).

41. 656 A.2d 83 (Pa. 1995).

42. *See* Crawford and Covey, "Contribution of the Commonwealth," 161–66.

43. John P. McLaughlin and Patrick J. Harvey, "Municipal Unions and Municipal Grievances: *Betancourt* and the Narrow Certiorari Scope of Review of Appeals from Act 111 Grievance Arbitration Awards: Its Time Has Already Come and Gone," *University of Pennsylvania Journal of Labor and Employment Law* 5 (2003): 427.

44. 375 A.2d 1267, 1272–73 (Pa. 1967).

45. The Steelworkers Trilogy were three decisions rendered the same day in 1960 by the US Supreme Court and established that arbitration was the preferred means of resolving disputes arising under a collective bargaining agreement as a matter of federal labor policy. *See* United Steelworkers of America v. American Mfg. Co., 363 U.S. 564 (1960); United Steelworkers of America v. Warrior & Gulf Navigation Co., 363 U.S. 574 (1960); and United Steelworkers of America v. Enterprise Wheel & Car Corp., 363 U.S. 593 (1960).

46. *See* Enterprise Wheel & Car Corp., 363 U.S. at 597.

47. *See* Philadelphia Housing Authority v. Union of Security Officers, 455 A.2d 625 (Pa. 1983); Pennsylvania Liquor Control Board v. Independent State Stores Union, 553 A.2d 948 (Pa. 1989).

48. 743 A.2d 405 (Pa. 1999).

49. Ibid., 413.

50. Ibid.

51. 756 A.2d 1107 (Pa. 2000).

52. *See* Office of the Attorney General v. Council 13, AFSCME, 844 A.2d 1217 (Pa. 2004); Greene County v. District 2, United Mine Workers, Local Union 9999, 852 A.2d 299 (Pa. 2004).

53. 939 A.2d 855 (Pa. 2007).

54. Ibid., 865–66.

55. 52 A.3d 1117 (Pa. 2012).

56. Ibid., 1129 (Saylor, J., concurring).

CHAPTER 23

The Homestead Lockout of 1892 and Jurisprudence in Pennsylvania

MELVYN DUBOFSKY

Few industrial conflicts in American history have earned as much notoriety or iconic status as the lockout/strike that paralyzed the iron- and steel-making community of Homestead, Pennsylvania, in the summer of 1892. It pitted one of the late nineteenth century's leading industrial tycoons, Andrew Carnegie, and his loyal right-hand man, Henry Clay Frick, against perhaps the era's most powerful trade union, the Amalgamated Association of Iron, Steel, and Tin Workers (AAISTW). It radicalized a community then dominated by its American-born and Americanized skilled workers of northern European origin who led the local meetings of the AAISTW and also held the most important municipal offices. It caused the skilled, older-stock Homestead workers to ally with their more numerous, less-skilled brethren—newer immigrants from the east and south of Europe—in solidarity. And it led the wives, daughters, and sons of the mill's workers to join their spouses and fathers in battling the steel masters and the Pinkerton agents Carnegie hired to escort strikebreakers into the plant and break the union. As the title of a book about the battle proclaimed, it made "the river (Monongahela) run red," mostly with the blood of wounded and slain Pinkertons.[1]

There is no need here to recapitulate the events of the struggle between workers and the Carnegie corporation, a conflict that began with the breakdown of negotiations between the company and the union; climaxed with the bloody battle between the strikers and their supporters and the Pinkertons along the banks of the Monongahela; and dragged on nearly to the end of 1892, by which time the company had won a total victory and ousted the union. All this has been narrated and analyzed in great detail in excellent books and essays.[2] Suffice it to say that Carnegie consciously precipitated the lockout and ensuing strike in an effort to eliminate what he deemed a union tax on production and infringements on managerial authority. Carnegie absented himself from the scene of the struggle, moving for the summer to his Scottish castle while allowing Frick to put into practice their mutual plans for eradicating union power.

Carnegie and Frick were able to achieve their aims because, by the last decade of the nineteenth century, the United States had been transformed from de Tocqueville's land of relative social and economic equality for its white citizens to one that nearly matched its European counterparts in its level of inequality as described by Henry Demarest Lloyd and Gustavus Myers.[3] With the enormous wealth and economic power that the corporate tycoons had amassed by the late nineteenth century, they were able not only to rule their workers relatively unchallenged but also to influence legislatures, executives, and courts. Nowhere in the summer of 1892 was the power and influence of wealth and capital displayed as graphically as in the Commonwealth of Pennsylvania.

At first, however, labor power seemed to reign supreme in Homestead. The workers and their union defeated the Pinkertons, took them prisoner, and marched them through the streets of Homestead, where men, women, and children showered the captives with imprecations, bricks, stones, and other injurious missiles. After the initial bloody battle along the riverbank, the workers kept the strikebreakers out of the mill, maintained their solidarity, and restored order to the community that they governed. Unfortunately for them, their power did not extend beyond the town of Homestead. The Carnegie Corporation's power did, reaching into the governor's office and the state's courts. Convinced by the company's leaders that anarchy reigned in Homestead and that the union exercised illegitimate power, Governor Robert Pattison, a Democrat, dispatched eight thousand state militia to restore "law and order" in Homestead, reopen the mill, and enable strikebreakers to produce steel. In the meantime, local courts tried union leaders for rioting, homicide, and even treason.

I. LEGAL CULTURE AND INDUSTRIAL CONFLICT

Pennsylvania jurists, like other state and federal judges, sought to adjust common law and statutory law that had originated to manage conflicts among independent proprietors, autonomous professionals, and skilled craftspeople and that relied on the individual's ability to bargain equally in a society in which impersonal, professionally managed corporations exercised power over masses of workers who lacked both skill and collective strength. Federal, state, and local jurists repeatedly weighed how to accommodate a legal regime based on pure, competitive markets and the right of each and every individual to contract for himself or herself with an economy in which concentrated capital sought to regulate markets and individual employees lacked the power to ensure their contractual rights. In the late nineteenth century, courts continually had to weigh the rights of private property against the interests of the larger community.[4]

More often than not in cases that pitted the rights of corporate capital against those of its employees, the power of property prevailed over the interests of human labor. Over the course of the first half of the nineteenth century, the law had evolved to liberate laborers from the older master/servant categories of the common law and to create the archetype of the free laborer able to contract freely on his or her own behalf. The law also came to recognize trade unions as legitimate institutions insofar as they respected the rights of property, the rules of the market, and governmental authority.[5] By the late nineteenth century, however, the concept of the autonomous free laborer appeared anachronistic in an economy dominated by aggregated capital, while trade unions appeared to challenge the rights of property, the rules of the market, and even public authorities.

For jurists and public officials in the late nineteenth century, the issue of how to accommodate the growing disparities in social and economic power and the rise of economic inequality proved nearly insoluble. The law's stress on property rights and individual free will to contract collided regularly with the interests of the broader community. In Homestead, for example, the workers who toiled at the Carnegie Works sustained their community through the wages earned by their labor, and their rights at work were protected by their union. If their wages, job security, bodies, and even lives were left subject to the power of the corporation without the countervailing presence of a union, the town of Homestead—as a stable, sustainable community of working people—remained at the mercy of Carnegie and Frick. That is why, in July 1892, the union resisted Carnegie's attempt to eliminate its power and instead sought to keep the furnaces banked until the corporation recognized its workers' collective rights. This was a struggle that repeated itself in the United States from the 1870s through the 1930s, including the nationwide 1877 railroad strikes, the McCormick Harvester Strikes of 1885 and 1886 that precipitated the infamous Haymarket Riot, the great Burlington Railroad Strike of 1888, the struggles in Colorado and Idaho hard-rock mining communities that occurred from 1886 to 1899, and the famous Pullman Strike and Boycott of 1894. In all these cases, public authority and the law intervened, with federal troops and state militias securing the rights of private corporate property and jurists subordinating union rights to corporate power. Homestead was not an outlier in this pattern of industrial conflicts.[6]

During the 1880s and 1890s, the law, as explicated by judges nationally, wove a mixed tapestry for employers and employees. Most judges practiced what Daniel Ernst calls a Victorian legal culture that deified individualism, demanded personal rectitude, policed private practices in the interest of community well-being, and lauded natural law. The Victorian legal code forbade employers and employees from diminishing the rights of others; group or collective interests lacked standing in the law. Businesspeople could not restrain competition, impair free markets, or exact monopoly prices from consumers. The free-labor doctrine and its concomitant, employment at will, denied workers the right to withhold their labor (i.e., strike or boycott) if such action infringed on the equal rights of other workers, harmed the community, or "illegally" diluted the value and use of employers' private property. Courts issued rulings and injunctions that restrained both employers and workers from acting to injure others through combinations that violated the rules of the marketplace. Finally, judges schooled in Victorian legal culture insisted that public actors lacked the authority to enact legislation that violated natural law.[7]

In practice, however, Victorian legal culture operated inequitably, exacting a far higher price from workers than employers. In a series of cases brought by railroads in receivership, federal courts ruled that private parties must not usurp the law. For many judges, strikes, by definition, harmed the community and unlawfully interfered with management in stark contempt of court.[8] Most judges believed that they had no choice but to protect employers, nonunion employees, and the public at large from the power to call strikes "by any set of irresponsible men under the sun."[9]

During the late nineteenth century, federal court decisions limiting collective action multiplied and hardened. Judges acted in what they deemed to be the "public interest" and on behalf of fundamental constitutional and natural rights. In theory, workers remained free to withdraw their labor voluntarily, whether individually or collectively. To decide otherwise would be to legitimate involuntary servitude and thus to violate the free-labor doctrine and the results of the Civil War. Yet judges persistently ruled that if a strike harmed the community, improperly infringed an owner's right to use his or her property freely, or violated the rights of nonparticipating workers, it could be ruled illegitimate. Many federal judges rarely hesitated to use their equity power to offer injunctive relief to parties allegedly injured by strikers. Judges decided if and when strikes infringed basic rights. The closed shops and boycotts to enforce it, judges ruled, ceded to unions the power to limit managerial authority and damage economic enterprises that refused to accede to union demands. Society, represented by the judicial arm of the state, must neither concede to nor tolerate such class-motivated behavior.[10] To allow unions the right to determine whom employers might hire (the closed shop), declared one court, would cause enterprises to cease and idleness to replace activity. In this country, proclaimed the court, "every owner of property may work it as he will, by whom he pleases, at such wages, and upon such terms as he can make; and every laborer may work or not, as he sees fit, for whom, and at such wages as, he pleases; and neither can dictate to the other how he shall use his own, whether of property, time, or skill. Any other system cannot be tolerated."[11]

"Neither law nor morals can give a man the right to labor or withhold his labor when such rights work harm on other innocent parties," declared Judge William Howard Taft, whether themselves workers, employers, or members of the community. Strikes and boycotts that required union members to quit work in solidarity with union brothers, Taft ruled, rendered unions "a criminal conspiracy against the laws of their country."[12]

Federal judges saw themselves as guardians of the public interest against the depredations wrought by battles between employers and employees. Judges insisted that it was not their role or function to participate in struggles between capital and labor; but courts must act, they said, to restrain warring factions from disrupting society and invading its peace and, most importantly, to ensure "that individual and corporate rights may not be infringed." "Liberty and license," a court declared, "must not be confounded. Liberty is not the exercise of unbridled will, but consists in freedom of action, having due regard for the rights of others." Strikes, asserted several judges, represented license, not liberty, for they coerced the community and innocent nonunion workers in order to achieve goals that the strikers could not win fairly.[13]

Judicial rulings and rhetoric in the late nineteenth century associated organized labor and strikes with incendiary images.[14] Certainly, most judges assumed that unassailable natural rights encompassed employers' freedom to use their property as they chose, provided no irreparable harm was done to the community. They likewise assumed that individual workers could labor on whatever terms they preferred, even if such choices diluted the equally legitimate right of other workers to withdraw their labor, and that the public had a right to be protected when labor and capital clashed.

Without the police power represented by municipal law officers, sheriffs, state militia, federal marshals, and ultimately the US Army, however, judges were impotent to enforce their decisions. Elected public officials implemented court rulings because they shared judicial values and assumed that most citizens did as well. Noted labor historian David Montgomery was absolutely correct when he wrote that "it would be misleading . . . to depict the judiciary as the bulwark of capitalists' interests, single-handedly protecting the unfettered marketplace against persistent attempts by elected officials to aid the workers."[15]

Judges, elected public officials, and the citizens they claimed to represent shared a common commitment to principles of "civic republicanism," which implied that the community had rights that must be protected against the selfish claims of organized private interests. A corollary principle held that individuals retained inalienable rights that neither the community nor the state could impair. Politicians who defended the right of workers to combine into unions in order to bargain with their employers asserted that the same principle demanded "that an equal right be secured to those workmen who desire to keep aloof from the combination and dispose of their labor with perfect individual freedom." Neither trade unionists nor capitalists should have the power to restrain free choice among individual workers.[16] Senator Henry Teller of Colorado expressed the "free labor" doctrine emphatically and in more popularly appreciated language than any judge. His words deserve attention:

> No power should interfere to prevent the free exercise of this right [free contract], and no laboring man for a moment should surrender that right, either to the State, to his fellow-workmen, or to capital. His labor is valuable to him only as it is at his uncontrolled disposal, both as to whom he will sell it, and when he will sell it. Any interference by his fellow workmen of the same trade or any other in the disposal of his labor is an invasion of his right. . . . The difference between a slave and a freeman consists mainly in the fact that the freeman may freely dispose of his labor . . . on the terms fixed by himself.
>
> What the American laborer needs is individualism, freedom from the control of others . . . what the American laborer wants is freedom from control, either

of capital or his fellow workmen, independence, individuality, the right and disposition to take care of himself untrammeled, either by legislation, the rules of guilds, associations, trades unions, or other conditions that deny him the free control of his labor.[17]

II. PENNSYLVANIA JURISTS AND CONFLICT IN HOMESTEAD

Pennsylvania jurists faithfully reflected such attitudes and values during the Homestead strike and lockout. Indeed, Chief Justice Edwin M. Paxson, who indicted and tried Homestead's union leaders, not only charged them with using private power to usurp the rights of the community but also accused them of treason against the state, a charge that far exceeded those commonly leveled against "criminal union conspiracies." It is also important to recall that in the late nineteenth century, governmental responses to labor actions did not separate Democratic and Republican officeholders. Differences of opinion and policy about unions existed more within the parties than between them. A Republican president, Rutherford B. Hayes, dispatched US troops to break the 1877 nationwide railroad strikes; a Democratic president, Grover Cleveland, acted similarly in ending the 1894 Pullman Strike. At the state level, a Republican governor, Frank Steunenberg of Idaho, requested federal troops to break the 1892 strike of hard-rock miners in northern Idaho, while a Democratic governor in Pennsylvania, Robert Pattison, dispatched state militia to Homestead after the confrontation between Pinkertons and locked-out union members exploded in violence.

The arrival of state troops in Pennsylvania accomplished what the employment of Pinkertons failed to achieve. Homestead's steel workers, supported by their community and its elected officials (also themselves often union members), had stymied Frick and his Pinkerton-protected strikebreakers, but they failed to neutralize a state militia authorized to enforce martial law. Protected by troops, strikebreakers entered the town's steel mill and production resumed. As smoke poured once again from the mill's smokestacks, nonunion workers drifted back to work followed in turn by less-loyal union members. As the number of returning steelworkers grew and production approached normal levels, the union surrendered in late November, ending the strike and ceding power to the company. For the next three decades and more, the Amalgamated Association would lack an effective presence at the Carnegie Corporation and its successor, United States Steel. Over the ensuing decade and a half, other iron and steel companies would oust the Amalgamated from their mills, creating what another noted labor historian, David Brody, labeled the "nonunion era." And in a town once governed by workers, the social investigator John Fitch discovered in 1909 that Homestead's citizens had grown so cowed by the company that their public voices rarely rose above a plaintive whisper.[18]

Clearly, then, events in Homestead proved that by the end of the 1800s, corporate power had come to prevail. If corporations lacked the ability to tame workers and defeat their unions owing to labor solidarity and community support, they could rely on the state and the law to buttress corporate power. In Homestead's case, the decision by Governor Pattison to declare martial law and dispatch the state militia served the Carnegie Company's purposes, subordinating worker rights and union power to the claims of private property. State intervention could also restructure local public power by criminalizing union officials and their sympathizers who held public office, ousting them and their allies from power and transforming Homestead from a worker-dominated community into a company town. All this and more found favor with Pittsburgh-area criminal court judges and the chief justice of Pennsylvania, who allied to inflict punishment on strikers and union leaders.

After the mill resumed production and the strike was on its way to being broken, the courts in September 1892 acted to punish the defeated workers. The state indicted numerous union members who had been present during the battle against the Pinkertons for assault and murder. Criminal court judges generally instructed juries that the evidence against the defendants had been well established and that the crimes they had been charged with were serious and merited punishment. Yet local juries invariably found the defendants not guilty, revealing clearly the gap that remained between community sentiments and corporate and state authorities.[19] Corporations, bolstered by the law and the state's coercive power, could break strikes and smash unions, but they could not convince local citizens to find fellow citizens guilty of assault or murder.

III. CHIEF JUSTICE PAXSON AND THE CHARGE OF TREASON

More remarkable still was the legal action initiated by Chief Justice Paxson. Acting at the behest of the commanding officer of the state militia assigned to restore law and order in Homestead, who had consulted with Carnegie Company officials, Paxson chose to assume personal charge of local judicial proceedings, an action that would have been legitimate had local Allegheny County courts been unable to function. In fact, however, local courts had tried scores of union members charged with numerous counts of riotous behavior, criminal assault, and murder. The trials proceeded without exception in orderly fashion, producing verdicts that pleased the defendants (all were found not guilty) and displeased their adversaries. Paxson thus took it upon himself to compensate for jury members' failures to convict their local peers. He decided to charge the members of the union's strike council, thirty-three men in all, with treason against the Commonwealth, conflating the Carnegie Company and the Pinkerton Detective Agency with the authority of the state where the actions occurred. Yes, the strikers had acted against the interests of the company and the detective agency and did so violently, for which a goodly number had been tried and acquitted. One wonders, however, how the unionists had committed treason against Pennsylvania. After the state militia arrived in Homestead to enforce the martial law proclaimed by the governor, the strikers never openly questioned the authority of the troops, did nothing to interfere with the imposition of martial law, remained impotent to act against the strikebreakers who began to replace them in the mill, and submitted to a legal process that brought many before local courts on the charge of homicide. Yet Paxson, who not only filed the charge of treason but also assumed control of the grand jury that considered the evidence, convinced its members that treason had in fact occurred. But the riotous behavior for which Chief Justice Paxson indicted the strike leaders occurred before the state interposed its coercive power between the strikers and the corporation. For Paxson, the timing did not matter because, in his mind and in his charge to the grand jury, "when a large number of men arm and organize themselves by divisions and companies, appoint officers and engage in a common purpose to defy the law, to resist its officers, and to deprive any portion of their fellow citizens of the rights to which they are entitled . . . it is a levying of war against the State, and the offense is treason." Not only had the union members declared war against the state, according to Paxson, but they had also violated the "free labor doctrine" under which an employer cannot compel an employee to work a moment longer than the latter sees fit but under which an employee cannot compel an employer to give him work or to deny another worker the right to such employment.[20]

What might have led Chief Justice Paxson to go to such an extreme, especially when, by the time that the treason charges were filed (September 1892), the Carnegie Company had won its battle against the Amalgamated? An address that he delivered in 1888 to attorneys recently admitted to the Pennsylvania Bar hints at his motivations. The speech hit hard on the dominant chords of nineteenth-century legal culture, respectability, personal rectitude, moderation, respect for governmental authority, law as one of the highest callings, and perhaps most of all, an individual's responsibility for his or her own fate. In some respects, Paxson's admiration for the legal profession and the law allowed no tolerance for human foibles or for external constraints on individual actions. Imagine a High Court judge in the year 1888 condemning a legislative act of 1842 that eliminated imprisonment for debt. In Paxson's judgment, the abolition of imprisonment for debt relieved profligate individuals from their responsibilities and thus encouraged improvident behavior. Not only had individuals been pardoned for their bad debts, but young attorneys had lost what once had been a large part of their income, representing clients facing debtors' prison. In the same speech, Paxson bemoaned the passing of an idyllic, pastoral nation in which individuals rose and fell as a result of their personal behavior and actions into one in which corporations and collectivities (large cities as well) limited individual volition. He advised the young attorneys in his audience never to spend more than they earned (debt remained for him a sin of the highest order) and at all costs to avoid the "demon rum."[21]

How, then, did this nineteenth-century Democratic Party stalwart and devotee of impartial justice defend the sort of corporation that he had condemned in his 1888 address and create out of whole cloth the charge of treason against thirty-three union members who had sought to check corporate power? Chief Justice Paxson's decision flowed logically from another part of the late nineteenth-century legal tradition. However much business corporations might have limited individual initiative, they nevertheless enjoyed legal standing and enjoyed property rights that the law held sacrosanct so long as such rights were not employed to harm the broader Commonwealth. Unions and their members, by way of contrast, enjoyed a more ambiguous place in the law. By 1892, unions had attained legal legitimacy, and their members' right to strike appeared justifiable. Yet the actions of unions and their members remained constrained in ways that business corporations did not. If a strike caused irreparable harm to a business, it might be ruled as illegitimate, and a union restrained from doing so. If strikers acted to bar other workers from taking their places, that too could be condemned as illegitimate, and courts might authorize local authorities to protect the replacements. If local authorities failed to heed such orders, as happened in Homestead, then the state might intervene and dispatch troops. If the state failed to act or was unable to do so, then the federal government, as happened during the 1877 railroad strikes, the 1892 and 1899 industrial conflicts in Idaho's Coeur d'Alenes, and the 1894 Pullman Strike, might dispatch the US Army to maintain order. For many state and federal jurists in the late 1800s, unions—by resorting to collective action—threatened to subvert established authority and violate the inalienable rights of US citizens.

For jurists such as Chief Justice Paxson, union rules and codes threatened to usurp the power of legally established authorities and create an alternate political reality. The right of a corporation and its individual employees to contract freely "in regard to wages, and the character of employment, whether by the piece or day, whether for ten hours or less," he declared, "is as fixed and clear as any other right which we enjoy under the constitution and laws of this state." For Paxson, then, "it is a right which belongs to every citizen, laborer or capitalist, and it is plain duty of the state to protect them in the enjoyment of it." Hence the decision by the Amalgamated to interdict the Pinkertons and the strikebreakers amounted to establishing an illegitimate government that, by denying citizens their contractual and constitutional rights, subverted the authority of Pennsylvania and thus amounted to treason.[22] That he could convince a grand jury to indict the union members proved that a select group of private citizens shared similar sentiments about collective actions undertaken by union members. Yet just as happened in the cases of union members tried for homicide in local courts and acquitted by juries composed of twelve ordinary local citizens, the jury that heard the treason cases acquitted the defendants. Events in Homestead proved that powerful corporations could eliminate unions but failed to criminalize the behavior of their members.

NOTES

Melvyn Dubofsky is a distinguished professor of history and sociology emeritus at Binghamton University, SUNY.

1. David P. Demarest Jr., *"The River Ran Red": Homestead 1892* (Pittsburgh: University of Pittsburgh Press, 1992).

2. Demarest, *"River Ran Red"*; Leon Wolff, *Lockout: The Story of the Homestead Strike of 1892: A Study of Violence, Unionism, and the Carnegie Steel Empire* (London: Harper & Row, 1965); Paul Krause, *The Battle for Homestead, 1880–1892: Politics, Culture, and Steel*

(Pittsburgh: University of Pittsburgh Press, 1992), esp. chs. 19–22; Joseph F. Wall, *Andrew Carnegie* (Oxford: Oxford University Press, 1970), 537–82 and *passim*; David Nasaw, *Andrew Carnegie* (New York: Penguin Books, 2006), ch. 23.

3. Henry Demarest Lloyd, *Wealth Against Commonwealth* (New York: Harper & Brothers, 1894); Gustavus Myers, *History of the Great American Fortunes* (Chicago: C. H. Kerr, 1936). For a more contemporary and quantitatively more precise analysis of the process of widening material inequality, *see* Thomas Piketty, *Capital in the Twenty-First Century* (Cambridge, Mass.: Brilliance Audio, 2014).

4. William J. Novak, *The Peoples Welfare: Law and Regulation in Nineteenth-Century America* (Chapel Hill: University of North Carolina Press, 1996).

5. Karen Orren, *Belated Feudalism: Labor, the Law, and Liberal Development in the United States* (Cambridge: Cambridge University Press, 1991); Christopher L. Tomlins, *The State and the Unions: Labor Relations, Law, and the Labor Movement in America, 1880–1960* (Cambridge: Cambridge University Press, 1986); C. Tomlins, *Law, Labor, and Ideology in the Early American Republic* (Cambridge: Cambridge University Press, 1993); Robert J. Steinfeld, *The Invention of Free Labor: The Employment Relation in English and American Law and Culture* (Chapel Hill: University of North Carolina Press, 1991).

6. For a brief treatment of this pattern of conflict, *see* Melvyn Dubofsky, *Industrialism and the American Worker, 1865–1920* (Arlington Heights, Ill.: Harlan Davidson, 1996), ch. 2.

7. Daniel R. Ernst, *Lawyers and the Labor Trust: A History of the American Anti-boycott Association* (Urbana: University of Illinois Press, 1995); *cf.* Haggai Hurvitz, "American Labor Law and the Doctrine of Entrepreneurial Property Rights: Boycott, Courts, and the Juridical Reorientation of 1886–1895," *Industrial Relations Law Journal* 8 (1986): 307–61; Herbert Hovenkamp, *Enterprise and American Law, 1836–1937* (Cambridge, Mass.: Harvard University Press, 1991).

8. In re Wabash Railroad Company, 24 Fed. 217 (C.C.W.D. Mo. 1885); *see also* Donald L. McMurry, "The Legal Ancestry of the Pullman Strike Injunctions," *Industrial and Labor Relations Review* 14 (1961): 235–56.

9. Chicago, Burlington, & Quincy Ry. v. Burlington, C.R. & N. Ry. Co., 34 Fed. 481 (C.C.S.D. Iowa 1888).

10. Casey v. Cincinnati Typographical Union No. 3, 45 F. 135, 135–47 (C.C.D. Ohio 1891).

11. Coeur D'Alene Consolidated Mining Co. v. Miners' Union of Wardner, 51 F. 260, 260–68 (C.C.D. Idaho 1892).

12. Toledo, A.A. & N.M. Ry. Co. v. Pennsylvania Co. et al., 54 F. 730, 736–39 (C.C.D. Ohio 1893).

13. Farmers' Loan and Trust Co. v. Northern Pacific Ry. Co., 60 Fed. 803 (C.D.E.D. Wis. 1894).

14. *See, e.g.,* Dianne Avery, "Images of Violence in Labor Jurisprudence: The Regulation of Picketing and Boycotts, 1894–1921," *Buffalo Law Review* 37 (Winter 1988–89): 3–117.

15. David Montgomery, *Citizen Worker: The Experience of Workers in the United States with Democracy and the Free Market During the Nineteenth Century* (Cambridge: Cambridge University Press, 1993), 152.

16. "Investigation of Labor Troubles in Missouri, Arkansas, Kansas, Texas, and Illinois," 49th Cong., 2nd Sess., House Report 4174 (Washington, D.C.: Government Printing Office, 1887), xxii–xxiv.

17. Congressional Record, 49th Cong., 2nd Sess. (Washington, D.C.: Government Printing Office, 1887), 2375–76.

18. John Fitch, *The Steel Workers* (Pittsburgh: University of Pittsburgh Press, 1959); *see also* Margaret Byington, *Homestead: The Households of a Mill Town* (Pittsburgh: University of Pittsburgh Press, 1974), esp. ch. 1; David Brody, *Steelworkers in America: The Nonunion Era* (Cambridge, Mass.: Harvard University Press, 1960).

19. Wolff, *Lockout,* 210–11; Krause, *Battle for Homestead,* 348–50; Arthur G. Burgoyne, *Homestead: A Complete History of the Struggle of July, 1892 Between the Carnegie Steel Company, Limited, and the Amalgamated Association of Iron and Steel Workers* (digitized by the Internet Archive in 2010 with funding from the University of Pittsburgh Library System), 204–6; Myron R. Stowell, *"Fort Frick," or the Siege of Homestead* (Pittsburgh: Pittsburgh Printing, 1893), chs. 29–30.

20. Wolff, *Lockout,* 212–13; Demarest, *"River Ran Red,"* 192–93; Krause, *Battle for Homestead,* 348–50; *Homestead: A Complete History,* 204–6; Stowell, *"Fort Frick,"* chs. 29–30.

21. Edward M. Paxton, "The Road to Success, or Practical Hints to the Junior Bar: An Address Delivered Before the Law Academy of Philadelphia," 1888, reprinted in *Green Bag* 16, no. 3 (2013), http://www.greenbag.org/v16n3/v16n3_from_the_bag_paxson.pdf.

22. *Homestead: A Complete History,* 206.

CHAPTER 24

Defining the Role of the Legislature in Regulating the Economy

VINCENT C. DELIBERATO JR.

I. REGULATORY AUTHORITY AND ITS OVERSIGHT

Given Pennsylvania's historic prominence as the keystone in America's industrial arch, its Supreme Court has long confronted contentious questions about whether and to what extent the legislature can regulate the economy. The rise of laissez-faire economics in the United States coincided with Pennsylvania's industrial prominence in the early 1900s. Proponents of laissez-faire believed that the economy operated on its own moderating rules of supply and demand, which should not be restrained by law.[1] This is a valid proposition in a truly competitive market: as to products and services that are provided by a large range of people and desired by a large range of people, the economic principles of supply and demand are superior to any rules set forth in legislation or jurisprudence. This is a questionable, and indeed harmful, proposition, however, if there is no competitive market: as to products and services that are provided by a small range of people but are needed by all the people, the principles of supply and demand might properly yield to economic regulation for the benefit of the entire society.

Some of the Pennsylvania Supreme Court's most important work has been in mediating between a free-market ideal and the government's interest in regulating the excesses that can result from such a market. This chapter focuses on foundational aspects of the Court's work in this regard and considers the origins, development, and use of judicial review, the once-controversial authority of courts to examine the constitutionality of legislation.

The initial aspect is recognition of a government of checks and balances. The doctrine of judicial review establishes the ascendancy of the judicial branch over both the legislative and executive branches in determining the constitutionality of governmental action. Recognition of the power and influence of the federal judiciary nationally and the Pennsylvania Supreme Court provincially leads to an exploration of the roots, expansion, and directed focus of judicial oversight of economic legislation. The origin of such oversight is found in the struggle between vested rights and the police power. Pennsylvania jurisprudence foreshadowed federal jurisprudence on this subject.

Judicial review in economics expanded nationally on the basis of protecting vested property rights and contract rights. Pennsylvania went a step further with the concept of special legislation. The rise of the natural rights philosophy directed judicial focus toward more stringent oversight of economic legislation under the concept of substantive due process, nationally and in Pennsylvania. This approach continued until the threat to the national economy and the general welfare forced a modification.

II. ESTABLISHMENT OF JUDICIAL REVIEW

A. The Federal Model

One of the most famous cases in American history is *Marbury v. Madison*.[2] The underlying legal dispute arose out of an attempt to force the sitting Jeffersonian-Republican secretary of state, James Madison, to deliver a commission to a "midnight appointment" made by the former Federalist president, John Adams. The case invoked the original jurisdiction of the Supreme Court to grant mandamus under a federal statute, and this grant of jurisdiction was questioned by the Court as conflicting with the grant of original jurisdiction in Article III, Section 2, Clause 2 of the US Constitution.[3] The conflict was resolved in favor of the constitutional provision. A statute cannot expand the original jurisdiction of the Supreme Court beyond what is set forth in the Constitution.[4] *Marbury* was the first case to recognize the federal judicial power to invalidate legislation.[5] The Court cited two sources of this power: the essence of the constitutionally conferred judicial authority is review for constitutionality,[6] and the Supremacy Clause, Article VI, Clause 2 of the US Constitution, demands review for constitutionality.[7]

Marbury's holding is the primary jurisprudential source of the overwhelming power of the judicial branch in the federal government. President Thomas Jefferson himself characterized this power as despotic, asserting that no language in the Constitution conferred such a power.[8] His criticism of Marshall's decision was emphatic: "[T]he Chief Justice says, 'there must be an ultimate arbiter somewhere.' True, there must; but does that prove it is either party? The ultimate arbiter is the people of the Union, assembled by their deputies in convention, at the call of Congress, or of two-thirds of the States. Let them decide to which they mean to give an authority claimed by two of their organs."[9]

B. The Pennsylvania Model

It is not unusual for state constitutional jurisprudence to influence its federal counterpart.[10] This was especially true in the early days of the American republic with respect to the constitutional jurisprudence of the original thirteen states. The doctrine of judicial review fits into this model. In Pennsylvania, judicial power to invalidate a statute on the basis of unconstitutionality predated *Marbury*.[11]

Pennsylvania's first state Constitution was established by a convention in 1776 pursuant to a resolution of the Second Continental Congress.[12] It was extensively revised by a convention in 1790.[13] When Thomas Mifflin was proclaimed governor under the Pennsylvania Constitution of 1790, members of the Supreme Court addressed transition of various executive officers.[14] On the question of whether the individual serving as register general could continue in office pursuant to legislative appointment prior to the Pennsylvania Constitution of 1790, the justices stated, "We think the *Constitution* to be paramount to the Acts of the legislature, and that the appointment of the Register General is *thereby* vacated upon the complete organization of the Executive Branch of Government: a new appointment . . . is now vested in the Governor."[15]

In 1792, a statute was enacted to regulate the procedure for occupying vacant lands. In a dispute under the statute, constitutionality was contested by the litigants.[16] Although the case was resolved without applying the statute, the Court specifically addressed the doctrine of judicial review: "We possess also the power of declaring a law to be unconstitutional, and such power has heretofore been exercised."[17] In 1797, nearly seventy years before the abolition of slavery under the US Constitution, an argument was made in the Pennsylvania Supreme Court on the constitutionality of slavery under the Commonwealth's Constitution.[18] The case was a habeas corpus action against a slaveholder. The defendant relied on two eighteenth-century Pennsylvania statutes permitting registration of slaves depending on residency. Although the case was resolved by determining residency against the slaveholder and thus holding the statutes inapplicable, the Court recognized the significance of the constitutional arguments.[19] Counsel for the slaves was eloquent on the constitutional authority of the courts to review legislation impairing human freedom:

> [T]he act of . . . 1782, so far as it respects . . . slaves . . . is unconstitutional. It contains a most extraordinary principle. It affects to return back to a state of slavery certain human beings, who were legally free. Will it be said, that the legislature at their pleasure can transmute a freeman into a slave, by directing the performance of a few ceremonial acts? . . . .
>
> The people of America are the real sovereigns of the government. They are represented by the executive, legislative, and judicial branches; but each branch is limited by the boundaries of the constitution. When the legislative authority infringes on the judicial, their acts cease to be the will of the community, and the judiciary will be prompt in declaring their opinions thereon.[20]

Even counsel for the slaveholders recognized the constitutional principle of human freedom but concentrated on the constitutional protection of property: "[O]n elementary principles, slavery itself might be questionable under the 1st section of the 9th article of the state constitution, which declares, that 'all men are born equally free and independent'. . . . But the same clause guards and secures property, and regards the right of acquiring, possessing and protecting it, as inherent and indefeasible. The slaves among us were no parties to this compact. The general practice of mankind, in most of the civilized ages of the world, evinces, that there may be a property in slaves, which in this state is not abolished, but only restricted *sub modo*."[21] Counsel for each side recognized the primacy of the state Constitution over any particular legislative enactment; the Court, however, was reluctant to enter the conflict over slavery.

At the end of the eighteenth century, in a prosecution under a Philadelphia ordinance proscribing erection of specified buildings, the defense challenged the authority of the General Assembly to delegate to a municipal corporation the authority to adopt criminal ordinances to accomplish building requirements.[22] The Supreme Court addressed the argument in a precise analysis. A municipal corporation has no authority on its own, the Court explained, to impose a criminal penalty, but the General Assembly may grant this authority to a municipal corporation.[23] In upholding the constitutionality of the delegating statute and the dependent ordinance, the Court characterized the function of judicial review as both a power and a duty: "[A] breach of the constitution by the legislature, and the clashing of the law with the constitution, must be evident indeed, before we should think *ourselves at liberty* to declare a law void and a nullity on that account; yet if a violation of the constitution should in any case be made by an act of the legislature, and that violation should unequivocally appear to us, we shall think it *our duty* not to shrink from the task of saying such law is void."[24]

In two cases decided after *Marbury*—*Emerick v. Harris* in 1808 and *Eakin v. Raub* in 1825—the Supreme Court best articulated its power of judicial review. The issue in *Emerick* was whether a jurisdictional statute for justices of the peace to determine small claims violated the constitutional right to trial by jury. The key debate involved whether the Court was empowered to declare a statute unconstitutional.[25] Speaking through Justice Yeates, the Court began its analysis by invoking the constitutional principle of separation of powers.[26] The role of the judiciary, it explained, is central to this principle.[27] This fact led the Court to an inevitable conclusion: "[T]he courts of justice must necessarily possess and exercise the power of judging of the constitutionality of all laws, brought before them judicially. . . . It cannot be denied that entertaining an argument on the constitutionality of a legislative act by the judiciary, implies necessarily in itself a power to judge and determine on its validity, on a fair comparison of it with the powers granted to the former branch of the government, by a solemn act of the people, sanctioned by the oaths of those who are delegated to act in the three branches."[28]

The language of *Eakin*, a famous decision that continued to divide the Court seventeen years later, is equally instructive. According to the majority, the duty of the judiciary to invalidate a statute passed in violation of the Constitution derives from the oath of each jurist, the litigants in each case, and the people who formed the Constitution.[29] In short, deciding the constitutionality of legislation is a crucial judicial function.[30] Yet the majority's embrace of judicial review is not what makes *Eakin* famous. Rather, the decision has gone down in history because of the dissent of Justice John Bannister Gibson, which is widely viewed as the most effective attack on *Marbury* and judicial review ever authored. Justice Gibson's powerful judicial opinions were widely quoted throughout the United States and in England. Judicial review, he believed, was nothing more than "dogma," widely held but baseless:

> I am aware, that a right to declare all constitutional acts void, without distinction as to either constitution, is generally held as a professional dogma; but, I apprehend, rather as a matter of faith than of reason. I admit, that I once embraced the same doctrine, but, without examination, and I shall therefore state the arguments that impelled me to abandon it, with great respect for those by whom it is still maintained. But I may premise, that it is not a little remarkable, that although the right in question has all along been claimed by the judiciary, no judge has ventured to discuss it, except Chief Justice MARSHALL, (in *Marbury v. Madison*, 1 Cranch 137,) and if the argument of a jurist so distinguished for the strength of his ratiocinative powers be found inconclusive, it may fairly be set down to the weakness of the position which he attempts to defend. . . . Instead, therefore, of resting on the fact, that the right in question has universally been assumed by the *American* courts, the judge who asserts it ought to be prepared to maintain it on the principles of the constitution.[31]

What followed was a point-by-point critique of the rationale supporting judicial review, in which Justice Gibson flatly rejected the notion that the Constitution vested in the judiciary a special power to superintend the acts of independent branches of government. "It is the business of the judiciary to interpret the laws," he wrote, "not scan the authority of the lawgiver."[32] Judicial review, Gibson believed, was a usurpation of both the legislative prerogative to make laws and the sovereign power of the people "to correct abuses in legislation, by instructing their representatives to repeal the obnoxious act."[33] While Justice Gibson agreed with US Supreme Court Chief Justice Marshall that the will of the people must be supreme, the two men differed on the fundamental question of how that will was expressed. Chief Justice Marshall believed that the people speak through the Constitution, whereas Justice Gibson believed that the people speak through the ballot box.

Despite the enduring power of Justice Gibson's dissent, the battle over judicial review had already been lost, as Gibson himself recognized, and it has been a jurisprudential article of faith ever since. As the nineteenth century progressed and America emerged from her agrarian roots to become a world industrial power, economic issues took center stage in legislatures across the country. Proliferating economic regulations spurred the increasing exercise of judicial review.

III. ROOTS OF JUDICIAL REVIEW IN ECONOMICS

A. The Federal Model

Judicial review of economic regulations requires courts to balance competing interests, including the rights vested in private actors in the marketplace and the rights of government to protect the citizenry under its police power and levy taxes.[34] The reconciliation of these competing interests was considered by the US Supreme Court in *Brown v. Maryland*.[35] The dispute in that case involved the authority of Maryland to require licensure in order to sell goods imported from a foreign country. A group of importers challenged the licensure statute as violative of the constitutional prohibition against states laying import duties without congressional approval. Chief Justice Marshall decided the issue in favor of the importers, holding that a state tax on the occupation of importing is, in effect, an unconstitutional state tax on importation.[36] In reaching his conclusion, Marshall had to deal with Maryland's argument that the constitutional ban on state import duties must end when goods enter the country, or else states would have no power to tax and no police power.[37] The opinion dealt with both state powers.

Taxation was treated first, with the Court recognizing the distinction between an import tax on personal property in the packaging and form in which it is originally brought into the country and other taxes on personal property after its packaging or form have been altered. The former violates the constitutional stricture; the latter does not.[38] The police power was treated next. The removal or destruction of dangerous material is comprised by the police power and is exempt from the constitutional ban on state import duties.[39]

B. The Pennsylvania Model

The clash between vested rights and the police power was apparent in Pennsylvania even before the *Brown* decision. At the end of the eighteenth century, the Pennsylvania legislature authorized Philadelphia to prohibit, by ordinance, the erection of specified wooden buildings in a defined geographic area.[40] The city passed such an ordinance, an individual violated it, and a successful prosecution was then appealed to the Supreme Court.[41] The defendant argued that a municipal corporation may regulate but not restrain trade unless warranted by particular custom.[42] In opposition, the Commonwealth argued that the balance between individual liberty and public protection had to be struck in favor of the latter.[43] In that context, the Court posited the authority of the Commonwealth to allow a political subdivision to regulate dwelling heights.[44] The Court ultimately valued the collective interest in public safety more than the individual right to deal with private property.

IV. EXPANSION OF JUDICIAL REVIEW IN ECONOMICS

A. The Federal Model

Early federal jurisprudence focused on the procedural component of due process of law.[45] There was substantive review in the area of vested rights of property, particularly as derived from contract, and this was review over state, as opposed to federal, action.[46]

The US Constitution, in its original and current form, speaks to property rights derived from contract: "No State shall . . . pass any . . . Law impairing the Obligation of Contracts."[47] The so-called Contracts Clause prohibits state legislation that impairs property rights under a contract.[48]

B. The Pennsylvania Model

1. Contracts Clause

The Pennsylvania Constitution's language on impairment of contract is virtually identical to the federal language: "No . . . law impairing the obligation of contracts . . . shall be passed."[49] The current language dates back to 1790.[50]

The Pennsylvania Supreme Court has been careful about using the Contracts Clause to invalidate legislation. For instance, in determining whether to invalidate a bankruptcy law under the Contracts Clause, Chief Justice Tilghman, in an opinion joined by Justice Gibson, stated,

> But, it may be asked, by what rule shall the meaning of these words "*impairing the obligations of contracts*," be restricted or limited, if they are not taken in their full extent? I confess that to lay down a rule which would decide all cases, appears to me to be very difficult, perhaps impossible[.] One may be certain, that particular cases are not within the meaning of a law, without being able to enumerate all the cases that are within it. To attempt such enumerations, is unnecessary and dangerous, lest some should be omitted. It is safer to decide on each case, as it arises.[51]

Following this case-by-case approach, the Court upheld the statute, which authorized bankruptcy in Philadelphia upon collection and distribution of a debtor's assets. In so holding, the Court applied the Contracts Clause in terms of the basic contract law principle of mutuality of rights and obligations of all contracting parties. A tender law, forcing a creditor to take a debtor's assessed property in satisfaction of a debt, would violate the clause because it alters a contract solely for the benefit of a debtor; but a bankruptcy law discharging a debt upon surrender of all the debtor's property would not violate the clause because it alters a contract for the benefit of both parties.[52] Since the case at bar involved a bankruptcy statute, there was no need to invalidate it under the Contracts Clause.[53]

A similar situation arose in *Evans v. Montgomery*.[54] An 1840 statute limited passage of title on improved property subject to lien on the title of the possessor of the property at the time the improvement was commenced.[55] *Evans* addressed the application of this statute, and the sequence of events was complex: In March 1839, the plaintiff owned the land, and she leased it to a tenant. In February 1840, the tenant improved the land, and a mechanic's lien was filed against the land. After the statute took effect, the defendant purchased the land from the tenant in fee simple. The plaintiff attempted to reenter under the lease, and the defendant demurred on the basis of her ownership in fee simple.[56] The case turned on whether application of the statute to improved property subject to a lien filed prior to the effective date of the statute would impair vested rights.[57] The Court addressed the issue squarely when it held that alteration of contract *remedies* was not within the proscription of the Contracts Clause.[58]

The Court did, however, use the clause to invalidate legislation where warranted. When the legislature had properly enacted all corporate charters, that of the initial corporation and that establishing two new corporations, the Supreme Court nonetheless invalidated subsequent legislation dividing the corporations under the federal Contracts Clause: "[T]he supplementary act is, as regards original stockholders who have not consented to be arranged to either of the new incorporations, in direct collision with the tenth section of the first article of the constitution of the United States, which . . . prohibits the enactment of laws impairing contracts: and notwithstanding our deference to the legislature, we are bound to give effect to the constitutional provision, though at the expense of our common law."[59]

Even in validating a corporate stock tax, the Court recognized that "it is not to be questioned that the original and subsequent charters granted . . . are contracts within the meaning of the constitution, and entitled to its protection. Any law, therefore, impairing their obligation, or materially interfering with their fundamental conditions, is destitute of binding efficacy."[60]

2. Special Legislation

The earliest constitutional provisions on special legislation dealt with marriage contracts[61] and special privileges.[62] Even before special legislation was introduced as a constitutional principle, the Supreme Court recognized its significance.[63]

A nineteenth-century statute authorized municipal commissioners, upon application of a majority of affected property owners, to undertake curbing and paving in minimal areas but to assess all property fronting the improvements.[64] The commissioners, however, went beyond the minimal areas in making improvements and assessments. An affected property owner who did not apply for the improvement challenged the assessment against the property fronting the improvement and lost at trial. On appeal, the Supreme Court framed the issue in terms of an abuse of power inherent in legislation imposing the expense of an improvement on property owners not seeking the improvement.[65] Proper resolution of the issue required invalidation of the statute, the Court held, insofar as it authorized assessment beyond the minimal areas where voluntary application was made.[66]

Judicial concern with special legislation did not dissuade the legislature from enacting it; a constitutional amendment was required.[67] In 1874, the prohibition of special legislation was added to Pennsylvania's Constitution.[68] Twenty-one years later, the Court addressed the parameters of the prohibition.[69] Legislation had been enacted to extensively regulate anthracite mines.[70] In a negligence action brought against a coal company under the vicarious liability provision of the statute, the defendant attacked the constitutionality of the entire act as special legislation. The heart of the argument was that the legislation targeted only anthracite mines in the areas of employment regulation and tort liability.[71] Although ruling for the defendant on the constitutional invalidity of the vicarious liability provisions,[72] the Court refused to invalidate the entire statute as special legislation.[73] It held that a legislative definition of a regulated business that excludes only operations that are too small to be subject to general regulation does not violate the proscription against special legislation.[74]

V. DIRECTED FOCUS OF JUDICIAL REVIEW IN ECONOMICS

A. Natural Rights Philosophy

In the nineteenth century, the rise of natural rights philosophy, which holds that all human beings are born with certain inalienable rights, prompted American courts to focus on the substantive component of due process of law.[75] Substantive due process began to take hold at the state level with particular force in the decade prior to the Civil War[76] and continued throughout the remainder of the nineteenth century.

In state jurisprudence on labor reform, the police power began to give way to deprivation of liberty or property without due process of law.[77] A noted historian has characterized the judiciary in the second half of the nineteenth century as a "dike against which the surging tides of welfare legislation beat in vain."[78] Against this inequitable backdrop, legal reformers began to not only apply a due process analysis to legislative procedure but also to test the reasonableness of the legislation in court. Under this analysis, legislative action that restricts vested rights or violates natural law exceeds the bounds of the social compact between government and the governed, and such action denies substantive due process to those it affects.[79]

Economic, social, and intellectual thought of the late nineteenth century urged the US Supreme Court to do more to protect business interests from encroaching governmental control.[80] The Court agreed, and many states followed suit.

Among the targets of strife between capital and labor in this period was the "company store," a retail establishment owned by the employer that accepted only script issued by the employer.[81] In Pennsylvania, the legislature required the mining industry to pay wages in legal tender only and prohibited price-gouging at company stores.[82] This statute represented the ultimate struggle between the police power and substantive due process. The Supreme Court addressed the struggle in *Godcharles v. Wigeman*.[83] The Court came down on the side of substantive due process, holding that legislative regulation of the compensation and merchandising between employer and employee abridged freedom of contract.[84]

In its holding, the Court interpreted freedom of contract as a liberty or property element of due process, enabling a man in need of a job to support himself and his family by bargaining away his labor on terms he chose, even if those terms were onerous. The Court's language is disingenuous in characterizing the legislation as "an *insulting* attempt to put the laborer under a legislative tutelage, which is not only degrading to his manhood, but subversive of his rights as a citizen of the United States."[85] The legislature was protecting, not insulting, the laborers.

The Court's understanding of labor relations was built on the notion that a laborer "may sell his labor *for what he thinks best*, whether money or goods," and any "law that proposes to prevent him from so doing is an infringement of his constitutional privileges, and consequently *vicious* and void."[86] In truth, the laborer might have no choice at all in assessing the value of his or her labor. The legislature recognized the lack of choice but did not attempt to deal with it; the legislation did no more than address legal tender and price-gouging of employees. Consequently, such legislation was not vicious but benevolent. There can be no police power to protect public welfare if it cannot even regulate the method or basic value of compensation. Modern jurisprudence recognizes that an illusory freedom of contract without realistic bargaining power results in poverty and degradation.[87]

By the turn of the twentieth century, the US Supreme Court had generally accepted the substantive due process doctrine as a viable basis on which to void economic or social legislation that (the Court believed) unreasonably infringed upon freedom of contract.[88] This jurisprudential period, which spanned well into the Great Depression, has been known ever since as the *Lochner* era, based on the infamous 1905 decision of the US Supreme Court that struck down, under liberty of contract, a New York law limiting the number of hours that bakery workers could be compelled to work in a week to sixty.[89] In a similar case decided eighteen years later, the US Supreme Court used liberty of contract to invalidate federal minimum wage legislation in the District of Columbia.[90]

However, the prevailing *Lochner*-era concept of liberty of contract was never fully embraced by the Pennsylvania Supreme Court. For instance, in *Commonwealth v. Wormser*,[91] the defendant was charged with violating a statute that prohibited employment of minors in excess of specified hours. Rejecting the defendant's argument that the statute violated liberty of contract, the Court held that legislative regulation of the employment of minors is a valid exercise of the police power that is not incompatible with freedom of contract.[92]

B. The Depression and the New Deal

1. The Federal Model

President Franklin D. Roosevelt responded to the Great Depression with the New Deal, a sweeping legislative and executive program built on federal regulation of industry and social welfare legislation.[93] However, the US Supreme Court and other federal courts invoked *Lochner*-esque notions of substantive due process to invalidate New Deal legislation. This precipitated a constitutional crisis.[94] In an effort to circumvent judicial opposition to his programs, President Roosevelt attempted to "pack" the US Supreme Court by proposing to add a new justice for each justice who had reached a certain age.[95]

The constitutional crisis was averted when the Supreme Court reversed itself.[96] Justice Owen Roberts, who had previously opposed the New Deal on liberty-of-contract grounds, abandoned the conservatives and aligned himself with the liberals and moderates.[97] In *West Coast Hotel Company v. Parrish*,[98] the new five-to-four majority rejected the prior view of substantive due process and liberty of contract:

> The Constitution does not speak of freedom of contract. It speaks of liberty and prohibits the deprivation of liberty without due process of law. In prohibiting that deprivation the Constitution does not recognize an absolute and uncontrollable liberty. Liberty in each of its phases has its history and connotation. But the liberty safeguarded is liberty in a social organization which requires the protection of law against the evils which menace the health, safety, morals and welfare of the people. *Liberty under the Constitution is thus necessarily subject to the restraints of due process, and regulation which is reasonable in relation to its subject and is adopted in the interests of the community is due process.*[99]

This 1937 ruling sounded the death knell for substantive due process as a basis on which to invalidate economic regulation.[100] Since then, courts have routinely applied so-called rational basis review, which upholds government action so long as there is a reasonable relationship between that action and a legitimate government purpose in the areas of allocating welfare benefits, restricting use of property, and regulating business.[101]

2. The Pennsylvania Model

Like its federal counterpart, the Pennsylvania Supreme Court was confronted with constitutional challenges to economic regulations throughout the *Lochner* era. The most important of these cases fell within one of four categories: poverty relief, price control, impairment of contract, and fair trade.

a. Poverty Relief

Even before the Great Depression, the Pennsylvania Supreme Court recognized the critical governmental function of expending state money to care for the poor.[102] The Court, however, was scrupulous in interpreting this function in conformity with the constitutional prohibition of direct legislative appropriations to charities. At that time, the prohibition appeared in Article III, Section 18 of the 1874 Pennsylvania Constitution.[103]

For instance, in 1923, the legislature enacted a statute providing state assistance to aged individuals with limited resources.[104] The legislation was challenged as an unconstitutional direct charitable appropriation.[105] In invalidating the legislation, the Supreme Court held that any state assistance must be paid to governmental districts organized to aid the poor rather than paid directly to poor individuals.[106]

A similar fate befell an appropriation to the welfare department to pay privately owned hospitals for treatment of indigent persons.[107] Justice Kephart interpreted the constitutional prohibition as follows:

> There should be no doubt as to the comprehensiveness of this provision in the Constitution. It states in short (and this is the real thought underlying the constitutional provision) that the *people's money shall not be given for charity, benevolence or education to persons or communities, or for any purpose to sectarian and denominational institutions, corporations, or associations.* This mandate comes direct from the people. It is placed on those in authority, to be followed without exception or reservation of any character. It is to be obeyed as a command. *It represents a right or power expressly withheld by the people and as such it transcends the judicial, legislative, and executive authority.* The provision forces recognition as a part of our scheme of government; it is a limitation on authority, and, with the other affirmative powers, forms the basis of our social organization. It is an exemplar of one of the most fundamental concepts of our government. It is then the imperative duty of judges to hold strictly to the fundamental law, and prevent any violation of it whether through a direct effort by legislation peacefully to rewrite any part of it, or an indirect one coming through an act of charity of a state-created agency.[108]

Once again, the Court was adamantly opposed to using public money to directly fund charities. While this jurisprudence was consistent with the view of courts nationally, it gave way as courts across the country began to recognize the social consequences of unprecedented poverty stemming from the Great Depression. The Pennsylvania Supreme Court was at the forefront of that change.[109]

In the midst of the Great Depression, Governor Gifford Pinchot summoned the legislature into special session to consider taxation, borrowing, and spending to create jobs and provide poverty relief.[110] Legislators responded with poverty relief only, authorizing each poor district to spend appropriated money for food, clothing, fuel, and shelter for individuals who could not support themselves.[111] Attorney General William A. Schnader advised Governor Pinchot that the measure violated the constitutional provision against direct charitable contributions.[112] The governor agreed but allowed the bill to become law without his signature.[113] Attorney General Schnader authorized a mandamus action against state welfare officials, ordering them to comply with the new law, and then undertook to represent the officials.[114] This led to the seminal case of *Commonwealth ex rel. Schnader v. Liveright*.[115]

Justice Kephart, the author of prior decisions that struck down legislative efforts to aid the poor, announced a new approach to the central issue of poverty relief. He defined poverty as the status of being without means of support and concluded that prohibiting aid to the poor impeded the Commonwealth's self-preservation.[116] The relief of poverty, he held, is to be treated not as charity or benevolence but as a proper function of government.[117]

Justice Maxey's concurrence on this point was succinct: "[A]n appropriation of state money to combat widespread poverty arising from unemployment can no more justly be characterized as 'charity' or 'benevolence' than could an appropriation of state money with which to combat a plague sweeping over Pennsylvania."[118] While aid to the poor had previously been viewed as charity, the new formulation viewed poverty relief as a key governmental function designed to support the citizenry and thus preserve the Commonwealth itself.

b. Price Controls

As with the Supreme Court's rulings on poverty relief, its position regarding price controls reflected the realities of the Great Depression and the need for increased governmental intervention into the economy.

Among the legislative responses to the Great Depression was the Milk Control Board Law, a 1934 statute that established a board to regulate and license the sale of milk.[119] This regulatory scheme was quickly challenged as a violation of liberty of contract and property rights. While the Superior Court panel had deemed the statute unconstitutional,[120] the Supreme Court embraced the rationale of the Superior Court dissent and upheld the law on the basis that there exists no constitutional freedom to conduct business in a manner that inflicts injury on the public in general or a substantial group of people.[121] Moreover, the price-control legislation could be upheld on the apparent findings of the legislature that industry practices had failed to protect consumers, wasted public resources, threatened to eliminate access to a necessary commodity, and/or threatened the industry itself.[122]

c. Fair Trade

As with poverty relief and price controls, the Supreme Court upheld fair trade legislation passed as part of the New Deal. For instance, the Court considered the validity of the Fair Trade Act, which permitted a manufacturer to contract with retailers for minimum pricing of manufacturers' trademarked products and provided penalties for violation of such pricing even for nonparties to the contracts.[123] Although the statute restricted the competitive rights of retailers, the Court upheld it on two separate occasions.[124]

In 1955, after the Second World War and the Great Depression, the Fair Trade Act was upheld as a valid exercise of the police power. In *Burche Co. v. General Electric Company*, the Supreme Court held that with regard to fair trade legislation, the police power overrides substantive due process.[125] Although *Burche* was overruled within ten years of its pronouncement, the basis for the later decision was not substantive due process but the invalidity of delegations of legislative authority to private citizens or organizations.[126]

d. Impairment of Contract

Although Pennsylvania judicial philosophy on poverty relief, price controls, and fair trade came to reflect the realities of the Great Depression, the Supreme Court nonetheless continued to adhere in some cases to the liberty of contract ideal of the *Lochner* era. For instance, in 1936, the Court invalidated the Mortgage Deficiency Judgment Act,[127] which was passed during the height of the New Deal to provide debt relief to homeowners.

The act essentially limited foreclosure to a judicially determined fair value of the mortgaged property,[128] and opponents challenged its application to mortgages executed before its enactment.[129] Relying on traditional liberty-of-contract principles, Justice Stern concluded that a mortgage is a contract within the protection of the Contracts Clause.[130] Because the statute changed the procedure to enforce preexisting mortgages, it unconstitutionally impaired a contractual obligation.[131]

VI. SCOPE: FEDERALLY AND IN PENNSYLVANIA

The work of the Pennsylvania Supreme Court, similar to its federal counterpart, has reflected the struggle between the legitimate desire of citizens to engage in unfettered economic pursuits and the government's equally legitimate interest in protecting the public from the deleterious effects of unrestrained capitalism. While the clash between vested rights and the police power was recognized on the federal level early in the nineteenth century, the Pennsylvania Supreme Court addressed that clash, and exercised the formidable power of judicial review, even earlier.

On the federal level, the substantive component of due process was originally limited to vested property rights, especially as derived from contract. The Pennsylvania Supreme Court, on the other hand, recognized those substantive due process considerations but invoked them sparingly to invalidate legislation as impairing contract rights and as special legislation. The development of the natural rights philosophy gave rise to jurisprudence on substantive due process. Judicial analysis deemed regulation of business a danger to be avoided or controlled. To be sure, courts in Pennsylvania and beyond struggled to balance freedom of contract and substantive due process against the protection of health, safety, morals, and welfare lying at the heart of the police power. On the federal level, in most states and in Pennsylvania, jurisprudence favored due process protection of liberty or property over the police power. This led to stringent judicial oversight of economic and social legislation. The Pennsylvania exception related to wage regulation for minors.

The Great Depression and the New Deal dramatically changed the nation's economic landscape. The result was an ideological battle pitting judicial principles of substantive due process and freedom of contract against legislative and executive programs designed to regulate industry and protect social welfare. On the national level, the latter prevailed. In Pennsylvania, the situation was similar but more restrained, with poverty relief enshrined as an essential function of government and price controls and fair trade validated but mortgage relief invalidated as an impairment of contract rights.

By drawing these distinctions, the Pennsylvania Supreme Court carefully enunciated a state jurisprudence that was different in important ways from the prevailing view of courts elsewhere and faithfully recognized and accounted for the Commonwealth's unique place in the American economy.

NOTES

Vincent C. Deliberato Jr. is the director of the Pennsylvania Legislative Reference Bureau and an adjunct professor at Widener University Law School.

1. Matthew J. Lindsay, "In Search of 'Laissez-Faire Constitutionalism,'" *Harvard Law Review Forum* 123, no. 5 (2010): 61; Samuel E. Morison, *The Growth of the American Republic*, vol. 2 (Oxford: Oxford University Press, 1970), 79; William G. Sumner, *What Social Classes Owe to Each Other* (New York: Harper & Brothers, 1883), 120–21.

2. 5 U.S. (1 Cranch) 137 (1803).

3. Ibid., 173.

4. Ibid., 176.

5. William J. Rich, *Modern Constitutional Law*, vol. 3 (Eagan, Minn.: Thomas Reuters, 2011), § 39:12.

6. Marbury, 5 U.S. (1 Cranch) 178.

7. Ibid., 180.

8. XI *The Writings of Thomas Jefferson*, 51 (Library ed. 1903); XIV Ibid., 303–4.

9. XV *The Writings of Thomas Jefferson*, 451.

10. *See, e.g.*, Lawrence v. Texas, 539 U.S. 558, 577 (2003); *cf.* New State Ice Company v. Liebmann, 285 U.S. 262, 311 (1932) (Brandeis, J., dissenting).

11. *See* Respublica v. Duquet, 2 Yeates 492, 501 (Pa. 1799); Respublica v. Blackmore, 2 Yeates 234, 238–39 (Pa. 1797) (per curiam); Hubley's Lessee v. White, 2 Yeates 133, 146 (Pa. 1796) (per curiam).

12. Kenneth G. Gormley, *The Pennsylvania Constitution: A Treatise on Rights and Liberties* (Philadelphia: George T. Bisel, 2004), § 1.1; Legislative Reference Bureau, *Constitutions of Pennsylvania, Constitution of the United States* (Harrisburg, Pa.: Legislative Reference Bureau, 1986), 413.

13. Legislative Reference Bureau, *Constitutions*, 365.

14. "Judges of Supreme Court—Tenure of Office, 1790," reprinted March 4, 2014, in XII *Pennsylvania Archives* (1856): 30, http://www.fold3 .com/image/#734132.

15. Ibid., emphasis in original.

16. Hubley's Lessee, 2 Yeates at 144.

17. Ibid., 147.

18. Respublica, 2 Yeates 235.

19. Ibid., 239–40.

20. Ibid., 238–39.

21. Ibid., 235.

22. Duquet, 2 Yeates at 494–96.

23. Ibid., 501.

24. Ibid., emphasis added.

25. Emerick v. Harris, 1 Binney 416, 416–17 (Pa. 1808).

26. Ibid., 419.

27. Ibid., 421.

28. Ibid., 422–23.

29. Eakin v. Raub, 12 S. & R. 330, 339 (Pa. 1825), emphasis in original.

30. Ibid., 359.

31. Ibid., 345–46 (Gibson, J., dissenting), emphasis in original.

32. Ibid., 348.

33. Ibid., 355.

34. *See generally* Ronald D. Rotunda, *Treatise on Constitutional Law*, vol. 2 (Eagan, Minn.: Thompson Reuters, 2012), § 15.1(c).

35. 25 U.S. 419 (1827).

36. Ibid., 444–45.

37. Ibid., 443.

38. Ibid.

39. Ibid., 444.

40. Pa. Pub. Act. No. 15, § 1 (April 18, 1795).

41. Respublica v. Duquet, 2 Yeates 492, 492 (Pa. 1799).

42. Ibid., 493.

43. Ibid., 499.

44. Ibid., 501.

45. Rotunda, 2 *Treatise on Constitutional Law*, § 15.1(e).

46. Ibid., § 15.1(a).

47. U.S. Const. art. I, § 10, cl. 1.

48. Trustees of Dartmouth College v. Woodward, 17 U.S. 518, 628 (1819).

49. Pa. Const. art. I, § 17.

50. Legislative Reference Bureau, *Constitutions*, 386.

51. Farmers' & Mechanics' Bank v. Smith, 3 S. & R. 63, 71 (Pa. 1817), emphasis in original.

52. Ibid.

53. Ibid., 72.

54. 4 W. & S. 218 (Pa. 1842).

55. Pa. Pub. Act. No. 185, § 24 (April 28, 1840).

56. Evans, 4 W. & S. at 218.

57. Ibid., 219.

58. Ibid., 220.

59. Indiana and Ebensburg Turnpike Road Company v. Phillips, 2 Pen. & W. 184, 196 (Pa. 1830).

60. Easton Bank v. Commonwealth, 10 Pa. 442, 449 (1849).

61. Legislative Reference Bureau, *Constitutions*, 315.

62. Ibid., 339.

63. Commissioners of the District of Kensington v. Keith, 2 Pa. 218, 219 (1845); *cf.* Lycoming v. Union, 15 Pa. 166, 168 (1850) (statute held to be of general application).

64. Pa. Pub. Act. No. 86, § 2 (March 19, 1828).

65. Commissioners of the District of Kensington, 2 Pa. at 219.

66. Ibid., 221.

67. Robert E. Woodside, *Pennsylvania Constitutional Law* (Sayre, Pa.: Murrelle, 1985), 321.

68. Legislative Reference Bureau, *Constitutions*, 179–80.

69. Durkin v. Kingston Coal Company, 33 A. 237 (Pa. 1895).

70. Pa. Pub. Act. No. 177 (June 2, 1891).

71. Durkin, 33 A. at 239.

72. Ibid.

73. Ibid., 204.

74. Ibid.

75. Rotunda, *Treatise on Constitutional Law*, § 15.1(e).

76. Ibid.

77. Morison, *Growth of the American Republic*, 79, 99.

78. Ibid.

79. Rotunda, *Treatise on Constitutional Law*, § 15.1(e).

80. Ibid., § 15.2.

81. Morison, *Growth of the American Republic*, 100.

82. Pa. Pub. Act. No. 173, §§ 1–4 (June 29, 1881).

83. 6 A. 354 (Pa. 1886).

84. Ibid., 356.

85. Ibid., emphasis added.

86. Ibid., emphasis added.

87. *Cf.* Spierling v. First American Home Health Servs., Inc., 737 A.2d 1250, 1256n14 (Pa. Super. 1999) (Schiller, J., dissenting).

88. Rotunda, *Treatise on Constitutional Law*, § 15.3(a).

89. Lochner v. New York, 198 U.S. 45 (1905).

90. Adkins v. Children's Hospital, 261 U.S. 525, 545, 560 (1923).

91. 103 A. 500 (Pa. 1918).

92. Ibid., 502.

93. Morison, *Growth of the American Republic*, 485.

94. Rotunda, *Treatise on Constitutional Law*, § 15.3(b).

95. Morison, *Growth of the American Republic*, 513.

96. Rotunda, *Treatise on Constitutional Law*, § 15.3(b).

97. Morison, *Growth of the American Republic*, 515.

98. 300 U.S. 379 (1937).

99. Ibid., 391, emphasis added.

100. Rotunda, *Treatise on Constitutional Law*, § 15.4(b).

101. Ibid., § 15.4(e).

102. Collins v. Martin, 139 A. 122, 125 (Pa. 1927); Busser v. Snyder, 128 A. 80, 84 (Pa. 1925).

103. Legislative Reference Bureau, *supra*, 182. The current provision is Pa. Const. art. III, § 30.
104. Pa. Pub. Act. No. 141, §§ 7–11 (May 10, 1923).
105. Busser, 128 A. at 82.
106. Ibid., 86.
107. Collins, 139 A. at 127.
108. Ibid., 124, emphasis added.
109. Woodside, *Pennsylvania Constitutional Law*, 321, 590–91.
110. Ibid., 589–90.
111. Pa. Pub. Act. No. 7-E, § 4 (December 28, 1931).
112. Ibid. (governor's statement); Woodside, *Pennsylvania Constitutional Law*, 589.
113. Pa. Pub. Act. No. 7-E, § 4 (December 28, 1931); Woodside, *Pennsylvania Constitutional Law*, 590.
114. Woodside, *Pennsylvania Constitutional Law*, 590.
115. 161 A. 697 (1932).
116. Ibid., 709–10.
117. Ibid.
118. Ibid., 715.
119. Pa. Pub. Act. No. 37, § 10A (January 2, 1934).
120. Rohrer v. Milk Control Bd., 184 A. 133, 147 (Pa. Super. 1936) (en banc).
121. Rohrer v. Milk Control Bd., 186 A. 336, 358 (Pa. 1936).
122. Ibid.
123. Pa. Pub. Act. No. 115, §§ 1–2 (June 5, 1935), as amended in Pa. Pub. Act. No. 66 (June 12, 1941) and Pa. Pub. Act. No. 589 (May 25, 1956).
124. Bristol-Myers Co. v. Lit Bros., 6 A.2d 843, 847 (Pa. 1939); Lentheric, Inc., v. F. W. Woolworth Co., 13 A.2d 12, 15 (Pa. 1940).
125. 115 A.2d 361, 363 (1955); *see also* Gulf Oil Corp. v. Mays, 164 A.2d 656, 658 (Pa. 1960); Olin Mathieson Chemical Corp. v. L. & H. Stores, Inc., 139 A.2d 897, 898 (Pa. 1958).
126. Olin Mathieson Chemical Corp., 199 A.2d at 267–68.
127. Act of January 17, 1934 (1933 Sp. Sess. 1, P.L. 243, No. 59), continued July 1, 1935 (P.L. 503, No. 197), 21 P.S. §§ 806, 807, Historical Note (2001).
128. Section 1, ibid. (1933–34 Sp. Sess. 1, P.L. 243–44); Beaver Cnty. Bld'g & Loan Ass'n v. Winowich, 187 A. 481, 485 (Pa. 1936).
129. Beaver Cnty. Bld'g & Loan, 187 A. at 483.
130. Ibid.
131. Ibid., 486–94.

Administrative Law

CHAPTER 25

The Supreme Court and Administrative Law

JOHN L. GEDID

I. INTRODUCTION: WHAT IS ADMINISTRATIVE LAW?

Administrative law consists of the standards and principles that (1) form the structure or guide for the branches and agencies of government in conducting their business and (2) define the relationship and actions of government and citizens in transactions between them. Because the Pennsylvania Constitution was drafted in general terms, one important function of administrative law is to create a template or operational guide for the conduct of government consistent with the general instructions of the Constitution. To that end, the three branches of government act to fill gaps in the operation of government: the legislature creates administrative law by enacting statutes, the judiciary interprets and explains the general provisions of the Pennsylvania Constitution and statutes, and executive agencies decide cases and enact regulations that interpret statutes regarding the conduct of government. Administrative law is a major part of government law—the law by which, or under which, the government operates.

II. THE SUPREME COURT'S ADMINISTRATIVE LAW JURISPRUDENCE

The Pennsylvania Supreme Court has made significant contributions to administrative law in a number of areas. Those areas include (1) cases in which administrative statutes and regulations operated unfairly and violated the Pennsylvania and US Constitutions; (2) cases in which the Supreme Court interpreted and applied new principles of administrative and constitutional law within the Pennsylvania court system; (3) cases in which the Supreme Court used the concept of separation of powers to define the boundaries between, and the powers of, the executive, legislative, and judicial branches of government, a process that frequently involves cases relating to governmental agencies; (4) cases asserting the doctrine known as the inherent power of the judiciary, for which the Court has received national recognition;[1] and (5) cases in which the Court improved the body of law on the scope and standard of judicial review of agency action by reintroducing the standard of "capricious disregard of evidence."

Agencies carry out the commands of the legislature. When an agency renders a decision, it is acting as an agent of the legislature or the executive. When a claimant appeals from an agency decision to a court, the claimant in effect asks the court to overturn an action of the legislature or an action of the executive. However, the legislature, executive, and judiciary are coequal branches of government under the Pennsylvania Constitution. This coequal status means that the Supreme Court cannot simply retry a decision that comes to it from an agency, because to do so would be setting aside a legitimate action of a coequal branch of government. So the Supreme Court, like the federal courts and the supreme courts of other states, has adopted a standard of review that protects citizens from arbitrary or unconstitutional agency action but at the same time respects the constitutional status and power of the legislature and executive.

A. Fair Procedure: The Procedural Due Process Doctrine

The Pennsylvania and US Constitutions guarantee procedural due process to citizens when the government takes action that affects life, liberty, or property.[2] By definition, a major part of administrative law includes cases between a citizen and a government agency, a type of interaction that falls within the guarantees of Article I, Section 1 of the Pennsylvania Constitution.[3] The Supreme Court has actively developed this area of the law. In several instances, the Court has also created law that anticipated similar action by the US Supreme Court and the supreme courts of other states.

At its most basic level, the concept of procedural due process implements the concept that when governmental action affects a citizen's life, liberty, or property, the government must use a procedure that is fair. As will be seen, the basic concept of fairness embodied in procedural due process has evolved over the years through judicial precedents focused on answering several general questions. First, since not all government action that affects citizens is subject to the requirements of procedural due process under the Constitution, is the particular government action affecting a citizen subject to the protections of procedural due process? This determination turns on whether the action involves life, liberty, or property rights or interests. Earlier law provided that procedural due process was implicated only if a citizen's life, liberty, or property *right* was taken or adversely affected. Second, if the first question was answered in the affirmative (i.e., a life, liberty, or property right is involved), then what procedure does due process require?

The Supreme Court's answers to these questions have often been consistent with US Supreme Court precedents. Generally, a citizen must receive adequate and timely notice of the action that the government is going to take, the citizen must have a fair opportunity to be heard (essentially, to tell his or her side of the story), and the hearing must be conducted by a neutral, unbiased, and unprejudiced official.

B. Early Procedural Due Process

For many years, the Supreme Court followed the traditional, so-called right/privilege analysis in order to determine whether the protections of procedural due process were available to a claimant.[4] Under this test, the Court characterized the subject matter of the proceeding as either a right or a mere privilege. If the Court decided that it was a right, then the protections of procedural due process attached; if a privilege, procedural due process did not apply and the government did not have to provide a hearing. Traditional items of property easily satisfied this test. For example, where a hunting license was to be revoked or taken away, the Supreme Court, like the courts in many other states, held that a license to hunt is a mere privilege.[5] Under this earlier approach, a license was not property like, for example, a parcel of real estate or an automobile. Therefore, because a license was not a species of property to which a person has an absolute right, the state had the power to suspend or revoke the license without a hearing. Procedural due process simply did not apply. On the other hand, if the government action affects something that qualifies as a property, life, or liberty *right*, procedural due process applies. For example, before the state can take a citizen's bank account, due process entitles the citizen to notice and an opportunity to be heard before a neutral tribunal.

The right/privilege test was criticized by many scholars and judges.[6] The basis for the criticism was that the test was subjective and did not provide any guidance; there were no standards or objective criteria that differentiated a right from a privilege. Each judge simply characterized or classified the right or injury asserted based on a subjective understanding of what constituted a right. A second criticism was that many of the disputes involved dealings with the government. It was thought that such dealings had become a major source of income and wealth for many in our society. The right/privilege test did not recognize what was asserted to be a form of property.

The right/privilege test answered the first of two questions that arose in connection with a claim of procedural due process protection. The first question was, Is this claimant eligible for the protections of the procedural due process doctrine? If the answer was affirmative according to the right/privilege doctrine, then the second question was, What are the procedures that due process requires? As noted, the answer was generally notice and an opportunity to be heard before a fair tribunal.

Most of the cases on this subject involved examination of what action would satisfy each of the procedural requirements. For instance, although there is no set form of notice, the Supreme Court held that the notice must be sufficient for the citizen to present his or her position to the tribunal.[7] Also, the state must inform the citizen with "reasonable certainty of the substance of the charges against him so that he may adequately prepare a defense."[8] The Supreme Court held that the second requirement—opportunity to be heard—means that the claimant must be given the opportunity to hear the evidence, cross-examine witnesses, present evidence on the claimant's own behalf, and present argument.[9]

With some minor modifications, the requirements of notice and an opportunity to be heard remain the essential requirements of procedural due process in Pennsylvania.

C. The Federal "Due Process Revolution"

In 1970, the US Supreme Court decided *Goldberg v. Kelly*,[10] which began what has since been called the "due process revolution."[11] The gist of *Goldberg*, and two later decisions explaining *Goldberg*,[12] was that procedural due process applied to the deprivation of *both* rights and interests. The term *interest* in this context was described as a "legitimate claim of entitlement"[13] against the government. According to the US Supreme Court, this concept recognized that in modern times, government has much more contact with its citizens and many forms of wealth come from government. State employment, welfare, and disability payments, for instance, might create a "legitimate claim of entitlement."[14] What *Goldberg* and its progeny meant was that government benefits such as disability payments and welfare, as well as expectations created by a statute or a citizen's contract with the government, were henceforth subject to the protection of procedural due process.[15] This approach was a substantial expansion of the doctrine.

The description in *Goldberg* of these "interests" was general and left open the question of which types of government contacts or connection created a legitimate claim of entitlement. As a result, after *Goldberg*, individuals brought thousands of cases claiming the procedural due process right to a hearing as holders of an interest in life, liberty, or property.[16] Because the protections of the federal Due Process Clause apply to the states, this revolution took place in both state and federal courts.

D. Procedural Due Process in Pennsylvania

The Pennsylvania Supreme Court played a key role in interpreting procedural due process both before and after *Goldberg*. First, the Court decided cases prior to *Goldberg* that recognized procedural due process protections for those "interests" that its federal counterpart later described in the *Goldberg* case. Second, the Court extended procedural due process protections to situations beyond those recognized in *Goldberg*.

An example of the first type of case, where the Supreme Court anticipated *Goldberg*, was *Man O'War Racing Association v. State Horse Racing Commission*,[17] a case decided in 1969, one year before *Goldberg*. There, the Court recognized that some situations not involving property rights nevertheless merit the protections of procedural due process. An unsuccessful applicant for one of four state-issued horse racing licenses brought an action seeking judicial review of the state agency's denial of its application. In an opinion authored by Justice Samuel J. Roberts, the Court reasoned that although the racing license sought was not property, the "stakes" involved were "very valuable" because they would enable the licensee to make large sums of money and also pay significant taxes to the state. The expense of the application fee and cost of preparing the extensive application, taken together, constituted a substantial financial stake that should be reviewable by a court.[18] The Supreme Court's decision rejected the right/privilege lockstep, which would have held that the award of the license was not a property *right*, and prepared for the transition to the property *interest* approach to procedural due process ushered in by *Goldberg*.

In *Pennsylvania Coal Mining Association v. Insurance Department*,[19] decided seven years after *Goldberg*, the Court recognized *Goldberg*'s "new property" in a factual situation where it was not obvious.[20] In that opinion, Justice Roberts explained that the new property concept meant that the old right/privilege dichotomy was no longer the law.[21]

The real significance of *Pennsylvania Coal Mining Ass'n* is its application of *Goldberg* in a situation where there was no *express* statutory grant or claim created by the text of the applicable statutes, as some argued that *Goldberg* required in order to create a property "interest."[22] In *Pennsylvania Coal Mining Ass'n*, Pennsylvania statutes required all mining companies to purchase workers' compensation insurance.[23] Under the applicable insurance statute, the rates for workers' compensation insurance are set once each year by a rating agency. But that statute did not provide an opportunity for any input from the mining companies.[24] Thus they were required to purchase workers' compensation insurance (at substantially increased rates, they claimed) with no opportunity for input on the need for, or amount of, the rate increases.

Employing the *Goldberg* analysis, the Supreme Court concluded that the mining companies had a property interest. Justice Roberts explained that a property interest exists even when there is no express statutory creation of a right or entitlement. He opined that such a limited definition of property interest (namely, express recognition in a statute) amounted to reliance on the old right/privilege characterization.[25] Instead, determining whether due process protections extend to a situation, even in the absence of an express statutory creation, requires a court also to examine the nature of the government activity and the extent of legitimate citizen reliance on that activity.[26] Justice Roberts then applied this new formulation: First, the regulation was comprehensive because it bound every mining company in Pennsylvania. Second, rates for insurance set by the rating bureau were binding on all mining companies. Third, the coal companies had no opportunity for input on rate increases. This combination of required insurance, binding rates, and lack of notice and an opportunity to be heard enabled the mining companies to claim the protections of procedural due process.[27]

There are several important features of the *Pennsylvania Coal Mining Ass'n* opinion. First, it understands that a new property interest can arise in many different, flexible, and diverse ways. Justice Roberts found that although there is no explicit entitlement, it is difficult to argue that the right to do business competitively had not been substantially impaired or taken away by the regulatory scheme applicable to the miners. The case creates a precedent for the proposition that dealing with government agencies can involve widely divergent relationships, many of which do not neatly fit traditional property categories, yet such dealings should still be subject to procedural due process protections. That approach is one of the defining characteristics—and advances—of the "new property" approach fashioned by the Supreme Court.

1. An Opportunity to Be Heard

The Supreme Court has also addressed and resolved one of the major recurring problems involving the opportunity of a claimant to be heard: the irrebuttable presumption. The term refers to the idea that some regulations or statutes, usually aimed at public safety, create a presumption of incapacity that the affected citizen is prohibited from challenging or rebutting. For example, the Pennsylvania Department of Transportation (PennDOT) has adopted a regulation that suspends a driver's license for one year upon a required report from a doctor that the driver has suffered an epileptic seizure. Under this regulation, the suspension is immediate upon notice of the seizure, and the driver is not permitted to testify, argue, or introduce evidence such as doctors' reports or depositions that medical treatment has controlled the seizures.[28]

In *PennDOT v. Clayton*,[29] David Clayton had suffered a grand mal epileptic seizure for which he sought and received medical treatment. His doctor reported the seizure to PennDOT, as required, but his report stated that it was safe for Clayton to drive because his seizures were controlled by medication. PennDOT nevertheless suspended Clayton's license for one year pursuant to its standard regulation. PennDOT took this action unilaterally without giving any type of hearing to Clayton, and he appealed. On consideration, the Supreme Court found that a driver's license is a property interest protected by procedural due process under the *Goldberg* test. Before it can be taken away, the Court held, the state must provide an opportunity for the driver to show that the epilepsy is controlled. This ruling limited the use of irrebuttable presumptions in favor of due process protections, and subsequent cases followed suit.[30]

2. A Fair and Neutral Judge

Although our constitutional structure is premised on a separation of powers between the three branches of government, agencies often perform all three functions themselves: legislation,[31] execution (or carrying out of the laws), and adjudication. In a situation involving enforcement of a regulation, for instance, the same agency not only helps promulgate the regulation but also identifies, prosecutes, and adjudicates violations. Uniting these functions in the same agency creates two potential problems. First, it creates the appearance of unfairness: persons litigating with the agency often believe that they cannot receive a fair hearing when the prosecutor and judge are part of the same company or government entity. In particular, such persons believe that the judge employed by the agency bringing the prosecution will be more likely to side with the prosecutor representing the same agency rather than remain neutral. This belief is not based on actual prejudice or bias but on the *appearance* of bias. Second, uniting separate functions might actually lead to a temptation on the part of the agency adjudicator to act in a biased or prejudiced fashion because, after all, the agency pays his or her salary.

The Supreme Court examined these problems in a series of creative decisions that go far toward eliminating both actual bias and the appearance of bias. In *In re Schlesinger*,[32] a committee appointed by a trial court made the decision to bring an action to disbar Schlesinger, an attorney. The same committee then heard evidence and recommended disbarment to the trial court, which accepted the recommendation without hearing or review. On appeal, the Supreme Court held that mingling prosecutorial and adjudicatory functions in the same committee violated Schlesinger's due process right to a fair hearing by a fair tribunal. Similarly, in *Dussia v. Barger*,[33] the Supreme Court found a due process violation where the commissioner of the state police both initiated the prosecution and then adjudicated the employment termination of a subordinate officer. According to the Court, "The decision to institute a prosecution . . . is a decision which requires a judgment as to the weight of the evidence against the accused, a judgment which is incompatible with the judicial function of providing an impartial forum for resolution of the issues presented."[34]

In *Gardner v. Repasky*,[35] a member of a local civil service board brought a complaint against a tenured employee. The same member then sat on the board and voted at the hearing on the complaint. The Supreme Court held that commingling the prosecutorial and judging functions violated the employee's right to a fair trial because even the appearance of unfairness was improper.

The Supreme Court rendered its most important decision in this area in the 1992 case of *Lyness v. State Bd. of Medicine*.[36] In *Lyness*, a subcommittee of three members of the state medical board decided to prosecute a physician for unethical behavior toward patients and then sat on the medical board when it decided to revoke the physician's medical license. The physician appealed, arguing that he had a property right in his license and his due process right to a fair hearing was violated when the same board members both prosecuted him and decided his fate. The Supreme Court agreed. First, in addressing the question of whether due process protections were available to the physician, the Court concluded that he had a property *right* in his professional license. Relying on the Pennsylvania Constitution,[37] Justice Cappy, citing *Soja v. Pa. State Police*,[38] opined that the holder of a license to practice a calling or profession has a property *right* to that license and is therefore protected by due process constitutional guarantees. Note that this is an extension of the federal approach from *Goldberg*,[39] which described individual relationships with the government such as licenses as property *interests*. This was a significant step because it emphasized that full procedural due process protections apply to all licenses that involve a job, calling, or profession.

The Supreme Court's resolution of the second issue—which procedure should have been provided to the physician—was another major step forward in the development of procedural due process law in Pennsylvania. In particular, the Court noted that actual bias is not necessary so long as the *appearance* of bias arises from the comingling of functions, as it did when the medical board suspended the physician's license. This too was a significant advance because of the difficulty of proving actual bias unless the state official has been careless enough to make public statements that demonstrate prejudice. Justice Cappy cited both *Dussia v. Barger*[40] and *Gardner v. Repasky*[41] as supporting his conclusion that the appearance of bias in the tribunal is a violation of the requirements of procedural due process. This holding broadened the due process right of a fair tribunal.

Yet the *Lyness* Court also recognized that many agencies inevitably continue to simultaneously prosecute and adjudicate. To accommodate this reality, the Court held that agencies must separate the two functions.[42] As the Court put it, the agency must erect "walls of division" that eliminate the appearance of bias as well as the threat of actual bias.[43]

In *Stone & Edwards Insurance Agency v. Department of Insurance*,[44] the Court held that the action of the insurance department in assigning the investigation and prosecution functions to the deputy insurance commissioner while retaining the adjudicative/judging function in the commission was a sufficient separation to satisfy *Lyness*.[45] Also, the Court has held that *Lyness* is not offended where an agency board member makes the decision to prosecute a licensee but then plays no role in the adjudication of that case.[46]

III. SEPARATION OF POWERS / INHERENT POWER OF THE JUDICIARY

The Separation of Powers doctrine, which identifies distinct roles for each branch of government, was included in the Pennsylvania Constitutions of 1790, 1838, 1873, and 1968.[47] The Supreme Court has developed and refined an extensive body of case law regarding the doctrine in the context of Pennsylvania's unique history.

The purpose of separating powers is to prevent the accumulation of absolute power in a single body, for that, as James Madison said, would constitute the "very definition of tyranny."[48] Separation of powers consists of two different components: (1) each branch must only exercise the power that the Constitution assigns to it, and (2) each branch may defend itself by bringing a suit to stop another branch's encroachment. This is Madison's system of "checks and balances."[49] The second (or checking) power means that when one branch invades the power assigned to another, the invaded branch has an incentive to protest and to bring suit to have the invasive action declared unconstitutional.

Despite the theoretical clarity of the doctrine, the Supreme Court has acknowledged that the boundaries between the branches of Pennsylvania government are "indistinct and probably incapable of any precise or exact definition."[50] As a result, frequently one branch will challenge the action of another branch, alleging a violation of the doctrine.[51] The lack of exactness includes, or might be caused by, some "overlap" between the powers of the various branches of government.[52]

It is important to note that clashes over separation of powers among the branches of government have become a key part of administrative law. The Pennsylvania Constitution contains general terms that define the structure of government. But because the Constitution's terms are indefinite, they provide only a general guide or outline for the structure and operation of state government. This means that provision for the actual operation of the government must occur through legislation. The vehicle that the Pennsylvania and federal legislatures use to fill the gap is the creation of agencies to perform governmental functions. As a result, the Pennsylvania Constitution and the statutes that deal with agency creation and jurisdiction define the structure of government in Pennsylvania. This structure often implicates separation of powers issues. Such issues arise, for instance, when the legislature attempts to assign to one branch of government a function that the Constitution vests in a different branch.[53]

Commonwealth v. Mockaitis[54] is an example of this problem. In that case, the legislature assigned to the judiciary the task of verifying whether ignition interlock devices were installed on the cars of drivers repeatedly convicted of driving under the influence (DUI). In *Mockaitis*, the Supreme Court struck down that delegation on the basis that executive authority must be exercised by the governor, not the courts.[55]

One pervasive problem arising from the separation of powers involves the "nondelegation doctrine." For example, the Pennsylvania Constitution provides that the legislature is to make laws.[56] Often the legislature creates a new agency to deal with a problem and empowers that agency to take various actions, including enacting regulations, which have the force of law. The question that arises is whether empowering an agency to enact regulations improperly transfers or delegates the legislature's exclusive power to make law.

The Supreme Court addressed this issue in *Tosto v. Pennsylvania Nursing Home Loan Agency*.[57] In that case, the legislature created an agency to provide low-cost loans to nursing homes to enable them to improve their physical plants and thereby meet new federal guidelines. The agency possessed the power to make rules to govern eligibility and the distribution of loans. The plaintiff, Tosto, made the classic nondelegation argument that the legislature could not delegate this power to the agency because it amounted to transferring the power to make laws to the agency, a function exclusively assigned to the legislature.

The Supreme Court held that there was no violation of the nondelegation rule. The rule means only that the basic policy choices must be made by the legislature, the Court held, and the legislature had properly made the choice to provide loans to nursing homes. Because the legislature's policy choice furnished identifiable standards that limited the agency's discretion, there was no violation of the nondelegation rule. *Tosto* stands for the proposition that the Constitution is not offended when an agency is merely carrying out the command of the legislature or filling in details of the legislature's policy choice.[58]

Another separation-of-powers problem arises from the nature or extent of the delegation of power. For example, in an attempt to fully discharge its duties, an agency might attempt to exercise its jurisdiction in areas where there has been no express delegation of jurisdiction. Analogously, one branch of government might attempt to exercise a power that does not fit easily within the definition of the power assigned to it in the Constitution. Are there any powers not enumerated—that is, not expressly included in the text of the Pennsylvania Constitution—that an agency or branch of government is permitted to exercise?

The Supreme Court has described this issue as whether agencies and branches possess any *implied* powers in addition to the express powers spelled out in the Constitution.

In several cases, the Supreme Court has stated that agency authority must be "clear and unmistakable, and that the agency must act within the exact limits defined."[59] However, the Court has also decided many cases in which it found implied power that was not conferred in express language. The express language requirement is "tempered" by a rule of legislative construction recognizing that an agency possesses such implied powers as are necessary to carry out its legislative mandate or mission.[60] As the Supreme Court has explained, "[W]e recognize that the General Assembly has prescribed that legislative enactments are generally to be construed in such a manner as to effect their objects and promote justice . . . and, in assessing a statute, courts are directed to consider the consequences of a particular interpretation, as well as other factors enumerated in the Statutory Construction Act."[61] For example, although the Constitution assigns the function of making laws to the legislature, judicial rulemaking (the creation of procedural rules) is a form of legislation. Nonetheless, the Supreme Court has held that procedural rules are so closely linked functionally and historically to judicial action that an exception exists for such rules.[62]

Clashes between the judiciary and the legislature have also spawned issues involving the separation of powers. The Pennsylvania Constitution assigns the power to tax and provide the money to support the judiciary to the legislature, and it assigns the power to decide cases to the judiciary. Thus, in a sense, both the legislature and the judiciary share the task of rendering justice in cases: the legislature provides the money to fund the judiciary, and the judiciary actually hears the cases and renders judgment. But the area of judicial funding has been a source of problems in Pennsylvania for many years. In particular, the legislature and the courts have differed sharply over the amount of money needed for the courts to operate.

A Pennsylvania statute creates a system of funding trial courts at the county level. Under this statute, local trial courts submit budgets to the county commissioners, and the commissioners fund the courts.[63] However, there have been disagreements over the number of employees the courts need,[64] employee salaries,[65] and whether the county must pay the expenses of jurors required to sleep over in capital cases.[66] In one leading case, the Supreme Court described the number of cases involving deadlock between the courts and the county commissioners to be so numerous that it had led to "fragmentation"[67] of the judicial system.

In order to deal with this problem, the Supreme Court drew on the concept of the inherent power of the courts, a doctrine that is an important part of separation of powers. Early inherent judicial power cases involved situations where the legislature attempted to reduce the salary of a judge during his or her term in office. In the case *Commonwealth ex rel. Hepburn v. Mann*,[68] the legislature imposed a specific tax on trial judges after enacting a statute setting the amount of their salaries. The judges then brought an action in which they argued that under the Pennsylvania Constitution of 1790, then in force, the legislature could not lower the salaries of judges during their terms in office.

The Supreme Court agreed. Its decision was based in large part on lessons learned in the past and enshrined in the Pennsylvania Constitution to preserve the independence of the judiciary. The Court reasoned that long experience has taught that, in every type of government, it is necessary to safeguard the rights of citizens from encroachment or invasion by government.[69] Specifically, the basis for separation of powers flows from the recognition that the judiciary is the weakest branch and therefore must be carefully protected from the "encroachments" of the other branches.[70] The purpose of separation is that all branches—and especially the judiciary—would remain "unbiassed, uninfluenced and independent," and "power over a man's subsistence amounts to a power over his will."[71] Moreover, "the complete independence of the judiciary is a fundamental principle of the Constitution, designed mainly for the protection of public and private rights. . . . [and] [t]his independence of the Judges is equally requisite to guard the Constitution and rights of individuals."[72]

In the more recent case of *Leahey v. Farrell*,[73] the Supreme Court again gave a clear explanation of the rationale for separation of powers in the Pennsylvania Constitution. The judicial power of the Commonwealth is vested in the judiciary. The doctrine of separation of powers means that the legislature cannot interfere with the exercise of the judicial power; for example, the legislature cannot attempt to overrule a decision of the courts or mandate that a statute be construed in a certain way.[74] On the other hand, the power over state finances belongs to the legislature, subject to constitutional limitations.[75] Thus the judiciary and the legislature share the duty to make a system of justice available to the citizenry: in the normal course, the legislature has the duty to provide funds for the judiciary to operate[76] and the judiciary has the duty to hear cases and deliver judgment. If the legislature does not, or assigns an amount that is insufficient for the administration of justice by the judiciary, then the judiciary may exercise inherent jurisdiction to order payment of money sufficient for the efficient operation of the judiciary out of the public fisc.[77] However, the judiciary must establish the reasonable necessity of the funds it demands.[78]

IV. JUDICIAL REVIEW OF ADMINISTRATIVE ACTION

Does a citizen have an opportunity to seek the protection of the judiciary when an administrative agency (state or local) takes action that harms him or her? For example, if an agency takes action that affects a citizen's right or interest, does the citizen have the right to seek to overturn the agency action by an appeal to the courts? This question is answered in the Pennsylvania Constitution of 1968, which expressly gives jurisdiction to the courts to review most types of agency action.[79] The language of Article V, Section 9 of the Constitution requires the legislature to enact a statute that includes the power of a citizen to appeal to the courts from an adverse administrative decision. The legislature has done so in a statute known as the Administrative Agency Law (AAL),[80] which provides that a "person aggrieved" by a decision of a "Commonwealth Agency" has the right to appeal to a court of record.[81]

Although this language appears to be clear, the fact that it appears in a Constitution based on a separation of powers creates a serious problem. When the legislature creates an agency, it intends the *agency*—not the courts—to make decisions in that area.[82] There is also good reason for judicial deference to agency action because the agency brings particular expertise to the area of its jurisdiction.[83]

Yet citizens must also have recourse, through judicial review, for agency actions. The constitutional right to judicial review of agency action is not only well established by judicial precedent[84] but, as noted, expressly guaranteed by the Constitution. If there were no judicial review of agency action, there would be no check on the power of the legislature, for it could act through its creature, the agency.[85] For example, if the legislature enacted a statute that empowered an agency to interfere with the right of free speech, then without judicial review it would be difficult to check the agency to protect freedom of speech.[86] Moreover, what if an agency oversteps its jurisdictional boundaries? For example, what if an agency created to maintain the price of milk attempted to control the price of gasoline? Such hypotheticals indicate the necessity of judicial review, which allows the judicial branch to act *cooperatively* with the legislature by forcing the agency to carry out the mission, and only the mission, that the legislature assigned to it.

But the judiciary also faces a dilemma when it reviews administrative action. If the courts give too much deference to agency decisions, then the right of a citizen to judicial review, the separation of powers, and the duty of the courts to review legislative actions for constitutional violations are watered down or nullified entirely. If the courts give too little deference to agency action, then the courts have substituted themselves as the decision maker in a situation where the legislature has indicated in the agency charter or in another statute that the agency, not the court, should be the decision maker.

The Pennsylvania legislature and the judiciary have resolved many of these problems. The legislative contributions to the solution are the AAL provisions dedicated to judicial review.[87] Since the terms of this judicial review statute are general, it has been necessary for the judiciary to construe the statutory language. The reasons for which the courts may overturn agency action are set forth in Section 704 of the AAL: "[T]he court shall affirm the adjudication unless it shall find that the adjudication is in violation of the constitutional rights of the appellant, or is not in accordance with law, or that the provisions of Subchapter A of Chapter 5 (relating to practice and procedure of Commonwealth agencies) have been violated in the proceedings before the agency, or that any finding of fact made by the agency and necessary to support its adjudication is not supported by substantial evidence."[88]

Over the years, the Supreme Court has addressed each of these concepts of judicial review of the AAL (violation of constitutional rights, violation of procedural requirements not in accordance with law, and lack of substantial evidence).[89] More recently, the Supreme Court clarified one area of judicial review that had spawned significant confusion. That clarification affected the "arbitrary and capricious" standard as well as the "lack of substantial evidence" standard of review. It was a distinct clarification and an advance in the area of judicial review.

Wintermyer v. Workers' Compensation Appeal Board (Marlowe) precipitated this change.[90] There, an employee sought workers' compensation benefits based on carpal tunnel syndrome. The workers' compensation judge (WCJ) found for the employer and denied benefits on the basis that the injury had begun long before the claim, despite the fact that the employee alone presented medical expert testimony. Two subsequent levels of appellate review, in the Workers' Compensation Appeal Board (WCAB) and the Commonwealth Court, reversed the WCJ, finding that its decision was made in capricious disregard of the evidence. The employer appealed to the Supreme Court, arguing that the capricious disregard standard was no longer relevant because it had been removed from the AAL when it was amended in 1978.[91] The Supreme Court held that despite the change to the statute, the capricious disregard standard is still appropriate, particularly where recovery has been denied. But because the WCJ's decision was not made in capricious disregard of the evidence, it was reinstated.[92] This case clarified confusion regarding what the capricious disregard standard means and, further, confirmed that the standard remains applicable.

It is now well established that in areas where the legislature has delegated discretion to agencies, it would be a violation of separation of powers[93] for a court to substitute its judgment as to reasonableness for that of the agency. The only exception occurs if the agency action is arbitrary and capricious or in capricious disregard of the evidence presented to the fact finder. In that situation, the reviewing court's inquiry is not "What is the more or most reasonable outcome?" but "Is the agency action *unreasonable*?" In order to make certain that lower appellate courts understand that permitting capricious disregard review is not a license to adopt a generalized reasonableness test that permits a court to substitute its own judgment about what is more reasonable, the *Wintermyer* Court emphasized that capricious disregard review is "limited" and "deferential."[94] The Court concluded with the caution that capricious disregard review is intended only to "assure that the agency adjudication has been conducted within lawful boundaries—it is not to be applied in such a manner as would intrude upon the agency's fact-finding role and discretionary decision-making authority."[95]

V. CONCLUSION

This discussion illustrates the Supreme Court's careful approach to developing Pennsylvania's body of administrative law. In the area of delegation, the Supreme Court has kept the Commonwealth abreast of developments in the federal and other state courts. In the area of separation of powers, Pennsylvania has been at the forefront of defining the proper constitutional balance between the branches of government. The Supreme Court has also led the way in several areas that, when decided, were unique. Its approach to providing a fair tribunal is an advance over the federal approach, which allows more leeway to the agency in providing tribunals that have participated in earlier parts of a case. The Supreme Court has also led the way in the area of the inherent power of the judiciary, an important characteristic in this age where many persons and entities are attempting to lessen the independence of the judiciary and where fiscal weapons are commonly used for this purpose. Finally, the Court's thoughtful balancing of the needs of the citizenry and the prerogatives of government is reflected in its development of the capricious disregard standard of review, a unique and positive approach to the problem created when agencies irrationally ignore evidence. In all of these areas, the Supreme Court has substantially improved administrative law in the Commonwealth.

NOTES

John L. Gedid is a professor emeritus at Widener University School of Law.

1. *Inherent power* means that when the legislature refuses to fund or takes other action that impedes the basic operations of the Pennsylvania judiciary, the court may assert a power to defend itself as a coequal branch of government in a lawsuit and order the other branch to take appropriate action to fund the judiciary.
2. Pennsylvania Constitution, Article I, § 1 provides, "All men are born equally free and independent, and have certain inherent and indefeasible rights, among which are those of enjoying and defending life and liberty, of acquiring, possessing and protecting property and reputation, and of pursuing their own happiness."
3. Ibid.
4. *E.g.*, Cement Nat'l Bank v. Dep't of Banking, 230 A.2d 209 (Pa. 1967); Del. Cnty. Nat'l Bank v. Campbell, 106 A.2d 416, 421 (Pa. 1954).
5. Pennsylvania Game Comm'n v. Marich, 666 A.2d 253 (Pa. 1995).
6. William W. VanAlstyne, "The Demise of the Right-Privilege Doctrine in Constitutional Law," *Harvard Law Review* 81 (1968): 1439; Edward L. Rubin, "Due Process and the Administrative State," *California Law Review* 72 (1984): 1044; Donald A. Dripps, "Delegation and Due Process," *Duke Law Journal* (1988): 657.
7. Dep't of Transp. v. McCafferty, 758 A.2d 1155 (Pa. 1999).
8. Dep't of Transp. v. Sutton, 400 A.2d 1305 (Pa. 1979).
9. Callahan v. Pa. State Police, 431 A.2d 946, 948 (Pa. 1981).
10. 397 U.S. 254 (1970).
11. *See* Henry J. Friendly, "Some Kind of Hearing," *University of Pennsylvania Law Review* 123 (1975): 1267, 1268.
12. Those cases are Perry v. Sindermann, 408 U.S. 593 (1972); and Bd. of Regents of State Colls. v. Roth, 408 U.S. 564 (1972).

13. Perry, 408 U.S. at 602; Roth, 408 U.S. at 577.
14. Roth, 408 U.S. at 577–78.
15. Charles A. Reich, "Individual Rights and Social Welfare: The Emerging Legal Issues," *Yale Law Journal* 74 (1965): 1255.
16. Some descriptions of the cases can be found in Jason Parkin, "Adaptable Due Process," *University of Pennsylvania Law Review* 160 (2012): 1309, 1323–25; Fred O. Smith Jr., "Due Process Republicanism and Democracy," *New York University Law Review* 89 (2014): 599–606; Wright S. Walling and Gary Debele, "Private Chips Petitions in Minnesota," *William Mitchell Law Review* 20 (1994): 800; Karen H. Flax, "Liberty Property and the Burger Court," *Tulane Law Review* 60 (1986): 889.
17. 250 A.2d 172 (Pa. 1969).
18. Ibid., 176.
19. Pennsylvania Coal Mining Ass'n v. Ins. Dep't, 370 A.2d 685, 691 (Pa. 1977).
20. Charles Reich, "The New Property," *Yale Law Journal* 73 (1964): 733; Paul R. Verkuil, "Revisiting the New Property After Twenty-Five Years," *William and Mary Law Review* 31 (1990): 365.
21. Pennsylvania Coal Mining Ass'n, 370 A.2d at 689.
22. The applicable statutes were the Federal Coal Mine Health and Safety Act of 1969, § 423, as amended, 30 U.S.C. § 933 (Supp. 1976); Pennsylvania Workmen's Compensation Act, Act of June 2, 1915, P.L. 736, § 305, as amended, 77 P.S. § 501 (Supp. 1976), as explained in *Pennsylvania Coal Mining*, 370 A.2d 688n1.
23. Pennsylvania Coal Mining Ass'n, 370 A.2d at 689.
24. Ibid., 688–89.
25. Ibid., 690.
26. Ibid.
27. The Court also examined the issue of what process was due, but the resolution of that question is straightforward.
28. PennDOT took this action under the authority of a statute, 75 Pa.C.S. § 1519 Determination

of Incompetency, by enacting a regulation that required a physician to report treatment of an epileptic seizure and providing for immediate surrender of the patient's driver license. The regulation provided the following: "A person who has a seizure disorder will not be qualified to drive unless a licensed physician reports that the person has been free from seizure for at least 6 months immediately preceding, with or without medication. A person will not be disqualified if the person has experienced only auras during that period."

67 Pa. Code § 83.4(a).

29. 684 A.2d 1060 (Pa. 1996).
30. D.C. v. Sch. Dist. of Philadelphia, 879 A.2d 408 (Pa. Cmwlth. 2005); Volk v. Unemp. Comp. Bd. Rev., 49 A.3d 38 (Pa. Cmwlth. 2012).
31. Agency legislation is referred to as regulation.
32. 172 A.2d 835 (Pa. 1961).
33. 351 A.2d 667 (Pa. 1975).
34. Ibid., 674.
35. 252 A.2d 704 (Pa. 1969).
36. 605 A.2d 1204 (Pa. 1992).
37. Ibid., 1207. Justice Cappy cited the following sections of the Pennsylvania Constitution:

Art. 1, § 1, which provides, "Inherent rights of mankind. All men are born equally free and independent, and have certain inherent and indefeasible rights, among which are those of enjoying and defending life and liberty, of acquiring, possessing and protecting property and reputation, and of pursuing their own happiness."

Art. 1, § 9, which further provides, Rights of accused in criminal prosecutions. In all criminal prosecutions the accused hath a right to be heard by himself and his counsel, to demand the nature and cause of the accusation against him, to be confronted with the witnesses against him, to have compulsory process for obtaining witnesses in his favor, and, in prosecutions by indictment or information, a speedy public trial by an impartial jury of the vicinage; he cannot be compelled to give evidence against himself, nor can he be deprived of his life, liberty or property, unless by the judgment of his peers or the law of the land. The use of a suppressed voluntary admission or voluntary confession to impeach the credibility of a person may be permitted and shall not be construed as compelling a person to give evidence against himself.

Finally, Art. 1, § 11, which provides, "Courts to be open; suits against the Commonwealth. All courts shall be open; and every man for an injury done him in his lands, goods, person or reputation shall have remedy by due course of law, and right and justice administered without sale, denial or delay. Suits may be brought against the Commonwealth in such manner, in such courts and in such cases as the Legislature may by law direct."

38. 455 A.2d 613, 615 (Pa. 1982).
39. 397 U.S. 254 (1970).
40. 351 A.2d 667 (Pa. 1975).
41. 252 A.2d 704 (Pa. 1969).
42. 605 A.2d at 1209–10.
43. Ibid., 1209.
44. 648 A.2d 304 (Pa. 1994).
45. Ibid., 308.
46. Office of Disciplinary Counsel v. Duffield, 644 A.2d 1186 (Pa. 1994).
47. *See* Beyers v. Richmond, 937 A.2d 1082, 1090 (Pa. 2011).
48. James Madison, *Federalist* No. 47, in *The Federalist Papers*, ed. Clinton Rossiter (New York: New American Library, 1961).
49. Jefferson County Court Appointed Employee Ass'n v. Pa. Labor Rel. Bd., 985 A.2d 697, 706 (Pa. 2009).
50. Stander v. Kelly, 250 A.2d 474, 482 (Pa. 1969).
51. Commonwealth ex rel. Jiulante v. County of Erie, 657 A.2d 1245, 1249 (Pa. 1995).
52. Beckert v. Warren, 439 A.2d 638, 643 (Pa. 1981).
53. Commonwealth v. Mockaitis, 834 A.2d 488 (Pa. 2001) (legislature assigned executive function to judiciary).
54. Ibid.
55. Mockaitis also reasoned that the action of the legislature was in interference with the independence of the judiciary because judicial employees were being commanded to perform acts by the legislature rather than the judiciary. Such action took away control of employees from the judiciary and thus constituted an interference with the power and independence of the judiciary.
56. "The legislative power of this Commonwealth shall be vested in a General Assembly, which shall consist of a Senate and a House of Representatives." Pa. Const. art. II, § 1 (1968).
57. 331 A.2d 198 (Pa. 1975).
58. Ibid., 202.
59. Pa. Human Relations Comm'n v. St. Joe Minerals Corp., 382 A.2d 731 (Pa. 1978); Volunteer Firemen's Relief Ass'n. v. Minehart, 227 A.2d

632 (Pa. 1967); Green v. Milk Control Comm'n, 16 A.2d 9 (Pa. 1940).

60. Ins. Fed'n of Pa., Inc. v. Dep't of Ins., 889 A.2d 550, 554 (Pa. 2005).

61. Commonwealth v. Beam, 788 A.2d 357, 359 (Pa. 2002).

62. In re 42 Pa.C.S. § 1703, 394 A.2d 444 (Pa. 1978).

63. 42 Pa.C.S. §§ 101–9913 (judiciary and judicial procedure).

64. Beckert, 430 A.2d 638.

65. Leahey v. Farrell, 66 A.2d 577 (Pa. 1949).

66. Comm'rs v. Hall, 7 Watts 290 (Pa. 1838).

67. Allegheny Cnty. v. Commonwealth, 534 A.2d 760 (Pa. 1988).

68. 5 Watts & Serg. 403 (Pa. 1843).

69. Ibid., 406.

70. Ibid., 407.

71. Ibid., 407, 408.

72. Ibid., 411.

73. 66 A.2d 577 (Pa. 1949).

74. Ibid., 579.

75. Ibid.

76. Ibid.

77. Ibid., 579–80.

78. Commonwealth ex rel. Carroll v. Tate, 274 A.2d 193 (Pa. 1971).

79. "There shall be a right of appeal in all cases to a court of record from a court not of record; and there shall also be a right of appeal from a court of record or from an administrative agency to a court of record or to an appellate court, the selection of such court to be as provided by law; and there shall be such other rights of appeal as may be provided by law." Pa. Const. art. V, § 9.

80. 2 Pa.C.S. §§ 101, *et seq.*; *see* 2 Pa.C.S. § 702 ("Any person aggrieved by an adjudication of a Commonwealth agency who has a direct interest in such adjudication shall have the right to appeal therefrom to the court vested with jurisdiction of such appeals by or pursuant to Title 42 [relating to judiciary and judicial procedure].").

81. The AAL defines a "commonwealth agency" as "[a]ny executive agency or independent agency." 2 Pa.C.S. § 101. It defines an "executive agency" as "[t]he Governor and the departments, boards, commissions, authorities and other officers and agencies of the Commonwealth government, but the term does not include any court or other officer or agency of the unified judicial system, the General Assembly and its officers and agencies, or any

independent agency." Ibid. Independent agencies are "[b]oards, commissions, authorities and other agencies and officers of the Commonwealth government which are not subject to the policy supervision and control of the Governor, but the term does not include any court or other officer or agency of the unified judicial system or the General Assembly and its officers and agencies." Ibid. The AAL defines local agencies as "[a] government agency other than a Commonwealth agency." Ibid.

These definitions of the AAL draw a line between most Pennsylvania agencies with statewide jurisdiction (Commonwealth agencies) and agencies that are part of local government (local agencies). Similar, but not identical, provisions govern appeals from the two different types of agency under the AAL.

82. Charles H. Koch and Richard Murphy, *Administrative Law Treatise*, § 9.14.

83. Ibid.

84. Hume Cofer, "Judicial Review of Agency Law Decisions on Scope of Agency Authority," *Baylor Law Review* 42 (1990): 255; Sarah H. Ludington, "Simplifying the Standard of Review in Appeals," *Journal of the National Association of Administrative Law Judiciary* 33 (2013): 585; Robert Force and Lawrence Griffith, "The Louisiana Administrative Procedure Act," *Louisiana Law Review* 42 (1982): 1227.

85. Alfred C. Aman Jr. and William T. Mayton, *Administrative Law*, 3rd ed. (Eagen, Minn.: West Academic, 2014), § 13.1.

86. Ibid.

87. 2 Pa.C.S. §§ 701–4, 751–54.

88. Ibid., § 704.

89. Detailed explanation of each of those standards is beyond the scope of this chapter.

90. 812 A.2d 478 (Pa. 2002).

91. Ibid., 485.

92. Ibid., 488.

93. For example, the legislature has made the agency its agent for the particular action. For a court to substitute its judgment for the agency's because the court believes that its resolution is more reasonable involves the court interfering with a power (delegation to an agency) of the legislature. Such interference is a violation of separation of powers.

94. Wintermyer, 812 A.2d at 486–87.

95. Ibid., 486–87.

Afterword

On behalf of my colleagues on the Supreme Court of Pennsylvania, past and present, I wish to express our great appreciation for the efforts of the many academics and legal professionals who have contributed to this historical portrait of the Supreme Court of Pennsylvania. In particular, the Court owes a special debt to John Hare and Dean Phillips for their vision and perseverance in shepherding this undertaking to fruition.

As an afterword to this first comprehensive history of this Court, I thought it appropriate to close with an overview of the work of the modern Court. The institution's current framework traces its roots to the most recent iteration of the Pennsylvania Constitution, consummated in 1968, which comprehensively revised the judiciary article. The Unified Judicial System (UJS) was created, and the Supreme Court was afforded general supervisory and administrative power over that system, from the tier of local magistrate district courts through the intermediate appellate courts. The 1968 Constitution also reposed rulemaking power in the Supreme Court, as well as the responsibility to regulate the practice of law.

From a decisional perspective, the centerpiece of what we do is select and resolve discretionary appeals involving matters of statewide importance, issues of first impression, or conflicts among decisions of the intermediate appellate courts. Each year, litigants across the Commonwealth file thousands of petitions for allowance of appeal, seeking the Court's review. From those, the Court selects about seventy to one hundred cases annually to be considered on their merits.

Given the heavy volume of requests for discretionary review, the case selection function is time consuming. The many petitions are divided equally among the chambers of the seven justices, who prepare internal reports offering a recommendation about whether each petition should be granted or denied. Thus on an average annual basis, each justice is responsible for the preparation of three to four hundred of these reports. Once a report is circulated, it is reviewed by all justices. The Court then votes to grant or deny the petition for allowance of appeal, and it takes only the affirmative vote of at least three of seven justices—less than a majority—to support a discretionary grant.

When considering the Supreme Court's screening function, I think it is important to remember that the litigants already have secured direct appellate review from an intermediate court, thereby vindicating the constitutional entitlement to an appeal. Accordingly, any additional appellate review is a matter of grace. Furthermore, in light of the way the Court is organized and attendant resource constraints, it simply could not handle thousands of appeals per year. For these reasons, the intermediate appellate courts—with decisional units often composed of three-judge panels—are tasked with discharging the appellate function in the vast majority of cases. This is very similar to the US Supreme Court, which receives some ten thousand certiorari petitions each year but entertains only seventy-five to eighty cases on their merits.

In terms of the kinds of matters that arise on the discretionary appeals docket, I note that our Supreme Court's jurisdiction is very broad, and thus, by charge, we are generalists. The cases we consider for review cover the gamut from criminal to civil to administrative matters and everything in between. Of course, the Court does not select all the appeals we must consider; there are a number of matters where we serve as the court of original appellate jurisdiction. Capital cases are a ready example.

I cannot overstate the impact that the death penalty cases have had on our workload during my tenure over the past two decades. In the discretionary-appeals arena, the Court can narrow and tailor the issues, whereas in direct appeals, we take the cases as they come to us. Moreover, given the stakes involved and the great commitment of legal professionals in the capital arena to their respective roles, each case generally has entailed resolution of a proliferation of issues. Legislative measures put into place in the 1990s, which were intended to limit the number of serial appeals, also had the effect of increasing the number of filings and expanding the individual presentations, since the appeals became more likely to serve as the exclusive vehicle permitting access to state postconviction review.

Our direct review also encompasses matters arising within the original jurisdiction of our intermediate appellate courts, such as certain suits against the Commonwealth. The General Assembly has more frequently taken to "fast-tracking" matters it considers to be important by allocating the responsibility for direct review immediately to our Court—for example, the licensure disputes arising in the 2000s pertaining to a fledgling gaming industry. Every ten years, the Court has the task of considering appeals from the final plans of legislative reapportionment commissions obliged to establish the boundaries of Pennsylvania voting districts.

In terms of the appeals slated for oral argument, the Supreme Court sits six times a year: twice in Philadelphia, twice in Pittsburgh, and twice in our state capitol in Harrisburg. These sessions are now videotaped, and gavel-to-gavel coverage of each session is later broadcasted by the Pennsylvania Cable Network.

In addition to the allocatur and appeal dockets, the Court also maintains a large miscellaneous docket, with many matters arising there also implicating the decisional function. These cover the range of petitions for review, original jurisdiction matters, petitions for

King's Bench review, and petitions from the federal courts for certification of questions of law. Last year, about 520 of these matters arose on the miscellaneous docket.

The other broad category of the Supreme Court's work encompasses its responsibilities for administrative and supervisory oversight. Overall, in matters of administration, the Supreme Court is responsible for maintaining a single, integrated judicial system and has supervisory power over all state courts. Much of this work is conducted with the assistance of the Administrative Office of Pennsylvania Courts (AOPC). The AOPC has offices across the state, but we now have a judicial center in the capitol complex in Harrisburg, where much of the administrative work is centralized. Considering the number and scale of its tasks, the AOPC is divided into units, a few of which I will mention to provide context.

The Research and Statistics Department keeps data on caseloads of county and local courts, including the numbers and types of matters and the ages of cases awaiting disposition. This information primarily serves as a tool to assess and implement policy initiatives, making the best use of the resources of the judicial system to ensure the timely and just disposition of cases.

The Judicial Programs Department has been involved in a number of interesting projects. For instance, through the department, an Office of Children and Families in the Courts has been created under the leadership of Justice Baer. The main objective is to protect children and promote strong families, with the corollary effort to shorten the length of time displaced children must wait for safe, permanent homes.

The Judicial Programs Department also assists judicial districts in the creation of special problem-solving courts, such as drug courts. Drug courts combine judicial supervision, drug treatment, and incentives in an effort to curtail drug addiction and crime. Similarly, mental health courts partner with policy makers to provide judicially supervised and community-based treatment programs for those afflicted with mental and emotional difficulties. Veterans' courts have been created to address the special circumstances of those who have served in our armed forces. More specifically, these tribunals assist veterans charged with nonviolent crimes through volunteer mentor training and the use of specialized probation officers. In terms of specialty courts, Justice Todd recently worked with the Allegheny County court system to create the first sex offender court, composed of judges with specialized knowledge in handling criminal proceedings against adult defendants charged with and convicted of Megan's Law offenses. This specialty court's overriding goal is increased community safety through a reduction in recidivism among sex offenders.

The AOPC also has units covering media communications, judicial security, judicial education, human resources, and judicial automation, which was overseen by Justice Eakin. Court finances are always an issue in these challenging budgetary times for government, and through legislative affairs and finance departments in the AOPC, we continue to work toward ensuring the availability of the necessary resources to fund our constitutional responsibilities and ensure the ends of justice. The AOPC publishes an annual report, which is available on the UJS website and offers a great deal more information about the Court's work performed through and with the AOPC.[1]

The *Thomson Reuters Pennsylvania Rules of Court* book[2] contains collections of the work the Court performs with the assistance of our eight rules committees: Appellate, Civil, Evidence, Criminal, Domestic Relations, Juvenile, Minor Court, and Orphans' Court. Within the procedural realm, these committees endeavor to maintain comprehensible, current, and workable rules to further the interests of the courts and the citizenry they serve.

The work of the Supreme Court also encompasses the supervision of six advisory boards. The Board of Law Examiners reviews applications for admission to the practice of law and administers bar examinations. The Continuing Legal Education Board, obviously, is responsible to administer the requirement for attorneys to continue their legal educations. The Disciplinary Board considers and investigates potential violations of professional standards by anyone subject to the Rules of Disciplinary Enforcement. The Lawyer's Fund for Client Security helps clients recover some or all of the losses occasioned by attorney misappropriations and nonperformance. The Interest on Lawyers Trust Account (IOLTA) Board distributes interest on attorney trust accounts to legal service organizations throughout Pennsylvania and clinical programs at the Commonwealth's law schools. Finally, the Committee for Proposed Standard Jury Instructions works to revise jury instructions to make them more understandable to lay jurors.

The broad range of the Court's responsibilities also provides opportunities to collaborate with other dedicated professionals within the system, many of whom have contributed to this book. Like other institutions, ours is not a perfect one, but we do strive toward the goal of protecting and enforcing Pennsylvanians' rights through the most effective system of judicial administration we can realize.

The current justices are always cognizant that we are but the latest in a long line of men and women who have had the privilege of serving on Pennsylvania's court of last resort.

Thomas G. Saylor
Chief Justice of Pennsylvania

NOTES

1. *See* the reports here: "Reports," *Pennsylvania Judicial System*, http://www.pacourts.us/news -and-statistics/reports.

2. *Pennsylvania Rules of Court: State and Federal*, rev. ed., vols. 1 and 2 (St. Paul, Minn.: Thomson Reuters, 2017).

Appendix A

The Reports of the Supreme Court of Pennsylvania

JOEL FISHMAN

The publication of Pennsylvania court cases began with Alexander James Dallas, who in 1790 published only the second set of state court reports in the country after Edward Kirby's *Connecticut Reports*. This first volume had the title *Reports of Cases Before the Revolution* and contained both Supreme Court and Philadelphia County court cases from 1754 to 1788. Dallas continued to publish three more volumes of reports, which from 1789 onward had a new title that included cases from the US Supreme Court and circuit court cases, as well as the state appellate and county cases: *Reports of Cases Ruled and Adjudged in the Several Courts of the United States and of Pennsylvania, Held at the Seat of the Federal Government* (1797, 1799, 1807). These four volumes became the first four volumes of the *United States Reports*. The first volume had four editions, the second volume had three editions, and the third and fourth volumes had only two editions.

From 1790 to 1845, there were sixty volumes of Pennsylvania Supreme Court cases,[1] known as nominative reports for the names of the reporters: Alexander James Dallas (1754–1806), Jasper Yeates (1791–1808), Horace Binney (1808–14), Thomas Sergeant and William Rawle Jr. (1814–28), William Rawle Jr. (1828–36), Charles Penrose and Francis Watts (1829–32), Thomas I. Wharton (1835–41), and Frederick Watts and Henry J. Sergeant (1841–45). Some of these reports were reprinted during the nineteenth century in later editions with additional notes, such as volume 1 of Dallas's *Reports* updated in four editions down to 1882.

Because the reports appeared to some to decline in content and prestige, the General Assembly passed the Act of April 11, 1845, P.L. 374–75,[2] which introduced an official court reporter and an official set of court reports, *Pennsylvania State Reports*. It is from this act that our current set of official court reports (up to 625 volumes) emerged. The governor appointed the court reporter until 1951, when statutory law gave the Supreme Court the right to hire a court reporter as one of its personnel.[3] The earlier act made provisions for a reporter to receive opinions from the justices in order to prepare the synopsis for each report and for only two volumes to be published each year. There was a 550-page limit in each volume, which had to be published in calf binding.[4]

Because of the volume limitation on the publication of the court's cases, five additional sets of nominative reports were later published, known as *Grant's Reports*, *Walker's Reports*, *Pennypacker's Reports*, *Sadler's Reports*, and *Monaghan's Reports*. The authors and their coverage were as follows:

Reporter	Volumes	Years on Book Spines
Benjamin Grant	3 vols.	1814–63
Lewis B. Walker	4 vols.	1855–85
Samuel Pennypacker	4 vols.	1881–84
Sylvester B. Sadler	10 vols.	1885–89
James Monaghan	2 vols.	1888–90

Benjamin Grant (1822–1878) was a successful lawyer in Erie, Pennsylvania, when he compiled his reports.[5] Lewis Walker (1855–1903) edited *The Burd Papers* (1897–99).[6] Samuel Pennypacker (1843–1916) was the best-known reporter, having served as a judge of the Philadelphia Court of Common Pleas (1889–1902), the twenty-third governor of Pennsylvania (1903–7), the president of the Historical Society of Pennsylvania (1900–1916), and a trustee of the University of Pennsylvania (1886–16).[7] Finally, Sylvester Sadler (1876–1931) taught at Dickinson Law School before becoming a judge on the Cumberland County Court of Common Pleas (1915–21) and then an associate justice of the Pennsylvania Supreme Court (1921–31).[8]

The official reports had eighteen reporters from 1845 to 1976. Most served only one five-year term, but several—Boyd Crumrine, William Schaffer, C. Brewster Rhoads, and Laurence Eldredge—served more. Lawrence Eldredge published eighty-six volumes, while Joseph Pringle just published two in completing the work of the first reporter, Robert Barr, who died before the volumes were completed. Boyd Crumrine and James Monaghan had a suit against each other over the publication of reports,[9] while Laurence Eldredge was the only court reporter sued by a Supreme Court justice (Michael Musmanno) over the failure to publish an opinion in the official reports.[10] Joseph W. Marshall was the last-named reporter before West Publishing Company took over the publication of the *Reports*.[11] The list of reporters follows:

Volumes	Reporter	Years of Service
1–10	Robert Barr	1845–48
11–12	J. P. Jones	1849
13–24	George Washington Harris	1849–55
25–36	Joseph Casey	1855–60
37–50	Robert Emmet Wright	1860–65
51–81	Persifor Frazer Smith	1865–76

(*continued*)

Volumes	Reporter	Years of Service
82–96	Alexander Wilson Norris	1876–80
97–110	Albert Albouy Outerbridge	1881–85
111–15	Lemuel Amerman	1885–86
116–46	Boyd Crumrine	1887–92
147–65	James Monaghan	1892–95
166–94	Wilson C. Kress	1895–1900
195–262	W. I. Schaffer	1900–1919
263–309	Albert B. Weimer	1919–33
310–44	C. Brewster Rhoads	1932–42
345–431	Lawrence Howard Eldredge	1942–68
431–52	Norman Lindenheim	1968–73
453–58	Joseph W. Marshall	1973–74

The twentieth-century reporters were lawyers who were well known to the Pennsylvania Bar. James Monaghan (1854–1949) edited a *Cumulative Annual Digest of Pennsylvania Law Reports (1899–1927)* and was the first editor of the *Pennsylvania County Court Reports* and *Pennsylvania District Court Reports*, predecessor reports to the *Pennsylvania District and County Reports* (1918 to present).[12] Wilson Kress (1836–1920) was the first state reporter for volumes 1–12 of the *Pennsylvania Superior Court Reports* and the oldest member and president of the Pennsylvania Bar Association (PBA) in 1920.[13] William I. Schaffer also was state reporter for volumes 13–70 of *Superior Court Reports*. Albert Weimer (1857–1938) was the assistant state reporter and then state reporter of volumes 71–106 of the *Superior Court Reports* and author of two treatises on corporations and railroads.[14] Laurence Eldredge (1902–82) was a law professor at the University of Pennsylvania Law School and later at Hastings Law School in California. He was an assistant reporter for the *Restatement of Torts* and author of *Modern Tort Law* (1941), *Law of Defamation* (1978), and other articles.[15] Joseph Marshall taught for more than thirty years at Temple Law School.

From the late nineteenth century, the George T. Bisel Company was the chief—but not the only—publisher of the court reports. In 1976, West Publishing Company took over the publication with volume 459. Between 1845 and 2015, there were 625 volumes published. The numbers broken down by each hundredth volume including the first and last volumes are as follows:

Volume	Year
1	1845
100	1882
200	1901
300	1930

(continued)

Volume	Year
400	1960
500	1982–83
600	2009
625	2014

Beginning with volume 459, the West series contains the same material as the *Atlantic Reporter* second and third series, including digest topics and headnotes at the beginning of each case. The bound volumes follow the standard format of other West court reports: a title page, list of judges, list of cases reported, list of statutes and rules construed, and words and phrases preceding the cases reported followed by the digest topics at the end of the volume. The official reports contain introductory materials such as court rules, calendars for the court, notices of meetings, appointments to the various committees under the Supreme Court, inductions, memorials, and picture presentations that can number several hundred pages.[16]

Supreme Court opinions were also published during the nineteenth century in the Philadelphia and Pittsburgh legal newspapers the *Legal Intelligencer*[17] and the *Pittsburgh Legal Journal*,[18] respectively. The *Intelligencer* cases were later reprinted in the *Weekly Notes of Cases* (forty volumes) covering October 1874 to December 1899. There might be opinions found in this publication not published in either the official reports or the later nominative reports. The *Pittsburgh Legal Journal* published Supreme Court cases into the early twentieth century.

Nineteenth-century opinions were also published in various legal periodicals. Pre-1860 journals, including the *American Law Journal*, the *American Jurist and Law Magazine*, and the *Pennsylvania Law Journal / American Law Journal*, reprinted the full text of cases and digests of cases from multiple states. The *American Law Register*, one of the best-known legal periodicals of the second half of the nineteenth century, digested cases in each issue.[19]

Two other nineteenth-century volumes of court reports also published Supreme Court cases. First, Frederick C. Brightly published *Brightly's Nisi Prius Reports*,[20] covering 1809 to 1851. F. Carroll Brewster published four volumes of Pennsylvania reports (1856–73), with volumes 3 and 4 covering the Pennsylvania Supreme Court.[21]

The reports contain various events in the Court's history—mostly the inductions, memorials, and portrait presentations of the justices of the Court.[22] These begin in the early nominative reports and carry through to the most recent volumes; for example, volume 600 contains the installation of Chief Justice Ronald D. Castille. In addition, publication includes events such as the celebration of the 200th (vol. 273) and 250th anniversaries of the Court (vol. 448); the reports of seven of the eight judicial conferences that met in the late 1920s and early 1930s (vols. 292–383); Pennsylvania Rules of Civil Procedure (vol. 331), Rules of Criminal Procedure (vol. 412), Appellate Procedure (vol. 461), and Evidence (vol. 550); the Model Rules of Professional Responsibility (vol. 438); and later, the Model Code of Professional Conduct (vol. 515). The publication of court rules has only increased since 1968, when, under Article V, Section 10 of the Pennsylvania Constitution, the Supreme Court increased its administrative control over the Unified Judicial System (UJS) to include the regulation of attorneys through its rules for admission to the bar, rules for disciplinary enforcement (vol. 446), and Continuing Education Board (vol. 527), as well as the appointees to all Supreme Court committees.

These publications have provided an invaluable record of the work of the continent's oldest court, and as other state supreme courts begin to eliminate bound volumes in this electronic age, the use of paper reports should continue in the Commonwealth.

LIST OF INDUCTIONS, MEMORIALS, AND PICTURE PRESENTATIONS

Like their counterparts in other states, Pennsylvania's court reports publish memorials (and more recently inductions) of justices who served on the Court. The following lists have been compiled from the three appellate court reports. I = Induction/Investiture; M = Memorial.

Pennsylvania Supreme Court Justices

Arnold, John C., 394 Pa. xxiii (M)

Baer, Max, 579 Pa. lxxxvii (I)

Baldwin, Cynthia A., 589 Pa. cxliii (I)

Barnes, H. Edgar, 339 Pa. xxxv (M)

Bell, John C., 405 Pa. xxiii (I)

Bok, Curtis, 408 Pa. xxiii (M)

Bradford, William, 1 Yeates 496 (M)

Cappy, Ralph J., 525 Pa. ccxiii (I)

Cappy, Ralph J., CJ, 572 Pa. clxiii (I)

Castille, Ronald D., CJ, 600 Pa. (I)

Chidsey, Thomas McKeen, 392 Pa. xxiii (M)

Clarke, Silas M., 144 Pa. xxi (M)

Cohen, Herbert B., 388 Pa. xxi (I)

Dean, John, 211 Pa. xxx (M)

Drew, James B., 374 Pa. xxi (M)

Eagen, Michael J., 397 Pa. xxiii (I)

Eagen, Michael J., 520 Pa. cxli (M)

Eakin, J. Michael, 571 Pa. lxv (I)

Fox, Edward J., 325 Pa. xxxi (M)

Frazer, Robert S., 322 Pa. xxxiii (M)

Gibson, John Bannister, 19 Pa. 9 (M)

Green, Henry, 197 Pa. xix (M)

Greenspan, Jean Cutler, Pa. (I)

Hughes, Howard W., 352 Pa. xxiii (M)

Hutchinson, William D., 500 Pa. xxxix (I)

Jones, Benjamin R., 388 Pa. xxi (I)

Jones, Benjamin R., CJ, 446 Pa. xcvii (I)

Jones, Charles A., 387 Pa. xxi (I)

Jones, Charles A., 423 Pa. xxix (M)

Kauffman, Bruce W., 487 Pa. Ii (I)

Kennedy, John, 4 Barr 5 (M)

Kephart, John W., 350 Pa. xxiii (M)

Ladner, Grover C., 380 Pa. xxi (M)

Lamb, William H., 573 Pa. clxiii (I)

Linn, William B., 366 Pa. xxiii (M)

Manderino, Louis L., 447 Pa. 1 (I)

Maxey, George W., 365 Pa. xxiii (M)

McCollum, J. Brewster, 207 Pa. xx (M)

McDermott, James T., 497 Pa. xlvii (I)

McDermott, James T., 532 Pa. cxlvii (M)

Mercur, Ulysses, 116 Pa. xix (M)

Moschzisker, Robert von, 336 Pa. xxxi (M)

Musmanno, Michael A., 433 Pa. xxxv (M)

Nestrezat, S. L., 261 Pa. xxxv (M)

Nix, Robert N. C. Jr., 447 Pa. 1 (I)

O'Brien, Henry X., 406 Pa. xxiii (I)

O'Brien, Henry X., CJ, 494 Pa. cxxi (I)

Parker, William M., 348 Pa. xxiii (M)

Penrose, S. B., 271 Pa. xxxii (M)

Potter, W. P., 261 Pa. xxxv (M)

Roberts, Samuel J., 409 Pa. xxxvii (I)

Roberts, Samuel J., 499 Pa. cxlvii (I)

Roberts, Samuel J., 516 Pa. lv (M)

Roberts, Samuel J., 518 Pa. lxxiii (M)

Sharswood, George, 88 Pa. xv (I)

Sharswood, George, 102 Pa. 601 (M)

Simpson, Alex Jr., 319 Pa. xxix (M)

Stern, Horace, 434 Pa. xcv (M)

Stearne, Allen M., 384 Pa. xxxix (M)

Stewart, John, 267 Pa. xxv (M)

Stout, Juanita Kidd, 519 Pa. cxcv (I)

Thompson, James, 72 Pa. xiii–xxvi (M)

Tilghman, William, 16 S&R 437–54 (M)

Wilkinson, Roy Jr., 493 Pa. xxxv (I)

Williams, Henry W., 82 Pa. xx (M)

Zappala, Stephen, 501 Pa. clxvii (I)

NOTES

Joel Fishman is the associate director for lawyer services at the Duquesne University Center for Legal Information/Allegheny County Law Library and an adjunct professor at Duquesne University School of Law. This chapter draws on the following articles: Joel Fishman, "The Reports of the Supreme Court of Pennsylvania," *Law Library Journal* 87 (Fall 1995): 643–93; Fishman, "History of the Court Reporter in the Appellate Courts of Pennsylvania," *Widener Journal of Public Law* 7 (1997): 1–37; and Fishman, "Celebrating 600," *Pa. Lawyer* 32 no. 6 (2010): 46–48.

1. This list omits Alexander Addison's court reports of the Fifth Circuit that included cases from the Pennsylvania High Court of Appeals and Errors (1780–1806), which served as the highest court in Pennsylvania during these first decades after the Revolution. Cases from this court are also found in Binney's *Reports.*

2. Laws of Pennsylvania (1846), 374–75.

3. Laws of Pennsylvania (1951), 1236.

4. Laws of Pennsylvania (1846), 281–83.

5. Fishman, "Reports," 670n145.

6. Ibid., 670n146.

7. Ibid., 670n147; Hampton L. Carson, "An Address on the Life and Services of Samuel Whitaker Pennypacker," speech delivered in the Hall of the Historical Society, January 8, 1917 (Philadelphia: Historical Society of Pennsylvania, 1917).

8. Fishman, "Reports," 670n148.

9. In re State Reporter, 24 A. 908 (Pa. 1892); *see* Fishman, "History," 12–17.

10. Fishman, "History," 17–34.

11. Ibid., 11; *see Pennsylvania Bulletin* 5 (1975): 1811, 1837.

12. Fishman, "History," 667n128.

13. Ibid., 667n129.

14. Ibid., 667n131.

15. Ibid., 667n132.

16. A bibliographic record of the introduction can be as much as a single-spaced full page. For instance, volume 568 had 272 pages, volume 574 had 211 pages, volume 577 had 273 pages, volume 582 had 379 pages, volume 584 had 323 pages, and volume 591 had 251 pages.

17. The *Legal Intelligencer* was first published in 1842 and became the official publication of the Philadelphia courts. It started as a weekly newspaper, but in the twentieth century it became a daily publication.

18. The *Pittsburgh Legal Journal* (1853–) began as a weekly newspaper. From 1910 to 1963, the *Journal* published weekly advance sheets, followed by monthly issues from 1963 to March 1999. In 1963, the Allegheny County Bar Association took over the publication of the *Journal.* There was also a daily publication of the *Pittsburgh Legal Journal* from the early twentieth century that contained the trial list information for federal, state, and local courts and courts of Allegheny County.

19. Examples of Pennsylvania cases digested in the *Register* can be found at *American Law Register* (1868): 358, 578, 781; (1869): 583; (1869–70): 193–94, 401; and (1877–78): 188–89, 402–3, 610–12.

20. Frederick C. Brightly, *Brightly's Reports of Cases Decided by the Judges of the Supreme Court of Pennsylvania, the Court of Nisi Prius, at Philadelphia, and also in the Supreme Court, with Notes and References to Recent Decisions* (Philadelphia: J. Kay, Jun & Brother, 1851).

21. The four volumes had different titles. The first two volumes contained cases dealing with

equity, elections, and other important cases. Volumes 3 and 4 had the title *Reports of Cases Decided in the Supreme Court, and Other Courts of Pennsylvania*. Fishman, "History," 675–76.

22. A list of the inductions, memorials, etc., follows this chapter. The paragraph is based on Joel Fishman, "Bibliography of State Court Reports: Pennsylvania" (unpublished manuscript), which contains the bibliography of all volumes of the Pennsylvania Supreme, Superior, and Commonwealth Court reports.

Appendix B

Historical List of Supreme Court Justices

Justice	Start Year	End Year	Chief Justice
Nicholas Moore	1684	1685	1684–85
William Welsh	1684	1684	
William Wood	1684	1685	
Robert Turner	1684	1685	
John Eckley	1684	1685	
William Clarke	1685	1705	1703–5
James Claypoole	1685	1687	
Arthur Cooke	1685	1693	1686; 1690
John Simcock	1686	1692	1690–92
James Harrison	1686	1687	1685–87
John Cann	1686	1694	
Joseph Growden	1690	1715	1707–15
Peter Alrichs	1690	1690	
Thomas Wynne	1690	1690	
Griffith Jones	1690	1690	
Edward Blake	1690	1694	
Andrew Robeson	1692	1699	1693–99
William Salway	1693	1694	
Anthony Morris	1694	1698	
Cornelius Empston	1698	1701	
Edward Shippen	1695	1701	1699–1701
William Biles	1699	1701	
Robert French	1701	1701	
Caleb Pusey	1699	1701	
Thomas Masters	1701	1704	
Samuel Finney	1702	1711	
John Guest	1701	1706	1701–3; 1705–6
Roger Mompesson	1706	1707	1706–7
Jasper Yates	1704	1720	
William Trent	1704	1720	

(*continued*)

Justice	Start Year	End Year	Chief Justice
Richard Hill	1711	1729	
Jonathan Dickinson	1711	1717	
George Roche	1715	1716	
Robert Assheton	1716	1726	
David Lloyd	1717	1731	1717–31
Jeremiah Langhorne	1726	1742	1736–37, 1739–42
Dr. Thomas Graeme	1731	1743	
James Logan	1731	1739	1731–39
Thomas Griffits	1739	1743	
John Kinsey	1743	1750	1743–50
William Till	1743	1750	
Lawrence Growden	1750	1764	
William Allen	1750	1774	1750–74
Caleb Cowpland	1750	1757	
William Coleman	1758	1769	
Alexander Stedman	1764	1767	
John Lawrence	1767	1773	
Thomas Willing	1767	1776	
Benjamin Chew	1774	1777	1774–77
John Morton	1774	1776	
William Augustus Atlee	1777	1791	
Thomas McKean	1777	1799	1777–99
John Evans	1777	1783	
George Bryan	1780	1791	
Jacob Rush	1784	1791	
George Bryan	1787	1791	
Edward Shippen IV	1791	1805	1799–1805
Jasper Yeates	1791	1817	
William Bradford Jr.	1791	1794	
Thomas Smith	1794	1809	
William Tilghman	1806	1827	1806–27
Hugh Henry Brackenridge	1800	1816	
John Bannister Gibson	1816	1853	1827–51
Thomas Duncan	1817	1827	
Morton Cropper Rogers	1826	1851	
Charles Huston	1826	1845	

(continued)

Justice	Start Year	End Year	Chief Justice
John Tod	1827	1830	
Frederick Smith	1828	1830	
John Ross	1830	1834	
John Kennedy	1830	1846	
Thomas Sergeant	1834	1846	
Thomas Burnside	1845	1851	
Richard Coulter	1846	1852	
Thomas S. Bell	1846	1851	
George Chambers	1851	1851	
Jeremiah S. Black	1851	1857	1851–54
Ellis Lewis	1851	1857	1854–57
Walter H. Lowrie	1851	1863	1857–63
George W. Woodward	1852	1867	1863–67
John C. Knox	1853	1857	
James Armstrong	1857	1857	
James Thompson	1857	1872	1867–72
William Strong	1857	1868	
William A. Porter	1858	1858	
Gaylord Church	1858	1858	
John M. Read	1858	1873	1872–73
Daniel Agnew	1863	1879	1873–79
George Sharswood	1867	1883	1879–82
Henry W. Williams	1868	1877	
Ulysses Mercur	1872	1887	1883–87
Isaac G. Gordon	1873	1888	1887–89
Edward M. Paxson	1875	1893	1889–93
Warren I. Woodward	1875	1879	
James P. Sterrett	1877	1878	
John Trunkey	1877	1888	
James P. Sterrett	1878	1899	1893–99
Henry Green	1879	1900	1899–1900
Silas M. Clark	1882	1891	
Henry W. Williams	1887	1899	
Alfred Hand	1888	1889	
J. Brewster McCollum	1888	1903	1900–1903
James T. Mitchell	1888	1910	1903–10
Christopher Heydrick	1891	1893	

(*continued*)

Justice	Start Year	End Year	Chief Justice
John Dean	1892	1896	
Samuel Gustine Thompson	1893	1894	
David Newlin Fell	1894	1914	1910–14
Jacob Hay Brown	1900	1921	1914–21
William P. Potter	1900	1918	
Stephen Leslie Mestrezat	1900	1918	
Samuel Gustine Thompson	1903	1905	
John P. Elkin	1905	1915	
John Stewart	1905	1920	
Robert von Moschzisker	1910	1930	1921–30
Robert S. Frazer	1915	1936	1930–36
Emory A. Walling	1916	1932	
Alexander Simpson Jr.	1918	1935	
Edward J. Fox	1918	1919	
Alexander Simpson Jr.	1919	1935	
John W. Kephart	1919	1940	1936–40
William I. Schaffer	1920	1943	1940–43
Sylvester B. Sadler	1921	1931	
George W. Maxey	1930	1950	1943–50
James B. Drew	1931	1952	1950–52
William B. Linn	1932	1950	
H. Edgar Barnes	1935	1940	
Horace Stern	1936	1956	1952–56
Marion D. Patterson	1940	1950	
William M. Parker	1941	1943	
Allen M. Stearne	1942	1956	
Howard W. Hughes	1944	1945	
Charles Alvin Jones	1950	1961	1956–61
John C. Bell	1950	1972	1961–72
Grover C. Ladner	1950	1952	
Thomas McKeen Chidsey	1950	1958	
Michael A. Musmanno	1952	1968	
John C. Arnold	1953	1958	
Benjamin R. Jones	1957	1977	1972–77
Herbert B. Cohen	1957	1970	

(*continued*)

Justice	Start Year	End Year	Chief Justice
Thomas D. McBride	1958	1960	
Curtis Bok	1958	1962	
Michael J. Eagen	1960	1980	1977–80
Anne X. Alpern	1961	1962	
Henry X. O'Brien	1962	1983	1980–83
Earl S. Keim	1962	1963	
Samuel J. Roberts	1963	1984	1983–84
Thomas W. Pomeroy Jr.	1968	1978	
Alexander F. Barbieri	1971	1992	
Robert N. C. Nix Jr.	1972	1996	1984–96
Louis L. Manderino	1972	1979	
Israel Packel	1977	1977	
Rolf Larsen	1978	1994	
John P. Flaherty Jr.	1979	2002	1996–2002
Bruce W. Kauffman	1980	1982	
Roy Wilkinson Jr.	1981	1982	
William D. Hutchinson	1982	1987	
James T. McDermott	1982	1992	
Stephen A. Zappala	1983	2003	2002
Nicholas P. Papadakos	1984	1995	
Juanita Kidd Stout	1988	1989	
Ralph J. Cappy	1990	2008	2003–8
Frank J. Montemuro Jr.	1992	1994	
Ronald D. Castille	1994	2014	2008–14
Russell M. Nigro	1996	2006	
Sandra Schultz Newman	1996	2006	
Thomas G. Saylor	1998–		2015–
J. Michael Eakin	2002	2016	
William H. Lamb	2003	2004	
Max Baer	2004–		
Cynthia A. Baldwin	2006	2007	
James J. Fitzgerald III	2007	2008	
Debra McClosky Todd	2008–		
Seamus P. McCaffery	2008	2014	
Jane Cutler Greenspan	2008	2010	
Joan Orie Melvin	2010	2013	

(continued)

Justice	Start Year	End Year	Chief Justice
Correale Stevens	2011	2015	
Christine Donohue	2016–		
Kevin Dougherty	2016–		
David Wecht	2016–		
Sallie Updyke Mundy	2016–		

Index

Page numbers followed by *f* and *t* refer to figures and tables, respectively.